(1998)

658.83 S491s

Servicescapes

ServiceScapes

The Concept of Place
in Contemporary Markets

John F. Sherry, Jr., Ph.D.

Editor

AMERICAN MARKETING ASSOCIATION

NTC Business Books
NTC/Contemporary Publishing Company

Library of Congress Cataloging-in-Publication Data

Servicescapes : the concept of place in contemporary markets / John F.
    Sherry, Jr., editor.
            p.   cm.
        Includes bibliographical references and index.
        ISBN 0-8442-3005-7
        1. Markets.   2. Marketing research.   3. Consumer behavior.
        I. Sherry, John F.
    HF5470.S48   1998
    658.8'3—dc21   97-41743
                                                                  CIP

Interior design by Precision Graphics

Published in conjunction with the American Marketing Association
250 South Wacker Drive, Chicago, Illinois 60606

Published by NTC Business Books
An imprint of NTC/Contemporary Publishing Company
4255 West Touhy Avenue, Lincolnwood (Chicago), Illinois 60646-1975 U.S.A.
Copyright © 1998 by NTC/Contemporary Publishing Company
Printed in the United States of America
International Standard Book Number: 0-8442-3005-7
    18   17   16   15   14   13   12   11   10   9   8   7   6   5   4   3   2   1

To the genius loci
 of marketplaces
  everywhere

CONTENTS

UNDERSTANDING MARKETS AS PLACES

An Introduction to Servicescapes

As the reader might well imagine upon digesting the title of the volume, this project has its origins in my longtime fascination with marketplaces and consumption sites, an interest shared in great measure with the colleagues whose efforts are collected between these covers. I have spent a large portion of my professional life, both here and abroad, immersed in such settings, observing the interactions of buyers and sellers with each other, with their surroundings, and with the goods, services, and experiences that are the focus of these environments. I have shopped, stocked, and shared with consumers, and strategized, shaped, and sold with marketers. I have talked at length with members of each of these groups about their lived experiences and probed them with projective tasks when my questions proved inarticulate in the face of their desire to express the ineffable. From settings whose structure and function range from primarily formal and economic to those whose are chiefly informal and festive (Sherry 1990, 16–17), I have haunted commercial precincts before and after actual marketing transactions have occurred. I have found myself drawn inexorably through these studies to the exploration of place, as designed by marketers and experienced by consumers, in the web of consumption. This anthology represents a playing out of this growing fascination, and a cocelebration of place with kindred spirits.

Let me illustrate the nature, scope, and tenor of our inquiry with a few personal observations on the placeways of markets:

For decades, I have observed parents, particularly mothers, perform an animated monologue that I call "cart-talk" as they and their children (who are often preverbal) wend their way around the aisles of a supermarket during shopping trips. Mothers provide a running account of individual family members' brand preferences, speculate aloud about price-quality relationships, employ packages as projective devices to divert and amuse their cart-bound charges, instruct their mobile children in search and selection principles, and generally socialize their fellow travelers into consumer culture during the course of the shopping trip. Indeed, cart-talk occurs even in the absence of shopping partners, yet the sight of solitary shoppers speaking aloud as they stock their carts is unremarkable to other consumers, although speaking to oneself in another context might be seen to push eccentricity into the realm of psychopathology.

What is it about supermarkets that promotes such disinhibition and encourages peripatetic discourse? While our literatures have occasionally probed the nature of grocery stores (Krugman 1967; Glaser 1985; Willis 1991), we actually know more about the placeways of submarines than we do about supermarkets (Gallagher 1993). Such disparity is remarkable, given the everyday nature of such shopping and the importance our discipline assigns to "place" in our comprehension of marketing. It is also suggestive of the range of everyday phenomena (infrastructural and superstructural) that escapes our disciplinary scrutiny. "Shopportunities" (Jukes 1990, 103) should become a focus of our inquiries.

Walking down North Michigan Avenue—Chicago's "Magnificent Mile"—one blustery fall evening, I find my wandering attention gradually begin to focus. In the gathering darkness, I watch images form directly on the building on the west side of the boulevard. I recognize them instantly as Absolut vodka ads and am captivated by the rippling effect created by their movement across the facades. As the physical landscape is transmuted to a symbolic one and back again, I find myself drawn along by the changing images, in tow with fellow pedestrians whose formerly purposive, directional strides have given way to a more leisurely ambling, as if we are all caught in some gentle, commercial tractor beam. I trace the traveling slide show to a projection machine mounted on the back of a flatbed truck. The truck is moving in the slow lane of rush hour traffic, allowing the projectionist plenty of time to play the images across the exteriors of upscale stores and galleries, to the amusement of commuters and passersby in the process of becoming conversational partners.

I am fascinated by the way the marketer has transformed *promotion*—in this case, yet again, as Absolut advertising has run the gamut from commissioned art (lowbrow through highbrow) to mobile museum exhibit to coffee-table book (Lewis 1996)— to *place* and has radically altered our immediate experience of the environment. For a moment, the product (and not only the experience it promises) is larger than life, a dominant form on the landscape, and, along with my fellow travelers, I am dwarfed by its presence. Meaning is *emplaced,* albeit transiently, and the ephemeral is made tangible.. Conversely the physical marketplace suddenly becomes an imagistic one, then, just as suddenly, resolidifies.

During my stay in Thailand, I grew accustomed to seeing the traditional greeting of respect (*wai*)—palms pressed together, fingers steepled, head bowed—extended not only to people, but to things as well. For example, it was not unusual to see an individual *wai* a musical instrument before picking it up, in deference to spirits inhabiting the crafted artifact. In Thailand, the landscape is alive with spirits, the more prominent of whom *(phii ruan* and *phra phum,* spirits of the household and of the land, respectively) have been induced to live in spirit houses. Spirit houses resemble small temples, and these dwellings are frequently laden with offertory gifts from supplicants seeking favors and sealing vows. Marketplaces in general, and retail stores in particular, feature spirit houses as part of their overall composition.

As I stood one afternoon outside the Brahmin shrine San Phra Prom, near the Grand Hyatt Erawan in downtown Bangkok, observing the devout hiring dancers and musicians to perform prayers, draping marigold garland gifts on the pedestal, and buying lottery tickets from street vendors surrounding the site, my gaze wandered across the highway to the enormous modern building that houses the Zen Central marketplace. Zen Central had its own shrine, which I felt compelled to explore. Crossing the street, I quickly became absorbed in contemplation of the shrine. Noticing my fascination, a Thai consumer told me that the shrine had come to occupy its present site just recently. When the marketplace had failed to prosper, geomancers—ritual practitioners of the local variant of *feng shui*—had been consulted, and the shrine relocated to a more auspicious space.

Thais recognize a numinous dimension in the landscape, and merchants feel obligated to propitiate the spirits of their market-places in order to ensure success. Their centuries-old recognition of cosmological marketing principles seems just dawning in Western retailing practices. My growing belief that Thai Buddhists are among the world's most avid materialists, and that they feel no particular doctrinal discomfort from this acquisitiveness, encourages me to continue rethinking our notions of materiality.

Considered as a whole, these "observations from the field" anticipate the issues raised throughout this book. Marketplaces have many extraeconomic facets. The consumer's experience of place is varied and often conditioned by role incumbency: the shopper's perspective differs from that of the flaneur. The negotiation of place is contingent upon the complicity of stakeholders. Place exhibits perception-shaping, behavior-inducing properties. The shape-shifting characteristics of place can be subtle or profound. Physical space embodies symbolic properties. Meaning is continually emplaced in consumers' experience. Place is by nature culture-, gender-, and class-bound in its manifestations. Each of this volume's authors undertakes the exploration of one or more of these aspects of the ambient environment of marketplaces.

ON METHOD AND PERSPECTIVE

While some of the volume's contributors use conventional market-ing research methods, the methodological thrust of the enterprise is guided by the suggestions of servicescape researchers who have called for a diversification of our tool kit. Klaus (1985, 28–29) advises inquirers to adopt techniques from social psychology and anthropology—notably structured interviews, participant observa-tion, ethnography, photography, and videography—to apprehend the service encounter more comprehensively. Zimmer and Golden (1988, 266) contend that despite the volume of research into retail store image, "prevailing approaches to measurement" don't attempt to capture the "gestalt" of that image; furthermore, such measurement is frequently incomplete and narrowly focused. Citing models by some contributors to this volume, Bitner (1992, 68–69) advocates the use of direct observation methods and the probing of symbolic meaning in future investigations of service environments. Lee and Vryza (1994) have stressed the need for phenomenological research into retailing and service environments. These cutting-edge admonitions are honored in the present volume.

The approaches our contributors have employed range from game theory to introspection. While quantitative measures are represented, qualitative ones predominate. Investigations unfold through the use of observation, interview, projective tasking, archival analysis, and photography. Most of the chapters are grounded in ethnography, and most have a phenomenological cast. Some of the findings have emerged through long-term field immersion and are presented in extended case study format. Other accounts are more introspective and take the reader on a richly elaborated interior journey. The tenor of the chapters is largely sociocultural and semiotic; contributors are concerned to explore the local experiences of consumers as they articulate with larger cultural themes.

Chapters range from conceptual through empirical to critical, with hybrid forms serving to remind the reader of the exploratory nature of this volume. Some chapters are more overtly managerial than others, though each of the authors is alive to the applications of disciplinary discoveries. Public and private consumption sites are investigated. Frontstage and backstage activity is explored in a number of marketplaces as well. Through a diversity of methods, perspectives, and foci, the volume seeks to capture the totality of the encounter that consumers have with servicescapes, by examining in detail the lived experience of consumers in the built environments that constitute contemporary marketplaces.

ORIENTATION OF THE FIELDS

The history of ideas from which this volume emerges can be briefly sketched. Our chapters contribute to a research stream that begins at the confluence of environmental psychology and cultural geography. This stream is being fed by a host of contiguous disciplines incorporating phenomenology into their conventional purviews. These disciplines examine the transformation of "space" to "place" and, in particular, explore the ways in which landscape functions as a major cultural product in our era (Zukin 1991). Still, Tuan's (1974, 246) observation that we are "largely ignorant of the quality and range of experience in different types of physical setting under different conditions" remains accurate today. Places of consumption are especially fertile fields for inquiring into the individual's sense of place, as these sites "interweave and alter elements of meaning, nature, social relations and agency," as well as perspectives (Sack 1992, 134). Marketers and consumer researchers are well positioned to combine the insights of phenomenological ecology broadly construed (Seamon 1993) with those of consumer-object relations (which examine the production of consumption) to disciplinary and managerial ends.

Places, as we experience them in everyday life, are "sensed in a chiaroscuro of setting, landscape, ritual, routine, other people, personal experiences, care and concern for home, and in the context of other places" (Relph 1976, 29). To account for our experience, Relph has distinguished between the geography of places, which is characterized by variety and meaning, and the geography of the placeless, which is characterized by a "labyrinth of endless similarities" (p. 141). He asserts that the latter is currently in ascendancy, resulting in the destruction and replacement of distinctive places, often with structures Augé (1995) has described as "nonplaces," and that the trend can be reversed through design practice attuned to the "lived-world" of significant places. Increasingly, marketers seek to transform the nonplaces that conventional marketplaces have threatened to become—the malling and chaining of America having contributed to a homogenized execution and lethargic reception of an all-too-familiar outlet—into the kind of differentiated places that Relph (1976, 43) believes "involve a concentration of our intentions, our attitudes, purposes and experiences." The strategies and sensory rhetorics driving such transformation are explored in this volume.

Our contributors draw heavily upon semiotics and phenomenology to help the reader reengage the marketplace. Semiotics is
essentially concerned with the creation, investment, divestment,
and transformation of meanings (Mick 1986; McCracken 1988;
Sherry 1991). Phenomenology has been called "the scientific study
of experience," insofar as it seeks to "describe consciousness in its
lived immediacy" before that experience (in all its manifold modal-
ities) is "subject to theoretical elaboration or conceptual theorizing"
(Jackson 1996, 2). Phenomenology "suspends inquiry into the hidden determinants of belief in order to describe the implications,
intentions and effects of what people say, do, and hold to be true"
(p. 11). In tacking between semiotic and phenomenological view-
points to capture the lifeworlds of the marketplaces they have studied, our contributors return us to the roots of marketing (Tucker
1967; Belk 1991). Sherry (1995, 439) describes the recent emergence
of a "marketing and consumption–based research tradition" that
he calls the "phenomenology of emplacement" as follows:

> On one level, this tradition is concerned with behavior on the
> ground and specifically addresses issues arising directly from
> institutions both formal and informal. On another more abstract
> level, this tradition is concerned with the kaleidoscopic indi-
> vidual "worlds" inhabited by stakeholders in the marketing
> transaction. The former aspect deals with the impact of the built
> environment on marketplace behavior; the latter deals with the
> individual elaboration of the environment as a projectable field
> for personal fantasy. Each aspect contributes to the experiential
> state we identify as "being-in-the-marketplace."

In this volume, as we focus on the psychocultural determinants of
this experience, we are guided by Camus's (1955, 88) observation
that "sense of place is not just something that people know and feel,
it is something people do."

Given the centrality of ethnography and introspection to the
depiction of marketplace lifeworlds in this volume, it is essential
to recognize that anthropological interest in place (Hirsch and
O'Hanlon 1995; Rodman 1992) is undergoing a shift in emphasis
toward understanding native perceptions and experiences of

locality (Feld and Basso 1996). While ethnographers are increasingly attentive to "the gritty and obscure drama of everyday life" (Wilshire 1990, 190), those places where consumer-object relations and geomantic principles (Stokols 1991; Anderson 1991) interact have gone surprisingly unexplored. Thus, our contributors focus on the site of the consumer's encounter with market forces—the servicescape itself—to launch a voyage of discovery.

These disciplinary influences have already provided ripples in the literatures of marketing and consumer research; predictably, these ripples have widened over time. Martineau's (1958) notion of a retail outlet possessing a distinctive "personality" matured into Kotler's (1974) more comprehensive conception of ambient influence described as "atmospherics," which in turn evolved into a more holistic and interfunctional design-centered model of engagement called "pathetecture," which Sherry and McGrath (1989) have brokered into the literature. The ascendancy of "integrated marketing communication" (Schultz, Tannenbaum, and Lauterborn 1994) as a unifying paradigm is itself a reflection of our gradual acknowledgment of the absolutely pervasive nature of the influence exerted upon consumers by the built environment of marketing. So also is our recent attention to servicescape dimensions and dynamics emblematic of this acknowledgment.

Bitner (1992, 57) coined the term *servicescape* in recognition of marketers' lack of "empirical research or theoretically based frameworks addressing the role of physical surroundings in consumption settings"; despite managers' willingness to manipulate store design, the impact of that manipulation upon consumers is rarely understood. In devising a typology of servicescapes that attempted to clarify relationships between users and environments, Bitner (p. 68) emphasizes the latitude still available to researchers for theory building, empirical testing, measure-and-method development, and application studies. While recognizing that all products have both tangible and intangible qualities, Bitner focuses on the relationship of physical complexity to action performance, and identifies three categories of tangible service evidence—people, process, and physical cues—that consumers experience in marketplaces (Bitner 1992, 1993). Accepting Bitner's challenge to extend our horizons, our contributors refine, extend, and refute some of these observations.

Prior to the late 1980s, despite awareness that consumers were present and involved in the production of services, models of servicescape dynamics made no provision for atmospherics (Czepiel et al. 1985). While researchers were advised to begin their inquiries "at the level of the most elementary behaviors and experiences" exhibited by participants in a service encounter, this so-called bottom-up approach has only recently been put into practice (Klaus 1985, 28). Designers have been criticized for being "unconcerned" for and "largely ignorant" of the wayfinding needs and habits of consumers (Werner 1985). Some researchers have even advocated deleting the term *design* from our marketing vocabulary, in favor of the more holistic term *situation creation,* which would focus our attention on all key design features and details that contribute to consumers' experience of marketplaces (Upah and Fulton 1985, 256). These issues of fundamental units of experience, cocreation of experience, and the delivery of projectable fields are explored in depth in this volume.

As we continue to examine marketplaces as "sites of social centrality" (Shields 1992, 103), observe the blurring of the rational and the ludic as shoppers and "postshoppers" confound and extend designers' intentions (Shields 1989), and realize that multiple experiences of a single marketplace are not only common (Williamson 1992) but inevitable (Bass 1996, 55), the need for individual accounts of *being-in-the-marketplace* of the kind we present in extended case study fashion in this volume will grow more pressing, both for disciplinary and managerial reasons. Design has been consciously marketed as a commodity in the United States since the 1920s (Reekie 1992) and may be reaching its apogee in the festival markets, themed environments, and cyberscapes our contributors describe in these pages. The importance of listening to the voice of the designer (Nixon 1992) rivals that of hearing the voice of the customer, once we accept that design is itself spectacle, in an era where more and more often stores *are* the brand and shoppers are flaneurs bent upon the acquisition of experience as much as goods.

THE PLAN OF THE BOOK

Our treatment of the role of place in the consumer's encounter with the market is organized according to four principal issues. The first part of the book deals with the built environment and explores some of the elements that atmospherics comprise. The second part of the book examines servicescapes familiar to the reader and investigates that experiential condition that we have called *being-in-the-market-place*. The third part of the book probes some less familiar alternative placeways projected to become increasingly meaningful to consumers in the near future. Finally, the fourth part of the book identifies some critical concepts and issues that render the context of servicescapes more accessible to scholars and practitioners. In the following pages, I briefly describe these sections and anticipate the significance of some of the contributors' findings for the reader.

I The Built Environment: Elements of Atmospherics

The contributors to Part I set the stage for the balance of the book by specifying some of the most significant parameters of the servicescape and by examining in detail some of the cognitive, material, cultural, and experiential dynamics that animate the built environment of the marketplace. Mark Gottdiener provides an initial overview of the volume's substance and tenor in his account of the semiotics of themed places. His chapter explores the rapidly escalating incidence of themed environments in the creation of consumer spaces. Using a sociosemiotic approach, he summarizes briefly the historical shift to reliance on themes in consumer spaces, examines major examples such as theme park malls, reviews recent extensions of the themed consumer space in the construction or renovation of restaurants, and charts the spectacular growth of themed gambling casinos. The sociosemiotic approach links recent changes in the political economy of late capitalism with the emergence of a symbol-dominated, media-culture environment as a way of explaining the rise of themed consumer spaces.

Employing a set of perspectives familiar to consumer researchers, Julie Baker assesses the informational value of store environments. While a number of studies have examined the affective influence of the store environment on consumer decision making, there is little consumer research that investigates the store environment from a cognitive perspective. Because store environments, like pricing and advertising, can provide critical information to consumers in the process of goods or services evaluation, it is important that a theoretical base be developed from which researchers can begin to study this important marketing variable. Her chapter examines several theories—information processing, categorization, inference making, semiotics, and information integration—to provide a basis for the development of research questions designed to stimulate thinking about the cognitive role of the store environment in consumer decision making. She also discusses the moderating influences of several situational and individual characteristics, before considering future research issues and managerial implications.

Mike Solomon focuses our attention on a particular aspect of servicescape negotiation, that of the "costume." Noting that servicescape design encompasses an array of sensory elements, ranging from signage to scents, he avers that the physical setting where the service is rendered is an important, yet largely ignored, dimension of the service encounter. From a dramaturgical perspective, the deployment of socially meaningful props, sets, and costumes instantiates the servicescape and creates a nexus of meaning for both customers and service providers. While some researchers have begun to examine the effects of architecture, signage, and other tangible environment cues, very little attention has been paid to the role of costume in the service experience. His chapter deals specifically with the functions of apparel and other aspects of employee appearance in the engineering of the servicescape.

In the concluding chapter of the section, John Sherry weaves a number of the preceding contributors' concerns together in his investigation of a particular site: the servicescape that is Nike Town Chicago. Tracing his own encounter with the built environment, he focuses on the design elements that contribute to consumers' experience of being-in-the-marketplace. His account describes in detail the dynamics by which the Nike brandscape becomes emplaced for consumers and the particular placeways exhibited at a localized servicescape. In his meditation on design, he interprets both the cultural significance of the commoditization of sport and the ritual nature of retail theater.

Familiar Servicescapes:
Being-in-the-Marketplace

Part II presents a series of extended case studies. Our contributors range across time, culture, sector, and industry to provide meticulous, thick descriptions of servicescape placeways. These chapters capture something of the breadth of servicescape dynamics and illustrate both the generalizable and ineluctably local dimensions of marketplaces frequented by our readers. In their chapter on "Gorilla Marketing," Melanie Wallendorf, Joan Lindsey-Mullikin, and Ron Pimentel demonstrate how, rather than simply warehousing inventory for sale, retail stores are designed to provide particular kinds of consumer experiences to those who come into the store. As the regional context in which a store is embedded changes, so must the store environment change to respond to these population changes. The authors illustrate how relocation is a time when such adjustment in store environment may be made. The authors dwell on how physical features of a retail space serve as the basis for consumer animation, how changes in location and store design challenge retailers with a broadened market that may contest the previous bases of consumer animation and therefore store image; and how temporal shifts in store design and its accompanying forms of consumer animation are embedded in and constitutive both of patterns of regional development and global development of hypermarkets.

In her chapter on Japanese servicescapes, Millie Creighton takes an in-depth look at one major retailing store in Tokyo, Seibu SEED (designed by Japan's trendy and often avant-garde department store chain Seibu Saison Group) to analyze what has been designated *seibu-realism*. The store's architecture, design, layout, and art all attempt to engage customers not just in shopping, but in an experience of personal development. Shoppers enter as "seedlings" at the first level, proceed through store levels as levels of consciousness, and emerge at the summit of their journeys as "sophisticated shoppers" and "creative human beings." The store is situated within the current cultural and historic conditions of contemporary Japan. Having emerged from its post–World War II destruction and poverty to realize the "economic miracle," with affluence, westernization, modernization, and the full flowering of the "consumer society," Japan and the Japanese are discovering disillusionment with these successes, nostalgia for the lost past and forgotten community, and a need to reestablish meaning in human life outside of consumerism or purely economic relations. Stores like SEED address these concerns by offering shoppers philosophic statements of ultimate meaning. Creighton's chapter reveals the extent to which Japan is now enmeshed in its self-identity as a consumer society, and explores the paradoxes involved in the ultimate consummation of this consumer orientation, as stores like SEED philosophically proclaim that consumerism provides the modern path *(michi)* that will allow Japanese to transcend material goods and regain touch with their essential humanity.

The bridal salon is the subject of Cele Otnes's inquiry, and her chapter explores the various roles that women expect the bridal salon to fulfill as they engage in wedding planning. Interviews and shopping trips undertaken by Otnes with brides engaged in selecting their wedding dresses reveal six such roles: the salon as clearinghouse, "one-stop" shop, school, storehouse, dressing chamber, and singularizer. Although salespeople are vital to the successful (or unsuccessful) expressions of these roles, physical aspects of the store such as lighting, dressing room size, music, and decor also are important in their successful articulation.

Annamma Joy pursues her inquiry into servicescapes by examining the role Canadian art galleries play in the circulation of art. The focus of her chapter—its title, "Framing Art," a play on the idea of the frame—is, at a broad level, on the space between the work of art and the viewer and, more specifically, on the role of commercial and parallel galleries as channels of art distribution.

While commercial art galleries promote and sell the artist and his or her works, parallel galleries are more concerned with exhibiting artworks, particularly those of a more experimental nature. The mandate of most parallel galleries is to diffuse and expose the artist. In this respect, parallel galleries are similar to museums. However, they cannot hope to parallel the seal of approval and value that museums bestow on the artists and their work. Nonetheless, parallel galleries perform an important service by providing space for unknown or up-and-coming artists to show their work. "Seeing" or "being seen" is the first step toward the recognition of the artist in the art world. But this is not enough—the objet d'art needs to be seen and exchanged several times before the artist's career is decisively launched. Every time the artist's work is sold, its importance is reinforced and its value rises. Each resale also contributes credibility to the artist's career and artistic complexity to the object via the currency that art critics and dealers offer for a given piece. Oral and written discourses and exchanges circulating with the object further entrench its value and bestow status (and wealth) on its owner(s). The longer this circulation process persists, the greater the depth/history and status that the object acquires. Joy demonstrates how the circulation of art and the long-term promotion and sale of the artist and his or her works are central to the functioning of commercial art galleries.

The concluding chapter of this section, by Ozlem Sandikci and Doug Holt, provides a semiotic appraisal of the shopping mall, grounded in an introspective, ethnographic account of a particular mall. The authors examine the relationships between the distinctive structural and atmospheric characteristics of the mall environment and the way in which the mall is experienced by shoppers. They analyze both the existing typologies of mall shopping behavior in the marketing literature and descriptions of the mall consumption experience in postmodern literature. Their chapter is a comprehensive analysis describing how the mall environment structures shopping experiences. They add empirical rigor to what has been an impressionistic postmodern literature on the mall, and also extend theoretically the empiricist marketing literature to include insights from theories of postmodernity.

Alternative Placeways:
Visiting the Undiscovered Country

In Part III, the contributors probe the geographic frontiers of our knowledge of servicescapes by exploring unconventional sites of marketplace activity of emerging interest. These sites are found in the ether, in the outdoors, in the home, and in consumers' imaginations. They mark the movement of marketing and consumption into important new venues. For example, Alladi Venkatesh adopts a critical posture to evaluate what he terms "cybermarketscapes" and consumer behaviors unfolding in cyberspace. The recent developments in computer, information, and telecommunication technologies, according to some, have begun to herald a new cultural order, known as cyberculture. Venkatesh believes we are witnessing a major development whose impact will be quite dramatic and far reaching. His chapter provides an overview of current developments, anticipated trends, and implications for the configuration of consumer spaces in the cyberculture. While his approach cannot help being somewhat speculative—for what is being developed here is a picture that has not emerged yet but is unfolding—it is grounded in his own ten-year research effort in the area of social impacts of information technologies with particular reference to individual consumers and households. His chapter gives rise to a number of intriguing questions. What new consumer spaces are being generated in this emerging electronic world? Given that the cyberculture is being described in terms of interactivity, virtual reality, hyper- and multimedia, how are these spaces configured and negotiated? What will be the nature of marketing–consumer transactions in the cyberculture? What will be the nature of service encounters in this electronic space? What kind of theorizing should we engage in to articulate consumer behavior in the cyberculture? He examines the technological imperative that requires marketing scholars and practitioners to take into account the new technologies.

In their chapter on "brandfests," Jim McAlexander and John Schouten present an ethnography of brand-centered festivals designed to cultivate brand loyalty and celebrate preference. They examine mechanisms and processes integral to building relationships between owners and brands, as well as between consumers themselves. Endowing the brand with a distinctive mystique and facilitating consumers' achievement of optional experience are two functions of brandfests that the authors consider. They focus on brandfests that occur outdoors.

The American wilderness is the servicescape interpreted by Eric Arnould, Linda Price, and Patrick Tierney. Their ethnographic study of commercial white-water rafting explores the interplay between culture and nature occasioned by marketing. The authors tap multiple participants' perspectives on the peculiar tensions and ironies that surface during river trips. Service encounters in natural settings confront a primitive conflict between the near-biological human propensity to appropriate and exert control over a space and time (i.e., human territoriality) and a desire for a primal contact with the combined forces of nature. The typical managerial approach to the servicescape is to manage the features of the marketing environment to influence behavioral outcomes. Yet here there is an ironic tension, because what brings customers into the natural setting is a search for the mysterious and unforeseeable elements often denied us by the controlled orderliness of rationalized marketing environments. Indeed, multiple ironies prevail. The authors describe how participants may seek an escape from spatial routinization, but may nonetheless look to the products of industrial civilization to aid their escape. Further, a central element of the drama of river rafting is that uncertainty about conditions and outcomes prevails. This provides a departure from scripted service delivery text and an opportunity for authorship in a way not available through many leisure activities in such controlled marketing environments as theme parks. Yet commercial outfitters need to control uncertainty: the "religion" of commercial boating is the "smooth run." Finally, the authors illustrate how lack of control creates a social leveling effect on all participants, since no one is totally "in control," and how the fantasy of equality becomes an important aspect of the service encounter.

In her discussion of servicescape as an ideal type, Mary Ann McGrath employs a projective storytelling methodology to elicit consumers' fantasies of an ideal retail environment. She also probes the ideal level of service they desire. She finds that men and women converge upon a similar ideal that includes cornucopian abundance, an individualized phenomenology of a pleasant retail ambience, playful shopping, pleasurable self-indulgence, and specialized service that is invisible yet instantaneous. Perhaps ironically, she notes that price and value considerations are not articulated priorities in an ideal service venue.

Part III concludes with Kent Grayson's inquiry into commercial activity conducted in the home, which he envisions as a "private" servicescape. He observes that, since the home is not generally built for commerce, and may in many cases be hostile to commercial activity, those who wish to use the home as a marketing environment must strike a careful balance between pursuing selling goals and respecting the dwelling's central purpose and values. Network marketing (sometimes called multilevel marketing or pyramid selling) has made particularly extensive use of the home as a selling space. Network marketing products are offered solely through neighborhood distributors, who are encouraged to run their business from their home. In fact, distributors are just as likely to give sales presentations in their own home as in the homes of others. Grayson's research, based on interviews with network marketing distributors in the United Kingdom, identifies several strategies used by network marketers as they ply their wares in their own homes.

Servicescape Context: Concepts and Issues

Part IV emphasizes the contextual essence of servicescapes from a kaleidoscopic variety of perspectives. Our contributors apply widely divergent methods in their inquiries and demonstrate the differential accessibility to key concepts that particular approaches afford. Social class, ethnicity, gender, and personality are among the dimensions impinged upon by servicescapes. Privacy, dissatisfaction, and discrimination are among the conditions affected by servicescape design.

Perhaps the most provocative exploration of the interaction between consumer behavior and the servicescape to be found in this book is Morris Holbrook's introspective account of his own passionate involvement with music. He presents a phenomenological account of the shopping experience stemming from service encounters associated with retailers in general and with record stores in particular. Toward that end, he adopts an approach referred to as subjective personal introspection, bolstered by a consideration of some recent literature on artistic performance (especially the theater) as a kind of service, and on service (especially retailing) as a kind of performance. His narrative begins with some historical background on his experiences as a jazz-oriented refugee from the football field seeking shelter in the piano studio and finding solace in the purchase of recordings. From there unfolds an account of his personal encounters with the retail environment in shopping for jazz records over the past forty years, focusing on how record stores have evolved and on the subjective meanings connected with these changes. Finally, some insights borrowed from the recent literature on theater as service and on retailing as theater suggest interpretations concerning the interpenetration of art and commerce in the potential communion between performers and their audiences.

Dawn Iacobucci returns us to the use of conventional consumer research tools in her treatment of a critical design flaw in the servicescape: the failed service encounter. She takes the theoretical perspectives of game theory, which is known to have clear prescriptives for enhancing the quality of social interactions, and applies it as a metaphor to the fairly pervasive problem of poor service interactions between a customer and a service provider. The purpose of her inquiry is not so much to assess the fit and applicability of this particular theory to this particular phenomenon. Rather her orientation is more managerial; lack of fit between the theory and properties of the phenomenon is diagnostic for the customer service manager. Given that it is known how to enhance socially beneficial behavior in the framework of game theory, she argues that one solution to poor customer service is to increase the extent to which the customer-service provider interaction resembles a game, because then the normative implications would be clear.

One of the most pervasive and pressing practical and ethical concerns confronting marketers—the consumer's right to privacy—is addressed in Cathy Goodwin's chapter. She suggests that the privacy construct offers a novel and interesting way to classify service experiences. Recent research has emphasized that consumers appear to evaluate experiences holistically rather than according to specific attributes. Retail environments represent an aspect of experience. Services, which are delivered in public places, force interactions among strangers, yet often address the customer's most private concerns. This potential for conflict derives from the historical development of services. Many commercial services were originally enacted in a home setting, and privacy represents a relatively recent phenomenon in social history. Desired privacy levels often come at a price (e.g., first-class air travel), yet services also offer anonymity and refuge in the urban setting. Goodwin provides directions for future research and practice as well.

An equally compelling issue is raised in the chapter by Eileen Fischer, Brenda Gainer, and Julia Bristor: the gendered nature of servicescapes. The authors begin their inquiry with an ambitious question: What makes a servicescape "gendered," and what are the implications of a servicescape being gendered? To explore these issues, they elicit responses to a series of scenarios describing people of one gender entering retail environments we might normally associate with the other gender. Their analysis of the responses reveals that very few tangible physical cues other than the gender of customers and service providers consistently denote a "male" versus a "female" environment; rather, stereotypes associated with the expected gender of people in the setting foster deep-seated beliefs about how a servicescape is gendered. Their analysis also suggests that changing assumptions regarding the gender of a servicescape would require direct confrontation of widespread stereotypes. Simple manipulation of cues in the physical design of space would probably be inadequate.

Our examination of contextual dimensions of the servicescape concludes with Elizabeth Chin's sobering description of the ways in which consumption itself is implicated in perpetuating social inequality. By focusing relentlessly on the perspectives of minority consumers, and those of the stakeholders shaping the experience of these children, she allows us to hear the voice of the "other" over and beyond the literatures in which it is all too often muted. Blending insights from ethnography, history, and political economy, she embeds our understanding of the servicescape in the larger nexus of social institutions and reminds us that our inquiries are the poorer for their failure to explore the landscape of moral geography.

CONCLUDING COMMENTS

This volume unfolds along the lines of an ambitious agenda. The contributors are committed to a discovery-oriented, theory-building program of research into servicescapes. They are motivated by a desire to get substance into play. By providing a range of empirically grounded, conceptually driven, extended case studies, the contributors offer future researchers the kind of critical mass of exemplary studies that will catalyze disciplinary progress. Through thick description and rich interpretation, they expand our current understanding of the minimal parameters of the servicescape in a way that will facilitate future measurement and theory testing. Those chapters tied more loosely to data—the thought-pieces by Baker, Venkatesh, and Iacobucci in particular—provoke exactly such frontier applications, bracketed as they are between studies of particular sites. The thorough documentation of placeways in these markets, and the exploration of these placeways as they ramify throughout consumers' experience, is a novel contribution to our literature. The authors are attuned to the phenomenological crosscurrents in contiguous disciplines that are diffusing gradually into consumer research (Thompson, Locander, and Pollio 1989, 1990; Thompson 1996) and channel this exciting line of inquiry into their quest to understand consumers' experience of place. Beyond their contribution to marketing and consumer research, the authors stand to influence the investigations into placeways afoot in these contiguous disciplines.

The contributors are also wedded to the notion that empirically rigorous and theoretically significant inquiry is indispensable to managerial practice. As we move into the new millennium, it is apparent that "stronger conceptual links between the human sciences and environmental design" are desperately required (Perrin 1970, 107). So also is it apparent that traditional marketing research practices are ineffective in discerning and responding to unarticulated consumer needs (Hamel and Prahalad 1994; Leonard-Barton 1995). In the process of capturing and representing consumers' experiences in a variety of servicescapes, our contributors reveal a wealth of managerial implications and suggest a range of practical applications. Perhaps more importantly, by depicting the experiential dimensions of the servicescape so comprehensively and vividly, they have provided managers with a projectable field for imagining more effectively how particular, local servicescapes might be redesigned not only to enhance consumers' satisfaction but also to prompt delight.

We invite the reader to conduct a dialogue with the authors in the margins of these pages. We encourage the reader to tack between disciplinary and managerial perspectives and to transfer insights from one venue to another as each new servicescape is unpacked. As we celebrate the ingenuity (or lament the illegibility) of servicescape design and the variety of consumption experience, we hope this volume will serve as a stimulus for the reader to become a more introspective, multimodal apprehender of marketplace ambience. In aspiring to return a *sense* of place to the marketing mix, we emphasize that every servicescape is the cocreation of designer, marketer, and consumer.

BIBLIOGRAPHY

ANDERSON, RICHARD. 1991. "Geomancy." In *The Power of Place: Sacred Ground in Natural & Human Environments,* edited by James A. Swan. Wheaton, IL: Quest Books, 191–200.

AUGÉ, MARC. 1995. *Non-places: An Introduction to an Anthropology of Supermodernity.* New York: Verso.

BASSO, KEITH. 1996. "Wisdom Sits in Places: Notes on a Western Apache Landscape." In *Senses of Place,* edited by Steven Feld and Keith Basso. Santa Fe, NM: School of American Research Press, 53–90.

BELK, RUSSELL, ED. 1991. *Highways and Buyways: Naturalistic Research from the Consumer Behavior Odyssey.* Provo, UT: Association for Consumer Research.

BITNER, MARY JO. 1992. "Servicescapes: The Impact of Physical Surroundings on Customers and Employees." *Journal of Marketing* 56(2):57–71.

———. 1993. "Managing Evidence of Service." In *Service Quality Handbook,* edited by Eberhard Scheuing and William Christopher. New York: AMACOM, 358–370.

CAMUS, ALBERT. 1995. *Noces Suivi de l'Eté.* Paris: Editions Gallimard.

CZEPIEL, JOHN; MICHAEL SOLOMON; CAROL SUPRENANT; AND EVELYN GUTMAN. 1985. "Service Encounters: An Overview." In *The Service Encounter,* edited by John Czepiel, Michael Solomon, and Carol Suprenant. Lexington, MA: Lexington Books, 3–15.

FELD, STEVEN, AND KEITH BASSO, EDS. 1996. *Senses of Place.* Santa Fe, NM: School of American Research Press.

GLASER, MILTON. 1985. "I Listen to the Market." In *On Signs,* edited by Marshall Blonsky. Baltimore: Johns Hopkins University Press, 467–474.

HAMEL, GARY, AND C. K. PRAHALAD. 1994. *Competing for the Future: Breakthrough Strategies for Seizing Control of Your Industry and Creating the Markets of Tomorrow.* Cambridge, MA: Harvard Business School Press.

HIRSCH, ERIC, AND MICHAEL O'HANLON. 1995. *The Anthropology of Landscape: Perspectives on Space and Place.* Oxford: Clarendon Press.

JACKSON, MICHAEL. 1996. *Things as They Are: New Directions in Phenomenological Anthropology.* Bloomington: Indiana University Press.

JUKES, PETER. 1990. *A Shout in the Street: An Excursion into the Modern City.* Berkeley: University of California Press.

KLAUS, PETER. 1985. "Quality Epiphenomenon: The Conceptual Understanding of Quality in Face-to-Face Encounters." In *The Service Encounter,* edited by John Czepiel, Michael Solomon, and Carol Suprenant. Lexington, MA: Lexington Books, 17–33.

KOTLER, PHILIP. 1974. "Atmospherics as a Marketing Tool." *Journal of Retailing* 49(4): 48–64.

LEE, JINKOOK, AND MARIA VRYZA. 1994. "The Paradigm of Retailing Revisited: Directions for Theory and Research Development." *Journal of Retailing and Consumer Services* 1(1):53–55.

LEONARD-BARTON, DOROTHY. 1995. *Wellsprings of Knowledge: Building and Sustaining the Sources of Innovation.* Boston: Harvard Business School Press.

LEWIS, RICHARD. 1996. *Absolut Book: The Absolut Vodka Advertising Story.* Boston: Journey Editions.

MARTINEAU, PIERRE. 1958. "The Personality of the Retail Store." *Harvard Business Review* 36 (January–February): 47–55.

MCCRACKEN, GRANT. 1988. *Culture and Consumption: New Approaches to the Symbolic Character of Consumer Goods and Activities.* Bloomington: Indiana University Press.

MICK, DAVID. 1986. "Consumer Research and Semiotics: Exploring the Morphology of Signs, Symbols and Significance." *Journal of Consumer Research* 13(2): 196–213.

NIXON, SEAN. 1992. "Have You Got the Look? Masculinities and Shopping Spectacle." In *Lifestyle Shopping: The Subject of Consumption,* edited by Rob Shields. New York: Routledge, 149–169.

PERRIN, CONSTANCE. 1970. *With Man in Mind: An Interdisciplinary Prospectus for Environmental Design.* Cambridge, MA: MIT Press.

REEKIE, GAIL. 1992. "Changes in the Adamless Eden: The Spatial and Sexual Transformation of a Brisbane Department Store 1930–1990." In *Lifestyle Shopping: The Subject of Consumption,* edited by Rob Shields. New York: Routledge, 170–194.

RELPH, EDWARD. 1976. *Place and Placelessness.* London: Pion Ltd.

RODMAN, MARGARET. 1992. "Empowering Place: Multilocality and Multivocality." *American Anthropologist* 94(3):640–656.

SACK, ROBERT. 1992. *Place, Modernity, and the Consumer's World.* Baltimore: Johns Hopkins University Press.

SCHULTZ, DON; STANLEY TANNENBAUM; AND R. LAUTERBORN. 1994. *The New Marketing Paradigm: Integrated Marketing Communications.* Lincolnwood, IL: NTC Business Books.

SEAMON, DAVID, ED. 1993. *Dwelling, Seeing and Designing: Toward a Phenomenological Ecology.* Albany: SUNY Press.

SHERRY, JOHN F., JR. 1990. "A Sociocultural Analysis of a Midwestern American Flea Market." *Journal of Consumer Research* 17(1):13–30.

————. 1991. "Postmodern Alternatives: The Interpretive Turn in Consumer Research." In *Handbook of Consumer Behavior,* edited by Thomas Robertson and Harold Kassarjian. Englewood Cliffs, NJ: Prentice Hall, 548–591.

————. 1995. "Anthropology of Marketing and Consumption: Retrospect and Prospect." In *Contemporary Marketing and Consumer Behavior: An Anthropological Sourcebook,* edited by John F. Sherry, Jr. Thousand Oaks, CA: Sage, 435–445.

SHERRY, JOHN F., JR., AND MARY ANN MCGRATH. 1989. "Unpacking the Holiday Presence: A Comparative Ethnography of Two Gift Stores." In *Interpretive Consumer Research,* edited by Elizabeth Hirschman. Provo, UT: Association for Consumer Research, 148–167.

SHIELDS, ROB. 1989. "Social Spatialization and the Built Environment: The West Edmonton Mall." *Environment and Planning D: Society and Space* 7: 147–164.

————. 1992. "Spaces for the Subject of Consumption." In *Lifestyle Shopping: The Subject of Consumption,* edited by Rob Shields. New York: Routledge, 1–20.

STOKOLS, DANIEL. 1991. "People-Environment Relations: Instrumental and Spiritual Views." In *The Power of Place: Sacred Ground in Natural & Human Environments,* edited by James A. Swan. Wheaton, IL: Quest Books, 347–360.

THOMPSON, CRAIG. 1996. "Caring Consumers: Gendered Consumption Meanings and the Juggling Lifestyle." *Journal of Consumer Research* 22(4):388–407.

THOMPSON, CRAIG; WILLIAM LOCANDER; AND HOWARD POLLIO. 1989. "Putting Consumer Experience Back into Consumer Research: The Philosophy and Method of Existential Phenomenology." *Journal of Consumer Research* 16(2): 133–146.

————. 1990. "The Lived Meaning of Free Choice: An Existential Phenomenological Description of Everyday Consumer Experiences." *Journal of Consumer Research* 17(3):346–361.

TUAN, YI-FU. 1974. *Topophilia: A Study of Environmental Perception, Attitudes, and Values.* New York: Columbia University Press.

TUCKER, WILLIAM. 1967. *Foundations for a Theory of Consumer Behavior.* New York: Holt, Rinehart and Winston.

UPAH, GREGORY, AND JAMES FULTON. 1985. "Situation Creation in Service Marketing." In *The Service Encounter,* edited by John Czepiel, Michael Solomon, and Carol Suprenant. Lexington, MA: Lexington Books, 255–263.

WERNER, RICHARD. 1985. "The Environmental Psychology of Service Encounters." In *The Service Encounter,* edited by John Czepiel, Michael Solomon, and Carol Suprenant. Lexington, MA: Lexington Books, 101–112.

WILLIAMSON, JANICE. 1992. "Notes from Storyville North: Circling the Mall." In *Lifestyle Shopping: The Subject of Consumption,* edited by Rob Shields. New York: Routledge, 216–232.

WILLIS, SUSAN. 1991. *A Primer for Daily Life.* New York: Routledge.

WILLSHIRE, BRUCE. 1990. "Resistance to Tolerance and Pluralism in World-Community: Otherness as Contamination." *Public Affairs Quarterly* 4(6):189–201.

ZIMMER, MARY, AND LINDA GOLDEN. 1988. "Impressions of Retail Stores: A Content Analysis of Consumer Images." *Journal of Retailing* 64(3):265–293.

ZUCKER, SHARON. 1991. *Landscapes of Power: From Detroit to Disney World.* Berkeley: University of California Press.

PART I

THE BUILT ENVIRONMENT: ELEMENTS OF ATMOSPHERICS

In this section, we lay the groundwork for the kind of interdisciplinary habit of mind required for a holistic inquiry into the built environment of marketplaces. We espouse a hybrid orientation that, while case driven (Lovelock 1984; Bateson 1989), is both theoretically significant (Dunnetal 1992; Lusch et al. 1990) and sensitive to application (Albrecht and Zemke 1985). The chapters are animated by an ethos emerging at the confluence of investigations into environmental psychology (Bonnes and Secchiaroli 1995) and place attachment (Altman and Low 1992). The authors are concerned to wed these inquiries by beginning to integrate a psychosocial view of place with an understanding of person–place interactions. The shift to a more sociocultural comprehension of atmospherics characteristic of the balance of this volume begins in this section.

In providing a practically managerial semiotic primer, Mark Gottdiener reminds marketers that, no matter how exquisitely or erratically humankind may evolve, each consumer embodies the soul of the original *homo narrans* that sets humans apart from other creatures. As hungerers after meaning, people are drawn to the telling of stories; we invest the landscape with meaning and elicit that meaning back again in pursuit of wisdom and entertainment (Basso 1996). Gottdiener speaks of the further differentiation of differentiated places and shows how a process of what might be called "metabranding" makes beacon products and site magnets out of particular locales. In an era of parity products, the symbolic dimension of goods becomes a powerful determinant of choice. The themes and theming process he describes are cultural artifacts beyond their apparent commercial allure. A close reading might reveal them to be a type-and-motif index of contemporary cultural concerns.

Julie Baker demonstrates persuasively how "place" becomes a brand in our era, and emphasizes the irony behind our relative ignorance of the role of environment in shaping preference patterns. She advances the field by showing how a semiotic approach to atmospherics might link productively with more currently mainstream research approaches, and provokes us to imagine the role that simulation techniques might play in our semiotic understanding of marketplaces. Her musings constitute a marketing bridge to the sociological concerns of Gottdiener and the neofuturistic issues raised by Venkatesh later in the volume.

Mike Solomon weaves a semiotic perspective into his account of some of the phenomenological underpinnings of atmospherics. The human body is ultimately the nexus from which our notions of place emerge, and from whence our strategies of directed intervention go forth. Taking a systemic view of the servicescape, Solomon shows how clothing functions semiotically to help integrate messages the marketer sends to consumers. In this regard, he anticipates issues raised by Wallendorf, Lindsey-Mullikin, and Pimentel later in this book. His dramaturgical model allows him to explore the propping of the larger symbolic scene that is the servicescape, and leads him inevitably to consider what may be the most pressing issue in postmodern consumer research: the production of consumption.

Finally, John Sherry explores a phenomenon he calls "emplacement" in his account of a particular local marketplace. Employing phenomenological notions of "brandscape" and "marketworlds" in his discussion of the ways in which marketers and consumers cocreate the environment, Sherry uses ethnography to illustrate the ways in which consumer and servicescape interact. He pays particular attention to the enactment of the built environment and shows how retail theater derives from the interplay of intentional design and emergent behavior. In keeping with the orientation of this section, his chapter grounds the insights of previous chapters in a particular site and anticipates themes and issues raised later in this volume.

It is interesting and ironic to note that, while our understanding of the psychological and ecological contexts of vandalism matures, and as our insights into the motives that inspire destructiveness toward place are translated into intervention strategies (Goldstein 1996), we still have not fielded a comprehensive theory of being-in-places that is essentially prosocial. Nor do we have a set of guidelines that represents the mirror image of the demarketing directives (from target hardening to counseling) employed to safeguard places. Marketers and consumer researchers are poised to contribute to the refinement of "deep" design and "aikido engineering" (Wann 1996) principles by making use of context sensitivity to promote successful person-place interactions that stem from nonresistance to essential properties of the place. Such refinement will occur only when we have accumulated a critical mass of observations of consumers as they currently dwell in marketplaces and consumption sites of the varieties captured in the present volume.

BIBLIOGRAPHY

ALBRECHT, KARL, AND RON ZEMKE. 1985. *Service America! Doing Business in the New Economy.* Homewood, IL: Dow Jones–Irwin.

ALTMAN, IRWIN, AND SETHA LOW, EDS. 1992. *Place Attachment.* New York: Plenum.

BASSO, KEITH. 1996. "Wisdom Sits in Places: Notes on a Western Apache Landscape." In *Senses of Place,* edited by Steven Feld and Keith Basso. Santa Fe, NM: School of American Research Press, 53–90.

BATESON, JOHN. 1989. *Managing Services Marketing.* Hinsdale, IL: Dryden Press.

BONNES, MIRILIA, AND GIANFRANCO SECCHIAROLI. 1995. *Environmental Psychology: A Psycho-Social Introduction.* Thousand Oaks, CA: Sage.

DUNNE, PATRICK; ROBERT LUSCH; MYRON GABLE; AND RANDALL GEBHARDT. 1992. *Retailing.* Cincinnati, OH: South-Western.

GOLDSTEIN, ARNOLD. 1996. *The Psychology of Vandalism.* New York: Plenum.

Lovelock, Christopher. 1984. *Services Marketing.* Englewood Cliffs, NJ: Prentice Hall.

Lusch, Robert; Patrick Dunne; and Randall Gebhardt. 1990. *Retail Marketing.* Cincinnati, OH: South-Western.

Wann, David. 1996. *Deep Design: Pathways to a Livable Future.* Washington, DC: Island Press.

I

THE SEMIOTICS OF CONSUMER SPACES

The Growing Importance of Themed Environments

M. GOTTDIENER

In 1994 over 700,000 people took a tour through Graceland, Elvis Presley's home in Memphis, Tennessee. At the opposite end of the state, in Pigeon Forge, a place hard to find on the map, Dolly Parton enjoyed the visit of the nine-millionth customer to her theme park, Dollywood. These figures represent consumer visits to lesser-known but increasingly significant themed destinations. More familiar examples are the hundreds of millions of tourists passing through the Disneylands and Disney Worlds around the globe, the thirty million people a year visiting Las Vegas casinos, and the large numbers of customers attracted by themed, fully enclosed shopping malls, such as the mega Mall of America located in a suburb of Minneapolis.

Themed environments seem to be everywhere, and most of them are successful as commercial enterprises. There are themed restaurants, malls, airports, hotels, gambling casinos, fast-food courts, sports

M. Gottdiener is Professor of Sociology at the State University of New York at Buffalo. This chapter excerpts and revises material from Chapters 1 and 5 of his book *The Theming of America: Dreams, Visions and Commercial Spaces* (Boulder, CO: Westview/Harper Collins, 1996).

stadiums, and, lately, even themed museums or monuments, like the Holocaust Memorial in Washington, D.C. Personal celebrations, such as weddings, anniversaries, and vacations, increasingly rely on themes. Symbolic motifs vary across a full spectrum, drawing from popular culture in a variety of ways. Sometimes pure themes like the "Wild West" or "tropical paradise" define commercial spaces. At other times, motifs are mixed together in a postmodern pastiche of new combinations, like the decor of the themed restaurant chain Ruby Tuesday's, which features an implosion of popular culture images from the 1920s to the 1940s that might be called "olde-tyme kitsch."

The growing reliance on themes for commercial spaces is relatively recent. Until the 1970s shopping places were recognized by their prestige names or their associations to reputable products or designers, but buildings were, on the whole, austere affairs that stressed functionality and efficiency, not symbolic motifs. People shopped at Gimbel's in downtown New York City because it was a well-known, full-service department store. Today, Manhattan's Gimbel's is gone, and people are as likely to travel to suburban malls for shopping as they are to the central city. In fact, the major portion of retailing sales now occurs in suburban shopping malls, many of which are fully themed environments.

This chapter examines the important shift in commercial spaces to themed milieus. I will show how the dynamics of selling increasingly relies on the help of symbols and images derived from popular culture and mass-media advertising. I will also suggest some reasons why the use of themes is so important today. Cultural and economic factors are both involved in this societal change. To understand the way themes operate in the built environment, it is useful to review the approach of semiotics and some of its key terms, because that approach provides an efficient way of analyzing the role of themes in commercial space (see Gottdiener 1995, 1996).

THE SEMIOTICS OF CULTURE

The subject of semiotics, an inquiry started around the turn of the century, concerns itself with aspects of meaning production and consumption as a function of social processes (see Barthes 1967, 1972; Eco 1976; Peirce 1931; Saussure 1966; Baudrillard 1983; Greimas 1966, 1972; Gottdiener 1995). The basic unit of semiotics is the *sign,* defined conceptually as something that stands for something else and, more technically, as a spoken or written word, a drawn figure, or a material object *unified* in the mind with a particular cultural concept. The sign is this unity of a word/object, known as a *signifier,* with a corresponding, culturally prescribed concept or meaning, known as a signified. Thus, our minds attach the word *cat* or the drawn figure of a cat, as a signifier, to the idea of "cat," that is, a domesticated feline species possessing certain behavioral characteristics. If we came from a culture that did not possess cats in daily life, however unlikely, we would not know what the signifier "cat" means.

Analysts of contemporary society consider our culture increasingly as a *signifying culture* (Baudrillard 1983; Featherstone 1988). This shift can be explained using semiotic analysis. When dealing with objects that are signifiers of certain commodities, cultural meanings, or ideologies of belief, we can consider them not only as signs, but *sign-vehicles.* Signifying objects carry meanings with them. They may purposefully be constructed to convey meaning. Thus, Disneyland, as a theme park, is a large sign-vehicle of the Disney ideology and forms the semantic universe within which the many objects of merchandising with the Disney theme make sense. The sale of such merchandise could *not* proceed without a common subscription to the larger Disney semantic field.

The concept of objects as sign-vehicles, however, has two aspects that are often a source of confusion. When we use a signifier to convey simple information, usually of a functional nature, we *denote* meaning. The word *train,* for example, denotes a mode of transportation or movement. Objects that denote a particular function are called *sign functions.* Every material form within a given culture is a sign of its function and denotes its use. When we approach a building that is a bank, we understand its meaning at the denotative level in terms of its sign function as a repository and transaction space for money.

In addition, every signifier, every meaningful object, conveys other meanings that exist at the *connotative* level; that is, it *connotes* some association defined by social context and social process beyond its denotative sign function. The word *train,* which denotes a mode of transportation, also connotes old-fashioned travel, perhaps "the nineteenth century" by association, maybe a sort of romanticism of travel, even mystery, exoticism, and intrigue as in the Orient Express train. Or, in another vein, it may connote slowness, noise, pollution, crowds, and the like. The bank building, which is the sign function for the activity of "banking" also connotes a variety of socially ascribed associations, including wealth, power, success, future prospects, college educations, and savings for vacations or Christmas. In short, while every sign denotes some social function and conveys a social meaning at the denotative level, each also connotes a variety of associations that have meanings within specific cultural contexts. Control of these different interpretations is made possible by an underlying structure or symbolic universe that ties together signifiers and associated meanings.

Semioticians refer to this underlying interpretive domain as the *code.* The code is a commonly held ideology that legitimates the valorization of objects or discourse. It is especially important to the process by which material artifacts are turned into objects of desire and commodified by advertising discourse and the mass media. The codified ideology, or semantic field, defined by media and advertising discourse creates a social context for consumption and entices people to participate in some larger lifestyle that is fashionable or desirable by association with the commodified object. Thus, behind both consumption and our popular, mass culture lies a society whose everyday life depends on active signification and the conversion of objects or discourse into sign-vehicles of desire.

Thus, sign-vehicles that are material objects and their respective codes can operate on many social levels. The restaurant chain Planet Hollywood articulates diner food with the entire symbolic world of the American cinema. This is a form of connotation writ large that helps explain the popularity or appeal of the chain, as well as its more specific association to particular Hollywood superstars, like Sylvester Stallone. Thus, the themed environment draws on the code of Hollywood by association, thereby valorizing its location as a desirable place. Customers of the chain not only consume typical diner fare such as hamburgers, but are situated in a larger phenomenological universe of fantasy with the aura and cachet of Hollywood super-stardom. All of these semantic operations are performed with an economy of concept by the multilayered aspects of signification unified by codified ideology that underlies the system of connotation.

Understanding the dual nature of signs and their function as sign-vehicles for semantic fields or codes provides an appreciation for the rich cultural life of objects. It also means that we can understand how material objects are used as signs in the construction of consumer environments that are experiential milieus for consumption. Rather than considering objects as signs, that is, as existing exclusively in the mind of the interpreter, we also consider signs as objects, as material forms that are used and manipulated by social processes, especially advertising and commercial marketing. The first is associated with the act of consuming a themed environment, while the latter two concern the way business interests use themes that can have many interpretations as the overarching shell for comfortable places to spend money. Both processes operate simultaneously depending on the point of reference. Given a large enough semantic field, such as the world of high fashion, rock music, or Hollywood, commercial representations deriving their decor from these sources can both stimulate and accommodate a wide variety of personal fantasies responded to by consumers—another reason for the success of themed environments.

THEMED MILIEUS: SOME EXAMPLES

Theming of built environments is important in applications from restaurant franchising to fully enclosed shopping malls, theme parks, and Las Vegas casinos. In these latter cases, uses for motifs are realized in the creation of a consumer space on a large scale with multiple functions.

The Themed Restaurant

Until quite recently, Americans rarely ate in restaurants. The norm was to cook meals at home. Dining out was reserved for special occasions. Eating at the local community diner was an exception to this practice, because it offered a substantial breakfast or meat-and-potatoes lunch at a reasonable price. Frequenters of diners were mainly people on the move, such as truck drivers, traveling salespeople, and deliverymen, or single adults, especially males or "bachelors," who did not have families. The roadside diner was an important place during the 1930s and '40s, at the first blossoming of our now-mature automobile culture.

Many of these structures were simple affairs that restricted their advertising to the daily specials. They counted on traffic and the sparsity of competition to bring customers their way. Nevertheless, a few of these establishments exploited advertising in competition for business, and some managed to develop thematic devices. One classic case was the original McDonald brothers' roadside hamburger stand located on Route 66 just west of San Bernardino, California. The brothers embellished their simple diner with a golden logo in the shape of a large *M*. Over the years, as the original stand grew into a multinational, multibillion-dollar corporation under new, franchise-thinking owners, this arched logo would undergo many stylistic transformations as it melded with the *theme* of the "McDonald's" experience.

As Venturi, Brown, and Izenour (1972) observed, the diner is essentially a simple shed adorned with symbols. The *decorated shed* became the forerunner of many of the fast-food franchises of today. Now competition among franchises or restaurants, increasing affluence, and new consumer norms that support frequent meals outside the home have pushed eating establishments into the use of thematic devices in more complex ways. Not simply decorated sheds anymore, some restaurants offer totally themed environments where the exterior and interior all draw signs from the same code. Typical of the new trend are the dining places constructed by the Specialty Restaurant Corporation (Wright 1989). That company often renovates failed factories, such as the one that housed the Cannery Restaurant of Newport Beach, California, which operated from 1921 to 1966 preparing seafood until pollution from suburbanization forced it to closure. The interior of the factory was gutted and converted into a restaurant. Instead of throwing out the original machinery, however, the designers recycled it as sculpture. Artifacts from the manufacturing process have become part of the decor. Thematic elements unified around the motif of the local fishing industry, such as photographs, ships' compasses, and navigational equipment, are pinned to the walls. Employees dress in uniforms that recall a version of the 1920s. Aspects of the cannery motif therefore pervade the entire space as a totally themed environment. Of course, the current cannery is only a simulation—not a real fish-processing plant, but a fish restaurant disguised as a factory.

Perhaps the best-known fully themed franchise is the Hard Rock Cafe concept, which started in England. Catering to young adults and serving comparatively simple meals centering on the staple of hamburgers and french fries, this restaurant chain has become so successful that it can be found in the capital cities of several countries, and recently a Hard Rock Hotel and Casino opened in Las Vegas. The thematic motif of this franchise derives from codes of the rock music industry, including nostalgic elements from its origins in the 1950s. The distinctive theme, fed constantly by the connection to popular music, is developed further by ambitious merchandising made available at all restaurant locations, including sales of Hard Rock Cafe jackets and tote bags, as well as T-shirts with the location on the logo.

Because the totally themed environment proved successful for the Hard Rock Cafe franchise, its form has been copied more recently by other operations, such as Planet Hollywood and the Fashion Cafe. The former derives its theme from Hollywood glitz, while the latter articulates with the world of its supermodel owners. The codified ideology of mass-media industries, such as fashion, cinema, and rock music, are powerful semantic fields that valorize the act of eating simple diner fare. This conversion of space into a sign-vehicle for some valorized, desirable location through theming has now been extended to individual eating places as well.

In the last few years, renovations of existing restaurants by noted interior designers have spawned a new type of theming called "imagist architecture" ("Feast Your Eyes" 1994). One of its exponents, Chicago designer Jordan Mozer, is known for his fantastic, kinetic interiors that turn restaurants into representations. His

Vivere restaurant in Chicago has been described as "a dizzying baroque symphony of dancing mosaics, huge sculpted copper spirals, custom-blown glass lamps, and a squid shaped iron gazebo that houses the host station" (Allen 1994, 93). For all its powerful Gaudi-influenced shapes, Mozer's design logic for Vivere was based on a single theme, the rise to prominence of the restaurant's owners as represented by a spiral motif that is repeated throughout the interior. "It's the basis for columns, chandeliers and other light-fittings, for an entry gazebo and as inlays in the granite bartop" ("Feast Your Eyes" 1994, 18). Similarly, his Iridium restaurant in the Lincoln Center area of Manhattan was inspired by the theme of music as represented synesthetically in forms deriving from kinetically portrayed musical notes, as well as instruments and the ballet.

In short, while there have always been restaurant interiors that took their corporate symbols, such as the arches of McDonald's, and converted interiors into representations referencing these logos, now there are more ambitious and better-developed examples of eating places that consciously mine popular culture forms from Hollywood, the rock industry, fashion, or the kinetic world of cartoons for thematic inspirations that are consistently carried out from the exterior to the interior. Or as architect Mozer states, "It's all about an image. There are totally different types of images appropriate for a business. . . . The design makes these people money" (Allen 1994, 93).

The marketing of a restaurant as a thematic environment also deploys aspects of merchandising to attract customers. Fast-food places often run promotions by providing special gifts that reflect corporate motifs or representative characters. Even when not engaging in special promotions, themed restaurants carry through their coordinated designs down to their napkins, plates, cups, and table decor. As we have seen for the Hard Rock Cafe or Planet Hollywood, they may also extend merchandising to clothing such as T-shirts and jackets, which become lucrative areas of sales in their own right. In addition, stores play themed background music that may match the connotations of their motifs. They spruce up menus with designs that represent restaurant symbols or logos, like illuminated medieval manuscripts. And, finally, they may carry interior design to the extremes of imagist architecture, as in Mozer's Vivere and Iridium.

The Themed Mall

Like the restaurants I have discussed, malls vary by the extent to which they carry through thematic designs. Yet they, too, increasingly use overarching motifs, as some codified ideology, to coordinate design schemes within the large space. As we have seen, restaurants compete with each other for cash customers. Malls began, however, not in competition with other malls, because only recently have they proliferated, but with the downtowns of cities that once were the sole centers of department store retailing. Consequently, they had to advertise themselves as a place to go within the expanding metropolitan region, and they still do. This kind of advertising for a particular space or site within an urban region is aimed at attracting customers to the location within the metro area of the mall itself. As a particular destination, malls require some overarching means of identification. Consequently, they often adopt an image meant to be attractive to potential consumers, who always have the choice of where to shop. In this way they are different from the city downtown, which is not a unified commercial space and rarely advertises itself as a location.

There is another reason why malls adopt a unified image. While the central city remains a public space that allows free interaction among a variety of people for any number of purposes, the mall is a highly regulated, private commercial space that is expressly designed to make money. This instrumental function of the mall, for realizing capital, must be disguised because it would not be attractive to consumers. As a result, almost every mall has an overarching motif that attempts to portray it as a unique and desirable location for its own sake. As with restaurants, the mall theme is a simulation, a facade, but as a motif for the entire space, it sets the symbolic tone for the interior and becomes a codified ideology to which other store designs can refer.

Malls have been very effective as commercial spaces. They account for over half of all retailing sales in the United States. In many metropolitan areas, competition from malls has been so severe that they forced downtown shopping districts out of existence. Buffalo, New York, for example, has several large, successful suburban malls ringing the central city, but the last big department store located downtown closed in 1995. During the 1960s, suburbanization and mall development were so devastating to central cities that they required large infusions of cash from federal government renewal programs to float schemes that would bring customers back to the downtown. Few of these efforts succeeded.

Suburban malls have changed the nature of retailing competition by introducing the dimension of space. In the past, when central-city department stores dominated all commerce, only individual stores had to advertise. Once suburbanization reached a mass level after World War II and malls were introduced as retailing outlets dispersed within the larger metropolitan region, the downtown of the city became only one location among several alternate destinations for shoppers. Each retailing center, suburban or urban, had to compete with every other center as a specific destination of commuters. Advertising that expresses competition among stores was therefore joined by mall advertising, which expresses competition among the alternate locations of retailing centers. The latter kind of promotion takes the form of thematic appeals that project a special image of their own. Thus, retailing competition over the years has taken on a dimension of spatial competition, and it leads to a greater use of themes. This place competition brought about by the growth of *regional* metropolitan areas is a principal reason for the elaboration of themes in our built environment. In addition, because of place competition, developers have tended to build bigger and bigger malls so that more store possibilities are offered to potential visitors.

The largest mall in the United States is the Mall of America, located in Bloomington, Minnesota, outside Minneapolis. This "megamall" which opened for business on August 21, 1992, is in many ways a separate small city itself. Developers pushed the total environment form a step further by constructing a closed and immense interior space—sometimes called a "hyperspace" because of its size and disorienting qualities (see Jameson 1984). The Mall of America covers seventy-eight acres with over 4 million square feet of floor area, including 2.5 million square feet of actual retailing space. It has over four hundred specialty shops, four large department stores, a fourteen-screen movie theater, nightclubs, bars, nine areas of family entertainment, over twenty-two restaurants, and twenty-three more fast-food outlets. But that is not all. At the center of this three-story complex, beneath an immense hyperspace of skylights, mall developers located a seven-acre theme park that is run by Knotts Berry Farms of southern California. The park has trees and bushes, a controlled climate, twenty-three amusement rides including a roller coaster, fourteen places to eat, high-tech virtual reality simulations, and an overarching theme of "Camp Snoopy," which was imported from the Knotts Berry Farm theme park.

Promotional literature for the megamall claims that it is as big as eighty-eight football fields, can contain twenty of Rome's St. Peter's Basilicas, and is five times as large as the famous Red Square in Moscow. According to its Canadian developers, the megamall site in Minnesota was chosen among alternatives in several states because of key factors including the presence of 27 million people in the surrounding region and a household income that is above the national average. In addition, local governments put up over $100 million in transportation upgrades for the surrounding area, including the construction of large multistoried parking ramps.

The Mall of America cleverly ties its overarching theme to the grand symbol "America." Developers made up the exterior facade in stars and stripes with a color scheme of red, white, and blue. This patriotic motif functions as a grand form of codified ideology that can mean many things to many different people. Consequently, it serves as a consummate mass-marketing device. Ironically, the original developers of the mall were Middle Eastern immigrants to Canada, but that did not prevent them from feeding an "all American" simulation to the hungry United States consumers of the Minneapolis–St. Paul region.

The interior of the megamall articulates the polysemic patriotic theme with others shaping the major shopping sections. Hence the interior space consists of an implosion of codes ranging from the overarching motif to the individual themes of franchise shops.

Restaurants within the immense space are also often like the ones analyzed in the last section with individual themes of their own. Most of them are chain franchises such as Hooters (featuring skimpily clad waitresses), Tony Roma's (a chain of rib restaurants), Ruby Tuesday's (discussed earlier), Fat Tuesday (a Mardi Gras motif emphasizing frozen drinks), the Alamo Grill (Southwestern food), the California Cafe (a simulation of southern California style), and Gators (another diner food chain), among others. Each of these themes relates to the others only in the loosest possible sense, but they have in common a source in the mythologies of mass media and advertising that have valorized over the years certain distinct images, such as "California," "the Southwest," and "home-style cooking," which are sign-vehicles that differentiate in representation one franchise from another, even if the food they all offer remains roughly the same.

Retailing activities within the mall subdivide space into four main areas. Each one encodes a particular overarching motif. However, as a constructed space, they all have in common a re-creation of some version of an urban milieu as the referential codified ideology of their sign systems. The motif of city, pedestrian life pervades the symbolic visions of the different mall sections. It seems that malls cannot escape from their main competitor—the downtown, public space of the classic central city. The four shopping areas of the Mall of America are North Garden: Main Street, USA; West Market; South Avenue; and East Broadway.

The mall's inaugural brochure describes the North Garden area as follows:

> This lushly landscaped, serpentine walk extends from the venerable Sears to the eagerly awaited Nordstrom. With plant-covered balconies, wooden trellises, gazebos, bridges and airy skylights, North Garden is Main Street, USA (Mall of America 1992, 10).

Why North Garden is like a typical main street of the United States is not at all clear from the brochure's description, but the mall promoters make that connection anyway because their underlying referent is the ideology of pedestrian, city life.

The second area, West Market, is a simulated representation of a European-style marketplace: "From Nordstrom to Macy's, West Market bustles like an old-fashioned European marketplace. You'll make your way past a variety of carts, street venders, shops and eateries to the fancifully painted shop fronts" (Mall of America 1992, 11).

In the brochure's description of the third area, South Avenue, the urban metaphor continues. The brochure says, "This upscale promenade between Macy's and Bloomingdale's just might become the Rodeo Drive of the Twin Cities. Its sophisticated storefronts recall the great shopping streets of Europe" (Mall of America 1992, 12). With this description we reach the realm of postmodern, mixed references and geographical confusion, as South Avenue implodes Beverly Hills and European streets. More importantly, it is possible to ask whether the place in the mall called South Avenue is that distinct from another place in the mall called West Market, and whether, in fact, the entire mall description as recalling or representing a type of place or specific "placeness" of some kind merely exists as advertising discourse with no real basis in reality. Like other malls that manufacture a sense of place using simulated facades, spatial difference is a creation of discourse rather than true changes in physical location. Hence, the mall interior is an excellent example of the way interior simulations function to create a culture dominated by the process of signification in the production of difference.

Finally, the last area of the mall is known as East Broadway: "From Bloomingdale's to Sears, this upbeat district features sleek storefronts, bright lights and the latest looks from the hottest shops" (Mall of America 1992, 15). At last we have escaped the European street. What we find ourselves in, however, is just as amorphous in description and just as hard to pin down as the other sections.

It is clear, in fact, that the ambience of the Mall of America is produced less by careful simulation of city street scenes from the United States or Europe than by general designs meant to create an urban ambience of pedestrian traffic within a marketplace. The motifs of the different sections are only vague simulations of places, such as European streets, but they fit in with the style of stores located in each of the four sections. Hence they have a second purpose: to serve as the underlying thematic code referencing the individual stores within the separate areas of the gigantic hyperspace. Thus, two large department stores, Sears and Nordstrom, dominate North Garden; West Market contains several small shops and places to eat besides the department stores; South Avenue is denoted as the "upscale" section of the mall with the most expensive stores; and East Broadway possesses shops specializing in glitter, current fashions, and more youthful clothes. A semiotics of this mall, then, points to thematic space as serving two functions: First, it is a grand metaphor for the re-creation of a pedestrian, urban milieu. Second, it is a series of overarching codes that organize through some vague associations the different retailing sections of the mall.

Despite its sometimes overreaching metaphors that try to connect with urban spaces in real cities, this mall's decor is only a thinly veiled disguise for what is essentially an immense indoor commercial shopping area. This is true of other malls, too. The grand themed environment of the mall functions as a sign-vehicle that aids its role as a container of many commercial enterprises because it is also attractive as a desirable destination itself. What makes the Mall of America different are its large scale and overabundance of family entertainment opportunities, including the seven-acre theme park. The mall represents a consummate linkage between retailing and the effort to attract families in competition with the downtown of the city, which has little family entertainment of its own. This mall is a totally themed environment, but its motifs, as is the case for other malls as well, are subservient to the principal need of conformity with the decors of its tenant shops. Commercialism, not the overarching themes of the classical city (i.e., religion, cosmology, or politics), dominates the *contemporary* mall form.

Las Vegas

Recently, marketing analysts have become interested in the growth of a signifying environment and the way it is changing the consumer experience. In the preceding discussions, I have explained this emergence as principally a consequence of the regional development of our urban areas and the resulting increase in *spatial* competition among competing commercial interests in a society that is automobile-oriented and dominated by mass culture. Some consumer analysts, such as Firat and Venkatesh (1995), however, see something much larger at work, namely, a fundamental shift in the entire social structure from a "modernist" to a "postmodernist" epoch. While these authors correctly identify the present as a condition where cultural, symbolic, and signifying practices are as important to an understanding of daily life as political and economic concerns, they contradict themselves when they also define the present in terms of epochal change based strictly on cultural transformations.

Since the original publications heralding the emergence of the postmodern turn in culture (Jameson 1984), in philosophy (Lyotard 1984), and in architecture (Jencks 1987), there has been a veritable cottage industry of academic production proclaiming the new age of the postmodern (for some examples, see Borgmann 1992; Featherstone 1991; Nicholson 1990; Harvey 1989; Hirschman and Holbrook 1992; Lash 1991; Seidman 1991). Adding to this chorus, Firat and Venkatesh are Johnny-come-latelies. More curiously, their argument is self-contradictory. They claim that postmodernist ways of thinking are more useful than the modernist approach it has superseded because the latter always framed ideas in overly drawn dichotomies, such as subject/object, production/consumption, and the like. Firat and Venkatesh prefer postmodernism because it subverts dichotomies and dwells on complexities that cannot be expressed as clear antinomies. But their argument extolling the virtues of postmodernism not only ignores many important criticisms of its features that have been published since the 1980s (see Dickens and Fontana 1994; Norris 1990; Best and Kellner 1991; Baumann 1992, to name just a few), it also relies on a strictly drawn dichotomy of its own. Namely, in a very *un*postmodern argument, Firat and Venkatesh use a totalizing discourse to draw a strict distinction between some alleged historical period, called the "modern," that has been superseded at present by another epoch, called the "postmodern." Most cultural analysts, in distinction to these authors, now argue that there are many manifestations of modernism, just as there are of postmodernism, and that it is neither justifiable to periodize social development through cultural changes in these terms, nor to suggest, as they do, that some totalizing complex called postmodernism should be privileged over modernism. The modern and the postmodern interpenetrate and are realized materially in society only in varying degrees and with varying results, some good, some bad.

Furthermore, the principal attractiveness of many contemporary aspects of the built environment is not that they are conscious efforts at expressing some totalizing ideology that might be called "postmodern" in contradistinction to another epochal aesthetic called "modern," but that they have consciously ignored the tenets of high modernism entirely because of a practical need to explore the functional use of symbols and signage in material space simply for commercial purposes. In this sense, themed environments may be termed antimodern or nonmodern (see Gottdiener 1995, Ch. 6), rather than encoding an intentional propagation of some "postmodern" aesthetic.

Perhaps the example par excellence of a nonmodernist environment is Las Vegas, because it has been constructed since the 1940s as if modernism never existed. Las Vegas architecture used signs and themes long before they were ever identified as harbingers of a new environmental "postmodernism." Its casinos are perfectly functional spaces for the accumulation of cash that also celebrate popular culture themes in a thoroughly signifying milieu. The purpose of Las Vegas architecture has always been commercial, and its forms are all functional adaptions to the need of attracting customers in a strip-zoned highway culture.

According to modernist architectural theory, structures express meaning through the characteristics of form rather than through symbol and allusion. Buildings are sign-vehicles of their social function. In their spectacularly prescient book *Learning from Las Vegas,* Venturi, Brown, and Izenour (1972) observe that Vegas architecture represents a vernacular idiom based on commerce, the automobile, and the need to advertise from the roadside because the struggle for customers is highly competitive.

The Las Vegas casino environment is a multidimensional system of signs drawing inspiration largely from the symbols of Hollywood kitsch. The entire city is saturated by theming. Both the built forms and the messages they intend to convey are highly developed and articulated as intentional symbols. Signs exist everywhere. They direct traffic off the main interstate highway to the streets on which the various hotel/casinos are located. They advertise individual casinos and their attractions, such as food and headliner entertainment. The signs also amuse through computer-generated electronic light displays. Unlike the "hyposignificant" urban spaces produced by modernism, the built environment of Las Vegas is overendowed with signification and meaning, but its signs are always functionally connected to its commercial goals.

This symbolic environment fits the needs of an automobile-dominated landscape with immense distances and high-speed travel "where the subtleties of pure architectural space can no longer be savored" (Venturi, Brown, and Izenour 1972, 153). The vast spaces of the desert-dominated Southwest with its fast-paced interstate highways require a commercial environment with "explicit and heightened symbolism" composed of "watts, animation, and iconology" (p. 19). The function of the Las Vegas themed environment is rather straightforward, namely, the seduction of the consumer. Las Vegas is a multidimensional experience of seductive pleasures—money, sex, food, gambling, nightlife. Vegas constitutes a specialized space; it is one of several global "pleasure zones," such as Monte Carlo, the French Riviera (Riviera and Monte Carlo are also the names of Las Vegas casinos), the Greek islands, Rio de Janeiro (also the name of a Las Vegas casino), Walt Disney World, Marienbad, and the Taj Mahal. According to Venturi and associates,

> Essential to the imagery of pleasure-zone architecture are lightness, the quality of being an oasis in a hostile context, heightened symbolism, and the ability to engulf the visitor in a new role: vacation from everyday reality (p. 53).

Las Vegas as a whole signifies a contrast from the blandness of Southwest suburban environments, such as Los Angeles, and the heat of the desert:

Signs in Las Vegas use mixed media—words, pictures, and sculpture—to persuade and inform. A sign is contradictorily, for day
and night. The same sign works as polychromic sculpture in the
sun and as black silhouette against the sun; at night it is a source
of light. It revolves by day and becomes a play of lights at night.
It contains scales for close up and distance. . . . Day is negated
inside the casinos and night negated on the Strip (pp. 51, 77).

Beyond the uniqueness of Las Vegas as a fully themed environment, the individual casinos develop motifs and possess concor-
dant sign systems that express some of the most vivid fantasies of
American culture. Advertisements for Las Vegas casino/resorts
develop these fantasy themes through signs, sculptures, and three-
dimensional light and sound shows that are often incredibly elaborate. Fantasy themes are developed through language and pictures
that connote a specific ideology or set of cultural meanings relating to the announced theme. The metaphorical relation is both
declared as a unifying motif exploited within the interior of the
casino and developed as a particular set of connotations by the
design of the exterior or facade of the casino/hotel. The various
themes of Vegas casinos derive, for the most part, from underlying
codes that are inspired by visions from the Hollywood cinema.
Thus, there are Wild West casinos (the Golden Nugget, the Four
Queens, the Frontier), an Arabian code (the Dunes, the Sands, the
Sahara, Aladdin), a tropical paradise code (the Rio, the Tropicana,
the Mirage), and a classical code (Caesars Palace, the Luxor), among
others.

Most hotel/casinos are totally themed environments. For example, Caesars Palace has an exterior designed as an immense Roman
villa. This motif is carried forward throughout the interior design
elements, which always refer to a fantasy version of Rome. Even the
cocktail waitresses wear a uniform that recalls that style. Both the
interior and exterior, therefore, are themed by one motif. Near Caesars is the Mirage Hotel and Casino, another place with a totally
themed environment, namely, "tropical paradise." The motif is
developed by the re-creation of a tropical rain forest in the lobby
and a large exploding volcano display that occurs outside every fifteen minutes. The tropical theme seems a contradiction because the

resort's name, Mirage, signifies a desert phenomenon. But, in Las Vegas, no one seems to care.

The literal signs and themed exteriors of Las Vegas economically convey to both pedestrians and the occupants of passing cars the complexity of fantasy motifs and the rapid-fire transmission of distinct messages that simultaneously denote specific forms of information, such as the contents of a meal and its price, and connote thematic associations, such as the invitation to participate in a Hollywood fantasy. In this milieu, the close connection between commercial competition that is spatially structured and the explicit need for themes, which I have discussed in the case of restaurants and malls, becomes clearest.

The Las Vegas gambling economy is situated within structures that are combinations of casinos, hotels, and, often, resorts. Most of the spectacular resort/casinos are located on the north-south route of Las Vegas Boulevard, also known as "the Strip," because of the need for sprawling space. The downtown area, or "Glitter Gulch," is dominated in contrast by casinos specialized for gambling, or hotel/casinos, like the Golden Nugget, that exploit the original theme of Las Vegas as a Wild West paradise.

According to Venturi, Brown, and Izenour (1972), the casino structures are examples of the "decorated shed." They are simple buildings designed for gambling or hotel occupancy that are overlaid by elaborate signs. Decorated and lit up with neon graphics, the Las Vegas casino functions, in fact, as one big sign. Each casino possesses a separate theme, that is, some overarching code or ideology that reflects some desirable fantasy aspect of American culture. The varied thematic devices, with the casino functioning as one large sign of itself, creates an emergent system of signification through difference. Each differentiated casino, as a separate theme, standing juxtaposed against other casinos, produces an overarching intertextuality that is the grand text of Las Vegas, a system of difference at the level of casinos themselves. This grand text does not intend to convey any particular message, but instead becomes the profusion of signs that is the environmental experience of Las Vegas. As owners alter individual casino themes, or when they build new casinos, the system of difference also changes, and the Las Vegas experience becomes more varied and deeply modulated. In this way, the signage of Vegas is similar to that of the mall interior as each commercial establishment competes for customers.

FROM SALES TO MARKETING: THE ECONOMIC BASIS OF THEMING

The preceding examples of restaurants, malls, and casinos show the strong connection between economic needs of retailers deriving from increased competition and the reliance on themed environments in the marketing of commodities. This link is very important in understanding both the function and the increasing use of themed milieus in our society. What is true for restaurants, malls, and casinos also holds for the sale of other commodities. Increasingly, suppliers of all types of consumer products compete with each other through symbolic differences. During the period of early capitalist industrialism, in the eighteenth and nineteenth centuries, economic competition meant competition through production, that is, the need simultaneously to reduce costs and manufacture products in quantity. Today these production criteria remain important, but in addition there is a second aspect—thematic competition or competition through variation in symbols among products in any particular market that are virtually the same.

Clearly, the ability to afford commodities rules the act of consumption, but the use of thematic appeals in marketing also regulates the social process of consuming. Thus, besides the relation of consumers to prices and budgets, which has always underlain individual behavior in a capitalist system, the consumption process also involves the relation between consumers and the motifs of commodity purchasing. Furthermore, the importance of the *symbolic* value of commodities, provided by the social context of mass marketing, has grown considerably over the years. At present, then, the price-consumption link that once dominated consumer choices, is now joined by the symbolic value-consumption link, which involves considerations of a personal, sign-oriented nature in the purchase of consumer goods (Baudrillard 1983). Nineteenth-century, modernist, industrial capitalism has thus evolved from a hypo-significant system, with attenuated or limited symbolic encoding of the environment, to a "postmodern," late capitalist, information and service economy that produces a themed culture whose material manifestation is a themed environment (Harvey 1989; Baudrillard 1983; Gottdiener 1996). Due to the importance of motifs in marketing, the current economy is quite different from what it was one hundred years ago. The present global relation between economic processes and the use of themes reflects significant historical changes because of fundamental shifts in the organization of capitalism itself, although epochal change cannot be periodized in terms of culture alone, as some advocates of postmodernism have suggested.

The Role of Symbols or Themes in the Circuit of Capital

A nation of consumers must be fed by appeals to consume even when the goods they are presented with have dubious use-values. Basic human needs are relatively simple and consist, as every third-grade child can attest, mainly of food, clothing, and shelter, not to mention a job that can provide these necessities. The needs pumping up a consumer society, however, extend much beyond these basics, and even the basics are elaborated by the practice of consumption almost beyond recognition from the picture painted for schoolchildren. For example, shelter for most people in the United States means a basic three- or four-bedroom suburban house complete with a fully equipped kitchen and recreation room. Consumers also view the commodities that stock such a "basic" home as "necessities." They desire dishwashers, refrigerators, microwave ovens, conventional ovens, stoves, and assorted electric gadgets in the kitchen, and television sets, videotape players, stereo equipment, CD players, portable phones, leisure furniture, and TV sets in the family room and bedrooms. Many of these commodities are either manufactured abroad or contain components manufactured abroad. The principal task of U.S. consumers, as the economy has shifted away from industrial production, has become one of desiring these goods as necessities that we cannot do without in our daily life.

Thus, as the United States has shifted to a nation of service and information-processing industries, the function of consumption has persisted and grown in importance.

For the most part, the production of desire for such commodities at the intense level that exists in our society depends directly on symbolic mechanisms. Signs and themes play a central role in the proper priming of the consumer society. We have matured into a society possessing a fully themed mass culture. Mass advertising fuels the spending activities of our society through the production of desire. Today's marketing procedures encompass not only the appeals made by advertising, such as those found on TV or in magazines, but also appeals within the built environment itself, that is, in the suburban and city consumerscapes, or the stores and malls that remain responsible for the realization of capital. The key economic relation of the consumer society is not the exchange of money for goods as it was in the nineteenth century, but the link between the promotion of desire in the mass media and advertising, and the commercial venues where goods and services can be purchased. Store environments are but an extension of TV, magazine, and newspaper advertising. They provide material spaces for the realization of consumer fantasies primed by movies, rock videos, the record industry, and commercial advertising; lifestyle orientations from religious, ethnic, racial, or class origins; and even political ideologies propagated in community discourse or at the place of work.

Recently, researchers of consumer behavior have incorporated these societal shifts into their analysis of the new grounds of consumption (Sherry 1995; Costa and Bamossy 1995; Firat and Venkatesh 1995). In particular, the view of consumers as passively manipulated by advertising, and of consumption as a largely destructive process secondary to production have been abandoned in favor of a perspective that appreciates the creative aspects of consumption, given the new realities of a media-driven, image-driven society:

> Consumption is not the end, but a moment where much is created and produced. It is not a personal, private act of destruction by the consumer, but a very social act wherein symbolic meanings, social codes, political ideologies, and relationships are produced and reproduced (Firat and Venkatesh 1995, 251).

In short, the changed view of consumer behavior relies on a changed view of society—one that emphasizes the semiotic nature of social life.

The new economic realities of a consumer-oriented economy derive from the crisis base of capitalism that is, above all, a crisis in the realization of capital among highly competitive global producers. While most of the countries in the world possess immense productive capacity, their development depends on the ability of corporations to sell goods and services after they are produced. Increasingly, the problem of capital realization is solved through the creation of image-driven, themed environments that are attractions themselves but also contain outlets for the sale of commodities. People today consume symbols and environments along with goods and services. For the most part, this commercial universe melds seamlessly with the mediascape of popular culture programming on TV and in magazines, advertising, Hollywood films, and the rock music industry.

If the increasing use of themed environments can be explained as a response to the realization problem of capital, its implementation has occurred through changes in marketing since the 1970s. Retailing was once dominated by prestige department stores centrally located in the downtown sections of cities. As cities themselves have declined since the 1950s as places to live for the affluent middle class, the commercial functions of their downtowns have also deteriorated. Suburban malls, in contrast, have enjoyed remarkable success during this same period.

Malls are themed consumer environments that attract people to their location in competition with other locations, and not necessarily to specific stores. They provide a certain experience that derives from our highly developed, image-driven, commodity-driven, popular culture. The environment of the mall is an engineered extension of mass advertising and mass media; so, too, are theme parks, like Disneyland, and the many Las Vegas casinos that derive their inspiration from the most hackneyed clichés of Hollywood cinema. In this sense, commercial retailing, advertising, and mass media meld together to produce our contemporary culture. The world of commerce increasingly transpires within mass-mediated settings that are thematic and entertaining in their own right, although competition between separate locations remains.

Themed environments work not only because they are connected to the universe of commodities, but because they offer consumers a spatial experience that is an entertaining attraction. People may go to the mall to shop, but they also go there to see and be seen. For this reason future changes will not only involve fashionable shifts in the content of desirable images, but also changes in the types of environments offered to consumers as entertainment in conjunction with retailing.

BIBLIOGRAPHY

ALLEN, T. 1994. "The Shapes of Things to Come." *Chicago Magazine* (December): 93–95, 124–126.

BARTHES, ROLAND. 1967. *Elements of Semiology.* New York: Hill and Wang.

———. 1972. *Mythologies.* New York: Hill and Wang.

BAUDRILLARD, J. 1983. *Simulations.* New York: Semiotext(e).

BAUMAN, Z. 1992. *Intimations of Postmodernity.* London: Routledge.

BEST, S. 1991. *Postmodern Theory.* New York: Guilford.

BORGMANN, A. 1992. *Crossing the Postmodern Divide.* Chicago: University of Chicago Press.

COSTA, JANEEN, AND GARY BAMOSSY. 1995. *Marketing in a Multicultural World: Ethnicity, Nationalism and Cultural Identity.* Thousand Oaks, CA: Sage.

DE SAUSSURE, FERDINAND. 1966. *Course in General Linguistics.* New York: McGraw-Hill.

DICKENS, D., AND A. FONTANA. 1994. *Postmodernism and Social Inquiry.* New York: Guilford Press.

ECO, UMBERTO. 1976. *A Theory of Semiotics.* Bloomington, IN: Indiana University Press.

"Feast Your Eyes." 1994. *Designweek* (April): 18–19.

FEATHERSTONE, M. 1991. *Consumer Culture and Postmodernism.* London: Sage.

FIRAT, A., AND A. VENKATESH. 1995. "Liberatory Postmodernism and the Reenchantment of Consumption." *Journal of Consumer Research* 22 (December): 239–267.

GOTTDIENER, M. 1995. *Postmodern Semiotics: Material Culture and Signs of Postmodern Life.* Oxford: Blackwell.

———. 1996. *The Theming of America.* Boulder, CO: Westview.

GREIMAS, ALGIRDAS. 1966. *Semantique Structurale.* Paris: Larousse.

———. 1976. *Semiotique et Science Sociale.* Paris: Seuil.

HARVEY, D. 1989. *The Condition of Postmodernity.* Oxford: Blackwell.

HIRSCHMAN, E., AND M. HOLBROOK. 1992. *Postmodern Consumer Research: The Study of Consumption as Text*. Newbury Park, CA: Sage.

JAMESON, F. 1984. "Postmodernism, or the Cultural Logic of Late Capitalism." *New Left Review* 146:53–92.

JENCKS, CHARLES. 1987. *What Is Postmodernism?* New York: St. Martin's.

LANGDON, P. 1994. *A Better Place to Live*. Amherst: University of Massachusetts Press.

LASH, S. 1991. *Sociology of Postmodernism*. London: Routledge.

LYOTARD, J-F. 1984. *The Postmodern Condition*. Minneapolis: University of Minnesota Press.

MALL OF AMERICA. 1992. *Guide*. Minneapolis: Mall of America.

NICHOLSON, L. 1990. *Feminism/Postmodernism*. New York: Routledge.

NORRIS, C. 1990. *What's Wrong with Postmodernism*. Baltimore, MD: Johns Hopkins University Press.

PEIRCE, CHARLES S. 1931. *Collected Papers*. Edited by P. Weiss and C. Hartshone. Cambridge, MA: Harvard University Press.

PIORE, M., AND C. SABEL. 1984. *The Second Industrial Divide*. New York: Basic Books.

SEIDMAN, S. 1991. "The End of Sociological Theory: The Postmodern Hope." *Sociological Theory* 9 (Fall): 131–146.

SHERRY, JOHN F., JR. 1995. *Contemporary Marketing and Consumer Behavior: An Anthropological Sourcebook*. Thousand Oaks, CA: Sage.

VENTURI, R.; D. S. BROWN; AND S. IZENOUR. 1972. *Learning from Las Vegas*. Cambridge, MA: MIT Press.

WEISS, M. 1988. *The Clustering of America*. New York: Harper and Row.

WRIGHT, T. 1989. "Marketing Culture, Simulation and the Aesthetization of Work and War." Unpublished manuscript, Department of Sociology and Anthropology, Loyola University of Chicago.

2

EXAMINING THE INFORMATIONAL VALUE OF STORE ENVIRONMENTS

JULIE BAKER

A few years ago Motherhood Maternity, a national chain of maternity boutiques, remodeled several of its stores. According to the national sales director, customers she spoke with perceived that the remodeled stores had all-new merchandise. In reality, however, the stores contained essentially the same inventory they had before the remodeling effort ("Motherhood Adopts a Fashion Look" 1985).

The Motherhood Maternity example highlights that consumers' evaluations and decisions are based upon their perceptions, and what they perceive is heavily influenced by the informational cues that marketers communicate to them (Tom et al. 1987). One entity that allows marketers to provide these cues to consumers is the physical environment of goods and services retailers (hereafter referred to as the store environment). Since many consumers make decisions at the point of purchase (Keller 1987), the store environment is a critical aspect of the decision-making process. Indeed, point-of-sale creativity is considered a must for retailers who want to remain competitive (Pierce 1985).

Julie Baker is Assistant Professor in the Department of Marketing, University of Texas at Arlington.

Since Kotler (1973) introduced the "atmospherics" concept, a number of researchers have empirically examined the effects of the store environment. Most of these studies have taken an affective perspective, which assumes that consumers' emotional reactions to a store environment influence their browsing or purchasing behavior (e.g., Bellizzi and Hite 1992; Donovan and Rossiter 1982; Donovan et al. 1994; Hui and Bateson 1991). A few studies have examined the cognitive aspects of way finding, which focus on how consumers find their way through retail environments (e.g., Mittelstadt, Grossbart, and Curtis 1977; Titus and Everett 1995), and several have addressed the behavioral consequences of varying store environment elements such as color (Bellizzi, Crowley, and Hasty 1983), music (Milliman 1982; 1986), and scent (Spangenberg, Crowley, and Henderson 1996).

Few studies, however, have investigated the store environment from an informational perspective, one category of internal consumer response to the environment suggested by Bitner (1992). Because store environments, like price and advertising, can provide critical information to consumers in the process of evaluating goods or services (hereafter referred to as products), it is important to develop a theoretical base from which researchers can begin to study this important influence on decision making.

The purpose of this chapter is to examine a number of theories that support the informational value of store environments. The moderating influences of several situational and individual characteristics are also explored. The chapter ends with a discussion of research issues and managerial implications.

THE INFORMATIONAL VALUE
OF THE STORE ENVIRONMENT

For purposes of this chapter, the store environment is defined as a building or physical structure and all that is contained within that structure. Store environment elements (cues) can be categorized as ambient cues (background elements such as scent, music, temperature), aesthetic-design cues (color, architectural style, decor), functional-design cues (layout, signage), and social cues (customers and employees in the store) (Baker 1986).

Five theoretical frameworks were chosen as appropriate for studying the informational value of the store environment. These theories all suggest, in similar yet unique ways, the processes by which consumers mentally convert physical stimuli in the store environment into information that will help them in decision making. These theories—information processing, categorization, inference making, semiotics, and information integration—are reviewed to provide a basis for the development of research questions that may stimulate thinking about the cognitive role of the store environment in consumer evaluation.

Information Processing

The information-processing perspective of consumer behavior proposed by Bettman (1979) suggests that individuals engage in external search during a purchasing situation. External search occurs when consumers look for information outside of memory that will help them evaluate product alternatives.

There is conceptual support for the notion that the physical environment supplies important informational cues to consumers (Olson 1977). Mazursky and Jacoby (1986) empirically validated this notion, finding that a picture of a store's interior was the second most heavily accessed type of information respondents used to evaluate merchandise quality. Interestingly, they found that store environment information was used more heavily than was price, a more commonly investigated informational cue in the decision-making literature.

Because an individual is subject to limitations in processing capacity, the attention given to external stimuli is selective; i.e., some stimuli are attended to in preference to others (Bettman 1979). Consumers in an increasingly complex marketplace may not take the time to learn about product attributes, or information about attribute values may not be available. Therefore, by necessity or by choice, they rely on simple, easy-to-examine cues. These cues do not provide specific product information, but consumers use them as the basis for forming inferences about product quality and value (Bloom and Reve 1990). The retail store environment offers a multitude of easily accessible cues to consumers seeking an information-processing shortcut. For example, a luxuriously decorated jewelry store like Corrigan's may cue consumers to expect the merchandise sold there to be of high quality and to be expensive. On the other hand, consumers may expect jewelry sold in a spartanly decorated store like Service Merchandise to be of lower quality and to be correspondingly lower priced.

According to Kahneman (1973), a person's attention can be either voluntary (allocation of processing efforts related to current goals) or involuntary (based on automatic mechanisms). Thus, consumers who attend to store environment cues may do so because they consciously recognize, based on past experience, that these cues offer reliable information about product-related attributes such as quality or price. Alternatively, because the attention process does not always require conscious control, occurring whenever a particular stimulus is present (Bargh 1984), the simple act of entering a store may trigger involuntary attention to environmental cues. Either way, it is important for store managers and designers to understand what these environmental cues are "saying" to consumers.

The information-processing framework suggests some direction for studying the influence of the store environment on decision making. Several illustrative research questions include the following:

- The use of the store environment to aid external information search, while an intuitively appealing concept, has not been well documented empirically. Do consumers use environmental cues to predict and evaluate product offerings? If so, under what conditions are consumers most likely to use these cues?

- How are environmental cues processed and utilized in the decision-making process? Do consumers process the environment holistically, do they process only some key elements (e.g., music or decor), or do they use a combination of the two approaches?

- How important are store environment cues in relation to the other cues consumers may use in the purchase process (e.g., price, location, advertising)?
- What cues in the environment do consumers attend to, and what kind of information do these cues provide?

Categorization

Categorization, a type of knowledge structure, involves the process of comparison between a target stimulus and categorical knowledge that is stored in memory (Cohen and Basu 1987). Categorization is important to consumers' decision-making ability because grouping together objects that are similar not only can enhance information-processing efficiency but can give meaning to novel items or situations. This in turn allows individuals to draw inferences about features and outcomes and to make causal or evaluative judgments (Alba and Hutchinson 1987; Cohen and Basu 1987; Nisbett and Ross 1980).

Once consumers have given some level of attention to store environment cues, they use a mental matching process to place a retail facility into a category (e.g., "high priced") based on a comparison of that facility with a representative example stored in memory (Ward, Bitner, and Barnes 1992). This categorization process may be automatic (Alba and Hasher 1982) and may not provide any strain on mental capacity. The comparison may result from remembering a particular, previously encountered instance (exemplar) or a single prototype that corresponds to the "central tendency" of those instances (Alba and Hutchinson 1987; Cohen and Basu 1987). The categorization process thus enables consumers to use information that is available to them (e.g., environmental cues) as a basis for drawing inferences about possibly missing information (e.g., price, quality) by comparing the target stimulus with their category knowledge.

Representations of product-defined categories and the resulting comparison processes can be shaped by the contextual influences of the choice environment (Cohen and Basu 1987). For example, Grewal and Baker (1994) found that store environment cues influenced consumers' categorization of the price of a product as acceptable or unacceptable.

The notion that consumers structure information in memory in terms of categories has implications for how they evaluate products under conditions when store environment cues and product cues are incongruent. The schema-triggered affect model (Fiske 1982) suggests that when a specific instance (e.g., a product) is congruent with a category (e.g., a store), evaluation will be consistent with the valence of the affect that was originally stored with the category. In turn, positive affect will result from a successful fit between a focal object and a category (Cohen and Basu 1987), resulting in a more positive evaluation of the focal object. For example, a high-quality product sold in an upscale store environment will produce a positive evaluation, as will a lower-quality product sold in a discount store environment.

However, how might a consumer evaluate a high-quality, brand-name product, such as Lancôme cosmetics, displayed in a discount store like Kmart? In this situation, product cues are incongruent with store cues. Would consumers feel good that they are getting the cosmetics at a bargain, or might they feel that these cosmetics are somehow not the same as those sold at Bloomingdale's?

Taylor and Crocker (1981) suggest that categorization schemas serve an interpretive function that defines information that is incongruent. Because categorization reduces uncertainty, incongruent cues may make an individual unable to categorize an object, which may result in negative affect (Cohen and Basu 1987). In addition, when a consumer receives conflicting information from an external source and what is stored in memory, processing is interrupted (Bettman 1979), and the consumer has to expend effort to resolve the inconsistencies, which may lead to negative affect.

Fiske (1982) has shown that under conditions where a schema is evoked but the fit is poor, an ambivalent combination of positive and negative affect about the focal object results. How consumers resolve this ambivalence depends to a large extent on their familiarity with the focal product. "Expert" consumers have more-developed product category knowledge, and they tend to use piecemeal processing, focusing on product- and attribute-related thoughts when faced with a discrepancy between incoming and category information (Sujan 1985). Similarly, Rao and Monroe (1988) found that consumers who are familiar with a product tend to focus on product attributes in their evaluations.

In contrast, "novice" consumers rely on category-based processing more than do experts, regardless of whether the incoming and category information are consistent or discrepant (Sujan 1985). If novices do not have well-developed product category knowledge with which to evaluate the product, they may rely on external cues that are more accessible and understandable (Rao and Monroe 1988). Store environment cues (e.g., bright lighting, linoleum flooring, crowded aisles) may trigger a store category (e.g., discount store) that novice consumers can use to evaluate the products sold there (e.g., low quality).

A number of research questions about the store environment can be derived from categorization theory:

- How do consumers categorize store environments?
- Upon which store environment elements do these categorizations depend?
- What is the process by which consumers categorize products based on the store environment?
- How do consumers evaluate products when there is incongruity between elements of the product and store environment?

Inference Making

Categorization theory suggests that consumers may draw inferences about product offerings based on what they experience in the store environment because it provides an efficient means for them to integrate internal and external information without expending much cognitive effort. Monroe and Krishnan (1985) posited that buyers who lack complete information about product attributes must make choices based on inferences from informational cues that are available to them. Nisbett and Ross (1980) concur, noting that classification of a physical object permits one to confidently predict additional properties of the object, reiterating the importance of category structures in the choice process.

Alba and Hutchinson (1987) proposed that one type of inference that individuals make is based on "correlational rules." Correlational rules form when the perceived correlation between two attributes is so high that the presence of one leads to the strong belief about the value of the other. When a firm rule is formed, an attribute-to-attribute inference is made almost automatically. In the context of the store environment, consumers may believe that when they see Persian rugs on the floor and crystal chandeliers hanging from the ceiling, the store offers expensive, high-quality products, or they will always receive good service. Likewise, a restaurant company discovered that rest room cleanliness was an important factor influencing consumers' perception of the overall quality of its food (Heath 1995).

There is empirical support for the notion that people make inferences from environmental stimuli. Marketing studies have shown that consumers make inferences about the quality, currency, and selection of products based on store information in the form of color, scent, music, and social environment elements (Baker, Grewal, and Parasuraman 1994; Bellizzi, Crowley, and Hasty 1983; Spangenberg, Crowley, and Henderson 1996). Results of a study by Bitner (1990) suggested that when a service failure occurred at a travel agency, consumers more often blamed the agency if its facility was disorganized.

Research in environmental psychology also supports the inference-making role of the physical environment. Sadalla, Vershure, and Burroughs (1987) found that subjects were able to correctly infer a homeowner's self-concept from pictures of that person's dwelling. Similarly, contemporary judges were able to discriminate appropriately among the nineteenth-century homes of different socioeconomic groups, identifying the status of the original owners from photographs of their houses (Cherulnik and Wilderman 1986). Variations in office decor were discovered to influence student evaluations of a faculty member (Campbell 1979), suggesting that respondents are basing their perceptions of an individual upon inferences made from the environment created by that individual. Even people's perception of zoo animals depends upon the environment in which the animals are seen (Finlay, James, and Maple 1988).

The inference-making perspective suggests several avenues for future research:

- Do consumers make inferences about product offerings based upon store environment cues?

- If inferences are made, what are the relationships between specific inferences generated and specific store environment cues (or combinations of store environment cues)?

Semiotics

Semiotics and inference making are related concepts in that both deal with the construction of meaning that goes beyond what is explicitly given. The focus of semiotics, however, is on the analysis of the structures of verbal and nonverbal meaning-producing events (Mick 1986). Sebeok (1976, 1) declares that the scope of semiotics includes "the exchange of any messages whatever and of the systems of signs which underlie them." Consumers may form inferences about product attributes, and possibly even about product use, based on the symbolic meaning they associate with certain store environment cues.

Much of the semiotics-related work that has been done in marketing has focused on product symbolism. Levy (1959) suggested that people purchase and use products for symbolic as well as functional reasons. The symbolic interactionist paradigm in social psychology also acknowledges the symbolic importance of products (Goffman 1959). With this emphasis on the product itself, the meaning associated with where the product is purchased (or consumed, as is the case with many services) has been virtually ignored in the marketing literature.

The semiotic view would propose that the store environment provides symbols that represent what Kotler (1973) calls a "silent language" in communication. These symbols may characterize not only product attributes, but also a broader way of life. For example, a store with marble floors, sparkling light from crystal chandeliers, and muted, fashionable colors may symbolize an elegant lifestyle; consumers buying products in this store can thus vicariously participate in this lifestyle. A Land Rover dealership on Long Island, New York, created an environment that reflects a lifestyle and suggests product use. Sales staff dress in khaki clothing, vehicles rest on slate-and-wood floors accented with compass markings, and a ledge along the ceiling is full of artifacts of the country gentleman—bridles, saddles, and fly rods. The effect is that of an exclusive Ralph Lauren shop. Videotapes of Land Rovers taking on the wilds of Africa play on a large-screen television, even though only 5 percent of four-wheel-drive vehicles ever leave the pavement (Naughton 1995). Customers who buy a Land Rover are "buying" an upscale gentleman's outdoor adventure.

Environmental psychologists provide conceptual support for the symbolic nature of the physical environment (Russell and Ward 1982; Steele and Jenks 1997). For example, the Navajo culture attributes religious significance to the location and orientation of a house (Snyder, Stea, and Sadalla 1976); thus, a place can stand for an idea (Moore 1979).

Empirical research in organizational behavior also supports the symbolic role of the physical environment. Zalesny and Farace (1987) found that a symbolic meaning paradigm explained employees' reactions to changes in their physical work environment from a traditional to an open-plan office: physical surroundings appeared to communicate information about organizational culture and expectations about behavior. Research done by Konar et al. (1982) verified that certain elements in the office environment (such as carpeting) may have a relatively low functional value, but that their importance to worker satisfaction is manifested in the form of symbolic value. A number of environmental features, such as office size and location, have been empirically associated with symbolic status in the workplace (Duffy and Worthington 1976; Halloran 1978; Manning 1965; Sundstrom, Burt, and Kamp 1980).

In marketing, Morrow and McElroy (1981) found that the appearance of a professor's office communicated messages about that professor to students. Bitner (1990) discovered that a disorganized physical environment in a travel agency symbolized lack of efficiency, unprofessionalism, and a lack of care to study respondents. Baker, Berry, and Parasuraman (1988) reported that customers thought an expensive-looking facility meant a bank was inappropriately spending the customers' money.

The semiotic perspective suggests the following research questions:

- What symbolic meanings do consumers associate with various types of store environments?
- How is meaning in the store environment transferred to the products offered in that store?
- Under what conditions do consumers "buy the image" exemplified by the store environment (e.g., for what products, what types of consumers, what types of store environment)?
- How might the symbolic meaning in store or service environments influence employee attitudes and/or behavior?

Information Integration

In Bettman's (1979) information-processing theory, the stage in which consumers acquire and evaluate information is followed by the process of decision making. This stage involves combining and integrating the various pieces of information that consumers have obtained in the search process. Anderson (1981) proposed that thought and behavior depend on the simultaneous action of multiple stimuli. He focused on the cognitive algebra that explains how people combine or integrate psychological information about a stimulus to produce a response.

One issue that can be addressed within the information integration framework is how consumers will weigh various cues in the choice process. Two aspects of cues that will determine how they are weighed in the integration process are their predictive value and their confidence value (Olson 1977). Predictive value (PV) is the degree to which a consumer perceives that a cue is related to or indicative of a product characteristic. Confidence value (*CV*) is the degree to which a consumer is confident of his or her ability to accurately perceive and categorize that cue. Olson (1977) suggests that high *PV* and *CV* cues are likely to be chosen by consumers and to have strong effects on product judgments.

The store environment is likely to provide consumers with cues that are high in *PV* because of category schemas. For example, individuals are likely to predict that a store with linoleum tile floors, exposed fluorescent lighting, and narrow aisles will carry inexpensive, low-quality merchandise, based on their past experience with similar stores. This category schema could even extend across categories of goods or services. A doctor's office with a "discount look" may result in patients expecting a low level of service and low prices.

Store environments are also likely to have high *CV* cues due to the pervasiveness of the store environment that surrounds consumers, aiding attention and perception as they make purchase decisions. Mazursky and Jacoby's (1986) finding that subjects relied more heavily on store environment cues than on several other available cues (including price) in their assessments of product quality suggest that these cues had high *CV.*

Thus, consumers' weighing of store environment cues may depend on the *PV* and *CV* of both environment cues and other information cues that are available to them. Moreover, if store environment cues are perceived to have a high *PV* and *CV,* they may eventually become heuristics that consumers use to shorten information-processing time.

Research questions suggested by the information integration framework include the following:

- How do consumers weigh various store environment cues in the evaluation and choice process?
- How do consumers weigh store environment cues in relation to other marketing cues (price, advertising, etc.) that are available? Because store environment cues are available at the point of purchase, are they weighted more heavily because of recency effects?

- Are there particular store environment cues that have higher *PV* and/or *CV* than others? Do these cues vary across consumers or buying situations?

SITUATIONAL AND INDIVIDUAL DIFFERENCE FACTORS

The interpretation and use of store environment cues depends to some extent on consumers' situational and individual characteristics. Because it is beyond the scope of this chapter to review all possible factors that may moderate use of store environment cues, several will be highlighted: consumer goals, product familiarity, whether the consumer is purchasing a good or a service, and some individual difference characteristics.

Consumer Goals

Canter (1983) proposed that a critical aspect of an individual's "place experience" is the degree to which that place contributes to the objectives that individual might have. Certain physical cues in the store environment will thus have more importance because they are more central to an individual's goals. In terms of goal orientation (i.e., the expected outcomes of a shopping trip), two broad categories of shoppers can be drawn from the work of Bloch, Ridgeway, and Sherrell (1989):

1. Purchasers, who are oriented toward buying merchandise or services
2. Browsers, who are oriented toward recreation and/or gathering information

Given these two categories, it is reasonable to expect that each group may be attuned to different sets of environmental cues. The importance and use of specific sets of cues may depend on the goals of the consumer. Recreational shoppers (browsers), for instance, have been found to care a great deal about the sensory characteristics of shopping (Bellenger and Korgoankar 1980). The aesthetic-design and ambient components of the store environment would represent the more sensory-oriented aspects of the store environment. Jansen-Verbeke (1987) found store decor to be an important determinant of activity levels for browsers. Also, heavy browsers reported more positive perceptions of environmental factors in a clothing store than did either nonbrowsers or light browsers (Bloch et al. 1989), suggesting that recreational and/or information-gathering consumers may pay more attention to design and ambient components in the store environment.

In contrast, purchasers are likely to be more concerned with the functional-design and social aspects of store environments. This is due to the relatively more time-conscious aspects of a purchase situation vis-à-vis a browsing situation. Purchasers would be interested in quickly getting in and out of a store, which would be facilitated by store layout and an adequate number of service personnel. By the same token, ambient factors would be less important to purchasers than to browsers because they are likely to spend less time in a store and thus may be less likely to notice characteristics such as temperature or noise.

Given that these arguments have not been empirically tested, future research should explore the relationship between consumer goals and the role the store environment plays in inhibiting or enhancing these goals.

Product and Store Familiarity

The extent to which consumers weigh store environment cues likely depends on product and store familiarity. Zeithaml (1988) distinguishes between extrinsic cues (not a part of the physical composition of the product) and intrinsic cues (part of the product itself). As discussed earlier, extrinsic (store) cues are more likely to be used by consumers when they are unfamiliar with a product, while intrinsic cues tend to be used more by those who are familiar with a product.

In terms of store familiarity, when individuals become accustomed to an environment, habituation may become an issue. This is a process that takes place when subsequent exposures to a new stimulus over time cause that stimulus to become decreasingly effective in eliciting focal attention (Greenwald and Leavitt 1984). Deasy and Lasswell (1985) propose that when people enter a new building, they do so in an exploratory manner, searching for environmental cues, but that once they become accustomed to the setting, they move habitually. Thus, habituation would suggest that people play less attention to the store environment as they grow used to it. Research is needed to examine the effects of environmental habituation in the choice process.

Purchase of Goods or Services

Whether consumers are purchasing a good or service may determine the degree of informational value of the store environment. The environment is likely to have a more pivotal role in the purchase of services for two reasons. First, because a service is intangible, judging its intrinsic attributes is difficult (Zeithaml 1988). Wyckham, Fitzroy, and Mandry (1975, 61) note that with services, consumers "desire the security of evaluating something tangible, and do so by analyzing what they can: the appearance of the physician's waiting room, the venue of the travel agent's office, the color of the aircraft." Second, because a service involves simultaneous production and consumption (Zeithaml, Parasuraman, and Berry 1985), in many cases an individual has to enter the service facility. Therefore, this facility not only provides extrinsic cues to consumers, it also can become an intrinsic cue that is part of the total service experience.

Researchers agree that the physical environment is critical for services retailers. Parasuraman, Zeithaml, and Berry (1988) discovered that tangibles (one of which is the store environment) make up one of five components of perceived service quality. Rys, Fredericks, and Leury (1987) concluded that environmental factors are more important cues to restaurant quality than product-related attributes such as size of portions or type of menu offerings. The design of the physical environment had a significant effect on respondents' intentions to return to a travel agency (Bitner 1990). The research question to be addressed, therefore, is whether consumers are more likely to depend on the store environment for informational cues when purchasing services than when purchasing goods.

Individual Difference Characteristics

Demographic or psychographic characteristics such as age, gender, income, culture, and lifestyle may be critical determinants of how consumers interpret and use cues in the store environment. For example, Saegert and Winkel (1981) noted that the home holds different meanings for men and women. For women the home means self, family, and social relationships, while for men it means ownership and childhood memories. Evidence indicates that culture is a moderating factor in perception of crowding (Gillis, Richard, and Hagan 1987; Hall 1969). The symbolic meaning of color differs across cultures. For example, yellow flowers suggest infidelity in France, while in Mexico they represent death (Hitchings 1976).

Social class differences may determine how people view the environmental experience. For example, working-class immigrant groups view their homes in urban villages (perceived as slums by some) as friendly, secure places that support an interlocking set of social and cultural networks (Fried and Gleichner 1961; Rainwater 1966). In contrast, the home of the suburban upwardly mobile middle and upper class is a symbol of status and the presentation of self (Duncan and Duncan 1976).

Work done by Grossbart and his colleagues (1979; 1989) suggests that personality factors, such as sensation seeking, influence an individual's sensitivity and response to store/service environments. One who is sensation seeking, and thus more attuned to the environment, is likely to make more effort to draw information from a greater number of sensory cues than is one who is less sensation seeking. Consequently, the informational value of the store environment may differ depending upon the number and type of cues used in processing by consumers with varying levels of sensitivity and involvement with that environment.

Research is needed to explore how these consumer characteristics (as well as others) may moderate any relationships found between the store environment and consumer evaluation and choice processes.

RESEARCH ISSUES

For goods and services retailers and store planners to make facility design decisions that convey the appropriate information to consumers, more systematic research needs to be done to explore the topics outlined in this chapter. Studying the store environment presents a number of interesting challenges that researchers in other areas of marketing, such as pricing or advertising, do not face. These challenges include the difficulty and expense of manipulating elements of the environment in a real store setting, the demand bias inherent in field studies of specific stores, and the questionable realism of using two-dimensional pictures or slides to represent a three-dimensional space. This section will examine a number of methods that are available for researching store environment issues.

While each method in and of itself has limitations, field studies, field experiments, and laboratory experiments all can make important contributions to a store environment research program. Factors that influence the choice of research strategies include the researchers' access to field sites, cost, ability to provide adequate experimental controls, and ease of manipulating environmental conditions. For example, music is a variable that is easy and inexpensive to manipulate in a field experiment, and it has been studied repeatedly in actual service settings (e.g., Milliman 1986; Smith and Curnow 1966). In contrast, variables such as lighting, color, and temperature are more difficult to control and manipulate in actual store settings, and retailers may be less willing to allow systematic manipulation of these elements in their facilities. This may explain why many environmental studies utilize laboratory experiments (e.g., Baron 1990; Bellizzi et al. 1983).

Several forms of simulated environments such as photos and slides have been used in experimental studies (e.g., Bitner 1990; Hui and Bateson 1991). The advantages of these techniques are convenience, low cost, and the opportunity for systematic manipulation of the environment. However, two-dimensional simulations may have limited external validity.

A simulation method that would allow researchers to easily manipulate environmental conditions in an experimental study is computer-aided design (CAD). With CAD, a technique familiar to architects and designers, a computer is used to generate drawings quickly and inexpensively. Taking this one step further, and overcoming the two-dimensionality limitation, is the use of virtual reality. However, both of these techniques are relatively new, so their full potential for experimental purposes has yet to be tapped ("New CAD Software" 1990).

Another relatively inexpensive and quick approach is to use a laboratory experiment in which subjects respond to verbal descriptions of a store (Gardner and Siomkos 1985). This approach has been used to examine the effects of the retail store environment on consumers' brand evaluations (Akhter, Andrews, and Durvusula 1994). However, the external validity of this approach has limitations because the descriptions can be value laden.

Video technology can overcome the limitations of two-dimensional pictures. This method is also low cost and relatively simple to use in gathering data from multiple respondents. Video technology in an experimental setting has been used effectively in several environmental studies (e.g., Baker, Grewal, and Parasuraman 1994; Carpman, Grant, and Simmons 1985).

To explore the inference-making and semiotics issues in depth, more qualitative techniques such as verbal protocols or thought-listing tasks would allow researchers insight into consumers' thought processes and the meaning generated by store environments. For example, one of my friends, upon entering an expensive department store, commented that the aisles were so wide that the store would "have to" charge higher prices. Her reasoning was that wider aisles meant less merchandise could be displayed, thereby necessitating higher unit prices.

MANAGERIAL IMPLICATIONS

The literature reviewed in this chapter suggests that the store environment is a critical component in modeling consumer decision making. Consumers make many decisions at the point of purchase, where they are surrounded by environmental cues, and the evidence reviewed provides conceptual support that these cues may offer them important information.

The managerial implications of this chapter are, until more research can be conducted, necessarily broad. The evidence reviewed strongly suggests that how managers design their store facilities may have an important impact upon consumer perceptions of the products they sell. Research has also shown that perceptions of the store environment influence consumer behaviors (e.g., how long they stay, purchase behavior) while in the store (e.g., Spangenberg et al. 1996). Therefore, managers need to ensure that their store environments are communicating the appropriate information to consumers.

The issue of cue congruence is important in designing store environments. A retailer is likely to derive maximum benefits from the store environment when all cues (ambient, design, and social) are congruent with each other and with the retailer's overall image, to project the correct information to consumers. For example, a retailer trying to project a high-quality image may spend a lot of money on store decor. However, if the music played in the store is inappropriate, or if there are too few employees on the floor (suggesting poor service), that investment may be wasted. Similarly, the use of expensive carpeting or music that connotes a high-quality image in a discount store may communicate that the products in this store are beyond the means of the targeted consumer groups.

The semiotic perspective suggests that the store environment may symbolize a lifestyle to consumers. When they buy a product in a store like Banana Republic, Eddie Bauer, or Nordstrom, consumers are taking a bit of this lifestyle home with them. In fact, the lifestyle more than the product may be the key factor in the choice process, and the store environment becomes an intrinsic rather than an extrinsic product attribute. Retail managers who understand this can design their store environments to be unique and exciting enough that consumers will want to "take the experience home."

Store managers need to make sure their stores are designed to appeal both to browsers and to purchasers. For example, in many department stores, the layout is designed to force the consumer to walk around the perimeter of the store. While this layout may be fine for browsers, it is an annoyance for purchasers who are in a hurry.

Finally, it is important that store managers understand how the demographic and cultural makeup of the store's target market may influence the consumers' use and interpretation of store environment information. For example, the growth in numbers of Asian and Hispanic consumers in the United States has implications for retailers who target these groups. The way these consumers interpret store environment cues may be much different from that of other ethnic or regional segments in the United States. Thus, it is necessary that store managers conduct research to determine what their store environments are communicating to consumers with different cultural backgrounds.

BIBLIOGRAPHY

AKHTER, SYED H.; J. CRAIG ANDREWS; AND SRINIVAS DURVASULA. 1994. "The Influence of Retail Store Environment on Brand-Related Judgments." *Journal of Retailing and Consumer Services* 1:67–76.

ALBA, JOSEPH W., AND LYNN HASHER. 1983. "Is Memory Schematic?" *Psychological Bulletin* 93(2):203–231.

ALBA, JOSEPH W., AND J. WESLEY HUTCHINSON. 1987. "Dimensions of Consumer Expertise." *Journal of Consumer Research* 13 (March): 411–454.

ANDERSON, NORMAN H. 1981. *Foundations of Information Integration Theory.* New York: Academic Press.

BAKER, JULIE. 1986. "The Role of the Environment in Marketing Services: The Consumer Perspective." In *The Services Challenge: Integrating for Competitive*

Advantage, edited by John A. Czepeil, Carole A. Congram, and James Shanahan. Chicago: American Marketing Association, 79–84.

BAKER, JULIE; LEONARD BERRY; AND A. PARASURAMAN. 1988. "The Marketing Impact of Branch Facility Design." *Journal of Retail Banking* (July): 33–42.

BAKER, JULIE; DHRUV GREWAL; AND A. PARASURAMAN. 1994. "The Influence of Store Environment on Quality Inferences and Store Image." *Journal of the Academy of Marketing Science* 22(4):328–359.

BARGH, JOHN. 1984. "Automatic and Conscious Processing of Social Information." In *Handbook of Social Cognition,* vol. 3, edited by Robert S. Wyler, Jr., and Thomas K. Srull. Hillsdale, NJ: Erlbaum, 1–43.

BARON, ROBERT A. 1990. "Lighting as a Source of Positive Affect." *Progressive Architecture* 71 (November): 123–124.

BELLENGER, DANNY N., AND PRADEEP KORGOANKAR. 1980. "Profiling the Recreational Shopper." *Journal of Retailing* 58 (Spring): 58–81.

BELLIZZI, JOSEPH A.; AYN E. CROWLEY; AND RONALD W. HASTY. 1983. "The Effects of Color in Store Design." *Journal of Retailing* 59(1) (Spring): 21–45.

BELLIZZI, JOSEPH A., AND ROBERT E. HITE. 1992. "Environmental Color, Consumer Feelings and Purchase Likelihood." *Psychology and Marketing* 9(5) (September/October): 347–363.

BETTMAN, JAMES. 1979. *An Information Processing Theory of Consumer Choice.* Reading, MA: Addison-Wesley.

BITNER, MARY JO. 1990. "Evaluating Service Encounters: The Effects of Physical Surroundings and Employee Responses." *Journal of Marketing* 54 (April): 69–82.

———. 1992. "Servicescapes: The Impact of Physical Surroundings on Customers and Employees." *Journal of Marketing* 56 (April): 57–71.

BLOCH, PETER H.; NANCY RIDGEWAY; AND DANIEL SHERRELL. 1989. "Extending the Concept of Browsing: An Investigation of Browsing Activity." *Journal of the Academy of Marketing Science* 17(1):13–21.

BLOOM, PAUL N., AND TORGER REVE. 1990. "Transmitting Signals to Consumers for Competitive Advantage." *Business Horizons* (July/August): 58–66.

CANTER, DAVID. 1983. "The Purposive Evaluation of Places." *Environment and Behavior* 15(6) (November): 659–698.

CARPMAN, J. R.; M. A. GRANT; AND D. A. SIMMONS. 1985. "Hospital Design and Wayfinding: A Simulation Study." *Environment and Behavior* 17:296–314.

CHERULNIK, PAUL D., AND SCOTT K. WILDERMAN. 1986. "Symbols of Status in Urban Neighborhoods: Contemporary Perceptions of Nineteenth-Century Boston." *Environment and Behavior* 18(5) (September): 604–622.

COHEN, JOEL B., AND KUNAL BASU. 1987. "Alternative Models of Categorization Toward a Contingent Processing Framework." *Journal of Consumer Research* 13 (March): 455–472.

DEASY, C. M., AND THOMAS E. LASSWELL. 1985. *Designing Places for People.* New York: Whitney Library of Design.

DONOVAN, ROBERT J., AND JOHN R. ROSSITER. 1982. "Store Atmosphere: An Environmental Psychology Approach." *Journal of Retailing* 58(1) (Spring): 34–57.

DONOVAN, ROBERT J.; JOHN R. ROSSITER; GILIAN MARCOOLYN; AND ANDREW NESDALE. 1994. "Store Atmosphere and Purchasing Behavior." *Journal of Retailing* 70(3):283–294.

DUFFY, F. C. CAVE, AND J. WORTHINGTON. 1976. *Planning Office Space.* London: Architectural Press.

FINLAY, TED; LAWRENCE R. JAMES; AND TERRY L. MAPLE. 1988. "People's Perceptions of Animals: The Influence of the Zoo Environment." *Environment and Behavior* 24(4) (July): 508–528.

FISKE, S. F. 1982. "Schema-Triggered Affect: Applications to Social Perceptions." In *Affect and Cognition: The 17th Annual Carnegie Symposium on Cognition,* edited by M. S. Clarke and S. T. Fiske. Hillsdale, NJ: Erlbaum, 55–78.

FRIED, M., AND P. GLEICHER. 1961. "Some Sources of Residential Satisfaction in an Urban Slum." *Journal of the American Institute of Planners* 27:305–315.

GARDNER, MERYL P., AND GEORGE J. SIOMKOS. 1985. "Toward a Methodology for Assessing the Effects of In-Store Atmospherics." In *Advances in Consumer Research,* edited by Richard Luts. Chicago: Association for Consumer Research, 27–31.

GILLIS, A. R.; MADELINE A. RICHARD; AND JOHN HAGAN. 1987. "Ethnic Susceptibility to Crowding." *Environment and Behavior* 18(6) (November): 683–706.

GOFFMAN, ERVING. 1959. *The Presentation of Self in Everyday Life.* Garden City, NY: Doubleday.

GREENWALD, A. G., AND C. LEAVITT. 1984. "Audience Involvement in Advertising: Four Levels." *Journal of Consumer Research* (June) 2:581–592.

GREWAL, DHRUV, AND JULIE BAKER. 1994. "Do Retail Store Environment Factors Affect Consumers' Price Acceptability? An Empirical Investigation." *International Journal of Research in Marketing* 11:107–115.

GROSSBART, SANFORD; DOUGLAS AMEDO; AND DAVID CHINCHEN. 1979. "The Influence of Retail Environments on Consumer Cognition and Feelings." In *American Marketing Association Educator's Conference Proceedings,* edited by Neil Beckwith et al. Chicago: AMA, 268–273.

GROSSBART, SANFORD; RONALD HAMPTON; B. RAMMOHAN; AND RICHARD S. LAPIDUS. 1989. "Environmental Dispositions and Customer Responsiveness to Atmospherics." Paper presented at the Symposium on Patronage Behavior and Retail Strategy, May, at Louisiana State University, Baton Rouge, LA.

HALL, EDWARD T. 1969. *The Hidden Dimension.* Garden City, NY: Doubleday.

HALLORAN, J. 1978. *Applied Human Relations: An Organizational Approach.* Englewood Cliffs, NJ: Prentice Hall.

HEATH, REBECCA PIIRTO. 1995. "Fuzzy Results, Fuzzy Logic." *Marketing Tools* (May): 6–11.

HITCHINGS, BRADLEY. 1976. "Personal Business." *Business Week* (December 6): 91–92.

HUI, MICHAEL K., AND JOHN E. G. BATESON. 1991. "Perceived Control and the Effects of Crowding and Consumer Choice on the Service Experience." *Journal of Consumer Research* 18 (September): 174–184.

JANSEN-VERBEKE, MYRIAM. 1987. "Women Shopping and Leisure." *Leisure Studies* 6:71–86.

KAHENEMAN, DANIEL. 1973. *Attention and Effort.* Englewood Cliffs, NJ: Prentice Hall.

KELLER, KEVEN LANE. 1987. "Memory Factors in Advertising: The Effect of Advertising Retrieval Cues on Brand Evaluations." *Journal of Consumer Research* 14 (December): 316–333.

KONAR, ELLEN; ERIC SUNDSTROM; CHRISTINE BRADY; DANIEL MANDEL; AND ROBERT W. RICE. 1982. "Status Demarcation in the Office." *Environment and Behavior* 14(5) (September): 561–580.

KOTLER, PHILIP. 1973. "Atmospherics as a Marketing Tool." *Journal of Retailing* 49(4) (Winter): 48–64.

LEVY, SIDNEY J. 1959. "Symbols for Sale." *Harvard Business Review* 37 (July–August): 117–124.

MANNING P., ED. 1965. *Office Design: A Study of Environment.* Liverpool, England: University of Liverpool Press.

MAZURSKY, DAVID, AND JACOB JACOBY. 1986. "Exploring the Development of Store Images." *Journal of Retailing* 62(2) (Summer): 145–165.

MICK, DAVID GLEN. 1986. "Consumer Research and Semiotics: Exploring the Morphology of Signs, Symbols and Significance." *Journal of Consumer Research* 13 (September): 196–213.

MILLIMAN, RONALD E. 1982. "Using Background Music to Affect the Behavior of Supermarket Shoppers." *Journal of Marketing* (Summer): 86–91.

———. 1986. "The Influence of Background Music on the Behavior of Restaurant Patrons." *Journal of Consumer Research* (September): 286–289.

MITTELSTADT, ROBERT A.; SANFORD L. GROSSBART; AND WILLIAM CURTIS. 1977. "Consumer Perceptions and Retail Mapping: Research Findings and Preliminary Theory." In *Consumer and Industrial Buying Behavior,* edited by Arch G. Woodside, Jagdish N. Sheth, and Peter D. Bennett. New York: Elsevier–North Holland, 95–110.

MONROE, KENT B., AND R. KRISHNAN. 1985. "The Effect of Price on Subjective Product Evaluation." In *Perceived Quality,* edited by J. Jacoby and J. Olson. Lexington, MA: Lexington Books, 209–232.

MOORE, GARY T. 1979. "Knowing About Environmental Knowing: The Current State of Theory and Research on Environmental Cognition." *Environment and Behavior* 11:33–70.

MORROW, PAULA C., AND JAMES C. McELROY. 1981. "Interior Office Design and Visitor Response: A Constructive Replication." *Journal of Applied Psychology* 66(5):646–650.

"Motherhood Adopts a Fashion Look for the Eighties." 1985. *Chain Store Age Executive* (April): 31.

NAUGHTON, KEITH. 1995. "The Ralph Lauren of Car Dealers." *Business Week* (November 20): 153–156.

"New CAD Software for Retail Designs." 1990. *Visual Merchandising and Store Design* (October): 72–73.

NISBETT, RICHARD E., AND LEE ROSS. 1980. *Human Inference: Strategies and Shortcomings of Social Judgment.* Englewood Cliffs, NJ: Prentice Hall.

OLSON, JERRY. 1977. "Price as an Informational Cue: Effects on Product Evaluations." In *Consumer and Industrial Buyer Behavior,* edited by Arch G. Woodside, Jagdish Sheth, and Peter D. Bennett. New York: Elsevier–North Holland, 267–296.

PARASURAMAN, A.; VALARIE A. ZEITHAML; AND LEONARD L. BERRY. 1988. "SERVQUAL: A Multiple-Item Scale for Measuring Consumer Perceptions of Service Quality." *Journal of Retailing* 64(1) (Spring): 12–40.

PIERCE, MAURICE. 1985. "The Future Ten Years in Retail Design and Construction." *Texas Retailer* (Fall): 17–18.

RAINWATER, L. 1966. "Fear and the House-as-Haven in the Lower Class." *Journal of the American Institute of Planners* 32:23–31.

RAO, AKSHAY R., AND KENT B. MONROE. 1988. "The Moderating Effect of Prior Knowledge on Cue Utilization in Product Evaluations." *Journal of Consumer Research* 15 (September): 253–264.

RUSSELL, JAMES A., AND LAWRENCE M. WARD. 1982. "Environmental Psychology." In *Annual Review of Psychology,* vol. 33. Palo Alto, CA: Annual Reviews, 651–688.

RYS, MELANIE E.; JOAN O. FREDERICKS; AND DAVID LUERY. 1987. "Value = Quality: Are Service Value and Service Quality Synonymous: A Decompositional Approach." In *Add Value to Your Service,* edited by Carol Suprenant. Chicago: American Marketing Association, 25–28.

SADALLA, EDWARD K.; BETH VERSHURE; AND JEFFERY BURROUGHS. 1987. "Identity Symbolism in Housing." *Environment and Behavior* 19(5) (September): 569–587.

SAEGERT, S., AND G. WINKEL. 1981. "The Home: A Critical Problem for Changing Sex Roles." In *New Environments for Women,* edited by G. Wekerle, R. Peterson, and D. Morley. Boulder, CO: Westview.

SEBEOK, THOMAS A. 1976. *Contributions to the Doctrine of Signs.* Bloomington: Indiana University Press.

SMITH, PATRICIA CAIN, AND ROSS CURNOW. 1966. "Arousal Hypothesis and the Effects of Music on Purchasing Behavior." *Journal of Applied Psychology* 50(3):255–256.

SNYDER, P. Z.; D. STEA; AND E. K. SADALLA. 1976. "Socio-Cultural Modifications and User Needs in Navajo Housing." *Journal of Architectural Research* 5:4–9.

SPANGENBERG, ERIC R.; AYN E. CROWLEY; AND PAMELA HENDERSON. 1996. "Improving the Store Environment: Do Olfactory Cues Affect Evaluations and Behaviors?" *Journal of Marketing* 60 (April): 67–80.

STEELE, F. I., AND S. JENKS. 1977. *The Feel of the Workplace.* Reading, MA: Addison-Wesley.

SUJAN, MITA. 1985. "Consumer Knowledge: Effects on Evaluation Strategies Mediating Consumer Judgements." *Journal of Consumer Research* 12 (June): 31–46.

SUNDSTROM, E.; R. BURT; AND D. KAMP. 1980. "Privacy at Work: Architectural Correlates of Job Satisfaction." *Academy of Management Journal* 23:101–117.

TAYLOR, SHELLEY, AND JENNIFER CROCKER. 1981. "Schematic Bases of Social Information Processing." In *Social Cognition: The Ontario Symposium,* vol. 1, edited by E. T. Higgins. Hillsdale, NJ: Erlbaum, 20–32.

TITUS, PHILLIP A., AND PETER B. EVERETT. 1995. "The Consumer Retail Search Process: A Conceptual Model and Research Agenda." *Journal of the Academy of Marketing Science* 23(2):106–119.

TOM, GAIL; TERESA BARNETT; WILLIAM LEW; AND JODEAN SALMANTS. 1987. "Cuing the Consumer: The Role of Salient Cues in Consumer Perception." *Journal of Consumer Marketing* 4(2) (Spring): 23–27.

WARD, JAMES C.; MARY JO BITNER; AND JOHN BARNES. 1992. "Measuring the Prototypicality and Meaning of Retail Environments." *Journal of Retailing* 68(2) (Summer): 194–220.

WYCKHAM, R. G.; P. T. FITZROY; AND G. D. MANDRY. 1975. "Marketing of Services: An Evaluation of the Theory." *European Journal of Marketing* 9(1): 59–67.

ZALESNY, MARY D., AND RICHARD V. FARACE. 1987. "Traditional versus Open Offices: A Comparison of Sociotechnical, Social Relations and Symbolic Meaning Perspectives." *Academy of Management Journal* 30(2):240–259.

ZEITHAML, VALARIE. 1988. "Consumer Perceptions of Price, Quality and Value: A Means-End Model and Synthesis of Evidence." *Journal of Marketing* 52 (July): 2–22.

ZEITHAML, VALARIE; A. PARASURAMAN; AND LEONARD BERRY. 1985. "Problems and Strategies in Services Marketing." *Journal of Marketing* 49(2):33–46.

3

DRESSING FOR THE PART

The Role of Costume in the Staging of the Servicescape

MICHAEL R. SOLOMON

Apparel and the meanings it conveys influence three interrelated domains of service delivery:

1. *Corporate identity*—As one component of the overall promotional mix, dress influences perceptions of the firm's market position and unique character in the minds of customers, employees, vendors, stockholders, and the general public.

2. *The customer*—Perceptions of service quality are mediated by the costume of service providers. Appearance cues play a significant role in inferences regarding competence, professionalism, caring, and a host of other interpersonal attributes.

3. *The employee*—In addition to its impact on various audiences, costume also affects the morale, self-definition, and performance of service providers themselves.

Michael R. Solomon is Human Sciences Professor of Consumer Behavior at Auburn University, Auburn, Alabama.

CORPORATE IDENTITY

The business community acknowledges that corporate image is a key point of competitive advantage. Wally Olins, chair of Wolff Olins Ltd. (a corporate identity firm), has made these observations:

> An organization's corporate identity can inspire loyalty, shape decisions, aid recognition and attract customers. It is vital to effective employee recruitment and to the way people work together inside a company. And it is directly related to profitability. A corporation's identity, if it is perceived negatively, can work against even the best marketing innovations and strategic initiatives (Olins 1990).

Increasingly, the company is itself being recognized as a brand:

> Criteria such as *appearance,* performance, trust, and value are applied to virtually every brand shopping decision, from a new car to a new computer to a can of shaving creme [sic]. These criteria should also be applied in the management and marketing of a corporate brand (Vick 1993).

This perspective is especially relevant to service industries, where the company name (and the corresponding image it elicits in the minds of customers and potential customers) serves as an umbrella for the set of attributes constituting the service experience. These attributes embrace such diverse variables as reputation, modernity of equipment, and employee demeanor. The uniform allows the marketer to give concrete expression to a distinctive positioning or repositioning strategy (as in the case of the gold blazers worn by Century 21 Realtors). It is one very important part of service design, a part that can and must be integrated with other design aspects.

This integration, by the way, is at the heart of the communications revolution under way in the advertising industry. The integrated marketing communications philosophy recognizes that *any* aspect of a company, from its stationery and the architectural design of its headquarters to its advertising messages and the appearance of its representatives, is potentially an important piece of information used by others to form an impression of the company. Federal

Express, for example, recently revamped its entire design program and worked hard to be sure that the same design principles were carried out in everything from its television commercials to the hats worn by its drivers. The employee, then, has to be regarded as more than a mode of service delivery—he or she is also a part of the firm's communications strategy (Solomon and Englis 1994; Schultz et al. 1993; Solomon and Stuart 1997).

The role of the employee as an embodiment of corporate identity is particularly well recognized in the airline industry, a high-contact, high-risk service where most major carriers focus on reducing risk and perpetuating an image of competence to maintain competitive parity. United Airlines, for example, maintains appearance standards for its flight attendants that mandate acceptable accessories, skirt and pants length, hair styles, and cosmetics usage (Airline Pilots Association v. United Air Lines 1979). According to the carrier, "The purposes of the appearance standards are to achieve a tasteful uniformity among the flight attendants as representatives of United, and to project a quality image of the flight attendants as clean, healthy, attractive individuals who take pride in themselves and their job" (p. 612).

The Service System

A service business can be conceived as a system (see Lovelock 1991). This system can in turn be roughly demarcated into two areas: service operations, where the service "product" is created, and service delivery, where this product is delivered to the customer. Some parts of the service (the "technical core") are hidden from the customer, while other parts are visible. The service delivery system includes physical support and personnel, as well as exposure to other patrons of the business, who have been termed "co-consumers" (Solomon 1996). The customer's perceptions of the service system are determined by the character of the service delivery system, in addition to advertising, word of mouth, and other miscellaneous interactions with the company (e.g., billing statements). While the technical core may be flawless, "it is how customers *perceive* the organization that determines their decisions to select one service rather than another" (Lovelock 1991, 17, italics in original).

Unlike the selection and purchase of a good, buying a service is the consumption of an experience. A copious literature delineates the many important differences between goods and services (see Czepiel, Solomon, and Surprenant 1985; Lovelock 1991). For the purposes of this discussion, a few of these dimensions are particularly pertinent to the notion that costume is a key mediator of corporate identity for services:

- Since services tend to be labor-intensive, consumers' images of a service business often depend upon the person who actually delivers the service. An airline may invest millions of dollars in providing top-quality planes, devising efficient route systems, training pilots, and so on, but a passenger's experience with the company will be soured (perhaps permanently) by one nasty encounter with a rude flight attendant (Czepiel, Solomon, and Surprenant 1985).

- Many services are delivered repeatedly, and there tends to be less consistency in the nature of the service act from T_1 to T_2. This means that it is harder to maintain quality-control standards relative to the manufacture of goods. It also implies that when consumers evaluate service quality, they search for common cues that span consumption occasions.

- In contrast to goods, consumers' evaluations of the quality of an intangible, ephemeral service experience often focus on what have been termed "credence qualities"—post hoc, subjective assessments based on peripheral cues provided by the provider and the service environment (Zeithaml 1991). For this reason, tangible cues of professionalism, such as an appropriate appearance, diplomas, or an organized office, often are critical to purchase satisfaction. For example, a study that elicited subjects' evaluations of a travel agency office that was either cluttered or organized demonstrated that consumers partly base their assumptions about the competence of a service on the environmental cues that are salient while the service is being delivered (Bitner 1990).

It is not surprising that a common strategy in service businesses is to create tangible symbols of service excellence, or "physical evidence" (cf. Shostack 1977), to serve as material proxies for latent characteristics (e.g., the Dreyfus lion, the Prudential rock, the Travelers umbrella). Physical evidence takes many forms, including the firm's building and equipment, its employees, and its advertising.

THE CUSTOMER

The image of the company among outside audiences is largely shaped by those inside. . . . Employees wear two hats—one is the work they perform, the other is the image they convey as ambassadors for the company.

—Chajet (1992, 19)

A recent survey reported that 68 percent of customers stop purchasing a product or service due to dissatisfaction with an employee (Jenkins 1992). It is clear that customers' perceptions of service providers matter. These assessments are partly based on how well the employee performs his or her function, of course, but an array of other peripheral cues also affect these judgments. These cues include physiognomy, verbal abilities, and the many pieces of apparel and grooming data that aid in the classification of the employee in terms of subcultural memberships, physical attractiveness, and so on.

The pivotal role played by the service provider in the delivery of many services cannot be overemphasized. Indeed, the individual who represents the service may well be the single most important aspect of the business, insofar as he or she physically embodies the service and represents its character to customers:

The product tangibility will be judged in part by who offers it—not just who the vendor corporation is but also who the corpo-

ration's representative is. The vendor and the vendor's representative are both inextricably and inevitably part of the "product"
that prospects must judge before they buy (Levitt 1981, 64).

A study conducted in a restaurant setting attests to the potential primacy of subjective factors in mediating service satisfaction.
Conjoint analysis revealed that objective variables, such as price,
play a relatively minor role in influencing service expectations and
selection of a service. To the contrary, more personal sources of
information, particularly the behavior of employees and the opinions of friends and relatives, had the greatest influence on ratings of
service (Sweeney, Johnson, and Armstrong 1992). Another study
employing the critical incident technique in an airline setting found
that the perceptions of 320 business passengers of factors leading to
dissatisfaction differed from those of 80 front staff employees, with
the implication that subjective factors (e.g., communication with
passengers) are more pivotal to service satisfaction and dissatisfaction
than many industry operatives realize (Edvardsson 1992); similar
findings are reported in Kloppenborg and Gourdin (1992).

Given the centrality of employees in many service situations,
it is essential to consider how these individuals may affect customers' overall perception of the servicescape. Put more simply, how
can we evaluate the character of a service setting without paying
attention to the actors who populate that environment?

One helpful way to address this issue is grounded in the dramaturgical perspective as initially articulated by Goffman (1959),
which offers us the construct of the *performance* to help explain the
dynamics of human behavior (i.e., an individual's activity before a
set of observers, or *audience*). To deliver a believable performance,
the actor can employ a variety of expressive techniques and objects
(collectively termed the *front*). The front includes both the *setting*
(objects in the performance space such as furnishings and decor)
and the *personal front,* which includes the actor's manner and appearance. This approach is grounded in the dramaturgical perspective on
human behavior. The basic premise is that people's interactions are
based upon their interpretations of symbols in the behavioral set-

ting. Thus, social reality is *constructed* by participants, based upon their prior experiences, socialization, expectations, and so on (Solomon 1983).

The dramaturgical approach relies heavily on the work of sociologist Erving Goffman, who adapted the metaphor of the theatrical performance to ground his study of human social interaction (Goffman 1959). When applied to services marketing, this perspective stresses that the deployment of socially meaningful props, sets, and costumes instantiates the servicescape and creates a nexus of meaning for both customers and service providers (Solomon et al. 1985).

One facet of Goffman's analysis is the notion of a performance, an individual's activity before an audience, using the variety of expressive techniques and objects that constitute the front. Often, a "troupe" of actors must cooperate to communicate a consistent social reality; together, they form a *performance team*. A successful performance requires *dramaturgical discipline,* meaning actors must do their best to maintain the actions and appearances associated with their roles, and all parties to the interaction must be motivated to maintain the front. This perspective is especially relevant to service businesses that perform for multiple audience members and involve high contact between provider and customer (Grove and Fisk 1991).

As is ably recognized by other contributors to this volume, servicescape design can and should embrace an array of sensory elements, ranging from signage to scents. The physical setting where the service is rendered is indeed an important, yet largely ignored, dimension of the service encounter. While a few researchers have begun to examine the effects of props and settings on customers' perceptions of service quality (e.g., Bitner 1990), very little attention has been paid to the parallel role of the actor and his or her appearance in the service experience (for some exceptions, see Solomon 1985b; 1987b).

To be sure, the actions and utterances of service providers are well recognized as being crucial determinants of service satisfaction, and a rich literature attests to the importance of salesperson behaviors in the personal selling process. However, the role of non-verbal behaviors—including but not limited to appearance—has received only a small fraction of this attention. Since it has been estimated that up to 80 percent of the meaning in a social encounter is transmitted on nonverbal channels, this gap should be addressed.

Apparel is tremendously rich in symbolic meaning, and an abundant literature attests to the impact of clothing cues on person perception (see Kaiser 1997; Solomon 1985a). On the other hand, the interpretation of these cues often is a complex and indeterminate process. Clothing is in a sense semiotically muddy; its ability to convey information about the wearer typically can be viewed as a code, but *not* as a language (Barthes 1983; Davis 1985). That is, apparel meanings are usually somewhat ambiguous—or undercoded, in semiotic terms—which makes the decoding process an interesting interaction of cultural context and idiosyncratic experience.

Nonetheless, clothing cues are among the most visible and most utilized information sources employed in the process of impression formation. As one simple example, subjects in a study who were shown photos of nurses in traditional uniforms judged them to be more neat, organized, reliable, competent, and pleasant than those wearing either modern or scrub uniforms (Franzoi 1988). This basic pattern has been replicated empirically in many occupational domains, including evaluations of therapists, executives, and even criminal defendants (see Sproles and Burnes 1994; Kaiser 1997; Solomon 1985a).

This communicational function of contact employees is recognized by United Airlines. The carrier has stated that (in addition to safety), "Flight attendants are present on airplanes to perform additional functions, including passenger service and *projection of an image*" (Airline Pilots Association v. United Air Lines 1979, 611, emphasis added). United makes additional claims:

> Flight attendants are the most important public contact employees of United, and their overall job performance influences customer choice in the selection of a flight. Apart from flight schedules, flight attendants are the most important factor in influencing customer choice (p. 611).

On the other hand, undue emphasis on projecting a coordinated, "preprogrammed," and/or artificial image may have deleterious effects (see Surprenant and Solomon 1987a; Hochschild 1983).

Appearance as a Mediator of Social Perception

"Clothes make the man."
—Thomas Carlyle, nineteenth-century philosopher

For better or worse, ours is a visual society. Service users make decisions based on the messenger as well as the message. *Person perception* refers to the study of the factors that affect one's impressions of the self and of others. It is concerned with such issues as the inferences we draw from what we observe and remember about a person (Bromley 1993; Hastie et al. 1980; Jones 1990). Many of these observations are based on first impressions, snap judgments of people that depend upon integrating perceptual information regarding facial characteristics, clothing, etc., with an extant frame of reference brought about by experience. A distinguishing feature of these judgments is their tendency to persist over time, even in the face of subsequent, disconfirming information.

Physical attractiveness, typically the most accessible information available, is used to make initial categorizations. People (often unconsciously) sort others into cognitive categories based on appearance cues. The evaluative aspects of these categories (called *prototypes*) mediate assumptions about a person's character and capabilities (for reviews, see Cash and Pruzinsky 1990; Hatfield and Sprecher 1986; Patzer 1985; Solomon 1985a).

The bulk of attractiveness research has focused on facial appearance, though some researchers have also examined how body type, clothing, and accessories affect person perception (e.g., Solomon, Ashmore, and Longo 1992; for a compilation of studies pertaining to clothed appearances and person perception, see Solomon 1985a). The extensive literature on person perception attests to the powerful impact of appearance cues during the social categorization process. A person's assessments of others are strongly influenced by their level of physical attractiveness.

Good-looking people (however defined) often benefit from a "What is beautiful is good" stereotype (Berscheid and Walster 1974). This assumption has been summarized as "We like beautiful and handsome people better than homely people, and we attribute all kinds of good characteristics to them" (Aronson 1972, 216). A positivity bias toward attractive people is apparently caused by the implicit personality theories held by perceivers (Schneider 1973). These "lay theories" (i.e., assumptions drawn by typical observers) of personality consist of learned associations between physical cues and (inferred) personality attributes.

A corpus of research spanning more than a twenty-year period has generally been supportive of the "What is beautiful is good" stereotype. One bibliography compiled more than a decade ago included roughly five hundred studies done by that time (Cash 1981). A review of this literature reached the following conclusion:

> Physically attractive people . . . are judged by audiences as more sexually warm, responsive, curious, complex, sensitive, perceptive, kind, interesting, confident, assertive, strong, poised, happy, amiable, sociable, modest, candid, serious, outgoing, pleasure-seeking, and flexible, and they are expected to procure better jobs, to marry better, and to live happier, more fulfilling lives (Schlenker 1980, 270).

Relevant to the present discussion, attractive people appear to have an advantage because they are accorded greater social power. Observers are more likely to be persuaded by the words of, or to model their behaviors after, attractive versus unattractive stimulus persons (Tedeschi, Schlenker, and Bonoma 1973). In one typical study of this genre, 30 male and 30 female university students viewed the videotaped professional self-descriptions of a female counselor who was either physically attractive or unattractive. Subjects indicated their impressions of the counselor on 12 traits and their expectancies of her helpfulness for 15 personal problems. Relative to the physically unattractive counselor, the attractive counselor was perceived more favorably by the female subjects, especially with regard to her competence, professionalism, assertiveness, interest, relaxation, and ability to help with problems of general anxiety, shyness, career choice, sexual functioning, and inferiority. Two control groups (30 subjects) who listened to the tapes but were unaware of the counselor's appearance generally did not differ in their ratings of the two tapes (Lewis and Walsh 1978).

Employee Appearance in the Workplace

The plethora of ads featuring highly attractive men and women attests to the emphasis placed on physical appearance by manufacturers, marketers, and advertisers. Indeed, abundant research evidence in the marketing literature attests to the effectiveness of employing attractive rather than unattractive spokespersons and models in advertising and promotions (e.g., Baker and Churchill 1977; Belch, Belch, and Villareal 1987; Bloch and Richins 1992; Caballero and Pride 1984; Courtney and Whipple 1983; Joseph 1982; Kahle and Homer 1985; Reid and Soley 1983; Richins 1991).

Limited evidence also speaks to the ramifications of appearance for the ability of retail salespeople to successfully promote merchandise to shoppers. A recent study investigated the effects of the physical attractiveness stereotype in the context of personal selling. It was hypothesized that if persuasion targets behave according to the physical attractiveness stereotype, they should perceive attractive salespersons more favorably, treat them more cordially, and respond to their requests more readily than they do to unattractive salespersons. A series of three experiments confirmed that more favorable selling skills were attributed to highly attractive salespersons, buyers treated ostensibly attractive sellers more cordially, and attractive persons got more when soliciting for a charitable organization (Reingen and Kernan 1993).

The pivotal nature of physical appearance in the workplace is also reflected in the emphasis on clothing and grooming echoed by the popular press (e.g., Molloy 1975) and in the proliferation of "personal image consultants" who specialize in managing the appearance of professionals and businesspeople. The *Directory of Image Consultants* includes over 250 consultants who specialize in honing the personal images of executives (Wiesendanger 1992; for additional empirical data on this industry, see Solomon 1987b).

A typical example of this emphasis is a recent article in *Working Woman* observing that hands and fingernails are constantly on display in the workplace, and that a handshake often is the first physical evidence a person uses to make judgments of character. This article reports (without attribution) that a study conducted by Lancôme found that 55 percent of all communication is nonverbal, conveyed through gestures or appearance. Dirty nails indicate that a person is not detail-oriented and does not have much self-esteem. Long nails can send a negative signal, perhaps implying narcissism and a lack of professionalism (Sterne 1993). Regardless of its veridicality, the plethora of articles in this genre attests to the emphasis such cues are given in the popular press.

Dress Codes

A realization that the image of employees can influence perceptions of an organization is evidenced by the common business practice of mandating appearance regulations for employees. In a recent Gallup poll, 74 percent of 750 U.S. employees surveyed said they work for companies that have some kind of dress code ("Leave the Muumuu at Home" 1994). A survey of 60 British companies, most in the service sector, revealed that 18 provide dress codes with detailed rules for the majority of employees. Another 20 make shorter generalized references to appearance in employee handbooks and codes of conduct ("Dress Codes à la Mode" 1993).

Traditionally, corporate dress codes have been dictated more by unwritten culture than by a policy manual; even nontraditional or progressive firms exhibit norms that tend to reflect underlying organizational culture and values. Thus, even if a service business does not adopt a formal dress code, implicit appearance norms are likely to be created and perpetuated over time. While there may not be explicit dress requirements in "laid-back" service operations (such as an academic department!), the unwritten rules regarding deviation from prevailing standards (however scruffy) may be every bit as salient. An art professor who shows up to class in a staid business suit may attract as much attention as the business professor who shows up without one.

The importance of the dress code issue is illustrated by the current practice of instituting a "Casual Friday" policy in many workplaces, where the dress code is deliberately relaxed for at least one workday. This trend supports the notion that apparel reflects, if not creates, the culture of a business. According to research conducted by Levi Strauss, 75 percent of businesses now permit their employees to dress casually at least once a week, compared to 37 percent in 1992.

Ironically, this attempt at relaxation has provoked stress in many circles. One problem is that many workers simply don't possess the appropriate script once the traditional costume requirement is removed—complaints abound regarding "liberated" employees showing up for work in scruffy shorts and T-shirts. People in positions of authority grope for ways to maintain their control once they emerge from behind the armor of a business suit. Levi Strauss is leading the charge to "educate" people about acceptable alternatives (usually involving one or more Levi's products . . .). The company has advised more than 22,000 corporations on dress policy and recently launched an $8 million advertising campaign to promote casual attire in offices (Himelstein 1996; J. Solomon 1996).

Uniforms

Many corporate dress codes only go so far as to delineate certain boundaries vis-à-vis mufti (civilian clothing), such as mandating ties for men or prohibiting the wearing of slacks for women. However, other firms have adopted entire career apparel programs, where clothing is specially designed for employees (either as distinct uniforms or in the form of color-coordinated jackets, shirts, pants, etc.) and is often provided to them on a subsidized basis. As one representative example, BellSouth Corporation recently instituted a uniform program for its 25,000 "outside contact" employees. Technicians are now given the choice between khaki and navy trousers and a collection of golf shirts emblazoned with the company logo.

BellSouth has undertaken this initiative to allay customers' apprehensions about letting strangers into their homes, as well as to promote a more identifiable corporate image in the face of increasing competition (Thompson 1996).

Because a service company's image is only as good as the image communicated by its people, management must use all available means to ensure that the service provider communicates the company's attributes. This is one reason that many companies are concerned with correctly packaging their employees (Solomon 1985b). Company uniforms, for this reason, can be an important part of the services mix. Service apparel performs several functions for service delivery that are performed by packages in the case of goods: it affects how service quality is assessed, implies consistency of service, and differentiates the provider from its competitor (Solomon 1985b). In addition to such traditional users as nurses, police officers, and employees in the airline industry, large companies such as Hertz Corporation, McDonald's Corporation, and the Coca-Cola Company have initiated extensive career apparel programs (Solomon 1996). The National Association of Uniform Manufacturers and Distributors estimates that 4.5 million workers wear uniforms on a regular basis, and it has been predicted that a majority of the 21 million new jobs created by the year 2000 will require standardized apparel.

The uniform is a notable exception to clothing's semiotic ambiguity, insofar as it consists of a set of symbols that formally identify, make tangible, and express the culture of a recognized organization (cf. Davis 1985). While most clothing derives its interest value from its ability to create nuance, the goal of a uniform is to eliminate the potential for misinterpretation (part of the logic behind BellSouth's decision as noted previously).

This clarity permits service apparel to serve several communicational functions that are performed by packages in the case of consumer goods: It affects how service quality is assessed, implies consistency of service usage across occasions, and differentiates the firm from its competitors (cf. Solomon 1985b). In addition, the uniform reinforces the authority of the sponsoring organization. When airline flight attendants in the late 1960s and early 1970s insisted on replacing traditional, military-inspired uniforms with more casual, fashionable versions, they subsequently found that the respect they received from passengers diminished. By the early 1980s most airline uniforms had returned to a more traditional style (Collins 1989).

Having said that, however, it is worth noting that interpretations of uniforms can indeed be malleable, especially those that carry the social baggage of political, gender, or racial issues. For example, the authoritarian meaning of American military uniforms was inverted by the counterculture of the 1970s, even to the extent that some traditional symbols such as the Army jacket were co-opted and transformed to represent contempt for governmental authority. And gender identity may be affected by uniform design, as when the accepted dress for female executives is a potential handicap to career mobility or when the mandated dress for female service personnel in hotels, restaurants, and bars is calculated to arouse the sexual interest of customers. Finally, some service uniforms have even been co-opted as fashion items. Clothing issued by UPS, Federal Express, and the U.S. Postal Service has become a "hot" style among some young people (Frank 1994, 1995).

It is clear that many view appearance as an issue with commercial ramifications. Physical attractiveness is an important consideration in the choice of spokespeople in advertising, and some evidence indicates that it also affects the efficacy of retail salespeople. The concerted efforts by companies in many industries to regulate the appearance of their employees through the development and enforcement of dress codes and/or the provision of career apparel attests to the recognition among many managers that the service provider's appearance does influence customers' perceptions.

THE SERVICE PROVIDER

A less obvious—but perhaps equally robust—facet of employee appearance in the servicescape concerns the attitudinal, emotional, and even behavioral effects on the individual service provider. A social constructionist perspective is a reminder that the creation and interpretation of the servicescape is a joint function of both parties—the server and the served. Thus, the enactment of a successful service encounter often requires that all parties buy in to the script (see Solomon et al. 1985).

The self-definition and role performance of the service provider plays a vital part in this process, and clearly that individual's appearance has the potential to affect his or her ability to successfully play the required role. One potent testimonial to the power of uniform cues to influence wearers' behavior is found in a study that reported a significantly greater incidence of penalties incurred by sports teams whose players wore black; the aggressive connotations of this color apparently have been taken to heart by these "service providers" (Frank and Gilovich 1988). On another front, several major school districts, including Long Beach, California; Baltimore; and New York City, have implemented or are seriously considering school uniform requirements as a way to reduce disciplinary problems ("School Uniforms Growing in Favor" 1994).

Certainly the lay public is well aware of the likely link between employee appearance and the attainment of such instrumental goals as professional recognition, career mobility, and even initial employment. The dramaturgical perspective underscores the importance of the various dimensions by which an audience infers the believability of an actor's performance and responds accordingly with rewards for a credible act and punishments for a sloppy one. No aspect of appearance, from body shape to grooming, has escaped the scrutiny of image specialists, media pundits, co-workers, and the like. These "critics" emphasize that even very subtle cues can exert a dramatic impact on social perception, perhaps to the extent that minor slipups can torpedo an otherwise successful career or job interview.

Appearance and
Organizational Socialization

Personal career success aside, an employee's appearance has other ramifications for the organization as a whole. This dimension also is related to the process of organizational socialization, where a person learns the values, norms, and required behaviors that permit participation as a member of an organization—and thus permit the organization to function effectively. Clothing and other possessions, for example, are commonly modified to symbolize a "novice's" change in identity as he or she takes on member status in a group. That explains why inductees in many organizations, whether soldiers, prisoners, nuns, or fraternity initiates, first divest themselves of "civilian" clothing to reinforce their new status. The adoption of a new look emphasizes the solidarity of group identity, creating a distinction between "we" versus "they" that often is useful to build identification with the new organization.

This process involves several stages, beginning with the decision to enter the organizational context (accompanied by an implicit or explicit agreement to adhere to that group's regulations and norms) and culminating in the attainment of "insider" status, where one has internalized the organization's objectives and is motivated to conform to its culture. The role of clothing in socialization has been well documented in many contexts, ranging from large bureaucracies (see Whyte 1956) to a simulated prison environment; clothing manipulations were an integral part of the false reality created by experimenters in Philip Zimbardo's classic prison study (Zimbardo 1973).

Company Identity: "We" Versus "They"

Clothing plays a key role in the creation of a company identity, where service providers internalize their employee roles. Organizational differentiation is a prerequisite for uniforms; there must be some reason to distinguish wearers from nonwearers. A testimonial from the copy of a recent advertisement for a uniform company nicely illustrates this function: A plant manager at a boat factory observes, "Anytime you can make people feel a part of the company, even if it's a simple thing like a hat or a jacket or whatever, you've really accomplished a lot. I think uniforms give people a sense of pride and a feeling of being a part of our organization."

This type of differentiation tends to occur late in the history of organizations as their group structures begin to crystallize. For example, the American naval force originated on an ad hoc basis early on; individuals were recruited when a ship was ready to sail, and the same men served on both naval ships and merchant ships. It was not until late in the nineteenth century that the need arose for a pool of specialized individuals. At that point, a distinctive naval uniform began to appear (Joseph 1986).

Embodying Organizational Metaphors

The symbolism of a uniform helps to communicate the priorities of the sponsoring organization. Uniforms often serve as a metaphor for ideologies, such as militarism, science, or religion, that reflect the fundamental values of the group. For example, the Salvation Army adapted military-style uniforms because the public was favorably disposed toward this type of authoritarian ideology at the time the uniforms were created.

If a business values consistency and homogeneity (as in the case of fast food or mail delivery services), this message might be conveyed through dress code standards (Rafaeli and Pratt 1993). In another context, hotel surveys indicate that safety and security are guests' top priorities. Accordingly, plain suits for hotel security guards are being replaced with paramilitary-style uniforms to ease guests' anxieties about security—a deliberate invocation of the military metaphor to communicate organizational priorities (Marshall 1994). It has also been suggested that low-status service providers, such as hotel doormen, may be used as pawns in a game of vicarious consumption. Issuing these employees elaborate, ostentatious, and even gaudy uniforms in a sense transforms them into mannequins in order to flaunt the organization's wealth and power (see Joseph 1986).

Another manifestation of this communicational function is found in health care servicescapes. The traditional symbol of the physician is the sterile white coat, which connotes a laboratory setting. This garment symbolizes "science" and imposes a rational perspective on what can be for patients an irrational and scary situation. The significance of the color white is vital here. White relates to life, purity, superhuman power ("cleanliness is next to godliness"), and even candor or justice (Blumhagen 1979). This color is also chaste and thus implies a lack of sexuality; it depersonalizes the internist. Such symbolism may ameliorate the anxieties of women who must submit to intrusive physical contact by male strangers. In contrast, some psychiatrists and pediatricians have taken to wearing either street clothes or pastel medical smocks to reduce the formality of the doctor/patient relationship.

Rewards of Membership
Apparel can also serve as a reinforcer by symbolically indicating the successful transition from outsider to insider. It is thus a potent form of internal marketing insofar as it helps to build esprit de corps. For example, Xerox issues a company blazer to employees upon their completion of some technical classes. In the New York City Police Department, promotion from probationary status is accompanied by a change from a gray uniform to the regular blue attire, a transition recruits call "moving up to the blues" (Joseph 1986).

Conflict Management and Status Denotation
Uniforms can also play a valuable role in clarifying status structures within the service environment and in ensuring that expectations of the occupational role remain dominant when the role occupant is tempted to stray from the firm's grasp. For example, the military encountered problems with pregnant soldiers who were having difficulty reconciling the role demands of military bearing with those of childbearing. The policy of allowing these women to wear mufti once their pregnancies advanced past the six-month stage had to be abandoned after excessive disciplinary problems were reported. The military's eventual response was to design and mandate the wearing of maternity uniforms throughout the pregnancy. Behavioral problems subsequently abated.

While the military uniform provides the most clear-cut example of the use of apparel to reinforce role membership, many service businesses also need to reduce the ambiguity inherent in defining employees' duties and prerogatives. Uniforms can be used either to create or diffuse internal competition among units, or to make it easier to identify employees who perform different service functions. For example, stratified dress in restaurants reduces confusion. It minimizes the extent to which waiters are questioned about seating arrangements and hostesses are queried about dinner specials.

A case study of organizational culture at Disneyland provides a telling illustration of the use of appearance standards to connote the employee's position in the status hierarchy. The researchers found that status at the park is expressed less by monetary means than by access to different uniforms. High-status jobs for men include "the crisp, officer-like monorail operator . . . the swash-buckling Pirate of the Caribbean, the casual cowpoke of Big Thunder Mountain." These members of the Disney "cast" thus appear to internalize the symbolism of their costumes. A quite different dynamic was observed for female employees, who apparently vied for the right to wear the sexiest uniforms. When high-status female tour guides found they were being upstaged by the more revealing outfits that were issued to the operators of the "It's a Small World" attraction, they lobbied against this policy and succeeded in having their rivals' skirts lowered and necklines raised (van Maanen and Kunda 1989).

The Legality of People Packaging

As service businesses continue to recognize the strategic value of exerting greater control over employees' appearance, the legal and ethical ramifications of these decisions must be carefully considered. To what extent does the company have the right to mandate how employees will groom themselves, or what they are allowed or not allowed to wear? For example, in 1994 employees of music stores owned by Blockbuster Entertainment were informed that they must adhere to grooming guidelines, including the prohibition of long hair and earrings for males ("Male Workers Ordered to Cut Hair" 1994). It is not uncommon for service organizations ranging from major corporations like Disney to locally owned cleaning businesses, restaurants, and so on to impose appearance requirements on their employees.

The legality of these rules is a matter of some debate among legal scholars. The current consensus appears to be that dress codes are legally enforceable if they meet three criteria: (1) they are not discriminatory; (2) they are reasonable; and (3) they are based on business necessity. This means that the code must be integrally related to the communication of a specified image, or that some type of apparel is required for safety or functional purposes.

An organization may establish differences in dress codes for male and female employees if this decision is based on community standards, but it should proceed with caution when prohibiting clothing, jewelry, etc., that could result in a claim of racial, ethnic, or gender discrimination (Hass and Moore 1990). Discrimination can be an issue, for example, when members of ethnic or religious minorities are prohibited from exhibiting distinctive apparel or grooming styles. One example is hair braiding among African-American women, and another is a ruling by the government of France barring the wearing of head scarves by Muslim students on the grounds that this practice violated a tradition of secular education (Ibrahim 1994).

The majority of legal and moral objections to dress policies have been raised in the context of sex discrimination, where it is argued that the same standards typically are not upheld for both sexes equally. A J. C. Penney store reversed a policy forbidding women employees to wear slacks after management encountered a firestorm of public opposition to the rule (Kunde 1993). Similarly, a Continental Airlines ticket agent was fired for failing to wear lipstick and foundation, but she too was reinstated following a media uproar (Ziemba 1993). On the other hand, the courts upheld a ruling in favor of a policy that bars male employees from wearing facial jewelry, including earrings, but that allows women to wear jewelry that is not "unusual or overly large" (Bartlett 1994). Another court denied a claim of handicap discrimination by a transsexual who was fired for wearing "excessively feminine" attire, including a strand of pink pearls (see Bartlett 1994).

One recent discussion in the legal literature of the implication of appearance standards as a vehicle for sex discrimination is instructive. This case involves the Hooters restaurant chain, which deliberately hires only women servers, bartenders, and hostesses and requires its female employees to wear skimpy attire. According to an attorney who specializes in these issues, to justify this policy in light of Title VII (which addresses sexual subordination in the workplace), Hooters would have to establish that the essence of its business is the sale of sexual arousal rather than food and drink. If the chain could do this, subordination would be permitted. She summarizes this ironic situation as follows: "The rule of thumb . . . is simple: sex bars may subordinate women, but airlines and restaurants may not" (Bartlett 1994, 2,579).

CONCLUSIONS

The concerted efforts by companies in a range of services businesses to regulate the appearance and dress of their employees attests to the intuitive recognition by management of the power of costume in the servicescape. Despite widespread acknowledgment of this power, the field of services marketing suffers from a paucity of research that more systematically examines how clothing and grooming cues contribute to the creation of meaning in service settings. These issues need to be addressed to provide a better understanding of the intersection between the physical environment and the phenomenology of the service encounter.

In addition to the work that is needed to identify how specific manipulations of clothing styles, designs, insignia, etc. affect perceptions of corporate identity and of service quality, other issues also cry out for attention. For example, as "themed environments" are gaining in popularity among servicescape designers (e.g., Fashion Cafe in New York, Ed Debevic's diner in Chicago, Jimmy Buffett's Margaritaville in Florida and New Orleans, Disney theme parks everywhere), the role of apparel symbolism in creating these "realities" needs more attention. As a matter of semiotic consistency, apparel design must be coordinated with the remainder of the physical environment. More needs to be known about the relative salience of different servicescape dimensions—do costumes, settings, and/or props carry the bulk of the meaning communicated to patrons?

Another issue that has not been addressed is how the appearance of other customers in the servicescape affects perceptions of it. To paraphrase Groucho Marx, "I would never join a club that would

class

have me as a member." To what extent does the clothing of other "co-consumers" affect the servicescape gestalt (see Solomon 1996)? For example, numerous restaurants and nightclubs enforce dress codes for the purpose of excluding both the sloppy and the "unhip." How are these criteria established, and what effect does this mandated exclusivity have on the image of the service establishment— among the admitted or among the rejected?

Finally, a host of legal and ethical issues arise from organizations' attempts to "package" their employees. As service providers become objectified by managers and are forced to fit into a "theme," conflicts inevitably will arise between the need to standardize service delivery versus the employee's right to self-expression. Should every aspect of the play be tightly scripted, or should individual actors be allowed to ad-lib by improvising unique identities on the service stage? This will become an even more important issue as service businesses continue to expand into franchising and "turnkey systems," where every aspect of the servicescape is engineered for maximum efficiency and consistency. Careful attention to these questions and, in more general terms, to the overlooked power of the built environment to create and perpetuate meaning in the servicescape will be needed to ensure that service performances are satisfying and productive for all concerned: the theater (service business), the audience (customers), and the troupe of actors (employees).

BIBLIOGRAPHY

AIRLINE PILOTS ASSOCIATION, INTERNATIONAL V. UNITED AIRLINES, INC. 1979. *FEP Cases* 26 (June 12): 607–629.

ARONSON, ELIOT. 1972. *The Social Animal.* San Francisco: Freeman.

BAKER, MICHAEL J., AND GILBERT A. CHURCHILL, JR. 1977. "The Impact of Physically Attractive Models on Advertising Evaluations." *Journal of Marketing Research* 14 (November): 538–555.

BARTHES, ROLAND. 1983. *The Fashion System.* Translated by Matthew Ward and Richard Howard. New York: Hill and Wang.

BARTLETT, KATHARINE T. 1994. "Only Girls Wear Barrettes: Dress and Appearance Standards, Community Norms, and Workplace Equality." *Michigan Law Review* 92 (August): 2,541–2,582.

BELCH, GEORGE E.; MICHAEL A. BELCH; AND ANGELINA VILLAREAL. 1987. "Effects of Advertising Communications: Review of Research." In *Research in Marketing,* vol. 9. Greenwich, CT: JAI Press, Inc.

BERSCHEID, ELAINE, AND ELAINE WALSTER. 1974. "Physical Attractiveness." In *Advances in Experimental Social Psychology,* vol. 7, edited by Leonard Berkowitz. New York: Academic Press.

BITNER, MARY JO. 1990. "Evaluating Service Encounters: The Effects of Physical Surroundings and Employee Responses." *Journal of Marketing* 54 (April): 69–82.

BLOCH, PETER H., AND MARSHA L. RICHINS. 1992. "You Look 'Mahvelous': The Pursuit of Beauty and the Marketing Concept." *Psychology & Marketing* 9 (January): 3–15.

BLUMHAGEN, D. W. 1979. "The Doctor's White Coat: The Image of the Physician in Modern America." *Annals of Internal Medicine* 91:111–116.

BROMLEY, D. B. 1993. *Reputation, Image, and Impression Management.* West Sussex, England: John Wiley & Sons Ltd.

CABALLERO, MARJORIE J., AND WILLIAM M. PRIDE. 1984. "Selected Effects of Sales-person Sex and Attractiveness in Direct Mail Advertisements." *Journal of Marketing* 48 (January): 94–100.

CASH, THOMAS F. 1981. "Physical Attractiveness: An Annotated Bibliography of Theory and Research in the Behavioral Sciences." *Psychological Documents* 11:83 (Ms. No. 2,370).

CASH, THOMAS F., AND THOMAS PRUZINSKY, EDS. 1990. *Body Images: Development, Deviance and Change.* New York: Guilford Press.

CHAJET, CLIVE. 1992. "Employees as Image Shapers." *Executive Excellence* (October): 18–19.

COLLINS, JULIA M. 1989. "Off to Work." *Harvard Business Review* (September–October): 105–109.

COURTNEY, ALICE E., AND THOMAS W. WHIPPLE. 1983. *Sex Stereotyping in Advertising.* Lexington, MA: Lexington Books.

CZEPIEL, JOHN A.; MICHAEL R. SOLOMON; AND CAROL F. SURPRENANT, EDS. 1985. *The Service Encounter: Managing Employee/Customer Interaction in Service Businesses.* Lexington, MA: Lexington Books.

DAVIS, FRED. 1985. "Clothing and Fashion as Communication." In *The Psychology of Fashion,* edited by Michael R. Solomon. Lexington, MA: Lexington Books, 15–28.

"Dress Codes à la Modes." 1993. *Industrial Relations Review & Report* (March): 5–9.

EDVARDSSON, BO. 1992. "Service Breakdowns: A Study of Critical Incidents in an Airline." *International Journal of Service Industry Management* 3:17–29.

FRANK, MARK G., AND THOMAS GILOVICH. 1988. "The Dark Side of Self- and Social Perception: Black Uniforms and Aggression in Professional Sports." *Journal of Personality and Social Psychology* 54(1):74–85.

FRANK, ROBERT. 1994. "Tired of Lacing Up Work Boots? Why Don't You Try a UPS Shirt?" *The Wall Street Journal* (November 21): B1.

———. 1995. "In the UPS Man, Some Women Find a Complete Package." *The Wall Street Journal* (February 8): A1.

FRANZOI, STEPHEN L. 1988. "A Picture of Competence." *American Journal of Nursing* 88(8):1,109–1,112.

GOFFMAN, ERVING. 1959. *The Presentation of Self in Everyday Life.* Garden City, NY: Doubleday.

GROVE, STEPHEN J., AND RAYMOND P. FISK. 1991. "The Dramaturgy of Services Exchange: An Analytical Framework for Services Marketing." Reprinted in Christopher H. Lovelock (1991), *Services Marketing,* 2d ed. Englewood Cliffs, NJ: Prentice Hall, 59–68.

HASS, MARSHA E., AND DOROTHY P. MOORE. 1990. "Company Uniforms: Vulnerability in People Packaging." *Employment Relations Today* (Spring): 37–43.

HASTIE, R.; T. M. OSTROM; E. B. EBBESEN; R. S. WYER, JR.; D. L. HAMILTON; AND D. E. CARLSTON, EDS. 1980. *Person Memory: The Cognitive Basis of Social Perception.* Hillsdale, NJ: Erlbaum.

HATFIELD, ELAINE, AND SUSAN SPRECHER. 1986. *Mirror, Mirror . . . The Importance of Looks in Everyday Life.* Albany, NY: SUNY Press.

HIMELSTEIN, LINDA. 1996. "Levi's vs. the Dress Code." *Business Week* (April 1): 57–58.

HOCHSCHILD, ARLIE R. 1983. *The Managed Heart: Commercialization of Human Feeling.* Berkeley: University of California Press.

IBRAHIM, YOUSSEF M. 1994. "France Bans Muslim Scarf in Its Schools." *New York Times* (September 11): 4.

JENKINS, KEVIN J. 1992. "Service Quality in the Skies." *Business Quarterly* 57 (Autumn): 13–18.

JONES, E. E. 1990. *Interpersonal Perception.* New York: W. H. Freeman.

JOSEPH, W. BENOY. 1982. "The Credibility of Physically Attractive Communicators: A Review." *Journal of Advertising* 11(3):15–24.

KAHLE, LYNN R., AND PAMELA M. HOMER. 1985. "Physical Attractiveness of the Celebrity Endorser: A Social Adaptation Perspective." *Journal of Consumer Research* 11 (March): 954–961.

KAISER, SUSAN B. 1997. *The Social Psychology of Clothing: Symbolic Appearances in Context,* 2d ed. rev. New York: Fairchild Publications.

KLOPPENBORG, TIMOTHY J., AND KENT N. GOURDIN. 1992. "Up in the Air About Quality." *Quality Progress* 25(2) (February): 31–35.

KUNDE, DIANA. 1993. "Firms Finding Dress Codes Turning into Battleground." *Arizona Republic* (March 15): E4.

"Leave the Muumuu at Home." 1994. *Business Week* (February 7): 8.

LEVITT, THEODORE. 1981. "Marketing Intangible Products and Product Intangibles." *Harvard Business Review* (May–June): 97.

LEWIS, KATHLEEN N., AND BRUCE W. WALSH. 1978. "Physical Attractiveness: Its Impact on the Perception of a Female Counselor." *Journal of Counseling Psychology* 25 (May): 210–216.

LOVELOCK, CHRISTOPHER H. 1991. *Services Marketing,* 2d ed. Englewood Cliffs, NJ: Prentice Hall.

"Male Workers Ordered to Cut Hair, Drop Earrings." 1994. *Asbury Park Press* (May 23): A4.

MARSHALL, ANTHONY. 1994. "Hotel Security Team Confronts New Challenges." *Hotel & Motel Management* (July 25): 11.

MOLLOY, JOHN. 1975. *Dress for Success.* New York: Warner Books.

OLINS, WALLY. 1990. "How a Corporation Reveals Itself." *New York Times Forum* (October 14): F13. Quoted in Marion G. Sobol, Gail E. Farrelly, and Jessica S. Taper. (1992), *Shaping the Corporate Image: An Analytical Guide for Executive Decision Makers.* Westport, CT: Quorum Books, 136.

PATZER, G. L. 1985. *The Physical Attractiveness Phenomena.* New York: Plenum.

RAFAELI, ANAT, AND MICHAEL G. PRATT. 1993. "Tailored Meanings: On the Meaning and Impact of Organizational Dress." *Academy of Management Review* 18 (January): 32–55.

REID, LEONARD N., AND LAWRENCE C. SOLEY. 1983. "Decorative Models and the Readership of Magazine Ads." *Journal of Advertising Research* 23(2):27–32.

REINGEN, PETER H., AND JEROME B. KERNAN. 1993. "Social Perception and Interpersonal Influence: Some Consequences of the Physical Attractiveness Stereotype in a Personal Selling Setting." *Journal of Consumer Psychology* 2(1):25–38.

RICHINS, MARSHA L. 1991. "Social Comparison and the Idealized Images of Advertising." *Journal of Consumer Research* 18 (June): 71–83.

SCHLENKER, BARRY R. 1980. *Impression Management: The Self-Concept, Social Identity, and Interpersonal Relations.* Monterey, CA: Brooks/Cole.

SCHNEIDER, DAVID J. 1973. "Implicit Personality Theory: A Review." *Psychological Bulletin* 79:294–309.

"School Uniforms Growing in Favor in California." 1994. *New York Times* (September 3): 8.

SCHULTZ, DON E.; STANLEY I. TANNENBAUM; AND ROBERT F. LAUTERBORN. 1993. *Integrated Marketing Communications: Putting It Together and Making It Work.* Lincolnwood, IL: NTC Business Books.

SHOSTACK, G. LYNN. 1977. "Human Evidence: A New Part of the Marketing Mix." *Bank Marketing* (March): 32–34.

SOLOMON, JOLIE. 1996. "Why Worry About Pleat Pull and Sloppy Socks?" *Newsweek* (September 30): 51.

SOLOMON, MICHAEL R. 1983. "The Role of Products as Social Stimuli: A Symbolic Interactionism Perspective." *Journal of Consumer Research* 10 (December): 319–329.

———. 1985a. *The Psychology of Fashion.* Lexington, MA: Lexington Books.

———. 1985b. "Packaging the Service Provider." *Service Industries Journal* 5 (March): 64–72.

———. 1987a. "Standard Issue." *Psychology Today* (December): 30–31.

———. 1987b. "The Wardrobe Consultant: Exploring the Role of a New Retailing Partner." *Journal of Retailing* 63 (Summer): 110–128.

———. 1996. *Consumer Behavior: Buying, Having, and Being,* 3d ed. Englewood Cliffs, NJ: Prentice Hall.

SOLOMON, MICHAEL R., AND BASIL G. ENGLIS. 1994. "The Big Picture: Product Complementarity and Integrated Communications." *Journal of Advertising Research* 34 (January/February): 57–63.

SOLOMON, MICHAEL R., AND ELNORA W. STUART. 1997. *Marketing: Real People, Real Choices.* Englewood Cliffs, NJ: Prentice Hall.

SOLOMON, MICHAEL R.; CAROL SURPRENANT; JOHN A. CZEPIEL; AND EVELYN G. GUT-
MAN. 1985. "A Role Theory Perspective on Dyadic Interactions: The Service
Encounter." *Journal of Marketing* 49 (Winter): 99–111.

SOLOMON, MICHAEL R.; RICHARD ASHMORE; AND LAURA LONGO. 1992. "The Beauty
Match-Up Hypothesis: Congruence Between Types of Beauty and Product
Images in Advertising." *Journal of Advertising* 21 (December): 23–34.

SPROLES, GEORGE B., AND LESLIE DAVIS BURNS. 1994. *Changing Appearances: Understanding Dress in Contemporary Society.* New York: Fairchild Publications.

STERNE, HILARY. 1993. "Hand Signals." *Working Woman* (January): 60–62.

SURPRENANT, CAROL F., AND MICHAEL R. SOLOMON. 1987. "Predictability and Personalization in the Service Encounter." *Journal of Marketing* 51 (April): 86–96.

SWEENEY, JILLIAN C.; LESTER W. JOHNSON; AND ROBERT W. ARMSTRONG. 1992.
"The Effect of Cues on Service Quality Expectations and Service Selection
in a Restaurant Setting." *Journal of Services Marketing* 6 (Fall): 15–22.

TEDESCHI, J. T.; B. R. SCHLENKER; AND T. V. BONOMA. 1973. *Conflict, Power and
Games: The Experimental Study of Interpersonal Relations.* Chicago: Aldine.

THOMPSON, RICHARD. 1996. "BellSouth Installs Uniform Program." *Montgomery
Advertiser* (October 2): 12A.

VAN MAANEN, JOHN, AND GIDEON KUNDA. 1989. "'Real Feelings': Emotional
Expression and Organizational Culture." In *Research in Organizational Behav-
ior,* edited by L. L. Cummings and Barry M. Straw. 43:58–70. Greenwich,
CT: JAI Press.

VICK, EDWARD H. 1993. "The Corporation as a Brand." *Directors & Boards.* (Summer): 57–58.

WHYTE, WILLIAM H., JR. 1956. *The Organization Man.* New York: Simon and
Schuster.

WIESENDANGER, BETSY. 1992. "Do You Need an Image Consultant?" *Sales & Marketing Management* (May): 30 (5).

ZEITHAML, VALERIE A. 1991. "How Consumer Evaluation Processes Differ Between
Goods and Services." In *Services Marketing,* 2d ed., edited by Christopher H.
Lovelock. Englewood Cliffs, NJ: Prentice Hall, 39–47.

ZIEMBA, STANLEY. 1993. "Worker Rights Debate Is Back." *Chicago Tribune* (April
18): 7.

ZIMBARDO, P. G.; C. HANEY; W. S. BANKS; AND D. JAFFE. 1973. "A Pirandellian
Prison: The Mind Is a Formidable Jailer." *New York Times Magazine* (April 8):
38–60.

4

THE SOUL OF THE COMPANY STORE

Nike Town Chicago and the Emplaced Brandscape

JOHN F. SHERRY, JR.

But before there could be wonder (or theory, or philosophy, or architectural treatises), there had to be the well-made thing.
—McEwen (1993)

[Nike Town Chicago is] built as a theater, where our consumers are the audience participating in the production. Nike Town gives us the opportunity to explore and experiment with innovative ways to connect with our consumers.
—NTC (1992a)

Fuck the world. Fuck the numbers. Air feels right. Air feels like Nike.
—Strasser and Becklund (1993)

If we acknowledge the existence of an "ancestral blood tie between architecture and philosophy" (McEwen 1993, 2), then Nike Town Chicago (NTC) is surely the embodiment of the corporate dictum

John F. Sherry, Jr., is Professor of Marketing at the J. L. Kellogg Graduate School of Management, Northwestern University, Evanston, Illinois. The author would like to thank Jennifer Chang, Morris Holbrook, Sidney Levy, and Victor Margolin for their helpful comments on earlier versions of this manuscript.

"Just Do It." As this tagline—part New Age mantra, part secular ejaculation—has been embroidered into the fabric of adcult (Twitchell 1996), so also has the building expanded our notion of alternative translations of retail space. With the exception of pricing strategy, every designed element of the servicescape encourages impulsive behavior and invites instant gratification.[1] NTC is perhaps the most current incarnation of a retail theater alive to the liturgical roots of drama. A paean to design, NTC crosscuts genres of experience to evoke in consumers a range of synergistic thoughts, emotions, and behaviors that encourages active engagement with its servicescape. NTC is not merely the site of "commercial athleticism" (Agnew 1986), nor is it solely a "spiritual gymnasium" (Mandel 1967, 16) or "cathedral of consumption" (O'Guinn and Belk 1989). Neither is it primarily an amusement-centered themed environment (Gottdiener 1996) nor a megaboutique. While this chapter explores the polysemous possibilities the site affords, I begin, as is my custom, with a vignette drawn from my field notes, which I regard as a revelatory incident (Fernandez 1986) opening a window onto the phenomenology of this marketplace:

> Even in the company of key informants, I find myself shifting from the role of social scientist to flaneur [perhaps tending toward *dériveur?*] and back again, as I watch consumers watch me watch them watch their surroundings [note: revisit Benjamin's optical unconscious], trying all the while to attend to the observations of my interviewees without allowing my own engagement with the place to mute their comments.
>
> Don and Larry, two entrepreneurs in their midthirties, have invited me to accompany them on their visit to Nike Town Chicago, even though we have just met here on the spot. Each is an industrial designer, and together they create, restore, and market religious goods. As we wander, Larry speaks of the "mystical" quality of the setting, and compares NTC to a "basilica."

[1] And yet, when your sales receipt is presented to you in a small logo-emblazoned upscale envelope, ennobled by its package and giftlike in greeting card–esque aspect (the slip may even approximate a stock certificate or deed of ownership), the premium you've paid feels less like self-indulgence and more like wise investment. Ironically, the most elemental form of everyday retail theater—haggling—is absent from NTC (Sennett 1976).

Don compares his experience of NTC to being in a "museum," observing that "when you 'do' Chicago, you go to the Museum of Science and Industry, the Art Institute, and Nike Town." [Many of my informants are quick to proclaim the "accepted fact" that Nike Town is the "biggest tourist attraction" in the city.] Building on this remark, Larry allows that the building is more than a museum: "It's a museum of the future. You never have to remodel. George Jetson could pull up outside and never tell the difference!" Don supports his contention with an expansive arm gesture: "Look at all these parents showing their kids around; they're *teaching*. Just like a museum."

The two have come to NTC today not to shop, but to study the store, in particular its products and their merchandising. They are keenly aware of the synergies between their own enterprise and Nike's. They've come for "inspiration" and "ideas." Beyond their reverence for the sacral tones of the ambience lies an even more intriguing respect for the products on display. In Don's estimation, "This all speaks to the integrity of their products. If you spend so much effort to showcase your product, it must be really good. They've paid attention to every detail—from door handles and railings to sound effects. They try to reach all your senses. Even the salespeople are low-key. There's no sales pressure." As if to sum up his evaluation of the NTC servicescape, Larry concludes, "There's a carryover effect. Next time I see Nike products in a regular store, I'll recall this good experience." As our conversation unfolds, I notice each of them actively engage the environment, handling products, touching fixtures, closing eyes, and cocking heads to discriminate background sounds, and scanning constantly. They are curiously hypervigilant and yet relaxed, as they absorb the grand design.

I have selected this introductory vignette because it resonates with my own experience of the store and intuitions about the affecting nature of servicescapes. The field note addresses the influence of the designed environment on brand equity in general and on the more numinous dimensions of brand identity in particular. Elsewhere (Sherry 1995a, 36), I have called attention to an obverse strategy of the one McCracken (1988, 105–106) has called "meaning displacement." I think of this strategy as one of *emplacement,* whereby culture instantiates the mundane "by encoding its folkways in holographic fashion into the material vehicles of social life, to be recovered discontinuously, and often outside conscious awareness" (Sherry 1995a, 36). Emplacement is at work on a molecular level as well, when a corporation embodies its vision not only in the product it makes, but also in the other elements of its marketing mix. Integrated marketing communication (Schultz, Tannenbaum, and Lauterborn 1994), for example, is a manifestation of the emplacement process writ small.

The delight inspired in consumers by their discovery of the larger significance of a corporation's attention to detail—the "aha" experience or epiphany that occurs in the unwrapping of unanticipated added value—shapes relationships developed with a brand. Emplacement is especially intriguing in an era of eroding brand loyalty and "cereal monogamy" (Sherry 1985), when place increasingly becomes (de facto if not de jure) the brand (Sherry 1995b). So it is with NTC, where brand is both a noun and a verb. Consumers are invited to enhance their brandscape through engagement with this polysemous environment.

A brandscape is a "material and symbolic environment that consumers build with marketplace products, images and messages, that they invest with local meaning, and whose totemic significance largely shapes the adaptation consumers make to the modern world" (Sherry 1985). Brandscaping is one of the ways in which consumption is actively produced by consumers. Emplacement and brandscaping act in tandem to ground or root a consumer's experience in the artifact, while at the same time allowing the artifact to become a projectible field or projective vehicle for culturally mediated idiosyncratic meaning. The cocreation of experience by marketers and consumers—the performance of negotiated meanings—is engendered in NTC by design.[2] Whether or not they are shoppers, once inside the doors of NTC, consumers become flaneurs and *bricoleurs.*

In this chapter, I explore the interaction of emplacement and brandscaping by focusing on the experience that design conspires to elicit from visitors to NTC. By attending to design cues and affordances provided by the marketer, and observing the effects their

---

[2] The "performance" motif emphasized in current NTC merchandising, emblazoned on signage and free-floating in air via optical illusion in the video theater, is both an ironic and reflexive reminder to consumers that their in-store behavior, whether scripted or improvisational, is ultimately theatrical.

reception exerts upon consumers, I highlight aspects of the NTC servicescape that are illustrative of the affecting presence (Armstrong 1974) that all marketplaces become when extraeconomic issues are considered.

METHODOLOGY

This account is a lineal descendant of the wave of ethnographic investigations of periodic markets and upscale specialty stores (McGrath 1989; McGrath, Sherry, and Heisley 1993; Sherry 1990a, 1990b; Sherry and McGrath 1989) that has contributed to the rejuvenation of retailing studies in recent years. It is a collateral relative of the renewed exploration of museums and galleries (Duhaime, Joy, and Ross 1995; McCracken 1990) that is helping consumer researchers better understand the experiential dimensions of servicescapes. After Buttimer (1993, 202), I attempt to "read" vernacular architecture "as text to be decoded in terms of the values of its human inhabitants." In temperament, this account is a hybrid effort that seeks to combine something of the studied alienation of ethnographic inquiry (Sherry 1995) with something of the disciplined reflexiveness of introspection (Gould 1991; Holbrook 1988a, 1988b; Rose 1995; Sherry 1996). I intend the result to lie somewhere between the unreflectively critical, idiosyncratic tradition of cultural studies and the conventionally dispassionate stakeholder-focus of ethnographic consumer research. What I strive to produce in this chapter is a phenomenological account of my own engagement with a particular marketplace hedged about with observations and interpretations drawn from other participants in process of enacting the servicescape. In tacking between self and other, I construct an account that is at once "producerly" (Sherry 1996b) and grounded in "reader-response" (Scott 1994). In conveying my own experience of "being-in-the-marketplace" (Richardson 1987; Sherry and McGrath 1989) in tandem with that of fellow consumers, I offer a perspective that is comparative rather than privileged, and probative rather than definitive.

I began this investigation in the summer of 1992 and have continued to visit the site through the autumn of 1996, the time this chapter was written.[3] During this prolonged engagement, I immersed myself in the round of life at the marketplace, gaining an appreciation for the seasonal flux of activity and variety of stakeholder perspectives (Sherry 1990). I employed participant observation extensively throughout the study. I conducted intercept interviews with fifty consumers and observed hundreds of others in their encounter with the servicescape. Interviews ranged from ten minutes to an hour, and from highly unstructured to structured. I shopped with consumers (Otnes, McGrath, and Lowrey 1995) and loitered with intent among clerks and cashiers, interviewing in context. Structured interviews were conducted with the store manager, marketing manager, and various staff members. I photographed dimensions of the servicescape and conducted autodriving interviews (Heisley and Levy 1991; Rook 1989) with some consumers.

Concurrently with the ethnography, and cognizant both of the risks (Wallendorf and Brucks 1993) and rewards of intraceptive intuition (Murray 1943; Sherry 1991), I practiced what Holbrook has called "subjective personal introspection" (Holbrook 1988a, 1988b), in an effort to capture my own experience of NTC. Thus, what follows is a composite account, and an inevitable confounding of emic and etic perspectives, of the NTC servicescape. While it may well be that the lawyer who defends himself has a fool for a client, I suspect that many social scientists resonate with poet Gary Snyder's (Tarn 1972) discovery that he'd rather be an informant than an anthropologist. In this essay, I attempt just such a shift in perspective.

MANAGERIAL PRÉCIS

NTC, the second in a series of seven company stores launched to date, opened in Chicago in the summer of 1992. Designed in-house

---

[3] Thus, while I employ the ethnographic present tense, my account is actually diachronic, which produces some distortion in synchronic accuracy. For example, exhibits and merchandising displays change over time, rendering some descriptions and photographs anachronistic. Yesterday's *Batman* exhibit becomes today's *Jurassic Park* exhibit. Wherever significant, I note such change in the text.

by Gordon Thompson, the 68,000-square-foot store boasts three selling floors and eighty feet of frontage on the "Magnificent Mile" of Michigan Avenue. The store is designed to deliver a "landmark experience," comparable to "enter[ing] Wrigley Field or hop[ping] on a ride at Disneyland" (NTC 1992a). The NTC "retail theater" concept is intended to combine "the fun of Disneyland and FAO Schwarz, the museum quality of the Smithsonian Institution and the merchandising of Ralph Lauren with the sights and sounds associated with MTV" (NTC 1992b). The store comprises eighteen pavilions that display products related to twenty different sports. Before I present an ethnographic overview of the built environment and experiential dimensions of NTC, it may be instructive to provide an account of the store from the perspective of its principal managers.

Marketing managers envision NTC as a "showcase" for the range of Nike products local dealers are not able to stock as comprehensively or merchandise as effectively. NTC dramatizes the breadth and depth of the Nike product mix. This presentation is expected to benefit dealers. NTC observes a policy of "noncompetition" with dealers, in an effort to be "sensitive" to their livelihoods. NTC does not run sales, does not have exclusive or advance availability of product, and offers training in merchandising to dealers in an effort to export the essence of Nikeworld. NTC exists strategically to enhance the brand without alienating dealers.

Consumers appear to respond to this strategy. Among the most common unelicited product-related consumer comments in my field notes reflect amazement both at the range of products and the premium pricing at NTC. Variations of "I didn't know Nike made this much stuff or was into this many sports!" compete with "Do you believe this [price]? I can get this much cheaper at home!" in my record of emic evaluations. Customers and staff readily acknowledge that "new" products encountered in NTC are eventually ordered through local dealers. Marketing managers describe their concession to dealers—the emphasis on equity building over sales—as a "museum" (versus a "warehouse") strategy.

While headquarters ultimately dictates objectives and evaluates end results, the regional Nike Town marketing managers are encouraged to innovate within a standardized pattern. Designers of these servicescapes eschew a cookie-cutter approach to design, and are invited to combine common elements and modules with local touches to "fit the space" the stores must occupy. At NTC, marketing managers have "wide parameters" for meeting "budget constraints" and revel in the "individual initiative" that the "loose organization" of their "creative company" permits. "Just Do It" is treated as a mandate for "entrepreneurial initiative." Managers and clerks alike speak of "shooting from the hip" in pursuit of servicescape refinement.

A NOTE ON BRAND EQUITY: MYTHOLOGY AND SOUL

At the time of this writing, the Nike "swoosh" logo has become so thoroughly identified with the brand that it is iconic. The company name no longer must accompany the mark to achieve recognition among consumers. The symbol and the brand are one. Serendipity and heroic marketing have conspired to produce this iconicity.

The "swoosh" name is derived from the Japanese nylon fabric that gave the company its original distinctive edge. The swoosh symbol—commissioned for thirty-five dollars from a young artist—was designed to combine structural functionality with visibility. Initial corporate reception of the logo was lukewarm. The Nike name was adopted after the logo was designed, as an expedient compromise in the face of deadline pressure. The name was inspired by an awakening dream of a company salesman—an anthropology graduate student turned social worker—and again received a lukewarm initial response (Strasser and Becklund 1993). The correspondence of name and symbol with mythology—the wings of Victory, the talaria (winged sandal) of Hermes—and of mythopoeia with onomatopoeia, has been achieved through marketing.

Over time, the logo has been refreshed to emphasize the company's commitment to quality and innovation in design. The company's "discovery" of marketing, and its pursuit of integrated marketing communication (of the "There Is No Finish Line" kind) dates from the historic brand-from-a-brand launch of the Air Jor-

dan line—complete with the Jump Man trademark, which itself has
achieved global iconicity—that was commemorated by the launch
director (and author of this chapter's third epigraph) in these prescient words: "On this rock . . . we will build a church" (Strasser
and Becklund 1993, 455). While the marketing director was eventually exorcised from the firm before the building of NTC, his New
Testament diction was strategically prophetic. Principal among the
many meanings of NTC is that of sacred space. NTC is not merely
emblematic of the sacralization of sport in America, nor of our
recently recovered awareness of its eroticization (Guttmann 1996).
It is a basilica of basketball, complete with reliquaries, and monumental witness to the apotheosis of Michael Jordan.[4]

ETHNOGRAPHIC OVERVIEW

In the following pages, I provide an ethnographic overview of NTC
phenomenology. I begin with a description of the larger retail environment of the store and devote attention to the building's exterior.
I then undertake a sort of "walking tour" of the interior of the
store, discussing the ambient surroundings and exploring reactions
to them. I employ the pontifical *we* and address the reader rhetor-
ically, as a fellow traveler. Finally, I offer an interpretive summary
of the NTC experience.

Let me begin this section with another field note excerpt, to
remind the reader of the emic input that has shaped my own
perceptions:

> So many informants profess to have come to NTC "not to buy
> something," but to "see" it, whether on their own, with family

---

[4] Upon returning to his career as hard-court demigod shortly before Easter at the
United Center (the House that Jordan built, and site of his statue), after having
undertaken the archetypal heroic journey involving great challenges, personal sacrifice, and wondrous encounters—enduring the murder of his father and a sojourn
as a baseball player—Jordan was greeted by a multistory banner hung from NTC,
proclaiming "He's back!!" Part Christ, part poltergeist (like Muhammad Ali before
him), Jordan is revered by Chicago as its current patron saint.

and friends, or with out-of-town guests, because it is "more than just a store." A teenage boy describes the "peaceful feeling" elicited by the "music and colors" of the surroundings and likens his experience to being in an "amusement park" or "museum." He tells me he "sees things [products] here [he] doesn't see in other stores." "Maybe I'll buy something, but I came here because Dad wanted to see it." Consumers seem not to search or browse so much as inspect the store. [Note: explore the commercio-aesthetic dynamic of the visual at NTC. Revisit Urry on the tourist gaze.]

Marie and Anna, two "out-of-town" women in their early twenties, have come to NTC specifically to buy sports shoes in their "hard to find" sizes, and graciously allow me to shop with them. "I come right to the source," proclaims Marie, a former basketball player, in describing her decision to shop NTC. "It's amazing how they draw you up four stories," Anna offers. "The open heights, the use of space. . . . You're *up* here, on the same level. . . . It's like a fantasy. There's the player, there's the player's shoe, there's the shoe for sale—it's all together. It's like a shrine." The immediacy produced by such vertically integrated merchandising is palpable for these two shoppers. Notes Marie, "The store changes with the sports. If there's a development in the sport, it shows up in the store. They constantly change the pictures and exhibits." As we continue to examine shoes, Anna concludes, "It's amazing. It's hard to verbalize. It makes you feel like you can 'do it.'" "Yeah," agrees Marie. "I was a player. I like the court. You can pretend to dunk." Even though physically present with me and their purchases, the women each wander a field of dreams, dwelling in an Erehwon of athletic accomplishment not bounded by the walls of NTC.

Cultural Geography of NTC: Location, Location, Location

A significant measure of the experience NTC affords consumers derives from its prestigious location on "the Boule Mich," a celebrated stretch of North Michigan Avenue also known as "the Magnificent Mile." NTC is flanked by a range of upscale retail outlets and galleries. The art-and-commerce ambience of this setting is not reflected solely in discrete and distinctive offerings by specialized shops. Rather, the effect is heightened by the kind of hybridized merchandising that gives NTC its own particular appeal, and the architectural diversity for which Chicago is renowned.

Facing north from the NTC entrance, the consumer's gaze takes in the Water Tower district of fine shops (including the vertical mall Water Tower Place) and assorted architectural wonders (the Old Water Tower, the Hancock Building, and the like). Directly across from the entrance, facing west, consumers encounter an architectural pastiche: the majestic Chicago Place, an enormous vertical mall designed in an agglomeration of styles and reminiscent of a European arcade. The Terra Museum of American Art also is prominently visible from the entrance. As if to challenge the primacy of the gaze, the visually unobtrusive Garrett Popcorn Shop, whose door is always open to accommodate the long line of consumers snaking into the extremely narrow shop, emits a pleasingly intense aroma of popcorn, caramel corn, and cheese corn onto the boulevard and into the surrounding stores. Passersby slowing to negotiate the queue or savor the scent often create something of a bottleneck on the sidewalk, giving pedestrians occasion to notice itinerant vendors and street musicians in their wandering orbit.

Facing south, and immediately next door to NTC, consumers are greeted by the Sony store. Sony has also affected a museum-cum-gallery servicescape, which allows consumers to admire state-of-the-art electronics while field-testing them in the store. On the corner southwest of the NTC entrance, Crate and Barrel has a flagship store, conveying, in its cylindrical glass facing, the essence of many of the wares it offers for sale.

Thus, as one looks up and down the boulevard, this urban marketplace resembles nothing so much as a canyon of consumption, its glass and concrete walls reigning over a river of pedestrian and vehicular traffic. As a transparently designed canyon, its cultural ecology is characterized by spectacle and desire. The energy and pace of this urban setting contribute to the immediacy of NTC's external presence and mirror the phenomenal realms contained within the building.

The exterior of the NTC building is fairly unremarkable, concealing its internal wonders in a fashion reminiscent of the way the outers of Nike footwear conceal their own internal engineering marvels. A landscaped parkway—whose concrete abutments invite consumers to sit and rest, observe and ruminate—gives the store an initial curb appeal. The facade is strongly reminiscent of an old gymnasium. Banners hang between the windows in columns on the middle stories. Two entranceways flank a bank of windows at street level. In those windows, consumers see not only product offerings and vestibule merchandising, but also reflections of their own images and the surrounding streetscape. Reflection is an activity greatly encouraged by the NTC servicescape. Above this central glassworks, the corporate name and logo are centered on a filigree grillwork. On the four structural columns bracketing the entranceways, bas-relief sculptures executed in material resembling aluminum are framed above eye level. These sculptures depict the body parts of athletes engaged in sport—a cyclist's torso, a runner's trunk and limbs, basketball players' arms, torso, and head, the profile of a female enacting aerobics. These sculptures appear to be emerging from the building (or merging with it), and the functions they embody make them suitable genius loci for this marketplace. If we allow the temple or shrine conceit to shape our interpretation, the fixity of these cult statues is not simply appropriate, it is also essential to the shaping of experience the consumer will undergo upon crossing the threshold. (Indeed, the *nikai,* or victories [McEwen 1993, 104] themselves, embodied in all the offerings of the corporation, from whence its name was derived, alight in this building.) That threshold crossing marks the entrance of the consumer into an alternative phenomenal realm, an existential condition of being-in-the-marketplace, a participation in a lifeworld just shy of a total institution.

Inside the Building: A Walking Tour

Because space limitations make it impossible to describe all the pavilions in sufficient detail, I limit my discussion to those interior structures that both give the reader an overall sense of the enterprise and reflect the degree of consumer interest that promoted my own initial introspection. That is, I confine my treatment more to the remarkable than the mundane as communicated to me by intuition and the enthusiasm of informants. I employ a bottom-up approach, describing phenomena encountered in ascending the building.

Vestibule

The vestibule has undergone considerable change since I began this investigation. The original window display consisted of a large rimless paddle wheel whose spokes terminate in athletic shoes, giving the impression of perpetual motion sustained by the product. Over this display, a banner proclaims, "There Is No Finish Line," reminding exiting visitors that true athletes remain suspended in an existential present of achieving, and that Nike will support them in their Sisyphean pursuit. Mounted on a side wall are framed covers of *Sports Illustrated*—each bearing the picture of a Nike celebrity endorser—that look like pictures in an exhibition.[5] An accompanying plaque pays tribute to the performance of "great athletes," the accomplishments of which confraternity the cobranding sponsors enable the customer to experience vicariously.

The performance motif conjoined with the opportunities for touching greatness (O'Guinn 1989) are impressed upon the consumer at the very outset of the visit. Consumers walk across a set of inlaid embossed concentric circles, at the center of which is the globe (North America featured prominently), ringed about with the Nike Town trademark. This same design, adorned with cardinal compass points, is also reproduced on what appear to simulate manhole covers on street-level floors inside the building. Crossing these globes gives us the impression that we are standing at the

[5] This concept has recently been reinterpreted in an upstairs wall-of-fame gallery that features photographs of area amateur athletes and accounts of their achievements, while the original vestibule exhibit has been retired. Whether the removal of these covers coincides with the end of history, or the corporation's transcendence of the historic into the realm of the fantastic, if not mythic, is interesting to consider. It may enable viewers to enter more easily into a culture-bound delusional system if they are not reminded so graphically of the firm's historical situatedness. Perhaps history has been "captured totally by the spin-doctors of market forces" (Fjellman 1992, 308).

epicenter of athletics. As if to confirm this impression, a statue of Michael Jordan stands[6] at the center wall of the vestibule. Accompanying signage identifies him as "The Man," and as a "good guy" who plays "great ball." Consumers read of Jordan's accomplishments while they touch the exhibit. In the background, the sounds of ringing mauls and hammers and the noises associated with the basketball court merge with ethereally atonal New Age music, as we ponder the relationship between effort and reward, and marvel at the retailer's attempt to forge an identity between them.

First Floor

Crossing the threshold of the vestibule, we enter NTC proper and step directly into a spectacular illusion. Walking through NTC's "Town Square" simulates the feel of strolling outdoors through a small-town shopping district. The open-air feel is enhanced by the vaulted ceiling, the brick-faced and window-studded exteriors of the pavilions, the street-paved flooring complete with sewer grates, the birdsong soundscape, and booths that simulate vendor carts. This feeling is further enhanced later on during consumers' meanderings to other floors, where you can look out of pavilion windows, over balconies, and down to the "street" below.

The initial sensory rush consumers experience is delightfully overwhelming. "Oh my God!" "Pretty cool!" "Gorgeous colors!" "Boy, I like this!" These and other spontaneous exclamations in many languages other than English can be captured by the casual auditor standing in Town Square. Hushed voices are audible as well. Poster-size photographs of athletes of varying renown—local, national,

---

[6] Once suspended like other NTC statues, now encased in a tubular transparent time capsule not unlike a vertical analogue of the resident of Lenin's tomb, this white plaster sculpture—part museum specimen, part gallery exhibit—invites veneration. A charitable reading of the "whiteness" of the bleached black statues throughout NTC marks this homogenization as an homage to classical antiquity in the service of projection and visibility. Though these be giants, they are self-made Everymen whose greatness we all can emulate, if not appropriate, through purchase.

international—adorn some walls, where their accomplishments are documented. Exhibit cases containing products and memorabilia proliferate, confounding the boundary between the categories and reinvigorating the notion of commodity aesthetics.

The sheer verticality of the Town Center brick facade reinforces the "Flight" motif signage at its pinnacle. The consumer's gaze is drawn upward to encounter the suspended white plaster statues of athletes in motion—some recognizable as basketball players Scottie Pippen and David Robinson; others, like the nameless cyclists, as anonymous as ghost riders in the sky—and the Nike footgear they wear. Where Sergey Bubka's vaulting effigy once soared at the beginning of my field study, now stands the soccer pavilion sign, a merchandising tribute to the waxing and waning of celebrity.

At ground level, the open sight lines reinforce feelings of expansiveness and connectivity. Visible everywhere are colorful escalators, catwalks, transparent delivery tubes, and hordes of roaming consumers. People and goods move in concert, passing each other numerous times in transit. These delivery tubes in particular (as well as their associated terminals) fascinate consumers, as shoe boxes whiz along, almost pneumatically, from stockroom to sales floor, visible to all throughout the journey. "Can you ride in them?" children wonder, as their parents reminisce to them about "The Jetsons." It is a sanitized scene from *Blade Runner,* a transmogrified *Our Town.* Black-and-white murals of athletes, executed in the socialist realism style of wood engravings of the kind sponsored during the Depression by the WPA and FAP, and made commercially viable by artists such as Rockwell Kent, adorn some walls, giving sport the heroically populist cast the corporation seeks to foster. The waffle-patterned sole—the firm's original innovation, showcased in floor exhibits[7]— is prominently featured in these murals. Macro-photographs of Nike

---

[7] These exhibits and others displaying the evolution of footgear through time, however simulated, give viewers the feeling of being in the presence of the original, perhaps even the Ur-shoe, thus facilitating reflection upon the ownership of one's own shoes and resonance of "original" with "own." Sensory rhetoric helps link primal and unique aura to ownership.

endorsers mounted on a wall are shielded by vertical blinds painted in neo-impressionist style to resemble athletes, creating an optical illusion that weds present with past, technology with art, and fantasy with reality, again in the service of corporate vision. All art at NTC is performance art.

A curious effect is achieved by signage mounted over the ground floor elevator. A directory for the three showroom floors of NTC gives specific pavilion information. The sign calls attention to the uninterestingness of the fourth-floor "Command Center" of the building in a way that intrigues consumers. Consumers are prohibited from visiting this floor. The attractiveness of a back-stage area in what is apparently a completely transparent front-stage is almost irresistible to consumers, and the corporation piques this interest strategically. Images of an inner sanctum—part holy of holies, part behind the curtain of Oz—pepper consumers' commentaries as they ride the elevator. We are in a high-tech tabernacle.

Perhaps the most compelling consumer experience on the ground floor of NTC is achieved on water. Two liquid media engage our attention here. The more apparent of the two is the large aquarium that provides the backdrop for shelving units full of sandals and Aquasocks. A tankful of exotic fish, color-coordinated to products (Katz 1994), draws consumers toward the outdoor-gear boutique. Adults rush children to "see the pretty fish," lifting the children for a better view and a chance to touch the glass. "Are they real fish?" is a frequent question, as children try to discriminate the fantasy-reality boundaries of the NTC environment.

Even more alluring is the video pond set off in a grotto flanked by lava lamp lighting and wave-contoured shelving, hard by a set of wave-contoured benches with acrylic swoosh inlays. The pond is a bank of nine video screens set in the floor, which projects the illusion of water and underwater scenes. Children flirt with its visual cliff appeal, while adults joke about "walking on water." Kids, often lost to the biblical subtext but not the fantasy feeling of such walking, are as apt to respond that they've never "walked on TV before." Consumers often gather around the pond, either standing or sitting, and gaze deeply into the video screens. Cast by design as Christ and Narcissus, we imagine perhaps that the brand will work miracles for us, and mask our self-absorption as reflection. Now literally bathed in the glow of the electronic hearth, perhaps we feel that Nike Town is Our Town. This transformation is especially relevant in our postmodern era, where "third places" (Oldenburg 1989) are as likely as not to be retail "drop-in centers" (Katz 1994, 271).

Second Floor

Riding the escalator to the second floor, consumers continue to cock and swivel their heads to absorb the sights and sounds of NTC, pointing out discoveries, calling out observations, and anticipating what they are likely to encounter next. Their curiosity whetted by having seen display cases of heroes' relics, corporate sacra, public-service projects, and products themselves, consumers take direction from the engaging signage—sometimes neon, sometimes contoured to follow the building's angles, sometimes varied typographically to suit the pavilion—as they debark.[8] Indeed, the escalators have something of the feel of an amusement park ride or monorail shuttle, and encourage a festive attitude among riders. Their fluorescent lights and transparency intensify this feeling.

Roaming the floor, we soon encounter benches built to resemble the air-support technology that has given Nike one of its distinctive competitive advantages. The bench is in effect a deliciously visual oxymoron that renders the corporation's distinctive technology transparent: we experience visible air. By encouraging consumers to see and feel on a grander scale what benefits design delivers to them, NTC facilitates a *being-in-the-shoe* experience. Consumers are quick to seize on the cue, and they grow increasingly alert to the affordances designers have built into merchandising fixtures. They are pleased to discover shelving that consists of basketball goals and backboards, or to recognize and learn from the

---

[8] Those riding the elevator—itself summoned by logo-emblazoned buttons—encounter display cases within as they shuttle between floors. Even the bathrooms contain exhibits, such as the Hollywood-style shoes made by Nike for Elton John.

head-to-toe merchandising strategy that dictates sartorial propriety from sport to sport. Squeals of delight and a summoning of witnesses accompanies the discovery by children and adults alike of door handles and railing support struts cast in the shape of the distinctive swoosh. Almost universally, this visual detection prompts a fondling of these fixtures, as if a palpable grasping of brand essence were to make the experience of NTC tangible. Design promotes the hands-on philosophy that corporate vision seeks to instill in consumers. Such tangibility is self-consciously showcased at the pinnacle of the consumer's journey, as I describe in the upcoming section.

While other sports such as aerobics, tennis, and golf are featured here (captured often enough in the soundscape itself), and while the memorabilia of Nike celebrities from sports such as baseball are on display, the focus of the second floor, and arguably of NTC at large, is the half-court basketball unit that serves a number of functions. As a sales floor, it periodically houses temporary shelving for shoe displays. It provides a realistic opportunity for customers to field-test footwear under consideration for purchase. It is the site of the occasional pep rally to celebrate the victories of the Chicago Bulls basketball team. Indeed, the team introduction music is audible in the background. Perhaps most importantly, its scale and soundscape encourage the mystical participation of visitors in the lifeworld of Michael Jordan.

As consumers wander the court, or sit on benches whose seat pads bear the jersey numbers of Nike endorsers, or jump, feint, and pivot, they are dwarfed by a multistory fantasy photograph of His Airness soaring through the clouds behind the net, in his iconic Jump Man pose. A caption appended to the photo is an epigraph taken from William Blake:

> No bird soars too high,
> If he soars with his own wings.

The epigraph ceremonializes Jordan's near-mythic abilities and legendary work ethic while at the same time encouraging the projective fantasy in individual consumers of infinite perfectibility, of effort rewarded by success.[9] The words are a denial of hubris, the image one of a divine messenger, if not an avenging angel.

More than one young consumer advised me, as we gazed at this picture, that "Michael Jordan is God." Adults would often murmur, "Amazing!" in response to both the built environment and Jordan's presence. That Jordan embodies "flight" is ironically, and perhaps even mechanically, undeniable. That he embodies the virtuous face of "pride" is also apparent. Consumers' behaviors in this half-court room range from hushed reverence as they regard the wall display, to noisy exuberance as they squeak soles on the hard court and leap for the rim. The disinhibiting effect of the servicescape extends to adults as well as children. Sometimes it's irresistible to laugh in church. Especially, in the reflexively self-referential adcult (Goldman and Papson 1995; Twitchell 1996) instant where we try to "be like Mike."

The second-floor experience is encapsulated for consumers in their being surrounded by the memorabilia displays and their attaining the same physical heights as the suspended statues of the superstar endorsers. We are literally immersed in a milieu of accomplishment, whether we make eye contact with the soaring

---

[9] "God bless the child that's got his own," goes one song. "Angels in the architecture," goes another. The allusions in this wall display are dizzying in their multistrandedness. The biblicality of Blake's poetry and the woodcuts gives the display a cosmological significance. Jordan's ethnicity gives the display a sociopolitical presence. Jordan as bird. Jordan as angel. Michael the Archangel. Blackbird. Jim Crow. Stealth bomber. Basketball as a black man's game. Mobility tied to athletics. Even the dangling statues commingle in this cosmology. Alabaster African-Americans homogenized in obverse minstrelsy and hanged in effigy in parodic lynching, hover as so many marionettes on the strings of the felt yet unseen presence of the corporation. And still, recall that binding animated cult statues of the archaic world, the bonds making manifest the divine life in the images (McEwen 1993, 5). Jordan sacra—golf clubs, clothing worn in commercials, images, etc.—are everywhere on display. Jordan products are NTC's bestsellers. At the time of this writing, the athlete has breached the boundaries of the cosmetics industry to launch a fragrance labeled—what else?—"Michael Jordan," to remind us of the revival of interest in the synergy between sexuality and athletics (Guttmann 1996). Chrism? Holy water? Aqua vitae? Ergodisiac? Whether we invoke P. T. Barnum or David Copperfield to account for brand extension, we can only marvel at the oxymoron that is Jordan's bottled essence: liquid air.

likenesses of Scottie Pippen and David Robinson or place our own hands and feet into the casts of those of Charles Barkley and Penny Hardaway. Consumers tell me that NTC is the best place to "learn" about NBA superstars, that "the history is important," and that here "it feels like you get to know them [the players] personally." A momentary merging of consumer with consumed is achieved. Looking back into the half-court room, where other consumers become a tableau for us, allowing us to enjoy a bit of the improvisational theater that we had only moments before provided for others, we are reminded by design of the interactive nature of the products the corporation desires us to desire. We are literally the stuff of which dreams are made.

Third Floor

The pinnacle of the building is notable for the aerial views of the store it affords, its birdsong soundscape, and its diorama-like sign fixtures. The Air Jordan Pavilion—a shrine to the Jump Man—is here. The kids' pavilions are here. Consumers can prowl the catwalks, gaining a perspective of all they have seen, or contemplate a ceiling display of our solar system, composed of orbiting planets tricked out as sports balls. Sports become the fabric of the universe. On this floor, exhibits of sports memorabilia and cinema paraphernalia confound the distinction between athletics and movies, work and leisure, and artifact and experience.[10] T-shirts and posters, framed like prints and displayed as if in a gallery, give some pavilions the feel of a museum gift shop. In these pavilions reside the most affordable of NTC artifacts, to which consumers are drawn in search of a souvenir to commemorate their pilgrimage. It is in these pavilions that products are perhaps most dramatically aestheticized. But the most public proclamation and visible enactment of commodity aesthetics at NTC takes place at two third-floor sites in particular: the design exhibit and the video theater.

---

[10] It will come as no surprise that *Space Jam*, the first genre-bending movie-made-from-a-commercial, starred Michael Jordan and Bugs Bunny.

In a cased exhibit resting atop a large cut-block-letter acronym N.T.C., "The Dimension of Nike Design" is displayed in elaborate fashion. The case holds three-dimensional architectural models, artists' renderings and blueprints, early merchandising concepts, and other assorted artifacts that illustrate the corporation's commitment to an integrated design philosophy. Graphics inform the viewer that every element of Nike Town is consciously *designed*. Everything the corporation produces—products, fixtures, displays, buildings, and all—springs "from the Mind of Nike Design"[11] and is intended to embody a corporate vision. Nike artifacts are described as "tangible examples of innovation" and a "testament to team thinking," resulting from the teamwork that is the collective "effort of every Nike employee." The exhibit is an explicit recognition and promotion of the role of design to the distinctiveness of the corporation. It is also an affirmation of the heroism of production reflected in wall murals viewed earlier by consumers. It is ultimately a dramatic staging of the "Just Do It" attitude that drives heroic performance to great achievement.

The exhibit both reminds and reveals. Consumers (re-)discover what NTC is designed to produce in them: a confluence of cosmology and technology that inspires faith in the brand and enflames desire in the direction of purchase, no matter how delayed. Insightful design captures the ways in which artifacts mediate between mythological and material worlds (Krippendorf 1989).

Adjacent to the design exhibit is the video theater, built to simulate an open-air structure more like a drive-in or living room than a conventional cinema. The video screen curves to follow the contour of the wall in which it is embedded. Advertising for Nike products plays almost continuously across the screen, as some consumers linger to watch and listen, while others amble through en route to the next pavilion. Signage notifies us that the commercials portray products "in their natural habitat," working for and through athletes who pulse with a "primitive rhythm" that the corporation

---

[11] Not like Athena, full-blown from the head of Zeus, but rather painstakingly and incrementally evolving through the "ambition" of architects and the integrity of the "design process."

has sought to embed in its offerings. A rock video format is used to help capture this pulse. "Products in action" are enfolded over time into the "performance" motif that the theater's signage now proclaims. Once again, as in any museum or gallery, visitors are reminded in text of what they've (not) experienced in person. Further, the setting produces discussion among viewers. At any given moment, parents classify images for children, as do children for parents. Presentation sets didacticism in motion, here just as at the display cases.

As consumers move across the catwalks and wander through the setlike pavilions, the frontstage/backstage contrast of wandering through a dramatic production is reinforced. The music, the visuals, the soundscape, the vantage points, and the constant parade of other consumers taking in these same servicescape elements makes the third-floor experience both a summary or closure occasion and an opportunity to make further discoveries upon descent. By the time we have attained the third floor, we are used to seeing sales personnel interact with consumers, joking with them, providing tourist as well as product information, allowing children to push delivery tube buttons, and in general contributing to the built environment of the store.

Interpretive Summary

The Nike Town concept has been described as a "brand-building, 3-D commercial" whose theatrical embrace is reminiscent of a "1939 World's Fair" and whose inspiration stems in part from "The Jetsons" and *Back to the Future* (Katz 1994, 95, 272). It is, however, much more than just a curious hybrid of infomercial and edutainment, jointly produced by marketers and consumers. In Table 4.1, I characterize the mythopoeic merchandising that makes the NTC servicescape so engaging. In Table 4.2, I unpack some of the design features that contribute to this engagement. The intent of these efforts is to reveal the world as a company store (Idris-Soven, Idris-Soven, and Vaughn 1978), that is, to describe a phenomenological lifeworld contained in microcosm by a local marketplace, and to explore the mechanisms that animate that microcosm.

TABLE 4.1 Mythopoeic Merchandising at NTC: Experience by Design

Phenomenal Realm	Experiental Dimension*	Servicescape Venue	Analogues and Variants	Cues and Affordances
"Supernatural"			Pantheon	Nike Spirit
			Cathedral	Invisible fourth floor
			Basilica	Windows/lighting
			Church	Suspended statues
			Shrine	Vestibule
			Reliquary	Lamps/altars
			Grotto	Memorabilia/sacra
	Sacred	Museum		Interactive exhibits
				Bas-relief sculptures
				Display cases
				Diagrams
				Statues
				Extramural banners
		Gallery		T-shirt displays
				Poster displays
				Banner/blind paintings
				Geographic location
			Theater	Frontstage-sets
			Cinema	Backstage—catwalks/lights
			(TV/living room)	Improvisation
				Living tableaux
				Video screen
design				Commercials

← (design, directional arrow)

131

TABLE 4.1 *(continued)*

Phenomenal Realm	Experiental Dimension★	Servicescape Venue	Analogues and Variants	Cues and Affordances
"Cultural"		Playground	Stadium/arena Ball court	Hardwood court Basketball goal Jordan photo Soundscape arena
			Theme park Mall Category killer	Cross-promotion (Warner Bros.) Spot merchandising
		Marketplace	Boutique Gift shop Open-air market	Booths Kiosks Displays Design exhibit Socialist realism murals
			Factory of the future	Ethereal music Transparent escalators Computer terminals Soundscape: hammers
		Street	United Airlines terminal *Our Town* "Sesame Street" "Mr. Rogers' Neighborhood" "Toon Town" "Wacky Warehouse"	Pneumatic tubes Neon lighting Escalators

design

Phenomenal Realm	Experiential Dimension*	Servicescape Venue	Analogues and Variants	Cues and Affordances
↓	Profane		Epcot Center Gotham City *Blade Runner* Town square	Rough brick facades Windows Balconies Sewer covers
"Natural"		Outside	Water Aerie Heights Promontory	Pond Aquarium Vertical space Open sight lines Clouds Natural light Soundscape: birdsong

★This is less a continuum than a dialectic, since all dimensions may be sacralized. It resembles more a Möbius strip, where the "natural" may be either base or exalted.

TABLE 4.2 Discovering Delight

Servicescape Artifact	Design Feature	Sensory Engagement	Experiential Impact
Doorknobs	Swoosh logo	Visual/tactile	Threshold fantasies; tangibility of brand essence
Railing supports	Swoosh logo	Visual/tactile	Brand stability and integrity
Bench cushions	Air support; shoe skeuomorph; endorser numbers	Visual/tactile	Transparent tool; *being-in-the-shoe*
Signage	Sport-specific	Visual	Draw flaneur through pavilions; naturalism
Artwork	Socialist realism; macro-photography	Visual	Labor-value musings; WPA-esque inherent dignity of work and effort
Sewer covers	Nike logo	Visual/tactile/aural	Groundedness; permanence
Aquarium fish	Color-coordinated with products	Visual/tactile	Aesthetic engagement; wonderment, speculation
Video theater	Nike commercials	Visual/aural	Edutainment
Merchandising fixtures	Pavilion-specific decor (shelves, sport benches, etc.)	Visual	Organic unity; muted didactics
Statuary	Celebrity sculptures; body parts	Visual	Veneration; cathexis
Soundscapes	Birdsong; music; street noise; court noise	Aural	Immediacy

134

Servicescape Artifact	Design Feature	Sensory Engagement	Experiential Impact
Exhibit displays	Museum cases; local material	Visual/tactile	Historical grounding; sacral–aesthetic engagement
Sales personnel	Youthful; knowledgeable; athletic attire	Visual/aural/tactile/olfactory	Humanity; relationship
Video pond	CRT hard water	Visual/tactile	Awe; Christ/Narcissus
Catwalks/lights	Interrupted sight lines; inaccessible scaffolding; spot–/klieg–light effect	Visual/tactile	Theatricality (director/performer/audience)
Ball court	"Jordan"	Visual/tactile/aural	Physicality; biblicality
Sports Illustrated covers	Celebrity endorser champions	Visual/tactile	Historicity; veneration
Blinds/banners	Optical illusion	Visual	Stability/change dialectic
Delivery tubes	Transparency; velocity	Visual/tactile	Atemporality

NTC, like the ancient city, is a symbol of the cosmos (Tuan 1974, 247). Perhaps more vividly than many buildings, it "condenses culture in one place" (Casey 1992, 32). Its theatrical underpinnings draw from ancient and contemporary dramaturgy (Fletcher 1991). Its architecture is a merger of Hestian and hermetic traditions—centered, self-enclosed curvilinear space abuts rectilinear, decentered, outward-reaching space, inviting simultaneous experience of the stationary and the mobile—that foster empathic connection (Casey 1993, 132–142). NTC is an interesting example of "design that begins and ends with the lived-experience of the users for whom the place is being transformed" (Dovey 1993, 260). More often than immediate sales, its ambience promotes alternation between a hypervigilant mode of exploration and a species of meditative bliss that has been christened "commodity Zen" (Fjellman 1992, 310, 401).

If we understand marketing to mean primarily the shaping of consumer experience, and consumption to mean the creative interpolation of marketing mix variables with extraeconomic concerns, then NTC is kind of a commercial Biosphere II of cosmological significance. NTC is a world where children hopscotch on water and ride or resist stairways to heaven, while products emerge from some invisible source of plenty and fly through inside/outside space in transparent arteries, in sync with the music of the spheres. It reminds children of their favorite television haunts: "Toon Town," the "Wacky Warehouse," "Mr. Rogers' Neighborhood," "Sesame Street." It is a world where adults worship athletic idols, pontificating and proselytizing as they wander about, fondling fixtures, brailling product, vetoing extravagant economic demands, and occasionally feeling sheepish about living in a culture that appears to have too much time on its hands. It reminds adults of Gotham City and Epcot Center. NTC is ultimately an unfolding experience, where regression and exaltation work in tandem in the service of brand equity. NTC is both surreal and hyperreal. NTC is "awesome," "amazing," "fantastic," "futuristic," "incredible," "unbelievable," and positively "cool," but most especially, it is *here*. It is Nike Town *Chicago*, where the word is made flesh and dwells among *us*.

Given his belief that "being number one is not very cool" because it breeds risk aversion, Gordon Thompson, the force behind

Nike design (and the author of this chapter's second epigraph), has become "obsessed with going beyond Nike Town" and intends to explore the "new frontier of retailing" by creating such outlets as "hands-on sports environments," "sports bars inside digitized environments," and "interactive TV technologies" that would permit customers to measure their feet on a home screen and place orders for digitally customized shoes (Katz 1994, 273–274). Nike is in the process of building a global "event marketing" division charged with the task of "possessing control of how its brand is presented and perceived," and intends to explore opportunities "from the sublime to the ridiculous" for "creating experiences that will tangibly communicate the brand's values and U.S. mystique" (Jensen 1996a, 2). As the corporation seeks increasingly relevant vehicles for tangibilizing the brand's essence—emplacing it in vessels consumers will in turn decant—the strategy of building local showcases remains firmly entrenched.

Nike Towns have recently arisen at the intersection of Rodeo Drive and Wilshire Boulevard (the "spiritual center" of Beverly Hills) and in the Union Square area of San Francisco, as the "entertainment retail" trend spreads to more traditionally "chic" shopping districts (Pacelle 1996, B1). The newest Nike Town at the time of this writing has been installed in New York (Lefton 1996). As history attests (Leach 1993; Monod 1966), such retail spectacle is linked as inextricably to the growth of consumer culture in the United States as it has been in Europe (Sack 1992). We can imagine exporting Nike Towns to other international centers of commerce, as we have witnessed the cross-cultural diffusion of McDonald's, Disney World and the Hard Rock Cafe.[12] It seems quite likely that

---

[12] Whether Michael Jordan's persona would prove crucial to international success, it appears not to have driven domestic diffusion of Nike Towns. Local heroes are featured locally, as emplacement might dictate, and as quick-turnover merchandising might demand. While Jordanworld may be rooted in Chicago, its essence may travel well to emerging sports markets outside the United States, as basketball, entertainment genres, and fashion diffuse globally. Where Al Capone's persona all too recently caricatured the city for its foreign visitors, Michael Jordan's now promises a semiotic urban renewal (Gallagher 1993). Worldwide, Nike strives to "make the brand part of the cultural fabric" (Jensen 1996b, 16).

Nike Towns will be the outposts from which the frontiers of retailing will be exploited. In that sense, NTC is both a site magnet and a beacon product (Sherry 1996, 359), drawing consumers to the source of the brand's production.

Let me conclude this section with a final field note excerpt that returns the reader to informants' perspectives:

> I have encountered relatively few skeptics or ardent critics over the course of these interviews. Most of these seem to be young women or mothers acting as family financial officers. [Note: Is the masculine feel of NTC as gendered space my own idiosyncratic reaction, or does it reflect a corporate reading of U.S. cultural sportways?] And still, even criticism is muted, or framed in terms of the sunk cost of delight. "They spent a lot of money on this place—I wonder if it was worth it," speculates one young woman on a sight-seeing stroll. "Do you think they spent too much money on all this?" a teenage boy wonders aloud to his mates, as they take a break from Rollerblading down the boulevard to explore the building. "Can this spectacle be profitable?" is the unspoken subtext of these queries.
>
> Prices for most items—T-shirts excepted, given their unique designs and parity prices—are contrasted with those found in less opulent settings, and suffer in comparison. "Get your ideas here, but buy stuff at Sportmart" is a common observation. One mother advises, "It's like FAO Schwarz. You go there to look, but you buy at Toys 'Я' Us."
>
> Metacriticism—of capitalism, commercialism, materialism— seems similarly restrained, transmuted perhaps through the aura of Michael Jordan. Again, it is young women who have told me things like, "It [NTC] doesn't impress me too much, but I like the Jordan posters," and, "It's strange . . . I don't see why people get so excited about a brand name. But I do like Michael Jordan, and I like to see the exhibits."

CONCLUSION

Let me return finally to the notion of emplacement to summarize my experience of the NTC servicescape. Nike brand essence is both embodied in the built environment and realized in apprehension, in an act of cocreation transacted by the firm's stakeholders. Consider some of the root meanings of *technology:* to build, to give birth, to allow to appear (McEwen 1993). Consider as well how meanings are gathered to an artifact. In Heideggerian perspective, a thing "things" in a provisive carrying out of itself; it is a genuine happening. When we dwell in the world, we experience the "living out of openness specifically in relation to things" (Lovitt and Lovitt 1995, 173, 187). The design of NTC conspires to imbue artifacts with the "particulate sensuosity" that gives goods their "fetish quality" in consumer culture (Taussig 1993, 23).

Like drama, sport has its roots in religious ritual, but sport has long been suffused with a sense of erotic pleasure (Guttmann 1996, 172), which arguably makes athletics and its requisite equipment the most eminently suited vehicles of sublimation that retail theater/ therapy could imagine. Consumption at NTC is ultimately about "tactile knowing" and "proprioception"; the servicescape engages what Benjamin called our "optical unconscious" (Taussig 1993, 25, 97). Our imaginative fondling of the sacra/erotica that these props of retail theater have become—branded products, exhibits, fixtures, and the like—impels their literal handling. NTC evokes the kind of "simultaneous perception"—utter watchfulness, split-second attention to innumerable variables, fluid body boundary—that disrupts and alters our everyday consumer experience by encoding in its servicescape such dimensions as legibility and mystery, refuge and prospect (Hiss 1990). Not only is the superfluous stuff of consumer culture fetishized at NTC (Debord 1983), the retail inscape of NTC works to invest all objects housed there with enduring cultural values. Not only has Nike harnessed air, it has transmuted this base element into gold by designing its quintessence into every aspect of the servicescape.

The conflation of commerce with other domains of cultural experience—the transformation of commodities or brands into increasingly complex polyvocal artifacts and back again by filtering them through novel cultural institutions—is at the heart of the NTC servicescape. Our experience of consumption is recodified in ways that ramify beyond exchange but bear ultimately upon exchange. The aura of the outlet (like the spirit of the gift) drives future sales at other outlets; a species of immersion advertising works to recontextualize, validate, and sacralize products at a distance. NTC becomes a numinous link in the distribution chain, part of the totemic circuitry that makes the brand iconic. The sensory rhetoric of the place, and its confounding of categories, keeps stuff interesting.

At the time of this writing, the architecture critic of the *Chicago Tribune* is lamenting the fall from grace of the Magnificent Mile to the "Mediocre Mile," as designers seek ineffectually to transcend the "mold of the sterile urban mall" by razing hallowed older structures and replacing them with "mixed use behemoths" that repeat the "overdesigned" and "garish" mistakes of trendy redevelopment without capturing any of its "extraordinary" triumphs (Kamin 1996, 12). The 600 block in particular is the site of contested meanings, as the forces of historic preservation clash with the demands of marketplace immediacy. In the critic's estimation, the "showroom approach" to retail design is destroying the aesthetic appeal of the Nike Town neighborhood.

During the course of my fieldwork, companies such as Eddie Bauer and Levi Strauss have established flagship brand sites on this block, providing consumers with the spectacle so central to the being-in-the-marketplace experience that entertainment retail engenders (Debord 1983). An inversion of guerilla theater, retail theater becomes a public enactment of retail therapy (Cushman 1990). Where mise-en-scène is merchandising, search is sensually choreographed. Consumers are encouraged to cathect commodities, infusing them with a kinetic libidinal energy summoned from energy's dormant potential as much by the built environment as by desire itself. If the external edifice of the Michigan Avenue marketplace is in decline, its internal artifice is in ascendancy.[13] Being-

---

[13] A young female informant provides the following anecdote:

> The essence of Nike Town definitely follows you out the door. I bought my brother's fiancée a Michael Jordan T-shirt at NTC. The salesperson wrapped it in nice Nike Town–emblazoned tissue and put it in a shopping bag. Feeling completely accomplished, I strolled down Michigan Avenue carrying the Nike Town shopping bag on my wrist as if it were a Louis Vuitton handbag. Anyhow, when I got home, I had to pack the T-shirt in my suitcase for San Francisco. I pretty much

with-brands in situations simulating the natural through the super-natural, under cultural conditions from low- through highbrow, is the experience this artifice invokes, in the service of secular prayer. Like a latter-day Euhemerus, we realize at some deep level that toys *are* us. I have titled this chapter (with apologies to Tennessee Ernie Ford) in ironic and allusive recognition of the reciprocal relation-ship of commodity fetishism to self-actualization.

Economists have estimated that Michael Jordan's presence annually generates in excess of $600 million for Chicago's economy (McCarthy 1993). One-third of these dollars is linked to tourism. I have described NTC as a site magnet for secular pilgrims. Among the retail trends afoot in Chicago that have drawn popular atten-tion—destination merchandising, service-with-a-smile, clutter bust-ing, designer private label, next-generation shopping, novel promotions, and surprising product placement (Spethman 1995)—each is in evidence at NTC. Just as revealing, a recent *Brandweek* sur-vey of 12 influential young (under 40) marketers identifies Nike as the "favorite marketer" of 5 of these managers, who cite such fac-tors as iconic equity, risk taking, authenticity, attention to details, execution, and consumer identification in their admiration of the brand (Khermouch 1996). Each of these factors is also in evidence at NTC. Where an entire line can be merchandised in ways that designers intend (Kuntz 1995), marketers can influence the shape of consumer brandscapes more precisely than in the past. Further, sheer abundance, if not cornucopian display (Sherry and McGrath 1989) of products, contributes to the immediacy of the marketplace. As a

refused to take the shirt out of the bag for fear that some of the essence would escape. Somehow I packed it in my suitcase completely intact.

When I got to San Francisco, I gave the intact gift to my brother, who was packing his own suitcase to visit his fiancée. Then he did the unfathomable. He proceeded to pull the T-shirt *out* of the bag and *out of* its nice Nike tissue paper and put it in his suitcase. Not only had he unwrapped the gift for her, but he had stripped her of the Nike Town-ness of the gift. Of course, I told my brother he was completely wrong and that it must be rewrapped (a minor consolation). Unfortunately, you see, my brother is an engineer. It was a question of utility (a lighter suitcase—by a whole two ounces), and I was irrational. I think we ended up settling on putting the tissue around the shirt.

stage for such merchandising, NTC is unparalleled. The company itself has been honored as the 1996 Marketer of the Year by *Advertising Age,* which claims the brand to be a "cultural icon" more "recognized and coveted" than "arguably any brand" (Jensen 1996b, 16).

Nike. Mikey. Mike. Here prosody prevails. By aural rhyme and by sight rhyme, the words and their adcult essences (Twitchell 1996) converge upon one another at NTC. The site is, after all, Mike Town.[14] He is the soul of the company store. Let me conclude by returning to the emplacement conceit with which I began this chapter. Once meanings are emplaced in artifacts, these artifacts in turn contribute "to our definition of the spatial situation, and the reciprocal amplifying effects that occur when artifacts resonate with space" (Sherry 1995, 360). As work in environmental and architectural phenomenology suggests (Seamon 1993; Walter 1988), our relationship to objects is often geomantic. Artifacts situate us in a "moral geography of culturally significant quality space" and help foster among visitors—in this case, liminoid pilgrims sharing a communitas of psychophysical, commercio-aesthetic origin—a groundedness rooted in air. While the essence of Nike Town is ineluctably local, the experience of *Nike World* travels as far as the products and images of the firm diffuse.[15]

As marketers attempt to forge a retailing agenda for the twenty-first century (Peterson 1992), it is painfully apparent that we lack both a theory that comprehends the obvious world and a chorography that accounts for and taps the spirit of the place (Walter 1988). In our era of hyperconsumption and image-driven search, where the boundaries between marketplaces and other public forums blur, we are beginning to understand "cognitive acquisition," but we have no true feel for its ethos, which may simultane-

---

[14] Again, allusions are alluvial. Boys Town. Boyz'N the Hood. The Island of Wayward Boys. Boys will be boys. Boy toys. Here in this commodity kiddie land, play is the thing. Regression in the service of fantasy enables us to be like Mike. For one brief, shining moment, life is nothing but net.

[15] Like seeds, spores, starter dough, or the theft of fire (Sherry, McGrath, and Levy 1995), Nike will be everywhere you want to be. Whether its brand equity—in this case, the authenticity of any particular Nike *Town* as a pilgrimage site—is diluted in extension remains to be seen.

ously stimulate and sedate (Crawford 1992, 13–14). Venues such as
NTC are especially fertile field sites for the kinds of discovery that
humane social scientific inquiry can facilitate. Perhaps this chapter
will provide encouragement for just such discovery.

BIBLIOGRAPHY

AGNEW, JEAN-CHRISTOPHE. 1986. *Worlds Apart: The Market and the Theatre in Anglo-American Thought.* New York: Cambridge University Press.

ARMSTRONG, ROBERT. 1974. *The Affecting Presence.* Urbana: University of Illinois Press.

BUTTIMER, ANNE. 1993. *Geography and the Human Spirit.* Baltimore, MD: Johns Hopkins University Press.

CASEY, EDWARD. 1993. *Getting Back into Place: Toward a Renewed Understanding of the Place-World.* Bloomington: Indiana University Press.

CRAWFORD, MARGARET. 1992. "The World in a Shopping Mall." In *Variations on a Theme Park,* edited by Michael Sorkin. New York: Noonday Press, 3–30.

CUSHMAN, PETER. 1990. "Why the Self Is Empty: Toward a Historically Situated Psychology." *American Psychologist* (May): 599–611.

DEBORD, GUY. 1983. *Society of the Spectacle.* Detroit: Black and Red.

DOVEY, KIMBERLY. 1993. "Putting Geometry in Its Place: Toward a Phenomenology of the Design Process." In *Dwelling, Seeing and Designing: Toward a Phenomenological Ecology,* edited by David Seamon. Albany, NY: SUNY Press, 247–269.

DUHAIME, CAROLE; ANNAMMA JOY; AND CHRIS ROSS. 1995. "Learning to 'See': A Folk Phenomenology of the Consumption of Contemporary Canadian Art." In *Contemporary Marketing and Consumer Behavior: An Anthropological Sourcebook,* edited by John F. Sherry, Jr. Thousand Oaks, CA: Sage, 351–398.

FJELLMAN, STEPHEN. 1992. *Vinyl Leaves: Walt Disney World and America.* Boulder, CO: Westviers Press.

FLETCHER, RACHEL. 1991. "Ancient Theatres as Sacred Spaces." In *The Power of Place and Human Environments,* edited by James Swan, Wheaton, IL: Quest, 88–106.

GALLAGHER, WINIFRED. 1993. *The Power of Place: How Surroundings Shape Our Thoughts, Emotions and Actions.* New York: Praeger.

GOLDMAN, ROBERT, AND STEPHEN PAPSON. 1996. *Sign Wars: The Cluttered Landscape of Advertising.* New York: Guilford.

GOTTDIENER, MARK. 1996. *The Theming of America: Dreams, Visions and Commercial Space.* San Francisco: Westview Press.

GOULD, STEPHEN. 1991. "The Self-Manipulation of My Pervasive, Vital Energy Through Product Use: An Introspective–Praxis Approach." *Journal of Consumer Research* 18(2):194–207.

GUTTMANN, ALLEN. 1996. *The Erotic in Sports.* New York: Columbia University Press.

HEISLEY, DEBORAH, AND SIDNEY LEVY. 1991. "Autodriving: A Photoelicitation Technique." *Journal of Consumer Research* 18(2):257–272.

HISS, TONY. 1990. *The Experience of Place.* New York: Knopf.

HOLBROOK, MORRIS. 1988a. "The Psychoanalytic Interpretation of Consumer Behavior: I Am an Animal." *Research in Consumer Behavior* 3:149–178.

———. 1988b. "Steps Toward a Psychoanalytic Interpretation of Consumption: A Meta-Meta-Meta-Analysis of Some Issues Raised by the Consumer Behavior Odyssey." In *Advances in Consumer Research* 15, edited by Michael Houston. Provo, UT: Association for Consumer Research, 537–542.

IDRIS-SOVEN, A.; E. IDRIS-SOVEN; AND M. K. VAUGHN, EDS. 1978. *The World as a Company Town: Multinational Corporations and Social Change.* The Hague: Mouton.

JENSEN, JEFF. 1996a. "Nike Creates New Division to Stage Global Events." *Advertising Age* (September 30): 2, 62.

———. 1996b. "Marketing of the Year." *Advertising Age* (December 16): 1, 16.

KAMIN, BLAIR. 1996. "Mediocre Mile." *Chicago Tribune* (November 10): sec. 7, p. 12.

KATZ, DONALD. 1994. *Just Do It: The Nike Spirit in the Corporate World.* New York: Random House.

KHERMOUCH, GERRY. 1996. "Marketing's Most Wanted: 1997's Hot Marketers." *Brandweek* (November 4): 35–76.

KRIPPENDORF, KLAUS. 1989. "On the Essential Context of Artifacts, or On the Proposition that 'Design is Making Sense (of Things).'" *Design Issues* 5(2):9–38.

KUNTZ, MARY. 1995. "These Ads Have Windows and Walls." *Business Week* (February 27): 74.

LEACH, WILLIAM. 1993. *Land of Desire: Merchants, Power and the Rise of a New American Culture.* New York: Pantheon.

LEFTON, TERRY. 1996. "Nike uber Alles." *Brandweek* (December 9): 25–36.

LOVITT, WILLIAM, AND HARRIET LOVITT. 1995. *Modern Technology in the Heideggerian Perspective,* vol. 1. Lewiston, NY: Edwin Mellen Press.

MANDEL, DAVID. 1967. *Changing Art, Changing Man.* New York: Horizon Press.

MCCARTHY, MICHAEL. 1993. "Jordan's Retirement Will Make No Cents to Chicago Economy." *The Wall Street Journal* (October 7): B12.

MCCRACKEN, GRANT. 1988. *Culture and Consumption: New Approaches to the Symbolic Character of Consumer Goods and Activities.* Bloomington: Indiana University Press.

———. 1990. "Marketing Material Cultures: Person-Object Relations Inside and Outside the Ethnographic Museum." In *Advances in Nonprofit Marketing* 3, edited by Russell Belk. Greenwich, CT: JAI Press, 27–49

———. 1996. "Culture and culture at the Royal Ontario Museum: A Ghost Story." Working paper, Department of Ethnology, Royal Ontario Museum, Toronto, Ontario, Canada.

MCEWEN, INDRA. 1993. *Socrates' Ancestor: An Essay on Architectural Beginnings.* Cambridge, MA: MIT Press.

MCGRATH, MARY ANN. 1989. "An Ethnography of a Gift Store: Trappings, Wrappings and Rapture." *Journal of Retailing* 65(4):421–449.

McGrath, Mary Ann; John Sherry; and Deborah Heisley. 1993. "An Ethnographic Study of an Urban Periodic Market Place: Lessons from the Midville Market." *Journal of Retailing* 69(3):280–319.

Monod, David. 1996. *Store Wars: Shopkeepers and the Culture of Mass Marketing, 1890–1939.* Toronto: University of Toronto Press.

Murray, Henry. 1943. *Thematic Apperception Test Manual.* Cambridge, MA: Harvard University Press.

Nike Town Chicago. 1992a. "Nike Town Comes to Chicago." Press release, Nike Town Chicago, Chicago, July 2.

———. 1992b. "Nike Town Chicago Fact Sheet." Press release, Nike Town Chicago, Chicago, July 2.

O'Guinn, Thomas. 1989. "Touching Greatness: The Central Midwest Barry Manilow Fan Club." In *Highways and Buyways: Naturalistic Research from the Consumer Behavior Odyssey,* edited by Russell Belk. Provo, UT: Association for Consumer Research, 102–111.

O'Guinn, Thomas, and Russell Belk. 1989. "Heaven on Earth: Consumption at Heritage Village." *Journal of Consumer Research* 16(1):147–157.

Oldenburg, Ray. 1989. *The Great Good Place.* New York: Paragon House.

Otnes, Cele; Mary Ann McGrath; and Tina Lowrey. 1995. "Shopping with Consumers: Usage as Past, Present and Future Research Technique." *Journal of Retailing and Consumer Services* 2(2):97–110.

Pacelle, Mitchell. 1996. "Razzmatazz Retailers Jolt Chic Shopping Streets." *The Wall Street Journal* (October 4): B1, B10.

Peterson, Robert, ed. 1992. *The Future of U.S. Retailing: An Agenda for the 21st Century.* New York: Quorum.

Richardson, Miles. 1987. "A Social (Ideational-Behavioral) Interpretation of Material Culture and Its Application to Archaeology." In *Mirror and Metaphor,* edited by Donald Ingersoll and Gordon Bronitsky. Lanham, MD: University Press of America, 381–403.

Rook, Dennis. 1989. "I Was Observed (*In Absentia*) and Autodriven by the Consumer Behavior Odyssey." In *Highways and Buyways: Naturalistic Research from the Consumer Behavior Odyssey,* edited by Russell Belk. Provo, UT: Association for Consumer Research, 48–58.

Rose, Dan. 1995. "Active Ingredients." In *Contemporary Marketing and Consumer Behavior: An Anthropological Sourcebook,* edited by John F. Sherry, Jr. Thousand Oaks, CA: Sage, 51–58.

Sack, Robert. 1992. *Place, Modernity and the Consumer's World.* Baltimore, MD: Johns Hopkins University Press.

Schultz, Don; Stanley Tannenbaum; and Robert Lauterborn. 1994. *The New Marketing Paradigm: Integrated Marketing Communications.* Chicago: NTC Business Books.

Scott, Linda. 1994. "The Bridge From Text to Mind: Adapting Reader-Response Theory to Consumer Research." *Journal of Consumer Research* 21(3):461–480.

Seamon, David. 1993. *Dwelling, Seeing and Designing: Toward a Phenomenological Ecology.* Albany, NY: SUNY Press.

SENNETT, RICHARD. 1976. *The Fall of Public Man.* New York: Vintage.

SHERRY, JOHN F., JR. 1985. "Cereal Monogamy: Brand Loyalty as Secular Ritual in Consumer Culture." Paper presented at the 17th annual conference of the Association for Consumer Research, Toronto, Ontario, Canada.

————. 1990a. "A Sociocultural Analysis of a Midwestern American Flea Market." *Journal of Consumer Research* 17(1):13–30.

————. 1990b. "Dealers and Dealing in a Periodic Market: Informal Retailing in Ethnographic Perspective." *Journal of Retailing* 66(2):174–200.

————. 1991. "Postmodern Alternatives: The Interpretive Turn in Consumer Research." In *Handbook of Consumer Behavior,* edited by Thomas Robertson and Harold Kassarjian. Englewood Cliffs, NJ: Prentice Hall, 548–591.

————. 1995a. "Bottomless Cup, Plug-In Drug: A Telethnography of Coffee." *Visual Anthropology* 7(4):351–370.

————. 1995b. *Contemporary Marketing and Consumer Behavior: An Anthropological Sourcebook.* Thousand Oaks, CA: Sage.

————. 1996. "Reflections on Giftware and Giftcare: Whither Consumer Research?" In *Gift Giving: A Research Anthology,* edited by Cele Otnes and Richard Beltramini. Bowling Green, OH: Bowling Green State University Popular Press, 217–227.

SHERRY, JOHN F., JR., AND MARY ANN MCGRATH. 1989. "Unpacking the Holiday Presence: A Comparative Ethnography of Two Midwestern American Gift Stores." In *Interpretive Consumer Research,* edited by Elizabeth Hirschman. Provo, UT: Association for Consumer Research, 148–167.

SHERRY, JOHN F., JR.; MARY ANN MCGRATH; AND SIDNEY LEVY. 1995. "Monadic Giving: Anatomy of Gifts Given to the Self." In *Contemporary Marketing and Consumer Behavior: An Anthropological Sourcebook,* edited by John F. Sherry, Jr. Thousand Oaks, CA: Sage, 399–432.

SPETHMAN, BETSY. 1995. "Shopping for Answers." *Brandweek* (February 27): 30–32.

STRASSER, J. B., AND LAURIE BECKLUND. 1993. *Swoosh: The Unauthorized Story of Nike and the Men Who Played There.* New York: Harper Business.

TARN, NATHANIEL. 1972. "From Anthropologist to Informant: A Field Record of Gary Snyder." *Alcheringa* 4 (Fall): 392–401.

TAUSSIG, MICHAEL. 1993. *Mimesis and Alterity: A Particular History of the Senses.* New York: Routledge.

TUAN, YI-FU. 1974. *Topophilia: A Study of Environmental Perception, Attitudes and Values.* New York: Columbia University Press.

TWITCHELL, JAMES. 1996. *Adcult U.S.A.: The Triumph of Advertising in American Culture.* New York: Columbia University Press.

WALLENDORF, MELANIE, AND MERRIE BRUCKS. 1993. "Introspection in Consumer Research: Implementation and Implications." *Journal of Consumer Research* 20(3):339–359.

WALTER, EUGENE. 1988. *Placeways: A Theory of the Human Environment.* Chapel Hill: University of North Carolina Press.

PART II

FAMILIAR SERVICESCAPES: BEING-IN-THE-MARKETPLACE

In this section, we explore servicescapes with which the reader will have appreciable familiarity: malls, department stores, specialty stores, and galleries. In these kinds of everyday environments, our lived experiences ordinarily go unexamined analytically, yet these settings thoroughly condition our thoughts, emotions, and behaviors. While we have some intriguing accounts of this unexamined conditioning at the macro level of the city (Whyte 1988) and at the micro level of the home (Wood and Beck 1994), there are relatively few examinations of the kinds of consumption sites—restaurants being a notable exception (Fine 1996; Leidner 1993; Reiter 1991)—that most concern marketers. We narrow this gap in the following chapters.

Taking advantage of a critical incident—store relocation—to analyze a servicescape holistically, Wallendorf, Lindsey-Mullikin, and Pimentel provide a comparative ethnography quite different from available precedents (Sherry and McGrath 1989) in that they examine the same outlet over time. They explore a commercial variant of "homeyness" (McCracken 1989), which they term a "consumption dreamworld," and describe the ways in which servicescape design animates consumer behavior. They focus in particular on theming issues discussed by Gottdiener earlier in this volume. As the ambience of their site evolves from a nostalgic Victorian homeyness to postmodern Hollywood glitz, the authors track the shift in the nature of consumer animation that the design encourages. They also explore the alienation or disaffection of existing customers that renovation is bound to produce even as the consumer franchise expands. Whether the servicescape dreamworld is a literal toy box or a projective playground, it is an important component in the production of children's culture (Kline 1993).

Cultural forces are at the center of Creighton's inquiry into the extraeconomic dimensions of a Japanese servicescape. Her account reminds us that retail ambience is ultimately a gift from marketer to consumer, no matter how latent the recognition might be. In unwrapping this ambience, she discloses the struggle ongoing in Japanese culture to reconcile escalating materialism with traditional spirituality. This disclosure underscores our disciplinary need for a comprehensive theory of materiality or a cultural poetics of desire that mediates between acquisitiveness and metaphysics (Sherry, McGrath, and Levy 1995). In Creighton's study, the servicescape functions ritually to transform materialism from a debased drive to a vehicle of transcendent spirituality not entirely unlike the melting pot graduation ceremony that symbolically transformed Henry Ford's immigrant employees into productive American workers. She describes consumers' mental, emotional, and physical engagement with the servicescape, resulting in enhancement of both self- and corporate identity in the service of nation building. Shopping becomes the medium of this metaphysically nationalist construction project.

The exploration of bridal servicescapes by Otnes is unique to the retailing literature, insofar as the institution underlying such a fundamental cultural ritual of transformation and representing such a significant proportion of initial household provisioning expenditures seems to have gone undetected by earlier marketing scholarship. This omission is even more surprising given the apparently bimodal nature of the shopping experience reported by consumers: Exhilaration and disappointment are the most common outcomes resulting from this servicescape encounter. Otnes describes variations of the cornucopian display and bundling practices (in this case, of both goods and services) we have examined in earlier chapters, but she examines them in light of individual and group preference dynamics. Her account of the role of surrogate consumers and market mavens in servicescape realization is instructive. So also is her discussion of merchandising strategies, in an era of sales force downsizing and passively managed service encounters. Finally, her account of singularizing rituals that occur in servicescape settings should be a powerful reminder to marketing managers that substrate behaviors beneath rational calculation often determine choice outcomes, and intervention directed against this ritual substratum can assist the consumer in cocreating the marketer's larger offering.

Joy's chapter on gallery servicescapes weds concerns in consumer-object relations to those in commodity aesthetics, as she examines extension and incorporation dynamics as a kind of tension between containment (or boundedness) and liberation (or unboundedness); that galleries deal in subversion animates their servicescape in novel fashion. Her investigation tracks the conversion of space to (enculturated) place, as she follows the circuit of the object from artifact to art.

I have placed Sandikci and Holt's chapter on malls as places at the conceptual center of the volume. These authors synthesize and integrate a host of issues raised in earlier chapters and prefigure many that the reader will encounter in subsequent pages. The mall instantiates and encapsulates our modern experience of marketplaces at the same time that it shapes our emerging postmodern consumer sensibilities. The mall is a limen, or threshold, across which we pass on our journey from shopper to postshopper (Urry 1990). It is at once a familiar and a strange place; it is an inevitable staging ground for our disciplinary forays into marketplaces more and less mundane. The authors focus on servicescape design features and mall consumption practices in evidence at a particular local site, as dictated by their evaluation of positivist and postmodern mall literature shortfalls. The authors examine the sensuous and social nature of search, as it is helped and hindered by the servicescape. They help consumers articulate a *premodern* marketplace ethos whose design potential would appear to be profound. Perhaps a (so-called) paraprimitive approach to servicescape design is warranted in the future. As the authors suggest, facilitating the performance of community might be the single greatest benefit designers could deliver to consumers, who view the mall as a source of communitas. Figuring out how to deliver communal space to impoverished consumers, or, more properly, developing public space for all consumers, may be the greatest challenge social marketers of the immediate future will face.

BIBLIOGRAPHY

FINE, GARY. 1996. *Kitchens: The Culture of Restaurant Work.* Berkeley: University of California Press.

KLINE, STEPHEN. 1993. *Out of the Garden: Toys and Children's Culture in the Age of TV Marketing.* New York: Verso.

LEIDNER, ROBIN. 1993. *Fast Food, Fast Talk: Service Work and the Routinization of Everyday Life.* Berkeley: University of California Press.

LEVY, SIDNEY. 1978. *Marketplace Behavior: Its Meaning for Management.* New York: Amacom.

McCRACKEN, GRANT. 1989. "Homeyness: A Cultural Account of One Constellation of Consumer Goods and Meanings." In *Interpretive Consumer Research,* edited by Elizabeth Hirschman. Provo, UT: Association for Consumer Research, 168–183.

REITER, ESTER. 1991. *Making Fast Food: From the Frying Pan into the Fryer.* Montreal: McGill-Queen's University Press.

SHERRY, JOHN F., JR., AND MARY ANN McGRATH. 1989. "Unpacking the Holiday Presence: A Comparative Ethnography of Two Gift Stores." In *Interpretive Consumer Research,* edited by Elizabeth Hirschman. Provo, UT: Association for Consumer Research, 148–167.

SHERRY, JOHN F., JR.; MARY ANN McGRATH; AND SIDNEY LEVY. 1995. "Monadic Giving: Anatomy of Gifts Given to the Self." In *Contemporary Marketing and Consumer Behavior: An Anthropological Sourcebook,* edited by John F. Sherry, Jr. Thousand Oaks, CA: Sage, 399–432.

URRY, JOHN. 1990. *The Tourist Gaze.* Newbury Park, CA: Sage.

WHYTE, WILLIAM. 1988. *City: Rediscovering the Center.* New York: Doubleday.

WOOD, DENIS, AND ROBERT BECK. 1994. *Home Rules.* Baltimore, MD: Johns Hopkins University Press.

5

GORILLA MARKETING

Customer Animation and Regional Embeddedness of a Toy Store Servicescape

MELANIE WALLENDORF,
JOAN LINDSEY-MULLIKIN,
AND RON PIMENTEL

The relocation of a retail business often involves the physical expansion of selling space as well as an associated expansion of the customer base. Expansion of the customer base may simply mean attracting more of the same type of customers, by retaining the same store image and general design but in a new location that is more convenient to a larger group of people. However, more often,

Melanie Wallendorf is Professor of Marketing and of Comparative Cultural and Literary Studies, and Joan Lindsey-Mullikin is a Ph.D. student. Both are in the Department of Marketing, College of Business and Public Administration, at the University of Arizona, Tucson. Ron Pimentel is Assistant Professor of Marketing at the University of Central Florida in Orlando.

This chapter is titled and written with apologies and appreciation to Jay Levinson (author of *Guerrilla Marketing*) and William (Tom) Tucker (author of *Foundations for a Theory of Consumer Behavior*). We wish to express deepest appreciation to the owners of Mrs. Tiggy-Winkle's Toy Store for their cooperation and encouragement, without which this project would not have been possible. Their openness and continued commitment to this project reflect the core of their individual personalities and a core value embodied by the store.

retail relocation and expansion include a change in store image and design in an attempt to broaden the customer base by diversifying the target market through simultaneous retention of some original customers and recruitment of new (types of) customers. The resulting heterogeneity of the target market poses challenges to store owner/managers who are forced to move beyond what previously worked for them in personal selling, pricing, inventory mix and turnover, display, interior design, employee training, and promotion. It is this retail situation that interests us in this chapter.

Relocation is both an exciting and frustrating time for retail store owners. They choose a new location, design a store interior, and order inventory for an as-yet-undetermined mix of old and new (types of) customers. They notify their existing customers of the move and reassure them of continuity of services, while simultaneously courting new customers. Salespeople must simultaneously adapt to the new store, new systems, and new types of customers. Ultimately, owners can answer the question of whether bigger is better in terms of profitability.

Relocation is also a time of both excitement and frustration for the store's original customers. They must learn where the new store is located and develop new heuristics for approaching its layout and inventory (Tversky and Kahneman 1974). They may need more assistance from salespeople than they have sought in recent store visits. Of substantial interest in this chapter, old customers are called upon to adapt to the new image and new product mix chosen by the owner/managers. Upon coming into the new store, they look to cues in the physical and social environment to form judgments about whether it is still "the same." As a consequence of these processes, which may take only minutes, they decide whether "the drive" to the new location is "worth it."

METHODOLOGY

Participant observation of retail activity in a toy store that has recently relocated and doubled its size forms the empirical basis for this chapter. Three ethnographers spent considerable time over 18

months at a locally owned retail toy store in roles ranging from simply watching activity at the store to more actively serving as unpaid
sales staff (sometimes costumed in fairy wings or angel halos) and
as occasional merchandisers, shelf stockers, gift wrappers, window
dressers, and clean-up crew, as well as on- and off-site sympathetic
listeners when problems arose. In-store observations extended
beyond daily retail store activities to include assistance and participation in special workshops and evening concerts held at the store,
staff completion of inventory taking during nonretail hours, and
preparation of photographs for entries in national trade magazine
competitions. Observations extended outside the store context to
trips to the store's competitors to observe similarities and differences in inventory and display, meetings with the store owners at
the owners' as well as the researchers' homes, focus groups with
two categories of store customers held in a university setting, in-
home in-depth interviews with three customers, attendance at a
luncheon/fashion show with store customers, delivery of Easter baskets to customers' homes while dressed in an Easter Bunny costume, follow-up telephone interviews with 12 Easter-delivery
customers, attendance at a national trade association conference with
the store owners, and preparation and mailing of the store's newsletter to 3,000 customers.

Through these membership roles (Adler and Adler 1987), the
researchers documented their observations of human behaviors in
the retail setting in computer text files of field notes and tracked
the financial success of the store through accounting data on sales,
inventory, and expenses. Photographs were taken at the former store
location (in its last weeks of operation) and at the new store location (over the 18 months of fieldwork) to serve as a record of temporal changes in the physical environment. In total, this fieldwork
resulted in 535 single-spaced pages of computerized field notes, 225
photographs, and 3 videotapes. To further refine our ethnographically grounded understandings, mail survey data about consumer
impressions and experiences in the old store, the new store, surrounding businesses, and competitive businesses were collected
from store customers using a survey insert in the store's monthly
newsletter.

ISSUES ADDRESSED

Three interconnected issues are of focal interest in this chapter.

1. How physical features of a retail space serve as the basis for consumer animation

2. More dynamically, how changes in location and store design challenge retailers with a broadened market that may contest the previous bases of consumer animation and store image

3. How temporal shifts in store design and consumer animation are embedded in and constitutive of patterns of regional development and global development of hypermarkets.

Each of these is elaborated below.

Store Design and Consumer Animation

A retail store is more than a place for storing products before customers decide to purchase them. Effective retail space is carefully designed not only to warehouse products efficiently but, more importantly, to create an intangible gestalt that animates customers to have a particular kind of shopping experience. Effective retail store design evokes a particular consumption dreamworld for a consumer, whether it is the deliberately cluttered bins of sale merchandise in a department store basement that animate some customers to dig hands-on in hopes of unearthing a possible hidden bargain or the deliberately sparse boutique displays of high-priced sweaters exhibited in museumlike glass cases that animate some customers to experience the rarity, high price, and desirability of each item. Consumers choose whether the dreamworld presented in the retail space fits their current fantasies or their worst nightmares.

The dreamworld offered by a retail space, theoretically impoverished in our literature by the cognitively laden attribute-based concept of store image, transfers cultural meaning (à la McCracken

1986) to objects purchased there. Enormous plastic bags of popcorn purchased at a warehouse club open to consumers only part of the day "must" be a bargain; their situatedness in the effectively created dreamworld proves their low price to consumers so convincingly that they forgo the need to do comparison shopping at other stores. Soft, cashmere sweaters so delicate that layers of tissue paper protect their inner surfaces "must" be of high quality, or they would not be displayed in the polished wood dreamworld of the boutique, protected from the touch of unqualified customers by vigilant, well-heeled sales staff who hover over the glass cases like museum security guards.

In this chapter, we examine how the physical features of a store and the shopping context in which it is embedded (e.g., shopping center, regional mall, or office and shopping complex) create this dreamworld. In particular, we probe how store environment features that consumers may not be able to cognitively identify nonetheless create consumer expectations and meanings that transfer even to commodity products available in competing stores. In contrast to our literature's prevailing metaphors for buying behavior, this analysis sees potential motivation, or consumer animation as it is called here (after Sherry 1990), as emanating significantly from the design of retail space, rather than as either an unpredictable impulsive moment or as a preexisting goal that initiates product search in the complex behavioral sequence glossed as consumer decision making.

Relocation, Market Broadening, and Shifts in Consumer Animation

A relocated retail store is pushed to accommodate increased variety in customers in what is called market broadening. Customers who have very different ideas and expectations about the store are now brought together to shop in the same retail environment. For instance, retail toy store customers of different classes hold different beliefs about what kinds of toys are "appropriate" for certain children and different expectations of what product benefits toys should deliver (Kline 1993). Customers express these expectations in terms of how much "fun" the toy is, its "educational" nature, its durability or cost, or whether it is "suitable for" or "popular with" a child of a particular age or gender. Toy purchasers, who are typically not the toy users themselves, are especially receptive to sales staff who can suggest "appropriate" toys (despite the salesperson's lack of familiarity with the intended recipient) or show potential purchasers how a toy "works."

With increased variety of customers in a new location, store image may become temporarily diffuse and even contested. Old customers come in search of the dreamworld of the "old" store, only to find it has changed without their consent. They may find the infusion of "new" customers troublesome; the(ir) store has been "discovered" and "isn't the same anymore." They express concern that the owners have "sold out" or "gotten too commercial." On the other hand, new customers are excited at their discovery of a dreamworld in the new location, unaware of their intrusion into the preexisting relationship between the store and its old customers. The store's owner/manager, whose own personal dreamworld is reflected in the new store design, must mediate the contest over store meaning waged by these two groups.

Individual customer purchases become the tangible expressions, and points scored, in this contest. Choosing a birthday present of rubber he-man Stretch Armstrong rather than an illustrated children's book on Greek mythology, or a Christmas present of a Disney-licensed stuffed Lion King rather than this year's Muffy VanderBear dressed in a Mozart-era costume, affects not only sales and profits, but also retail direction and dreamworld evolution. We employ our data to document the conflicts that emerge between "new" and "old" customers as their patronage determines the store's future orientation.

Embeddedness in Regional and Global Development

Beyond the empirical context of the toy store in this study, this chapter delves deeply into issues that are central to regional patterns of development and the shift at a global level from markets to hypermarkets. Individual consumer behaviors that make sense to

TABLE 5.1   Characteristics of Store Environments

Ambient Factors	Design Factors	Social Factors
Music	Floor and wall coverings	Salespeople
Lighting	Display and fixtures	Other shoppers
Smell	Color	
	Cleanliness	
	Ceilings	
	Dressing rooms	
	Aisles	
	Layout	
	Signs	

Source: Baker, Grewal, and Parasuraman (1994).

the persons enacting them are plumbed for their deeper cultural consequences and broader social implications. Individual purchases are regarded as not just embedded in, but also constitutive of, regional patterns of development and the emergence of global hypermarkets.

As a precursor to our analysis of these three issues, we begin with detailed contextual descriptions of the former store location and the new relocated site. We incorporate into our description of the two locations the ambient, design, and social factors of store environment identified by Baker, Grewal, and Parasuraman (1994) and shown in Table 5.1.

ETHNOGRAPHIC DESCRIPTION OF STORE HISTORY AND PREVIOUS LOCATION

Mrs. Tiggy-Winkle's Toy Store was opened in 1978 by a husband-wife team. Initially the store sold both new and used toys, as a means of limiting the young owners' financial investment in inventory, and occupied a tiny space encompassing 500 square feet of selling area. Over time, the store gradually expanded as the business was ready to grow, but without ever physically moving. Instead, walls were knocked out when adjoining store space became available. Until just before its move to a new location, the store occupied five adjoining retail spaces, with 1,800 square feet of space and inventory of $25,000 to $60,000, depending on the season. Since much of the character of this servicescape was determined by the shopping center in which it was embedded, we turn to a description of that shopping center before resuming our description of the former store location.

Broadway Village Shopping Center

Broadway Village is the oldest shopping center in town, but more than age makes it distinctive. It has been described as the "venerable grande dame of shopping centers" (Schensul 1981). One local writer claimed that "calling the gracious potpourri of shops and arches and patios at Broadway and Country Club Road a shopping center is a little like calling the *Queen Mary* a boat" (Henry 1989). It is a low-key environment, softly lit, without a parking structure, and without numerous directories pointing out "You Are Here."

Construction on Broadway Village Shopping Center began in 1939 at the corner of what was previously a golf course, adjacent to two affluent Anglo neighborhoods that were nonetheless given Spanish names. The shopping center was considered then to be on the eastern outskirts of town and served local residents and visitors at small, outlying guest ranches and resorts. A 1947 aerial photograph shows sparse development around the shopping village (Glinski 1995). Since the shopping center's construction, the metropolitan area's population has increased by roughly 2,000 percent in a residential relocation pattern that is nationally salient (Garreau 1981). Heavy dependence on private automobiles (Flink 1970) has allowed the city limits to be extended ten miles further east, nearly to Mountain National Park, which marks the geologic edge of the city valley.

The shopping center was developed by local builder John W. Murphey and designed by the Swiss architect Josias T. Joesler. They began working together in the 1920s and developed a reputation for constructing commercial and residential Southwestern buildings that exhibited both grace and practicality, incorporating function and design with the environment (Schensul 1980). Included in the center's design were statues and building materials brought back by Murphey and Joesler from their frequent trips to nearby Mexico. Even today, residential real estate designed by Joesler is advertised and proudly referred to by owners as "a Joesler."

Originally built to hold eight shops, the shopping village has since expanded several times to now include space for twenty-four. A local journalist has described Broadway Village as a "homey, neighborhood shopping center" (Schensul 1980). The incongruous use of the adjective *homey* to describe a shopping center points the way to instructive juxtapositions, particularly when guided by McCracken's (1989) ethnographic penetration of the components of homeyness (see Table 5.2 for a summary). We highlight these components of homeyness in our description of the ambient, design, and social features of the shopping center, and then the store itself.

In stark contrast to the massive regional mall located half a mile away (itself constructed on the site of a former resort hotel), shops in the shopping village are small in number and in size, displaying the *diminutive* property of homeyness. The stores are different from those in the nearby mall in that they are locally owned specialty shops and boutiques. While the mall has an outlet of the nationally pervasive B. Dalton, Bookseller, Broadway Village has Coyote's Voice Books, an owner-run bookstore specializing in Southwest books, and Footprints of a Gigantic Hound Ltd., a mystery bookstore owned and run by two women. While a mall shopper can snack on a regionally invariant Orange Julius, Broadway Village customers can eat a tuna salad sandwich served with rippled potato chips and several dill pickle slices, followed by a scoop of chocolate-chip ice cream or orange sherbet that is "homemade" (on the premises) at adjoining Austin's, locally owned and apparently unchanged in its basic decor since it opened in the late 1950s. Mall shoppers can run their children by Cost Cutters for an inexpensive haircut by whichever stylist is available first; shopping village customers can make an appointment to have "the usual" or "something new" done to their hair by either of the two sons of the now-deceased founder of Chez Josef Salon, while simultaneously

TABLE 5.2   Properties of Homeyness

Symbolic Properties

Diminutive property	Low ceilings, small windows and doors. The space is divided and filled. Gives a simplifying power.
Variable property	No symmetry, balance, or premeditated order. Not uniform or consistent. "Rubble-stone" rather than cut stone.
Embracing property	A pattern of descending enclosure, as in successive enclosure by the neighborhood, the yard, the ivy, roofline/awnings, external wall, books, furnishings of room. Psychologically like a parental embrace: security.
Engaging property	Engages, welcomes the observer. Opens to new arrivals.
Mnemonic property	Items, mementos that constitute a sort of "family archives."
Authentic property	Real, natural, not contrived or artificial.
Informal property	Warm, friendly, "puts people at their ease."
Situating property	The occupant becomes part of the arrangement.

Pragmatic Properties

Status corrector	High-standing groups must set aside homeyness to achieve status. Middle-standing groups embrace homeyness as a defense against status competition.
Marketplace corrector	Strips possessions of their commercially assigned meanings.
Modernity corrector	Contends with the cold, severe nature of modern designs.

Source: McCracken (1989).

catching up on the latest developments in each of their lives. Toddlers brought here for their first haircut will encounter a hairstylist who lovingly recalls the day he "did" the mother's hair for her wedding, or how little time there is for the father to ride mountain bicycles with him since this child was born.

An informant who is a longtime business operator in the area believes that the differences between the stores at the two locations are sufficient that the regional mall does not represent real competition for Broadway Village. Other informants make social distinctions between those who shop at Broadway Village and "mall shoppers," who are disparaged as showing less sophistication and taste. In fact, those who shop at Broadway Village are likely to also shop at the mall, but for different categories of merchandise.

The rambling, asymmetrical layout of the shopping village resonates (McQuarrie 1989) with variations in the natural building materials used to construct it: slightly varying types of brick in different sections, with tiers of mission tile roof surfaces made of red clay, decorative Mexican tile accents in several different patterns, and brick paving of varying layout designs. While these materials are characteristic of Southwestern architecture of that era, they also enhance the homeyness of the center by simultaneously manifesting the *variable* and the *authentic* properties of homeyness. The fact that the paving surface of the walkway is uneven from being lifted by tree roots makes it both treacherous and charming. The rambling layout and quaint irregularities force shoppers to stroll rather than dart, creating a leisurely rather than bustling pace.

Characteristic of Southwest residential architecture, the shopping village is built around a patio featuring two planters. Olson's Restaurant and Stacia's Bakery-Cafe (both named for local owners) each have tables and chairs set on the patio. Delicious bakery aromas complete the sensory experience of homeyness, which makes the individual feel welcomed by the open patio, cared for by beautiful apron-clad Stacia, and also embraced by the surrounding buildings—simultaneously displaying the *engaging* and *embracing* properties of homeyness. This dual effect is reinforced by the several archways that welcome and embrace those who pass through. In particular, the arched covered walkway at the back of the center is constructed in a layered, embracing style: a low-slung mission tile roof covers it, while delicate vines hug the surface of the arch with their green tendrils.

Remnants of past configurations of the shopping center remain in evidence and provide the *mnemonic* property of homeyness. The words *Broadway Village* are faintly visible in worn black paint on the brick wall above one of the stores. Holes in the wall indicate that a sign once covered this wall but was later removed. Those who have shopped at the center for many years recall that today's planter on the patio was once a decorative fountain with sprays of water bursting forth; decades of change in local and global concerns about water usage have altered this feature. Variation in the paving and window structures near the corner location serves as a physical reminder that this was recently a bank and, much earlier, a gas station. Some informants are able to relate not only the entry, exit, and movement of stores in the center, but also the names of the store owners.

There has been a concerted effort to retain the original charm despite substantial changes in the size and tenants of the shopping village. The style represented is unlike the more recent infusion into the national aesthetic lexicon of a pastiche of Southwestern design elements (e.g., turquoise and pink wooden-cutout howling coyotes wearing pastel bandannas, and chunky, whitewashed wooden furniture with stylized Zia-design padre cross cutouts across chairbacks), all of which represent a folksy updating of what is more appropriately referred to as "authentic" Santa Fe style (see Mather and Woods 1986). Instead, this shopping center represents authentic construction styles from Arizona and northern Sonora of 1939, when it was designed. By remaining faithful to its original style and not updating to conform to the invented tourist version of Southwestern style (Babcock 1990), Broadway Village displays the pragmatic property of a *modernity corrector,* adding to its homey effect.

Yet, for all of the architectural properties that contribute to its homeyness, Broadway Village remains a shopping center, a venue for commercial activity. Although it is homey to many, it is home to none. It is this juxtaposition that provides the opening for understanding the connections among retail store image, customer animation, and regional development that are a focus of this chapter. But before exploring these linkages, we complete the picture by providing contextual details of the toy store itself and its temporal changes.

Mrs. Tiggy-Winkle's Toys
at Broadway Village

Along with the rest of the shopping center, Mrs. Tiggy-Winkle's Toys displays an exterior of Southwestern architectural style with brick construction, archways over doors and windows, Mexican tile, exposed wooden beams, and brick paving pushed upward by the roots of a row of mature olive trees. Mexican ceramic tiles giving the suite number for each of the five original store spaces are still attached to the exterior: 11, 12, 13, 14, and 15. The store entrance is next to number 13. Former entryways have either been converted to bay windows or marked, "Please use other door." Exterior signage conforms to the variable property of homeyness. The sign above the entrance features a logo of a large spotted dog kissing a little French schoolgirl in a long dress and matching cap with tied chin strings. The logo is based on the flat, delicate drawings of the turn-of-the-century French illustrator Louis-Maurice Boutet de Monvel. In contrast, a small A-frame sign outside the front door displays the Union Jack and promises "English Garden toys."

Store Layout and Design

Mrs. Tiggy-Winkle's is a particularly homey store in this homey shopping center. Informants consistently describe the store as "quaint" or "charming." The store's name is a little-understood (by customers) literary reference to a 1905 Beatrix Potter children's story. In the story, a laundress hedgehog named Mrs. Tiggy-Winkle is visited in her cozy cottage cut into a hill by a small girl from Littletown searching for her lost pocket handkerchiefs and pinafore; Mrs. Tiggy-Winkle invites the girl to stay for tea and gives her (without requesting payment) her missing possessions, now nicely laundered. The story ends with questions leading the reader to ponder whether the meeting actually occurred or was the girl's dream.

Unlike some other Potter stories, such as *The Tale of Peter Rabbit,* this story is not well known (Carpenter and Prichard 1984); as a result, the store name is the source of some confusion for customers. Some customers confuse the store name with more familiar terms such as Mrs. Piggly-Wiggly, after the southern grocery chain, or Mrs. Tiddly-Winks, after a classic children's game. Not surprisingly, given the names of other stores in the shopping village, some people mistakenly believe the store is named for its owners, who are named Joey Beck and Barb Gilder rather than Mr. and Mrs. Tiggy-Winkle. This mistaken belief resonates with the homeyness of the store by situating a real married couple at its center. Further adding to its homeyness is the fact that the couple have borne two daughters over the years of running the store, a fact shared with customers through the store's newsletter and through their caring for these babies tucked under the counters in the store.

The diminutive property of homeyness pervades the store, which is, by national chain standards, quite small. Remaining architectural features from the former five retail spaces enhance the diminutive effect by dividing the store into a rambling assortment of distinct rooms and alcoves, each crowded with merchandise. The rambling traffic pattern is reminiscent of that of an old house with multiple successive additions, and roughly forms the shape of a backward L. The single functioning entrance is at the corner of the L through a single wooden door with a paned glass window at the top.

The front counter and register near the entrance serve as the active, bustling geographic and social center of the store. The initial impression upon entering is visual overload from the bright primary colors of merchandise that not only fills the small store, but seems to threaten to burst it. Illumination from bay windows crowded with merchandise on shelves and overhead track lighting is insufficient, so a large number of clip-on lamps have been added. The front counter is crammed with small bins of low-priced items that customers can keep exploring while the salesperson writes the paperwork for the financial transaction.

The slightly elevated open-beam ceiling in the entry room appears low, since the overhead space is filled with shelves that overhang the room, and colorful large items of merchandise hang from the center of the ceiling. The interior brick walls and wooden shelves have been painted white with a small amount of purple trim. A narrow passageway for customers is flanked by the cash register counter on one side and a wall-hugging display of greeting cards on the other.

This passageway leads to an area where the ceiling drops to seven feet and then opens to eight feet. In this space there is a wooden Brio train on a table low enough for toddler play, and a bay window displaying collectible Muffy VanderBear and her accessories. Above the window is a shelf holding a toddler push cart and other toys. Purple wooden dinosaur cutouts (not TV character Barney) form a shelving unit holding a variety of items including grotesque crushable puppets. Across the aisle is a half wall displaying small items such as packets of "fairy dust," rubber stamps, plastic animals, Mary Englebreit bath items, little purses, and play jewelry. Behind the half wall is a small room featuring preschool toys on shelves to the ceiling. An irregularity in the wall creates a small alcove for infants' toys. Another small space is created by a shelving fixture topped with a pink and purple striped canopy. Since the space above cannot be spared, a hockey game is displayed on top.

Proceeding back from the entrance of the store, one enters the largest room, where the ceiling rises to ten feet. The space is divided by an awning-covered alcove at one side displaying stuffed animals and various kinds of dolls: realistic baby dolls, Madeline dolls (a product spin-off based on the 1939 children's book by Ludwig Bemelmans about a French girl in boarding school; see Bemelmans 1939), and Mary Englebreit dolls (a product spin-off based on nostalgic, quaint figures from greeting cards by a contemporary St. Louis graphic artist; see Englebreit 1994). Some merchandise is displayed on a dark wood antique cabinet. Other merchandise is displayed on wooden shelves painted white with turquoise trim. Two child-size wooden chairs, made of particleboard and painted white, with the seats in accent colors, provide a place for children to sit and play.

The rest of the room is devoted mostly to children's clothing. Four wooden wardrobes shaped like houses and painted white with pink and green accents display some clothing, but a large amount hangs from racks along the wall. An old wooden trunk in the corner is filled with fairy wings, feather boas, and other fantasy dress-up clothes. Since space is at a premium, all available space is used to display merchandise. There are no dressing rooms where parents could have children try on clothes, and a tricycle is displayed on top of one of the wardrobes.

If one turns left at the store entrance instead of proceeding forward, a ramp leads up to a small room described by one informant as "Joey's special room," where Joey "expresses himself." To be more accurate, Joey expresses himself wherever he is. He is a naturally effervescent person, and it is not uncharacteristic to find him jumping around the store on spring-soled moon shoes, wearing fairy wings. Wherever he is, he gleefully demonstrates toys and entices customers to play with him in a selling effort convincingly disguised as spritely play. His engaging, playful approach results in informant descriptions of him as a "child at heart" or "tall elf." Nonetheless, steady customers see this room as particularly expressive of his character. More stereotypically masculine than other areas of the store, the room contains interesting science-based toys, monster and grotesque fantasy toys, racing car sets, magic tricks, and games. Merchandise is displayed on an antique cabinet and in a bay window.

Beyond this room is the book room. It is visually busy, with shelves showing the faces of colorful books, bracketed by two large cutout palm trees; nonetheless, this is the most serene room. A customer can sit in a little particleboard chair or an antique schoolroom chair, and browse through books. Stuffed animals and dolls representing book characters are displayed here. This room is seen by customers as more expressive of the interests of Joey's wife, Barb. With graduate degrees in creative writing and social work, she is keenly attuned to the role of children's literature in child development and social change and is concerned about contemporary parenting and family issues. The books she selects humorously and compassionately reflect these profound concerns, as do the first-person articles she writes for the store newsletter she publishes.

Symbolic Properties of Homeyness

As this description illustrates, Mrs. Tiggy-Winkle's Toys at Broadway Village is eclectic in a way that produces homeyness. The store fixtures simultaneously represent the variable and mnemonic properties. Shelves in the preschool area are constructed differently than shelves in other parts of the store. Similarly, the combination of displays for clothing defies conventional understandings of a comprehensive and integrated store design. Nonetheless, these variations cement longtime customers' connection to the store by serving as a visual mnemonic of the customers' pivotal role in the store's gradual growth and success. The shelves, chairs, and fixtures, many of them simplistically constructed of particleboard, appear whimsically "homemade," adding to the *informal* property of homeyness.

The store is also eclectic in its pastiche of geographic and temporal referents (see Jameson 1984). Its homeyness is nostalgic, but not with reference to a particular time or place (Davis 1979; Lowenthal 1985). The exterior is 1930s Southwestern, while the store name derives from turn-of-the-century English literature. The A-frame sign on the sidewalk uses both text and graphics to claim English heritage. A more continental influence is present in the store logo based on French children's story illustrations, and featured European toys such as Brio trains (from Sweden) and Ravensburger puzzles (from Germany). Furthermore, the influences include the New World; 1930s French schoolgirl (Madeline) dolls mingle with contemporary, St. Louis, nostalgic (Mary Englebreit) dolls. English Victorian walnut and rural American oak antiques cohabit with "homemade" painted particleboard display fixtures.

The store's features also manifest the embracing property of homeyness. Tight passageways are formed by shelves packed with merchandise hugging the walls and filling the overhead space. Other embracing layers form the exterior of the store. Walls are accessorized with decorative tile and protected above by a low-slung covering of exposed-beam roofing. Mature trees on the west side of the store overhang the roof and shelter the bay windows from the harsh afternoon sun, a welcomed landscape design in this desert environment.

Mrs. Tiggy-Winkle's sustains its homeyness by the means it uses to engage customers through the liminal space of the front door. The A-frame sign outside directs customers to the entrance and invites them in. The sign's impermanence speaks of the store's informality and dynamism. Above the front door, a neon sign gleefully declares "TOYS" with off-center letters, each in a different color. Immediately upon entering, customers are greeted by multiple sensory experiences including rollicking children's music and the explosion of primary colors described earlier. In these ways, the store is an authentic place where real fun is happening right now, and also a *situating* environment that pulls the consumer into that experience of fun.

In creating the engaging atmosphere that is constructive of homeyness, the social factors of the store environment may be more important than the ambient and design factors mentioned to this point. Customers become unpaid barkers harking their coshoppers into the store. The displays and initial impact of the store convert children into excited but unwitting accomplices who do what every store owner would love to do: extend a hand that literally pulls adults into the store. Upon entering, customers receive a friendly greeting or seemingly spontaneous product demonstration from one of the owners or employees. Before even asking what kinds of product interests or "needs" brought customers to the store, the salesperson or owner demonstrates toys, selected for their personal appeal, in a way that engages customers in playing with the merchandise. This greeting socially constructs an informal and situating environment for the customer. The surprising lack of apparent selling intent serves as a subterfuge for animating customers. Customers are nonverbally informed that they are expected to discard the distance and formality of "no touching," and even to temporarily put aside the goal-directed consumer search that prompted this shopping trip. The store becomes a place to play, with salespeople or alone, as well as an institution of commerce. In selecting one of their own favorite toys to demonstrate, owners and salespeople demonstrate a bit of themselves as they share the play experience with customers, as if they were just standing around playing when the customer arrived. This is not an impersonal institution.

In this respect, the store is authentically homey. For a home to be authentically homey means that it seems real or natural, and that it seems as if someone lives there. When the store owners or salespeople welcome customers inside, show them some of their favorite toys, and entertain them, the customers learn that this is not just a place for storing things until they are purchased. This store is inhabited by real people, and, thus, customers' experiences of going to the store take on some similarities to a visit to the owners' home.

However, like the shopping village in which it is situated, Mrs. Tiggy-Winkle's is homey but not a home. The back room is not a cottage where Mr. and Mrs. Tiggy-Winkle settle down for a cozy cup of tea at the end of the day; instead, it is a dimly lit, small space for unpacking boxes of new merchandise and pricing it. At the end of a long day of working at the store, the owners in fact long to go to their home for dinner. Unlike customers' children, who pull their parents into the store, the owners' children beg to be taken home.

Nonetheless, McCracken's articulation of the concept of homeyness in domestic environments is enormously instructive in helping us understand this servicescape. The symbolic components of homeyness resolve how its eclectic assemblage of ambient, design, and social factors "works" to create a cohesive store environment. However, the pragmatic properties of homeyness, unplumbed as yet, are useful not only in explaining how this store "works"—how it animates consumers (Sherry 1990)—but also in explaining how it was reworked to respond to its embeddedness in larger patterns of regional and global development. We thus complete our description of the former location by examining how the store addresses the final category in McCracken's (1989) deconstruction of homeyness: how it incorporates the pragmatic properties, operating as a marketplace corrector, status corrector, and modernity corrector.

Pragmatic Properties of Homeyness

This store creates the dreamworld of an old-fashioned, homey, non-work, play environment. It is a corrective to the pervasive encroachment of a marketplace mentality throughout postmodern life in which everything is for sale (Belk, Wallendorf, and Sherry 1989; Sherry 1990). The store momentarily suspends disbelief in customers and convinces them that the owners and salespeople are here to abandon the worries of the adult world in favor of playing and having fun with them. Rather than being the rational motivation that guides their behavior through this servicescape, buying is an outcome of customers' fascination with the playthings and playtime they come here and discover. Purchases are as much souvenirs (Stewart 1984) of the visit to the store as they are solutions to preexisting product needs. Somehow objects purchased are infused with the dreamworld created by being in this space.

In this respect, the store has an important advantage over a visit to someone's home: one can take home from the store (for a price) the enjoyable things found there. The store also has an advantage over competitors who display their merchandise warehouse style: at Mrs. Tiggy-Winkle's, the boxes of Brio trains, otherwise identical to those at other stores, are presumed by customers to have absorbed some of the homeyness and fun of the store. That absorbed fun and previous embeddedness in homeyness make these toys better able to serve as a *marketplace corrector;* they are expected to more readily lose their commercial meanings and instead become companionable objects within their destined homes. Whether the somewhat higher prices at Mrs. Tiggy-Winkle's are sufficiently justified by that contamination (Belk, Wallendorf, and Sherry 1989) is unquestioned by some customers, but a perplexing and restraining dilemma for others. The phenomenology of the dreamworld's economic value is a competitive component of so-called store image that has not yet been sufficiently researched.

This selection and display of inventory supports the marketplace corrector component of homeyness. Price tags are handwritten stickers, defying SKU numbers and scanner technology. Conspicuously absent are popular toys from Mattel (e.g., Barbie dolls), Coleco (e.g., Cabbage Patch Kids), Nintendo (e.g., Super Mario video games), and generally, toys advertised during Saturday-morning television shows. "Where did you find such a wonderful toy?" is more likely the response to receiving a Mrs. Tiggy-Winkle's gift than is, "Oh, I saw that on TV and wanted it for a long time." These toys and the store are correctives to the mass distribution of heavily advertised, licensed spin-offs that convince children they "must" have the toy today, only to discard it tomorrow (see Kline 1993). It is as if customers have a real "find" when they go on what one informant aptly referred to as a "treasure hunt through the various rooms" to locate these toys. The treasure hunt takes place not just in the store's cluttered rooms, but also in the regional and national retail context in which this store is embedded.

It is not just the homey shopping experience that transfers to the object, but also its prior embeddedness in a homey store. This helps explain why Mrs. Tiggy-Winkle's serves many adult customers buying gifts for children: parents as well as grandparents, parents of children going to a birthday party, and adult friends of children. Those with less direct experience with the specific child can count on Mrs. Tiggy-Winkle's to deliver not only the assistance they need, but also a toy imbued with homeyness that can make the transition to its new home effectively. Toys that come from a homey (marketplace corrector) store where owners and salespeople just like to play are regarded, especially by grandmothers, as more appropriate for expressing love and connection through gifts. Distinctive gift wrap of colorful tissue paper that whimsically rather than geometrically encases the item marks the gift's retail origin and sustains the quaint, homey touch.

This notion of the store as a marketplace corrector harks back to its early days when it sold even used toys, toys that literally were no longer available in the marketplace. Interestingly, this selling of used toys is affectionately recalled by longtime customers, although none lamented the current inclusion of only new toys in inventory, since they too can apparently serve as marketplace correctors. Through its inventory, design, display, and social encounters, Mrs. Tiggy-Winkle's homey store environment at Broadway Village served as a marketplace corrector, while it simultaneously functioned as a profit-making entrepreneurial venture.

However, in serving as a *status corrector* and a modernity corrector, Mrs. Tiggy-Winkle's paints a different picture, particularly when considered dynamically. The store at Broadway Village sold homey, nostalgic toys to a market of some longtime-resident, old-money families from the nearby affluent neighborhood who had every reason to preserve status quo; it also sold toys prized for being creative and developmental (but not "educational" in the schoolwork sense) to second-generation college-graduate, politically liberal, upper-middle-class families living in a nearby neighborhood adjoining the state university. Neither group shopped at Mrs. Tiggy-Winkle's to acquire social status. Old-money families have no need to engage in status acquisition; in fact, they have every reason to ensure that status cannot be purchased. Instead, their taste leads them to select items that subtly communicate and solidify their class position (Bourdieu 1984). Second-generation, upper-middle-class families pursue child development over the long term rather than status acquisition over the shorter term as a life project (Levy 1966; Coleman and Rainwater 1978; Mick and Buhl 1992). For both groups, shopping at this homey store served as a defense against the encroachment of status acquisition and competition into purchases of children's toys and clothing.

REGIONAL EMBEDDEDNESS AND THE DYNAMICS OF RETAIL RELOCATION

Despite demographic differences, Mrs. Tiggy-Winkle's at Broadway Village served as a modernity corrector for both groups of shoppers. Those who had moved to the area in the past decade often did so with a conscious desire to move westward away from the congestion and increasing pace of life in industrial-based urban areas. Delighted about their own relocation, they were critical of others who moved in after them. Longtime residents were embedded in work, leisure, and shopping patterns that developed in a previous time. Both groups were so fascinated by their face-to-face contact with preexisting local cultures that they often developed some specific knowledge about them and began adorning themselves and their homes with authentic, Native American and Sonoran art and jewelry. They delighted in the ways the area was unlike where they came from and learned about native plants as they hiked in local canyons. Both long-term residents and the large numbers who arrived in the 1970s and 1980s were immersed in local institutions (economic and political) based on personal connections. There was a sense that everybody knew everybody, although the area was already a large metropolitan center. During this time, Mrs. Tiggy-Winkle's at Broadway Village was part of a larger modernity-corrector social project that constructed the local area as a counterpoint to American urban life elsewhere.

What happened over time to the local community is not unlike what happens to any area when tourists enact the tautological desire to go where tourists don't go: unprecedented population growth was the consequence of hundreds of thousands of people longing to "get away from it all." Large destination resorts were built to attract hundreds of people at a time who wanted to "get away" for a few weeks of intense consumption of sun, golf, tennis, horseback riding, and "authentic" shopping. Areas at the entrance to federally protected canyons became prime real estate rather than remote, undeveloped natural areas to hike through en route to riparian areas. Having experienced the resorts on vacations, many tourists were attracted to relocate permanently. In contrast to the community visited by arthritic and asthmatic tourists during the winters in the 1930s and 1940s, air-conditioning in buildings and automobiles and ever-deeper pumping of groundwater now made year-round residence more attractive, even if it also placed an unmitigated strain on natural resources (see Reisner 1986 regarding Western water politics) and dramatically altered the nature of informal social connections between neighbors (Hinton 1988). Those who moved to the area now hoped to replicate not a simpler counterpoint to American urban life elsewhere, but the lush, upscale, intense recreational atmosphere of destination resorts. In microcosm, a staggering acceleration in population growth brought about through interstate and international migration moved the local community from *Gemeinschaft* to *Gesellschaft* in a few short years (Tonnies et al. 1871).

Those moving to the area from the mid-1980s to mid-1990s increased its population by 24 percent, producing a community very different in composition from the United States as a whole. The U.S. Census shows the three-mile trade area of the new store location to be well above the U.S. average in the percent of population with education beyond high school, and dramatically above the U.S. average for the percent with graduate degrees. White-collar and service occupations dominate, since growth was not precipitated by agricultural needs or industrial expansion. The resident population has a median age that is 3.7 years older than the nation's median age, primarily from having a smaller-than-average percentage of children under age 19 and a slightly larger percentage of people age 55 and older, especially who are retired. In addition, many people who are temporary residents during the winter are 55 and older, a phenomenon not captured by U.S. Census figures on permanent residents. Thus, the trade area of the new store location has a slightly lower percentage of residents who are children, but a large percentage of residents and temporary visitors who are in the age bracket of grandparents.

Those moving to the area during the mid-1980s to the mid-1990s were different from previous migrants. They were more likely to have come from southern California than from northeastern or Great Lakes states (Rex 1995). Company relocations of upper-level personnel in the computer and aircraft industries brought over ten thousand people in a few years. In selecting residences, they looked to outlying desert foothill areas near the destination resorts, rather than to the central city. Despite immense growth in total metropolitan population, the central city actually declined in population between 1980 and 1990. The new residents found they could afford much larger homes than in coastal California. They eagerly bought or built magnificent houses "with a view" of the mountains above and the ever-expanding city lights below, with fountains and swimming pools to replace the ocean they left behind in California. In addition, well-known entertainers and sports figures with newfound wealth bought second (or third or fourth) homes "tucked away" at the periphery of the area. The infusion of real estate capital escalated home prices, pushing many mountain foothill residential areas out of the economic reach of longtime residents.

The metropolitan growth pattern took the form of standard suburban development, with the location of most jobs requiring travel from the mountain foothill periphery into the valley center. In contrast to patterns developing in many other cities nationwide, the area did not yet develop Edge Cities that combine extensive office space, shopping areas, and some residential dwellings outside of the center city (Garreau 1991). In their daily commute, even those who live at the periphery still come "into town" for jobs and shopping, although increasingly at the edge of the valley nearest to their mountain foothill dwellings. Residential growth in peripheral areas that are increasingly distant from job sites, combined with local resistance to the construction of freeways, produced problems with traffic congestion and air pollution that are unlikely to diminish.

DESCRIPTION OF RELOCATION
AND NEW STORE SERVICESCAPE

Reasons for Relocation

As impactful as the store environment of Mrs. Tiggy-Winkle's at Broadway Village was in constructing homeyness, the pertinence of this concept to the cityscape in which it was embedded had diminished over time. New residents are less interested in cozy, nostalgic homeyness; they lack the basis to understand the mnemonic and authentic properties of homeyness represented by Mrs. Tiggy-Winkle's Toys at Broadway Village. They moved to the area because they were willing to forsake some nostalgic connections to another place in favor of something new and exciting. Rather than clinging to an idealized past, they focus on realizing their dreams in the present. Rather than moving to the area to "get away from it all" and learn about native desert plants, these new residents soon lamented their loss of southern California's greater variety and sophistication of consumer goods, services, and retail offerings.

Mrs. Tiggy-Winkle's Toys confronted the opportunity to respond to city growth of upscale households in the northern foothills and their different aesthetics. Tacitly aware of the opportunities accessible only through dramatic change, the owners eagerly decided to explore this possibility. Ever conscious of the store's tight space, they were again ready to grow, but in a more comprehensive way than by knocking out another wall. Worried about overextending and losing their ability to generate a profit, they took two years to formulate and implement relocation plans based on a difficult-to-accomplish balance of information and intuition. The contemplated store move paralleled their personal movement through the life cycle; having their children both in school allowed Barb to complete a graduate degree in social work as the starting point for a career beyond the toy store.

In an inversion of the classic retail gravitation model (Huff 1963), the store owners were pulled to relocate their store closer to the outlying mountain foothill areas. Yet simultaneously, they felt a gentler pull from current neighborhood customers in what was now dubbed "midtown." They knew they could not implement longtime customers' suggestion of continuing in the old store while also opening a second location. They chose a site in Crossroads Festival, a strip mall 3.5 miles northeast of Broadway Village, at the intersection of two major arterial roadways. The north-south street funnels traffic coming into town from the northern foothills areas with a daily traffic count of over 35,000 cars; the east-west street leads to other north-south funnels and residential building sites with a daily traffic count of over 49,000 cars.

The announcement of the decision to longtime customers was greeted with disappointment and dismay that they would be "leaving the neighborhood."

Crossroads Festival

Construction of Crossroads Festival began in 1986 on a site 1.5 miles south of the typically dry riverbed that forms the southern boundary of the mountain foothills area. A 1947 aerial photograph shows a horse trail running along what is now the four-lane north-south street (Glinski 1995); a contemporary aerial photograph in promotional materials from the leasing office shows almost complete development for miles around the center, with over 100,000 people living within 3 miles. The shopping center was designed by a Los Angeles architectural firm and developed by a real estate firm that has developed more than $7.5 billion of property in sixty-six markets. The original design included two phases of construction of 160,000 square feet of retail space and parking for 800 cars. Expansion beyond the original plans has produced a shopping center with eight restaurants and thirty-two retail stores, including a 30,000-square-foot supermarket, a bank, a national-chain video store, and a discount movie theater complex. The basic layout is L-shaped with shops aligned along a covered walkway, parking in front and in back, and four freestanding businesses along the major streets.

The basic building material—split-face concrete block—is a simpler version of that chosen in 1929 by Frank Lloyd Wright for a grand resort in the state's other major city. Lighter-colored concrete archways supported by unadorned round columns echo another large Wright-designed building in the state; here they serve to line the covered arcade over the sidewalk connecting storefronts. Nonnative fan palm trees, rounded river rock, and nonnative succulents decorate the south-facing parking lot without providing shade; median strips planted with grass offer tiny islands of green. Only a few native mesquite trees offer shade, but they stand away from the storefronts and parking area near the freestanding bank. Promotional materials from the leasing office describe the shopping center as being of a "contemporized Southwestern style" with a "high-energy ambiance." The terms *contemporized* and *high-energy* take on deeper meaning when employed in understanding the shift of retail servicescape brought about through the new location of Mrs. Tiggy-Winkle's Toys.

Rather than having established itself over time, Crossroads Festival is new construction, incorporating elements of now-classic buildings but in an updated, future-oriented style. No relics from trips to Mexico are included here; no quaint handworked ceramics decorate the walls. Instead, Crossroads Festival sets the stage for a faster pace and more intense shopping moment. Promotional materials distributed by the leasing office claim:

> The building architecture of the historic southwestern plaza is enlivened with a contemporary vibrance. With the jagged peaks and deep hues of the Santa Catalina mountains forming the backdrop, the unsurpassed beauty of the Crossroads Festival will be an enduring classic.

Rather than already being a classic, this shopping center aspires to attain that status. Even the descriptors chosen for the two shopping centers highlight their essential differences: *Festival* implies a fleeting, demarcated period of extraordinary conviviality and revelry by participants who are together for the moment, whereas the descriptor *village* is a nostalgic term for an ongoing, stable community with dense, historically rooted social connections.

Other stores in the shopping center reflect the contemporized, high-energy description. Crossroads Festival shoppers can lunch at the French Loaf Bakery and Cafe on a "California-Lite" green onion/dill bagel served open faced with white albacore tuna salad, with Dijon mustard, onions, and sprouts available on request. Lunch can be completed with a side order of vermicelli vinaigrette (made with pasta, celery, artichoke hearts, pine nuts, and raspberry vinaigrette) and a decaffeinated double cappuccino flavored with almond, hazelnut, raspberry, or vanilla Monin French syrup. For a snack later, shoppers can walk down the covered arcade to a shop next to Mrs. Tiggy-Winkle's called Marble Slab Creamery, to experience an ice-cream treat of their own invention, constructed before their eyes in a salesperson performance. Selected ice creams from a list of thirty-three flavors are made fresh daily in the store in small four-gallon production batches, including sweet cream, vanilla, vanilla bean, French vanilla, and vanilla cinnamon for those wanting something plain. Into the chosen ice-cream flavor can be added any combination of twenty-four "mixins" (including nuts, fresh fruits, and various crushed cookies and candies). Once the mixture has been folded together on a refrigerated marble slab, it is put into the customer's choice of freshly baked waffle cone, chosen either from the seven types dipped in various chocolate sauces and then rolled in nuts or crushed candy bars, or from the three types made for those wanting something plain (vanilla sugar, honey wheat, or vanilla cinnamon). The number of possible combinations ensures that each customer can create what the store calls a "unique experience"; the rotation of ice cream flavors infuses change and energizes the experience with positive tension in the creative process of constructing an ice-cream treat.

Alternatively, customers may spend an evening at the shopping center. They can combine local flavors with fish flown in daily from afar by dining at Buddy's Grill on mesquite-grilled fresh king salmon with cucumber dill relish or on mesquite-grilled fresh ruby trout with roasted red peppers and cilantro lime beurre blanc, accompanied by Southwestern au gratin potatoes and "homemade" zucchini muffins. The grill atmosphere allows diners time for a movie either before or after dinner. Alternatively, shoppers can dine at the contemporary Italian trattoria that is not named after its owner, despite the use of his family's names on two well-known Italian restaurants across town. Instead, the restaurant is named Vivace, an Italian word meaning lively, echoing the high-energy ambience descriptor used for the shopping center. In this sleek, starkly colored, Art Deco restaurant, diners sit on cantilevered, matte-black metal-frame chairs beneath framed abstract prints, and talk above the noise that enlivens the setting as it bounces around the many hard surfaces. Diners can begin with a first course of grilled shrimp and wild mushrooms in a baked filo cup served with fresh chopped tomato and basil sauce; followed by a spinach salad with warm pancetta–port wine dressing, pine nuts, and romano cheese; then a main course of filet of beef in green-peppercorn sauce with garlic-potato puree.

The largest retail space (34,000 square feet) is occupied by Bed Bath and Beyond, a national chain home-furnishings store with brightly lit white Scandinavian-type shelving extending twelve feet high in a massive display of uncluttered abundance that shoppers literally look up to. While reasonably priced, the merchandise is displayed using an updated, sleek aesthetic. There is a small section of toys and children's room furnishings, including bedding, safety devices, plastic interlocking blocks, and a few children's books. Occasionally, this store and Mrs. Tiggy-Winkle's simultaneously offer some of the same toys (especially plastic infant rattles with developmental intent). When the same item is found in both stores, invariably Bed, Bath, and Beyond offers it at a somewhat lower price, forcing the owners of Mrs. Tiggy-Winkle's to either respond or persevere.

No other direct competitors of Mrs. Tiggy-Winkle's are located in Crossroads Festival. A shop selling collectible dolls adjoins it, but these dolls appeal more to adult (often older women) doll collectors than to children. Little cross-shopping between the two stores occurs. More cross-shopping occurs between the store selling collectible dolls and another store in Crossroads Festival selling expensive dollhouses.

Other stores in the center are certainly contemporized, even while resisting a high-energy image. Mills-Touche retains a combination of two local family names and sells classic (read: simple but expensive) clothing in a boutique setting. Natural fabrics pervade in brand names such as Ruff Hewn jeans, in colors with evocative but nondescript names such as High Sierra and Aegean Tiles. Ralph

Lauren shirts, tagged as "becoming better and more personal with age" and adorned with an embroidered mounted polo player, are sold by carefully dressed salespeople who frown on customers shopping on the way home from jumping their horses and therefore still wearing authentic English riding apparel. The embroidered horses in this store are for those interested in representing themselves as having the status associated with polo horses, without ever touching an actual horse.

In contrast to Broadway Village, Crossroads Festival appeals to those who display status markers, rather than to those who seek a status corrector, and to those who seek change, rather than nostalgic constancy. These stores aim at the upper-middle- and lower-upper-class residents of swimming-pool-accessorized foothills homes, and to guests at the three major destination resorts in the foothills. The two busy streets make shopping here accessible for commuters between town and foothills; quick trips to one store are facilitated by the linear layout.

Mrs. Tiggy-Winkle's Toys at Crossroads Festival

The interior of Mrs. Tiggy-Winkle's Toys at Crossroads Festival is so dramatically different that several frequent shoppers at the former location were awed when entering the new store. Because the exterior sign was not yet hung when the store first opened, several "old" customers did not realize that they were in Mrs. Tiggy-Winkle's until it was time to write a check and they were told the store's name. The owner, who designed the award-winning new store interior, smiles as he assents that this is "no more a little European toy store." Even the exterior sign (when it was finally installed) and the new store logo set the stage for the construction of a very different dreamworld. The new logo features a baby-faced sprite popping out of a swirl-design cone. His face serves as the O in the most prominent word in the logo: TOYS. In much smaller letters above this character are the words *Mrs. Tiggy-Winkle's.* Below is a new slogan: "Letting the Joy Out of the Bag!"

In sheer size and layout, Mrs. Tiggy-Winkle's at Crossroads Festival is quite different. This retail space is roughly twice the size of the former location, with approximately 3,400 square feet and inventory of $68,000–100,000, depending on season. The store runs the width of the shopping center, with floor-to-ceiling glass doors and windows at both the front and back entrances to the open-plan L-shaped store.

Color and Light

Rather than simply being larger than the old store, this store has a completely different design. Upon entering, one is struck by the vivid colors and visual excitement. Colors of vivid chroma, inspired by the 1992 Robin Williams movie *Toys,* awaken the senses to a contemporary dreamworld of energized, free-floating fantasy. The movie, a modest success by Hollywood standards, has both visuals and a storyline that contextualize our understanding of this retail site. In the PG-13 movie, actor Robin Williams plays Leslie Zevo, the not-at-all-serious son of a toy manufacturer. When the jokester manufacturer dies, he bequeaths the whimsically styled toy factory to his three-star general brother rather than to his play-oriented son, whom he proudly calls a "flake" like himself. In opposition to the company's previous strategy, the general begins making items that look like military toys but are actually deadly military weapons launched by unsuspecting children. Williams's child-in-an-adult's-body character and his unusual, always-in-dreamland sister, Alsatia, are kept in the dark about this project for some time without much difficulty. When the pair finally realize what is happening, they employ a warehouse of windup toys to divert the military weapon "toys." The good guys win, and toy production resumes its peaceful purpose of providing "joy and innocence and squeezable fun for everyone."

Visually, the movie is set in a factory that is more of a fantasy playland than an industrial site. Alternate surfaces are painted different bright colors, making stairs look like children's blocks. Production machines with whimsical designs are powered by large orange and blue gears, making them resemble toys themselves.

Workers in colorful costumes dance in rhythm and sing "The Happy Worker" while working on the production line. The factory clock is the nose of a machine with a yellow head, orange horn-shaped ears, and a bright red mouth from which emerge newly produced toys. The ceiling is painted to resemble blue sky with white clouds. Yellow chairs with orange spots in the president's office are pulled around a bright blue table. Outside the factory sits a large gray elephant figure with blue ears, a red beanie with a windup key on top, and a moving trunk. This icon represents the factory's first toy product, called "Milton, the friendly elephant"; his image (in conservative white stone) is used as a headstone for Leslie's deceased father, complete with bubbles floating out of the trunk.

Reminiscent of the movie's factory, Mrs. Tiggy-Winkle's at Crossroads Festival comprises flat surfaces painted solid colors that change at each corner or surface change. The basic palette consists of saturated colors such as might exist in a tropical fish environment: periwinkle blue, aqua, sunshine yellow, goldfish orange, and bright white. Each is a deep tone rendered stronger by the use of gloss chroma enamel paint. There is a flatness to each single-color surface, enhanced by the absence of moldings. Sharp dimensionality and geometry are highlighted by the color change at each surface edge. Starting at the front of the store, the left side contains sunshine-yellow facings on aqua shelves, and the right side has aqua facings on white shelving. Goldfish-orange uprights nonverbally demarcate different merchandise areas in the store, much as the previous division into rooms provided architectural cues to customers. Between the two walls near the entrance are periwinkle display gondolas with white shelves. In the center at the front are four rectangular upright pillars with alternating sunshine-yellow and aqua surfaces, designed so display shelves can be easily rearranged. In the middle of these four pillars is a high skylight. Two settees covered in natural color canvas are framed by these pillars, and provide a neutral resting spot for overloaded grandparents.

The color alignments change as one moves back through the store, with different combinations of the same colors demarcating different thematic and functional areas. Using the bright colors as accents to plain white shelving for displaying products keeps the store's colors from competing with merchandise that often contains bright primary colors; the contrast use of white demonstrates tasteful restraint in an otherwise bold color scheme.

The ceiling surface has additional fantasy musings based on the factory in the movie: it is periwinkle blue dotted with wooden cutouts depicting white clouds. It is not sky blue; it is the blue of early twilight. Track lighting is hung among the clouds and is supplemented with recessed spot lighting in display soffits.

Whimsically interspersed among these solid-color surfaces are several strictly ornamental design elements that refer to contemporary popular and high culture; they point to this store being "contemporized" rather than "classic." From the movie *Toys* are two figures: Sprockethead and a beanie-clad elephant. Spherically surrounding two sides of one of the pillars is a figure referred to by the owners as Sprockethead. Fashioned after the machine head with a clock nose in the movie, he is done in the color palette of the store: sunshine-yellow face, a periwinkle gear forming spiky hair, white eyes with black centers lined in goldfish orange, red shapely lips, and nose and ears of goldfish orange with periwinkle-blue accents. On a facing column, aqua, goldfish, and periwinkle gears echo Sprockethead's hair and the movie's machine gears. Near the register sits a three-dimensional gray elephant head atop a five-foot, faux concrete Doric column. Reminiscent of Milton from the movie, the elephant head is the size of a large beachball, wearing a goldfish-orange beanie hat with a windup key and a yellow tie with orange polka dots. His eyes are black dots framed by white and aqua. His trunk is raised, but no bubbles come out. These two figures, vibrant and colorful in their own right, appear less vivid against the background of a store designed in the same palette and filled with brightly colored toys. Nonetheless, they refer to a dreamworld constructed by and through contemporary Hollywood, rather than derived from the diminutive drawings of turn-of-the-century French illustrators or English authors.

Much less vivid are several design ornaments in the book area that refer to literary culture rather than contemporary popular culture. Flanking the book area as one enters from the back door are two faux concrete floor-to-ceiling Doric columns intended to refer to those at the entrance to the New York City Public Library. The columns also define this space as a "room," much as the goldfish-orange uprights do elsewhere in the open-plan store. Their lack of bright color makes them unobtrusive, despite their size. Similar in color and even less noticeable is a figure hanging above the bright colors of the shelves displaying books: it is a stone-colored lion's head, intended to refer to the lion statues outside the entrance to the New York City Public Library.

The literary referents are rarely consciously understood or commented on by customers. These design elements nonetheless shape customers' visual understanding of this as a separate space in the store. In a less manifest way, the columns and lion's head contrast with the vividly colorful Sprockethead and Milton, the friendly elephant. Their lack of color makes them seem like timeless ghosts from a more literary past, a past that seems less vivid in contrast to the colorful but ephemeral referents of contemporary Hollywood.

Pattern

Although the store's visual impact comes primarily from alternating solid-color surfaces, a few patterns are employed as accents. Several are based on the work of graphic artist Mary Englebreit, whose work is also the basis of product spin-offs (e.g., cards, socks, dolls) sold in the store. The most prominent patterned accents appear on a canopied, wooden cart with two large spoke wheels, such as might be used by a street vendor. The cart's background is white, with its structural elements highlighted in periwinkle, sunshine yellow, goldfish orange, aqua, and glossy black. Pattern has been added to the cart's assemblage of alternating color surfaces. Goldfish-orange polka dots on a sunshine-yellow background echo the pattern of the necktie worn by Milton the elephant, which itself echoes the chairs in the president's office in the movie. Black-and-white checkerboard patterns and colorful stripes, stars, and floral motifs complete the effect, which is summed up by the inscription on the yellow ribbon painted on the back of the cart: "O Happy Day!"

Under the canopy of the painted cart sits a menagerie of stuffed animals and a multicultural assemblage of dolls: an Eskimo girl doll and a Red Riding Hood doll sit arm-in-arm near Muffy

VanderBear and her latest outfits. Also included are Mary Englebreit design dolls, adding additional surfaces of pattern to this display. Between the spokes of the cart's large wooden wheels are shiny, colorfully decorated balls.

Patterns used on the flower cart are also used as accents in other places in the store. Two paned windows at the side of the store are framed in the black-and-white checkerboard pattern with goldfish-orange accent blocks at the corners. This checkerboard pattern also resonates with the sharp geometry defined by the store's color changes at each surface edge. White stars have been painted on a periwinkle-blue soffit between the pillars around the skylight, and periwinkle stars have been painted on sunshine-yellow walls above the fantasy clothing area and the science toy area. Near the back entry, a sunshine-yellow soffit is the background for a popular Mary Englebreit pattern of pairs of red cherries joined by their stems and accented with aqua leaves. These patterns are playful by design and offset the austere geometry of the store's solid-color surfaces. Ultimately, they simultaneously reflect the whimsy of toys and the tasteful preferences of sophisticated customers.

Sound and Smell

Not only is the store visually vivid, it also provides lively stimulation for other senses as well. Children's songs from all over the world and from many ethnic origins are played loudly. Not only do the songs provide background music, customers frequently ask about them and buy a tape or compact disc. The owner's music selections are noted and appreciated even by internationally famous musicians who are part-time local residents. His childlike exuberance produces an active involvement in the music while it plays; he often walks around the store clapping and singing along with the music. Other employees and some customers frequently ask him to turn the music down. Soon, however, the music is loud again. It is as though he loves the music so much that he forgets that other adults may find it too loud.

Coincidentally, the store is also filled with strong aromas, evocative of childhood. The specialty ice-cream shop located next door fills the toy store with the aromas of waffle cones being baked and caramel sauce being kept warm. These sweet, delicious aromas arouse childhood longings and desires for a "treat" in an environment where they can only be immediately satisfied synesthetically through toy purchases.

Merchandise Display and Layout

As vivid and lively as the store environment is, its function is to display and highlight products, many of which are also very brightly colored. However, the dominant colors used in children's toys are primary colors of red, blue, and yellow, which are quite different from the palette used in the store's design. Thus, the geometric shape of the display surfaces, visually brought to the foreground through contrasting colors on adjoining surfaces, highlights rather than competes with product display.

As if floating in air, some displays are suspended from the ceiling: a Curious George monkey riding a bicycle across the store on a tightrope; a little girl's outfit stuffed with tissue, as if the dress has sprung to life and floated through the air; and, during the initial store opening, store shopping bags printed with the new logo in goldfish orange, sunshine yellow, and periwinkle blue, and stuffed with color-coordinated tissue paper.

Freestanding display gondolas are arranged in a way that avoids supermarket-style row organization with aisles. They are chest high, allowing access by children and visual openness for adults, who can peer or talk over them. Constructed on casters, they are rearranged as needed or even quickly pushed aside for evening workshops or concerts. Thus, few of the store fixtures are, in fact, fixed; instead, the store is poised for constant change.

Customers entering through the heavy glass front door are between two floor-level window displays accessible to shoppers. Freestanding deeply colored geometric pedestals raise the displayed toys from the floor. Two-dimensional black wire frame mannequins display clothing in the window among toys, typically along a theme such as toy horses among cowboy outfits, or gingham dresses at a picnic with teddy bears. Mannequins have no faces to distract from the clothing; instead, a two-dimensional drawing of a lion's or a child's head may be used as a face. Inside the entry, an easel (also for sale) announces special store events, such as book signings, evening "pajama party" concerts, or thematic workshops such as "Bugs," "Magic," and "Dreaming of Dragons."

On the side walls are girls' and boys' clothing, interspersed with toys that are thematically related to the clothing. Yellow T-shirts, khaki shorts, and safari hats are displayed near butterfly nets, magnifying glasses poised over plastic bugs, a book about bugs, and a ladybug-shaped backpack. Dresses with cherries and tomatoes embroidered on the bodices are displayed beside child-sized gardening tools in bright primary colors, stuffed bunnies dressed in gardening clothes, and straw hats accented with flowers. An alphabet book with a chimpanzee on the cover is displayed surrounded by gorilla puppets and stuffed chimps, a girl's dress with a wild-animal-print accent, a gorilla puzzle, and a humorous book entitled *Goodnight, Gorilla,* which is about animals escaping from the zoo.

Rather than warehousing items for sale, displays cross-merchandise items in a way that the owner describes as "telling a story." The stories told by these displays are children's dream experiences: a backyard bug safari, an afternoon with Mistress Mary tending the garden, or an imaginary swing through the trees with jungle primate friends. Cross-merchandising puts some items at two places in the store: the bug book is in the bug safari display and also in the book area; the gorilla puppet is on the ape display shelf near the clothing and also on the puppet rack near the back door. This duplication presents the item to two types of customers: one looking at books and the other assembling a bug safari gift. Cross-merchandising allows salespeople to easily suggest tie-in items to gift purchasers, bundling the merchandise into a thematically organized gift. Unlike conventional carefully arranged tabletop displays with inventory stocked below, these in-store displays contain multiples of items so that customers can help themselves to items contained within the display without denuding it.

Almost all toys have at least one demonstration item with packaging removed that is intended for in-store play. Because these toys are played with by many customers, almost any display soon shows some disorder. This does not concern the store owners, who commented: "See, some employee has stacked these up like what we are trying to do is stack things neatly on the shelf. So some employee came along and thought they were straightening things up. But we're not trying to stacks things on the shelf! We're trying to put them out so customers can see them." Such displays require consistent maintenance, if not stacking. As in almost any child's room, after just a few hours, there are bits and pieces of games and toys and clothes and candy everywhere. From field notes: "A boxing puppet was missing his head, the bubble wrap from a pair of devil's eyeballs was left on the fountain, a wrapper from the Band-Aid gum was opened and left with the can."

Nonetheless, there is some organization of inventory, although it is not marked with signs for customers. Girls' clothing is on the right; boys' clothing is on the left. Toys for older children, including battery-operated toys and arts and crafts kits, are in between. Next to the girls' clothing are wooden train sets, with a low table containing a Brio train for in-store play. At the back of the selling space is the cash register, and behind it the back room and office. On the cash register counter is the new computer that organizes inventory by SKU number, the cordless telephone, and the direct line for charge card purchases. In front of the register counter is a gondola containing a blaze of red and pink plastic merchandise: cosmetic and jewelry trinkets appealing to school-age girls. Hanging from the front of the register counter are baskets of low-priced novelty items. Beside the register counter on the left are science-based toys and puzzles for adolescents and adults. This area contains merchandise that was included in "Joey's room" at the old store; its ineffective fluorescent lighting (leftover from a previous tenant) and its back corner location make it the area least frequented by customers.

If one turns right before reaching the register counter, the second leg of the L shape becomes visible. A breezeway and back door lead to the parking area and movie theater ticket booth. In this leg of the store, one first encounters a large stainless steel soda fountain topped with black plastic bins, some containing pump dispensers, all overflowing with novelty items, such as squirt guns, bubble guns, and windup toys. The bin arrangement and general lack of order invite customers to hunt and then dig in to see what treats they can find. These items and the larger ones on the nearby shelves are what is referred to with the double entendre *gag gifts*. Some are merely clever, such as bouncy balls that glow in the dark. Others play on older children's delight at being offensive: plastic dog feces, eyeballs fashioned out of a slimy rubberized product that sticks to walls when thrown, and products to simulate flatulence sounds.

Between the soda fountain and the back door is the new book room. Books are displayed face out, near small chairs, a cushioned settee, and an antique child's desk for those who want to sit and look. In the middle sits a round child's table and an assortment of small chairs and stools; some are for sale and some are store fixtures. Dolls and stuffed animals representing book characters are displayed beside the books. Classics such as *Anne of Green Gables* and *Kidnapped* are on shelves up high. Humorous books intended as much for adults as for children, such as *Politically Correct Bedtime Stories, The Paper Bag Princess,* and *Everybody Poops,* are prominently featured at the entrance to the room. Other books are grouped by children's age.

Near the back door is a display of soft, furry puppets ranging from adorable creatures such as hugging koala bears to abominable (but still soft and fuzzy) demons, such as dragons and Maurice Sendak's "Wild Things." Each puppet is perched upright on a salvaged medical instrument drying rack that makes each one appear to be already on someone's hand.

Across is an area devoted to fantasy clothes: fairy wings, angel halos, feather boas, ballerina tutus, glittery high-heeled shoes, princess hats, pirate caps, and soft plastic swords. These fantasy clothes spill out of an antique trunk that invites children to transcend time and reality and reach in for the accessories of a spontaneously constructed fantasy. A mirror and round step-up pedestal painted periwinkle and aqua invite children to display and admire their newly constructed fantasy. A dressing room is formed by a rounded goldfish-orange canopy with scalloped gold trim from which hangs a long periwinkle-blue canvas curtain painted with gold stars.

Taken as a whole, this store environment produces a servicescape quite different from the cozy, homey atmosphere drawn from nostalgic English literature referents that characterized Mrs. Tiggy-Winkle's Toys at Broadway Village. Instead, Mrs. Tiggy-Winkle's Toys at Crossroads Festival is the dreamworld of a Hollywood-inspired child's playroom. In it, the toys are already animated, already in action. They are interspersed with thematically relevant clothing, inducing a more complete dreamworld and thereby requiring less imagination and constructive effort from the customer. How would one wear this outfit? The mannequin shows us. How does one play with this toy? The display invites the customer to try it out. What would this toy look like if taken out of its box? One is already sitting on the shelf for us to see. Clothing and toys that might be used together are found together, much as they might be on the floor of a real child's room if parents are not allowed to impose their standards of cleanliness and order. This is clothing-in-action and play-already-happening.

CUSTOMER ANIMATION AND CONTESTS OVER STORE MEANING

To return to our initial themes, the location change of Mrs. Tiggy-Winkle's Toy Store is more than a simple geographic relocation; it is a sizable shift in the basis for animating customers. Whereas the old store animated customers through nostalgic, cozy security, the new store embeds them in a Hollywood-dream playroom permeated by energy and excitement with a sophisticated, contemporary aesthetic. Interestingly, these substantial changes in the store environment have been accompanied by amazing constancy in the lines of inventory carried. Certainly a store of double the size must have more inventory, both in breadth and depth. But both stores carried products from mostly the same manufacturers and suppliers of toys, books, music tapes, CDs, clothing, and cards. The most conspicuous changes are in store location and design, not in inventory categories or brands.

The mix of old and new customers at the new store broadened the market to include more of what the owner calls "Jeeps and minivans . . . yuppie foothills parents." Six weeks after moving, the owner estimated that only 60 percent of the customers were from the old store. During the initial retail cycle following relocation, the owners were challenged to retain old customers and assist them in adjusting to the new basis for customer animation, while simultaneously courting new customers who ventured into the store. Even before the move, some very good customers expressed disappointment upon hearing about the relocation plans. Their comments were summarized and conveyed to us by the owner in our first interaction with him, even before the move occurred:

> Some of our customers are happy, some aren't, with the change. Some have even said, "Oh, you are leaving the *neighborhood.* You should stay here and also open up over there." Right. Like I can handle rent on 3,400 square feet over there, and this too. But a different logo, a very different look. It's a big change for me after all these years.

In a focus group, a longtime customer said she was "mad at them for moving." Emotional reactions, such as this dismay and anger, go beyond utilitarian concerns with locational convenience, although all informants are quick to point to this cognitive attribute as a container for their emotional reactions. When we unpack that container, we see that their dismay comes from viewing this move as reflective of larger patterns of regional development that they feel powerless to change. Their dismay and anger is at the shifts occurring as their city grows; they see the global in the local and express their reaction through the emotional outlet of this store's relocation.

Upon seeing the new store and its impressive decor, old customers being "shown around" by the owners didn't know how to express their overall response. Most commonly, they simply said it is "different." Shortly after opening and having invested so much of themselves in the new store design, the owners were keenly sensitive to the reactions of longtime customers. Few were openly critical of the relocation in talking with the owners. Nonetheless, the owner described the hesitation she sensed in some longtime customers' responses:

> Some of them from the other store don't like it. Like that couple that was just in here, the ones who just left, they didn't like it. They like cozy. But the traffic here is incredible. I just have to get used to it.

The other owner took a longer-term perspective when he noted that customers also said "it isn't as cozy" when the store previously expanded from 500 to 1,800 square feet in Broadway Village. He therefore anticipated similar comments about the new store. Far from being completely put off by the new store, old customers acknowledged that the new store has a larger supply of toys and more space for children to play.

But in focus groups with the owners absent, old customers said, "It is just not the same." And, of course, they are literally and physically correct. But they are also speaking emotionally. They know that new customers haven't borne the pains as the owners grew from novices to successful entrepreneurs over the last sixteen years. Longtime customers are ambivalent because they are proud to be part of the success yet also dislike what success brings. They resent going into the new store and not getting "the attention" when the owner is busy with other customers. Necessarily the new store's larger size means a larger sales staff and owner interaction with a smaller fraction of customers. This is the customer's trade-off between intimacy and traffic, between cozy and lively.

Longtime customers refer to the owners by name and report in surveys that they prefer locally owned businesses where they know the owner. New customers do not have, and may not develop, that personal connection. The owner was surprised when she introduced herself to people in the new store and they didn't know who she was: "I'm not used to that. I'm used to people knowing me or knowing my name through the newsletter." Yet, after sixteen years of working with customers individually, she also wants to pull away from that role.

The life cycle of the owners is simultaneously cause and consequence of these business changes. Barb is launching a social work career that takes her out of constant involvement with the store. In response, some of the female aspect of *Mrs.* Tiggy-Winkle's has diminished. Joey now answers the phone simply, "Tiggy-Winkle's." Since the owners now have an additional source of income and dinnertime issues to discuss stemming from Barb's new career, Mrs. Tiggy-Winkle's has receded slightly in their family life/identity. Because their children are now budding young women, the owners' experience with toys and clothing for younger children is more purely professional and less an outgrowth of their personal lives.

So for old customers, disappointment in the new store is not just nostalgia for the old store's location, or color scheme, or displays, or even the strong connection to these owners. Instead, loss of the homeyness of the old store means the loss of an increasingly difficult-to-find marketplace corrector in their lives. The new store is more clearly a marketplace institution: it has a computerized cash register, SKU numbers, an inventory control system, and a customer database. In tandem with these institutional changes came the dysfunctional consequences of decreased personalized relations in commercial settings: more shoplifting and more bad checks. The commodified aspect of business growth was articulated by one longtime customer in saying the owners had "lost their soul" and "started trying to make money." Others made the curious comment that the store had become "too commercialized." Through these comments, longtime customers recognize that what they previously regarded as a sacred little toy store is now clearly a profane commercial enterprise (Belk, Wallendorf, and Sherry 1989).

These comments are metonymic expressions that have referents beyond the changes in this particular store: they literally refer to this store but simultaneously lament the fact that longtime residents' cozy little town (village) has become a booming city filled with consumption-focused newcomers (a consumption festival). Like tourists who want to go where no tourists go, customers want to discover creative, innovative, responsive businesses but don't want to become simply one of the masses of people who shop there for the same reasons.

Interestingly, despite their desires for exclusivity, consumers hegemonically shape the marketplace by introducing other consumers to the new store. For a few months after relocation, old customers brought local friends as well as out-of-town guests "to see the store." The ambient environment of the new store is sufficiently positively charged that it is a type of destination resort in itself. After making an initial trip to the new store and having the owners take the time to "show them around," longtime customers returned with friends and took on the role of self-made tour guides. On these later trips, they were able to provide a fun environment for their coshoppers, and also receive accolades from others for bringing them there. Old customers not only show off the new store in a gesture that is simultaneously generous and possessive, but also proudly explain to the new initiates that they knew the owners "years ago when they had a little cozy shop." Through their pride at recounting this history, they construct and solidify a distinction between themselves and those who are more recently arrived. As confirmation of their privileged position, they expect even more than previously to be recognized on a first-name basis by the owners. This poses a challenge to the owners, who thus are expected to provide intimacy even in the midst of heavy traffic. This personal contact with the owner simultaneously animates customers and limits the growth of the business.

So old customers have some reservations about the new store, but, in a world of hypermarkets, what alternatives do they have? Market forces are strong and pervasive; consumers seek ever more intense market experiences and weave consumption through their social relations and daily activities until it has become a leitmotiv of postmodern life. Tourists "spend" their time shopping for souvenirs, rather than experiencing a place. Some even spend their entire time at consumption venues, such as Disneyland or Sea World. People view shopping not just as a way to acquire utilitarian things, but as a hedonic experience they voluntarily seek. Like staunch liberals in a political climate in which all candidates strive to be perceived as moderate, consumers such as those who liked the homeyness of Mrs. Tiggy-Winkle's at Broadway Village have nowhere else to go to cast their vote. They are pulled along with the changing marketplace, although initially somewhat resentful.

If their resistance to commodifying forces emerges as reduced spending, they are subsequently given even less voice in the adjudication of the conflict; those who spend more increase in importance. Heavy spenders at Mrs. Tiggy-Winkle's (both new and old customers) are marked in the customer database as "star" customers. Much is done to cultivate their continued patronage. Some come into the store almost weekly, wondering what is "new." Some are big buyers of clothing (a pattern more characteristic of new customers); others are frequent buyers of toys, books, and music (more characteristic of old customers). Constant movement of merchandise around the store and new cross-merchandising displays give these big spenders the excitement of newness. Unlike grocery store shoppers who want to locate items on a list, frequent purchasers at Mrs. Tiggy-Winkle's come to the store for an experience of discovery that results in spending money to take their discoveries home: Star customers spend $25 to $400 on each trip to the store. Out-of-town stars come less often but spend more on each trip, partially to compensate for the guilt they feel at being away from their children, enjoying a week at a health spa or destination resort. Some out-of-town residents, especially those who have second homes in town or who are part of the national entertainment elite, place orders by phone for items to be sent. While the owners want to retain old customers, they cannot sacrifice the profits made from this type of new customer.

Old customers who want to resist the encroachment of hypermarkets are left with the dilemma of whether to continue shopping at Mrs. Tiggy-Winkle's. Compared to shopping at the gigantic, national chain toy supermarkets featuring an unending array of ever-changing, advertised-on-TV toys, even the new Mrs. Tiggy-Winkle's seems quaint. In this respect, shopping at the new Mrs. Tiggy-Winkle's is, for some consumers, similar to other types of consumption: buying organic produce at a greengrocer or freshly cooked meals at locally owned restaurants and enjoying respites at microbreweries and roasted-on-the-premises coffee shops. These are enacted forms of consumer resistance to homogeneity and commodification, sometimes without cognitive awareness beyond "it's better." Nonetheless, this resistance is hegemonic since it takes place within the commercial domain of licensed businesses engaged in generating a profit and is often accompanied by complaints about higher prices.

Despite its changes, longtime customers are still served by Mrs. Tiggy-Winkle's. The store's continuing provision of services that cut away at profits (e.g., mailing toys that are gifts, special-ordering items that require rush delivery fees) is intended to demonstrate that the personalized relations established over time are not eroded by commodifying forces. This service delivery juxtaposed with a Hollywood-inspired dreamworld may offer even greater proof of the enduring capability of such relations than they did when offered in the homey old store. Similarly, the fact that some classic toys (wooden German pull toys, Brio trains, Muffy VanderBear, Curious George, *Goodnight Moon,* and *Pat the Bunny*) are still carried in this new servicescape proves that they can fight off the threats of postmodernity and remain popular. Their embeddedness in this vibrant store standing beside the best of contemporary toys is more solid evidence of their capability as modernity correctors.

A scene from *Toys* is instructive in pointing to the deeper division between Mrs. Tiggy-Winkle's and its gigantic competitors. In calling the windup toys to battle against the electronic war toys, Robin Williams as the flaky son of the now-deceased president of the firm makes an improvisational speech containing these words:

> Four stores and many Christmases ago, my father brought forth a factory conceived in joy and innocence and squeezable fun for everyone. We determine today, in this warehouse, the future of toys as we know them: whether it will be toys of fun and innocence, or toys of total tot warfare. In the words of Mahatma Gumby, "We are toys of tolerance, but there is only so much a toy can tolerate." You simple gentle few, I would rather have you than any remote-control device. You, Alien Al, were never a big seller, but we stood by you. . . . Ask not what Zevo can do for you, but what you can do for Zevo.

Despite changes in location and servicescape, Mrs. Tiggy-Winkle's paradoxically serves as a continued outlet for hypermarket resistance by some customers, while simultaneously catering to other customers' desire for heightened levels of retail stimulation. The store's servicescape is a dreamworld in the true sense of projectives. Diverse, even oppositional, customers respond to the same environment with different dreams unfolding. In this respect, the vivid store design is sufficiently ambiguous in the dreamworlds it evokes to "work" as a psychological projective and economic directive for several types of customers. Mrs. Tiggy-Winkle's pastiche of inventory and interior design elements decontextualizes consumers in time and space and allows them to construct any number of dreamworlds through its evocative juxtapositions that are ultimately disassembled by purchases and then reassembled with new merchandise.

BIBLIOGRAPHY

ADLER, PATRICIA, AND PETER ADLER. 1987. *Membership Roles in the Field,* vol. 6, Sage Qualitative Research Methods Series. Newbury Park, CA: Sage.

BABCOCK, BARBARA. 1990. "Inventing the Southwest: Region as Commodity." Introduction to special issue, *Journal of the Southwest* 32 (Winter): 383–399.

BAKER, JULIE; DHRUV GREWAL; AND A. PARASURAMAN. 1994. "The Influence of Store Environment on Quality Inferences and Store Image." *Journal of the Academy of Marketing Sciences* 22(4):328–339.

BELK, RUSSELL W.; MELANIE WALLENDORF; AND JOHN F. SHERRY, JR. 1989. "The Sacred and the Profane in Consumer Behavior: Theodicy on the Odyssey." *Journal of Consumer Research* 16 (June): 1–38.

BEMELMANS, LUDWIG. 1939. *Madeline.* New York: Viking Press.

BOURDIEU, PIERRE. 1984. *Distinction: A Social Critique of the Judgement of Taste.* Cambridge: Harvard University Press.

CARPENTER, HUMPHREY, AND MARI PRICHARD. 1984. *Oxford Companion to Children's Literature.* Oxford: Oxford University Press.

COLEMAN, RICHARD P., AND LEE P. RAINWATER, WITH KENT A. MCCLELLAND. 1978. *Social Standing in America: New Dimensions of Class.* New York: Basic Books.

DAVIS, FRED. 1979. *Yearning for Yesterday: A Sociology of Nostalgia.* New York: Free Press.

ENGLEBREIT, MARY. 1994. *Over the River and Through the Woods.* Kansas City: Andrews and McMeel.

FLINK, JAMES J. 1970. *America Adopts the Automobile, 1895–1910.* Cambridge, MA: Massachusetts Institute of Technology Press.

GARREAU, JOEL. 1981. *The Nine Nations of North America.* Boston: Houghton Mifflin.

———. 1991. *Edge City: Life on the New Frontier.* New York: Anchor Books.

GLINSKI, JAMES. 1995. *Above Tucson: Then and Now.* Tucson, AZ: JTG Enterprise.

HENRY, BONNIE. 1989. "The Village Had a Corner on Its Market." *Arizona Daily Star* (February 22).

HINTON, LEANNE. 1988. "Oral Traditions and the Advent of Electric Power." In *Technology and Women's Voices: Keeping in Touch,* edited by Cheris Kramarae. New York: Routledge and Kegan Paul.

HUFF, DAVID. 1963. "A Probabilistic Analysis of Consumer Spatial Behavior." In *Emerging Concepts in Marketing,* edited by W. S. Decker. Chicago: American Marketing Association.

JAMESON, FREDERIC. 1984. "Postmodernism, or, The Cultural Logic of Late Capitalism." *New Left Review* 3:53–92.

KLINE, STEPHEN. 1993. *Out of the Garden: Toys and Children's Culture in the Age of TV Marketing.* New York: Verso.

LEVY, SIDNEY. 1966. "Social Class and Consumer Behavior." In *On Knowing the Consumer,* edited by Joseph W. Newman. New York: Wiley, 146–160.

LOWENTHAL, DAVID. 1985. *The Past Is a Foreign Country.* Cambridge: Cambridge University Press.

MATHER, CHRISTINE, AND SHARON WOODS. 1986. *Santa Fe Style.* New York: Rizzoli.

McCRACKEN, GRANT. 1989. "Homeyness: A Cultural Account on One Constellation of Consumer Goods and Meanings." In *Interpretive Consumer Research,* edited by Elizabeth C. Hirschman. Provo, UT: Association for Consumer Research, 168–183.

———. 1986. "Culture and Consumption: A Theoretical Account of the Structure and Movement of the Cultural Meaning of Consumer Goods." *Journal of Consumer Research* 13 (June): 71–84.

McQUARRIE, EDWARD F. 1989. "Advertising Resonance: A Semiological Perspective." In *Interpretive Consumer Research,* edited by Elizabeth C. Hirschman. Provo, UT: Association for Consumer Research, 97–114.

MICK, DAVID, AND CLAS BUHL. 1992. "A Meaning-Based Model of Advertising Experiences." *Journal of Consumer Research* 19 (December): 317–338.

REX, TOM R. 1995. "U.S. Migration Patterns Much Different in Early '90s." *Arizona Business* 42 (February): 5–7.

SCHENSUL, JILL. 1980. "Oldest Center Looks for New Life: New Tenants, Minor Surgery May Keep Broadway Village from Becoming Office Space." *Arizona Daily Star* (January 24): sec. H, p. 4.

———. 1981. "Stylish Old Shopping Mart Shows Signs of New Life." *Arizona Daily Star* (January 8): sec. H, p. 1.

SHERRY, JOHN F., JR. 1990. "A Socio-Cultural Analysis of a Midwestern U.S. Flea Market." *Journal of Consumer Research* 17 (June): 13–30.

STEWART, SUSAN. 1984. *On Longing: Narratives of the Miniature, the Gigantic, the Souvenir, the Collection.* Baltimore, MD: Johns Hopkins University Press.

TONNIES, FERDINAND; CORNELIUS BICKEL; ROLF FECHNER; AND HARALD HOFFDING. 1871/1989. *Gemeinschaft–Gesellschaft.* Reprint, Berlin: Dunker and Humbolt.

TVERSKY, AMOS, AND DANIEL KAHNEMAN. 1974. "Judgment under Uncertainty: Heuristics and Biases." *Science* 185:1,124–1,131.

6

THE SEED OF CREATIVE LIFESTYLE SHOPPING

Wrapping Consumerism in Japanese Store Layouts

MILLIE CREIGHTON

In this chapter, I explore one Japanese servicescape, embodied by the store SEED, which was designed and constructed by a retailing group organized around a major department store chain at the height of Japan's golden era of department store service orientation. Scholars of Japan studies have discussed the importance of "wrapping" in understanding Japanese society, both in ways items are physically wrapped to grant them cultural legitimacy and in ways actions or behaviors are wrapped in polite etiquette and expected

Millie Creighton is Assistant Professor of Anthropology in the Department of Anthropology and Sociology, University of British Columbia, Vancouver, Canada.

The portion of my research on department stores in Japan from 1985–1987 was supported by a Fulbright-Hays Scholarship (U.S. Department of Education). This essay has also benefited from subsequent research visits, including a 1990 visit to study consumer behavior among youth, under a UBC/HSS grant awarded through the Social Sciences and Humanities Research Council of Canada and administered by the University of British Columbia, and a research visit in 1991 to study advertising under a grant awarded by the Nakasone Foundation and administered by the Institute for Asian Research, University of British Columbia.

proper forms. I argue that in the case of the store SEED, the servicescape, in the form of the building and store layout, is itself the cultural wrapping, which wraps the goods for sale as well as the shopping experience. In this case the servicescape physically wraps the shopping experience within a sophisticated and sleek, aesthetically attractive building, while wrapping consumerism within philosophic statements of ideals that reaffirm Japanese spiritual values.

By providing this wrapping, SEED's servicescape addresses the contemporary conflict felt among Japanese between the desire to embrace the material benefits of their newly achieved economic affluence and the wish to uphold core cultural values promoting spiritualism over materialism. Sherry and Camargo (1987) assert that one of the critical functions of packaging in Japan is to allow the consumption of ever greater quantities of consumer goods by shifting the context of meaning away from "materialism." Drawing on insights from Oka's (1975) presentation of Japanese wrapping, they assert that Japanese "packaging is alleged to represent the triumph of a conservation ethic over a consumption ethic; . . . [teaching] that inner, spiritual satisfaction cannot be found merely in material abundance" (Sherry and Camargo 1987, 175). By wrapping the shopping experience with philosophic ideals about transcending materialism, SEED as servicescape redefines consumption in accord with these spiritual values of antimaterialism and thus promotes increasing consumption in two ways. It co-opts any negative sentiments toward the strong consumer orientation of modern Japanese society, redirecting this potential disillusionment with consumerism into further consumerism. It also allows the suggestion that increasing consumption, even of Western goods, fads, and lifestyles, can reaffirm Japanese core spiritual values against overt materialism and thereby reaffirms assertions of Japanese identity despite increasing consumption of the West.

This portrait of the servicescape SEED emerged from a larger study on Japanese department stores and retailing utilizing methods of cultural anthropological research. The bulk of this study was conducted between 1983 and 1987, a period representing the height of Japan's so-called bubble economy and department store retailing's ultra-service orientation, with follow-up visits providing additional insights over the next several years. Methods utilized in the study included participant observation, a period of work at a department store, interviews with store planners and personnel, and interviews or discussions with consumers. During the midst of this study, I also chose to do an ethnographic site mapping of SEED shortly after it opened in 1986. In writing this article, I have returned to my field notes of that ethnographic site mapping, employing reflexive techniques of engagement with field notes as text, as discussed by Sanjek (1990). In revisiting these field notes, I have paid particular attention to items that fall in the category of behavioral trace studies as a means of eliciting the retrospective voices of shoppers at SEED at that time. Behavioral trace studies are a method of soliciting people's ideas and patterns of behavior through the recordable traces of their actions. One advantage of such an approach is that it reduces response bias that creeps into people's direct responses to interview questions or survey questionnaires (Bernard 1994, 332–336). The design of SEED's servicescape helped facilitate this approach in its provision of specific venues of customer graffiti-type commentary.

According to a great deal of research on consumerism, generally labels and packaging embody attempts at communication and impression management (e.g., Kotler 1984; Gardner 1967; Dichter 1975). According to Sherry and Camargo (1987, 175), "the package is ultimately a drama, and its unwrapping has a particular psychology." To unwrap the packaging of this servicescape, I will provide a brief discussion of SEED's conception, a theoretical discussion of four ways a store such as SEED functions as a stage, a detailed mapping of SEED the store as an ethnographic site, followed by an analysis of the store layout presented in reference to the four suggested ways store servicescapes function as stages.

CONCEIVING SEED

In March 1986, the Seibu Saison Group, parent conglomerate of Japan's trendy and avant-garde Seibu Department Store chain, opened an innovative upscale store in the Shibuya district of Tokyo, called SEED. SEED exemplifies the concept of Seibu-realism; more than a store, the building purportedly embodies a philosophic statement of ultimate meaning in human existence. SEED's architecture, design, layout, and art all attempt to engage customers not just in shopping, but in a journey toward creativity and personal development. Shoppers enter the store as "seedlings," emerge as "spearheads" at the ground level, proceed through store levels as levels of consciousness, becoming "sensitive" shoppers along the way, and arrive at the summit of their journey as "creative" human beings.

SEED is partly the child of the intellectualism of Seiji Tsutsumi, chairperson of Seibu Saison Group, who contends that modern retailers must "go back to square one and rethink the absolute basics, such as the meaning of 'consumption'" (Seibu Saison Group 1985, 3). According to Tsutsumi,

> Consumption does not mean the use of goods to replenish energy needed for work—maybe that was so 300 years ago, but not in Japan today. Nor is consumption simply ostentation. Rather, consumption is a form of communication, a statement of worldview, an affirmation of existence. Consumption and retailing are therefore no longer problems solely for the economist, but for the sociologist and even the philosopher (p. 3).

SEED is also the child of contemporary Japan's cultural and historic circumstances. Japan emerged from the destruction and poverty of World War II to realize what the world would call its "economic miracle," with affluence, westernization, modernization and the full flowering of a "consumer society".[1] However, in the mid-1980s, having attained these goals, Japan and the Japanese began discovering disillusionment with these achievements, nostalgia for the lost past and forgotten community, and a need to reestablish

---

[1] The concept of consumer society suggests that consumerism, once a privilege of elites, has been extended to the mass of society, involving "mass consumption of mass-produced commodities by the mass of the public" (Fine and Leopold 1993, 69). It also suggests that most goods used in daily life are acquired through mass production and consumerism rather than more traditional craft processes, and that much of the operations of the economy are orchestrated around consumption.

meaning in human life outside of consumerism or purely economic transactions. The modern angst wrought by disenchantment with material affluence is expressed by Japanese journalist Honda Katsuichi (1993, 179), who writes, "Japan is populated by some of the most spiritually impoverished people in the world. How sad for the archipelago."

SEED is Seibu's attempt to address this sense of spiritual impoverishment. SEED philosophically proclaims that consumerism provides the modern path or way (*michi*) that will allow Japanese to transcend material goods and regain touch with their essential humanity. This paradoxical stance, which offers the promise of transcending consumerism through consumerism, is instead the consummation of commodification, showing the extent to which modern Japan is enmeshed in its self-identity as a consumer society.

STORE AS STAGE

Stores, like other institutions, are embedded in cultures, reflecting cultural predispositions and the ongoing processes of social life in a particular culture at a particular historical moment. Stores, however, do not just reflect culture; they are capable of affecting social change and shaping social trends. This is certainly true in Japan, where department stores have long been prominent among mass-culture industries which have often defined "commodified culture pretargeted and produced for large numbers of consumers" (Ivy 1993, 240). Throughout modern history, Japanese department stores have functioned as arbiters of the nation's fashions, tastes, and customs (Bestor 1989, 21; Creighton 1992, 45). In addition to selling merchandise, and in order to sell merchandise, they have also been involved in the creation of cultural meanings.

To explore the cultural meanings communicated through SEED, I adopt the stance taken by Seiter (1992, 233) that not only consumer goods, but the physical and ideational designations of space in store layouts constitute cultural objects. Definitions of space in a store establish a physical reality heavily imbued with symbolic meanings, which can, in Mukerji's (1983, 15) terms, "create a setting for behavior" that compels people toward certain forms of behavior, including both physical and intellectual activity.

There are at least four ways in which SEED represents the store as stage. The first of these reiterates my assertion that in the Japanese context the servicescape is the wrapping for everything inside. Modern stores are stages, spotlighting objects for sale, or as Featherstone (1982, 19) explains it, stages for "the field of commodities on display." Haug (1986) has extensively developed this idea, arguing that modern advertising and retailing no longer function to bring needed or useful goods to buyers but instead stage objects as aesthetically desirable, spotlighting the sensuality in these objects in order to induce the desire of buyers to possess. In this staging of the object, "the beautifully designed surface of the commodity becomes its package: not the simple wrapping for protection during transportation, but its real countenance, which the potential buyer is shown first instead of the body of the commodity" (p. 50).

The conflict Haug describes, whereby commodity aesthetics place greater emphasis on surface appearance and presentational wrappings than on the nature of the commodities themselves, may not be as great in the Japanese context because of the cultural role given to wrapping. Ekiguchi (1986, 6) points out that the concept of *tsutsumi,* or wrapping, "plays a central role in a wide variety of spiritual and cultural aspects of Japanese life." For example, in Japan greater importance is often placed on the wrapping of a present than on the object chosen in expressing the heart of the giver, or the social relationships involved (Creighton 1991; Clammer 1992). Hendry (1993) develops the thesis that Japan is a "wrapping culture," in which all aspects of life are "wrapped"—in layers of packaging, in layers of clothing, in layers of language, or in layers of etiquette. It is not the case that illusion is being cultivated by deflecting attention from the "real" meaning of the contents. Instead the "real" cultural meaning is located in the wrapping:

A Western perception of the practice prepares us to regard wrapping as a means to obscure the object inside, whereas in a Japanese view it would seem that the function of wrapping is rather to refine the object, to add to it layers of meaning which it could not carry in its unwrapped form (p. 27).

SEED in its designated role as a stage offers philosophic statements of meaning, exemplifying the wrapping of space with layers of symbolic meaning. With SEED, the store becomes the wrapping for all the objects for sale within it. Although to the Western view this might seem to epitomize commodity fetishism by further obscuring the nature of the commodities themselves, it is, however, consistent with the cultural importance given to wrapping in Japan, whereby cultural meaning is signified through the effort and care expended on the wrapping.

A second way that stores operate as stages is by creating settings for the participatory engagement of customers. Haug (1986) explains how consumers are transformed from purchasers to participants in well-designed store stages:

> The exhibition of commodities, their inspection, the act of purchase, and all the associated moments, are integrated into the concept of one theatrical total work of art which plays upon the public's willingness to buy. Thus the salesroom is designed as a stage, purpose-built to convey entertainment to its audience that will stimulate a heightened desire to spend (p. 69).

Elsewhere, I (Creighton 1994, 1995) have analyzed the Japanese children's market to show how large stores create stages designed to convey what I call edutainment (a combination of education and entertainment) while providing a setting where culturally appropriate behavioral roles for children and parents can be played, performed, and reinforced.

SEED as stage creates a setting for participatory behavior directed primarily at Japanese young adults, referred to in the 1980s as *shinjinrui,* a pun meaning "new faces" (*shinjin-rui*) or "new breed of human beings" (*shin-jinrui*) (Tetsuya 1986, 291).

Shinjinrui have been characterized as having very different values from previous generations. In particular, they have been associated with a shift by which younger Japanese, and Japanese in general, are less likely to define meaning in human existence through work, and more inclined to seek a meaningful life through leisure, hobbies, and consumer activities (see, for example, Hernadi 1990, 189–190). Seibu responded to this shift by designing SEED as a total theatrical consumer stage that would prompt the customer/ actor to physically engage in a spatial layout corresponding to the mental contemplation of ultimate meaning in human existence. SEED is a stage, but one not solely directed at entertaining its customers; it also seeks to engage them philosophically.

A third way that stores function as stages is as sites where identities are constructed and enacted by performing selves (see Goffman 1959). According to Featherstone (1982, 27), "Within consumer culture . . . the 'performing self' places greater emphasis upon appearance, display and the management of impressions." The construction of identities through consumerism is tied to the images associated with the goods people purchase, but also with the image positioning of the places and spaces of consumption (Urry 1990; Shields 1992, 6–13). Thus, the act of shopping at SEED, more than any items purchased there, involves the assertion of a self-identity statement. Similarly, SEED exists as a physical stage that brings the desired identity imaging of the interconnected corporate retailers Seibu Department Store and Seibu Saison Group into material form so people can look at it, touch it, walk through it—granting a physical reality to the idea of a Seibu self.

A fourth way in which stores function as stages is as sites for the socially constructed interaction between buyers and sellers. Expectations of socially defined economic conduct are related to cultural perceptions of space. According to many theorists, the transition from neighborhood merchant or seller to large-scale retailer corresponded to the shift from *Gemeinschaft* to *Gesellschaft*, with different definitions of the social relationships between buyer and seller. Chaney (1983) claims that the spatial parameters of large-scale retailing institutions played directly into cultural constructions of consuming relationships. He writes, "The physical demands of the department store therefore constitute a stage upon which a new dramaturgy of social and economic relationships can be developed and articulated" (p. 27). I suggest that SEED articulates the cultural definitions surrounding economic transactions between customers and retailers in Japan in the mid-1980s, an articulation revealing that *Gesellschaft* does not completely replace *Gemeinschaft*, even in the most modern of marketplaces. At the very least, *Gesellschaft* must appeal to the ideal of *Gemeinschaft* in order to be effective.

To Enter Through Seed Gate

Built in the upscale fashion and entertainment district of Shibuya, close to, but set apart from, the Shibuya branch Seibu Department Store, the new SEED building emanates a sleek and striking blackness.[2] The entire building is faced in tones of black, shading at times into gray. The impression of blackness is strengthened by the absence of windows anywhere on the building. SEED's sleek, black facade corresponds to designer concepts of sophisticated aesthetics in Japan during the mid-1980s. Like the hostess clubs during this period described by Allison (1994, 38), the spatial and aesthetic orientations of SEED produce a sense of luxury and sophistication appreciated by most Japanese seeking entertainment or a fun shopping outing. The slick facade immediately asserts that SEED provides a "polished yet hip environment" (Havens 1994, 180). SEED's facade also suggests meanings related to SEED's philosophic imaginings and its high-fashion positioning. Although slick and sleek, the windowless SEED is basically a black box, thus suggesting the frequently referred to Black Box of human existence, containing the unknown meanings and mysteries of life. The building shape and coloring also suggest a transmitter or transmitting cell. Store positioning plays on this idea, suggesting that SEED is not a store but a transmitter. For example, one Seibu pamphlet characterizes SEED as the "information transmitter on fashion" (*fasshon no jōhō hasshin o suru 'SEED'*)

---

[2] This description of SEED is based on its appearance the year it opened, particularly on one visit I made on May 30, 1986. Although I discuss the store in the present tense, this is the present tense of 1986; it can be assumed that, as in most retail stores, goods and messages at SEED are subject to continual repositionings. I want to present a portrait of SEED shortly after it opened because I feel this best reflects its intended image statement. The discussion later addresses how such imaging and positioning were related to Japanese society and marketing in the mid-1980s, and their connection to SEED's birth in 1986.

directed at those with a "high receptivity lifestyle" (*kōkando na seikatsusha*) (Seibu Saison Group 1986a, 15).

As one nears the entrance to SEED, one encounters a huge art piece, a black sculpture of a cat. It is a common custom in Japan, traced back to merchant traditions from the Edo era (1603–1868), to place a small statue of a cat in the windows of business establishments. The cat, known as *maneki nekko,* the "beckoning cat," stands on its hindlegs. One of its forepaws is stretched upward in a movement of waving, or beckoning, customers inside. *Maneki nekko* images, usually in white or red (happy or celebratory colors), and most commonly standing from six to twenty inches tall, are common features in small shops and restaurants in modern Japan. SEED's sculpture of the larger than human beckoning cat is its artistic rendition of the traditional *maneki nekko* concept. Before SEED opened, a contest was held to give this *maneki nekko* its own identity by naming it. The winning name chosen was Nanako—seventh child. Seven is considered a lucky and auspicious number in Japan, and the name also builds on the Western allusion of specialness attributed to the seventh child. However since Nanako is a woman's name, in contrast to the "seventh son," the name highlights the fact that modern consumerism is considered more the realm of women for whom shopping is both part of assigned domestic work and a form of leisure entertainment.

There are no display cases highlighting goods, such as one frequently finds at department stores, anywhere on SEED's storefront. There is, however, one large display case the customer encounters just before entering the store. The case contains a large, long brown pod, seemingly suspended in space, jiggling up and down in a rhythmic movement. The pod has cracked slightly, and the opening is larger toward the top. Through the crack, seed kernels interspersed along the pod are visible; a few have already dropped to the ground. With this view, the customer has reached SEED's first-floor doors and is ready to enter through SEED Gate.

SEED Gate is the designated name given to the ground-level entry floor of SEED, the level at which most shoppers will begin their encounter with SEED's internal layout. All floors of SEED are subtitled. Names of each level suggest a sense of shopping fun and entertainment to be experienced while at SEED. However, store pamphlets, guides, and indicators near escalators also suggest that customers travel through three different identity levels on their journey upward. The store layout emphasizes a sense of developmental journey upward from SEED Gate, but, in order to introduce the full range of the store, I will describe the floors beginning at the second basement (the lowest level) upward.

The second basement, or B-2 level, is, "The Wave." The Wave ripples with the current fads in entertainment. Records plus audio and video equipment are for sale on this level. One large sales area is devoted to magazines about fashions, popular entertainers, and rock music. The Saison ticket booth is located on this floor, as is a special *kissaten* (coffee and tea shop), directed at young adults. At various locations throughout the floor, video monitors show films and stereos play music. In contrast to those at many department stores, employee uniforms are neither serious nor businesslike. Clerks on this floor all wear tight-fitting black jeans topped with black T-shirts or black sweatshirts that say, "The Wave."

One of the men's rest rooms in the store is located on the B-2 level. All of the signs indicating rest rooms are holograms, which at first glance might be mistaken as trendy pieces of visual artwork. The "little man" hologram indicating the location of the men's lavatory is a floating adult-like form placed in a manner resembling depictions of developing fetuses—appropriate imagery, given the store's imaging of human development.

The first basement, or B-1 level, is called "The Microbeam." It has a limited range of goods, most of which are entertainment and fashion accessories. The goods here do not represent major purchases, but those that might instead encourage spontaneous or impulse buying. The Microbeam contains an underground passageway that links SEED directly to both the A and B buildings of the Shibuya Seibu Department Store. This is significant in that it allows customers to "travel the microbeam," or pass between the specialty store SEED and the department store, which is the mainstay of Seibu's business operations.

The first floor (at street level) is called "SEED Gate." SEED is located on Koen Street (*Koen-dori*), and SEED Gate is defined as a "communication space along Koen-dori for life designers" (SEED Shibuya Seibu 1986). SEED Gate is a pivotal interface between Seibu and the consuming public because, as indicated, this is the level at which most customers will enter SEED. Even those who enter SEED via the microbeam from Seibu Department Store must enter SEED Gate to proceed on their consumer journey of transcendence.

SEED Gate has very little for sale, although there are some displays of ethnic-influenced designer outfits. Instead, SEED Gate offers a space dedicated to message statements. These messages promise customers entertainment and advanced information access as well as philosophy. Situated at the "information area" are eight video screens which form an area called "message box." Information about the store is obtained via a touch screen system found on the bottom two videos. Some of the other monitors are showing current popular movies. The remaining screens can be used by customers for their own purposes. There is a computer area where customers can write, leave, or retrieve messages, which will appear on the screens, or compose their own artwork and graffiti and have these appear on the screens. A special copier attached to the computer allows customers to print out on paper the visual image on the screen. The instructions encourage shoppers to use these facilities for their own expressive needs. The floor guide explains these possibilities under the heading "Visual Message Board":

> A very useful visual message board for those who wish to meet others. You can make secret messages with your own secret numbers (Seibu Saison Group 1985b).

Although it is possible to secretly code messages so only intended viewers can retrieve them, some people wishing to be more openly expressive have left their computer-assisted graffiti visible on the screens. One drawing shows the caricatured portrait of a Japanese teacher of English. The teacher is shown with a squarish head, large-rimmed glasses, and a nose with large, overtly emphasized individuated nostrils. The gaping jaw, wide-open mouth, and huge, protruding tongue are, however, the most prominent features. On one side of the drawing, the caricature is identified as the

English teacher at Keiseijogakuen Junior High School (*kore wa kei-seijogakuen no eigo no sensei desu*). On the other side of the drawing, the speech balloon shows the teacher saying, "This is a pen." Another message was left by an apparently not so satisfied customer named Yumi on a store monitor for all to see. In this message, Yumi, who signs it, asserts, "I won't be beaten by Ticket Saison" (*chiketto Seison* [sic] *ni wa makenai zō. Yumi*).

Nearby is an area designated as "Grafty Spot" (*gurafuti supotto*), containing three television monitors on which customers can select programs they want to watch. "Grafty Spot" is arranged in conjunction with Television Tokyo.

In addition to these information- and entertainment-oriented messages, SEED Gate provides the philosophic messages that stage the background of the consumer's developmental journey. Most prominent among these messages is a full-wall mural located next to the escalator on the first floor. The mural carries out the thematic imagery of SEED and human development. The painting shows a garden setting, with human beings depicted as if they were plants in various stages of development growing up from the garden Earth. The newest shoot is the head of a human being that has just emerged above the ground level. Another person has grown up to about midbody level and has free use of the hands. Another is nearly fully grown with the entire torso and most of the legs evident, but one foot is still embedded in the soil. Although still growing and developing, a human plant is shown watering the newer seedling of the emerging human head. The mural depicts a set of messages about human growth and development. It shows an early dependent stage growing into greater competence and fuller range of expression. It suggests that development is lifelong, that as humans we are always in the process of creating ourselves, growing closer to our full creative potential. It also suggests that human existence means that while people are still enmeshed in their own process of growth, development, and overcoming struggles, they are responsible for nurturing and helping along those who have not yet come as far on this path.

After passing the jiggling seed pod, customers enter through SEED Gate as "seedlings." Standing near the mural about to ascend the escalator, they take on the ground-level identity of "spearhead." Like the emerging human head in the mural, the seed has broken through the earth and sprouted a bit. The information guide to the store floors located at the escalator details goods sold on each floor but also outlines the shifts in consumer identity as customers pass through store floors as though these were stages of development. The shopper is a spearhead in the lower levels, developing into "sensitive" shopper in the midlevels, and transcending to "creative" in the upper regions (SEED Shibuya Seibu 1986). The store layout prompts customers from the entrance through the information mall area toward the escalators to make this journey; the location of elevators is not immediately obvious.

The literal journey upward through each store floor is thus metaphorically linked to a journey of human development. Tobin (1992) points out that in Japan, "the process of growing up and becoming a person was thought to take place metaphorically if not literally on the road." To become a mature human being, a person needed to "embark on a journey" (p. 26). At SEED, the escalator becomes the vehicle of the shopper's journey. It is analogous to a train—which both Robertson (1988) and Ivy (1988) have discussed as a sign heavily imbued with sentimental and cultural meaning as the mediator of travel and journey in Japan. In addition to the suggestion that customers travel the escalator as they would a train on a journey, metaphoric associations to trains are made in other ways. For example, one corporate publication describing SEED claims it is the spot from which new designer goods will start their journey, using the expression *SEEDhatsu* (start off from SEED),[3] a takeoff on train lingo meaning to start off from a particular station (Seibu Saison Group 1986a, 15).

Adding to the allusion to trains, the second floor is called "The Express." The name also reflects the idea of consumption as a form of communication. The Express offers primarily high-fashion clothing. Mannequins on the floor are cast plaster in images reminiscent of Greek statues. Some are missing body parts. When one arrives

---

[3] The full statement in Japanese reads, "*Atarashii jidai no kansei o motsu deseinaa 21 mei ga sanka. 'SEEDhatsu' shōin o kaihatsu.*"

at The Express on the escalator from SEED Gate, one first encounters a headless white statue attired in an expensive leather outfit.

Third floor is "The Season." Displays depict beach life in Bali. In other areas mannequins, which appear to be made of granite, lounge in beachwear. In addition to beach and picnic fashions, the floor contains baskets and sales of souvenir-type items from Micronesia and Indonesia. Large plastic ferns decorate the floor, and two video screens show *Rocky III* for visual entertainment.

The fourth floor is "The Parts." This floor is decorated by more large ferns, only they are real this time. Where the third floor offers fashions for beach, sun, and fun, the fourth floor brings shoppers the accessories: sunglasses, parasols, umbrellas. There are several more video screens, where *Rocky III* reiterates again, and again, and again.

The shopper, until this point a growing spearhead, now develops into "sensitive" shopper. Alighting from the escalator, the shopper is greeted by living ferns on the fifth floor, or "The Closet." The Closet contains mostly women's designer fashions. One large area of the floor is a wall entirely made up of mirrors. Closer inspection shows that the mirrors are in panels that open outward. They are fitting rooms. As the shopper opens the outer mirror panel, she is greeted by herself on all sides while she enters this chamber of mirrors. The hologram indicating the toilets on this floor is a female analogue to the adult yet fetal-looking floating figure found near the men's room in the basement.

Floor six is "The Party." It is devoted largely to women's accessories—hats, jewelry, purses. There is a concert video playing on one video monitor, and the Uemura Story on another. The Party is a "dispatch center with the theme of 'Socializing'" (SEED Shibuya Seibu 1986).

Floor seven is "The Office." The Office is a "dispatch center with the theme of 'Career'" (SEED Shibuya Seibu 1986). The shopper is greeted by a display of three suits relaxing under the shade of ferns. These high fashion suits are positioned to contain their own embodiment; there are no mannequins. This floor is devoted to men's fashions, including suits. However, most of these designer suits are far removed from the conservative look expected at typical

Japanese workplaces. The video monitors on this floor show the movie *Picnic at Hanging Rock*.

The shopper is now moving beyond "sensitive" into the realm of "creative." Floor eight, "The Next," is defined as "an energetic stage for potential creators" (SEED Shibuya Seibu 1986). Women's fashions and contemporary home decorations are sold here. There is also a monitor devoted to the screening of contemporary Japanese art films.

Floor nine, "The Relation," has more video screens and is decorated with more potted ferns. The few goods for sale on this floor consist largely of ethnic-inspired women's fashions, and salesclerks all wear these ethnic-appearing designer clothes. Dressing rooms are shaped like stable stalls, but with an ornate appearance. There is a small cafe, done entirely in gray decor, surrounded by living ferns. A photography session and interview with a young Japanese female idol (starlet) is taking place, in full view of passing customers. The Relation is defined as a "contemporary space produced by active creators" (SEED Shibuya Seibu 1986).

The tenth floor, "SEED Hall," brings customers to the summit of their journey. SEED Hall is a theater for the visual and performing arts. As representative of these arts, it images the postulated ideal of "creative" that the consumer journey promised. SEED Hall suggests that our ultimate development as human beings is toward engagement in expressive and creative pursuits. It also underscores that consumerism no longer involves the consumption of objects, but of entertainment, experiences, involvement in one's own creative pursuits, and encounters with the creative processes or performances of other human beings.

"SEIBU-REALISM" AND THE MODERN JAPANESE MARKETPLACE

Utilizing the preceding description of SEED as a servicescape, I would like to explore Seibu's artistic and philosophical orientation (Seibu-realism) in relationship to the four aspects of stores as stages discussed earlier. On May 30, 1986, two months after SEED's opening, I discussed SEED with a *kachō* (section head) of the Shibuya Seibu personnel department who had been involved in planning SEED's development. He noted that SEED was a shift away from offering the complete range of daily and specialty goods typical of department stores, to "a totally high-fashion image," emphasizing a sophisticated fashion and entertainment lifestyle. However, he explained the essence of SEED as the philosophic meanings embodied in the store's spatial arrangement and artwork:

> SEED was an attempt to develop a new concept. The name is different and was selected to fit the image. We're trying to suggest the idea of "*tane*," or seed. A seed is something that grows, develops, and finally emerges into the new reality of tomorrow.

SEED as servicescape gives physical form to what has been called "Seibu-realism," a term showing that in Japan Seibu's image positioning is one associated with a high level of intellectualism. SEED as stage offers not just goods but cultural meanings and philosophic messages for consumption. The first aspect of store as stage discussed earlier elicited the servicescape's function in packaging consumer objects and the shopping experience. SEED defines a physical layout such that it provides the wrapping of space and all items in it, in a culture that heavily emphasizes the concept of wrapping. Where Lévi-Strauss discusses the distinction between what is considered cultural and what is not as the difference between the cooked (cultural) and the raw (natural), in Japan this distinction is better conceptualized as the difference between the wrapped and the unwrapped. In terms of consumerism, Clammer (1992) explains,

> The thing bought however, is not just "itself" and nor is it just the cluster of symbolic meanings attaching to it. It is indeed all of these too, but it is also transformed by one additional and quintessentially Japanese procedure: its wrapping (p. 206).

Although Clammer is discussing the cultural meanings surrounding the layers of packaging given to purchases in Japan, I contend that SEED the building likewise spatially wraps the consumer experience in layers of meaning. However, an important question to consider is why the wrapping of consumer space, transforming consumption into a cultural engagement, involves existential messages of human growth, development, and transcendence in Japan in the mid-1980s.

SEED was conceptualized, built, and opened in the mid-1980s at the height of what has been called Japan's bubble economy, an economy of prolonged growth. SEED was also conceptualized at a time when, overall, the Japanese populace had reached a high level of material affluence and was experiencing disillusionment with consumerism.

In the 1950s, Japan was still experiencing the poverty of the postwar era. Material goods were in short supply, and department store employees describe this as an easy time for retailers. As long as stores could provide goods for sale, people would buy them. In the 1960s Japanese, now emerging from the early postwar destruction and poverty, were influenced by a growing consumer society's promise of *akarui seikatsu,* the new "bright life," obtainable through the acquisition of modern consumer durables. Throughout the 1960s and 1970s, despite the setbacks of two oil shocks, incomes and the national economy were generally on the rise, and Japanese avidly set out to realize each new wave of consumer offerings. By the early 1980s, most Japanese found themselves materially well off. Their dwellings were saturated with material goods. Having achieved the long-sought goals of modernization, westernization, and an advanced consumer economy, Japanese were experiencing a disillusionment with it all. The 1980s also marked the height of various "retro" booms in Japan; the *dentōteki* (tradition) boom, which highlighted preindustrial crafts and craft processes, the *furusato* (hometown) boom, which highlighted small rural towns presumably less sophisticated and less westernized, and the search to discover a lost Japan (Ivy 1988; Martinez 1992) untouched by westernization. All of these movements suggested a need to reconsider materialism in order to recapture spiritual values. A Japanese end-of-year editorial in 1985 claimed that Japanese could no longer accept the premise that "human redemption proceeds from a cash register" ("By Bread Alone?" 1985).

Seibu flexibly responded to the mood of the times by proclaiming that consumerism would provide the means of transcending materialism. This was expressed by Chairperson Tsutsumi in a published interview as follows:

> At a time when material prosperity has grown, Japanese consumers are asking for more. They are looking beyond things to psychological self-fulfillment, aesthetic satisfaction and meaningful human relations. People want to discover something new. The term "breaking away from things" appears frequently in analyses of consumer trends in Japan. I interpret this to mean a transcendence of material values, and I believe the retail industry must provide the means to achieve this transcendence (quoted in O'Donnell 1982, 54).

SEED's layout pulses consumers on a journey toward this transcendence, while suggesting a consumer shift toward intangibles. The object of consumerism is no longer objects. Instead it is purchasing engagement in, or encounters with, entertainment and creativity. Akihiro Hayakawa, another spokesperson for Seibu, expresses this shift for Japanese consumers in the 1980s in this way:

> Now that most people have everything they need materially, they're looking for something mentally or spiritually appealing—and that means something in services, entertainment or other intangibles (quoted in Moffat 1985).

Recognizing that Japanese consumer society had entered a new phase, Japanese retailers coined the selling slogan *"mono igai no mono"*—selling "things other than things" (Creighton 1992, 53). SEED represents a shift in which the servicescape becomes less of a stage for the display of objects, and more of a stage for desirable lifestyles. As objects are wrapped by layers of meaning when purchased, the lifestyles staged at SEED are wrapped with philosophic messages about the nature of a meaningful human life.

SEED is also a stage in the second sense discussed of providing a site for the participatory engagement of customers. It offers them entertainment and leisure, but also purports to offer "something more." The entertainment is obvious in the form of currently popular movie and recording hits playing throughout the store, or the computers and screens available for shoppers' own expressive artwork. In a society that emphasizes harmony, conformity to proper form, and ritualized etiquette on expected occasions, SEED's message box allows an outlet for negative commentary, such as found in the joking caricature of one youth's junior-high-school teacher. The meanings attached to the spaces of SEED transform the shopping experience from merely entertaining to something, in Hayakawa's words, "spiritually appealing."

SEED as a stage engaging people philosophically in the contemplation of ultimate meaning in human existence can be related to McCracken's (1988) analysis of displaced meaning in consumerism. McCracken defines meaning as displaced because "it consists of cultural meaning that has deliberately been removed from the daily life of a community and relocated in a distant cultural domain" (p. 104). Cultures can project ideal values of the good life to some other time or place, making consumer goods the "bridges to these hopes and ideals" (p. 104). At SEED utopia is suggested as that time/place when humans are fully actualized to recognize their own potential and creative depths. Although there is a suggestion that consumer goods—sophisticated designer outfits, the latest audiovisual technology and products, tickets to artistic performances—are bridges to this ideal, at SEED these become secondary to the suggestion that the sites one chooses for consumerism are the bridges (or microbeams) to the ideal; SEED the servicescape is itself the projected bridge. The consumer who frequents SEED takes the first step toward the ideal not so much by the purchases chosen, but by the very act of shopping at SEED.

The third aspect of stores as stages mentioned is that they provide sites for the construction of identities, for both shopper and store. The consuming self as a foundation for identity is clear in Chairperson Tsutsumi's assertion that "consumption is a form of communication, a statement of world view, an affirmation of existence." As an affirmation of modern existence, consumerism transforms Descartes's "I think, therefore I am" into "I consume, therefore I am" (Falk 1994, xiii). Seibu's philosophical orientation as reflected at SEED tries to assert the unification of thinking, consuming, and being. Human beings both think and consume. SEED prompts people to consume but also to think; in thinking and consuming they create and re-create themselves. The end of the journey at SEED is the creative and re-created thinking/consuming human being.

In this regard as well, SEED suggests that the site of consumption is more relevant to the construction of identity than the consumer objects found in the servicescape. Shopping at SEED involves the self-identity assertion that one is a perceptive (*kōkando*), sophisticated, and creative human being.

SEED also embodies a physical reality for the idea of a Seibu self. Large retailers in Japan generally offer similar goods for sale and must therefore struggle for distinctive image positionings. In contrast to other department stores, Seibu tries to project its identity as an avant-garde, artistic, and highly intellectually oriented retailing chain.[4] Seibu does not deny that it is profit oriented, but also asserts a corporate identity of encouraging human creativity:

> The Seibu Saison Group aims not only to generate profit, but to balance material and mental well-being through a lively engagement in art and cultural activities. Awareness of the art and artifacts formed by [human] hands moves and encourages one to participate oneself in such activities. The Seibu Saison Group, via a wide range of creative and cultural involvements, tries to inspire that spirit in daily life (Seibu Saison Group 1985, 30).

Seibu attempts to assert this creative identity in various ways. One of its offshoot stores, Parco (from the word *park*), has a theater that stages theatrical and musical productions. Some of the Seibu department stores host legally designated art museums on the

---

[4] SEED has its own designer brands and in that sense can be said to offer different lines of goods from other stores. However, most department stores cultivate exclusive rights to certain designer-brand goods, so this category of stores in Japan offers similar types of goods in that sense. Image positioning is very important for department stores. All department stores strive for a high-class or upscale image, but with a different emphasis. For example, Mitsukoshi identifies itself as a traditional store, one with ties to the Imperial family and foreign royalty such as the British monarchy. Isetan positions itself as a family store and one emphasizing the female life course. Seibu, as a more modern entrant to department store retailing in Japan, tries to project an avant-garde, trend-setting, and even futuristic image.

upper floors.[5] The Seibu Saison Group has also opened museums totally independent of its stores, such as the Takonawa Museum situated in a natural mountain and forest setting at the resort area of Karuizawa.

SEED is an image statement asserting Seibu's desired self-identity. It offers entertainment, high fashion, and philosophy but contains a very limited line of goods compared to Seibu's department stores. Its rational profitability is not calculated through sales at SEED alone, because it is believed that if people are drawn to SEED, they might end up traveling the microbeam to shop at the Shibuya Seibu Department Store or other Seibu stores, even if they forgo the trend-setting but expensive designer goods staged at SEED. When I asked a Seibu design staff member about the purpose of store concepts like SEED, her answer reiterated an emphasis on the creation of a sophisticated Seibu identity:

> It's to get people to think, "Wow, so Seibu is this kind of place." I think that is the whole point. Even if it doesn't make enough money immediately, for the future it builds a good corporate identity.

SEED's intellectual assertion of a human developmental journey toward creativity is a projection of Seibu's own desired self-identity positioning as Japan's intellectual and creative retailer.

The fourth aspect of stores as stages, discussed previously, involves the dramaturgical setting of interaction between buyers and sellers. It is often suggested that in a *Gemeinschaft* community, the seller is obligated to responsibly meet the needs of the shopper, and the shopper, by even entering a store, has some obligation to buy, but that with large-scale modern retailing, this interaction between sellers and buyers becomes an impersonalized *Gesellschaft*

---

[5] Most department stores in Japan host exhibits and art galleries. A few, such as Seibu and Isetan, have stores with legally designated *bijutsukan*, art museums. This is a legal designation that is difficult to obtain and defines the museums on the upper floors of these stores as in the same category as national public art museums.

relationship, where each can freely seek to maximize his or her own advantage.

Shoppers at SEED often usurp the layout and service offerings for their own purposes. Meeting friends and utilizing the entertainment possibilities at SEED is a cheap alternative to other forms of entertainment, such as paying to see a movie in the expensive central districts of Tokyo. Some shoppers, such as Yumi, appear to feel completely free of any obligation incurred by utilizing the facilities at SEED and can even use SEED's public screens to complain about the Saison corporation. However, many customers I interacted with stated that when they spend time at such special stores, utilizing the facilities and service offerings as leisure sites and pastimes, they feel an obligation to make some purchase, even if it is not an expensive one, before leaving. Perhaps these customers are also acting rationally, realizing that stores as pleasure sites cannot remain in operation if they do not ultimately make sales.

On the selling side, large-scale Japanese merchant houses appeal to an ideal of *Gemeinschaft,* suggesting that *Gemeinschaft* can be reintegrated into modern life. This is evident in Seibu's philosophic claim that "The Seibu Saison Group has to deal with this paradox, this responsibility to aim toward a post-modern industrial organization by acting like a non-industrial one" (Seibu Saison Group 1985, 3). Although large-scale marketing in Japan clearly attempts to maximize profits, the relationship of retailers to consumers is overlaid with an ideology of accountability to the social realm. This ideal historically developed during the Edo era (1603–1868), along with the development of Japan's large merchant houses. The merchant ethic of the period justified the pursuit of monetary gain but only if it was accompanied by a sense of social responsibility on the part of merchants. According to this ethic, since merchants made money off the public, they also incurred a debt to enhance the communities where they were located and Japanese society in general.

People within the retailing industry frequently expressed the belief that engaging customers in cultural, artistic, or intellectual activity was part of the merchant responsibility to respond to social needs. For example, the director of cultural events at Isetan

Department Store explains the purpose of department store art museums as a contribution to society:

> The art museum is considered a service to the customers. It also fulfills a sense of service to the society. Whether it's Shinjuku [a major central district of Tokyo] or Ikebukuro [another major center of Tokyo], there is no public museum. At Ikebukuro, Seibu has a museum and at Shinjuku, Isetan does. There are still few public museums in Japan compared to the U.S. or Europe, so it is department stores that take this role. . . . If lots of good public museums are made, perhaps the need for department store museums will diminish, but this hasn't happened yet (O'Donnell 1982).

The chairperson of Seibu also asserts that it is retailers who must take the lead in responding to social needs:

> When social needs develop faster than government can respond, the department store must take the lead in meeting these needs. It is part of our social responsibility and we aim to make these services pay for themselves in the long term (quoted in O'Donnell 1982, 54).

This statement again refers to social accountability, but another sentiment emerges. This is the belief that the pursuit of social welfare is compatible with a desire to increase profits. Department stores are not shy about the fact that they hope to attract people to their stores through their special service offerings, thereby increasing their sales. Department store museums and galleries are typically placed on upper floors as part of a strategic plan to encourage people to shop throughout the store. Putting a museum on the top floor is, according to one museum staff member, like putting in a shower:

> By getting more people to come to the exhibits, more people come to the store. So people might go to the exhibit first, but they must come down—through each floor—and maybe they'll buy something on the way down. We say it works like a shower. Think of a fountain. First the water goes up, but it must come down, and as it does, some of it splatters out at various places. It's just like that.

In a similar vein, to get to SEED Hall and realize the summit of one's journey toward becoming a creative human being, shoppers must go all the way to the top of SEED, rather than limiting their shopping to the lower floors.

It is possible that the ideology of merchant accountability simply "naturalizes" the profit incentive of large-scale retailers in Japan, by recasting their operations in the light of a social good. According to Barthes (1972), naturalization is the process by which behavior shaped by economic, political, and historical institutions is constructed as cultural and thereby made to seem natural. When a seller supplies the populace with art, culture, and philosophy, the profit motivation, while not denied, recedes to a backstage position. The seller, as spotlighted on stage, is there to improve the buyer's quality of life. The ideology of social accountability ultimately enhances the profitability of these stores, given the expectations of Japanese society. However, it was also clearly the case that many retailers I interacted with held these values strongly and believed that they were catering to public needs and serving an important social function as well as selling consumer goods. By adhering to these values, they were able to realize satisfaction and fulfillment in their work, which they could not have, as one said, if they were just there "to sell things."

CONCLUSIONS

SEED shows that not only advertising and consumer goods, but also store layouts constitute cultural objects. Servicescapes, like SEED, create settings for behavior that prompt people toward certain forms of physical and intellectual activity. As such, they define stages for human involvement, interactions, and the construction of identities, as well as for the display of goods. Pertinent to the Japanese context, where meaning is commonly found in the concept of *tsutsumi*, or wrapping, SEED as servicescape involves the wrapping of space with layers of meaning. It is this wrapping of space at SEED that transforms consumption into a cultural engagement. SEED shows how the sites of consumption can take precedence over items purchased in terms of defining the sophisticated and creative lifestyle shopper. SEED exemplifies how commodity aesthetics are transferred from the commodities themselves to the servicescapes as consuming spaces.

SEED's architecture, artwork, and store layout all seek to engage shoppers intellectually as well as economically. Definitions of space at SEED proclaim a journey of developmental growth from seedling, to spearhead, to sensitive shopper, and ultimately to creative human being. SEED embodies a philosophy of ultimate meaning in human existence as the pursuit and realization of creativity in daily life. This particular servicescape is the product both of Japan's cultural values and of the specific economic and historic circumstances surrounding its inception. From the level of ideology, SEED reflects the ethic of merchant accountability: the idea that in making a profit, merchants also have an obligation to contribute to the social good by responding to social needs. Paradoxically, the social need that SEED as a new consumer institution was designed to address was a renewed search for meaning in human life resulting from a growing disillusionment with materialism and the full attainment of Japan's consumer society. SEED was thus a result of the mood and economic circumstances of the mid-1980s, the peak of Japan's so-called bubble economy. Japanese, having struggled for decades to realize the long-sought-after post–World War II goals of modernization, westernization, and economic affluence, were, having achieved these, beginning to wonder what they had sacrificed in the process. At the height of national economic affluence, part of the service of SEED's servicescape involved refocusing Japanese goals to new ideals, suggesting that consumerism should not just be directed at survival, realizing economic growth, or enhancing work activity. Instead, SEED asserts that Japanese as well-off consumers, and Japan as an economically affluent society, should now redirect personal and societal goals to realizing a higher quality of life based on a creative human existence.

SEED enables many of its youthful urban target clientele to imagine themselves as creative lifestyle consumers. Some customers appreciate and respond to Seibu's philosophic messages, while others simply utilize store offerings for their own entertainment purposes or employ them to find new alternative nonconsumerist means of communicating with and furthering linkages among their own personal network groups. Whether SEED is a real appeal to enlightened consumerism or only a trendy marketing device, whether customers all realize SEED's proclaimed ideals, it is relevant that this was the packaging chosen to address Japan of the mid-1980s based on Seibu's own extensive consumer research into the mood of the country. By promising to help create the creative lifestyle shopper, SEED repackages materialistic consumerism into a return to spiritualism in an attempt to dissolve the contemporary conflict between desires to maintain a materially affluent existence and preservation of an identity of Japaneseness that prefers spiritual over material wealth. SEED as servicescape symbolically wraps consumer activity in spiritualism, intellectualism, creative development, and a traditionalistic code of merchant social accountability. In doing so, it wraps *Gesellschaft* in the metaphors of *Gemeinschaft* in order to co-opt disillusionment with consumerism and further propel Japanese society's increasing consumer orientation.

Postscript

Showing that the ongoing processes of social life reflected by consumerism and retailing activity are always subject to change, a few years after the construction of SEED, Japan's bubble economy burst, ushering Japan into the years of economic recession now referred to as Japan's "burst-bubble" or "post-bubble" economy. The burst-bubble economy has resulted in a conservative shift back toward more conventional expectations in both work and consumer activity. Thus, the *tane,* or seed, Seibu attempted in this servicescape did not have the best chance to emerge and grow into the new reality of tomorrow. It is questionable whether a servicescape such as SEED could even have been seeded in the post-bubble economy. In that sense, SEED as servicescape perhaps epitomizes Japan as an affluent consumer society of 1986, precisely at that moment in which Japanese society saw the economic bubble rise to its highest level.

BIBLIOGRAPHY

ALLISON, ANNE. 1994. *Sexuality, Pleasure, and Corporate Masculinity in a Tokyo Hostess Club.* Chicago: University of Chicago Press.
BARTHES, ROLAND. 1957/1972. *Mythologies.* Translated by Annette Lavers. Reprint, New York: Noonday Press.
BERNARD, H. RUSSELL. 1994. *Research Methods in Anthropology: Qualitative and Quantitative Approaches,* 2d ed. Walnut Creek, CA: Sage.
BESTOR, THEODORE C. 1989. "Lifestyles and Popular Culture in Urban Japan." In *Handbook of Popular Culture,* edited by Richard Gid Powers, Hidetoshi Kato, and Bruce Stronach. New York: Greenwood Press, 1–37.
"By Bread Alone?" 1985. *Japan Times* (December 19).
CHANEY, DAVID. 1983. "The Department Store as a Cultural Form." *Theory, Culture, and Society.* 1(3):22–31.
CLAMMER, JOHN. 1992. "Aesthetics of the Self: Shopping and Social Being in Contemporary Urban Japan." In *Lifestyle Shopping: The Subject of Consumption,* edited by Rob Shields. London: Routledge, 195–215.
CREIGHTON, MILLIE. 1991. "Maintaining Cultural Boundaries in Retailing: How Japanese Department Stores Domesticate 'Things Foreign.'" *Modern Asian Studies* 25(4):675–709.
———. 1992. "The Depaato: Merchandising the West While Selling Japaneseness." In *Re-Made in Japan: Everyday Life and Consumer Taste in a Changing Society,* edited by Joseph J. Tobin. New Haven: Yale University Press, 42–57.
———. 1994. "'Edutaining' Children: Consumer and Gender Socialization in Japanese Marketing." *Ethnology* 33(1):35–52.
DICHTER, ERNEST. 1975. *Packaging: The Sixth Sense.* Denver, CO: Cahners.
EKIGUCHI, KUNIO. 1985. *Gift Wrapping: Creative Ideas from Japan.* Tokyo and New York: Kodansha.
FALK, PASI. 1994. *The Consuming Body.* London: Sage.
FEATHERSTONE, MIKE. 1982. "The Body in Consumer Culture." *Theory, Culture and Society* 1(2):18–33.
FINE, BEN, AND ELLEN LEOPOLD. 1993. *The World of Consumption.* London: Routledge.
GARDNER, BURLEIGH. 1967. "The Package as a Communication." In *Marketing for Tomorrow . . . Today.* Chicago: American Association, 117–118.
GOFFMAN, ERVING. 1959. *The Presentation of Self in Everyday Life.* New York: Doubleday.
HAUG, WOLFGANG FRITZ. 1983/1986. *Critique of Commodity Aesthetics: Appearance, Sexuality and Advertising in Capitalist Society.* Translated by Robert Bock. Reprint, Minneapolis: University of Minnesota Press.
HAVENS, THOMAS R. H. 1994. *Architects of Affluence: The Tsutsumi Family and the Seibu Saison Enterprises in Twentieth-Century Japan.* Cambridge: Harvard University Press.
HENDRY, JOY. 1993. *Wrapping Culture: Politeness, Presentation and Power in Japan and Other Societies.* Oxford: Clarendon Press.
HERNADI, ANDRAS. 1990. "Consumption and Consumerism in Japan." In *Rethinking Japan.* Vol 2, *Social Sciences, Ideology & Thought,* edited by Adriana Boscaro, Franco Gatti, and Massimo Raveri. Sandgate, England: Japan Library, 186–191.

HONDA, KATSUICHI. 1993. *The Impoverished Spirit in Contemporary Japan: Selected Essays of Honda Katsuichi.* Edited by John Lie. Translated by John Lie, Eri Fujieda, and Masayuki Hamazaki. New York: Monthly Review Press.

IVY, MARILYN. 1988. "Tradition and Difference in the Japanese Mass Media." *Public Culture* 1(1):21–29.

———. 1993. "Formations of Mass Culture." In *Postwar Japan as History,* edited by Andrew Gordon. Berkeley: University of California Press, 239–258.

KOTLER, PHILIP. 1984. *Marketing Management.* Englewood Cliffs, NJ: Prentice Hall.

LÉVI-STRAUSS, CLAUDE. 1969. *The Raw and the Cooked: Introduction to a Science of Mythology.* Translated by John Weightman and Doreen Weightman. New York: Harper and Row.

MARTINEZ, D. P. 1992. "NHK Comes to Kuzaki: Ideology, Mythology and Documentary Film-Making." In *Ideology and Practice in Modern Japan,* edited by Roger Goodman and Kirsten Refsing. London: Routledge, 153–170.

McCRACKEN, GRANT. 1988. *Culture and Consumption: New Approaches to the Symbolic Character of Consumer Goods and Activities.* Bloomington and Indianapolis: Indiana University Press.

MOFFAT, SUSAN. 1985. "Trends in Year-End Gift Giving." *Japan Times* (December 25).

MUKERJI, CHANDRA. 1983. *From Graven Images: Patterns of Modern Materialism.* New York: Columbia University Press.

O'DONNELL, PETER. 1982. "Take a Lesson (and More) from Retailers in Japan." *Stores* (January): 49–54.

OKA, H. 1975. *How to Wrap Five More Eggs.* New York: Weatherhill.

ROBERTSON, JENNIFER. 1988. "The Culture and Politics of Nostalgia: *Furusato* Japan." *International Journal of Politics, Culture and Society* 1(4):494–518.

SANJEK, ROGER, ED. 1990. *Fieldnotes: The Making of Anthropology.* Ithaca, NY: Cornell University Press.

SEED SHIBUYA SEIBU. 1986. *Seed Shibuya Seibu Floor Guide.* Tokyo: company files.

SEIBU SAISON GROUP. 1985. *Seibu Saison Group 1985.* Tokyo: company files.

———. 1986a. *Nyūsha Annai.* Tokyo: company files.

———. 1986b. *SEED Floor Information Guide.* Tokyo: company files.

SEITER, ELLEN. 1992. "Toys Are Us: Marketing to Children and Parents." *Cultural Studies* 6(2):232–247.

SHERRY, JOHN F., JR., AND EDUARDO G. CAMARGO. 1987. "May Your Life Be Marvelous: English Language Labelling and the Semiotics of Japanese Promotion." *Journal of Consumer Research* 14:174–188.

SHIELDS, ROB. 1992. "Spaces for the Subject of Consumption." In *Lifestyle Shopping: The Subject of Consumption,* edited by Rob Shields. London: Routledge, 1–20.

TETSUYA, CHIKUSHI. 1986. "Young People as a New Human Race." *Japan Quarterly* 33(3):291–294.

TOBIN, JOSEPH. 1992. "Japanese Preschools and the Pedagogy of Selfhood." In *Japanese Sense of Self,* edited by Nancy R. Rosenberger. Cambridge: Cambridge University Press, 21–39.

URRY, JOHN. 1990. *Consuming Places.* London: Routledge.

7

"FRIEND OF THE BRIDE" —AND THEN SOME

Roles of the Bridal Salon During Wedding Planning

CELE OTNES

For many women, no occasion is more economically or sociologically significant in their lives than their wedding. As Cheal (1988) observes, the wedding is the only major rite of passage that has retained its original significance in postindustrial cultures. Moreover, Barker (1978) remarks that "weddings are the only major ceremonials organized by ordinary people, certainly by ordinary women" (p. 58). And while "everyday" women may be responsible for planning this rite of passage, the amounts of money involved in such an activity are typically far from mundane. For example, Dodds (1994) notes that the average cost of the American wedding is approaching $19,000, while Freise (1996) observes that the cost in the United Kingdom is comparable, at $16,500. In total, the cost of weddings, receptions, and honeymoons in the United States totaled

Cele Otnes is Associate Professor in the Department of Advertising and Fellow of the Cummings Center for Advertising Studies at the University of Illinois at Urbana-Champaign. The author gratefully acknowledges the assistance of Stephenetta Hoff, Tracey Lee, Elaina Joyce, and Catherine McDonald for their assistance in the data collection for this paper, as well as the financial assistance of the Summer Research Opportunities Fund at the University of Illinois.

more than $9 billion in 1990, "or 30 percent of all the money spent setting up households" (Waldrop 1990, 4).

For consumer researchers, the wedding in general—and wedding purchasing in particular—offers a rich venue from which to examine both highly salient and symbolic consumption. Scholars have explored this ritual in depth in other cultures (e.g., Charsley 1991, 1992). But given the significance of the wedding as consumer ritual (Rook 1985), it is surprising that studies of weddings in America have tended to focus upon relatively self-contained aspects of the ritual. For example, Casparis (1979) and Cheal (1988) have delved into the meaning of the bridal shower, and McGrath and her coauthors (McGrath and Otnes 1993; McGrath and Englis 1995) have explored the differences in wedding gift selection among different ethnic and generational groups.

More recently, a few researchers have begun to take a more holistic view in the study of wedding planning. For example, Lowrey and Otnes explored the actual wedding-planning process, focusing primarily upon the importance of artifact selection for the bride and groom (Lowrey and Otnes 1994, 1995; Otnes and Lowrey 1993). Likewise, Currie (1993) examined the role of bridal magazines and planners in shaping the ritual. In addition, Freise (1995) has recently examined the significance of wedding dresses for brides, by observing women shopping for these garments.

While much attention has been paid to consumer rituals in American culture, few have examined the role(s) of the retailer during these occasions (for exceptions, see McGrath 1990; Sherry and McGrath 1989). Indeed, a literature search resulted in no studies exploring the roles of either American bridal retail establishments or bridal salespeople during wedding planning. And only one scholar, exploring the meaning of wedding cakes in Britain (Charsley 1987a, 1987b, 1988, 1992), has integrated the perspectives of retailers (in this case, bakers) in his interpretation.

Yet the retailer's input and influence during wedding planning is worthy of study for several reasons. First, because weddings are typically rare events in a person's life, the "ordinary women" who plan them are often quite unfamiliar with the goods and services that need to be procured for the ritual. Thus, many rely on bridal retailers in the planning of these events, certainly more so than in the purchase of "ordinary" goods and services. Second, many key artifacts—especially the wedding dress—are often selected up to one year in advance (Barker 1978), and the procurement of this item often requires multiple visits to bridal salons for fittings and the purchase of related accessories. Thus, brides often develop relatively long-term relationships with retailers, especially when compared to those that develop (or do not develop) when these same women shop for most nonritual goods.

The last factor necessitating the involvement of the wedding retailer is the sheer transformational nature of the occasion. Brides often view their weddings as their "one day to be a princess" (Otnes and Lowrey 1993; Freise 1995) or their "one day in fairy land" (Currie 1993), and depend on family, friends, and retailers to facilitate this (albeit temporary) transformation. Add to this the fact that the wedding is typically a highly public rite of passage (Baker 1990; van Gennep 1960), and there can be little doubt that the personal and sociological risk surrounding wedding-oriented purchases is much greater than that incurred when more mundane goods and services are purchased.

Thus, this chapter explicates the roles expressed by bridal salons as they are used by women during the shaping of their weddings. Hopefully, it will encourage consumer researchers to expand their focus beyond that of customers and include the role of retailers and retail establishments when engaged in the exploration of consumer rituals.

METHOD

The text for this study was generated in two stages and during two distinct time periods. The first stage occurred in the summer of 1991, when brides participated in interviews and were accompanied on wedding-related shopping trips. This phase of the research focused on many issues related to wedding planning, and one of those was the ways brides utilized retail outlets while selecting wedding-related goods and services.

To explore this topic more fully, additional interactions with brides were conducted in July and August of 1995. During that time, 3 out of 4 bridal salons in a small Midwest city (population 100,000) were approached and asked if they would allow a researcher to observe brides as they shopped for wedding dresses. Two of the stores refused, citing as reasons space limitations and their desire to protect the privacy of their clientele. Therefore, to capture a range of experience at all stores in the city, the previous method of recruiting brides for interviews and shopping trips was repeated.

In both years, ads were initially placed in a campus and a local newspaper, informing brides that they would be paid for participating in a university study of wedding planning. The ad stated that brides should be willing to be interviewed twice and accompanied on two shopping trips. In 1991 nine brides were recruited as informants, and in 1995 four participated, for a total of 13 informants.[1]

The brides were all white lower-middle- or middle-class women, ranging in age from 21 to 35. It was the first marriage for all but one informant. All brides except one were using the services of a specialty bridal salon. All brides either worked full-time or were attending college.

The 1991 brides were not limited to shopping trips at bridal salons, but those participating in 1995 were accompanied only to those types of retail outlets. Consequently, 14 shopping trips were made to bridal salons across the two time periods. The 4 bridal salons where shopping with informants took place are described (with pseudonyms) in Table 7.1.

Interviews with the informants lasted 45 minutes to 1 hour. First interviews featured both "grand-tour" questions and carefully scheduled prompts (McCracken 1988; Spradley 1979; Fontana and Frey 1994). Informants were also encouraged to elaborate upon any other topics that arose related to wedding planning. Questions for the second interviews were created by the researchers, who asked

[1] The brides recruited in 1991—as well as grooms—also participated in focus groups during this phase of the research. For a description of these findings, see Otnes and Lowrey (1993) and Lowrey and Otnes (1994).

TABLE 7.1   Description of Bridal Salons Studied

"Bridal Fair" is a small discount salon that is part of a regional chain. Its selection was considered small by our informants, although one did observe that its franchise status allows the store to order a wide variety of merchandise. The store features tables and chairs where brides can browse through wedding-related catalogs and other merchandise (such as invitation samples). The store is rather dimly lit and quiet. It is located in a strip mall in a very heavily concentrated retail part of the city.

"Donny's" is a large, full-service salon that carries a wide range of products, including wedding gowns, tuxedos, bridesmaids' dresses, jewelry, shoes, crinolines and other lingerie, veils and other accessories. It is located on a major four-lane east-west artery in the city. The store retains an air of exclusivity by not allowing customers into the part of the store where gowns and other finery are kept until they complete a lengthy form that describes the particulars of their wedding. Donny's had a "mixed" reputation among our informants, with many loyal to its selection and service, and others relating horror stories about its snobbish approach to sales and its dishonesty. Donny's is the largest of all salons in the market and the most visible in terms of window displays. Donny's offers a promotion of a discount off of tuxedo rental if the wedding dress is purchased at the store.

"Monica's" is located approximately one-half mile from Donny's on the same east-west artery, in a small strip mall. It is brightly lit but does not feature many displays. The store is basically one large rectangle, featuring dresses on both the left and right sides. No tuxedos are available, and merchandise is basically limited to dresses for the bride and her attendants.

"Joanne's" is located in a converted Victorian house on a residential, tree-lined street. It is two-story and features three rooms downstairs and one below. The three rooms downstairs are the foyer, where displays are found, the main room that includes wedding and bridesmaids' dresses (both to buy and to rent) and other related merchandise, such as mothers' dresses. The final downstairs room consists of a counter where Joanne converses with her customers before and after the visit. Upstairs, brides find the necessary undergarments required when trying on their dresses, as well as dressing rooms. Because the store is an old home, it tends to seem rather crowded and cramped.

the informants to elaborate upon or clarify behavior that had been observed on a previous shopping trip.

Shopping with consumers has proven to be an effective means both of interacting with informants and generating credible, naturalistically based text (Otnes, Lowrey, and Kim 1993; Otnes, McGrath, and Lowrey 1995; Otnes, Lowrey, and Shrum 1997). Shopping trips lasted from 45 minutes to $1\frac{1}{2}$ hours. Researchers typically met informants at whichever salon the brides wished to visit, and when researchers actually accompanied brides to retail outlets, these interactions were also included in field notes. The format for all interaction with informants was as follows:

1. First interview
2. First shopping trip
3. Second (follow-up) interview
4. Second shopping trip

Informants were paid $40 for their participation.

The data were collected by four female undergraduate students, all of whom were trained participants in a minority summer research program at a large university in the city. Three students participated in this program in 1991, while one did so in 1995. Although racial differences might have led to social distance between informants and researchers, all informants were advised that students were members of the program, and all willingly participated in the study.

The author of this chapter created the research design, generated the structured interviews, trained the students in the process of interviewing and shopping with consumers, and oversaw text generation. All students conducted practice interviews and observation exercises before entering the field. Both the students and hired clerical workers transcribed the interviews. The researchers created detailed field notes of each shopping trip immediately after leaving the field. The transcripts of the interviews and shopping trips yielded over 180 pages of text that related directly to the role of the bridal salon during wedding planning.

Analysis and Interpretation

The author of this chapter also conducted all analysis and interpretation of the text. The procedure that I followed mirrors that of the "constant comparative method" described by Glaser and Strauss (1979) and Lincoln and Guba (1985). Namely, I began by sorting through the 1991 material in order to locate the text that related specifically to informants' attitudes toward, and use of, bridal salons while planning their weddings. After merging this material with that collected in 1995, I searched the entire text for patterns of usage across brides, that related to their experiences within, and expectations of, bridal salons. After completing this phase, I combined the emergent patterns into broader categories. At this point in the analysis, I decided that metaphors might best describe the ways in which brides relied upon salons during wedding planning. As Atkinson (1992) notes, the metaphor "provides conceptual apparatus and imagery through which we grasp generalities and make comparisons between one setting and another. . . . The analytic metaphor can thus be a condensation of sociological or anthropological understanding" (p. 12).

Once I decided upon that course of action, I reread the text, jotting down additional places where the metaphors I had previously identified—or those I had *not* previously observed—emerged. I conducted my final reading in order to select exemplars of each metaphor. The resulting analysis is both emic and etic, in that it features both what brides have said and done, as well as my interpretation of their thoughts and actions.

The remainder of this chapter explicates the six metaphors that emerged as related to either the bridal salon as a whole or to bridal salespeople in particular. As such, this chapter seeks to capture the roles our informants expected the salon to fulfill as they sought to acquire their wedding dresses and related merchandise. These roles reveal that not only bridal salespeople (whom one might assume would be important), but also physical aspects of the bridal salons, contributed to the ability of the store to fulfill these desired roles.

THE ROLES OF THE BRIDAL SALON

In the following interpretation, the names of the informants and the bridal salons have been changed to preserve anonymity.

The Bridal Salon as Clearinghouse

One of the metaphors that emerged the most consistently as brides shopped for the weddings was that of the "salon as clearinghouse"— or a store that is expected to offer merchandise that brides have, in actuality, *already* selected from other information sources. In other words, many brides enter the salon for the first time with a very clear idea of the type of dress (often even *the* dress) they wish to purchase.

Indeed, most of the brides reported following a two-step process of information search for their dress. Specifically, they perused national bridal magazines for the types of styles they wanted, and/or they had a previously established mental vision of how they wished to look on their wedding day.[2] Armed with this information, they entered the bridal salon, expecting it either to produce the exact merchandise they had preselected or to match a more abstract ideal they had already decided upon. Currie (1993), in discussing the influence of magazines on brides as they selected the gown, notes that "in many cases, women wanted their weddings to match what they saw in bridal magazines" (p. 411). Our informants also illustrated this tendency, as the following descriptions indicate:

> I like brides' magazines. . . . What I did is look in there and got a good idea of what I wanted and went from there. . . . I would look at the magazine and pick out what I wanted and then take it to the stores and say, "I want this right here. . . ." It is too much of a hassle to go to all of the bridal stores and then make a final selection. It's easier to flip through the magazines (Elaine, early 20s).

---

[2] The circulations of the top four bridal magazines for the first six months of 1991 were as follows: *Modern Bride,* 312,517; *Brides',* 304,538; *Bridal Guide,* 228,072; *Elegant Bride,* 164,885.

I used the brides' magazine more for a dress I saw in there, by the same designer, the same designer that had my dress, and I'd seen several of her items, so I kind of kept an eye open . . . for her designs when we went shopping (Jenny, late 20s).

I: What items for the ceremony did you spend the most time selecting?

J: I'd say my dress. . . . I mean, we had the perfect picture in our minds of what we wanted, but we just couldn't ever find it. . . . First of all, I went through all of the magazines, and I picked out, "Well I don't like this style," or, "I don't like this." And so then I had it down to, well, "I want sleeves off of this one, and the body off this one, and the skirt off this one." And so I walked in there, and I showed them all of the pictures of the ones that I wanted (Julie, early 20s).

Interestingly, this finding may explain why brides' dresses often seemed to "miraculously" appear to our informants in the stores, and why many informants often reported buying the first dress they tried on. For rather than the dress actually being magically "revealed" to them through the process of hierophany (Belk, Wallendorf, and Sherry 1989; Otnes and Lowrey 1993), perhaps it is more the case that because brides have conducted so much information search pertaining to the desired look and style of their wedding dress before entering the salon that they literally know it when they see it. This process makes the bridal dress no less sacred; rather, the sheer amount of time, money, and energy expended on bridal magazines attests to the importance of the wedding gown.

There are two interesting ramifications of the fact that our informants expect salons to act as clearinghouses for national, brand-name products. First, some were irritated with salons if these brand names were masked somehow or if salons did not "allow" them to have access to style numbers of dresses, so that selection and shopping could be facilitated:

What I really hate is that you look through the brides' magazines, right? And you see bridesmaids' dresses that you like, like Bill Westcox or New Image, and you're like, "OK, this is a national brand that my bridesmaids can try on wherever they are in the country." And so you go to these stores, and you say, "I would like to see this Bill Westcox dress," and the women, the salespeople are like, "Oh, well, we don't know which ones are Bill Westcox dresses because we code all our dresses. . . ."

So if you were to find a dress in a magazine and go to one of the local shops, you basically have to go through every single dress until you find, like, that same one. . . . And my bridesmaids are in New York City and Austin, Texas. And I don't want them to have to go to a bridal salon and have to dig through all those dresses to find the right one from just a picture. So that really irritated me (Belle, mid-20s).

I went to [Joanne's] because the people at [Monica's] were like, "Oh, we don't give out brand names," because . . . what I'm doing is going around and seeing who has the cheapest price. And so I went to . . . [Joanne's]. They let me look at their book, and I found the exact dress . . . and it's by Venus, and they had the style number on it, so I photocopied it across the street, and so I have that with me, and now I, when I went to [a large market], this one place . . . said they could go [from $850 retail] down to $640 (Kate, early 20s).

Thus, if brides are unable to link brand-name products with a particular bridal salon, their mental image of that particular store may suffer accordingly. This evidence extends a finding by Zimmer and Golden (1988), who conclude that association with brand-name goods is one characteristic consumers use when conceptualizing store images. And in this case, our informants' *inability* to associate brand-name goods with bridal salons hampered the images they held of these retail establishments.

The second implication of the salon-as-clearinghouse metaphor is that brides expect these salons to carry a large selection of wedding dresses. This feature has ramifications for the atmospherics of the salon, as one bride even stated she would rather see a store "stuffed" with dresses than one with a less crowded appearance:

[Donny's] had good store displays with the mannequins. And everything seemed a little, not as spread out or in the open . . . like a little more crowded with racks of dresses and it just seemed that [Bridal Fair] was kind of empty, you know.

Like there was a lot of dead space. Where at [Donny's] and [Monica's], there are a lot more displays and things to make the store look fuller and more presentable (Belle, mid-20s).

Thus, the salon-as-clearinghouse metaphor means that brides not only expected to be able to find brand-name merchandise they had already chosen, but that they believed they should have the "right" to acquire the brand names and style numbers of the merchandise, as is the case when purchasing more mundane products.

The Bridal Salon as "One-Stop Shop"

Not surprisingly, the majority of the merchandise at the four bridal salons consisted of bridal gowns. This fact clearly supports the assumption that the dress is the single most important purchase for the wedding ceremony (Frese 1991; Otnes and Lowrey 1993). However, brides were also quite willing to make other wedding-related purchases at salons, if these items were available. Indeed, brides rewarded retailers who simplified their shopping with displays of related merchandise:

They also have tuxes [at Donny's]. That was really cool. And they set up a deal where if you buy your tuxes there, you can get your dress at a discount, as well as your bridesmaids' dresses (Belle, mid-20s).

[At Monica's] they had some very nice dresses, and I ended up getting mine there. And now we're having to try to get the tuxes there as well. Since you get a certain percentage off if you do everything at the same salon, which is like all the salons have that same deal (Gail, late 20s).

I: For what purchases did you use in-store materials?

E: Well, the flowers, for sure. I used the setup that [the salon] had already done. And I'm going to go back for the napkins and the invitations, and the cake topper, and all of the little extras that you need at the reception. I'm going to go back to [Bridal Fair] because their display was so impressive . . . and they had a very big selection of all kinds of things (Elaine, early 20s).

Many factors have probably contributed to brides' expectations that salons should offer a broad line of merchandise. For example, changes in American society have resulted in the fact that most brides now either work or attend school, and do not have either the desire or the time to go from one bridal specialty store to another. Moreover, the general rise in one-stop shops in the retail industry as a whole seems to have had an agenda-setting effect on women shopping for wedding-related items. Retail outlets themselves clearly recognize this trend, with the major salons located inside department stores in Chicago now reporting that they offer dresses, garters, ring-bearer pillows, and an assortment of other related merchandise (Gill 1988). In addition, a new chain titled We Do, which was specifically created around the concept of a wedding superstore, opened in November 1995—with forty stores and sales in the range of $180 to $200 million forecast in five years (Wilson 1995).

Thus, our informants tended to reward bridal salons that are stocked not only with dresses, but with invitations, tuxedos, bridesmaids' attire, and party supplies as well. Of course, this has direct implications for atmospherics. Bridal salons that set up displays resembling dioramas, as opposed to those that merely place in their windows mannequins wearing wedding gowns, can communicate convenience and breadth of selection more immediately. Moreover, the product bundling achieved through multiple-purchase discounts often necessitates the presentation of a wider array of goods than is available at the traditional bridal salon.

The Bridal Salon as School

Even with the high divorce and remarriage rates in the United States, 65 percent of all weddings feature *both* men and women who have never previously been married (Magiera 1993). Moreover, the complexity of the wedding ritual means that the bride must acquire a great deal of information in order to successfully "pull off" the event. This information ranges from the very specific (e.g., the cost of alterations) to the more far-reaching (the "proper" way a wedding dress should look). Because so many rules and regulations governing the wedding day involve the use of artifacts, brides often turn to salespeople and to displays in salons (as well as to bridal magazines and to members of their reference groups) in order to gain the knowledge they need.

Learning from Salespeople

The following examples of "teaching" by salespeople occurred in the bridal salon:

> [The saleswoman at Donny's] would [sometimes] take me out to a bigger room where there were mirrors where I could see the back part of the dress. . . . And along the way she would tell me the different styles and names of the different material. And after we had tried on all the dresses . . . she had marked down the style numbers and the prices of each one that I had picked out (Diane, early 20s).

> At [Donny's] they know dresses a lot better than I do. They do comparisons . . . oh, you know, "This dress has puffy sleeves and the other one you tried on didn't," or, "This dress has more decorations on the bodice, or you can do this and this. You can take off the bow." They make all kinds of suggestions. . . . That was really neat (Belle, mid-20s).

> I: What do you call "excellent help" [in the store]?
> G: Somebody who seemed . . . to be very honest and that, "This doesn't work, or this does work." They weren't just trying to sell me the dress and tell me I looked nice in whatever I wanted. They told me about the pros and cons and how things should fit (Gail, late 20s).

Furthermore, salespeople are also expected to serve as wellsprings of information about how to make wedding-related purchases for products their salons do *not* offer:

> At this point Kate decided to try on some other dresses. . . . Kate came out in the next gown. Neither she nor her mother were very excited about it. . . . As a result, instead of really looking at the gown, she spent this time chatting with Monica about area photographers. . . . [Later] they stood and chatted with Monica for a moment about ———'s, where the reception

would be held, and about a place to get a cake here in town. Monica gave her a name, and we left.

In these examples, the salesperson approximates what Solomon (1986) describes as the "surrogate consumer," or "an agent retained by a consumer to guide, direct, and transact marketplace activities" (p. 208). As such, the bridal salesperson wields more power and fulfills a more important educational role than a "typical" salesperson. Many of the criteria that Solomon suggests for determining surrogate usage—such as the inability of consumers to negotiate the marketplace on their own, the expectation that a surrogate can help secure needed goods or services, and the "presence of a meaningful preference hierarchy" (p. 210) during the selection of goods and services—clearly apply to the high-involvement (indeed, often high-stress) situation of selecting wedding artifacts.

Yet even while consumers may have higher expectations of bridal salespeople in terms of their educational functions, sometimes there appeared to be a fine line between "teaching" the bride and "bossing" her, as the following description indicates:

> I've heard many horror stories about this lady, that she had the entire wedding party in tears. . . . She said, "This looks horrible together, and you can't do that." So basically, I went in there and thought, I'm gonna go in there and if I see something I like, and if she says something unkind to me, then I'm either gonna walk out the door, or I'm gonna say, "Look, I'm paying for this. I mean, you can give me your opinion if you want, but don't tell me I can't buy it. I'm sure as heck gonna buy it" (Julie, early 20s).

Solomon et al. (1985) observe that in "any marketing situation in which personal interaction is an important part of the total offering" (p. 100), the interaction between salesperson and customer can be described as a series of role performances. As such, the expression of social roles has both positive and negative ramifications—especially if conflicts arise in role expectations (what each party expects the other to express) and role congruence (the amount of agreement between parties, in terms of each other's role). In the preceding example, Julie's role expectations of the retailer (as expert) were clearly in discord with the role the retailer wished to express (that of boss). As a result, Julie dismissed a priori any "teaching" that the salon owner might attempt.[3]

Learning from Displays

In addition to salespeople, displays in the stores often taught brides ways to combine and arrange the products to be used in their weddings:

> Jewelry . . . on the wedding gowns and bridesmaid dresses give me an idea of, you know, what to wear to a wedding. . . . I've seen a lot of flowers on display . . . what might look good. . . . I got the idea for spring flowers in a wedding shop, and it was just like a bunch of flowers . . . and there was a veil netting wrapped around it, with a bow that matched the dress, and it was so pretty (Kate, early 20s).

> A lot of the displays they have, like set up on the mannequins, are really good. The ones where I finally got my dress, they had a lot of their things out. . . . There was the bride and groom, and she had on a really pretty dress, and it just made you want to look, and you know, "Well, we could do this at my reception" (Elaine, early 20s).

This "teaching" function of bridal displays should not be overlooked by retailers, as it broadens the domain of retail factors influencing consumer socialization from beyond just interpersonal sources, and incorporates sensory experiences occurring within the confines of the store as well.

Finally, bridal salons and salespeople both performed a (not always positive) educational function for brides in helping them to realize what they did not want to include in their weddings. These decisions were as minute as Kate and her mother deciding that bride/groom champagne glasses were unnecessary items or as elaborate as the following types of decisions:

> As we entered Monica's, Diane first noticed the bridesmaids' dresses. While looking at each, she stated that she liked the "suit-style" dresses. As she was looking each dress up and

---

[3] For more on the effect of social role discord in the marketplace, see Otnes, Lowrey, and Shrum (1997).

down and one by one, she would pause for a very long time when she came in contact with a "suitlike" bridesmaid's dress. . . . Typical bridesmaids' dresses were not something Diane cared for. . . . Diane.was criticizing every bridesmaid's dress that she considered typical. For example, Diane saw an emerald green "typical bridesmaid's dress" and said, "What's that doing here?"

At [Joanne's,] I guess we were confused from the start. Because neither of us knew it was, like, a rental bridal salon. . . . And then it was just weird because we are getting married and we are willing to spend a lot of money on a dress. And it was weird (Belle, early 20s).

Given that 96 percent of all wedding dresses were bought in 1988, and given that Barker (1978) found that brides who rented dresses generally hushed up this information, the fact that the salon did not trumpet its rental policy is not surprising. However, the too-subtle way in which Belle learned of this service led Belle to experience discomfort and confusion.

In sum, bridal salespeople resemble other "surrogate consumers" such as interior decorators and financial planners, who are actively recruited by consumers for their advice and expertise. In all of these cases, consumers must rely on service experts to help them shape critical events. As such, consumers develop "an insatiable desire for information . . . with the anxiety-inspired insistence on knowing how things stand and how they are going to turn out" (Merton and Barber 1976, 23). Yet in all of these relationships, conflicts in role expectancy and role congruity can result in negative experiences for both the retailer and the customer.

The Bridal Salon as Storehouse

As previously mentioned, one of the reasons brides want to know the style numbers and brand names of wedding dresses is that they often shop around for the best prices. Given that the average cost of a wedding dress and veil was $782 in 1991 (Association of Bridal Consultants 1991), it is not surprising that brides elect to do so. One of the activities discussed—and often pursued—by our informants was shopping in a larger market where bridal stores are more competitive, in order to save money on their dresses.

However, the procurement of a dress far from the bride's home was not without its problems. For example, almost every wedding dress required alterations, which meant that the bride needed multiple fittings of the gown. For brides who purchased their dresses in other cities, this problem was solved by enlisting a local salon to provide alterations, cleaning, and storage for the dress until the wedding day. Interestingly, while studies have discussed the preservation of the gown for future generations after the wedding (Frese 1991; Otnes and Scott 1996), it appears that the gown also requires careful storing in the salon *before* the event as well. Kara observed that at Donny's, "I found that dress that I wanted . . . and they could store it for me since my wedding's a couple of years off." Likewise, two brides purchased their gowns in other markets and had them stored at local salons:

> What I think I'm going to do is, 'cause I'm going to be living down here and going to school, and it would be hard for alterations and stuff, so I'm probably going to get the dress at [a salon in a larger market] and then have my alterations done down here (Kate, early 20s).

> I didn't get my dress there [at Joanne's]. I mean, the only money I spent in the shop is for my veil, which is expensive. . . . So I haven't really spent a lot of money there at all, but she's holding my dress there. She's doing the alterations on it, which she by no means has to. She was going to dry-clean it for me, and she realized that if I took it over to the dry cleaner's, I would get it cheaper than what her price would be (Lynn, late 20s).

Thus, it appears that some brides regard salons not only as venues where wedding attire can be purchased, but also (and often separately) as places where these items can be altered and stored. Yet ironically, as is discussed in the next section, no bride wanted the salon to resemble a "storage tank."

The Bridal Salon as Dressing Chamber

The term *salon,* with its upper-class connotations of pampering and elitism, automatically sets bridal stores who incorporate it into their name apart from more mundane retail establishments, and reflects the distinctive nature of the merchandise carried. Moreover, one characteristic of the wedding dress is that in its length, weight, and complexity of attachments, it clearly does not resemble the everyday attire to which American women living in the 1990s are accustomed.

Indeed, our informants expected that salespeople would offer assistance with the physical aspect of trying on gowns, and that bridal salons (while paradoxically being stuffed with dresses) would also be bright and spacious enough so that brides could fully display and evaluate the dresses they were considering. As one salon owner has remarked, "These gowns have an awful lot of fabric, and the girls aren't used to getting in and out of that much material" (Gill 1988, 16).[4] However, our text records many instances where sales-people shirked these duties (typically when brides were accompanied on shopping trips)—often to our informants' irritation:

> Belle was having trouble getting into this particular dress. The saleswoman was not around, so zipping the dress up from the back was a hard task for Belle. With her head out, she then looked outside of the dressing room door for the saleswoman and said, "I'm abandoned. . . ." [The saleswoman came and] after having trouble getting the train's hook to attach to the dress, the saleswoman who was helping Belle called in another saleswoman to help. . . . [With another dress] Belle was having a hard time zipping the slip, so she yelled from the dressing room door, "Can you come here?"

> All of the dresses Diane chose to try on were long-sleeved beaded dresses with trains. After giving the saleswoman the last dress she was going to try on, Diane said, "God, these things are heavy. . . ." Every wedding dress that Diane tried on, she had the assistance of the saleswoman. As the saleswoman would help

---

[4] Moreover, some stores even offer an "attendant service"—either for a charge or for free—meaning that a store employee helps a bride with her wedding gown on the day of her wedding (Gill 1988).

her put on the wedding dresses, Diane's "job" would be to put both of her hands on her hips while she was being zipped and buttoned up.

Granted, not all informants were comfortable with the role of salesperson as personal dresser. After one shopping trip, Diane remarked:

> The one thing that took me aback . . . when we first came into the fitting room and I was gonna try on a dress . . . she gave me undergarments to put on . . . and she was gonna help me don those. I guess I was a little uncomfortable that she didn't ask if I wanted to go ahead and do it and she'd be back in the room to help me or come to see me if I wanted some privacy or something (Diane, early 20s).

Once again, these examples point to discrepancies in role expectation and role congruency between retail salespeople and customers. However, it is interesting to note that there is no consistency across brides. One was upset that too much privacy was given, while the other was uncomfortable with assistance in dressing!

As previously mentioned, brides also apparently expected to be surrounded by both decorative and practical physical characteristics of the salon (such as those found in ladies' dressing chambers of the past) as they selected their dresses:

> The better the mirrors in the larger dressing rooms made a difference. They had a place to sit for your entourage that comes with you. Everybody had a place to sit, I think. Except for [Bridal Fair] (Gail, late 20s).

> [Bridal Fair], it's just . . . it's not too fancy of a store, you know. It's got a couple of walls of dresses, and it doesn't have any real fancy decorations or any real fancy setups. So, you know, if they wanted to put a lot of money into it, they can make the store look really nice, and a lot more like an elegant bridal salon, instead of just . . . kind of like a discount store (Belle, early 20s).

Moreover, bridal retailers are not unaware of their patrons' desires for these amenities. One owner has described the remodeling of her salon as including "all ivory marble-look wall coverings, and lots of seafoam-green accents. We have Levelor blinds and wonderful lighting" (Gill 1988, 18). Even a new "off the rack" bridal chain is highly aware of brides' needs for the "dressing salon" atmosphere:

> Over the past two years, David's [where brides buy a dress in their size and leave with it the same day] has added an important ingredient to its superstore strategy: a service atmosphere. It has upgraded its prototype with better lighting, comfortable dressing rooms (20 per store) and stylish fixtures and displays. . . . "Our customers were telling us they wanted a degree of pampering and comfortable, service-oriented environment" (Wilson 1995, 34–35.)

In summary, the dressing room metaphor is probably the one most dependent upon the physical layout and design of the bridal salon—given that its connections to the "boudoirs of old" is best achieved through its physical design.

The Bridal Salon as Singularizer

The five metaphors discussed so far have all likened the salon to another type of place, such as a school or storehouse. The final metaphor that emerged was tied more to the ritual *function* of the salon and less to its resemblance to more mundane locales. For just as the transformation from single woman to bride begins with the acquisition of the engagement ring (Otnes and Scott 1996), so brides apparently expect the singularizing experience of selecting items for their weddings to begin in the bridal salon, months (perhaps even years) before they actually wear the items procured there.

This situation is in direct contrast to one that exists when women shop for non-wedding-related items. As Belle noted, "When you go shopping for regular clothing like jeans and stuff, you don't want people bothering you. . . . But I think for wedding gowns, it's completely different. People should really give good service." Moreover, one bride even distinguished between the service she expected to receive when shopping for her wedding dress and that she encountered when shopping for other wedding-related items:

> Those salespeople need to be more helpful when you're finding your wedding dress. Because you're the most important person on your wedding day. And you're the one that needs to look the best . . . so, it's more important than shopping for other wedding items, I think (Kara, early 20s).

Brides recounted many positive incidences of times when they experienced singularization in the retail salon:

> It's a lot of fun. They either do one of two things. They love you, or . . . they treat you like you don't know how to make any decisions but it's OK because they'll help you make them. . . . And this has just been amazing to me because you go to the store, and as soon as people find out that you're planning to get married, they just, they bond with you. It's interesting. And I'm real excited about that (Becky, mid-30s).

> I had excellent help at Donny's, and I had excellent help at Monica's. It made a difference to make an appointment. . . . And somebody that doesn't make you feel guilty for trying on eighteen dresses. Saying, "No problem, that is what you need to do." One problem at Monica's was that my appointment lasted longer than what they'd expected. . . . Then I had to share [salespeople], and I don't know how you fix that (Gail, late 20s).

Moreover, when singularization was *not* part of the bride's experience at the salon, the ramifications for the bride—and for her attitude toward bridal retailers—prompted feelings of ambivalence and negativity:

> I guess I wouldn't say that it should be like royalty or anything. That's what I expected it to be, but, you know, at these places you spend a lot of money, and on the prospect that you may buy, you know, an $800 dress . . . I guess that I would expect them to be a little more considerate of me. . . . I guess I didn't feel like I was getting any kind of personal touches. . . . I didn't see any kind of special, out-of-the-ordinary treatment that

separated the store from any other kind of store that I'd had experience with in the past (Diane, early 20s).

> L: There hasn't been anywhere other than where my dress is, that is in awe about a bride. . . . I think they've taken a lot of the joy away from it.
>
> I: What do you mean?
>
> L: . . . Well, I work with the public every day, and they are a nuisance. But yet, I think when you're dealing with a bride or a mother-to-be, or those kinds of special things, that they don't happen that often, and I think people should really go over, overboard with it (Lynn, late 20s).

I went in [to Donny's] and said I wanted to look at headpieces, which I was kind of in the market for. He told me I could not see them. I said, "Well, why not?" He said, "Because we're busy now." And I said, "I'll wait." He said, "No, you can't wait, you can't see the headpieces. Maybe if you come back tomorrow. But I don't know." And I was flabbergasted that this man told me I could not look at something in the store. So I told him I basically didn't think he should be open for business if he couldn't serve his customers, and walked out (Julie, early 20s).

In-Store Singularizing Rituals

One of the ways in which brides experienced singularization was through their participation in rituals within the bridal salon. Moreover, brides often incorporated aspects of the salons' atmospherics into the enactment of these rituals. Likewise, aspects of the store's design could also influence ritual participation in a negative way. In the following examples, observe how atmospherics both enhance and detract from brides' participation in such activities:

> Cheryl . . . decided to try on this dress because she automatically fell in love with it. When she came out of the dressing room, she looked absolutely beautiful with her glasses off. The first place she hurried to was the big mirror that was located next to the veils. While in the mirror, Cheryl was styling her hair . . . pulling her hair up. As her hair was held by her right hand, she asked her mom to bring the veil with the puff to her. As Cheryl was in the mirror, wearing her wedding dress and veil, she was modeling in her dress. She continued turning from

side to side, as well as striking poses. She would also smile and laugh about her actions. . . . Cheryl's bridesmaid joined her in the mirror. . . . As the music was playing, Cheryl and her bridesmaid were dancing together in the mirror in "their dresses."

"This is the dress I can afford," said Gale as she was putting [it] on. . . . While in this dress, Gale was doing the Chicken Dance because of the "flappy sleeves. . . ." She then said, "I forgot about the Hokey Pokey [often danced at receptions]" after her bridesmaid mentioned it. . . . While in the mirror, Gale stated that she felt this dress had a softer look to it. While she was getting off the pedestal, the bottom of her dress got stuck, and she said, "I hate their thing."

Through service in which brides receive the salesperson's undivided attention, and where physical accoutrements facilitate the experience of these special activities, salons can contribute to the process of "contaminating" the wedding with positive sacredness (Belk, Wallendorf, and Sherry 1989), by setting this type of shopping apart from all other types of shopping brides will ever experience. Yet paradoxically, salespeople are expected to individuate the retail experience, while also helping brides to select commodities chosen through mass-media channels laden with one of the most mundane cultural artifacts of all, advertising (Kopytoff 1986).

IMPLICATIONS FOR FUTURE RESEARCH

This study has several implications for consumer researchers and retailers alike. First, the fact that the atmospherics of the bridal salon contribute to the expression of many roles—especially those of the dressing chamber and singularizer—implies that salon managers should pay attention to the ways physical details contribute to, or detract from, consumer socialization and wedding purchasing. Paradoxically, brides apparently desire the convenience and selection available in a superstore but are unwilling to lose the intimacy of the traditional salon that is partially achieved through its atmospherics. Clearly, with new wedding "superstores" discovering that brides still want comfortable amenities and pampering surroundings, it appears that the label of "wedding" still carries more weight (in terms of desired atmospherics) than that of "outlet" in the minds of consumers. However, the ways consumers decide which roles they regard as imperative and which as optional in bridal salons still must be explored.

Moreover, many women regard shopping for wedding gowns as either one of their most exhilarating or one of their most disappointing retail encounters. While this chapter explored the experiences of women who were in the throes of wedding planning, it would be interesting to see if brides' experiences in these salons would remain as part of the narratives they create when recounting their wedding rituals, or whether the boundedness of shopping to the secular world of merchandising and marketing would cause this experience to diminish in significance when brides remember the wedding as an event. Obviously, this issue is important for retailers, because word of mouth is probably as important as (or even more important than) other information sources as brides consider their retail options. This assumption is no doubt particularly true when brides shop for wedding-related artifacts in the same locales as their married family members and friends. One example from the text illustrates this point:

> Donny's has a bad reputation for not following through the way they should have on things. I know specifically of a girl whose wedding dress was . . . almost ruined by [their] people altering it. And Donny's wouldn't fix it or help her out, and she had to take the dress away and find a completely different seamstress like a week before the wedding and have it altered so that it would work. . . . Several of my close friends and family said, "Oh, please don't buy your dress here." I mean, directly, "Don't buy your dress here" (Gail, late 20s).

Thus, the issue of how influential the retail establishment remains in determining brides' overall satisfaction levels with wedding shopping in particular, and their wedding experiences as a whole, should be examined.

A third implication stems from gaining a better understanding of the role of "others" in bridal-oriented retail outlets. As Solomon et al. (1985, 100) observe, "Not all service encounters are simple dyadic relations . . . [some are] more complex and involve a number of different actors." Many, if not most, of our informants were accompanied by family members and friends when selecting their bridal gowns, either on initial trips to the salon or on the crucial trip where a purchase decision was actually made. Some of these cohorts were no doubt what Feick and Price (1987) term "market mavens," or consumers who are sought out as experts in the wedding purchase experience. However, some (such as younger members of the bridal party) could be thought of more directly as being "in training" for their own weddings, and their role was not to dispense advice but to absorb information and offer opinions. Given that the purchase of a wedding dress often involves a large party of patrons and may often involve more than one salesperson, this context offers a rich opportunity to explore the nexus of influence that occurs in this context.

A fourth implication is the importance of exploring how these "purchase pals," such as mothers and other relatives, complement or detract from salespeople's performance in the bridal salon. For example, it appeared that some salespeople attempted to avoid the role of the salesperson-as-dresser when brides were accompanied by friends or family members. It would be interesting to determine how retailers adjust their roles depending upon the quantity and nature of the bride's entourage. For example, one informant remarked that when she went into a bridal salon by herself, no one "took her seriously," but when she returned with her mother, a salesperson immediately offered assistance. Thus, it would be interesting to compare the expectations of brides, purchase pals, market mavens, and the salespeople aiding them, depending upon the nature of the bridal party.

SUMMARY AND CONCLUSION

This chapter offers evidence that often brides enter salons after conducting extensive external information search (via bridal magazines) and/or internal search (tapping into their own vision of their wedding), and that many will actually decide upon their ideal or actual dress before entering the retail setting. During the process of actually purchasing a dress, many brides also peruse and select related merchandise such as jewelry, shoes, bridesmaids' dresses, and tuxedos. Moreover, brides often rely on word of mouth from salespeople, along with the advice of experienced members of their reference groups, to help them select suppliers for items that are not available in the store.

While in the salon, brides expect that shopping for a gown should be different from, and more special than, the type of shopping experience they encounter in other, more mundane retail outlets. Both physical aspects of the store—such as displays, mirrors, and lighting—and salespeople's interaction styles contribute to this singularizing experience. Moreover, brides expect to have some sense from the retailer that they are viewed as special, even if they use the salon only for alterations and storage of the gown.

This chapter therefore contributes to our understanding of the role of the bridal salon by articulating six roles that brides may expect from their experience in the bridal salon. Moreover, salespeople and retail atmospherics both can contribute to the successful expression of these roles. Given that the study of the wedding as consumption ritual in the United States is nascent, it is hoped this chapter will encourage exploration in this area. For as the only significant remaining rite of passage in American culture, the wedding—and the purchasing that accompanies it—is certainly deserving of further attention by researchers in consumer behavior, anthropology, and sociology alike.

BIBLIOGRAPHY

ASSOCIATION OF BRIDAL CONSULTANTS. 1991. "Statistics." New Milford, CT: Association of Bridal Consultants.

ATKINSON, PAUL. 1992. *Understanding Ethnographic Texts.* Newbury Park, CA: Sage.

BAKER, MAUREEN. 1990. "Mate Selection and Marital Dynamics." In *Families: Changing Trends in Canada,* edited by Maureen Baker. Toronto: McGraw Hill Ryerson Ltd., 41–66.

BARKER, DIANA LEONARD. 1970. "A Proper Wedding." In *The Couple,* edited by M. Corbin. New York: Penguin, 56–77.

BELK, RUSSELL W. 1975. "Situational Variables and Consumer Behavior." *Journal of Consumer Research* 2 (December): 157–163.

BELK, RUSSELL W.; MELANIE WALLENDORF; AND JOHN F. SHERRY, JR. 1989. "The Sacred and Profane in Consumer Behavior: Theodicy on the Odyssey." *Journal of Consumer Research* 16 (June): 1–38.

CASPARIS, JOHAN. 1979. "The Bridal Shower: An American Rite of Passage." *Indian Journal of Social Research* 20(1):11–21.

CHARSLEY, SIMON R. 1987a. "Interpretation and Custom: The Case of the Wedding Cake." *Man* 22 (N.S.): 93–110.

———. 1987b. "What Does a Wedding Cake Mean?" *New Society* 81 (July 3): 11–14.

———. 1988. "The Wedding Cake: History and Meanings." *Folklore* 99:232–241.

———. 1991. *Rites of Marrying: The Wedding Industry in Scotland.* Manchester: Manchester University Press.

———. 1992. *Wedding Cakes and Cultural History.* London: Routledge.

CHEAL, DAVID. 1988. "Relationships in Time: Ritual, Social Structure and the Life Course." In *Studies in Symbolic Interaction,* edited by Norman K. Denzin. Greenwich, CT: JAI Press, 83–109.

CURRIE, DAWN H. 1993. "'Here Comes The Bride': The Making of a 'Modern Traditional' Wedding in Western Culture." *Journal of Comparative Family Studies* 24 (Autumn): 403–421.

DODDS, KATHERINE. 1994. "Tales of Love and Money." *Ad Busters: Journal of the Mental Environment* 3 (Summer): 45–47.

DONATON, SCOTT. 1991. "Altar-ations Ahead." *Advertising Age* 62 (September 30): 43.

FEICK, LAWRENCE F., AND LINDA L. PRICE. 1987. "The Market Maven: A Diffuser of Marketplace Information." *Journal of Marketing* 51 (January): 83–97.

FONTANA, ANDREA, AND JAMES J. FREY. 1994. "Interviewing: The Art of Science." In *Handbook of Qualitative Research,* edited by Norman K. Denzin and Yvonna S. Lincoln. Thousand Oaks, CA: Sage.

FRESE, PAMELA R. 1991. "The Union of Nature and Culture: Gender Symbolism in the American Wedding Ritual." In *Transcending Boundaries: Multidisciplinary Approaches to the Study of Gender,* edited by Pamela R. Frese and John M. Coggeshall. New York: Bergin and Garvey, 97–112.

FRIESE, SUSANNE. 1996. "The Function of a Consumer Good in the Ritual Process: The Case of the Wedding Dress." Working paper, University of Hohenheim, West Germany.

GILL, PENNY. 1988. "Here Comes the Bride." *Stores* 70 (April): 12–20+.

GLASER, BARNEY G., AND ANSELM L. STRAUSS. 1967. *The Discovery of Grounded Theory.* Chicago: Aldine.

KOPYTOFF, IGOR. 1986. "The Cultural Biography of Things: Commoditization as Process." In *The Social Life of Things,* edited by Arjun Appaduri. New York: Cambridge University Press, 64–91.

LINCOLN, YVONNA, AND EGON S. GUBA. 1985. *Naturalistic Inquiry.* Newbury Park, CA: Sage.

LOWREY, TINA M., AND CELE OTNES. 1994. "Construction of a Meaningful Wedding: Differences Between the Priorities of Brides and Grooms." In *Gender and Consumer Behavior,* edited by Janeen Costa. Beverly Hills, CA: Sage, 164–183.

————. 1995. "Brides and Their Weddings: What's Advertising Got to Do with It?" Presentation at the 1995 Conference of the American Academy of Advertising, March, in Norfolk, VA.

MAGIERA, NANCY. 1993. "For Couple with Everything, Try Hardware Store." *Advertising Age* 64 (January 25): 27.

McCRACKEN, GRANT. 1988. *The Long Interview.* Beverly Hills, CA: Sage.

McGRATH, MARY ANN. 1990. "An Ethnography of a Gift Store: Trappings, Wrappings and Rapture." *Journal of Retailing* 65 (Winter): 421–449.

McGRATH, MARY ANN, AND BASIL ENGLIS. 1996. "Intergenerational Gift Giving in Subcultural Wedding Celebrations: The Ritual Audience as Cash Cow." In *Gift-Giving,* edited by Cele Otnes and Richard F. Beltramini. Bowling Green, OH: Popular Press, 123–141.

McGRATH, MARY ANN, AND CELE OTNES. 1993. "Communal Exchange in the Context of Intergenerational Giving of Wedding Gifts." Paper presented at the American Marketing Association Winter Educators' Conference, Newport Beach, CA.

MERTON, ROBERT K., AND ELINOR BARBER. 1976. "Sociological Ambivalence." In *Sociological Ambivalence,* edited by Robert K. Merton. New York: Free Press, 3–31.

OTNES, CELE, AND TINA M. LOWREY. 1993. "'Til Debt Do Us Part: The Selection and Meaning of Artifacts in the American Wedding." In *Advances in Consumer Research,* edited by Leigh McAlister and Michael Rothschild. Provo, UT: Association for Consumer Research, 325–329.

OTNES, CELE; TINA M. LOWREY; AND YOUNG CHAN KIM. 1993. "Gift Selection for 'Easy' and 'Difficult' Recipients: A Social Roles Interpretation." *Journal of Consumer Research* 20 (September): 229–244.

OTNES, CELE; TINA M. LOWREY; AND L. J. SHRUM. 1997. "Toward an Understanding of Consumer Ambivalence." *Journal of Consumer Research* (in press).

OTNES, CELE; MARY ANN McGRATH; AND TINA M. LOWREY. 1995. "Shopping with Consumers as Past, Present and Future Research Technique." *Journal of Retailing and Consumer Services* 2 (Spring): 97–110.

OTNES, CELE, AND LINDA M. SCOTT. 1996. "Something Old, Something New: Exploring the Interaction Between Ritual and Advertising." *Journal of Advertising* 25 (Spring): 33–50.

ROOK, DENNIS. 1985. "The Ritual Dimension of Consumer Behavior." *Journal of Consumer Research* 12 (December): 252–264.

SHERRY, JOHN F., JR., AND MARY ANN McGRATH. 1989. "Unpacking the Holiday Presence: A Comparative Ethnography of Two Gift Stores." In *Interpretive Consumer Research,* edited by Elizabeth C. Hirschman. Provo, UT: Association for Consumer Research, 148–167.

SOLOMON, MICHAEL R. 1986. "The Missing Link: Surrogate Consumers in the Marketing Chain." *Journal of Marketing* 50 (October): 208–218.

SOLOMON, MICHAEL R.; CAROL SUPRENANT; JOHN A. CZEPIEL; AND EVELYN G. GUTMAN. 1985. "A Role Theory Perspective on Dyadic Interactions: The Service Encounter." *Journal of Marketing* 49 (Winter): 99–111.

SPRADLEY, JAMES. 1979. *The Ethnographic Interview.* New York: Holt, Rinehart & Winston.

VAN GENNEP, ARNOLD. 1960. *The Rites of Passage.* Chicago: University of Chicago Press.

WALDROP, JUDITH. 1990. "Here Come the Brides." *American Demographics* 12 (June): 4.

WILSON, MARIANNE. 1995. "Wedding Stores Go Big." *Chain Store Age* (October): 31–35.

ZIMMER, MARY, AND LINDA GOLDEN. 1988. "Impressions of Retail Stores: A Content Analysis of Consumer Images." *Journal of Retailing* 64 (Fall): 265–293.

8

FRAMING ART

The Role of Galleries in the Circulation of Art

ANNAMMA JOY

Framing refers to the process of containment, of creating order, of maintaining boundaries, of exclusion and inclusion. When speaking of thinking itself or of the visual arts, the frame (the work) is essential whether the idea or the object is evident or not. The frame protects, regulates, reduces, forces, filters, cuts, and rejects. Framing a work implies a certain imposed direction whereby the viewer is persuaded to discard what is external to the frame and to focus instead on what is made visible (Goffman 1986; Hooper-Greenhill 1992; Ross 1995). It also allows the owner of the artwork to imprint his or her taste on someone else's genius. The frame circumscribes and creates and, in the process of doing so, calls into question the interference with its limits or edges (Becker 1982).

At the very heart of contemporary art today is the bursting of the frame, which assumes many forms from plays on the material frame surrounding a picture to plays on the idea of the museum itself (Joy 1993; Duhaime, Joy, and Ross 1995; Wolff 1993). Frames

Annamma Joy is Associate Professor, Department of Marketing, at Concordia University in Montreal and a visiting scholar in the Department of Marketing, Hong Kong University of Science and Technology, Kowloon, Hong Kong.

reinforce the autonomy of the work. The material object that surrounds the work; the pristine gallery wall or, for that matter, the
baroque setting; the art critic's discourse; or the museum's exhibit—
all guarantee that the work of art remains autonomous. The focus
in this chapter—a play on the idea of the frame—is, at a broad
level, on the space between the work of art and the viewer and,
more specifically, on commercial and parallel art galleries as channels of art distribution.

In particular, the concept of frame brings to the fore the question of ambience and physical space within which the art is exhibited and the context within which sales are made. In the marketing
literature there is much evidence to show that retail environments,
which include music, lighting, spatial arrangement, color, and scent,
significantly affect sales (Bitner 1986, 1990, 1992; Bruner 1990;
Crowley 1993; Milliman 1982; Spranberg, Crowley, and Henderson 1996). Psychologists suggest that people respond to environments with two generally contrasting forms of behavior: arousal
and avoidance. The former is a positive reaction that, from a marketer's perspective, allows the individual to spend more time examining products within retail contexts that are seen as pleasant. A
negative reaction leads to consumers leaving the retail contexts
considered unpleasant (Bitner 1992; Mehrabian and Russell 1974).
While the rituals of space and dispensation of knowledge are essential aspects of the framing process, the ambience and physical characteristics of the environment are central to the presentation of
the art.

The following are some excerpts from interviews with commercial and parallel gallery owners. These vignettes give us a
glimpse of how these types of galleries operate and, more specifically, the concerns of their owners and coordinators.

> Our clients include private collectors, museums, public galleries,
> and corporations. Each client is different based on taste, budget,
> and numerous other factors. Most of them are not interested in
> selling what they own, but rather wish to collect artworks. We
> do not promote aggressively. We encourage interest by provid-
> ing information when it is requested. We do not advertise.
> Reviews of our exhibits, word of mouth, and invitations to

openings are the means by which we inform our clients (Commercial gallery owner who specializes in abstract art).

We are able to buy less now than we were ten or fifteen years ago because many museums have opened up in the United States. Even museums in small cities in the States have their own African art department. The major trade of the art is among the collectors in New York, Chicago, Los Angeles, and other places that are more art conscious. Auction houses such as Christie's and Sotheby's have frequent exhibits and sales of ethnic art. I have people who come in here who say that they would not have this type of art in their house and yet others who have offered me $35,000 (for a rare and carefully crafted sculpture), and I have turned them down. So it is a question of taste, a question of education, a question of having seen things (Commercial gallery owner who specializes in African art).

At the auctions, I can obtain European works at a low price, which is an attractive investment for the gallery. I sometimes buy at auction houses. I also buy to inhibit works from being sold at ridiculously low prices. Because I specialize in prints, I work closely with European and Canadian editors, and I work directly with Quebec artists. When I exhibit their works, there is very little exchange with other local galleries (Commercial gallery owner who specializes in European and Canadian prints).

Visual art is an object not of consumption, but of reflection. It is like theater—it has to support reflection. I am against decorative arts because it confuses people who are not familiar with it. I sell an idea (Commercial gallery owner who specializes in photographs).

When we started out, there wasn't much. I had just noticed there was an interesting movement happening in glass. Glass was taken out of the factory and into the artist's studio. The beginnings were rudimentary, and artists had to fight with the material first. . . . It took a couple of years before the work could be called "art." The more the work is outside the mainstream, the more difficult it is to sell.

We had to maintain the fine craft section, which supports the gallery. We have two sections really: the present show section and the section which is part of the previous shows or works of our artists. Two and a half years ago, we formed another gallery with two associates who promote our artists who have outgrown our gallery because they are working on large pieces that we could not show in our small gallery. For artists who are working with hot glass, the size of our gallery is suitable, rather than for artists who use other materials in combination with glass (Commercial gallery owner who specializes in glass).

When we show young artists, it costs us thousands of dollars. We tell people that we are showing the best from the artist. When they do not buy right away, they have to pay more later because of storage and insurance costs. Sometimes, we buy back works from people or an art gallery, and that adds costs for transport, publicity, and catalogs. If, for instance, a piece of art costs $4,000 and if I choose to put it into the catalog, my costs are astronomical. This is going to be added to the price of the work. That's normal. Sometimes I have only one piece left where before I had ten. Therefore, I will sell it for more to make a profit (Commercial gallery owner who specializes in sculpture).

A considerable challenge is to please all of the artists. All demand equal billing or want several of their works displayed on the ground floor, or in the front window, or, if it is sculpture, maybe even in front of the gallery. All of them want exhibitions, and all want expensive catalogs. It is simply not possible. We must rotate our inventory, and often we are able to display only one work by an artist, since we have hundreds of names in our inventory and thousands of works. During an exhibit, a whole floor or two may be taken by an artist, leaving very little room for other exhibits (Commercial gallery owner who specializes in historical art).

The gallery caters to young, emerging artists as well as artists who are in midcareer, who have established themselves in the art market as well as on the international market. As one of the oldest organizations, we have had time to change and evolve. We have become more creative with the choice of exhibits. The gallery has built a reputation over the years and shows a fair number of established artists. The gallery also enjoys significant support from art critics, art historians, and other art institutions (Parallel gallery coordinator who specializes in paintings).

The gallery was started to give a space to artists to show, and to give the artist a chance to show what she or he chose, and to allow them to display it the way they wanted to. It is a multidisciplinary gallery. There are four rooms where exhibits hang. But, in addition, people who do contemporary dance, music, and theater also use the space. I am heavily involved in the administration of the gallery, and the organization does reflect my vision. I am very concerned about not merely showing dominant voices of artists in society. I am also interested in finding out what the other voices are saying as well (Parallel gallery coordinator who promotes all forms of contemporary art).

The repeated focus of these commercial and parallel art gallery owners on the framing process is critical, since all galleries are links in the circuit that defines art as distinct from all other aspects of society (Pearce 1992). These art institutions delineate the aesthetic as something that is set apart and highlight the creative process that leads to the creation of such artworks (Wolf 1993). Furthermore, galleries serve as vehicles maintaining an elaborate system that includes the creation, circulation, and consumption of art. Artists, curators, art dealers, art critics, art brokers, art banks, museums, and, more recently, corporations all participate in this process. This manuscript endeavors to understand this larger system by examining one of its most important component parts: the act of framing as it is exercised by commercial and parallel art galleries.

To Frame or Not to Frame

Certeau (1988, 17) makes a useful distinction between place and space:

> A place is the order of distribution and of relations between elements of whatever kind; it is an instantaneous configuration of positions. By contrast, space is composed of intersections between mobile elements and is actuated by the ensemble of movements deployed within it.

Space is manifested as the effect produced by the operations that orient, situate, temporalize, and make it function in a unity of conflictual programs or contractual proximities. A space is constantly being transformed by successive contexts and possesses none of the do we see thru ad'g msgs? of today?

how does service/a place is Casino
Servicescapes
support or not the ad'g claims?

stability of place (Delaney 1993). Thus, space can be thought of as a meaningful place.

We hardly think of an art gallery as a space for debate, as a site where differing voices and perspectives can be heard. Yet galleries are spaces rife with critical discourses (Hooper-Greenhill 1992). Like museums, they are places within which the visible is simultaneously contested and made understandable (Stretch 1992). McCracken (1988) defines galleries as way stations within which cultural meaning gets transferred from the artist to the viewer or as vehicles of meaning transfer where the artist is central to the transformative process. McCracken's "culturally-constituted world" is (re)created through critical works by artists, and this reconstruction and interpretation continues aided and abetted by curators and art critics. Galleries, in turn, take these new ideas located in artworks and frame them through exhibition and sales to private or institutional collectors. Furthermore, the educational and research processes conducted by galleries ensure that consumers ultimately accept the new notions they circulate. In the final analysis, galleries are central to the framing and dissemination of new ideas and worldviews in the larger social order.

Yet galleries are similar to museums only in very specific ways. Like museums, they too are social instruments for the fabrication of the social order. And like museums, especially ethnographic and historical art museums, galleries act as repositories of the past through the acquisition, classification, interpretation, and framing of art objects and ethnographic artifacts (Alpers 1991; Bal 1992; Belk 1994; Kelly 1987a, 1987b). Museums frame the past and present it as a preface to the present in a teleological sense. What is most manifested in a museum is the idea of the aesthetic as a "thing" with its own lineage (Baxandall 1991; Duncan 1991). Curatorial interpretation, collection processes, and displays of objects all use the space available to create and recount history—especially the history of art (Alexander 1983). However, unlike museums that evoke a sense of permanency and order, galleries have a more transitory and liminal role to play in the institutionalization of art and the creation of art history.

The entire network of art connoisseurship is a well-defined and well-defended hierarchy of authority, with galleries and museums as the linchpins of the fabrication process that recognizes art as a kind of "thing" separate from all other aspects of society. Galleries and museums both recognize the importance that art has in society, such as the role it plays in symbolizing the nation-state (e.g., Canadian art). Such art is replete with historical narrative. The complicated creation of such a structure is possible only because of the institutional network of circuits that create the trajectory of the artwork. In the final analysis, although the several levels of framing *create* such a grand edifice, the very process of framing itself calls into question the interference with its limits.

Given the foregoing, the critical study of galleries and museums must take into consideration not only the techniques and process of framing, but also all attempts to break away from the frame. In the end, the gallery, like the artwork it presents, subverts the very idea of the frame itself. This subversion is heightened when artworks are displayed in unconventional spaces.

Framing occurs in both formal, designated spaces and in informal, uncircumscribed spaces. Commercial, corporate, parallel, public, and museum galleries and cultural centers are all official spaces perpetuating the idea of the aesthetic as a thing. Even art banks are implicated in this process, because although they do not have official exhibit spaces, they purchase art to be displayed in government offices and buildings. Likewise, auction houses have more recently designated exhibit spaces (set apart from pre-auction displays) in order to attract a new group of collectors (Moulin 1987; Stretch 1994). In contrast to these designated spaces, uncircumscribed spaces are less official and more impromptu spaces such as warehouses, artists' studios, parks, and informal public city spaces temporarily created and used to exhibit works of art. While designated spaces possess formal "power" or status as regular spaces for "showing and seeing" art, these new informal spaces, as alternative circuits, are acquiring more prestige by subverting the process of framing.

This study primarily focuses on commercial and parallel galleries insofar as they play a central role in the framing process. However, from time to time I also make comparisons and contrasts to other formal and informal exhibit spaces.

Methodology

An Index of Galleries

For the purposes of this study, we were able to develop a master index of galleries in the city of Montreal based on various lists that were available to us. At the time of the study, there were 62 galleries in total. (Only commercial and parallel galleries are included in this figure.) We interviewed 52 owners of these galleries. While our aim was to interview them all, a few declined to participate, and the remainder were in the process of moving to new spaces in other cities. Having interviewed more than 80 percent of gallery owners in Montreal, we collected a great deal of information on various aspects of gallery ownership and maintenance that could not be included in this chapter.

This research was conducted over the course of $1\frac{1}{2}$ years and is a part of a larger study on the arts in Quebec. The approach was basically ethnographic and involved participant observation and in-depth interviews. Most of the research was done by the author and a research assistant who is an artist and possesses a master's degree in fine arts. Since this student was familiar with the art community, any queries, assumptions, or issues raised were dealt with immediately as they emerged. Both researchers maintained field notes and field journals, and there was a continuous interaction and development of ideas as they emerged in situ. Thus, triangulation of researchers was possible.

Coming to Terms with "Otherness"

A major issue in ethnographic research involves coming to terms with the "other" and interpreting "otherness." Traditionally, anthropologists have been confronted with otherness through their contact with cultures different from their own. In interpreting these cultures, anthropologists have posited that by defamiliarization, the "self" is made knowable through the other. This conscious attempt to understand "oneself" and "another," implicit in many of the ethnographies, arises out of the conviction that selfhood implies otherness to such an intimate degree that one cannot be thought of without the other (Ricoeur 1992, 3).

In our study, the other is a part of our own society. It is the art world and the artistic community. To the author, in particular, as a person who would like to be associated with art, this community is a world that is still very much "other." Coming to terms with it meant learning new ways of seeing and of experiencing art. Through the help of an assistant who was both "insider" and "outsider" (as researcher), it was possible to come to terms with the art world. Journals were particularly useful in this self-reflective process. Consequently, there is no doubt that constructing a narrative is an ideological process (Foucault 1980).

Narration and Reflexivity

In qualitative studies of this kind, what is observed and studied in situ is translated into field journals and notes, photographs, and audiotapes (Belk, Sherry, and Wallendorf 1988). The sifting of information gathered and the creation of field texts was done entirely by the two researchers. None of these artifacts speak for themselves, and none can be considered outside the context of the persons who shaped them. Over the course of the research, we remained acutely aware of the various types of texts that we had gathered (Joy 1991). These included oral histories, family histories, memories, catalogs, brochures, invitations for vernissages (art openings), conversations with artists, photographs, and other material artifacts. Since art is a valuable product and has a great deal of secrecy attached to it, certain information, such as gallery client lists, was difficult to obtain. However, notwithstanding such minor difficulties, we were able to gather a great store of information central to the design of this text.

Gathering data in the field raises other issues as well. The presence of a researcher can be intimidating and, in many instances, can overpower other voices, particularly the voices of those interviewed. The researcher can selectively present her or his own voice and balance it with the selective presentation of the voices of others (Fine 1994). A particular observation we made was that gallery owners were reticent. Unlike artists and visitors to a museum or gallery, who felt free to talk about their experiences, gallery owners expressed a heightened need for privacy and confidentiality.

Part of the gallery owners' reticence arose out of economic conditions in the art market. The recession of the early 1990s in Canada had a somewhat crippling effect on galleries. Consequently, competition among galleries in the city of Montreal has risen, while galleries outside the city confines, and particularly those overseas, have stressed cooperation as a survival strategy.

Clearly, a choice of whose voice and what message to embellish a text with is central to the legitimacy and credibility of that text. In this narrative, sometimes several quotes from various respondents are used to make a point. At other times, I use a single quote that represents the typical views of various gallery owners or dealers. Supportive documentation from other studies of art or galleries is mingled with the voices and identified as such in the text. Ultimately, as the author, I am the final arbiter of the narrative. Although I try to express the polyphony and the myriad permutations of this interactive process (Joy 1991), authority still rests with me.

Unlike conventional consumer research techniques, which require a priori reasoning and the development of a plan of action, naturalistic inquiry depends on emergent design. The whole concept of the frame and the bursting of the frame arose out of interviews with gallery owners and coordinators of various types of galleries: commercial galleries, auction houses, corporate galleries, public galleries, museums, and parallel galleries. Over the course of 18 months, we saw several exhibits in commercial and parallel galleries and attended many vernissages. Although the main sources of data for this manuscript are drawn from interviews with owners of commercial and parallel galleries, we also spoke with curators, artists, brokers, art critics, and the general public in all of these venues. The idea of the circulation and fabrication of art as a thing emerged from these many conversations and observations. In addition, we discussed our findings with many gallery owners, who offered useful suggestions and criticism. Since privacy and confidentiality were critical, we created pseudonyms for the owners.

FRAMING AND (DE)FRAMING

The Gallery Circuit

- Commercial galleries
- Corporate galleries
- Parallel galleries
- Public galleries
- Museums
- Informal exhibit spaces
- Auction houses

While all the spaces listed have one common mandate—to circulate and exhibit art—each also has other, more specific objectives. Commercial galleries, for instance, have as part of their mandate the sale of art in a manner unlike all other spaces in the circuit. While most of these designated spaces possess their own collections centered on a strategic focus, corporate galleries, owned and administered by corporations under the guidance of art curators, exhibit not only from their own collections (if they have them), but also from curated art. While sales may or may not result from an exhibit, these transactions are negotiated outside the purview of the corporate exhibit space.

The mandate of parallel galleries is different. Even though they do not have their own collection, their primary objective is to diffuse art. Although artworks may from time to time be sold on their premises, the sale of art is not a priority. Parallel galleries derive their major source of income from government funding, the volunteer work of artists, and private fund-raising endeavors.

Public galleries, on the other hand, are officially funded and run by the government (Rothman 1995). They are often associated with community centers or public libraries. Since they do not have their own collections, they exhibit curated art (Crane 1987). The major difference between public galleries and other types is that most of their exhibits are free and open to the public. Museums also exhibit curated art from their own collection or from collections of other museums or art institutes. The sale of art is not part of the museum's mandate, although it is central to the process of establishing value of artworks. Museums are the ultimate exhibit spaces, showing art that has already received acclaim and renown.

Informal exhibit spaces call into question all of the preceding circuits in that they don't have any, and they reject the discourse of all the foregoing spaces, particularly those of art museums.

Finally, auction houses sell art as part of their mandate. Their exhibits have historically been viewed as presale exhibits. However, auction houses have more recently organized exhibits in their own spaces in order to cultivate an art-buying clientele (Moulin 1987; Stretch 1994).

The Gallery as Ritual Space

Commercial galleries may be seen as small businesses operating with an owner/entrepreneur and perhaps one or two assistants. Although they specialize in and sell historical and/or contemporary art, commercial galleries may also sell art from other cultures. As Crane (1987) observes, commercial galleries take considerable risks with the art they own and exhibit because they are pretty much the gatekeepers of art at the entry level. They work closely with galleries and museums in other parts of the world in circulating and establishing the commercial value of artworks and the artist's reputation.

Commercial galleries are not quiet, neutral, open spaces where one can go to see art, nor is "seeing" art a neutral activity. O'Doherty (1976, 24) comments on the gallery as ritual space:

> Some of the sanctity of the church, the formality of the courtroom, the mystique of the experimental laboratory joins with the chic design to produce a unique chamber of esthetics.

Although galleries in general and commercial galleries in particular do not evoke the same sense of awe as museums do, both encourage a particular way of "seeing" and point of view. Indeed, successful galleries have a following composed primarily of individual collectors who have been persuaded by art dealers and/or art critics to "see" in a particular way. Most of these galleries hold a semipermanent collection, although the items in that collection are often up for sale. The collection is regarded as an investment for the future. From the point of view of many art dealers, the later they sell the artworks, the higher their accrued value.

The articulation of objects within galleries works in a fashion that is similar to the museum. Artworks are carefully marked off and culturally designated as special, reserved for a particular kind of contemplative learning experience demanding a special kind of attention (Goldin 1976). Victor Turner (1973, 19) uses the term *liminality* to refer to this. In this sense, the museum metaphor of a temple or shrine is also apropos to some galleries.

In all ritual sites, some kind of prescribed activity takes place. Visitors may see paintings, experience a drama, hear poetry, or listen to music. They may also follow a prescribed route or engage in activities that are appropriate to the site. Similarly, some individuals may use art space more knowledgeably than others because they are more educated in art and know what to do and how to behave around it. The greater the knowledge a client has, the greater the respect the gallery owner confers on him or her. Although the purchase of an artwork confers honor on the client, the high priests of art—gallery owners or dealers, in this instance—participate in the enactment of such rituals through careful manipulation of space, dispensation of critical knowledge, and rites of purchase.

MANIPULATION OF SPACE

A significant element of the manipulation of space within commercial and parallel galleries is the display and articulation of artworks. The organization of space within commercial galleries is designed to maximize sales, although it also mimics a museum. What is at stake is the presentation of the work as a "thing" of art, with a vitality of its own, capable of speaking for itself, and creating the illusion of the "inside" untouched by the "outside" through the framing process. Such an impression of artworks as capable of being judged on their own merit is achieved whether the gallery sells historical or contemporary art and regardless of the type of ambience it creates. However, more recently with exhibits of performing arts, installations, and video art, many galleries involve consumers in the production process. In other words, the simultaneous production and consumption of art occurs within the four walls of a gallery. The "artistic activity or product" thus does not stand by itself, nor is it capable of speaking for itself, as in the instances discussed earlier.

In any given year, between seven and ten exhibits are staged in all categories of galleries identified earlier. Since we identified 62 commercial and parallel art galleries in the city, this roughly amounts to at least 600 exhibits in a given year. These showings include solo, group, intentional, and, on occasion, thematic exhibits. Depending on whether these shows involve historic or contemporary art, galleries exhibit them in site-specific ways.

In Montreal, historical art is sold in galleries that are baroque in appearance and often located in three- or four-story townhouses, each level being allocated to a certain period or designated for art from a particular region or country. These galleries are often air-conditioned, have elaborate alarm systems, and are insured against theft and any form of damage.

Depending on what is displayed, their exhibit spaces may have ornate lighting and other lavish fixtures. Their overall architecture and exterior signage immediately convey to potential customers the impression of exclusive spaces. Indeed, some of these spaces are intimidating to the average customer merely because they are located on a particular street or perhaps beside expensive stores, hotels, or museums. Consider the following excerpt from an art lover:

> I love art, and I love to go to museums and art galleries in any of the cities I visit in the world. However, most of the established galleries in Montreal are located in one part of the city along with the expensive hotels, and of course the fine arts museum. It is rather intimidating to walk into any of these galleries, because you get the impression that it caters only to the very wealthy. The signage on the outside, the alarm systems in operation, the coldness of the exterior, and the lack of activity within the gallery are all barriers to entry as far as I can see.

The art displayed in gallery windows is often a clear indication of what the gallery sells and whom it intends to target. While the overall space may seem cold and alienating to a visitor, the owner often tries to create a cozy atmosphere by separating smaller spaces. The owner of a contemporary gallery in the city had this to say:

> To have the right place to exhibit artworks is at a premium in this city. However, once you have it, you want to set it up in such a way that it will attract the right clientele. Since most of the art I show is contemporary, I try to maximize the viewing space and create an open and friendly environment for viewing the art. My regular clientele are very happy with the spaces I create, but maybe this is not true of one-time visitors.

In the case of galleries that sell historical art, an attempt is made to make the space more like a museum, and in keeping with the new wave in museum thought, the gallery is broken up into more intimate spaces. Within each gallery level, for instance, enclaves are created through the location of room dividers, sculptures, and occasional pieces of furniture. The name of the artist and price are often discreetly identified next to an art object with the understanding that any further information is available upon the client's request. Sometimes these stone-townhouses-turned-galleries have skylights, which add to the charm of their surroundings and bring the outdoors inside.

Many of the commercial galleries selling fine art also have a stable of contemporary artists whose work represents the overall thrust of the gallery. Often the works of these artists are exhibited at the entrance, since these artworks are more accessible both in terms of price and ideas. Once the customer enters the gallery and becomes more familiar with it, then the other spaces (less accessible in terms of price, time, and history) become more accessible under the watchful gaze of the dealer or assistant.

Commercial art galleries selling contemporary art are similar to museums of contemporary art. Their neutral and quiet space mimics that of the museum, where the focus is on the object itself rather than on its context. The main galleries are often long and narrow, sometimes with additional exhibit and office spaces. The lighting is simple, functional, and discreet. Even though the art is often large and may fill up the gallery, the emphasis on its presentation is often minimal.

As short-term measures to guarantee long-term survival, many of the less-established commercial galleries also have sections reserved for selling smaller pieces (e.g., less expensive Inuit or Native American art and sculpture) or for custom framing in order to supplement their total revenues.

Many of the commercial art galleries sell on consignment, although many special contracts are drawn between the respective galleries and the stable of artists themselves. Selling art at the best of times is a difficult proposition, but during the years in which this study was done, it was especially hard. Thus, many gallery owners had to do outside consulting jobs in the field of art in order to survive.

To survive in the art world, many galleries were also nationally and internationally connected through mutually beneficial networks. Artists who were shown in various locations because of these arrangements thus received national and international exposure, so collectors came from cities other than Montreal. International and national exposure thus allowed artists to become established and acquire recognition. One artist who was interviewed for this art project observed:

> When I was younger, my mother's friends would buy my work. Then A. Y. Jackson [a well-known Canadian artist] bought one of my paintings. I thought this was incredible. Then, soon after, I sold a painting to the Vancouver Art Gallery. There is a whole mechanism for hitting the market. I sell a lot through international shows. More recently I have been working with art consultants. I am also in the Dominion Gallery, but I sell in smaller ones on the outskirts of the city. I used to be represented in well-established galleries such as Waddington and Martel. I left them only because I felt that they were not representing me as much as they could. I am also represented in galleries in other provinces in Canada, and I have had successful shows in Europe as well.

Parallel galleries, as their name suggests, are alternative circuits for artists to be seen and shown. First and foremost, they are research centers whose primary goal is to disseminate art. By their very mandate, they are subversive spaces because they show avant-garde art regardless of whether the works or the artist become known. They therefore consciously efface the framing process by questioning what is "contained" or what is "inside." They act as a check and balance in the circuitous system of institutions that fabricate art as a "thing." Moreover, they counteract the framing process carried out by commercial galleries, museums, and other exhibit spaces with the exception of informal exhibits. By virtue of being situated somewhere between museums and commercial galleries, parallel galleries question and subvert totalizing notions of cultural coherence, wholeness, and fixity. Their liminal status gives them the power and flexibility to define and reconstruct what is acceptable in art and within art circles. By showing political and controversial art, they subvert the established categories and inject new ones into the system.

Parallel galleries are generally owned and controlled by artists, who decide what is to be exhibited or performed within their space. Unlike museums, these artist-owned galleries are more avant-garde and risk-taking in their endeavors and are at least five to ten years ahead of other commercial galleries and museums respectively. As one commercial gallery owner ruefully admitted, "They [parallel galleries] were showing installations in the eighties which are only being currently sold in galleries." In addition, parallel galleries coordinate the research activity of their center and make it available to the public. They also participate in other diffusion programs, which may include the publication of books, articles for art magazines, and other related materials.

Parallel galleries are seen as the beginning rung for an artist, providing visibility for his or her work, which may eventually be exhibited in commercial spaces. The first step in establishing artist status is to be "seen," and this is what parallel galleries encourage:

> We have a particular place in the art market. We are a market without a market. Although we are not the establishment, yet we feed into established practices by being an involuntary supplier for commercial art galleries and eventually museums (Parallel gallery owner).

Due to the funding limitations of many parallel galleries, their exhibit spaces are not as attractive as those of museums, auction houses, and corporate or commercial gallery spaces. However, by being located close to other parallel galleries or contemporary art museums, these galleries have carved out a special and more collective space for themselves in the city. In terms of the actual availability and use of space and fixtures, they are akin to informal exhibits and public galleries.

DISPENSATION OF CRITICAL KNOWLEDGE

Galleries use many vehicles—vernissages and retrospectives, techniques of establishing value, relationships developed over the years with artists, and their strategic orientation—to dispense critical knowledge.

Vernissages and Other Public Events

Vernissages, or art openings, are held in all types of galleries with some minor variations. In commercial galleries focusing on historical art, they take place in the open space near the entrance, and a festive ambience is created with refreshments, fresh flowers, and ushers. In sharp contrast to parallel galleries, where Saturday afternoons are often reserved for vernissages and where children and adults are allowed to amble through the exhibits, commercial galleries discourage such a relaxed mode of viewing. Since they discourage children and limit attendance to those who have been invited (with fancy and expensive invitations), visitors tend to be either single men and women or couples.

Furthermore, since vernissages are held in the evening, they are seen as formal events requiring relatively formal attire and reserved behavior. Champagne or wine and cheese also add to the formality of the evening. On numerous occasions, we observed the dealer and his assistants conversing with as many guests as possible and often encouraging them to sign their name and provide an address for future invitations. Visitors primarily include private collectors, art critics, art dealers, brokers, curators, art students, and socialites who like to be associated with art.

Vernissages at commercial galleries selling historical art are occasions as much for being seen as for seeing. These events often bring visibility to the artist. Although colorful brochures with reproductions of selected works and excerpts from art critics are made available to interested viewers, the art provides a background against which social interaction occurs. More serious collectors and clients may have a preview or decide to take a more considered look at the artwork after the vernissage.

In commercial galleries selling contemporary art, vernissages are less flamboyant events often attended by a more specialized clientele of artists, art students, and art critics.

In parallel galleries, on the other hand, vernissages are seen as celebrations for the artist and occasions to invite the artists' friends. Often, the parallel gallery assumes the cost of printing the invitations and providing refreshments to guests. Vernissages are informal gatherings and are often held on Saturday afternoons, when entire families are welcome to participate and enjoy.

Vernissages in public galleries are similar to those in parallel galleries. In corporate galleries, vernissages are more formal events, closer to those held in commercial galleries and museums.

From time to time, commercial galleries also organize retrospectives of locally and internationally renowned artists. Dissemination is the primary motive of these showings, and sales often follow. The more prominent the artist, the greater the likelihood of a gala opening designed to attract a wide range of art critics and customers. Collectors who donate works of a specific artist for such occasions gain visibility through brochures and through the critical discourse that follows such a retrospective. Not surprisingly, the value of the works for sale is commensurate with the artist's reputation.

In the case of galleries specializing in a particular form of art (e.g., glassworks), a retrospective may be organized primarily to make people aware of this specific art form. One gallery owner who sells artworks had this to say:

> The Ontario Craft Council in Toronto made a big retrospective of glass ever since its inception as an art form [glass being a more recent form] and invited us to participate. For them, we put together a list of where the pieces have ended up including slides, addresses, and information, which creates an important feedback. Eighty percent of the gallery's work has nothing to do with direct sales; it is making people aware and collaborating wherever there is a readiness for promoting our artists.

Finally, most contemporary art galleries belong to the Association of Contemporary Galleries, from which they derive certain privileges as a result of working collectively. For example, once a year, the association organizes a large exhibit in which many contemporary art galleries participate. According to one contemporary art dealer, the annual exhibit "is not only getting bigger and more important every year, but now includes galleries from Toronto and from parts of western Europe as well."

Establishing the Value of Artworks

According to Pesando (1993b), the last fifty years have seen an unprecedented surge in art prices, and the price of artworks seems to have risen with an increase in the wealth of collectors. As Pesando's research (1993a, 1,375) demonstrates, it is not a coincidence that auction prices for artworks such as van Gogh's *Sunflowers* rose during a decade of unprecedented global stock investment. However, wealth is not the only arbiter for the price of artworks. Taste also is significant. Lamont (1992) argues that taste is cultivated and controlled through appropriate institutions and socialization. The globalization of art markets not only aids in developing strong international segments based on taste, but also is central to the rise in prices of artworks within these environs (Barker 1994).

The pricing of more historical works is often determined by the amount paid at previous auctions or for works of similar quality. If prices rise due to collector preferences, gallery prices also will rise. However, pricing is not primarily within the dealer's control, but rather depends on the value created in the art market. Quite often, the dealer relies on art historians, art critics, and, of course, her or his own knowledge of art history in order to set prices (Moulin 1987). However, the criteria for evaluating works are far from consistent.

In the pricing of contemporary art, demand and supply affect the prices of the art objects that are traded. According to Frey and Pommerehne (1989), the number of works produced by a living artist can be increased by further production, but it certainly depends on the cost of producing an artwork as well. The expectation of future prices will also affect the production process. Another factor in the calculation of costs is the raw materials used. The raw materials necessary for certain kinds of art such as sculptures are costlier than for paintings, although if materials such as gold dust are used in painting, then the cost of producing a painting is high as well. Other costs, including publicity and the promotion of the artist by specific galleries, add to the total costs and are recovered through higher prices. On the demand side, the income of the individual buyer and the predisposition of people to buy art are important. Likewise, artworks that have been recognized by art critics and art connoisseurs will attract more buyers and, therefore, command higher prices.

In the case of more contemporary art sometimes sold by these same galleries, the dealer has more discretion. Dealers often decide whether to sell art objects immediately or to hold them in inventory. Not surprisingly, some of their immediate considerations include the gallery's existing holding, its cash reserves, and the quality of the work itself. When these strategic concerns are evaluated, one finds that it is often advantageous for dealers to have been in business over generations because the family acts as a buffer against the tides of good fortune and misfortunes. In general, the larger the collection, the greater the capital reserves and the dealer's flexibility to acquire important collections as they enter the market.

While some of these galleries have permanent collections, most have art on consignment. The typical contractual agreement between the gallery and the artists exhibited may provide for a fifty-fifty or sixty-forty split on sale proceeds. Although their primary mandate is to sell art, contemporary galleries are also concerned with diffusing and promoting their artists both locally and internationally, since sales follow from the diffusion process. As one gallery owner observed:

> What we have been working on in the last four years is on exporting art. . . . We have gained exhibits for our artists in New York, Paris, and other major cities. Exporting art overseas builds the collectors' confidence in us and makes for sales.

Competition is especially fierce in the contemporary art segment because the demand for art in Montreal is limited in relation to its supply. As one dealer remarked:

> In Montreal, this is a small sector, and therefore if it is not active, it will become stagnant and dangerous for us. We have to think up new strategies, whether it means we associate with a New York gallery or not. I think New York is easier because of the proximity and similarity in cultural taste. Since Toronto is gaining in strength, Montreal will suffer the consequences.

Due to the intensity of the competition, contemporary art gallery owners fear and resent the activities of parallel galleries. One of them vociferously proclaimed:

> Parallel galleries were created at the beginning of the seventies to show experimental work because commercial galleries did not at that time exhibit installations. But in the last five years, they are doing what we are doing—exhibiting works that can be sold. I am against this because the government funds them. They do not work with artists in the long term and do not promote their artists as we do. Besides, they have more money than we do for such purposes. Their role should be different.

Finally, according to several contemporary art gallery owners, the pricing of artwork also depends on the amount of risk assumed by collectors. Gallery owners noted that Canadian collectors will take lower risks than their American counterparts. The lower the risk, the lower the possibility of circulating the artwork and promoting the artist's name. According to one dealer:

> In the United States, there is more opportunity for artwork to be invested several times, whereby a market will be created and its value will rise. Every time you resell the art, a supplementary value is added. In Canada, a collector will store it for years, and it will eventually end up in a museum. Whether it is donated or sold, the work would not have been seen for at least ten years. The biggest challenge is to encourage the collector to play with his or her acquisitions, whether it is to put works in the auction houses or to resell them. The goal is to make these objects circulate so that the artist can climb with his or her works as well.

Relationship to the Artist

Most commercial art dealers who had a stable of artists (fifteen to twenty at any one time) were very clear about their relationship to these artists. They made frequent studio visits, and most of them paid the artist to create a portfolio of work. One commercial art dealer described this close relationship as follows:

> They show me what they know and how they work. We teach each other. They direct me, and I direct them. We exchange ideas.

Several of the dealers interviewed echoed these sentiments.

Their impact on the artist is subtle but effective. While dealers all claim not to interfere with the creative process, the artist's interpretation of the dealer's recommendations often benefits both parties:

> I exhibit artists that I believe in, whom I personally like, and who will sell. I have created an image for the gallery through the works I exhibit, and my objective is to take work on consignment and receive 40 percent on the selling price. This is not based on a strict contract between the artist and me but by an informal verbal agreement. I am interested primarily in

professional artists who are capable of producing (Dealer specializing in prints).

Since the relationship between the gallery and the artist is, in many instances, a long-term one, it is in the interest of the gallery to make the artist's work more exportable. Consequently, many contemporary galleries have links with other galleries or museums overseas, mostly in Europe. The more international shows the artist participates in, the greater the value his or her works acquire. The circuit in which art objects move is thus central to their acquisition of value.

Sometimes the relationship between the artist and the gallery sours and comes to a painful halt. However, this closure opens up a slot for a newcomer wishing to be associated with a particular gallery:

> We generally subsidize the well-being of the artist, but we have sometimes ended up with artists who do not compromise at all. I found contracts for a sculptor, but he refused. After that, I found a contract for a painter. He even had carte blanche. But he also refused because he did not like the building. You cry, and then you make your personal blacklist. You tell yourself that these people [artists] live on grants and not on their sales (Parallel gallery coordinator).

In the case of galleries specializing in art from other cultures, the relationship with the artist is replaced by the relationship with other galleries or cooperatives selling this kind of art or with collectors who are knowledgeable about these forms of art:

> I go back to Vancouver once or twice a year. A lot of the native artists live in and around Vancouver and Victoria because that is where the market is. It is the same way that famous artists gravitated to Paris in the early part of the 1900s because that was where it was happening. I buy from anywhere where I can get credible pieces for a good price. I pick out every piece in the gallery. You cannot always buy from the artist (Dealer who sells North West Coast Indian art).

This view is echoed by another owner, who goes on trips lasting two to six weeks in order to pick the best for his clients in Montreal:

We try to get as close to the source as possible, to come into contact with the local indigenous people. In a country like Tanzania, they still have authentic pieces. When they know I am in town, they'll come to see what I say about a piece. I am constantly upgrading my knowledge, going to New York and Paris to speak with the experts there. The more you learn, the more you appreciate quality (Owner of gallery that specializes in African and Southeast Asian masks and artifacts).

Strategic Orientation

As noted earlier, commercial galleries may be classified as small businesses. Crane (1987, 111) observes, "Many of them are innovators because they have to take risks." They make the initial contacts with the artists, and with these chosen few, they organize exhibits in the absence of any critical appraisals by art critics, curators, or other dealers. This is particularly important in the case of avant-garde art, where the absence of other judgments can either make or break the risk taker.

Gallery owners scour the art studios for new styles and new talents. Without some form of exposure, artists rarely reach a wider audience. Without an exhibit, they cannot enter the circuit. Without entering the circuit, they cannot have a trajectory within which their work can be evaluated. And without an appraisal, they can hardly expect to have their work collected by either individuals or institutions.

As Appadurai (1986, 5) notes, we have to follow the things themselves, for their meanings are inscribed in their forms, their uses, and their trajectories. Ultimately, things-in-motion illuminate the human and social context. The trajectory is outlined by a successful artist in the following manner:

> I have been one of the lucky ones, and I have managed to sell—
> mostly to museums. Just lately, collectors are buying, but I am a
> museum artist, although not through choice. Belonging to a
> gallery association has also helped. You first show in galleries,
> and museum curators and art critics go to see the art in galleries. This is something that a young artist needs to do. The
> first big jump from being a student or an apprentice is to have

exhibitions—group or solo. So you have a string of exhibitions for many, many years, and then you finally get noticed. Only then will museums buy.

When I first came from Paris to Montreal, I had an exhibit at one of the university galleries. Then I began to show in established commercial galleries. I also have a gallery in Paris. It takes many exhibitions before you are recognized outside of your city or country. This is the next step for an artist—to be known internationally. More recently, I have received awards from the government as well as been consigned to create public pieces.

It is also a highly political thing—recognition depends on how many people you know, the power these people have in the world of art and so on. There is no question that there are *rites de passage* for every artist, and galleries play an important role in this transition.

Research has shown that in addition to an artist's style, the aesthetic evaluation is influenced by an artist's ouevre, or his or her artistic capital stock accumulated over time. Roughly speaking, this corresponds to the achievements of the artist as represented in a curriculum vitae. The greater the number of one-person or group shows, the presence of the artist's work in public and private collections, and the number of awards or forms of recognition that the artist has gained, the greater his or her reputation will be.

Frey and Pommerehne (1989) state that holding a steady reputation over a period of time is more valuable to an artist than gaining a high level of publicity. Further, the flexibility and versatility of an artist to work in different kinds of media, such as sculpture, painting, and graphics also enhances the reputation of the artist. Finally, the selling prices that have been achieved over a period of time signal the value of the artist as well.

Byrstyn (1989) also provides insight into the workings of galleries. She categorizes them broadly as those which encourage invention and those which encourage innovation. The first type is involved with the individual artist and nurtures the creative potential of artists. The second type encourages promising artists into the market and then promotes them heavily. The first type of gallery she further classifies as a cultural institution and the latter as an economic institution. Further, the first type of gallery acts as a gate-keeper and determines which artist has most potential. Once the artist has crossed over, then the second type of gallery markets his or her work. In the former, according to Byrstyn, there is a greater turnover of artists than in the latter.

Crane (1987, 113) argues that the second type of commercial gallery generally uses the following three strategies to succeed in the marketplace:

1. It increases the differentiation between its products and those of other sellers.
2. It increases the visibility of its products.
3. It establishes a leadership role in the market by its sheer size or its ability to represent the most prestigious and visible artists.

The pricing of art is another strategic concern. The absence of historical establishment of value makes contemporary art a high-risk venture. In contrast, galleries that sell historical art have an established measure to evaluate the artwork. Auction houses help in the determination of market value and facilitate the upward spiral of both objects and their value.

Most dealers do not consider the sale of art as akin to the sale of soap or automobiles. Any attempt to adapt the strategies applicable to the sale of commodities to the field of art is held suspect. Instead, more established galleries apply what Crane (1987) refers to as gatekeeping functions. These galleries typically represent artists who are successful—those who have had retrospectives and whose works are already included in private and public collections. To get there, however, galleries have had to assume risks and were the first, in terms of market entry, to "show and sell." They were also the first to initiate the acquisition of pedigree by the artwork. Establishing pedigree involves knowing previous owners and also the exhibits and publications in which the artwork has appeared, the sales at which the artwork has changed hands, and the prices paid at each transfer.

In addition to the foregoing strategies, commercial galleries, in particular, aim to encourage and show more international art. As one dealer said,

> I try to visit as many artist studios in as many cities and countries as possible. This constant monitoring of the world market allows one to evaluate what one is doing and helps one to prioritize.

For galleries that specialize in art from other cultures, such as African art, a strategy that works well is establishing a reputation and constant exchanges with specialists in New York and Paris:

> Our reputation is the most important factor. We are not aiming at making a quick buck; a long-term strategy is more important. We guarantee the authenticity of the items we sell. There's a certain approach required if you want your contacts to be fruitful. Though there are not too many collectors in the city, those that do are those who have developed a passion, who fall in love with ethnographic art, which they find exotic and intellectually stimulating (Owner of gallery selling African art).

Contemporary art galleries likewise monitor the art world very carefully. Many of them noted the difficulty not so much in making a sale as in diffusing and promoting the artist:

> What we have been working on in the last four years is exportation, which is difficult since we do not have a large external market for Canadian art and we are not strong enough to develop a demand. But we have managed to get exhibitions for our artists in New York, Paris, London, and other major cities. We travel to these places at least three times a year. Exporting [exhibiting internationally] on an international level builds our collectors' confidence in us because the artist goes outside the country (Contemporary art dealer).

Many of these dealers have masters' degrees in fine arts and are involved in various research on contemporary art forms. As one dealer noted:

I am the best one suited to make the choice of the artist and the artworks. I am the one who would know, because I see the works first, and I am the one who is best placed to decide. I do the promotions for the artist, and I can tell if an artist will succeed or not. Also, I cannot have too many collectors because I do not have enough production. In order [for me] to have a large clientele, my artists would have to produce many little pieces so that I can sell easily.

Parallel galleries consider greater collective efforts among themselves as essential to their future survival. They see themselves mainly as art centers, centers for research and documentation, with their primary mandate being to exhibit new and emerging artists:

Our first project is to move to a new location and stabilize a center for production, i.e., a multidisciplinary center for women with facilities for video shows and rehearsal space for performers—musicians, dancers, and actors. We also need to consider the myriad ways in which new technology affects art (Coordinator of a center specializing in women's art).

Since "buy now and sell later" is a strategy frequently used by successful art galleries, many commercial galleries hold large collections. Yet not many wish to show pieces or even sell from their collection, since the later they sell the artworks, the higher the value these pieces acquire. As one dealer noted:

We are not selling our collection right now, although we could. I know there are a few artists I could sell right now because it is time. However, if a collector walked in and was interested in a particular piece, I might be tempted to sell.

Many corporate galleries have collections associated with their establishment. The purchase of these collections is evaluated by a corporate committee, on the recommendation of art curators. In times of corporate financial crisis, many such galleries have gone under, only to resurface at later, brighter points in the corporation's history. Budgetary constraints have also affected other galleries. Since public galleries receive funding from the provincial and municipal governments, their survival is based on the indebtedness and cutback policies of these levels of government. While many of them have survived such economic ravages, they continue to operate on very limited budgets. Museums also have suffered budget cutbacks and have had to reduce their exhibits, their expenditures on artworks, and so on. As a result, many have chosen to promote blockbuster shows in order to subsidize other shows that might not appeal to the general public (Duhaime, Joy, and Ross 1995; Cooper-Greenhill 1992; Pearce 1992; Walsh 1992).

RITES OF PURCHASE

Since art is viewed as something set apart from all other productive activities in society, the techniques of selling art do not resemble the usual mechanisms by which goods and services are bought and sold in the marketplace. This is evident in the way art is viewed as a special product, the links galleries have with other galleries and with auction houses, and the type of visitors or clients that they encourage.

Art as Product

Most of the gallery owners and coordinators we interviewed referred to the importance of diffusing art, and those of commercial galleries in particular recognized the significance of marketing techniques. However, all of them unequivocally stressed the importance of differentiating art from all other products. While this is no surprise, the significant contributions institutions such as museums and art galleries make to the existence of such a thing as "art" is brought to the fore (Hirschman 1988). In a sense, what all these art factories perpetuate is the idea of the aesthetic as a thing and the spirit of craftsmanship. As one dealer noted:

> A work of art cannot be treated like other products. I choose every piece that is exhibited here, and ultimately I am the final arbiter of what this gallery shows and sells. I do not always buy

and show what will sell. Art is important to our culture; it is one of the essential traces of our culture after we have gone.

Even when the art objects refer to the banal and commonplace objects of consumption such as the soup cans in Warhol paintings, they are still set apart by the discourse of art. As Schroeder (1996, 9) observes, "Campbell's brand has meaning apart from that of a heavily advertised consumer product, because of Warhol's art and ensuing fame. . . . Through his international success, Andy Warhol became a major 'brand' himself."

In parallel galleries where sales are not central, art is truly celebrated. These galleries are committed to showing art that may not even be marketable:

> Art is more poetic, more mysterious. It confronts the individual to make an effort to understand it. It is not a practical object. I think it is necessary to lead a balanced life. You can buy a beautiful toothbrush, but it will always remain a toothbrush. You buy art for intellectual and aesthetic value. You also buy art because it is a good investment. That is not a sin (Coordinator of a parallel gallery).

Links with Other Galleries

Most dealers and coordinators spoke a great deal about their formal and informal links with other galleries and museums. While sometimes these links simply involve an exchange of information or a collaboration with others in order to mount a show, at other times there are also formal links through associations representing both commercial and parallel galleries. Furthermore, when a client is looking for a particular work, the dealer may research the object's availability and make an arrangement with the gallery that has the work in order to sell it to the client. All three parties will benefit from such an exchange.

For commercial galleries, continued linkages with their equivalents in other parts of the country or worldwide is essential for keeping abreast of the creation and circulation of value when objects are sold, for international collaborations, and for sales abroad. As noted earlier, contemporary galleries participate in international art fairs such as the one held annually in Germany. They also show foreign artists in their own exhibit spaces. As one dealer observed:

> We sell foreign artists very well. Already we have sold two pieces [referring to the current exhibit], and the exhibit has not yet begun. At the last show three years ago, we sold everything from the same artist.

Links to Auction Houses

Gallery dealers have differing opinions about the relative importance of auction houses in establishing art value. Commercial dealers were particularly negative about the impact of such institutions. Many commercial dealers, especially those who did not see their galleries as gatekeepers, felt that the art market was inflated because of auctions, regretfully acknowledging that at such auctions, artworks are sold for at least three to four times the price they go for in commercial galleries. Unlike auction houses in major cities such as London, Paris, and New York, auction houses in Montreal are fairly conservative and trade only in historical works. One dealer bemoaned the influence of auction houses: "Auction houses have created a monster—they are merchants. I will never give any of my gallery collections to be auctioned."

Types of Visitors or Clients

The type of clientele varies with the type of gallery and the art being shown and sold. Almost all commercial galleries identified two basic categories of clientele: the private collector and the institutional collector. Almost all these galleries also cited other types of clients, such as other art dealers and brokers, the general public, auction house representatives, and museum curators. In general, most commercial galleries preferred to focus on private collectors, although they did have dealings with clients from other categories.

Parallel, public, corporate, and museum galleries all target the general public. Since sales are not an important concern, reaching a wider audience allows them to diffuse art. Also, since parallel galleries act as research centers making resources available to the general public, their outreach effort is directed at the general public, with the artist and artist-oriented subsegment being a special focus.

Although collectors have multiple motives for purchasing art, general distinctions can be made between those who wish to be surrounded by aesthetic objects and those who see art acquisition as an investment opportunity (Belk et al. 1991). According to many dealers, most private collectors want to buy a name (a renowned artist) rather than the actual work because they know the artist is or is expected to become famous. Once these individuals know what to collect, they tend to request the most interesting and strongest piece made by the particular artist. Following this, collectors will research art, acquiring information by scouring newspapers and magazines or by talking to other dealers or art critics and historians. In general, experienced collectors begin to specialize in a few artists. While they may purchase larger pieces by preferred artists, they will also look into buying a little of everything from younger artists.

All in all, collectors wish to acquire a collection that is strong and, to some extent, specialized (Pearce 1992). The longer the collector is in the business of acquiring art, the more of a specialist he or she becomes. As one dealer explained:

> In private collections, there has to be a great deal of trust—it is a person-to-person dealing. It is you and the collector. At first it is a long process, because confidence has to be established between the client and the dealer. If, for instance, the private collector wants to buy works from a particular artist, he will look at other exhibits as well. You cannot sell under pressure; you are not selling an automobile, but a symbolic object with aesthetic and artistic value. Word gets around, and you lose your credibility if your collectors do not trust you.

When it comes to art from other cultures, visitors or collectors start with the familiar—something that they can recognize and begin to understand (Dobrovik 1993):

> The people who come in to buy African art are generally people who have, in the first instance, been struck by a particular

piece in a museum or elsewhere and who became intrigued by
it. They then start looking at these objects more carefully and
gradually become collectors. This art, unlike other forms of art,
does not redeem itself instantly. It's like a beautiful person—
you have to get close to it to know it. This is what happens to
a lot of visitors. They look around, hoping to see something
that they like, but it does not happen. It depends on how perceptive the person is and how curious they are to understand,
for instance, why the legs are short and the body so elongated
in a sculpture, or why the head is so large in proportion to the
rest of the body. It is like opening a door to a new experience
(Dealer specializing in African art).

Corporate collections are a more recent phenomenon in
Canada. They have only been around in the last thirty years (Joy
1993). Quite often, corporations specialize in contemporary Canadian art because the government encourages these collections
through tax breaks and other incentives. Some corporations also
have international collections. While corporations seem to hold safe
and uncontroversial pieces, the act of exhibiting art has a subversive
character because of the possibility of providing a venue for some
form of social or political critique (Joy 1993).

On the whole, however, a private collection is more risky and
challenging than a corporate one. While some dealers feel that corporate collections are just one more link in the circuit of diffusing
art, many others are skeptical about the value of such art. For private collectors, acquisition is a passion, not just an investment. The
private collector is preoccupied with the artist's name and career
and does not quit following up on the artist he or she is collecting.
Corporate collections, on the other hand, are less avant-garde and,
as in a museum, are usually managed by a curator. But, unlike
museum collections, corporate ones do not tell the history of art.
While adopting the role of a museum or a parallel gallery, corporate galleries have had to abide by company policies and project the
company's image. They may display contemporary art, but these
shows have to conform to a specific frame defined by the company's activities and corporate image.

From time to time, the company's art collection may be shown
in the gallery. Such an intimate connection between collection and

exhibit mimics the role of the museum. Corporate gallery curators, like those in other galleries, work closely with the artist in presenting his or her art work:

> Just yesterday an artist dropped by to talk about a proposal for an exhibit. I was completely seduced by the project and accepted it. The artist worked for three to four years, and the works were very good—both intellectually stimulating and emotionally satisfying. We worked very closely with him. He helped in the installation and lighting of the exhibit. He was there all the time and worked with every detail (Curator of a corporate gallery).

Corporate galleries, like others in the city, prepare the promotional materials and assume the cost of the show. A vernissage is held for every exhibit, and a large number of people from the business and art worlds are invited. The exhibits also draw people off the street. A corporate gallery curator proudly noted, "Since art is not sold on the premises and since we are not a museum, we are not so intimidating."

CONCLUSION

Art galleries, like museums, are central institutions in the circulation and exhibition of art. Through the circuitry of valuable objects, they contribute to the fabrication of the social order. Along with artists, curators, dealers, and art critics, they isolate and highlight the sanctity of the aesthetic as a "thing" separate from the rest of society yet with close links to other objects in a society, and they underscore the importance of skills and techniques necessary to the creation of such sacred and profane objects.

Galleries have a long history of participating in the creation and transformation of the culturally constructed world. The entire edifice of art connoisseurship is a well-defined and defended hierarchy of authority in which galleries and museums are assigned responsibility for recognizing the intrinsic beauty of masterpieces and others among us are expected to agree and to follow. While galleries do not have the same clout that museums do, they are seminal in the creation of such an illusion.

While all art institutions play a role in the creation of such an edifice, their specific mandates vary. The framing process I have described is represented conceptually in Figure 8.1. This paper examined more closely the similarities and differences between commercial and parallel art galleries. As noted earlier, parallel galleries stand in structural opposition to the commercial gallery. In essence, commercial galleries have as their mandate the sale of art, unlike parallel galleries, whose primary goal is to diffuse art. Consequently, commercial galleries create an ambience that implicitly promotes the sale of art while explicitly trying to mimic the museum. The display of artworks and the organization of exhibits all follow along the lines of the museum displays, although neither considers "seeing art" as a neutral activity.

Parallel galleries, while closer to the idea of a museum in terms of circulating art, nevertheless differ from the museum in terms of the risks they assume with the art they display. The act of showing

FIGURE 8.1   A Conceptual Model of the (De)framing Process

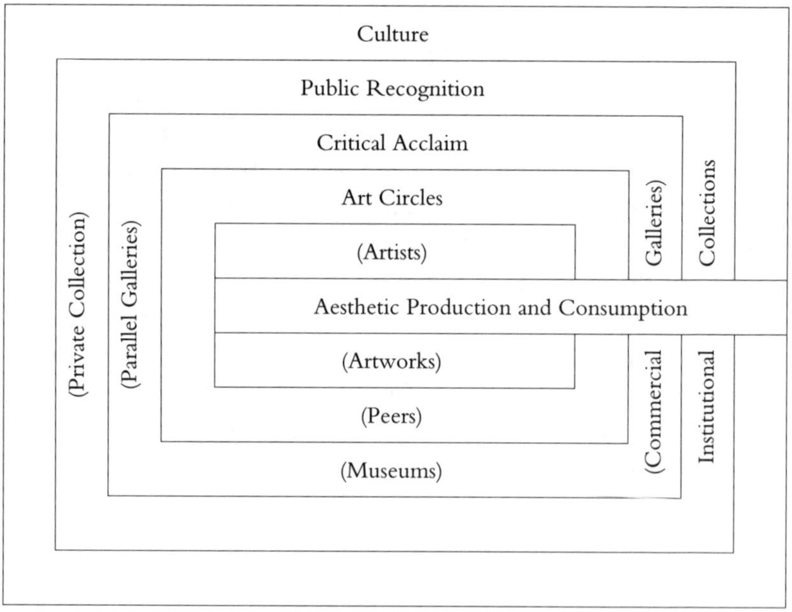

is more critical than what is being shown, and artists who gain a foothold in the system have a greater chance of survival and of building their reputation. While recognizing their role as suppliers to commercial galleries, parallel galleries question and subvert totalizing notions of cultural coherence and counteract the framing process carried out by museums and commercial galleries.

Another distinction between commercial and parallel galleries is manifested in the ways in which both organizations hold vernissages. Commercial galleries have openings that hope to establish the currency of the artist, with sales as the primary motive; parallel gallery vernissages celebrate the work of the artist and include the artist's family and close friends in this celebration.

Further, the pricing of artworks varies according to whether the art is historical or more contemporary. The former involves less discretion on the part of the dealer because gallery prices reflect previously established prices of artworks in the market (Crane 1987). Commercial galleries promote particular artists and develop long-term relationships with them in the hope that both parties will benefit financially from such an exchange. Parallel galleries, uninterested in the sale of art, do not promote any one artist, but rather facilitate the creation of specific trends in art which eventually lead to the popularity of particular art styles and, consequently, to the sales of such artworks.

The strategies adopted by most commercial galleries include differentiating their products from those of other sellers, assuming high risks in terms of establishing new styles in the marketplace, promoting international standing, and exporting their artists worldwide. Parallel galleries help to create an art style because they are the first exhibit space to promote a particular artist and his or her works.

Since the 1960s, a new art infrastructure has developed with special efforts made by corporations and various levels of government to provide financial support. This has meant a greater pluralism in the market and a greater democratization of the art world.

Today the public exhibition of art is necessary to establish its value. A style or an individual artist's work can become important because it is seen, and the confrontation of the work and the audience is held to be desirable in itself (Goldin 1966, 29).

This new focus on the viewer has opened up the marketplace for art and included other clients such as corporations. While artists, dealers, and art critics are not unanimous on the quality and the subversive content of art collections and exhibitions within corporations, these institutions are here to stay.

The mediation of the audience in the establishment of the value of artworks also is a more recent trend in the art world. Following this trend, galleries and museums are forced to eliminate the boundaries between high and low culture and to draw the public off the streets and into these exhibit spaces (Duhaime, Joy, and Ross 1995). Uneasy about such approaches, the public still seems to be in awe of institutions that sell or exhibit art. Confronting art, especially contemporary art, is viewed with distaste by many who do not want the responsibility of negotiating culturally constructed meanings with artists and artworks. Art, in this sense, is not viewed in the same manner as perfume, jewelry, homes, or furniture.

Furthermore, gallery owners and art dealers, while recognizing the centrality of marketing techniques, silently believe and reluctantly propagate the notion of the aesthetic as a thing in and of itself. The desacralizing process of selling is subdued, and more weight is given to gallery space as a "stage" where audience response is given high priority. Strategies used by galleries are thus more acutely aware of the delicate negotiations among artist, artwork, art institutions, and audience. Art, unlike other commodities, underscores the importance of studying "space" rather than "place" as central to the marketing mix (Sherry 1995).

Managerial and Marketing Implications

The creation of a space in which to sell art objects requires a particular way of thinking about sales and the way in which consumers buy art objects. Commercial galleries by definition promote and sell particular kinds of art. They may choose to promote the works of a few artists that they develop over time, or they may identify potential stars and promote them extensively. Either way, they have to create an ambience that is conducive to persuading customers to purchase art. The servicescape—in this case, the gallery—is critical to the accomplishment of this objective.

As Bitner (1992, 67) observes, the servicescape provides a visual metaphor for an organization's total offering. In this instance, the "surplus of the visual" is particularly interesting. The framing of the art object vis-à-vis the setting is crucial to the persuasion process. The spatial layout, the lighting, the color of the walls, and the warmth of the setting conveyed through any or all of these factors affect the interaction between the viewer and the work of art. The approach or avoidance behavior experienced by customers is very much a function of the image conveyed by the servicescape. While the "visual" is certainly emphasized, the comfort levels experienced by viewers are affected by their experience of the gallery space through their other senses.

According to Bitner (1992, 63), in general the pleasure and arousal that individuals experience increase their approach behaviors. She further argues that perceptions of greater personal control increase approach behavior, as does complexity in the servicescape, which leads to arousal. In the case of art, learning while viewing might provide this sense of personal control, and the encouragement of such activity through complex ordering of the servicescape might lead to positive evaluations of the artworks, the gallery, and the owners.

The gallery also conveys a total image that suggests the potential usage and quality of the service offered. Through this process they are able to signal the market segment they intend to target, and position themselves as different from their competitors.

Since art has to be viewed and meaning has to be generated and incorporated into the lives of customers, the purchase of art is often a long-term process. That is, the sales of art objects often result from much deliberation and knowledge search. Consequently, gallery owners must encourage a higher traffic of viewers and enhance the process of learning and acquisition of art by customers. They must therefore encourage viewing, which may not be followed by purchase, as well as encourage the purchase of art objects by a subsegment of these viewers. The servicescape thus has a critical role in the distribution of art.

BIBLIOGRAPHY

ADLER, J. E. 1979. *Artists in Offices.* New Brunswick, NJ: Transaction Books.

ALEXANDER, E. P. 1983. *Museum Masters: Their Museums and Their Influences.* Nashville, TN: Association of State and Local History.

ALEXANDER, VICTORIA. 1996. "Pictures at an Exhibition: Conflicting Pressures in Museums and the Display of Art." *Annual Review of Sociology* 101(4):797–839.

ALPERS, S. 1991. "The Museum as a Way of Seeing." In *Exhibiting Cultures,* edited by Ivan Karp and Steven D. Levine. Washington, DC: Smithsonian Institution, 25–32.

BAL, MICKE. 1992. "Telling, Showing and Showing Off." *Critical Inquiry* 18 (Spring): 556–594.

BARKER, GODFREY. 1994. "Wiser and Better." *ArtNews* (January): 121–124.

BAXANDALL, MICHAEL. 1991. "Exhibiting Intention: Some Preconditions of Visual Display of Culturally Purposeful Objects." In *Exhibiting Cultures,* edited by Ivan Karp and Steven D. Levine. Washington, DC: Smithsonian Institution, 33–42.

BECKER, H. 1982. *Art Worlds.* Berkeley: University of California Press.

BELK, RUSS. 1994. *Collecting in a Consumer Society.* Unpublished manuscript.

BELK, RUSS; JOHN F. SHERRY, JR.; AND M. WALLENDORF. 1988. "A Naturalistic Inquiry into Buyer and Seller Behaviour at a Swap Meet." *Journal of Consumer Research* 14:449–470.

BELK, RUSS; M. WALLENDORF; AND JOHN F. SHERRY, JR. 1989. "The Sacred and the Profane in Consumer Behavior: Theodicy on the Odyssey." *Journal of Consumer Research* 16 (June): 1–38.

BELK, RUSS; M. WALLENDORF; JOHN F. SHERRY, JR.; AND M. HOLBROOK. 1991. "Collecting in a Consumer Culture." In *Highways and Buyways: Naturalistic Research from the Consumer Behavior Odyssey,* edited by Russ Belk. Provo, UT: Association of Consumer Research, 178–215.

BERRY, LEONARD, AND A. PARASURAMAN. 1991. *Marketing Services: Competing Through Quality.* New York: Free Press.

BITNER, MARY JO. 1986. "Consumer Responses to the Physical Environment in Service Settings." In *Creativity in Services Marketing,* edited by M. Venkatesan, Diane Schmalensee, and Claudia Marshall. Chicago: American Marketing Association, 89–93.

———. 1990. "Evaluating Service Encounters: The Effects of Physical Surroundings and Employees Responses." *Journal of Marketing* 54(2):69–82.

———. 1992. "Servicescapes: The Impact of Physical Surroundings on Customers and Employees." *Journal of Marketing* 56(2):57–71.

BLATT, S. J. 1984. *Continuity and Change in Art.* Hillsdale, NJ: Lawrence Erlbaum.

BOURDIEU, PIERRE. 1993. *The Field of Cultural Production.* New York: Columbia University Press.

BRUNER, GORDON. 1990. "Music, Mood and Marketing." *Journal of Marketing* 54(4):94–104.

BYSTRYN, MARCIA. 1978. "Art Galleries as Gatekeepers: The Case of the Abstract Expressionists." *Social Research* 45 (Summer): 390–408.

CEMBALEST, ROBIN. 1993a. "The Ghost in the Installation." *ArtNews* (November): 140–143.

———. 1993b. "The Persistence of Philippe Montebello." *ArtNews* (December): 109–112.

CLIFFORD, J. 1985. "Objects and Selves—An Afterword." In *Objects and Others: Essays on Museums and Material Culture.* Vol. 3 of *History of Anthropology,* edited by George W. Stocking, Jr., Madison: University of Wisconsin Press, 208–245.

CONGRAM, CAROLE A., AND MARGARET L. FRIEDMAN, EDS. 1991. *The AMA Handbook of Marketing for the Services Industry.* New York: AMACOM.

CRANE, DIANA. 1987. *The Transformation of the Avant-Garde.* Chicago: University of Chicago Press.

DECKER, ANDREW. 1994. "Can the Guggenheim Pay the Price?" *ArtNews* (January): 142–149.

DELANEY, JILL. 1993. "Ritual Space in the Canadian Museum of Civilization." In *Lifestyle Shopping,* edited by Rob Shields. London: Routledge.

DERY, MARK. 1993. "Art Goes High Tech." *ArtNews* (February): 74–83.

DIAMONSTEIN, B. 1979. *Inside New York's Art World.* New York: Rizzoli International Publications.

DIMAGGIO, PAUL. 1986. *Nonprofit Enterprise in the Arts.* New York: Oxford University Press.

———. 1987. "Classification in Art." *American Sociological Review* 52 (August): 440–455.

DIMAGGIO, P.; M. USEEM; AND P. BROWN. 1978. *Audience Studies of the Performing Arts and Museums: A Critical Review.* Washington, DC: National Endowment for the Arts.

DIXON, B.; A. E. COURTNEY; AND R. H. BAILEY. 1987. *The Museum and the Canadian Public.* Published by Arts and Culture Branch, Department of the Secretary of State, Government of Canada. Montreal: Culturcan Publications.

DORNBERG, JOHN. 1993. "Things Are Moving." *ArtNews* (October): 134–136.

DOUGLAS, MARY, AND B. ISHERWOOD. 1979. *The World of Goods: Towards an Anthropology of Consumption.* London: Allen Lane.

DUBIN, S. C. 1979. *Bureaucratizing the Muse.* Chicago: University of Chicago Press.

DUHAIME, CAROLE; ANNAMMA JOY; AND CHRIS ROSS. 1990. "On the Appreciation of Art Objects and the Experiencing of Visiting an Exhibition in an Art Museum." In *Symposium Proceedings on Research and Marketing for the Arts.* Amsterdam: ESOMAR, 55–70.

———. 1995. "Learning to See." In *Contemporary Marketing and Consumer Behavior,* edited by John F. Sherry, Jr. Thousand Oaks, CA: Sage, 351–400.

DUNCAN, CAROL. 1991. "Art Museums and the Ritual of Citizenship." In *Exhibiting Cultures,* edited by Ivan Karp and Steven D. Levine. Washington, DC: Smithsonian Institution, 88–103.

FINE, MICHELLE. 1994. "Working the Hyphens: Re-inventing Self and Other in Qualitative Research." In *Handbook of Qualitative Research.* Thousand Oaks, CA: Sage, 70–86.

FREY, BRUNO, AND WERNER POMMEREHNE. 1989. *Muses and Markets.* London: Basil Blackwell.

GEERTZ, CLIFFORD. 1973. *The Interpretation of Cultures.* New York: Basic Books.

GLUECK, GRACE. 1981. "How Emerging Artists Really Emerge." *ArtNews* (May): 95–99.

GOFFMAN, E. 1983. "Felicity's Condition." *American Journal of Sociology* 89:1–53.

———. 1986. *Frame Analysis.* Boston: Northeastern University Press.

GOLDIN, AMY. 1966. "Requiem for a Gallery." *Arts* 40 (January): 25–29.

GRISWOLD, W. 1986. *Renaissance Revivals: City Comedy and Revenge Tragedy in the London Theatre from 1576–1980.* Chicago: University of Chicago Press.

GURIAN, B. 1991. "Noodling Around with Exhibition Opportunities." In *Exhibiting Cultures,* edited by Ivan Karp and Steven D. Levine. Washington, DC: Smithsonian Institution, 176–190.

HALL, JAMES. 1993. "British Art Now." *ArtNews* (September): 143–147.

HEINICH, NATHALIE. 1988. "The Pompidou Centre and Its Public: The Limits of a Utopian Site." In *The Museum Time-Machine,* edited by Robert Lumley. London: Routledge, 150–188.

HIRSCHMAN, E. 1986. "Humanistic Inquiry in Marketing Research: Philosophy, Method and Criteria." *Journal of Marketing Research* 23:237–249.

———. 1988. "A Sociology of Consumption: A Structural-Syntactical Analysis of 'Dallas' and 'Dynasty,'" *Journal of Consumer Research* 15:344–359.

HIRSCHMAN, ELIZABETH, AND MORRIS HOLBROOK. 1982. "Hedonic Consumption: Emerging Concepts, Methods and Propositions." *Journal of Marketing* 46 (Summer): 92–101.

HOOD, M. G. 1983. "Staying Away—Why People Choose Not to Visit Museums." *Museum News* 61(4):50–57.

HOOPER-GREENHILL, EILEEN. 1988. "Counting Visitors or Visitors Who Count." In *The Museum Time-Machine,* edited by Robert Lumley. London: Routledge, 168–180.

———. 1992. *Museums and the Shaping of Knowledge.* London: Routledge.

HOUSEN, A. 1983. "The Eye of the Beholder: Measuring Aesthetic Development." Unpublished doctoral dissertation, Harvard Graduate School of Education.

———. 1987. "Of Pluralism." In *Art Education Here.* Boston: Massachusetts College of Art, 29–39.

JONES, ANNA-LAURA. 1993. "Exploding Canons: The Anthropology of Museums." *Annual Review of Anthropology* 22:201–220.

JOY, ANNAMMA. 1991. "Beyond the Odyssey: Interpretations of Ethnographic Research in Consumer Behavior." In *Highways and Buyways: Naturalistic Research from the Consumer Behavior Odyssey,* edited by Russ Belk. Provo, UT: Association of Consumer Research, 216–233.

————. 1993a. "From Community Workshop to Professional Theatre: Audience Development and the Consumption of Art." In *Advances in Nonprofit Marketing,* edited by Russ Belk. Greenwich, CT: JAI Press.

————. 1993b. "The Corporate Medicis: Corporations as Consumers of Art." In *Research in Consumer Behavior,* edited by Russ Belk and Janeen Costa. Greenwich, CT: JAI Press, 29–54.

KELLY, ROBERT. 1987a. "Culture as Commodity: The Marketing of Cultural Objects and Cultural Experiences." In *Advances in Consumer Research,* vol. 14, edited by M. Wallendorf and P. Anderson. Provo, UT: Association of Consumer Research.

————. 1987b. "Museums as Status Symbols II: Attaining a State of Having Been." In *Advances in Nonprofit Marketing,* vol. 2, edited by R. Belk. Greenwich, CT: JAI Press, 1–38.

————. 1993. "Vesting Objects and Experiences with Symbolic Meaning." In *Advances in Consumer Research,* vol. 20, edited by L. McAlister and M. Rothschild. Provo, UT: Association of Consumer Research, 232–234.

KOTLER, PHILIP. 1982. *Marketing for Nonprofit Organizations,* 2d ed. Englewood Cliffs, NJ: Prentice Hall.

LINCOLN, YVONNA, AND E. GUBA. 1985. *Naturalistic Inquiry.* Beverly Hills, CA: Sage.

LUBAR, S., AND D. W. KINGERY. 1993. *History from Things.* Washington, DC: Smithsonian Institution Press.

LYNES, R. 1980. *The Tastemakers: The Shaping of American Popular Taste.* New York: Dover.

MARCUS, GEORGE, AND MICHAEL FISCHER. 1986. *Anthropology as Cultural Critique: An Experimental Moment in the Human Sciences.* Chicago: University of Chicago Press.

MARTORELLA, ROSANNE. 1990. *Corporate Art.* New Brunswick, NJ: Rutgers University Press.

MCCALL, SIMON, AND MALCOLM ELLENPORT. 1990. "The Production of a 'Consumer Based Strategy' Plan for the Museum of Victoria." In *Symposium Proceedings on Research and Marketing for the Arts.* Amsterdam: ESOMAR, 37–55.

MCCRACKEN, GRANT. 1986. "Culture and Consumption: A Theoretical Account of the Structure and Meaning of Consumer Goods." *Journal of Consumer Research* 13:71–84.

————. 1988. *Culture and Consumption: New Approaches to the Symbolic Character of Consumer Goods and Activities.* Bloomington: University of Indiana Press.

————. 1990. "Matching Material Cultures: Person-Object Relations Inside and Outside the Ethnographic Museum." In *Advances in Nonprofit Marketing,* vol. 3, edited by Russ Belk. Greenwich, CT: JAI Press, 27–49.

MCGRATH, MARY ANN; JOHN F. SHERRY, JR.; AND DEB HEISLEY. 1993. "An Ethnographic Study of an Urban Periodic Marketplace: Lessons from the Midville Farmers' Market." *Journal of Retailing* 69(3):280–318.

MICK, D. 1986. "Consumer Research and Services: Exploring the Morphology of Signs, Symbols and Significance." *Journal of Consumer Research* 13:196–200.

O'DOHERTY, BRIAN. 1967. *Object and Idea: An Art Critic's Journal 1961–1967.* New York: Simon and Schuster.

———. 1976. "Inside the White Cube: Notes on Gallery Space." *ArtForum* 14 (March): 24–30.

PERACCHIO, LAURA. 1993. "Young Children's Processing of a Televised Narrative: Is a Picture Really Worth a Hundred Words?" *Journal of Consumer Research* 20(2):281–293.

PESANDO, JAMES E. 1993a. "Art as an Investment: The Market for Modern Prints." *The American Economic Review* 83(5):1076–1089.

———. 1993b. "Accounting for Taste: Art and the Financial Markets over Three Centuries." *The American Economic Review* 83(5):1,370–1,376.

POSNER, ELLEN. 1988. "The Museum as Bazaar." In *Architecture*, 67–70.

PRICE, SALLY. 1989. *Primitive Art in Civilized Places*. Chicago: University of Chicago Press.

RICOEUR, P. 1992. *Oneself as Another*. Chicago: University of Chicago Press.

ROEDERER, BENOIT. 1990. "Socio-Cultural Trends and How They Affect the Public's Reactions to Art Museums." In *Symposium Proceedings on Research and Marketing for the Arts*. Amsterdam: ESOMAR, 71–78.

ROOKS, D. 1985. "The Ritual Dimension of Consumer Behaviour." *Journal of Consumer Research* 12:251–261.

ROSS, VAL. 1995. "Framing Matters." *Toronto Globe and Mail* (September 5): A13.

ROTHMAN, CLAIRE. 1995. "Thank Drapeau for the Maisons de la Culture," *Montreal Gazette* (September 17): F1.

SABBATH, LAWRENCE. 1989. "Landscape with Family." *Montreal Magazine* (November): 20–21.

SCHROEDER, JONATHAN. 1997. "Andy Warhol: Consumer Researcher." In *Advances in Consumer Research*, edited by Merrie Brucks and Debbie MacInnis. Provo, UT: Association for Consumer Research, 24:———.

SHERRY, JOHN F., JR. 1990. "Dealers and Dealing in a Periodic Market: Informal Retailing in Ethnographic Perspective." *Journal of Retailing* 66(2):174–200.

SHERRY, JOHN F., JR., ED. 1995. *Contemporary Marketing and Consumer Behavior*. Thousand Oaks, CA: Sage.

SHERRY, JOHN F., JR., AND MARY ANN MCGRATH. 1989. "Unpacking the Holiday Presence: A Comparative Ethnography of Two Gift Stores." In *Interpretive Consumer Research*, edited by Elizabeth Hirschman. Provo, UT: Association of Consumer Research, 148–197.

SHERRY, JOHN F., JR.; MARY ANN MCGRATH; AND SID LEVY. 1993. "The Dark Side of the Gift." *Journal of Business Research* 27(2):225–244.

SOLOMON, MICHAEL. 1988. "Building Up and Breaking Down: The Impact of Cultural Sorting on Symbolic Consumption." In *Research in Consumer Behavior*, edited by Jag Sheth and Beth Hirschman. Greenwich, CT: JAI Press, 325–351.

SOLOMON, MICHAEL, AND BASIL ENGLIS. 1994. "Reality Engineering: Blurring the Boundaries Between Commercial Signification and Popular Culture." *Journal of Current Issues and Research in Advertising* 16(2) (Fall): 1–17.

SOLOMON, ODILE. 1990. "Reversing the Usual Marketing Strategies to Market the Arts." In *Symposium Proceedings on Research and Marketing for the Arts*. Amsterdam: ESOMAR, 1–11.

SPANGENBERG, ERIC; AYN CROWLEY; AND PAMELA HENDERSON. 1996. "Improving the Store Environment: Do Olfactory Cues Affect Evaluations and Behaviors?" In *Journal of Marketing,* 60 (April): 67–80.

STRETCH, BONNIE B. 1994. "High Spirits, High Hopes." *ArtNews* (January): 136–141.

TORGOVNICK, M. 1991. *Gone Primitive.* Chicago: University of Chicago Press.

WAXMAN, SHARON. 1993. "The French Evolution." *ArtNews* (May): 96–99.

ZOLBERG, VERA. 1981. "Conflicting Visions in American Art Museums." *Theory and Society* 10:103–125.

9

MALLING SOCIETY

Mall Consumption Practices
and the Future of Public Space

OZLEM SANDIKCI AND DOUGLAS B. HOLT

Shopping malls now dominate the American consumer marketplace.
Mall transactions account for 50 percent of all retail sales dollars, and
there are more shopping malls than movie theaters in the United
States. Not only are malls the dominant retail form, they have also
become, de facto, one of the most important sites of social life in
advanced capitalist countries: 75 percent of Americans go to a mall
at least once a month, spending more time there than anywhere
else outside of home and work (Feinberg and Meoli 1991; Kowinski 1985; Stoffel 1988). Interrogating the particular characteristics of
this pervasive form of built environment, then, provides a critical
lens of both contemporary economic and social life.

In keeping with their blithe refusal of the popular, mainstream
intellectual traditions in both the social sciences and humanities all
but ignore the shopping mall. Instead, motivated respectively by a
pragmatic interest in malls and by the collapse of the high–mass
hierarchy, academic study of malls has fallen to marketing research

Ozlem Sandikci is a doctoral candidate in marketing and Douglas B. Holt is
Assistant Professor of Marketing at Pennsylvania State University, State College,
Pennsylvania.

and postmodern cultural criticism. These literatures together offer a platform from which we develop our study. In this chapter, we use a case study of a small mall in central Pennsylvania called the Nittany Mall to develop a holistic account of mall consumption that attends both to the semiotics of mall space and the consumption practices of those who participate in this space. Our interests are both descriptive and critical: we seek to document comprehensively what people do at malls and the ways in which these practices are structured by the built environment of the mall. Then we use these findings to consider how malls function as public space and how this use may evolve in the future.

CONCEPTUALIZING MALL CONSUMPTION

The Positivist View: Mall Consumption as Social Shopping

Most marketing research pursues positivist goals of developing nomothetic constructs and drawing causal relationships between them, so it views shopping as a generic activity. Studies conducted from this perspective develop typologies of the functions or benefits of shopping—much like "uses and gratifications" studies in communications (Kelley 1983; Bloch, Ridgway, and Nelson 1991; Bloch, Ridgway, and Dawson 1994). Studies argue that shopping is more than an economic activity; it also includes social interaction, break from daily routine, sensory stimulation, exercise, amusement, and fantasy (Downs 1961; Tauber 1972; Bellenger and Korgoankar 1980; Westbrook and Black 1985; Jansen-Verbeke 1987; Bloch, Ridgway, and Sherell 1989). Shopping to buy, browsing, eating, walking for exercise, socializing, and video/movie watching are reported as the major activities in which people engage in a mall. Attraction of the mall is attributed to the socially stimulating environment that it provides (Isogari and Matsushima 1972; Jacobs 1985; Feinberg et al. 1989). Consumers, as a result of their shopping orientation, differ in their degree of involvement in various types of activities provided and in the benefits they acquire from shopping at the mall, i.e., the social and affiliation benefits, relief from boredom and loneliness, exploration of new products and stores (Feinberg et al. 1989; Graham 1988; Lesser and Kamal 1991; Bloch, Ridgway, and Dawson 1994).

An oft-cited classificatory scheme of this type is economic versus recreational shopper (Bellenger, Robertson, and Greenberg 1977; Bellenger and Korgoankar 1980), termed utilitarian and hedonic in Babin et al. (1994). Economic shoppers desire convenience as well as lower prices and manifest a low interest in shopping as a leisure activity; recreational shoppers seek a ludic experience that provides satisfaction beyond the actual purchase of goods or services. Recreational shoppers tend to spend more time on an average trip, to have less of an idea about what they are going to buy before shopping, to shop with others, and to continue shopping after making a purchase. Browsing behavior is regarded as one of the main forms of recreational shopping, and profiles of browsers in the shopping malls are offered (Jarboe and McDaniel 1987; Bloch, Ridgway, and Sherell 1989; Bloch, Ridgway, and Nelson 1991). These studies suggest that, rather than making a special trip with the intention of making a specific purchase, browsers go to the mall with a mental list of possible purchases, not all of which are likely to be completed on the current trip, tend to report higher levels of purchase satisfaction and lower levels of dissonance, and enjoy and engage in shopping more often. In addition, browsers are more likely to be social while at the mall and appear to be younger.

To the extent that these studies acknowledge that retail experiences are structured by retail space, the built environment of the mall is described purely in functional terms. Features that draw consumers to malls for recreational reasons include the bigger size and broader assortment of stores available within the mall (Monitor 1988; Bloch, Ridgway, and Sherell 1989), the large variety of stimuli offered (Beard and Ragheb 1983; Tinsley and Tinsley 1986), the comfortable and safe environment (Bloch, Ridgway, and Nelson 1991; Monitor 1988), the low cost of entry (Bloch, Ridgway, and Nelson 1991), and opportunity for socialization and affiliation with others (Kelley 1983; Feinberg 1989; Bloch, Ridgway, and Dawson

1994). In sum, malls act as gathering sites allowing people to come with their families or meet with friends to recreate comfortably and safely by enjoying the display of a wide range of merchandise and participating in various activities unrelated to shopping.

These typologies provide a useful point of entry for the present study, roughing out important dimensions of the mall shopping experience. However, from the cultural perspective we advocate, these studies are in several ways impoverished. First, they grant little attention to our central research question: Why the shopping mall? Rather than pursue, idiographically, the particularities of consumption practices associated with the mall, these studies instead mostly abstract to nomothetic concepts that often erase the specificity of the mall. Shopping has always been economic and recreational, a source of escape and a site of sensory stimulation, as historical studies of shopping—in sites from department stores to arcades to public marketplaces—have shown.

To understand mall shopping requires, then, a cultural analysis that seeks to describe qualitatively the distinctive characteristics of economic and recreational practices as they are performed in mall spaces. Second, to the extent that these studies do attend to mall space and the consumption practices within it, the analysis is a brute materialist one that ignores both the extent to which malls are, like all spaces, symbolic environments. Thus, analysis of how consumers interact with mall space is reduced to the material and psychological benefits that accrue to them, rather than considering the embodied pleasures and cultural significance of being in mall space. Postmodern cultural criticism is more successful in addressing both of these issues.

The Postmodern View: Mall Consumption as Carnival, Spectacle, Dreamworld

Outside of marketing, the shopping mall is often cited as the paradigmatic site of postmodern consumption. Postmodern theorization of space and institutions emphasizes spectacle, hyperreality, and a focus on surface rather than depth (Jameson 1983; Baudrillard 1988;

Harvey 1990). In the marketplace hyperreality and spectacle often include elements of carnivalesque (Bakhtin 1968): an ordered disorder, an exaggeration of play, a borderline between reality and representation. With windowless spaces separated from the outside world, public squares simulating both nostalgic and futuristic city spaces, the side-by-side presence of a wide variety of stores with glittering designs, products, and ambience, and the diverse range of facilities and activities provided, the mall becomes the exemplar of the hyperreal, dreamlike, fragmented environment of the postmodern world (e.g., Baudrillard 1983; Fiske 1989; Featherstone 1991; Shields 1992; Gottdiener 1995).

The shopping mall attempts to combine two distinct principles. On the one hand, the mall is an economic space organized as an exchange-nexus where proprietors are motivated by the accumulation of capital. Its organizing structure depends on a continuous flow of goods and people. On the other hand, the mall disguises itself as a social arena that possesses characteristics of both leisure sites and public spaces. People come to participate in the various offerings of this quasi-public environment. Yet the dreamworld of the mall, while abundant with glittering surfaces and simulacra of the foreign and exotic, is physically isolated from the external world. The architectural design of the mall deemphasizes time and climate. While the mall attempts to simulate the public space, it rigorously controls the movement of people, display of commodities, and range of activities.

Faced with hyperreal spectacles and images coupled with contradictory definitions of time and place, the individual in the mall is fragmented, lonely, and depthless. As Langman (1992) argues, the shopping mall, lying in the pseudodemocratic twilight zone between reality and commercially produced fantasy world, enables the transformation of desire and self-images to a distinctive form of subjectivity: "a decentered selfhood has become a plurality of intermittent, disconnected, recognition-seeking spectacles of self-presentation." The self in the shopping mall is a fragmented and uncommitted one seeking to build an integrated self through consumption. The act of buying and consumption—the active appropriation of signs—becomes a means of self-realization, self-identification, and production of self-image. The consumer in this carnivalesque environment is no longer part of the "mass" but simultaneously the audience and performer of the show. While the shops and various activities offered within the mall are designed strategically for commerce, at the moment of encounter between the mall and the consumer, the organizing principles lose their determinacy; people are free to use the mall as they wish, thus producing their own ways of consuming the mall. Even the most disadvantaged and weak can find ways of appropriating the mall (de Certeau 1984; Fiske 1989). Teenagers use the mall as a stage, while older people converge on malls as shelter; many young artists and performers utilize the mall as a stage, while older people use the mall as an indoor exercise area.

Consuming Nittany Mall: Mall Semiotics

The semiotics of the mall are constructed from observations made by the first author over the course of 13 visits ranging from 1 to 2 hours in duration, to the research site, Nittany Mall, State College, Pennsylvania. Through these, she developed a close familiarity with the environment and also occasionally was able to have unplanned and unstructured conversations with shoppers. During some of these visits, the researcher was exposed to activities offered by the mall (e.g., crafts fair, exhibitions, fashion fair) and participated in their consumption while continuing to observe the surrounding shoppers. Eventually, in the course of data collection, the researcher's role shifted from an observer to a participating observer. Field notes taken during on-site visits consisted of observations made by the researcher both inside and outside of the mall and provided the input for the semiotic analysis.

We follow Gottdiener's (1995) materialist variant of Saussurean semiology developed to study built environments. For Saussure the linguistic sign derives out of an arbitrary relationship between the signified (the concept) and the signifier (the sound image). That is, the signifier in isolation possesses no intrinsic relation to the signified but refers to a meaning only within a system of signification that consists of oppositions or differences. Saussure proposes two ways to analyze how meaning is conveyed within a system. On the one hand, a sign or word conveys its meaning by its existence and placement within a context of other signs, that is, within a syntagmatic axis. On the other hand, the presence of any word or sign implies the presence of many absent words that could have been similarly employed. The absent but associated words constitute the paradigmatic axis of the meanings. Building on this idealist analysis, we then attend to the local social and economic conditions that help to structure these meanings.

Paradigm of the Nittany Mall

Rural central Pennsylvania, with its endless stripes of forested ridges dividing wide valleys that are not heavily farmed, conveys the feel of Appalachia, though its poverty is less extreme. Small towns wedded to increasingly obsolete economies dominate. State College, the only city in a county of 120,000 people, presents itself in stark contrast to this post–Rust Belt economy. Pennsylvania State University dominates not only the city landscape, but also the economic, social, and cultural life. The vast majority of residents are either students (40,000 strong), Penn State employees, or employees in the vast and diverse service economy that supports the university population. Most of the leisure activities available are either offered by the university (sports, films, theaters, concerts, fairs) or are oriented toward the student population (bars, restaurants, shops). The mutual existence of the town and the university manifests itself in the physical landscape. The downtown lies along the south end of the campus; when the campus ends, so does the downtown. Shops, cafes, bars, restaurants, bookstores, movie theaters, all geared toward the needs of the student population, shape the downtown. Because it is so easily accessible from the campus and is relatively safe, the downtown of State College is the focus of social life not only for students, but for some segments of the nonstudent population. Unlike large cities, State College is a modernist urban space with a single and ordered center.

The Nittany Mall is located three miles northeast of downtown State College. The mall is surrounded by a hodgepodge of businesses, a postmodern assemblage with no pretense of coherence: fast-food restaurants, retailers, light industries, a car dealer, a movie theater, a medium-security prison, a Wal-Mart, commercial suppliers, a utility, the local newspaper, and, after the fieldwork was conducted, an onslaught of category killer stores. Its geographical location in the midst of a business district confirms and signifies its instrumental logic—the accumulation of capital. However unlike large destination malls (e.g., Ye Olde Town in Orange County, California; Beverly Center in Beverly Hills; Mall of America in Bloomington, Minnesota), Nittany Mall's design does little to disguise its commercial function. It lies as a one-level, flat, and long building. The exterior design of the building resembles that of Wal-Mart and other major retail chains. Apart from the two main entrances, which are built as three-peak towers out of a mixture of red brick, glass, and steel, the exterior walls of the mall convey a monolithic pattern built out of pale, yellowish bricks. Overall the building stands in such complete harmony with the surrounding area that for a stranger, only the J. C. Penney and Sears signs and the big parking lot around the building cue the presence of a shopping mall.

Paralleling the architectural modesty and harmony, there is no overt attempt within the configuration of the Nittany Mall to disguise its functional logic. For those driving from downtown State College, the first commercial space to be confronted within the borders of the mall is the Sears Auto Center. The presence of an auto center stands uncomfortably with the notion of shopping mall as a simultaneous provider of consumption and leisure. The scattered existence of some common leisure places outside the mall further problematizes this. Some of the most popular restaurants, such as McDonald's, Pizza Hut, and Long John Silver, exist not inside the mall but either at the far end of the parking lot or in the surrounding area. Similarly, the movie theater—a common attraction of many malls—is located across the road. The stark physical separation of these common leisure sites from the mall signifies the emphasis on its instrumental and functional logic, and on the major concern for generation of profit through sale of merchandise, rather than provision of pleasure, fun, leisure, and fantasies.

Syntagm of the Nittany Mall

Nittany Mall, unlike the multistore, gallery-type malls described in the postmodern literature, is a flat and long rectangular building. The interior plan of the mall is in the shape of a tunnel, crowded with shops on both sides, with very few roads cutting the main pedestrian line. Overall it looks straight and long, almost without any curvature. This flat architectural design prevents the shopper from perceiving the mall from multiple perspectives—from top or bottom floor or from corners—and thus from observing many people and many parts of the mall simultaneously. In fact, most of the time, the gaze one is allowed to possess is directed only to the immediate surroundings.

There are two main entrances, one located toward the western edge of the building and the other toward the eastern edge. The western entrance is both larger and more monumental than the eastern entrance. Here the monotony of flat, pale yellowish brick walls gives way to a colorful, mixed-material design. The entryway is in the form of three peaks, with two exterior towers built out of red and tan brick walls and the in-between tower out of glass. Overall, the entryway evokes a church steeple. The glass ceiling on top of the side roads that link the two entrances to the main path provides a smooth transformation from outside to the enclosed and climate-controlled environment of the mall. A wide variety of stores are located at both entrances: banks, jewelers, small cafes and eateries, hairdresser, optician, amusement shop. While the banks at the very entrance of the mall connote the realization of capital as the organizational principle of the mall, the side-by-side presence of shops offering unrelated commodities and services confirms the identity of the shopping mall as an ideological vehicle of consumer culture—the provider of multiple goods and services. Both entrances open to a semicircular public area, decorated with a few plants and benches. Usually a car exhibition dominates these areas. However, because they are so small, these areas are hardly public spaces that allow people to gather around, gaze at each other, or sit down and talk. The few benches available are almost always inhabited by elderly people or mothers with small children, mostly sitting there to rest for a while.

Besides the semicircular areas, there is a main public area located at the center of the mall. This circular area, situated among Bon Ton, a jewelry shop, a couple of women's and men's apparel stores, and two snack food corners, is the most glittering part of the mall. One side of the area opens to the entrance of Bon Ton, filled with brightly lit cosmetics and perfume counters and their attractive sales representatives, stimulating the desire for the physically attractive bodies within the image-driven culture of consumption. A circular stage, elevated from the floor level by a couple of steps and surrounded by stage lights, occupies the center of this area. The stage, although very small, is utilized for occasional fashion shows, various expos and shows, and Christmas decorations.

Typical of shopping mall design, Nittany Mall has four anchor stores, of which two are strategically located on southern and northern ends and the other two in the midsection, one on the east and the other on the west side. Sears and Value City, are located at opposite ends, so shoppers desiring to shop at both must walk past all the lesser-known and smaller shops. However, unlike bigger malls in which the floor plan is constructed so that the linear walking paths are broken through various design elements to disorient the shopper toward other shops, the layout of the Nittany Mall, rather than demanding a detour, facilitates a straight-line flow of pedestrian traffic.

Overall, the interior design of the Nittany Mall is far from a postmodern architectural configuration. Rather, the tunnel-like layout, the geometrically shaped tiled floor, and the concrete ceiling, interrupted by glass only at the central and semicircular areas, suggest a modernist and industrial construction. In line with the overall design of the mall, the storefronts and displays also are modest. Except for Victoria's Secret—one of the most upscale shops in the mall, with minimalist solid wood exterior that stands distinct and more sophisticated than the rest of the shops, and so generates a slightly mystical and exotic desire of consumption—the other stores have utilitarian facades organized to display goods and announce sales rather than to create a more fantastic experience for the shopper through stylized design.

Unlike many malls, Nittany Mall does not have a food court. A dozen or so eateries, including a pizzeria, small fast-food Chinese and Italian restaurants, a couple of coffee shops, and other snack food stores, are dispersed all over the mall. Besides being disconnected, they are concealed; their sitting places are all inside, separated from the main path of the mall, thus preventing the shoppers from observing other people or store displays while eating. Apart from the occasional shows and exhibits, all of which are of small scale, and a few eateries, Nittany Mall offers only limited possibilities for leisure and recreation. It neither accommodates an ice rink, movie theater, or playground on its site nor provides carousels, marble fountains, clock towers, or any other such reproductions that resonate fantasies and exotica. Further confirming its existence as centered mainly around shopping, the mall closes early in the evening and leaves the task of providing entertainment and fun to the downtown.

Consuming Nittany Mall: Mall Consumption Practices

We use *mall consumption practices* as the unit of analysis to describe what people do at shopping malls (see Holt 1995). This term is intended to connote two distinctions versus other empirical studies of malls. First, in contrast to most marketing studies, we analyze types of practice rather than types of consumers. We do this because we found that, rather than fitting into a single orthogonal category, almost all of our informants engage in a variety of practices when they visit the mall. Second, people's practices at the mall are in no way constrained to types of shopping. In fact, for many informants, consummating an exchange is an afterthought. So, to understand people's activities in malls, it is necessary to analyze the full range of consumption practices that are performed. While some mall consumption practices are similar to those found in nonmall stores—some people sometimes go alone to the mall knowing what they want to buy, know what store carries the desired merchandise, and so come to the mall to visit a particular store to consummate a transaction—none of the informants use the mall solely in this manner. Rather, most report spending at least two hours on a visit, often in the company of others, and engage in activities that the mall facilitates compared to other shopping alternatives. We find five consumption practices that predominate during these extended visits.

Eighteen on-site interviews were conducted during June and July 1995. We selected a stratified random sample of mall shoppers to have about equal numbers of men and women and to vary widely in terms of age (the two variables that could be readily judged prior to contact). The informants were recruited by approaching shoppers at the mall, briefly describing the study, and asking whether they would be interested in participating in the research. On average, 1 out of 15 shoppers contacted agreed to participate. The interviews usually took place on one of the benches in the surrounding area or, occasionally, in one of the eateries. To ensure that both working and nonworking people were represented in the sample, the interviews were carried out both on weekdays and on weekends. The resulting sample comprised 10 females and 8 males, with ages ranging from 17 to 66. Participants were members of working, middle, and upper-middle class (see Table 9.1 for informant characteristics).

The semistructured interviews covered six major areas: descriptions of the mall trip, social interactions, activities, subjective feelings, images of the mall, and the ideal mall. Informants were encouraged to give detailed descriptions of their experiences and specific examples they have encountered in the mall. The interviews were transcribed, and the transcripts were analyzed to identify dominant themes. In the second stage of the analysis, we use these findings to interrogate and extend the marketing and postmodern literatures on the shopping mall. In addition to interviewing shoppers, we contacted and interviewed the marketing manager of the mall. Her information provided insight about the managerial and organizational aspects of the mall, its history, and business goals.

TABLE 9.1 Informant Demographics

Name*	Age	Sex/Number of Children	Marital Status	Education	Occupation	Years of Residence in Center County
Frank	66	M/3	Married	College	Photographer (retired)	32
Mary	27	F/0	Single	BA	Graduate student	1
Mark	32	M/1	Married	AA	Ground staff at the airport	5
Linda	38	F/1	Married	HS	Homemaker	38
Amy	41	F/2	Married	AA	Secretary	15
John	25	M/0	Single	BA	Graduate student	2
Tracy	29	F/0	Single	BA	Account executive	4
Alice	54	F/4	Widow	HS	Homemaker	21
Harry	42	M/2	Married	MA	Attorney	9
Scott	17	M/0	Single	HS	Undergraduate student	1
Doris	18	F/0	Single	HS	Undergraduate student	2
Ann	32	F/2	Married	BA	Teacher	6
Jerry	44	M/3	Married	Ph.D.	Professor	4
James	39	M/2	Married	AA	Technician	9
Ralph	62	M/3	Married	BA	Teacher (retired)	15
Melissa	61	F/4	Married	HS	Homemaker	21
Judy	28	F/1	Married	HS	Janitor	5
Kate	35	F/2	Married	BA	Administrative assistant	7

*Pseudonyms are used for all of the informants. All informants are of white/European/Caucasian descent.

Mall Shopping: Serendipitous Search

Echoing findings of previous studies, many informants characterize what they do at malls as "browsing." But of what does browsing actually consist? Based on specific descriptions and observations of shopping activities, we argue that what informants call browsing is actually two analytically distinct practices—serendipitous search and product foreplay—that are either pursued separately or commingled. In addition, we find a strong tendency for women to engage in the serendipitous search style of browsing, while both men and women engage in product foreplay.

Serendipitous searching falls somewhere between the instrumental logic structuring shopping visits to most stand-alone stores and the adventurous rummaging of shopping at informal markets (Sherry 1990), incorporating elements of each.

> I usually have something in my mind that I want to buy. But usually I just have a vague idea, like I know I need a top but I'm not sure about how it should be. So I walk around, browsing and trying. You see things in the magazines or ads. So you know what's cool and you just try to find the thing that will fit the image you have in your mind (Tracy, age 29).

Compared to Sherry's description of searching at flea markets, mall shoppers are more purposeful, usually focusing on a particular category of goods that they want to search around, with some fuzzy idea of what they want to achieve. Searching at the mall is also more instrumental. Whereas search at informal markets is structured by an ethos of adventure, the thrill of discovery, of finding something unexpected, mall shoppers expect generally to find something they want in the category they're shopping for. Thus, good malls have diversity and redundancy within a category of goods. The depth and variety of products available enable shoppers to engage in leisurely and opportunistic search even if they are highly familiar with the environment and know where they can find what they are looking for.

> If I am alone, I like to walk from one end to the other. I usually park my car next to Sears. So I first go to Sears, look

around, and then walk all over the mall till Value City. I have been shopping in this mall for the last five–six years, so I know the stores. I know where I can find the things that I am look-ing for. But I like to look around anyway (Ann, age 32).

Serendipitous search is adventurous, but this is a rationalized adventure for which market mechanisms have stacked the odds in the customer's favor. Rather than the one-of-a-kind find unearthed through search that could never be found in a shopping mall, mall shoppers search for unique goods that are available in malls because the small retail spaces allow for specialty shops that carry lines of idiosyncratic goods not found at mass merchandisers. Further, mall consumers often use searching purposively as a means to learn about styles, features, prices, and uses:

So my family tradition is that they make a lot of things on their own. So first I see whether I can do it on my own. If I see I cannot do it, then I go out in the marketplace and look. And I see what kinds of prices there are. I talk to different people to get an idea. When I come here I usually talk a lot with shop owners and get their opinions on which things are made the best, which have the best price. If I decide that I really need it, then I buy it (Linda, age 38).

Shopping as serendipitous search in all its manifestations demands a minimum size of facility and stores. Because it is small and has few upscale stores, the Nittany Mall provides a satisfactory space for serendipitous search only for certain categories, and only for a minority of our informants. Serendipitous searching is pre-dominantly a women's consumption practice. Some women will engage in this practice with women friends who also enjoy it. Many married women arrive at the mall with husband and/or children in tow but then split up, precisely because the serendipitous searching they enjoy is not favored by other family members. Still other women report coming to the mall alone because they know that their spouse will not enjoy shopping with them in their preferred manner. Men, on the other hand, uniformly comment that they hate to shop alone at the mall and so never do. Whenever they search, it is usually either economically oriented (i.e., to compare

prices and find the best bargain) or out of obligation (i.e., to purchase gifts for others).

Mall Hedonics: Product Foreplay

Consumer goods are not only instrumental resources that allow for
a variety of utilitarian benefits and symbolic uses; they are also sensuous objects that offer tactile, visual, aural, and olfactory pleasures
(see Chapter 4). As Haug (1987) suggests, commodity aesthetics
work through an artificially produced fascination, an enchantment
of the senses. Malls, from this perspective, are a hedonic cornucopia. Shoppers page through books, feel the weight and texture of
a new fabric, take in the smells of new shoe leather, play with pets,
handle power tools. Product foreplay is an individual and sensual
activity organized by a focused engagement with the commodity
at hand.

In our study we observed two different types of product foreplay. The first is the momentary indulgence in a specific commodity while shopping for other items. Here the commodity is
something that is not scrutinized for the purpose of purchase, but
looked at, touched, smelled for its momentary pleasure:

> And the pets. Always I am looking at least in the window. If I
> have a leisurely day, then I go inside and look at the animals. I
> never bought anything from there, but I love pets (Amy, age 41).

Sometimes the sensory characteristics of both the product and the
store stimulate the customers' sensual experiences. Victoria's Secret
offers one exemplar of such experiences:

> I like browsing in Victoria's Secret, too. It is really a very nice
> store. It is different. I mean, not exactly the things they sell.
> But the inside, the environment. I have never been to England
> or Europe, but it seems like a different place. The decor, the
> smell (Tracy, age 29).

Product foreplay often is practiced when people go in groups
to a mall. Because individuals in the group often have different

shopping interests and they are at the mall for extended periods, mall shopping creates a great deal of downtime—time to use up while a family member or friend finishes shopping. Mall spaces thus encourage sensuous play with goods because there is a sufficient variety of stores that most people can browse their favorite hedonically charged goods. Most of our male informants, who claim not to enjoy browsing with their wives or female friends, nonetheless mention that they like to browse in stores that display products they are interested in, for example, tools in Sears and electronic equipment in Radio Shack.

Product foreplay may take many forms and include a diverse range of senses, depending on the product and situation involved. Sometimes people prefer to walk directly to the section of the store where their favorite categories of goods are displayed and start playing with them: looking, touching, smelling, tasting, trying, and so on. Other times, product foreplay may resemble more the mating game: An unexpected initial encounter through a distant gaze followed by a more detailed, scrutinizing look. Usually, after visual interaction, the person starts touching the product, holding and eventually trying it. The following vignette illustrates one such instance in which we observed a young woman spending more than 10 minutes looking, touching, and trying jewelry:

> She walks around the store (B. Moss) rather quickly, with occasional touching to certain outfits. She doesn't seem to be particularly interested in the clothes at display. After strolling back of the store briefly, where discounted items are placed, she heads toward the exit. Just when she appears to be leaving the store, she notices the jewelry rack behind a column. She walks toward there while gazing at it. On top of the rack, a sign reads: Every Girl Loves Jewelry. She stands next to the rack and continues gazing at the earrings and bracelets. After a couple of minutes of visual inspection, she starts touching the jewelry. Her fingers hold an earring without taking it off. She feels the stone and the metal. She repeats this many times with other earrings.
>
> After a couple of minutes she finally takes an earring off its place, examines it more carefully, bringing it closer to her eyes. She finally holds the earring next to one of her ears and looks at herself in the mirror on top of the rack. After a couple of

seconds, she puts back the earring in its place. Her eyes go around the rack again. She then picks another pair and repeats the same acts. She puts that one also back in its place. She looks at the jewelry one more time and then heads toward the exit.

When playing with products, people leave the densely public space of the mall to dwell in an atomistic dream space whose intimate confines they share with products. When outsiders such as salespersons interrupt this hermetic interaction, people instantly become aware that they are in public space, so the foreplay usually ends:

> A young man in his early twenties browses in Radio Shack. He first spends a couple of minutes in the computer section, gazing at various computers displayed. Then he walks toward the other side of the store. He stands for a moment and looks around. He sees the section where cellular phones are displayed. He walks toward there. He stands in front of the phones for a moment. Then he grabs one of the phones that is being displayed—the most expensive model. He brings it closer to himself and carefully examines it. Then he turns it back and reads the label. He turns it back to its front and starts touching the keys as if he were dialing a number. Then he places the phone next to his ear for a second and pretends to be talking. He places the phone back on its stand.
>
> At that moment a salesperson approaches and asks whether he could help him. The man thanks him, says he is "just browsing," and leaves the store.

While mall spaces encourage sensual interactions with commodities, Nittany Mall suffers in comparison to other malls in this regard. A common complaint about Nittany Mall is that it lacks sufficient quality and quantity of goods that people like to play with, such as books, shoes, photography, hunting and fishing gear, sports gear, and tools.

Mall Play:
The Discreet Dance of Community

The most subtle and perhaps the most important practice that our informants describe is a particular type of social interaction distinctive to public spaces, which Georg Simmel terms *sociality*. Our analysis here gives empirical credence to the claim that the success of malls is based on their development as sites of social centrality (Kowinski 1985; Shields 1992) or social communion (Gottdiener 1995). But to what does sociality actually refer? Based on our informants' descriptions of both Nittany Mall and their ideal malls, we argue that social dimension of mall experience derives from two complementary but distinct practices—the discreet dance of sociality and accepted voyeurism.

The marketplace has traditionally played the role of communal meeting place. The idea of providing "public space" is as important to actual markets as the buying and selling activities per se. In an era in which public spaces have been either privatized or left to decay into criminal zones by their public benefactors, shopping malls today offer one of the few outlets to perform community. Performing community in the mall entails sharing the same physical space and time with a group of strangers but not necessarily interacting with them. The sense of community as experienced in the shopping mall derives mainly from the physical coexistence of a number of people, gathered together momentarily around an area of the mall that is not inhabited by shops but left for attractions, shows, or exhibitions. The design of Nittany Mall—its small scale, linear rationalized design, narrow range of public entertainment and recreational activities, and lack of public spaces in which to "hang around"—dramatically limits sociality compared to other malls. Nonetheless, our interviews provide strong evidence that mallgoers search out and find great pleasure in performing community in malls, both in how they seek to enact these practices, even in the impoverished social space of Nittany Mall, and also in their description of preferred malls and their idealized mall utopias.

The circular public space outside of the Bon Ton store is far and away the most desirable space in the mall because of the sociality it allows. Informants particularly like this space when there are activities such as fashion shows and Santa Claus that bring people together in this space:

> I guess the most prominent part is the big area in the middle . . . circular. There are places to sit. It is the only area that is big and open and centralized. It seems pretty bright.

Usually I am around that area, because I like that part (Mary, age 27).

I like the middle space, like circular. You can see the sky, and there are benches to sit. And there is usually a lot of people around there. Some nice, bright shops. I like when they put the Santa Claus during Christmas. It is like the heart of the mall. You can see people coming and going (Mark, age 32).

For almost all of our informants, sociality is understood as an autotelic activity—an end in itself. However, one informant spoke reflexively of its instrumental benefits, describing the "cultivation" that results, much as Simmel does:

We live in Belleville. There is nothing there. There is Amish people there. My sixteen-year-old stepdaughter goes to a small high school, doesn't really take her to anywhere. So I like to bring her here so that she can get culture, see different people, different styles, things. Can get ideas about what she might want to do. I want to put her in situations where she can learn what is out there. If I don't have anything to buy or find what I am looking for, I sit down on a bench, read a book, and wait for her (Linda, age 38).

While informants attempt to extract a modicum of community from the mall, these efforts often seem like extracting water from rock, given the design limitations of the mall space. These tensions between consumer desires and the mall's impoverished social space are most evident in their descriptions of alternative and ideal mall spaces:

There should be places to sit down and eat. But not very expensive ones. It should be bright and colorful. With some plants. Maybe an ice-skating rink or a movie. Some place that you can do something else besides shopping (Mark, age 32).

But if there were different activities, anything that would bring people together, I would be more interested and would spend more time. All the stores are offering things to buy. There is no exchange of ideas. There is no place that you can have diversity—a place that you are not expected to spend money. There is no community, no real social interaction (Linda, age 38).

There is much more fun downtown. In the mall, it's just a bunch of stores . . . I mean, you see much more interesting people and things in the downtown. So why should you go [to the mall]? There is nothing social there. You don't go there to hang around, look around, see some nice people, and talk with them. It looks cold. It's too long and straight. It is like you need to walk all the time. No place to stop and look around, hang around. There should be a real nice food place. Real good food, and nice cafes to sit down and talk and look around. And a gym or swimming pool; somewhere you can go and work out and meet people (John, age 25).

The importance of social space is clearly evoked in Mary's mall utopia. She separates spatially the economic and social functions of the mall, placing the stores on the first floor, organized for rational efficiency, and then allocates the entire upper level to public space devoted to hanging out, recreation:

There should be lots of outside cafes, coffee shops, and restaurants . . . eating and socializing at the food court, which I would like to have upstairs, just kind of a social area. They have to entertain little kids. . . . The lower floor should be all stores. Stores should be in sections like clothes, shoes. Downstairs should have easy access. Something like an ice-skating rink would be cool. You can go upstairs and sit for a while (Mary, age 27).

Mall Play: Accepted Voyeurism

The other dimension of sociality practiced in the mall setting is observing and being observed by strangers. While explicit and scrutinizing gaze directed toward strangers in other public places is not a socially accepted behavior, the commodity-based logic of the mall fosters such tendencies. The mall's structural elements—large, open public areas where one can sit and watch various attractions such as fashion shows and exhibitions, ice-skating rinks, food courts, playgrounds for children—create a social milieu in which both voyeurism and exhibitionism are acceptable (Belk and Bryce 1993). Like products, people become items of display. Our informants repeatedly express their desire to have spaces that would allow them to casually sit and observe passerbys. Such experiences usually entail a passive observation of other people while they are walking, talking, or sitting. Rather than interactional, those desires are spectatorial: scanning, glancing, and collecting different signs. Such uncommitted observing gaze resonates that of the postmodern person conceptualized by Denzin (1991): "a restless voyeur, a person who sits and gazes (often mesmerized and bored) at the movie or television screen" (p. 9; also see Urry 1990).

Nittany Mall performs poorly in providing public areas where people can gather and observe others. Nonetheless, the only area in the mall that comes closest to such a configuration generates voyeuristic and exhibitionist impulses at least for certain informants.

> I like the mid-area the most. In front of Bon Ton. It's circular and wide. . . . I love that part during Christmas when they put the Santa Claus. It's like the center. If you sit there for a while and look around, you see people moving up and down. Sometimes you see funny-looking people. Sometimes you see really cool-looking people. When I see a good-looking guy, I just tease my boyfriend. He gets so mad. Or you see someone with a really nice outfit. It makes you think about yourself, how you would look in such clothes. It gives you new ideas (Tracy, age 29).

The quest for a space that will allow watching others is also prominent in our informants' descriptions of their ideal shopping malls. Almost all descriptions involve architectural designs that will enable one to observe others while engaging in another activity, such as eating, sitting or skating.

> I like the two- or three-level malls. One thing I don't like here is that it is too long. I have been to bigger malls, and they were all two or three levels. It looks better. I mean you can go upstairs and look down and see all the people and stores.
>
> There should be a real food court. With cafes and different types of food where you can sit outside and see the shops and people. And it should be on the upper level with a glass roof so that you can see the sky (Tracy, age 29).

> I like when they have a food area and you sit down there and look at what is going on downstairs (Mark, age 32).

I like skating. So there should be an ice rink. Like in the middle of the mall. It should be three or four levels. And around the ice rink a circular area. And people on the other floors can look down and watch people skating (Doris, age 18).

People who take pleasure observing and being observed are *flaneurs* (Benjamin 1973): observers, spectators, gazers who view the urban scene as a spectacle and stroll through it as if it were a diorama. Flaneurs' experience is that of freely moving in the city, observing and being observed, but never interacting with others (see Weinstein and Weinstein 1991). A distinctive characteristic of mall sociality that is unanimously mentioned by our informants is that, unlike sociality in other public spaces such as coffee houses and bars, it seldom involves conversation. For all our respondents, engaging in conversation with those outside their shopping party is not desirable. None of them indicate that they initiate conversations with strangers and talk with them unless they ask something. Hence the mall functions as a peculiar public place: a space for the enactment of community not through conversation or joint activity, but through the noncommitted, open-ended, ephemeral dance of the marketplace.

Mall Aesthetics: Being-in-the-Bazaar

Retail spaces are sensuous aesthetic environments in which "being in" the space is an essential dimension of the consumption experience (Sherry 1990). Being-in-the-mall is a distinct experience that is shaped significantly by its architectural and aesthetic elements. Because of its nakedly economic organization, the Nittany Mall allows for little in the way of sensuous aesthetic experience. Among major complaints about the Nittany Mall is its aesthetically boring, depressive, and unexciting nature.

It is a boring mall. It is very small and very average. You can't do much. There are only shops, and if you are not really into shopping, there is nothing else here. It looks cold. It is too long and straight. It is like you need to walk all the time. No place to stop and look around, hang around. I never walk from one end to the other. It looks all the same. Maybe it is OK for this area. I mean this is not a big city; everything is on a small scale. There is much more fun in the downtown. In the mall, it is just a bunch of stores.

It looks old-fashioned, like something from the seventies or eighties. It looks old or for old people. I don't think that students go there to hang around. I see families mostly. You see much more interesting people and things in the downtown.

So why you should come here? There is nothing social here. You don't go there to hang around, look around, see some nice people and talk with them. It seems like people [are] there because they need to buy something (John, age 25).

When you go to King of Prussia Mall, you can always find what you want. I never mind going there and shopping. There it is more like a bazaar. They have little booths. The shops usually have one type of thing. . . .

There is really nothing that strikes me here. I don't like the way it is laid out. It is such a closed, controlled environment. I was at the Nordstorm Mall in San Diego. It had a roof. So when you were walking you were outside. It had trees and was really nice. Here you cannot do it. Before, they had a fountain here, but they removed it; I liked when there was the fountain. Maybe if they had a movie theater connected here. But this place is very orderly for me. It just goes straight up and down. There is no this way or that way and ups and downs. . . .

A lot of things I see here is stuff that they have maybe twenty of the same thing in stock. When somebody buys it, they put [out] another. That's why my daughter likes it here. Because what she buys here is accepted by the kids in her school, and so she would not stick out and be an individual, which she doesn't want. And that's why I don't like to shop here. I don't like mass-produced things (Linda, age 38).

Further, it is clear from informants' utopian desires for mall space that embodied aesthetics are a central mall consumption practice, even though desire for that type of consumption goes mostly unfulfilled at Nittany Mall. Descriptions of ideal malls often include amenities such as swimming pools, ice-skating rinks, and movie theaters scattered around a large, bright, multilevel space:

It would have a swimming pool in it. A clear one. So that you can see people when you are walking around. It would have movie theaters with armchairs and run imported films. There should be artisans. People with a unique craft. It could have an area where you can take little kids and leave them to play and you can go to shop.

I really like open air. You can do a glass ceiling. There should be many levels.

For the winter there should be an ice-skating rink. Whenever I come to the mall, I never have a lot of money, so there should be other activities besides just spending money. There should be musicians, too (Linda, age 38).

It should be three levels, at least. I like the way the place looks when you look from the ground floor upward or from the top floor downward. The architecture should be modern. Lots of glass and some metal construction. But it should not be just one style. Different construction for different parts. It looks like you have come to a different place. Maybe more circular or spiral; I like curvy designs (John, age 25).

It should be just glass so that during the wintertime you can still have the feeling of being outside. Maybe some waterfalls or just water—like fountains in the middle, but not fake. Some green would be nice, but [plants] should be real (Mary, age 27).

I think a two-level mall will be more interesting. In a two-level mall, you are more often looking around. Something might be going on in the middle; other people walk around. There would be more excitement.

I want lots of light. If you are inside and if you don't have time, it gets dreary. It should in pink or light green, maybe then it would look more warm and friendly.

An ice-skating rink would be nice. Even a bowling area. Then you would have things to do other than shopping (Amy, age 41).

I like small stands that sell interesting things that you cannot easily find. Or some handmade things. They are more like marketplaces. I would like to have them (Mark, age 32).

If there are exhibitions or craft fairs when I am here, I look at that stuff a little more closely. Because they are handmade, or have more craftsmanship. It's not punched out of machines (Linda, age 38).

While the utopian mall aesthetic described by informants overlaps with the postmodern description, it also has distinctive and even conflicting elements. Rather than situating in terms of postmodernity, we characterize our informants' desires in terms of the bazaar aesthetic. Informants seek out a variety of elements that recall preindustrial bazaars as well as informal markets in advanced capitalist economies: disorder, entertainments, unexpected juxtaposition, the cacophony of different people, sounds, goods, and personalized relationships between sellers and buyers. We read these descriptions as yearnings for the erasure of the rational organization of the marketplace, which is the structuring market principle of the post-Fordist era. These qualities have little to do with the artifice of postmodern simulacra. Just the opposite. As evidence, consider that informants reject the Nittany Mall as "fake" and ask for alternative design elements that are more natural, more real:

> It's not like downtown. I like downtown more because there is a different air about it. Maybe it's people, the students, the coffee shops. The mall seems different. I see things that I don't like. It is cold and depressing. It is, like, fake (Mary, age 27).

Contrary to the postmodern readings of shopping malls, which portray a lonely self adrift in a hyperreal dreamworld, our informants emphasize their desires for a marketplace that is culturally and socially a gathering place for crowds, offering diverse points of focus for diverse interests. This is a sense of market as a place of desire without obligation and containment of spectacle, of entertainment and play, of community and yet of anonymity.

MALL CONSUMPTION
AND THE FUTURE OF PUBLIC SPACE

Marketing researchers and postmodern critics alike urge that we examine malls as social and experiential spaces rather than merely as sites of economic exchange. But what kinds of experiences are produced in malls? And why? How are the noneconomic and economic dimensions of mall consumption related? Detailing what people do and what they want to do at malls allows us to conduct a grounded exploration of these questions. Even in the stripped-down economic space of Nittany Mall, we find substantial evidence for a variety of consumption practices often labeled postmodern. Our explication of mall practices supports and extends much of the postmodern literature on the mall. Malls are quasi-public spaces that allow for particular types of sociality with strangers that have otherwise been rationalized and privatized away by the logic of advanced capitalism. Malls also can simulate carnivalesque marketplaces—in our study more pronounced as utopian mall spaces than in the experience of the decidedly anti-ludic Nittany Mall—producing the vertiginous pleasures of ordered disorder, discontinuity, and disorientation.

However, our results do not support claims that malls produce interiorizing, aestheticized, consumerist fantasizing, or that atomistic "consumerist selves" are, momentarily, rejuvenated though engagement with the world of goods. While we do not deny that through their particular shopping activities people pursue and express individualizing visions of selves as consumers, we read this as a generic aspect of consumer capitalism not at all particular to mall consumption. Instead, in shopping at malls, our informants seek out a marketplace in which the public sphere is tantamount, in which the weak forms of ludic sociality that have always marked public marketplaces are re-created. Malls are liminal spaces that break up daily routines, that allow for ensemble improvisation. If such space has a ritual purpose beyond its obvious autotelic pleasures, it is to perform local community, to produce communitas in a privatized era that allows for little of this. Embodying disorder, in this case, can act to disrupt privatized, internalized lives, to transform experience from I to We.

The positivist marketing literature, ensconced in the ideology of the marketplace, assumes that malls are configured to optimize consumers' retail satisfactions (or else competition will lead to bankruptcy). Following the marketing concept, malls are understood as meta-retail offerings that offer a variety of benefits. People will choose to shop at malls to the extent that the package of benefits offered by malls fits their preferences better than other retail alternatives. So malls, in this literature, are conceived as integrated packages of economic, social, and experiential benefits that have been tailored to meet consumer preferences. To the extent that, as a retail genre, malls have concretized our shopping desires, we will happily use them.

Conceiving of mall consumption via the marketing concept presumes that developers' and mall consumers' interests perfectly align. Instead, we argue that mall consumption must be understood in terms of the tensions between owner interests and consumers' interests in the uses of retail space. Postmodern theorists view the shopping mall as an exemplary site of contemporary consumption because the economic function of the mall is occluded by its derationalized design elements and nonexchange activities. While some of these theorists believe either that mall consumption practices are ultimately dominated by the logic of capital (Gottdiener 1995) or that capitalist interests are readily subverted through oppositional practices (Fiske 1988), we argue that these practices are most appropriately construed in dialogic, dialectic terms as an unstable contested site in which the contradictions of advanced capitalism are everywhere evident.

The mall has emerged, and will continue to develop, as a particular form of built environment that negotiates between interests of capital in maximizing the profits generated by private retail space, and the interests of consumers in using retail space as a locus for particular forms of social rather than exchange practices. When mall owners seek to "meet consumer preferences" for mall space, they are not merely adding benefits to a market offering, they are also commodifying aspects of human life that have previously existed outside of the exchange nexus. That malls are organized to deliver public space as a marketable good creates an inherent tension between consumers' interests in consuming this space and owners' interests in maximizing the profits of the space. Mall developers do not simply provide what consumers desire. Rather, they integrate design elements only to the extent that they will pay out in attracting clientele to the mall and in generating incremental profits. Without focusing on this dialectic tension underlying the production of malls, it is difficult to explain why mall spaces have evolved as they have and to speculate in an informed manner on how malls will evolve in the future.

Mall developers do not attempt to create the ludic, carnival-esque spaces that people yearn for. Rather, through postmodern architectural veneer and the design of bazaar-like retail features (e.g., the "festival marketplace" concept with its restaurants and entertainments), mall owners mimic these spaces while maintaining rationalized control. Mall developers clearly understand people's interests in public social space and seek to build these interests into their malls. But their profit orientation leads them to provide only those features required to attract shoppers, creating shopping environments far removed from the ideals evoked by our informants. This explains why we find that sociality in malls is attenuated. Malls evoke the types of play, social communion, and carnival that non-rationalized marketplaces provide (see Sherry 1990), but these are only ephemeral glimpses, rather than lived experiences (see Belk and Bryce 1993).

Contradictions between these counterposing interests drive the dialectical evolution of retail space. Mall operators can minimize the space and architectural detail that sate sociality (e.g., the Nittany Mall), but in so doing they remove the raison d'être for mall consumption for many shoppers, baring the economic calculus of the space, a design that is objectionable to all except the most utilitarian of shoppers. Alternatively, operators can compete for customers by optimizing public space, hoping that retailers commingled will ride its coattails (much as do category killer bookstores with their cafes and reading spaces). But this competitive dynamic is ultimately a dead end for capital, since public space does not produce rents directly.

By this logic, then, the evolution of the mall should proceed as mall operators attempt to commodify their public spaces. That is, rather than providing space for sociality contiguous with shopping opportunities, operators will attempt to sell this space to consumers. This analysis provides an understanding of the recent evolution of mall space different than that offered by the dominant interpretations in the postmodern literature. Rather than the continuing elevation of the hyperreal spectacle, mall development is driven by the need to commodify social experience. Rather than sitting on benches looking upon an enchanting constructed space, why not visit Camp Snoopy? Instead of sipping a coffee amid the hustle and bustle of the market crowd, why not have a gourmet meal at California Pizza Kitchen? Through the commodification of the social, malls seek to develop "public" space that both draws clientele and makes a profit.

Malls have become, by default, the dominant public space in advanced capitalism. They are used by people from every sector of society to pursue different social practices. Shoppers pass power walkers on lunch break. The elderly escape the boredom and loneliness of retirement homes to grasp at a sense of belonging. Working-class kids rehearse the dance of sexuality in friendly environs.

If we are right that the economic-social dialectic is leading to the increasing commodification of public space, this raises a crucial and disturbing question. What will become of social life for those who cannot afford to be mall consumers? If the suburbanization of residential life—flowering most currently in the form of the gated community—has left behind impoverished public spaces for those who do not have the assets to participate in privatized social space, will malls follow suit, pricing the indigent out of one of the last communal sites available to them?

BIBLIOGRAPHY

BABIN, B. J.; W. R. DARDEN; AND M. GRIFFIN. 1994. "Work and/or Fun: Measuring Hedonic and Utilitarian Shopping Value." *Journal of Consumer Research* 20 (March): 644–656.

BAKHTIN, M. 1984. *Rabelais and His World*. Bloomington: Indiana University Press.

BAUDELAIRE, C. 1964. *The Painter of the Modern Life and Other Essays*. Oxford: Phaidon Press.

BAUDRILLARD, J. 1983. *Simulations*. New York: Semiotext.

———. 1988. "Consumer Society." In *Jean Baudrillard: Selected Writings,* edited by M. Poster. Stanford, CA: Stanford University Press.

BEARD, J. G., AND M. G. RAGHEB. 1983. "Measuring Leisure Motivation." *Journal of Leisure Research* 15(3):219–228.

BELK, R. W., AND W. BRYCE. 1993. "Christmas Shopping Scenes: From Modern Miracle to Postmodern Mall." *International Journal of Research in Marketing* 10:277–299.

BELLENGER, D. N., AND P. KORGOANKAR. 1980. "Profiling the Recreational Shopper." *Journal of Retailing* 58 (Spring): 58–81.

BELLENGER, D. N.; D. ROBERTSON; AND B. A. GREENBERG. 1977. "Shopping Center Patronage Motives." *Journal of Retailing* 53 (Summer): 29–38.

BENJAMIN, W. 1973. *Charles Baudelaire: A Lyric Poet in the Era of High Capitalism.* London: Verso.

BLOCH, P. H.; N. M. RIDGWAY; AND S. A. DAWSON. 1994. "The Shopping Mall as a Consumer Habitat." *Journal of Retailing* 70 (Spring): 23–41.

BLOCH, P. H.; N. M. RIDGWAY; AND J. E. NELSON. 1991. "Leisure and the Shopping Mall." In *Advances in Consumer Research,* vol. 18, edited by R. Holman and M. Solomon. Provo, UT: Association for Consumer Research, 445–452.

BLOCH, P. H.; N. M. RIDGWAY; AND D. L. SHERELL. 1989. "Extending the Concept of Shopping: An Investigation of Browsing Activity." *Journal of the Academy of Marketing Science* 17 (Winter): 13–21.

"Consumer Behavior in the Shopping Center." *Monitor.* 1988. 18:19–40.

DE CERTEAU, M. 1984. *The Practice of Everyday Life.* Berkeley: University of California Press.

DENZIN, N. K. 1991. *Images of Postmodern Society.* Newbury Park, CA: Sage.

DOWNS, A. 1961. "A Theory of Consumer Efficiency." *Journal of Retailing* 37 (Spring): 50.

FEATHERSTONE, M. 1991. *Consumer Culture and Postmodernism.* London: Routledge.

FEINBERG, R. A., AND J. MEOLI. 1991. "A Brief History of the Mall." In *Advances in Consumer Research,* vol. 18, edited by R. Holman and M. Solomon. Provo, UT: Association for Consumer Research, 426–427.

FEINBERG, R. A.; B. SHELLER; J. MEOLI; AND A. RUMMEL. 1989. "There Is Something Social Happening at the Mall," *Journal of Business and Psychology* 4 (Fall): 49–63.

FISKE, J. 1989. *Understanding Popular Culture.* Cambridge, MA: Unwin Hyman.

GOTTDIENER, M. 1995. *Postmodern Semiotics.* Cambridge, MA: Blackwell.

GRAHAM, E. 1988. "The Call of the Mall." *The Wall Street Journal* (May 13): 7R.

HARVEY, D. 1990. *The Condition of Postmodernity.* Cambridge, MA: Blackwell.

HAUG, W. F. 1987. *Commodity Aesthetics, Ideology and Culture.* New York: International General.

HOLT, F. 1995. "How Consumers Consume: A Typology of Consumption Practices." *Journal of Consumer Research* 22 (June): 1–16.

ISOGARI, H., AND S. MATSUSHIMA. 1972. *Market Places of the World.* This Beautiful World Series, no. 35. Palo Alto, CA: Kodansha International.

JACOBS, J. 1985. *The Mall: An Attempted Escape from Everyday Life.* Prospect Heights, IL: Waveland Press.

JAMESON, F. 1983. "Postmodernism and the Consumer Society." In *The Anti-Aesthetics: Essays on Postmodern Culture,* edited by H. Foster. Port Townsend, WA: Bay Press, 111–126.

JANSEN-VERBEKE, M. 1987. "Women Shopping and Leisure." *Leisure Studies* 6:71–86.

JARBOE, J. A., AND C. D. MCDANIEL. 1987. "A Profile of Browsers in Regional Shopping Malls." *Academy of Marketing Science* 15 (Spring): 46–53.

KELLEY, JOHN R. 1983. *Leisure Identities and Interactions.* London: George Allen.

KOWINSKI, W. S. 1985. *The Malling of America.* New York: William Morrow and Co.

LANGMAN, L. 1992. "Neon Cages: Shopping for Subjectivity." In *Lifestyle Shopping: Subject of Consumption,* edited by R. Shields. New York: Routledge.

LESSER, J. A., AND P. KAMAL. 1991. "An Inductively Described Model of the Motivation to Shop." *Psychology Marketing* 8 (Fall): 177–191.

SHERRY, JOHN F., JR. 1990. "A Sociocultural Analysis of a Midwestern American Flea Market." *Journal of Consumer Research* 17 (June): 13–30.

SHERRY, JOHN F., JR., AND MARY ANN MCGRATH. 1989. "Unpacking the Holiday Presence: A Comparative Ethnography of Two Gift Stores." In *Interpretive Consumer Research,* edited by Elizabeth C. Hirschman. Provo, UT: Association for Consumer Research, 148–167.

SHIELDS, R. 1992. *Lifestyle Shopping: The Subject of Consumption.* New York: Routledge.

STOFFEL, J. 1988. "Where America Goes for Entertainment." *New York Times* (August 7): 11: Fall.

TAUBER, E. M. 1972. "Why Do People Shop?" *Journal of Marketing* 36 (October): 46–59.

TINSLEY, H. E., AND D. J. TINSLEY. 1986. "A Theory of the Attributes, Benefits and Causes of Leisure Experience." *Leisure Sciences* 8(1):1–43.

URRY, J. 1990. *The Tourist Gaze.* Newbury Park, CA: Sage.

WEINSTEIN, D., AND M. A. WEINSTEIN. 1991. "Georg Simmel: Sociological Flaneur Bricoleur." *Theory, Culture and Society* 8:151–168.

WESTBROOK, R. A., AND W. C. BLACK. 1985. "A Motivation-Based Shopper Typology." *Journal of Retailing* 61 (Spring): 78–103.

PART III

ALTERNATIVE PLACEWAYS: VISITING THE UNDISCOVERED COUNTRY

In this section, we make a transition from investigating more traditional conventional marketplaces (Dorst 1989; Horwitz 1985; Kowinski 1985; Jacobs 1984; Prus 1989a, 1989b) to exploring emerging sites of increasing relevance to marketers. This requires a new typology of marketplaces. We can describe marketplaces along two dimensions, expediently defined as continua, although they are actually dialectical:

1. One dimension represents tractability or malleability of the marketplace. At one extreme, we encounter the *natural* environment, which is primordial, or "found." At the other, we encounter the *cultural* environment, which is designed, or "built." As we move from natural to cultural, marketplaces grow more plastic and shape-shifting; consumption sites become increasingly adaptable.

2. The other dimension represents the tangible or material quality of the marketplace. At one extreme, consumption sites are predominantly *physical*, or grounded quite literally. At the other extreme, consumption sites are predominantly *ethereal*, or metaphysical. As we move from physical to ethereal, marketplaces shift from an emplaced

"somewhere" to an unplaced "nowhere," their local geography becoming less charted as we proceed.

Inevitably, every marketplace will partake in every dimension, at some level.

Each possible combination can be defined as a different scape:

- A highly natural, physical marketplace is a *landscape.* It is realized through venues such as the wilderness and outdoor brandfest servicescapes described in this section.
- A highly cultural, physical marketplace is a *marketscape.* It may be expressed through retail- or home-based servicescapes as described in this section.
- A highly cultural and ethereal marketplace is a *cyberscape.* While realized through computer media described in this section, it also comprises direct marketing channels such as broadcast and narrowcast media.
- A highly natural and ethereal marketplace is a *mindscape,* a metaphysical inner space accessible via consciousness-altering techniques of bewildering psycho-socio-cultural-pharmacological (and, yes, bionic) diversity. With the exception of our tapping of consumer fantasy, the mindscape has gone lamentably unexplored in this volume, although not unconsidered in our literature (Belk 1987).

Consider this model a preliminary entry into the cartography of market placeways, and the following chapters our initial forays into uncharted placeways.

Alladi Venkatesh traces the growth and differentiation of markets in cyberspace, projects the nature of their possible future evolution, laments the co-optation of cyberspace by marketers, and challenges marketers to develop prosocial ideologies as they colonize this new world. His discussion of everyday life in consumer cyberspace is a lucid introduction to this unprecedented level of sociocultural integration. The new global cultural system in which cybermarket cultures are currently evolving celebrates "structures of common difference" that express locality in more widely intelligible ways (Wilk 1995, 18), which makes enclaves in cyberspace—ethnic, entrepreneurial, or otherwise—players in a transcultural dynamic that is not accurately described as either homogenization or fragmentation. That the principal pioneers of cyberspace are a bimodal lot (the relatively young and the relatively old) and that few viable cybermarkets have yet to emerge are just a few of the intriguing conditions for which we have yet to imagine consequences.

Jim McAlexander and John Schouten treat us to a fascinating account of a consumer ritual (grounded perhaps in subculture) that, while sharing surface similarities, is the virtual obverse of corporate-sponsored spectacle: the brandfest. Not quite a convention or trade show, not simply a variant of promenade or *flânerie,* the brandfest resembles most closely a pilgrimage and related *rites de passage.* The communitas arising from this liminoid encounter (Turner 1974; Turner and Turner 1979), grounded in a heroic tradition and emerging from ordeal, binds participants together in an organic relationship more significant than a segment. McAlexander and Schouten contribute to a growing literature that treats the animation of the brand (Loden 1992; Randazzo 1993), especially as it overlaps with elaboration of product constellations and brandscapes (Solomon and Assael 1987; Sherry 1986). The authors reveal something of the totemic circuitry (Plath 1987) that underlies product involvement in the United States.

Eric Arnould, Linda Price, and Patrick Tierney demonstrate that wilderness is culturally constructed, as marketers reposition natural grandeur even as consumers view it through postmodern-colored glasses. Via "communicative staging," marketers deliver a wilderness experience in conformance with their consumers' culturally conditioned expectations. The authors examine the brokerage of wilderness ideology over time in American society and show how marketers borrow from dominant historical interpretations to frame their own particular experiential offerings. We are challenged to reconsider our notion of authenticity in light of the authors' findings. Given the rise in the global significance of a tourism industry that seeks to deliver the experience of exotic difference with a minimum of discomfort to transnational travelers, the need to study "natural" servicescapes and their management grows more urgent.

Mary Ann McGrath draws upon her years of experience with ethnography and indirect elicitation in investigating marketplaces to sketch a picture of what consumers imagine to be an ideal servicescape. Her study, grounded in participant observation, interview, co-shopping, survey, and projective tasking, focuses on gender-based interpretations of "the ideal." Surprisingly, she finds greater commonalities than differences between men and women with respect to reception of retail ambience. Ironically, price appears to be a "nonissue" in these consumer idylls, which reinforces some of the insights Baker offers in Chapter 2. Her findings are suggestive for designers seeking to deliver at least the very minimal parameters of delight to prospective consumers.

In our final contribution to Part III, Kent Grayson examines the ways in which network marketers employ physical and procedural cues to transform domestic space into commercial space. Charismatic capitalism (Biggart 1989) demands that home become a sales floor, that private places become public. Grayson describes strategies geared toward fostering different types of consensus— business-oriented, home-oriented, and combined—that marketers invoke in the service of increased sales. His discussion recalls the dramaturgical perspective of servicescape dynamics developed by Solomon in Chapter 3. The proliferation of network marketing around the globe suggests that marketers must become hypervigilant in their assessment of the cultural variability of social consensus, if opportunity is to be realized.

BIBLIOGRAPHY

BELK, RUSSELL. 1987. "A Modest Proposal for Creating Verisimilitude in Consumer-Information-Processing Models and Some Suggestions for Establishing a Discipline to Study Consumer Behavior." In *Philosophical and Radical Thought in Marketing,* edited by A. F. Firat, Nikhilesh Dholakia, and Richard Bagozzi. Lexington, KY: Lexington Books, 361–372.

BIGGART, NICOLE. 1989. *Charismatic Capitalism: Direct Selling Organizations in America.* Chicago: University of Chicago Press.

DORST, JOHN. 1989. *The Written Suburb: An American Site, An Ethnographic Dilemma.* Philadelphia: University of Pennsylvania Press.

HORWITZ, RICHARD. 1985. *The Strip: An American Place.* Lincoln: University of Nebraska Press.

KOWINSKI, WILLIAM. 1985. *The Malling of America.* New York: Morrow.

JACOBS, JERRY. 1984. *The Mall: An Attempted Escape from Everyday Life.* Prospect Heights, IL: Waveland Press.

LODEN, P. JOHN. 1982. *Megabrands: How to Build Them, How to Beat Them.* Homewood, IL: Business One Irwin.

PLATH, DAVID. 1987. "Gifts of Discovery." *Liberal Education* 73(4):12–16.

PRUS, ROBERT. 1989a. *Making Sales: Influence as Interpersonal Accomplishment.* Newbury Park, CA: Sage.

———. 1989b. *Pursuing Customers: An Ethnography of Marketing Activities.* Newbury Park, CA: Sage.

RANDAZZO, SAL. 1993. *Mythmaking on Madison Avenue: How Advertisers Apply the Power of Myth and Symbolism to Create Leadership Brands.* Chicago: Probus.

SHERRY, JOHN F., JR. 1986. "Cereal Monogamy: Brand Loyalty as Secular Ritual in Consumer Culture." Paper presented at 17th Annual Conference of the Association for Consumer Research, Las Vegas, NV.

———. 1990. " A Sociocultural Analysis of a Midwestern American Flea Market." *Journal of Consumer Research* 17(1):13–30.

SOLOMON, MICHAEL, AND HENRY ASSAEL. 1987. " The Forest or the Trees? A Gestalt Approach to Symbolic Consumption." In *Marketing and Semiotics: New Directions in the Study of Signs for Sale,* edited by Jean Umiker-Sebeok. Berlin: Monton de Gruyfer, 189–217.

TURNER, VICTOR. 1974. *Dramas, Fields and Metaphor.* Ithaca, NY: Cornell University Press.

TURNER, VICTOR, AND EDITH TURNER. 1978. *Image and Pilgrimage in Christian Culture: Anthropological Perspectives.* New York: Columbia University Press.

WILK, RICHARD. 1995. "Learning to Be Local in Belize: Global Systems of Common Difference." In *Worlds Apart: Modernity Through the Prism of the Local,* edited by Daniel Miller. New York: Routledge, 110–133.

IO

CYBERCULTURE

Consumers and Cybermarketscapes

ALLADI VENKATESH

"Sorry, we're closed, the humans are temporarily down for maintenance."
> —sign on cyberstore front

Cybermarketscape may very well be the new story of marketing. We have just begun to create this new story. In this chapter, I undertake an analysis of the development of the cybermarketscape and some key issues concerning the conceptualization of the consumer in the cybermarketscape. Given how recent and undeveloped the topic is, the main focus of the chapter is to identify the issues and elaborate them, instead of trying to provide final answers.

In examinations of the issue of consumers in cyberspace, two narratives appear to recur. One refers to the unidimensional perspective of marketing and how marketing tries to colonize cyberspace and regards the consumer as fair game in its profit-seeking enterprise. The second narrative views consumers as trying to use cyberspace as a place to exercise their freedoms and establish their identities, and to use cyberspace as a "lifeworld" in a Habermasian sense (Habermas 1985).

Alladi Venkatesh is Professor of Management and Research Associate at the Center for Research on Information Technology in Organizations, University of California, Irvine.

We begin the chapter with a general introduction to cyberspaces. This will be followed by an elaboration of cybermarketscape as a derivative idea of cyberspace. Following this, I shall introduce the notions of cybercitizen and cyberconsumer as the true exemplars of human participants in the cyberspatial order. The chapter will conclude with suggestions for future directions.

CYBERSPACES AND CYBERMARKETSCAPES

Cyberspaces are spatial and temporal configurations formed out of electronic environments. They are usually described as parallel spaces to the physical spaces. Benedikt (1991), in his introduction to *Cyberspace: First Steps,* gives eleven descriptions/definitions of cyberspace, ranging from the technical to the metaphorical and the whimsical. The following definition is the most relevant to this chapter:

> Cyberspace: A new universe, a parallel universe [parallel to the physical universe] created and sustained by the world's computers and communication lines (p. 1).

It must, however, be noted that it was the science fiction writer Gibson (1984) who first coined the term *cyberspace* in his playful classic, *Neuromancer:*

> Cyberspace. A consensual hallucination experienced daily by billions of legitimate operators. . . . A graphic representation of data abstracted from the banks of every computer in the human system. Unthinkable complexity. Lines of light ranged in the nonspace of the mind, clusters and constellations of data. Like city lights, receding . . . (p. 51).

Clarity of purpose is not yet the goal of cyberspatial discourse, for cyberspace philosophy seems to suggest that pursuit of clarity may be a little premature and may indeed limit the horizons of possibility. Besides, cyberspace is still evolving and should be allowed to do so. This does not mean there are no attempts to introduce this clarity into this enterprise. But this is clarity of a different kind.

The media leader in this discursive formation of cyberspace is the magazine *Wired*. The magazine is a collage of advertising, short articles, long interviews, pictures, where every genre merges into the other. The cleverest feat of the magazine is that one cannot easily ascertain where the commercial space ends and the editorial space begins. This is because both are subsumed under the communal plurality of cyberspace. *Wired* is the realization in print of what cyberspace promises to be electronically. It is an amalgam of everything from art to science, praxis, and philosophy. If *Wired* represents anything, it is that cyberspace is a combination of chaos and clarity and the game playing between the two constantly goes on.

The point to remember, however, is that cyberspace is not a magic land; it is not created by a wave of an electronic wand, although such an image is plausible because of the powers of simulation and spectacle vested in cybertechnologies. Cyberspace is essentially a product *constructed* out of the new technologies of communication, information, and computerization. It is with these three technologies—or, more importantly, with their convergence—that we are concerned in cyberspace. It is in this constructed technological space that we have to envision the everyday life of the individual and the social/cultural order. This new social/cultural order has been labeled by Escobar (1994) as cyberculture:

> The study of cyberculture is particularly concerned with the cultural constructions and reconstructions on which the new technologies are based and which they in turn help to shape. The point of departure of this inquiry is the belief that any technology represents a cultural intervention, in the sense it brings forth a [constructed] world (p. 211).

Different people configure cyberspace differently. Cyberspace is a public space, a community space, as well as a private space. (For some recent elaborations of cyberspace, see Poster 1995; Shields 1996; Stone 1995; Turkle 1995.) It is a commercial space as well as an aesthetic space. It is a dimensionless space and a negotiated space. The transformation of public space into a commercial space means that the individual is both a citizen with civic identity and a consumer with desires and needs, making him or her a "target" for marketing—thus creating a simultaneous image of a private citizen immune from the market and a consumer par excellence under its direct influence.

Much reference is made to the multidimensionality as well as nondimensionality of cyberspace—that it is a space of information flows, databases, and networked/hypertextual links to people and places, that it is nurtured on the one hand by profit-seeking corporate presence and on the other hand by people driven by community concerns. At another extreme is the notion that it is also a place for humanoids, replicants, prostheses—in other words, a place where artificial life might emerge. It is a parallel space to the physical/Euclidean space but without its transparent certainty; for some others it is a pure Shangri-la, a never-never land. With so much going on in cyberspace, perhaps it makes sense for us to introduce some focus or crispness to the idea of cyberspace as we look at it from a marketing perspective.

Cybermarketscapes

As a first step toward this goal, I introduce the term *cyberscape* with the suffix *-scape* to signify its specific relevance to the discussion of this chapter. It was Appadurai (1990) who first employed a typology of scapes in his analysis of the global cultural economy. He identified the global cultural scene in terms of five scapes, which he called finanscapes, mediascapes, technoscapes, ethnoscapes, and ideoscapes. As used here, cyberscapes may be said to be a combination of mediascapes and technoscapes as enunciated by Appadurai and also something more that is created within the context of electronic environments.[1] The most dramatic manifestation of cyberscape is the Internet and its associated technologies, including various on-line services, Netscape, Explorer, and the like. For a comprehensive analysis of issues related to the Internet and user per-

[1] Reference must be made here to a similar term, *servicescape,* used by Bittner (1992) in a different context.

spectives, I refer to the special issue of *Communications of the* ACM
(December 1996), in particular, to the articles by Kraut (1996); Hoffman, Klasbeek, and Novak (1996); Venkatesh (1996); Kraut et al.
(1996); Franzke and McClard (1996); and Carrol and Rosson (1996).
For additional information on information technology and home
use, see Dholakia, Munsdorf, and Dholakia (1995). For previous
work in this area, see Vitalari, Venkatesh, and Gronhaug (1985) and
Venkatesh and Vitalari (1987, 1990).

A particular form of cyberscapes addressed in this chapter lies
at the intersection of electronic markets and consumers. I shall call
them cybermarketscapes. At this stage of evolution, there is a certain nebulousness and confusion about cyberscapes as viable marketscapes. There is simultaneously skepticism (White 1996) and
optimism (Flynn 1995; Balog 1996) regarding cybermarketscapes as
economic successes, suggesting the possibility that we are at an
experimental moment—the electronic terrain is still undeveloped,
and the gold rush has just begun. The literature on this subject
suggests that marketscapes are not a given but are being (need to
be) constructed, and they also need to evolve (Ellsworth and
Ellsworth 1996).

Marketscapes can evolve only when the elements of marketscapes evolve. The traditional marketscapes with which we are
familiar can be conceived in terms of the institutions of marketing
and advertising, shopping environments and shopping catalogs, and
a whole list of artifacts that constitute the marketing culture that
has evolved over a period of six or seven decades. The question facing the academic and the practitioner alike today is, What analogues
exist in the cybermarketscape so we can make sense out of the new
technological developments? One answer is that such analogues do
not in fact exist and must be and are being constructed for this as a
new territory ready for exploration and development. After all, contemporary marketing culture itself did not appear overnight but took
several decades to develop, with its origins going back to the early
telephonic era. It is this historical or Schumpeterean unfolding
which gives it its institutional strength, as well as its weakness—its
strength because it affords a reference point as new cultural signs and
institutions are introduced and get assimilated into the marketing

ethos; its weakness because the historical processes have been invested with certain adaptive inflexibility in the face of new forces.

An important element of the cybermarketscape is the consumer or, to be more precise, the "cyberconsumer," which is the main focus of this chapter. Just as "marketing" evolved over the last half a century and has now become part of our global cultural ethos, so has the category called the consumer evolved through a familiar cluster of meanings and practices. These meanings, as they refer to both the markets and consumers, are embedded in the traditional marketscapes that we take for granted. The consumer as a construct and product of this evolutionary process is essentialized through different conceptualizations appropriate to our definitions of marketscape. Any textbook on consumer behavior will provide a narrative appropriate to our contemporary view of the consumer (Solomon 1995).

THE CONSTRUCTION
OF THE CYBERMARKETSCAPE

The cybermarketscape is the product of the information revolution, whose full fury is just beginning to be felt. The technological dimensions of the cybermarketscape are changing so rapidly that it is difficult to keep track of all the developments. The changes occur daily, if not by the hour, with no definable horizons in sight. Figure 10.1 shows four key elements that encompass the cyberscape: the new and rapidly evolving cybertechnology [A], the larger social order [B], the cybermarketscape or the realm of marketing and commerce affected upon by cybertechnology [C], and the cybercitizen/cyberconsumer as the adopter of new technology [D]. In this simple schema, everything is in a dynamic state. The rapidly changing technology [A] has and continues to have an impact on the larger social order [B], and has also begun to make a similar impact on marketing institutions and processes, or commerce [C]. The technology and the marketing processes have an impact on the individual, both as a member of the social order (citizen) and as consumer [D].

Let us for a moment address the issue of the impact on the consumer. The consumer is not only a consumer of the new tech-

FIGURE 10.1   Key Elements of the Cyberscape

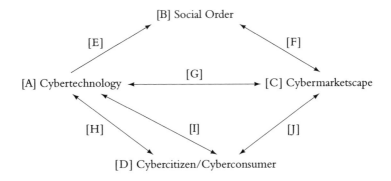

H = the broader impact of cybertechnology on the individual as cybercitizen
(doctor, lawyer, parent consumer, voter, etc.).
I = a *particular instance* of this impact on the individual as *consumer*.
Cyberconsumer is singled out because the focus of the chapter is the individual
as consumer. Other roles are not discussed here.

nology [H] and its products, but a consumer of the market processes, which are themselves affected by the new technology [J].
The consumer has a dual technological charge, as it were. He or she
has to become technologically literate in order to be able to function as an effective member of the social order, but he or she is also
required to respond to the market as the market attempts to incorporate new technological developments into its processes. So, for
example, the consumer has to decide what new computer to buy,
what new on-line service to acquire, what telecommunications connections to obtain, all of this in reference to the arrows designated
by H and I. At the same time, the consumer has to decide how to
negotiate the market exchange process [J], that is, how to order
goods and services in the cybermarketscape [C] and how to be
cybermarket literate. Obviously, there is a connection between how
consumers respond to technology [H/I] and how they respond to
the cybermarketscape [J]. This issue will be taken up later in the
chapter.

     To present a perspective to the discussion in the chapter, I
would like to present a "tale from the field" (with apologies to Van
Maanen 1988) that may very well describe the relationship between

the cybercitizen/cyberconsumer and the new technology [A] and cybermarketscape [C]. Of course, my main aim in the chapter is to develop the relationship between the consumer [D] and the market processes relating to the cybermarketscape [C].

Everyday Life of a Cybercitizen

Let us construct what I consider to be not an untypical day in the life of a cybercitizen in contemporary American society. Ms. K is a self-employed mother who works at home part-time. She gets up in the morning at 6:00 A.M. and makes coffee on her coffee machine, which has a built-in computer chip. While coffee is getting ready, she turns on her Web-TV for the latest morning news. As she is switching the channel, she finds on channel 6 a show about how to do business on the Internet. She also finds that her news channel has two commercials, one for the latest, fastest multimedia computer made by a new entrant into the field from a country half a planet away. She quickly logs on to check for E-mail messages and tends to urgent business mail. She will come back later in the day to attend to more routine personal and business mail.

At 6:45 A.M., her daughter, Ms. C, wakes up and goes through a rapid wash-change-of-clothes sequence in ten minutes, then dashes down to the kitchen for a glass of orange juice and a dried toast, all of which takes about seventeen minutes. She climbs back to her room where she finds the computer still running since last night when she went to bed at 1:00 A.M. after preparing her latest class report, titled "The Vanishing Tribes of Northern Utah." She makes last-second corrections and prints her report on the ink-jet printer that she recently inherited when her mother bought herself the latest laser printer. All of this takes an additional eleven minutes. She springs out of the door and off she speeds on her bike to her school, which is a six-minute ride.

At about 8:30 Ms. K makes herself a light breakfast and heats her coffee in the microwave oven, which also has a built-in computer chip. At 9:00 she is at her home-office desk, taking care of business correspondence and other details. At 11:00 A.M. she drives her car to the nearest strip mall, where she extracts some cash from a computerized ATM. She also attends to other banking business on a recently installed vending machine located next to the old ATM. She walks to the grocery store, negotiates the grocery cart—loaded with a computerized screen displaying special items on sale—through the aisles, and uses her grocery card, which she runs through a computerized cash register cum scanner machine. She is back home at about 12:30 P.M. and has a salad and yogurt for lunch.

After a short rest, she reads the daily electronic, personalized, newspaper on the Web and notices the flashing icon inviting her to examine new software. On a note of slight distraction, creature of habit that she is, she can't resist scanning the newspaper that is delivered to her home every morning by a speeding delivery van. The article on home offices catches her attention. She realizes that the mail must have just arrived, and as she examines it, she notices that it consists of business mail, personal mail, magazines, and junk mail. Most of the junk mail is computer oriented—subscriptions for a new Internet magazine, new software that does things quicker and better, new game software for children, an invitation from the local bank for a free trial of its computerized banking service, a diskette that gives her access to a database on "everything you wanted to know about the latest stocks," and similar material.

Not content with just looking at the mail, she decides to call an 888 number that lets callers access a lot of information just by pressing the appropriate numbers on the telephone keypad. A computerized voice guides her through some astonishing detail. Exactly five minutes later, she is a proud owner of a new computer service. . . .

This tale is slightly stylized but nevertheless a truthful caricature of the contemporary experience of a cybercitizen. All of this may not have happened on a single day but could easily happen within a matter of days. The telling point is how much we are surrounded by technology, in this case, the technologies of cyberculture.

More formally, I have presented this everyday experience in Figure 10.2. In the middle of the figure is the consumer, and in the first circle of the figure are a variety of activities performed by the consumer that have technological application or significance. In the outer circle is a set of technologies of cyberculture that are utilized in performing these activities. To interpret the figure, read a specific activity diagonally and refer to the associated technology indicated in the outer ring. To illustrate, let us take the activity of home shopping. The associated technologies are telephone, on-line ser-

FIGURE 10.2   Everyday Life of a Consumer in Cyberspace

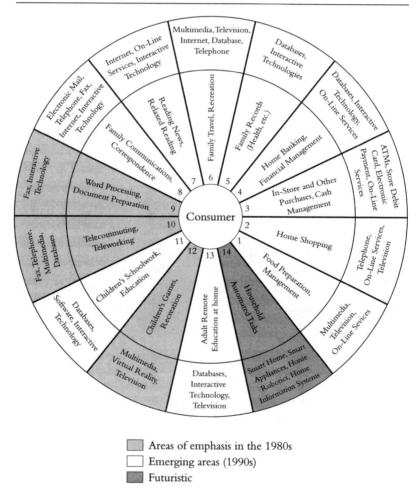

Areas of emphasis in the 1980s
Emerging areas (1990s)
Futuristic

vices, and television. While the figure is a static or a structural representation of a cybercitizen's activities, one can theorize about these relationships. For example, under what conditions does a consumer use a particular technology for home shopping? Or what type of consumers use TV for home shopping as opposed to the Internet? What happens when these technologies merge? Such questions will depend on specific research issues involved and the motivations of the researcher in understanding various phenomena under investigation. The purpose of the figure is to give an account of the ubiquitous nature of technology in the daily life of the consumer.

CONSUMER LIFE AND THE NEW TECHNOLOGIES

According to various industry sources and academic researchers, the following areas have been identified as having an impact because of the new technologies and electronic media: teleworking (telecommuting), home entertainment, education, cybershopping/home shopping, telecommunications, and home computing/home management. In no sense are these areas to be considered mutually exclusive or exhaustive. Here is a brief description of how these areas are developing and will continue to develop:

- *Teleworking*—This refers to work at home. Our own research (Venkatesh and Vitalari 1992) shows that this is a growing activity largely aided by computers at home. In our research, we identified five different types of teleworking: telecommuters, who substitute working at home for commuting to work; moonlighters, who work on different jobs from their primary employment during weekends or evenings; supplemental workers, who work at home in addition to full-time work; self-employed people, who use the home as their business location; and part-timers, who work at home for outside organizations on contract work.

- *Home entertainment*—This area includes two principal services: movies on demand and video games. Many industry

experts believe that this will be the most commercially
successful market among interactive services. The reason is
that home entertainment via TV and vcr is already well
established, and it involves a low-level effort by the user.

- *Cybershopping*—Not too long ago, a previous version of
  this was called "teleshopping" to signify home shopping
  via the telephone. A still previous version used the 800
  number. With the arrival of the on-line services and the
  Internet, home shopping involves a digital medium.

- *Telecommunications*—This is a rapidly growing area,
  especially with possible integration of the telephone,
  personal computer, and television. Some already existing
  facilities include computerized fax systems, electronic mail,
  and telemedicine.

- *Computing in the home*—This was a promised land in the
  eighties, and while the growth has been slow, it seems to
  be coming into its own. Currently, computer services such
  as Prodigy, America Online, and CompuServe are pushing
  their services aggressively.

- *Internet*—This refers to electronic networking of individuals with other individuals and organizations on a one-to-
  one basis or simultaneously.

- *Home management and intelligent home systems*—The user is
  granted convenience and control over appliances and elec-
  trical equipment in the home through interactive systems,
  thus minimizing manual operations. There are three functional categories in the home system: interactive smart
  products, intelligent subsystems, and central home automa-
  tion systems. This technology is at a very experimental
  stage and requires the integration of computers, fiber
  optics, and multimedia capabilities, which combine data,
  voice, and visual communications.

Recent studies have given us a glimpse of the behavior of
cybercitizens with respect to the new Internet-based technologies.
Table 10.1 is a recent report from *Wired* magazine (1997) indicating

TABLE 10.1   On-Line Activity by Women

Activity	Percentage of Women Selecting Activity as Their Top Use
E-mail	29%
Web surfing	24
Education/reference sources	13
News and information	9
Business/work related	8
Real-time chats	5
Entertainment	4
Computer/technical	2
Newsgroups	1
Other (miscellaneous)	5
Total	100%

Source: Wired (1997).

how women are using on-line services. Some other studies reporting on the Internet show a similar distribution. Of particular significance in this and similar studies is the result that as a cybercitizen, the individual in contemporary society is exposed to cybertechnology as part of his or her daily life (Figure 10.1, H and I), but that many of the activities of the cybercitizen do not yet represent active participation in the cybermarketscape in a major way. The cybercitizen is still in the process of becoming a full-fledged cyberconsumer. The most dominant use of on-line services is E-mail, which suggests that on-line services are being used as an interpersonal communication medium. A second major activity is Web surfing, which indicates an experimental behavior on the part of the cybercitizen, pointing to a potential participation in the market processes.

In a recent report in *USA Today* (Balog 1996), some statistics appear to suggest that on-line consumer buying is on the increase. Here are some pertinent developments reported in the study:

- Although on-line shopping makes up less than 2 percent of retail sales, the number of retailers offering that service tripled between 1995 and 1996.

- With some big-name retailers coming on-line and adding credibility to the distribution channel, on-line sales are estimated to reach $7 billion by the year 2000.

- As of December 1996, 14 percent of retailers were on-line, up from 4 percent a year earlier.

- Bad weather kept many people out of the malls in December 1996.

- Credit security does not seem to be as much of a problem as originally feared.

- Companies like IBM are taking a special interest in on-line shopping. Although not in the on-line business, they are interested in developing the technology that facilitates this new marketing practice.

- QVC, which runs a home-shopping channel, has stated that convenience is the reason for on-line shopping by time-strapped shoppers.

Since we are dealing with the potential development of the cybermarketscape, we need to identify implications of these new possibilities for various consumer-related issues. In the following sections, we provide some critical discussion regarding these issues.

NEW TECHNOLOGIES AND THE CYBERCONSUMER: SOME THEORETICAL ISSUES

No area of consumers' lives seems to escape the influence of computer technologies. We can consider computers at two levels—one implicitly when computerized technologies are built into an electronic system or machinery but not directly handled by the consumer, the other where the consumer is required to negotiate the technology directly. There is a continuum of user-oriented situations, ranging from one extreme where the consumer has to acquire a very specific set of sophisticated skills to operate the technology to the other where the consumer is the passive recipient of the benefits of technology.

Between these two extreme situations, there is a range of possibilities. Some technologies impose a burden on the consumer in terms of skills, but the same technologies might develop to a point where such skill requirements are minimized. In other cases, the skill requirements are low to begin with, but the benefits associated with the technology can be quite significant. An example of the latter is the ATM, which is easy to operate by a consumer with no special skills. The consumer deals only with the ATM screen and enters the data as prompted via the screen. Many automated systems are of this type, including microchip-based microwave ovens, house alarm systems, sprinkler systems, and so on. On the other hand, ATMs, although easy to operate, are backed up by extremely sophisticated technological infrastructure that is part of the banking system and has no bearing on consumers' ability to use the technology. If, however, the consumer decides to do home banking via the home computer, the situation gets complicated because the consumer has to know the basics of how to operate a home PC and the appropriate software.

What does this all mean to the relationship between the consumer and the computer? Conceptually, we would like to distinguish between *what the computer can do to the consumer* and *what the consumer can do with the computer.* These two concepts, although distinct, are mutually related. Of course, this is not purely a conceptual distinction. It has a great deal of practical significance because it is the customer who, as the user of the technology, ultimately determines its viability. What computers can do proclaims the potential of technology as well as its limitations, and what humans can do completes the picture from the other side. A second, perhaps more important aspect of this relationship is the social embeddedness of technology and the technological embeddedness of the consumer. This mutuality of technology and the user raises some important issues in the design of new technologies and in the strategies that consumers use in dealing with technologies to their own purposes. Another aspect of this relationship is the order effects of technology. The first-order effect of the technology is quite clear and usually is related to the functionality of the technology. The second-order effects go beyond the mere functionality of the technology as originally conceived by the producers and are shaped by consumers, who may use a form of technology for reasons totally different from the applications originally conceived, with unexpected results. Usually, this is referred to as the unintended consequences of the technology.

We shall now return to Figure 10.1 and discuss the technology/user issue as it unfolds in the context of the cybermarketscape. Figure 10.1 distinguishes between the impact of the information technology on the individual as a member of the social order (citizen, student, household member, educator, politician, office worker/manager, author, etc.) and as a consumer (member of the market system). This distinction is crucial to the focus of this chapter. An illustration of this point is in order. There is no doubt that as an author or a student or a worker, an individual does consume the technology directly. That is, as long as the individual buys a computer and related gadgetry to write a book (Figure 10.1, H), she is fulfilling her role as an author. Similarly, if the computer helps her pursue her profession as an educator, she would buy it for that reason. In cases such as these, she is a consumer (but) of technology that helps her perform her role (as author, educator, etc.) within the social order. We shall label this person the cybercitizen, as shown in Figure 10.1. There is also a second relationship between the individual as a consumer and the technology. It is this relationship that has recently captured marketers' attention or imagination. The marketing profession has become interested in this relationship because it opens more doors for direct consumer participation in the market-exchange system. It is one thing for an individual to buy a computer to pursue her profession. It is another thing to buy a computer so that she can buy a service, download a television program, record a recipe, gain access to information, open a bank account, purchase a holiday gift for a family member, or acquire a similar consumable item. In these examples, the individual is not using the technology to fulfill a social role but as a generalized cyberconsumer satisfying several of her daily needs. The ultimate irony of this relationship, of course, is that now one can buy a computer using a computer. When I use a computer, I am behaving like a cybercitizen, and when I am using a computer to buy a computer, I am behaving like a cyberconsumer. In the first instance, I am responding to cybertechnology (Figure 10.1, H), and in the latter instance, I am responding to the cybermarketscape.

Why has this relationship become so crucial to the current context? It has become crucial because as long as the individual is buying the technology directly to fulfill his or her role as a member of the social order or to practice his or her profession (Figure 10.1, H), the marketing paradigm is not affected drastically. That is, the conventional marketscape is still the reigning institutional order, although things may be done differently or more efficiently. However, if the new technology is not simply another means of doing things differently within the market system, but *itself represents a different market system,* then we may be anticipating a radical transformation of the marketscape. This is the reason why we have given it a special label, "the cybermarketscape."

The question facing us is whether the technology is drastically changing the marketscape or merely adding a technological dimension to the existing marketscape. At one end of the debate are the skeptics, who maintain that if the marketscape is changing, it is only at a technological level; the core of marketing is still the same, except perhaps there is more fragmented experimentation associated with the new technologies (Kling 1996). At the other end are the protechnology enthusiasts, who proclaim a new technological millennium that is poised to transform the very core of marketing (see several authors in Cronin 1996). (I must, however, admit that in this world of unmitigated hype, there are far fewer skeptics than enthusiasts.) The truth, as they say, lies somewhere in between. In this chapter, I have taken a position to pretend that a radical transformation is under way. There are certainly some key indicators pointing to this, not all of them very transparent. In pretending that such a transformation has begun to occur, I can develop a picture of what it would mean if indeed this were to occur.

Conceptually speaking, the market system is a system of exchange between the producer and the consumer, as well as a communication system between the same two entities. I shall contextualize and analyze this relationship with three technologies with which we are familiar, the telephone, the automobile, and the television. Using the schema in Figure 10.1, we might say that each of these technologies were acquired by individuals as consumers of the technology. What market impact do or did these technologies have? For example, as consumers, we do use the telephone to buy goods and services (e.g., airline reservations), sometimes seek information before the purchase of a product, and communicate problems if the good or service is not satisfactory. Similarly, on a limited basis, marketers do a certain amount of direct marketing via the telephone, when, for example, vendors make calls to households (especially at dinnertime) selling their wares. None of these behaviors prompt us to say that the telephone radically altered the principles of the consumer-oriented market system, although we can argue quite successfully that the telephone has had a revolutionary impact on the social order (Figure 10.1, B), and certainly on the workings of the business-market system (Figure 10.1, C).

Let us now take the example of the automobile. In a similar fashion to the telephone, the automobile has certainly transformed the society in fundamental ways, by creating new forms of suburban life and by introducing a new sense of freedom among youth. However, one cannot argue therefore that it has altered the market exchange processes.

The third technology is the television. In a similar fashion to the telephone and the automobile, the television has transformed our social order in unprecedented ways. However, in addition, and unlike the telephone or the automobile, the television has had a qualitative impact on the consumer-market system. The television is a technology of communication and entertainment, or mass medium. As a powerful medium of audiovisual communication, it has changed the way we consume entertainment and news as well as advertising messages. Television has had major impact on brand marketing and on the overall consumer culture. It has thus changed the content and delivery of marketing communication, created a new institution of advertising, and radically changed the practice of marketing.

In other words, the television seems to have had the most impact on the world of consumption and consumer behavior. Because television, unlike the automobile or telephone, is a major mass-media technology, its central role in the development and transformation of the global consumer culture is widely acknowledged. However, as powerful as television's role has been in changing the consumer culture or adding a new dimension to marketing practice, hitherto unprecedented, it did not alter the way we think about the marketscape.

The initial impact of the computer on marketing practice, although quite substantial, did not suggest that we should rethink the paradigm itself. Initially, it was positioned as a representation of information technology, and its first incarnation was as an information storage device. Indeed, computers were always likened to the human brain, yet they were considered one additional point in the technological spectrum. In the last few years, however, things began to change dramatically. What was considered the technology of information has now become a technology of communication—not communication in the ordinary sense, but as multiway communication. Terms such as *interactivity* and *connectivity* have further advanced our notions of what the new technology can do. Computers have also created a new space, cyberspace, and new communities of participants, or virtual communities. In other words, it is the recent convergence of communication and information that has created possibilities unthinkable only a few years ago.

Table 10.2 gives a brief comparison of all four technologies— the telephone, automobile, television, and computer—across some key dimensions.

TABLE 10.2   A Comparison of Four Technologies

Technology	Symbolism— Personal	Symbolism— Social	Symbolism— Spatial
Telephone	Speech communication	Time/space substitution, social participation	Temporal space
Automobile	Body motion	Suburban life, lifestyle, freedom	Physical space
Television	Feelings, emotion, pleasure	Instant entertainment, temporal entertainment, mass medium	Visual space
Computer	Mind/pleasure, information, alternative knowledge	Reasoning, information processing	Cyberspace

CONSUMERS AND CYBERMARKETSCAPES: ISSUES AND SCENARIOS

Consumers and Interactive Virtual Spaces

Virtual Reality: With the help of computer-aided design programs, home shoppers don't even have to set foot in a real structure. Michelle Tierney isn't an engineer or an architect, so why should she have to visualize the home she wants built from indecipherable blueprints and floor plans? She doesn't any more. With the help of computer-aided programs, Tierney can tour every detail of her future abode, right down to whether the family room looks better with an optional gas fireplace and what color carpet works best. And it can be done without setting foot in a model home.

—*Orange County Register* (June 6, 1996)

Cyberspaces provide a culture of simulation, signification, and communication as opposed to realism, representation, and objective participation. Cyberspaces create virtualities of all sorts. Where cyberspace is most effective in the electronic commerce world is in its ability to create a virtual environment where the consumer can experience as-if physical goods or actual services (Burke 1996).

A case in point is interactive retailing. Interactive retailing in virtual environments takes place when customers go through a sequence of steps leading to purchase of goods or services. One way to look at interactive retailing is to consider it as regular retailing but done with the help of computers. Interactive retailing may contain elements of store shopping and catalog shopping. In other words, the consumer is able to move through virtual Nordstrom in much the same way he or she can move through the real department store. Obviously, there are limitations to this, because consumers cannot touch or feel or smell objects in the virtual environment. But they can certainly see and hear. In other words, cyberspace is most powerful in the visual and audio dimensions.

This is very similar to TV advertising—but it is also different. TV advertising is usually in thirty- or sixty-second spots that have a very fleeting message content. TV advertising lacks interactivity or consumer feedback; it is just a one-way medium. Cyberspace is a virtual space where the product can be seen in its multidimensionality. The image can be replayed, and details of interest can be observed more closely. If a clothing item is of interest, one can examine the clothing more carefully. The three-dimensional image of the product gives a multidimensionality enabling the consumer to observe the products from different angles.

On the other hand, interactive retailing can contain additional elements that go beyond normal catalog or print-oriented shopping. These include walking through simulated aisles, examining products in three-dimensional spaces, and examining products of different colors, shapes, sizes, and other conditions of use, but all of this in a virtual setting. Consumers can enter shopping malls, walk through the aisles in a supermarket, and select the items of interest as they are doing a virtual walk. The customer can see the product, evaluate it, and buy it at the same time. In other words, the decision sequence and the purchase act are closely linked through virtual product experience.

Just as in catalog shopping, the market focus is on a single customer. However, generally speaking, interactive retailing contains more information than a catalog and more updated information because the construction of virtual catalogs and transmission of information can be achieved with greater ease and in less time. Interactive retailing gives rise to virtual environments that both mimic and extend beyond real physical environments.

The relationship between virtual and real environments can be represented in three possible scenarios, summarized in Table 10.3. At one extreme is Scenario A, where virtuality cannot be established and all actions are undertaken in physical surroundings. Scenario B

TABLE 10.3   Relationship Between Real and Virtual Environments

Scenario A	*Scenario B*	*Scenario C*
Unique real environment experience not possible in virtual space	Common experience space	Unique virtual environment experience not possible in real physical space

provides a situation where virtuality and physicality are substitutable. Scenario C is the new space completely ruled by virtuality.

Given this conceptual scheme, one possible goal of marketers in the cybermarketscape is to unburden themselves of the real environment as much as possible, that is, to decrease A and increase B, and ultimately, to consolidate a position in C, the cyberscape. I am not suggesting that it is necessarily a desirable goal, for that depends on the circumstances. I am merely stating that some existing technologies permit such a possibility.

What are the implications of a shift from physical space to cyberspace for consumers? Regardless of how we conceptualize cyberspace relative to physical space, several possibilities emerge. If cyberspace is a mirror image of physical space, we can think of access to cyberspace being available from any location in cyber- or physical space. For example, in a traditional context, a consumer may want to visit a shopping mall with an identifiable physical address. Unless the physical mall is physically accessible (for example, within driving distance), the customer is not likely to consider it as an option. Imagine that the shopping mall is now available in cyberspace. The customer can visit the shopping mall from anywhere in the world, from multiple locations. In other words, in this example, cyberspace multiplies the representation of physical space, an idea similar to watching a televised event from any corner of the globe. Here the concept of interactive retailing allows the customer to participate actively in the cyber shopping environment.

From the marketer's point of view, cyberspace may be less expensive to build and more easily changeable. Once the idea of a cyberspace shopping mall catches on, the next step is to do away with the actual physical location completely so that the shopping mall in a physical environment need not exist. This is represented by Scenario C above. A cyberspace shopping mall can be constructed with a similar impact as the physical mall.

Let us now analyze the development of a cyberspace shopping environment. We use a three-stage process, illustrated in Figure 10.3. In stage 1, cyberspace acts as an additional reinforcing environment but is considered just a reminder of the actual physical shopping mall. In stage 2, cyberspace is considered more proactive;

FIGURE 10.3 Development of a Cyberscape Shopping Environment

Stage 1
Physical shopping environment ——————— Cyberspace environment merely
is where all shopping occurs.   represents physical environment.

Stage 2
Physical shopping environment ——————— Cyberspace environment represents
is maintained as an alternative   physical environment but is kept more
to cyberspace environment.   updated.

Stage 3
Physical shopping environment ——————— Only the cyberspace environment
is considered redundant.   exists; no physical analogue is available.

for example, new design and decor not available in the real mall
can be created in the cyberspace model. Cost considerations may
make it difficult to introduce changes in the physical space as easily as in cyberspace. In stage 3, the physical mall is completely elim-
inated, and the entire shopping experience is possible only through
cyberspace.

Imagine that malls need not be built in the physical sense; there
is no need to worry about parking spaces, physical interiors, security, etc. There will not be any need to have staffing of sales
employees. For a class of products, this environment is entirely plausible. As the new cyberspace environments are developed, the
impacts will be quite profound. Fewer customers may visit real
shopping malls. Consider the implications of the electronic kiosk,
which is nothing but an information center that uses a TV screen
with graphics and menus. Usually a kiosk consists of a self-contained computer screen with media capabilities. Kiosks may also be
connected to network-based computers. Kiosks are available in
many public spaces, restaurants, malls, convention centers, hotels,
etc. Kiosks are the physical delivery system of cybermarket space.
Cybermalls can give more information in an instant than a conventional, physical mall could hope to deliver.

If cyberspace is a transformation of our concept of space, we
have to assume that there is a close relationship to our sense of time.
The greatest revolution in consumer marketing is in terms of

real-time marketing and customized mass marketing, both of which were inconceivable only a few years ago. In real-time marketing, the consumer is presented the material, some of his or her questions are answered right on the spot, and the consumer can then make product selections and payments. Many of the conventional steps in the consumer purchase sequence are collapsed. Of course, the general idea is not new, for we find some parallels in catalog shopping, where the consumer examines product information and immediately is able to order it. However, what is missing in catalog shopping is the notion of interactivity. The information is provided, but no queries can be answered. Also missing in catalog shopping is the updating of information in real time.

Consumer Identity

Another transformational idea of the cybermarketscape refers directly to the identity of the consumer. The concept of uniqueness—that is, to be treated as an individual with a unique self—is quite central to the consumer. The idea of personal identity goes hand in hand with not being treated as part of the mass market. This has also been one of the central problems of advertising over the last century, ever since mass advertising became a reality. Advertising is basically a mass enterprise. The historical challenge of advertising has been to create advertising messages that have a "mass appeal" yet treat each consumer as a unique person, as if the advertising were meant only for her or him and no one else.

With the emergence of virtual environments, the opportunity to make the individual consumer feel unique has become less daunting. Virtual environments are entered and exited by consumers as individuals. No other individuals are the virtual environments, at least not as they are in real shopping environments. When a consumer is sitting in front of the computer screen, trying to negotiate the virtual environment, the customer clearly is all by him- or herself. How is this different from watching a TV or reading a newspaper or magazine? It is different in the sense that the consumer is able to interact directly with the medium by using various digital controls. It is the response of the medium that renders the experience unique because the medium is interacting with the consumer. That is, the interactivity of the medium more than anything else makes the experience unique. This is what we mean by the one-to-many medium being transformed into one-to-one medium (Hoffman and Novak 1996).

Cyberspace and Consumer Freedoms

Food and Drink are allowed in the Cyberstore
You can shop naked, that is, if your parent doesn't mind it
The store never closes, never.

—Anonymous

At DreamShop mall, customers can browse Saks Fifth Avenue in their bathrobes.

—Balog (1996)

Consumer freedoms are aplenty in cyberspace. In a cyberstore, there are no behavioral norms that one normally encounters in a regular store. In the privacy of one's living room, what takes place is virtual shopping, and with free abandon. In this freest of spaces, there is no dress code and no regulation regarding food ingestion while shopping, for cyberspace ensures the personalization of the shopping environment. The consumer can wander from store to store without expending physical energy. Since time is the essence of contemporary life, the time savings is an important appeal that the consumer will appreciate.

There are also other issues here. Consumer fantasies can be exploited much more effectively in cyberspace. Consumers can be lured by spectacular promises via computerized images. Objects can be fetishized, colorized, and given phantasmagoric forms. The most effective way to appeal to consumers is interactive imaging. Consumers can test products in cyberspace. Since the cybermarketscape is limitless and boundless, it is also an appropriate candidate for tapping into the unbounded desires of the consumer. Cybermarketscape can turn the sovereign consumer into a desire machine. The home is not merely a place of casual chat or a simple private sphere, but the very site of the market, the site of electronic commerce. The consumer can peer into the market constantly, enjoy the delights of the market offerings, look at the wonders of the consumptive world, partake in the experiences that this world proffers. It is not just the cognitive mapping of a commodity space, but the very essence of simulated or virtual experience. The consumer delights in the shopping experience, hopping from store to store in a matter of seconds, examining products and making decisions about the products. In other words, in the hands of the consumer, the computer is a live medium in cyberspace.

Of course, what consumers can do is not the same as what they will actually do. It is too early to tell what consumers will do in and with cyberspace. Some behaviors have already surfaced, but their sustainability and future directions are not clear. Much will depend on what marketers will make them do. At this time we can only speculate on what the possibilities are.

THE INSTITUTIONALIZATION OF THE CYBERMARKETSCAPE

The institutionalization of the marketscape, the ways of doing business, the practices and the rituals, or what Bourdieu (1984) calls the habitus, are inscribed in our social memory. The crucial property of social memory is that new consumers can be socialized into market processes by exposing them to the market processes. Let us take as an example the inscription of the department store in our social memory. The origins of the department store can be traced to the midnineteenth century, when the first department store, Bon Marché, appeared in Paris. This was a truly historic moment, for it is the model that has been inscribed in our memory, a model for many stores that have evolved since that period. The concept of department store defines the "order of things." What is a department store? In reality, it is a permanent agglomeration of assorted goods and services under one roof, visited by customers, and facilitating mass distribution of goods at a retail level. For the past 150 years, the department store has become emblematic of the marketscape that continues today in several variations of the same theme, including the more recent version, the ubiquitous shopping mall. Of course, retail institutions over this period have changed in character, but what is a common characteristic of all the retail institutions in this evolution is their physical geography—that is, they are all physical structures that house consumer goods.

Another aspect of this social memory is catalog shopping, which also originated in the nineteenth century concurrently with the department store. Instead of the physical setting in which mass distribution of goods takes place, the meeting point of the customer and the marketer is the catalog. The catalog is a description of goods, not a storehouse of goods that the consumer can visit in a physical sense. The catalog represents another marketing institution in its own right, a tangible expression of direct marketing, which never attained a high status within the marketing discourse and had remained in the shadow of more mainstream marketing.[2] But it is part of the same marketscape that is part of our social memory.

How does social memory operate? The memory always resides with somebody or some institution. To draw upon the social memory, we can always appeal to this source, who is the repository of such memory. A second aspect of the social memory is that, by its very nature, it permits evolution. It operates not on the basis of surprises but through time-honored conventions.

What happens when there is no social memory or when existing social memory cannot be employed effectively? One such situation is represented by the emergence of the cybermarketscape. The cybermarketscape can be compared to the first appearance of the department store or catalog shopping or similar revolutionary moment in the history of commerce.

The only social memory that we have recourse to is the marketing-customer duality in the world of transactions or exchanges. The institution of marketing is still a valid category, and so is the category called the consumer. Somebody is producing the

[2] Things may be changing. The emphasis on and primacy of direct marketing seem to be suddenly on the ascendancy, in terms of both marketing practice and academic consciousness. Because of the new technologies of cyberspace, the very term *direct marketing* is now being replaced with a more fashionable synonym, *interactive marketing.*

goods and services that the society needs, and somebody is buying or consuming them. Behind the simple duality of exchanges lie some fundamental changes that cybermarketscape space represents.

When There Is No Social Memory or When Existing Social Memory Is Not Serviceable

One can view human societies as generational structures. The older generation leaves a legacy to the younger generation, and the young build on the legacy, changing it to suit the new circumstances and tastes. Imagine situations when young have no legacies to inherit. In certain cases, the memories have to be reconstituted, as in the case of war-ravaged societies. If there are no memories, societies build on histories. In the absence of histories, societies construct their histories or just start from scratch as a mass-scale social brico-lage—doing experiments that work on a trial-and-error basis. In any case, when social memories are obliterated, the burden falls on the new generation. For the new generation, this is both a challenge and an opportunity. It is a challenge because there is nothing to build on. It is an opportunity because something new can be built.

A second situation is when social memory exists but cannot be used. It gives rise to human intervention of a different kind—not because of warlike situations which destroy, but because of the emergence of new technologies or new ways of doing things that create social obsolescence. For example, the invention of the auto-mobile introduced some fundamental changes in family and work lives, physical mobility, and other second-order social arrangements. Existing social memories are of limited use because external forces have fundamentally altered the social landscape. The more radical the technological force, the less useful is the existing social memory.

Cyberscape as a Disjuncture with Social Memory

The emergence of cyberscape is of the second type—that is, it has made the existing social memory less serviceable. The older institutional arrangements have no pathways to negotiate in cyberspace. The old pathways can be followed analogically, but they do not always lead to the best results. In fact, whatever social memory exists appears to be a hindrance, and for the new generation, the social memory is a burden.

What does this mean in practice? Cyberculture is being nurtured by the young, the risk takers, and the uninitiated rather than the established guardians of the markets. The risk takers do not seem to carry the burdens of the past. The only burden they seem to be carrying is that of constructing the future. Since there are no foundational elements, everything becomes a foundation in its own right.

Let us take the fundamental notion of market exchange. Exchange is not a simple idea of transfer of assets. Whether it is potlatch or modern market system, exchanges are embedded in a complex array of institutional arrangements. The questions that need to be answered in cybermarketscape are the following:

- What are the institutional arrangements within which exchanges can take place?
- How can assets be transferred?
- How are people to examine each other's assets before exchanges can take place?
- How does marketing take place within the cybermarketscape?
- What new issues arise?
- How can we use existing knowledge or surpass it?
- What role does cyberscape play in determining the course of marketing activities?
- What kinds of communication can take place in the cyberscape?

These and similar questions are the ones that will keep coming up in the marketing discipline. In this chapter, given the limited space, we addressed some of them and will leave the discussion of the undiscussed topics for future writers on the subject.

CONCLUSION

The co-optation of cyberculture by marketing should come as no surprise to anybody who has followed the course of capitalist history in the last four or five decades. The simple truth is, for marketing, cyberspace represents a limitless commercial space. What is also interesting is the rhetoric of cyberspace that is now appropriated by marketing. In a series of articles, published from 1995 to 1996 in the *Harvard Business Review*, we have been exposed to the co-optation of cyberculture rhetoric by marketing writers. Thus, for example, the virtual community of Rheingold (1996) has now become a community of commerce in a piece by Armstrong and Hagel (1996). The title itself, "The Real Value of On-Line Communities," suggests that the cybermarketscape is borrowing from outside the marketing field for its imagery. As the footnote to the article indicates, this article is a slightly modified version of a previous article whose title is "Real Profits from Virtual Communities." That the *Harvard Business Review* substituted the word *value* for *profits* shows the extent to which the allies of marketing go to sanitize the practices of the discipline.

One should not, however, be misled by the term *virtual community* as used in the HBR article, for that is not what Rheingold had in mind. The first sentence of the article is, "The notion of community has been at the heart of the Internet since its inception." (p. 134). This is certainly true. However, the authors quickly move on to the business at hand by proclaiming, in what appears to be a parody of Rheingold (1993), "By creating strong on-line *communities,* business will be able to build *customer loyalty* to a degree that today's marketers can only dream of and in turn, generate *economic returns*" (italics provided). It should be obvious why the authors do not use a more accurate term, *markets,* and resort to the use of a rather innocuous but misleading word, *communities.* Their principal interest is no doubt customers and economic returns, not the shared experiences and common ideals that Rheingold's virtual communities are working hard to establish.

Why this euphemism? Why this appropriation? After all, any basic marketing textbook will tell us that marketing is about selling goods and services to customers based on economic exchange. But it is equally common knowledge that marketing practices also revolve around the circuits of power and potential exploitation of the customers. Obviously, the word *community* evokes a moral legitimacy that the word *markets* lacks.

It is well recorded that the origins of cyberculture are to be found among the early pioneers and scientists, who were not driven by greed or profit but by the pursuit of truth and pure enjoyment of human imagination that resides in the electronic space. In the later years, cyberculture was associated with fringe groups and support networks who established electronic communities far removed from economic exploitation and emphasized mutual help. When marketing recently began to eye cyberspace as its next frontier, it was facing a dilemma and treading a rather delicate ground—and did not want to dismantle the unsullied image of "communities" but was quick to appropriate it.

In sum, cyberspace began as an innocuous technological diversion, more as a "lifeworld" outside the "system," in a Habermasian sense, an unintended space for computer hackers who were the master tinkerers residing at the technological edge. Its very novelty and profundity were later converted into a marketing idea. At the present time, the marketing forces are trying to displace other community-based agencies to appropriate cyberspace.

What is the attraction of this cyberspace to the agents of marketing? Because cyberspaces are virtual, nevertheless nontrivial, they provide an alternative to the saturated world of traditional markets. As discussed earlier, cyberspace has become the global marketscape par excellence and has changed our conventional notions of time and space and human exchange. Clearly, marketing organizations are engaged in developing a transcultural ideology based on new communication technologies.

This critique is intended to give the marketing profession an opportunity to rethink its social role as the cybermarketscape emerges as the horizon of opportunity. Nobody denies the legitimate role of commerce in the world of social affairs, but the record of marketing has not always been one of great social pride in the history of modern capitalism. It is time to change this image.

BIBLIOGRAPHY

APPADURAI, ARJUN. 1990. "Disjuncture and Difference in the Global Cultural Economy." *Public Culture* 2(2) (Spring): 171–191.

ARMSTRONG, ARTHUR, AND JOHN HAGEL III. 1996. "The Real Value of On-Line Communities." *Harvard Business Review* 74(3) (May–June): 134–141.

BALOG, KATHY. 1996. "On-Line Cyber Shoppers Post Record Buying." *USA Today* (December 24): sec. B, p. 1.

BENEDIKT, MICHAEL, ED. 1991. *Cyberspace: First Steps.* Cambridge, MA: MIT Press.

BITTNER, MARY JO. 1992. "Servicescapes: The Impact of Physical Surroundings on Customers and Employees." *Journal of Marketing* 52(2) (April): 57–71.

BOURDIEU, PIERRE. 1984. *Distinction.* Translated by Richard Nice. Cambridge: Harvard University Press.

BURKE, RAYMOND R. 1996. "Virtual Shopping: Breakthrough in Marketing Research." *Harvard Business Review* 74(2) (March–April): 120–131.

CARROLL, JOHN M., AND MARY BETH ROSSON. 1996. "Developing the Blacksburg Electronic Village." *Communications of the ACM,* Special Issue on Internet@Home 39(12) (December): 69–74.

CRONIN, MARY J. 1996. *The Internet Strategy Hand Book.* Boston: Harvard Business School Press.

DHOLAKIA, R. R.; N. MUNSDORF; AND N. DHOLAKIA, EDS. 1995. *Information Technology in the Home: Demand Side Perspectives.* Hillsdale, NJ: Erlbaum.

ELLSWORTH, JILL H., AND MATHEW V. ELLSWORTH. 1996. *The New Internet Business Book.* New York: Wiley.

ESCOBAR, ARTURO. 1994. "Welcome to Cyberia: Notes on the Anthropology of Cyberculture." *Current Anthropology* 35(3) (June): 211–231.

FLYNN, LEISA REINECKE. 1995. "Interactive Retailing: More Choices, More Chances, and More Growth." In *Interactive Marketing: The Future Present,* edited by E. Forrest and R. Mizerski. Lincolnwood, IL: NTC Books.

FRANZKE, MARITA, AND ANNE McCLARD. 1996. "Winona Gets Wired: Technical Difficulties in the Home." *Communications of the ACM,* Special Issue on Internet@Home 39(12) (December): 64–66.

GIBSON, WILLIAM. 1984. *Neuromancer.* New York: Ace Books.

HABERMAS, JURGEN. 1987. *The Theory of Communicative Action,* vol. 2. (Translated by Thomas McCarthy.) Boston: Beacon Press, ch. 6, pp. 113–198.

HOFFMAN, DONNA L.; WILLIAM D. KALSBEEK; AND THOMAS P. NOVAK. 1996. "Internet and Web Use in the U.S." *Communications of the ACM,* Special Issue on Internet@Home 39(12) (December): 36–46.

HOFFMAN, DONNA L., AND THOMAS P. NOVAK. 1996. "Marketing in Hypermedia Computer-Mediated Environments: Conceptual Foundations." *Journal of Marketing* 60(3) (July): 50–68.

KLING, ROB. 1996. "Being Read in Cyberspace: Boutique and Mass Media Markets, Intermediation, and the Costs of On-Line Services." *Communication Review* 1(3):297–314.

KRAUT, ROBERT. 1996. "Introduction to the Special Issue on Internet@Home." *Communications of the ACM* 39(12) (December): 33–35.

KRAUT, ROBERT; WILLIAM SCHERLIS; TRIDAS MUKHOPADHYAY; JANE MANNING; AND SARA KIESLER. 1996. "The HomeNet Field Trial of Residential Internet Services." *Communications of the ACM,* Special Issue on Internet@Home 39(12): (December): 36–46.

POSTER, MARK. 1995. *The Second Media Age.* Cambridge, MA: Polity Press.

"Raw Data." *Wired.* 1997. (January): 76.

RHEINGOLD, HOWARD. 1993. *The Virtual Community: Homesteading on the Electronic Frontier.* Reading, MA: Addison-Wesley.

SHIELDS, ROB, ED. 1996. *Cultures of Internet.* London: Sage.

SOLOMON, MICHAEL. 1995. *Consumer Behavior,* (3d ed.) Boston, MA: Allyn and Bacon.

STONE, ALLUCQUERE ROSANNE. 1995. *The War of Desire and Technology at the Close of the Mechanical Age.* Cambridge, MA: MIT Press.

TURKLE, SHERRY. 1995. *Life on the Screen: Identity in the Age of the Internet.* New York: Simon & Schuster.

VAN MAANEN, JOHN. 1988. *Tales of the Field: On Writing Ethnography.* Chicago: University of Chicago Press.

VENKATESH, ALLADI. 1996. "Computers and Other Interactive Technologies for the Home." *Communications of the ACM,* Special Issue on Internet@Home 39(12) (December): 47–54.

VENKATESH, ALLADI, AND NICHOLAS VITALARI. 1987. "A Post-Adoption Analysis of Computing in the Home." *Journal of Economic Psychology* 8 (June): 161–180.

———. 1990. *Project NOAH: A Longitudinal Study of Computer Use in the Home.* National Science Foundation Report, 1990.

———. 1992. "An Emerging Distributed Work Arrangement: An Investigation of Computer-Based Supplemental Work at Home." *Management Science* 38(12) (December): 1687–1706.

VITALARI, NICHOLAS; ALLADI VENKATESH; AND KJELL GRONHAUG. 1985. "Computing in the Home: Shifts in the Time Allocation Patterns of Households." *Communications of the ACM* 28(5) (May): 512–522.

11

BRANDFESTS

Servicescapes for the Cultivation of Brand Equity

JAMES H. MCALEXANDER
AND JOHN W. SCHOUTEN

To succeed in an increasingly competitive market, it is imperative that managers act strategically to maintain or increase customer retention. The relationship between customer retention and the financial performance of firms is well documented and widely accepted (Bhattacharya, Rao, and Glynn 1995). For example, Reicheld and Sasser (1990) report that reducing customer defections by 5 percent can boost profits by as much as 85 percent. Thus motivated, managers have turned to programs, such as continuous improvement, in an effort to increase customer satisfaction and reduce flight to other brands. Customer retention, however, cannot

James H. McAlexander is Associate Professor of Marketing, College of Business Administration, Oregon State University, Corvallis, Oregon. John W. Schouten is Associate Professor of Marketing, School of Business Administration, University of Portland, Portland, Oregon. We wish to thank the people of Harley-Davidson, Bozell Worldwide, and Chrysler Corporation for their time and support in this project.

be guaranteed by the mere fact of customer satisfaction in a market filled with high-quality, appealing products. Retention requires the cultivation of customer loyalty and brand identification (Bhattacharya, Rao, and Glynn 1995; Schouten and McAlexander 1995; Webster 1994a).

One tool some marketers have used to cultivate customer loyalty is the sponsorship of brand-centered events, which we term *brandfests*. Brandfests are corporate-sponsored events provided primarily for the benefit of current customers. Their primary function is the celebration of brand ownership. Harley-Davidson's Harley Owners Group rallies and Camp Jeep, the foci of this research, are notable examples of such festivals. However, such festivals are not confined to expensive, recreational, or transportation-related brands. We have observed a wide variety of brandfests for products ranging from power tools to agricultural products to high-tech hardware to tourist destinations. For example, mobile power-tool demonstrations and parking lot tool-handling competitions for consumers have helped revive the once defunct DeWalt brand. Community events such as Oregon's Newport Crab Festival and Hood River Harvest Festival effectively promote entire towns as brand names for seafood, produce, and a host of tourist merchandise. Sokol-Blosser Winery combines outdoor rock and jazz concerts with wine tasting and case lot sales. The high-tech firm Sequent funds and supports conferences for a grassroots owners' group. Despite the apparent significance of such activities, brandfests have not yet been addressed in the academic literature.

In this chapter we report an ethnographic investigation of several brandfests. Among our most interesting emergent findings is the discovery that participation in such brand-intensive galas often leads consumers to extraordinary and memorable experiences with the brand—experiences that become virtual watersheds of attitude change and purchase intention. Another aspect of the brandfest with important implications for customer loyalty and long-term brand vitality is the opportunity for consumers to enter into or strengthen relationships with the brand, its various stewards, and other similarly devoted consumers. After a brief discussion of our ethnographic method, we examine the impact of brandfests on components of customer loyalty, and we elaborate on these issues as they relate to building brand equity.

METHOD

Our conclusions draw from ethnographic data collected over 5 years with owners of two quintessential American brands: Harley-Davidson and Jeep. Fieldwork included intensive participant observation at events sponsored by the Harley-Davidson Motor Company (see Schouten and McAlexander 1995 for a complete description of our ethnographic involvement) and the Chrysler Corporation's Jeep Division. Our first exposure to brandfests began five years ago as we immersed ourselves in the Harley-Davidson subculture of consumption. Research sites included the national motorcycle rallies at Sturgis, South Dakota, and Daytona Beach, Florida, and regional rallies of the Harley Owners Group (HOG). Two years ago we also began ethnographic research with Jeep owners. This work took us to Jeep Jamborees in Indiana and Colorado, and to Camp Jeep, a national Jeep event held near Vail, Colorado.

Our data collection consisted mostly of formal and informal interviews, nonparticipant and participant observation, and photography. Certain formal interviews we audiotaped or videotaped and transcribed. When taping was not practical, we jotted down skeletal notes during the interview and fleshed them out as soon afterward as possible. Observations or data gathered through informal interviews were reported into a microcassette recorder periodically during the course of a day's research activities; we then played back those recorded notes as prompts for creating more detailed field notes at the end of the day. We used photographs in the manner described by Hill (1991) to assist in "reliving the lived experience," and also as visual records of symbolism encountered in modes of dress, grooming, product customization, and other behaviors at the events.

We selected informants purposefully to reflect their diversity along the lines of such characteristics as age, gender, social class, and lifestyle preferences. We interviewed members of various clubs as well as participants who chose to remain unaffiliated with any organized groups. The diversity of the informants allowed us to challenge the validity and scope of emerging interpretations through triangulation of data across informants and through the search for limiting exceptions. We formed lasting relationships with several key informants, and they have contributed valuable longitudinal perspectives, as well as access to other formal and informal settings.

Our conclusions resulted from a constant, iterative process akin to puzzle building. In a variation of the processes described by McCracken (1988), Miles and Huberman (1984), and Glaser and Strauss (1967), we amassed, coded, compared, and collapsed specific data to form themes or categories. Then, treating each theme like a puzzle piece, we sought to devise conceptual frameworks that would unite them in a holistic fashion. The involvement of two researchers added another useful dimension to the data analysis, that of "devil's advocacy" (McAlexander, Schouten, and Roberts 1992). Individual interpretations of the data were advanced for discussion by either researcher, at which point the other developed counterarguments. This intentional skepticism forced scrutiny of the proposed themes and prevented premature closure. Themes that bore up under scrutiny remained open to further dialogue and development; those that did not were rejected or modified and advanced again.

RESULTS

Brandfests constitute marketer-created and controlled servicescapes (Bitner 1992) with unique power to contextualize and shape consumer attitudes toward a brand. They are special events, commonly associated with meaningful destinations. Moreover, they involve time set apart from the routines of everyday life, usually for leisure, but also for professional purposes. By their association with special times and places, brandfests grant marketers incredible access to consumer consciousness. Careful orchestration of a brandfest places the brand at the center of consumer activity in contexts that are relevant, or even central, to key aspects of the consumer's identity. We suggest that in several ways a brandfest is the ideal growth medium for customer loyalty. The following discussion deals with two very important mechanisms for cultivating customer loyalty through brandfests. First is the facilitation of extraordinary consumer experiences with the brand; second is the engineering of customer relationships at several levels, i.e., with their own possessions, with the brand, with the company, and with other customers.

Extraordinary Experience

From a consumer perspective, an important benefit of taking part in a brandfest is the satisfaction of basic hedonic needs (Holbrook and Hirschman 1982). Under the right circumstances, a brandfest can provide more than simple enjoyment; it can facilitate what we call extraordinary consumer experience. Arnould and Price (1993) discuss this caliber of experience in the context of white-water rafting, but it can occur in many activities in many different environments, including those engineered by marketers to showcase a brand. In our work at various brandfests, we have undergone personally or had reported to us several different types of extraordinary experience. We have felt and seen states of flow as described by Csikszentmihalyi and Csikszentmihalyi (1988). We have encountered nearly religious moments of discovery or self-discovery that resemble what Maslow (1961) called peak experiences. We have witnessed the emergence of communitas as described by Turner and Turner (1978).

While all these different types of experience vary phenomenologically, they nevertheless share certain important dimensions. They are emotionally intense, highly memorable, and personally significant, sometimes even to the point of transformation of the individual. What is particularly interesting among our findings is that each of these kinds of experience also can be linked strongly and positively in the consumer's mind to a facilitating product (good or service) and, ultimately, to a brand. For the sake of this discussion, we define an extraordinary consumer experience as one that yields feelings of personal growth or triumph, involves emotional intensity, is uniquely memorable, and becomes associated with a brand. Such experiences are understandably influential in shaping long-term brand impressions and are, in fact, instrumental to the development of brand loyalty.

In the context of the brandfest, extraordinary experience is linked to product usage in activities structured by the marketer for their inherently rewarding nature to consumers. Activities are chosen for their fit with consumer values and lifestyles and tend to present opportunities for participants to stretch their personal horizons of skill, knowledge, or experience. In addition, they frequently involve personal interaction in ways that enhance and reinforce the overall experience. In our studies we have identified three critical realms of action whereby brandfest sponsors can enhance the likelihood that consumers will have extraordinary experiences with their brands: (1) provide participants with opportunities for personal growth or triumph; (2) help manage their levels of perceived risk; and (3) facilitate community among them.

Opportunities for Personal Growth

A principal appeal of the brandfest for consumers is the opportunity to participate in novel or horizon-expanding experiences. To this end, the selection of the brandfest site is strategically important; it should resonate with the values and lifestyles of brand owners. To Jeep owners the Colorado Rockies are a destination valued for natural beauty and for suitability to outdoor activities. When asked why they had decided to come to Camp Jeep, many participants indicated they had always wanted to vacation in the Colorado Rockies and that the event gave them a perfect structure and excuse for doing so. Likewise, motorcycle rallies in general function as excuses for bikers to take road trips, often to places they have never visited or by routes they have never before taken. For Harley-Davidson owners, Sturgis, South Dakota, and Daytona Beach, Florida, are examples of brandfest venues valued for their complete embracement of biker culture during one week every year. What makes Sturgis and Daytona attractive as vacation destinations has little, if anything, to do with natural beauty and everything to do with the gravitational pull of hundreds of thousands of motorcyclists.

Travel to a brandfest may also enhance a participant's status within a relevant reference group. Jeep Jamborees on the Rubicon Trail in California and in Moab, Utah, are recognized by Jeep owners with off-road aspirations as particularly challenging to skills and machines. To have "done the Rubicon" is a badge of status. Similarly, the motorcycle rallies at Sturgis and Daytona serve as rites of passage to committed Harley-Davidson owners. The question "So, have you been to Sturgis?" arises frequently among Harley owners attempting to gauge each other's authenticity and status as bikers. The effort and expense involved in traveling to a brandfest and participating in the associated brand-centered activities both demonstrate and reinforce commitment to values held in common by owners of the brand. Through such items as souvenirs, photographs, and videotapes, brandfest veterans commonly take home a wealth of stories and artifacts for the entertainment and envy of interested friends.

Another important aspect of personal growth and triumph is the development of one's capabilities through enhanced skills and knowledge. In the design of the brandfest, marketers can provide attractive opportunities for such enhancement. At Camp Jeep, for example, Chrysler created a guided off-highway obstacle course, termed Jeep 101, which allowed registrants to tackle with an instructor a variety of hazards such as might be encountered on difficult off-highway trails. For most participants, this was the first time they had driven a Jeep over difficult terrain. Several novice off-roaders waited in anxious silence for their turns in the Chrysler-owned vehicles; others discussed the potential embarrassment of not successfully completing the course. Once in the vehicles, they concentrated as driving instructors explained techniques that would assist them in the course. Friends cheered them on as they focused their attention on each obstacle and tried out the techniques they had been taught. Drivers came away beaming from their maiden off-highway voyages as they proudly related their experiences to the waiting onlookers. Afterward, many participants went on to test their newfound skills and the capabilities of their own Jeep vehicles on the rugged roads of the surrounding Rocky Mountains.

In follow-up interviews, we have found that key brandfest experiences remain canonized in people's memories. Weeks or even months later, they still reminisce and relate tales filled (and sometimes embellished) with excitement, fears overcome, discoveries made, and friendships forged. They cast themselves clearly as the protagonists of their narratives, but at the heart of each experience is an important supporting character: the facilitating brand.

Management of Perceived Risk

Important to the emotional character of the extraordinary experience is the consumer's sense of engaging in risky behavior. Extraordinary experiences are much more likely to occur to a consumer actively involved in a challenging activity than a passive observer of someone else's risk-taking behavior. Risk plays a dual role. On the positive side, a certain level of risk heightens the stakes of participation and adds to a sense of challenge and adventure. On the negative side, excess risk may actually dissuade people from participating in certain key events or even from attending the brandfest at all. To maximize the probability that participants will have extraordinary experiences at the brandfest, it is important to manage their perceived risk, keeping it in the optimal range between boring tameness and frightening excess. The first principle of perceived risk for the brandfest is that there should be some. The second is that it should not be overwhelming.

One factor that moderates the perceived risk of participating in a brandfest is the legitimizing presence of corporate sponsors. There is a sense that corporate sponsors would not be involved in events that would be so risky as to place their customers in serious peril. Beyond their mere presence, however, there are other actions marketers can take to manage the different kinds of risk customers are likely to perceive.

Associated with participation in a brandfest are three particularly salient kinds of risk: social, financial, and physical. The financial and physical risk of participation in a Jeep Jamboree was underscored for us when we crashed a new Grand Cherokee into a tree on a mud-slicked road in the woods of Indiana. The damage was minor, but the lesson was profound: brandfest participants sometimes place personal safety and expensive property at risk when they engage in certain activities. Brandfest sponsors can help to manage such risks through such tactics as special staffing, instruction, and dissemination of information. At Camp Jeep, for example, instructors and Chrysler-owned vehicles reduced the perceived risks inherent in the Jeep 101 obstacle course. Special maps, trails graded by difficulty, and trained guides at trailhead helped manage the risks of trail rides on designated mountain roads.

As participants gain experience with a particular kind of activity, they become more comfortable with it and feel less at risk. Interestingly, participants tend not to relish the repetition of past experiences; instead they work through progressively more difficult obstacles, which has the effect of raising perceptions of risk. This suggests that the process of overcoming risk and the resulting feelings of personal triumph and efficacy ultimately are more rewarding than feelings of security and safety. It also suggests that consumers are themselves active participants in the risk management process. By maintaining their levels of risk and challenge within the margins of boredom to the one side and anxiety to the other, they create for themselves the conditions whereby they may optimize their experiences (Csikszentmihalyi and Csikszentmihalyi 1990).

Social risk at the brandfest includes a fear of "not fitting in" and the potential for embarrassment. Such perceptions are manifest in many facets of the brandfest experience, including the decision of whether to attend the event. One Grand Cherokee owner, for example, reported having the impression that the main body of Camp Jeep participants would likely be "those radical off-roaders with the super-modified Jeeps," and he feared he "would be stuck off in a corner with a handful of geeks in Cherokees." He nearly declined the invitation to participate because of that fear, and he considered his decision to go an act of courage. He was relieved upon arriving at the brandfest site to find that he was surrounded by people similar to himself. Sensitivity to consumer preconceptions and stereotypes about brand enthusiasts, coupled with corrective information, may significantly enhance the level of participation in a brandfest, especially an inaugural event that lacks history and the advantages of word-of-mouth communication.

Social risk is also inherent in many brandfest activities, which are engineered to be visible to an audience. For example, as bikers compete in field events such as "slow races" (wherein motorcyclists are challenged to cross a finish line in the longest time possible without putting down a disqualifying foot), they generally do so to the cheers and jeers of their peers. Tackling difficult obstacles on a Jeep Jamboree trail ride is a similarly public spectacle that exposes the driver to potential outcomes ranging from acclaim and kudos in the event of a respectable performance to frustration and humiliation in the event of a poor showing. Creating an atmosphere of cooperation through a friendly, helpful staff minimizes the chances or effects of the latter, more negative consequences. Furthermore, an empathic and encouraging audience gives validation and support to the participant who is attempting to negotiate a difficult challenge.

Facilitation of Community

The presence of peers with similar motivations, aspirations, and values leads to a sense of community and belonging among brandfest participants. The basis of community is shared experiences and values. Extraordinary experience is best shared in real time by people struggling to help each other toward a common goal, such as the joint negotiation of a particularly difficult obstacle in a trail ride. However, after-the-fact sharing through storytelling in social situations also brings people together and reinforces the value of each other's experiences. In its most heightened form, this sharing of experiences and values becomes the common bond of communitas as described by Turner and Turner (1978) and discussed by Celsi, Rose, and Leigh (1993) in the context of a skydiving community. Communitas can be thought of as a special quality of interpersonal bonding that arises from shared extraordinary experience.

We have observed that the emergence of community in the context of a brandfest can in itself constitute extraordinary experience. A high point for many of the bikers at Harley Owners Group (HOG) rallies and Jeep owners at Camp Jeep is the excitement of being in the company of so many others who share a common affinity for the brand and associated activities. Bikers eagerly await the parade that is such a visible part of the HOG Rally. Participation in this public show of numbers produces strong emotional responses, including feelings of self-affirmation and identification. Similarly, it is common for bikers to report feelings of exhilaration as they approach a brandfest site and converge with fellow pilgrims. They experience "chills" as they merge with larger and larger groups of riders destined for the rallies at Sturgis or Daytona. The excitement builds as a biker becomes one of ten, or twenty, or even hundreds who have descended upon a dot on the map in order to share in common activities, to see and be seen, and to validate one another in their mutual commitment to the brand event that has brought them together.

Summary

Extraordinary experiences are most likely to occur when consumers successfully complete tasks that challenge the limits of their personal skills or experience horizons. The emotional impact of these activities is enhanced by the inherently social setting of a brandfest. In cases we have studied, participants also find themselves testing the various capabilities of their relevant possessions—the ability of the Jeep vehicle to handle difficult terrain or the ability of the Harley-Davidson motorcycle to enjoyably transport its rider(s) and attract attention to the bike and its owner. Results of extraordinary experience go affirmingly to the heart of consumer identity and thus to positive and enduring changes in attitude about the product and brand. For the novice owner, these experiences are transformational in that they establish strong bonds to the product, where earlier there was simply ownership. For the committed owner, these experiences reaffirm the value of the already existing linkages.

The psychology of the extraordinary experience and its impact on consumer attitudes seems relatively simple: the emotional impact of personal growth or triumph becomes tied to the product that has been instrumental to the experience. If the experience also occurs in a particularly beautiful or otherwise meaningful setting removed from day-to-day concerns, it is even further enhanced. The end result may be an enduring mental picture with the product at the center of a virtual dreamscape, as if the owner were actually transported, however briefly, to the fantasy world created by advertising for the brand—except that it is real, personal, and unforgettable.

Building Relationships

Long-term commitment to a brand is enhanced by the development of key consumer relationships. We believe it is not only possible but essential to brand vitality for marketers to cultivate as much as possible customer relationships of four distinct types:

1. Between consumers and their own products of choice
2. Between consumers and the brand
3. Between consumers and the corporation behind the brand
4. Among consumers of the brand.

Finally, as a tactical issue, it behooves marketers to attend also to the relationship between the corporation and the communities in which brandfests are staged. In our research we have observed that brandfests influence each of these different kinds of relationships in powerful ways, for better or worse; the marketer's charge is to manage the relationships and make sure they are positive and edifying to overall brand equity.

Consumer-Product Relationships

This discussion advances and relies on the premise that a person can develop a relationship with a possession. Feelings that are important in the development and maintenance of interpersonal relationships, such as attraction, intimate understanding, sensual enjoyment, and feelings of attachment, security, comfort, stability, and self-worth (Drigotas and Rusbult 1992), may also manifest as important characteristics of people's relationships with valued possessions. Furthermore, the elements of interpersonal relationships that tend to give them longevity, such as investment, commitment, dependence, and integration in social networks (Lund 1985), may also constitute exit barriers to such consumer-object relationships. Though not as clearly dyadic as the interpersonal type, person-object relationships do exist and can be powerful. Belk's (1988) work on possessions as extensions of self describes some of the processes whereby relationships develop between consumers and commercial goods, and Fournier (1994) likens person-product and person-brand relationships to interpersonal relationships, not only in character but also in their manner of formation.

Both intimacy with the product possessed and loyalty to it are enhanced by memorable experiences that reinforce the connection between owner and possession. The brandfest can facilitate such extraordinary experiences. Well-planned and well-staged events provide consumers the opportunity to discover and experiment with product attributes of which they were aware, perhaps through advertising, but which they had not personally or fully explored. For example, prior to Camp Jeep, the majority of participants had never driven their Jeep vehicles off road, and the brandfest offered a way to ease into that experience. For many Harley-Davidson owners, a rally offers the first real glimpse of the scope of the biker subculture. By facilitating participation in quintessential product applications, the brandfest fosters deeper consumer appreciation for product capabilities and also for their own capabilities as owners. In the event of truly extraordinary experiences with the product, such discovery is personally transformational, granting the product "favorite possession" status and making it more central to the consumer's identity.

One woman we interviewed at the end of her first Jeep Jamboree described the change in her relationship to her vehicle as a result of discovering the increased efficacy and mobility she derived from it in the context of her brandfest experience, which included travel over particularly beautiful but intimidating mountain roads: "I've always liked my Jeep, but now I *love* it. . . . It's like now I have no limits as to where I can go and what I can do." In such cases the possession is viewed much as a friend who has helped the owner weather an important trial successfully. The consumer's personal identity is enhanced by the positive experience, which, in turn, is facilitated by the product possessed.

Participants also may have numerous less intense but certainly enjoyable encounters with their possessions in the course of a brandfest. For example, many of the participants in the Ouray, Colorado, Jeep Jamboree were impressed with the beauty of the mountains and the fall flora as viewed from trails that were accessible because of the technological features of their personal Jeep vehicles. Jeep owners frequently framed photographs of themselves and their vehicles with the mountain splendor as backdrop—pictures that, not coincidentally, resonate with Jeep advertising motifs. At home, such pictures serve as reminders of the experience for the participants themselves and as stimuli for relating the experience to others. More than that, they serve as graphic reminders of the close relationship between owner and vehicle.

Although less directly associated with the use of the product, other potentially pleasant brandfest activities may also strengthen the consumer-product relationship. At Camp Jeep, for instance, events such as an outdoor concert with musicians Kenny Loggins and Michael McDonald, fly-fishing clinics sponsored by Orvis, and an interactive health and fitness fair had little to do with Jeep ownership except in their exclusive availability to brandfest participants. The benefits of these activities constituted added and often unanticipated benefits of having purchased a Jeep vehicle. Through such activities, the possession is associated with special privileges of ownership that, if the product were replaced with another brand, would be forfeit. Consequently, the brandfest creates exit barriers that make product disposition more momentous and potentially difficult for the consumer.

Consumer-Brand Relationships

Brandfests also are valuable tools for strengthening the relationship between consumers and the brand. Essentially this occurs through personal identification with the brand and its connections to multiple facets of the owners' actual or desired lifestyles—connections that the marketer can deliberately underscore.

At the most superficial level, the owner-brand relationship is enhanced by the ubiquitous display of the brand. At Harley Owners Group rallies, the brand is displayed everywhere from banners and T-shirts to the sides of the corporate semitrailer that houses the traveling Harley-Davidson museum. At a recent rally in Reno,

Nevada, several casinos displayed Harley-Davidson motorcycles as prizes for progressive slot machines. Inside the rally site (available only to Harley Owners Group members) was a day-care facility, staffed by moonlighting local school teachers, which offered children Harley coloring contests and ridable miniature Harleys, among other supervised amusements. A class in food decoration featured watermelons carved elaborately in forms of Harley-Davidson logos and motifs. Yet another class instructed people in the customization of clothing to show off the Harley-Davidson brand. And these examples merely scratch the surface of the total amount of brand display. Similar brand ubiquity was evident at Camp Jeep, where even the fencing that separated exhibits bore the Jeep logo in large print at regular intervals. Significantly, at a brandfest, none of this display comes across as excessive, but it does have the effect of firmly positioning the brand in the consumer's mind.

Appropriate branded products and brand-related exhibits also serve to expand the consumer's understanding of an overall brand gestalt. Perhaps the most important message the brandfest can convey about the brand is its fit with owners' lifestyles and relevant role identities. Every aspect of the brandfest, from food and beverage selection to seminar content to the nature of activities, conveys symbolically something about the meaning of the brand and its compatibility with consumers' values and lifestyles. Naturally, the role of research in identifying what those values and lifestyles are cannot be oversold. For Jeep and Harley-Davidson owners alike, research has shown that a salient element of the gestalts of those brands is a strong sense of brand heritage and history. The importance of brand heritage is communicated at HOG rallies by the traveling museum and other devices such as photographic retrospectives. Camp Jeep also featured a Jeep museum that presented the evolution of the Jeep vehicle from its wartime youth all the way through to current models and futuristic concept vehicles. As owners grow in their understanding of a brand's cultural meaning, they also grow to appreciate it at a level much deeper than that of functional attributes.

Another function of the brandfest is to provide consumers with perspectives of the brand in use. It is valuable to consumers and marketers alike for consumers to see how other people have used, maintained, enjoyed, or customized their product. Ideas for product applications and personalization flow freely and naturally at a brandfest; however, there are techniques whereby marketers can enhance this natural process. HOG rallies routinely sponsor formal "ride-in shows," where interested participants display their customized motorcycles competitively, and spectators (also brandfest participants) cast votes for the best entries in each of several categories, all the while considering which modifications they might like to make to their own machines. Both Jeep and Harley-Davidson display current products customized with the addition of branded accessories.

The sharing of brand-related information is formalized even more in seminars, workshops, town meetings, and so on. For example, Harley-Davidson routinely conducts seminars on such topics as rider safety, motorcycle maintenance, and the care of leather riding apparel. These seminars not only educate consumers on the proper use, application, and maintenance of their Harley-Davidson motorcycles and related products, but in the process, they also expose consumers to additional branded products to be used. Armed with knowledge from these seminars, bikers are more likely to have satisfying experiences with Harley-branded products and to appreciate their advantages over aftermarket alternatives. Increased consumer knowledge of, intimacy with, and loyalty to the brand in its extended form constitutes only part of the benefit to the marketing firm of brandfest seminars and other such programs; their interactive nature makes these events veritable bonanzas of marketing information.

Finally, the impact of the brandfest on the consumer-brand relationship is evidenced by the brisk sales of branded merchandise at such events. As described by Holt (1995) in the context of professional baseball, branded merchandise such as apparel serves the dual purpose of enhancing affiliation with the brand and distinguishing the owner from others whose identification is less intense. While a broad range of branded products sell well at the brandfest, special-event merchandise is especially popular. At Camp Jeep, the sale of products adorned with the Camp Jeep logo exceeded expectations, resulting in temporary stock outages of some items. Event-related apparel and other merchandise allow participants to return home as virtual brand missionaries, displaying conspicuously the signs of having participated in an exclusive activity. The items serve as stimuli to conversation, increasing the amount and impact of word-of-mouth endorsement of both the brandfest and the brand.

Consumer-Company Relationships

Separate from the relationships they may form with a favorite possession or a trusted brand, positive relationships are also possible between consumers and the companies that produce and market those possessions. These relationships are made more immediate, real, and rewarding as owners learn of the company's true concern both for owner satisfaction and for the overall quality of the owner's life. Such concern is reciprocated by the brandfest participant as good will toward the company. The most truly interpersonal of the types of relationship we have yet discussed, bonds between the consumer and the company, are the direct result of a significant corporate presence at the brandfest.

Both Jeep and Harley-Davidson stage forums for interaction between interested customers and various product specialists, e.g., design engineers. Participants come away from those meetings feeling as if the company truly cares about them and their opinions. The "caring" can be communicated particularly well by a professional moderator trained in the skills of developing rapport, validating customer opinions, and making individual participants feel special. Each friendly face in corporate garb adds to customers' sense of belonging to a family of brand owners. Harley-Davidson masters this kind of familial relationship with policies encouraging top-level executives to ride and participate actively alongside customers and lower-level employees at key rallies and reunions. Many Harley-Davidson corporate leaders further reinforce such relationships outside the brandfest context by personally attending to all correspondence in their names from customers.

Direct involvement with brandfest participants also benefits the marketing company in another significant way. Company personnel, from engineers to advertisers and from assembly workers to warranty administrators, grow in their understanding and appreciation of the owners as flesh-and-blood people. Interviews with Harley-Davidson employees at all levels reveal that direct and empathic contact with customers at rallies helps them to keep in perspective the real importance of their jobs with respect to customer appreciation and service long after they have returned to their desks or workstations in Milwaukee, Wisconsin, or York, Pennsylvania. Mutual respect, trust, and perceived familiarity between customers and the corporation foster a cycle of loyalties. Company workers care more and give more when they can attach faces to once faceless customers, and customers reciprocate the improved product and service performance with more intense loyalty to the brand, along with all the benefits that loyalty implies, e.g., repurchase of the core product, increased purchase of product line extensions, more (and more favorable) word-of-mouth communication, and a higher tolerance for occasional product failures.

Interconsumer Relationships

Thus far, we have discussed certain brand-building benefits of interaction between the brandfest sponsor and the consumer. However, we also have found in our studies that many benefits of the brandfest accrue more particularly from interaction among participants themselves. At Camp Jeep we noted a transformation among the inexperienced Jeep owners that related to their experiences with other owners. One informant, who registered for Camp Jeep in order to briefly escape her household responsibilities, expressed some early skepticism regarding the social climate of the event. She commented to us that she was "not a Jeep person." As we spoke with her on a following day, she was enthusiastic about the people she had met and looked forward to attending similar Jeep-related events in the future.

Interconsumer relationships function as exit barriers to brand ownership. In some cases, such as among Harley owners and potentially among Jeep owners, they actually form the social fabric of a true subculture of consumers bound together by shared values, goals, and activities (Schouten and McAlexander 1995). To change brands is to abandon a significant and supportive social network.

Social ties among brand owners are strengthened by a number of phenomena, including shared extraordinary experiences and mutual validation or affirmation of brand ownership. These phenomena can be cultivated rather easily at a brandfest. One strategy (already discussed in the context of risk management) is to provide activities for which participants serve alternately as performers and as audience for others' performances. Extraordinary experiences are thereby cocreated and shared in real time. Social linkages can be encouraged even further by providing participants ample opportunity to mix and socialize with each other and relate the stories of their own extraordinary experiences. Friendships begun on the trail at a Jeep Jamboree, for instance, can be deepened later in a hotel hot tub or a local watering hole.

Another message participants take away with them from a brandfest is that many other people much like themselves share enthusiasm for their pet brand. At activities such as the engineering roundtables at Camp Jeep, they learn that other people have product passions and confront problems much like their own. The sense of fellowship and mutual understanding that comes from this sharing validates their brand choice.

Brandfest-Community Relationships

The fifth and final category of relationship is that between the brandfest itself and the community in which it is staged. In our experience, pride in brand ownership is enhanced significantly upon entry into a community that openly supports and appreciates the brandfest. Like all others, this relationship is enhanced by reciprocation of value. The most powerful lesson we have learned in this regard is the importance of leveraging local resources.

A clear advantage to utilizing local resources is that the economic benefit to community businesses is reciprocated as a welcoming attitude. Signs proclaiming, "Welcome Camp Jeep," were visible in several places throughout Vail, Colorado, as brandfest participants came and went. Such expressions help consumers to feel appreciated, a feeling that appears to spill over to their feelings about the brand via social reinforcement of the value of ownership. A welcoming community also provides a positive social environment for the development of the other kinds of relationships described earlier. Other practical benefits include the positive publicity that can be gained from friendly local and regional media and businesses.

Harley-Davidson also cultivates brandfest-community relationships in ways that leverage marketing dollars significantly. For example, by co-opting local businesses and tourist locations into its programs and activities, Harley-Davidson provides many participant perquisites at little or no marginal cost to the company. For example, at a Reno rally, riders made scheduled stops at businesses such as Virginia City's Bucket-of-Blood Saloon and the Ponderosa Ranch, where they received special deals but also tended to spend additional time and money. The same principle of leverage also applies to arrangements with nonlocal firms. At Camp Jeep, organizations such as Orvis, Ross Bicycles, and Rodale Press provided participants with seminars, equipment usage, souvenirs, and even free massages in exchange for the opportunity to be represented at the brandfest. Furthermore, such arrangements appeared to strengthen certain client relations at a business-to-business level and perhaps led to additional co-marketing opportunities.

Summary

In many ways a brandfest is the ideal servicescape in which to cultivate lasting relationships with customers. Extraordinary experiences enhance consumers' sense of appreciation and affection for the product. Activities and displays consistent with their values and lifestyles increase consumers' identification with the sponsoring brand. Interaction with caring corporate representatives builds mutual respect between the consumers and the firm. Furthermore, the entire positive experience of the brandfest is perceived as added value beyond that which is normally expected in conjunction with the purchase of a product; the principle of reciprocity suggests that in such circumstances, consumers will feel a debt of returned value, which they pay in loyalty to the brand. Consumers who already share certain commonalities of lifestyle and values are likely to be socially compatible; brandfests have the potential to knit them together into subcultures of consumption, facilitating social bonds that reinforce brand loyalties and form barriers to brand switching. The benefits to the firm of these combined loyalties include increased probability of customer retention, increased customer tolerance for imperfections in product performance, increased opportunity for successful brand extension, and increased word-of-mouth promotion of the brand.

Building Brand Equity

Brand equity grows through the cognitive and emotional connections consumers make between the brand and other constructs of value to them. The closer the brand resides to their important role identities, the more they are willing to embrace appropriate product line extensions and licensed goods. We contend that all marketing communications about a brand should be carefully weighed for their consistent congruity with a well-researched and clearly understood set of values associated with it in the consumer consciousness. Once it is understood how the brand articulates with consumer values and lifestyles, it is possible to develop a virtual litmus test for potential brand extensions.

Brandfests are valuable laboratories for reinforcing existing brand connections and testing the potential of new ones. Brandfest participants tend to be consumers who already value the brand and have some understanding, albeit latent, of what the brand means in the context of their lives and fantasies. In the controlled environment of a brandfest, those meanings can be both exploited and explored more ambitiously than in any other context. Where else can you expect consumers to participate eagerly, without compensation (feeling, in fact, that they are privileged for it), in focus groups or other research-intensive activities? Where else can you orchestrate such intense and memorable experiences with the brand and exposure to its many applications?

Keys to Success

Maximizing the potential of a brandfest as a tool for building brand equity requires consideration of certain principles. The following guidelines are not a precise formula, but rather a compilation of basic tactics that we have found to be effective, even critical, to the successful implementation of a brandfest.

The first principle for a successful brandfest is *exclusivity*. Limiting participation to current owners of the brand is crucial. In recent years marketers have become more attuned to the necessity of carefully targeting the "right customers" and providing unique benefits for them (Webster 1994a, 1994b). The brandfest creates added value of ownership and becomes a differential benefit in the minds of consumers. A properly managed brandfest will draw media attention such that nonparticipants, owners and nonowners alike, will be aware of having missed out on something special. At the same time, participants gain a badge of status and a topic of conversation whereby to cultivate the envy of friends and acquaintances. Another, equally important aspect of exclusivity is that all comparisons of product performance are limited to a within-brand set. There are no owners of competing brands to create dissonance; moreover, shared information among participants tends to reinforce and validate brand ownership as a value in and of itself.

Value and lifestyle compatibility of brandfest activities is important, partly because it enhances the likelihood that participants will have optimal experiences. It also reinforces positive cognitive and emotional linkages with the brand. When the consumer thinks about a favorite activity or a fond memory associated with the brandfest, the brand is perceived as instrumental to the enjoyment. Research, such as ethnography, that helps identify salient values and lifestyles is very valuable and should be undertaken prior to planning a brandfest. An additional benefit to the marketer of creating events with such compatible activities is the demonstration to the consumer that the marketer understands and is attuned to the needs and preferences of these valued customers. Such sensitivity is instrumental to building the types of relationships that yield strong customer loyalty.

In planning a brandfest, marketers should choose activities that challenge participants to develop new skills or to discover expanded capabilities of both self and the product. *Personal growth* is a critical component of extraordinary experience and, therefore, to the cultivation of brand loyalty. Aligned with this imperative is that of *risk management.* There is a therapeutic window of optimal risk associated with many aspects of a brandfest. Consumer experience is heightened by certain levels of risk but thwarted by that which is deemed excessive. Marketers should identify potential risks to consumer ego, person, and property, and generate information and safeguards to keep them within acceptable bounds.

Corporate presence at the brandfest serves many important functions. First and foremost, it conveys the message that the company cares about the consumer's well-being. Proactively seeking customer feedback through friendly, interpersonal means demonstrates a long-term commitment of the company to customer satisfaction, and such commitment invites reciprocity in the form of customer loyalty. Furthermore, such direct interaction with customers is a marvelous research tool for identifying new market opportunities. Committed customers are quite willing to provide feedback to company representatives regarding problems they have had, successes they have gained, and ideas they have cooked up for enhanced product usage. Even one good idea properly managed conceivably could pay for the entire investment in conducting a brandfest.

Follow-up research, to measure the impact of the brandfest on such phenomena as customer loyalty, word of mouth and referrals, and sales of branded accessories and licensed products, is also both doable and well advised. As marketers work in environments with constrained budgets, it is imperative to demonstrate the value of investment in events such as the brandfest.

Directions for Future Research

We readily concede that the brandfests we have studied have been limited to the celebration of high-involvement products. Harley-Davidson and Jeep are potent American brands that inspire loyalties and that facilitate activities that easily can form the basis for an enjoyable vacation. Future research might look at other product categories. We suspect that such events as rock concerts, wine tastings, Star Trek conventions, electronics shows, and other gatherings may also serve as brandfests with all the attendant merchandising of line extensions such as T-shirts, posters, books, tapes, key chains, and other branded items. The question of how to conduct a brandfest for somewhat less culturally entrenched brands is an interesting one.

Another fertile area for future research lies at the level of grassroots activities such as those of the myriad of users' groups, enthusiasts, and aficionados that regularly inhabit the Internet. Bulletin boards and home pages may well provide an ideal brandfest site for brands whose devotees are too diverse and too dispersed to come together in a single three-dimensional space. Currently, Internet-based groups focus on such brands as McDonald's fast food and Disney movies. Certain general principles of brandfests should also apply to these "virtual brandfests." For example, corporate presence (virtual and interactive) not only is possible but is likely to have the same benefits as physical attendance at a more literal gathering. Likewise, even a virtual brandfest can be constructed around opportunities for participants to learn and grow in meaningful ways. It is conceivable, for example, for a virtual brandfest to be created for aficionados of seemingly mundane brands such as Dole or Pillsbury to facilitate sharing of favored recipes and stories regarding their experiences with these products (compare Wallendorf and Arnould 1991).

BIBLIOGRAPHY

ARNOULD, ERIC J., AND LINDA L. PRICE. 1993. "River Magic: Extraordinary Experience and the Extended Service Encounter." *Journal of Consumer Research* 20 (June): 24–45.

BELK, RUSSELL W. 1988. "Possessions and the Extended Self." *Journal of Consumer Research* 15 (September): 139–168.

BHATTACHARYA, C. B.; HAYAGREEVA RAO; AND MARY ANN GLYNN. 1995. "Understanding the Bond of Identification: An Investigation of Its Correlates Among Art Museum Members." *Journal of Marketing* (October): 46–57.

BITNER, MARY JO. 1992. "Servicescapes: The Impact of Physical Surroundings on Customers and Employees." *Journal of Marketing* 56 (April): 57–71.

CELSI, RICHARD L.; RANDALL L. ROSE; AND THOMAS W. LEIGH. 1993. "An Exploration of High-Risk Leisure Consumption Through Skydiving." *Journal of Consumer Research* 20 (June): 1–23.

CSIKSZENTMIHALYI, MIHALY, AND ISABELLA S. CSIKSZENTMIHALYI. 1988. *Optimal Experience*. Cambridge: Cambridge University Press.

DRIGOTAS, STEVEN M., AND CARYL E. RUSBULT. 1992. "Should I Stay or Should I Go? A Dependence Model of Breakups." *Journal of Personality and Social Psychology* 62:62–87.

FOURNIER, SUSAN. 1994. "A Consumer-Brand Relationship Framework for Strategic Brand Management." Ph.D. Dissertation, University of Florida.

GLASER, BARNEY G., AND ANSELM L. STRAUSS. 1967. *The Discovery of Grounded Theory.* Chicago: Aldine.

HILL, RONALD P. 1991. "Reliving the Lived Experience: Photographs as an Aid to Understanding Consumer Behavior Phenomena." Paper presented at the Association for Consumer Research Conference, Chicago.

HOLBROOK, MORRIS B., AND ELIZABETH C. HIRSCHMAN. 1982. "The Experiential Aspects of Consumption: Consumer Fantasies, Feelings, and Fun." *Journal of Consumer Research* 9 (September): 142–154.

HOLT, DOUGLAS B. 1995. "How Consumers Consume: A Typology of Consumption Practices." *Journal of Consumer Research* 22 (June): 1–16.

LUND, MARY. 1985. "The Development of Investment and Commitment Scales for Predicting Continuity of Personal Relationships." *Journal of Social and Personal Relationships* (2):3–23.

MASLOW, ABRAHAM H. 1961. "Peak-Experiences as Acute Identity-Experiences." *American Journal of Psychoanalysis* 21(2):254–260.

MCALEXANDER, JAMES H.; JOHN W. SCHOUTEN; AND SCOTT D. ROBERTS. 1993. "Consumer Behavior and Divorce." In *Research in Consumer Behavior,* vol. 6, edited by Janeen A. Costa and Russell W. Belk. Greenwich, CT: JAI Press, 153–184.

MCCRACKEN, GRANT. 1988. *The Long Interview.* Beverly Hills, CA: Sage.

MILES, MATTHEW B., AND A. MICHAEL HUBERMAN. 1984. *Qualitative Data Analysis: A Sourcebook of New Methods.* Beverly Hills, CA: Sage.

REICHELD, FREDERICK F., AND W. EARL SASSER, JR. 1990. "Zero Defections: Quality Comes to Services." *Harvard Business Review* 68 (September/October): 105–111.

ROSENBERG, LARRY J., AND JOHN A. CZEPIEL. 1984. "A Marketing Approach to Customer Retention." *Journal of Consumer Marketing* 1 (Spring): 45–51.

SCHOUTEN, JOHN W., AND JAMES H. MCALEXANDER. 1995. "Subcultures of Consumption: An Ethnography of the New Bikers." *Journal of Consumer Research* 22 (June): 43–61.

TURNER, RALPH, AND EDITH TURNER. 1978. *Image and Pilgrimage in Christian Culture: Anthropological Perspectives.* Oxford: Blackwell.

WALLENDORF, MELANIE, AND ERIC J. ARNOULD. 1991. "'We Gather Together': Consumption Rituals of Thanksgiving Day." *Journal of Consumer Research* 18 (June): 13–31.

WEBSTER, FREDRICK E., JR. 1994a. "Defining the New Marketing Concept." *Marketing Management* 2(4):23–31.

———. 1994b. "Executing the New Marketing Concept." *Marketing Management* 3(1):9–16.

12

THE WILDERNESS SERVICESCAPE

An Ironic Commercial Landscape

ERIC J. ARNOULD, LINDA L. PRICE, AND PATRICK TIERNEY

Servicescapes are sites for commercial exchanges. They are also more or less consciously designed places, designed primarily to produce commercially significant actions. Like other places, servicescapes represent a subset of social rules, conventions, and expectations in force in a given behavioral setting, serving to define the nature and scope of personal experiences and social interactions (Bitner 1991, 61). But servicescapes, like other humanized spaces, often transcend their commercial intent, making manifest a smaller or larger range of social and personal potentialities of action and outcome. Servicescapes, like places generally, have meanings

Eric J. Arnould is an anthropologist and Associate Professor of Marketing, and Linda L. Price is Associate Professor of Marketing in the Department of Marketing, University of South Florida, Tampa. Patrick Tierney is Professor and Coordinator of the Commercial Recreation and Resort Management Program at San Francisco State University in San Francisco, California.
The authors would not have been able to complete this project without the amiable assistance of four outfitting companies, over a dozen river guides, and scores of multiday white-water river-rafting customers. We are deeply grateful to them for their time and effort.

and values for persons, indeed may serve as the foci for the production of socially and personally significant meanings, intentions, and purposes (Tilly 1994).

This study investigates a particular servicescape, making detailed accounts of environmental dimensions and the actual behaviors of the occupants. Our goal is to provide a "thick" characterization, mostly realist, partly confessional in tone (van Maanen 1995) of the specific nature of commercial activity and social interaction that take place in this servicescape. The servicescape we selected contrasts with many of the servicescapes examined in previous research, thus providing a unique location for investigation of the boundaries of current servicescape theory (Dubin 1976). This project provides a broadened conceptual framework of servicescapes as sites for the dramatic enactment of cultural scripts (Deighton 1992; Suprenant and Solomon 1995).

Our investigation focuses on a servicescape quite different from the kind described by Bitner (1991). For her, "the manmade, physical surroundings as opposed to the natural or social environment . . . is referred to . . . as the 'servicescape'" (p. 58). The servicescape that we discuss lies in the canyons where the Yampa and Green Rivers flow through Dinosaur National Monument (DNM) on the Colorado–Utah border. DNM is managed by the National Park Service and provides business opportunities for approximately half a dozen commercial white-water river-rafting operations. We can enumerate some critical empirical contrasts between our focal servicescape and the others discussed in this volume:

- It is predominantly natural rather than built.
- Limited managerial control is exercised over the site.
- The site is privileged over customer needs and wants, rather than subservient to customer needs and wants.
- It is in the foreground rather than the background of service delivery.
- Both service provider and customer access the servicescape from the outside together, rather than the customer entering an environment under the provider's control.

The data are drawn from a multiyear, multimethod investigation of service delivery in white-water river-rafting contexts. More methodological detail has been reported elsewhere (Arnould and Price 1993; Price, Arnould, and Tierney 1995a). Data reported here disproportionately represent insights drawn from 18 in-depth interviews with river guides, 10 days of participant observation, and over 50 posttrip surveys of rafting customers collected after their return home. All of the data reported here were collected during the summer of 1995 specifically for this project.

The first portion of the chapter considers the commercial mediation of the wilderness servicescape. Our data reveal that the primary instrument for producing this servicescape is *communicative staging*—the way in which the environment is presented and interpreted (Cohen 1989). River guides are sometimes aware of the communicative staging they engage in, but the staging is far from entirely strategic or fully systematized. In addition, guides and clients both assume a role in providing narrative framing for the service experience.

The cultural construal of the wilderness servicescape pervades the experience of river guides and customers, and is of central importance in understanding the narrative framing of the servicescape. Four meanings of American wilderness are articulated and highlighted in the data. Following a description of meanings associated with the American wilderness, we illustrate several themes apparent in the communicative staging of the servicescape. Our data reveal that what is communicated and when it is communicated are patterned rather than random, and are keyed to physical movement through a carefully selected servicescape. The experience evinces a narrative quality. Nevertheless, the experience is not fully scripted, as proposed in some models of the service encounter (Suprenant and Solomon 1987). Indeed, process and outcomes are moderated by situational factors often beyond the river guides' control; these contribute to a sense of freedom and possibility experienced on the river. These situational factors are central features of the servicescape and are negotiated and interpreted to buttress the four conventionalized American wilderness themes.

The proposed themes evidenced in this wilderness servicescape yield new insights for servicescape design, interpretation, and management. In the last portion of the paper, we summarize some of the central features of the experienced servicescape and outline some relationships among the service encounter, servicescape, situational factors, and the cultural blueprints that participants bring to the commercial interactions. Our summary highlights relationships that merit further investigation.

THE COMMERCIAL DELIVERY OF WILDERNESS

Wilderness experiences are mediated increasingly by specialized businesses. This commercial packaging and offering of wilderness is always colored with fundamental irony. For example, as Tuan says, "At the back of the romantic appreciation of nature, is the privilege and wealth of the city" (1974, 103). At the same time that wilderness visitors seek an escape from civilization, they are framed "within and against the civilization they sought to leave behind." As one guide notes, the packaging process is shifted from the product to the customer, providing them a cocoon of civilization through which to experience the wilderness:

> We prepare 'em with equipment, you know, food, shelter, all the basic necessities that we have in the civilized world. We teach them how to utilize those things that we give them, so they don't have a reason to be afraid of the wilderness, because they are self-contained (River guide, MWM in his 40s).

Wilderness businesses range from skill-building schools to packagers of eco- and ethnotourism adventures. Organizations vary substantially in the degree to which visitors are coddled and protected. For example, the sedate Lindblad Tours offers luxury cruises to the Galápagos Islands, while rustic trekking concerns in Thailand offer minimal amenities to young adventurers. Organizations also differ in the degree to which customers are spectators of the natural environment (packaged bus tour tourists shooting hasty snapshots of the Grand Canyon from a stop on the South Rim) or active participants in it (treks accompanying climbing expeditions on long and arduous journeys to base camps in the Himalaya Mountains).

The commercial offering of wilderness inevitably involves an ironic conversion of wilderness into a commodity to be marketed as a touristic spectacle like any historic relic, ruin, or touristic site (Cohen 1988; MacCannell 1973; Neumann 1993; Stanton 1989). Wilderness tourism requires human intervention that renders wilderness increasingly evaluated, managed, regulated and controlled. That is tamed.

In these wilderness settings, each outfitter distinguishes its servicescape with some *substantive staging,* that is, with some physical manipulation of the environment. For example, one guide claimed that his company had better toilet facilities than other companies. Another guide described the portable hot tub that one company carries on trips. Yet another company prides itself on not always having a campfire in the evening, under the thesis that watching a fire can be as mesmerizing as television, and thus distract clients from experiencing the wilderness. Sometimes river guides recognize the irony associated with substantive staging in the national monument setting in which they work:

> It's beautiful, it's there, it's, um, it's not buildings, it's not concrete. And to some extent, you know, I realize that it's to some extent controlled. I mean when you see the signs, and you see the paths. It has human impact on it. And there's no way to avoid that (River guide, swM in his 20s).

All in all, however, the wilderness servicescape involves relatively little substantive staging. Particularly in DNM, the mandate for all commercial operators is to minimize human impact on the land. Hence, *communicative staging* becomes the fundamental mechanism for delivering the wilderness servicescape. Moreover, it becomes the primary source of competitive differentiation. Communicative staging is embodied in the manner in which touristic sites are presented and interpreted to the participants by the commercial service provider.

Successful communicative staging is linked to the guides' construction of the wilderness environment as an appropriate place for experiences that clients desire. In contrast to most previous research on servicescapes, our research stresses the primacy of social construal in the perception and interpretation of the service environment. Four wilderness narrative themes that are prominent in American culture are fundamental to the experienced servicescape, and resonate in the fundamental themes that emerge as a part of the communicative staging in which guides engage. Understanding the American wilderness servicescape and the communicative staging of that servicescape requires knowledge of its cultural construction.

THE CULTURAL CONSTRUCTION OF WILDERNESS

In this section we describe and illustrate four cultural constructions of wilderness that are fundamental to the experienced servicescape. We begin with a short overview of the cultural invention of the American wilderness, then explicate four meanings of wilderness that are prominent in American culture. Each of these meanings is described briefly and illustrated in terms of data collected in the river-rafting context. Illustrations from our data highlight how guides, in their interactions with clients, explicate, interpret, and manage these cultural constructions of the wilderness.

The Cultural Invention of "Wilderness"

Wilderness is a complex and elusive concept freighted with changing personal and symbolic meanings. Wilderness is not really a geographically or biologically recognized place as one might imagine. Instead, it is an idea, a cultural invention that most often is celebrated by "city folks" (Cronon 1995; Tuan 1974). In popular imagination and discourse (literature, cinema, tourism), the "wilderness" is etched out as a contrast to civilized life. Henry David Thoreau, Charles Olson, John Milton, and other writers concerned with nature and the wilderness all suggest that civilization and wilderness require each other to have real meaning. Even the contemporary defense of wilderness forcefully argued by groups like the Nature Conservancy or the Environmental Defense Fund maintains that it is not in the best interest of civilization to eliminate wilderness— reasserting the reciprocity between the two (Nash 1982).

The American attitude toward wilderness is old and complex, with contradictory understandings vying for expression. For example, many have proposed that wilderness is a central symbol of American nationality, the "quintessential location" for experiencing what it means to be American (Cronon 1995, 42). But the contradictory ironies of the American construction of wilderness are captured vividly in the removal of the Indians from their native lands so that visitors to our national parks today can "safely enjoy the illusion that they are seeing their nation in its pristine, original state" (p. 42).

Illustrative of the multiple possible readings of the wilderness is a usually unremarked intertwining of North American wilderness attitudes with a Romantic subtext found in our popular (emic) models of emotion. The dominant psychological model of emotions employs adjectives like *innate, universal, biological, internal, unintentional,* and *context-independent.* Nevertheless, it is also true that emotions may be described in other terms, as they often are in North American popular vernacular. We employ adjectives like *energizing, true, unique, real,* and *shared*—i.e., public and performative (Lutz and White 1986; M. Rosaldo 1984; R. Rosaldo 1984). The dominant trope in this alternative emic paradigm, and the one that links the expression and experiencing of emotions to the wilderness servicescape, is that emotions are natural. All North American cultural constructions of wilderness include a strong narrative theme that associates wilderness and authentic emotional expression.

We review four of the most lucid visions of the wilderness in the following sections. They include the view of wild nature as a transcendental force; a molder of human character; a restorative, healing agency; and a refuge whose irreplaceability and complexity make it essential to conserve and preserve.

Wilderness as a Transcendental Force

One of the most pronounced visions of the wilderness anchors in the writings of Thoreau and other transcendentalists. They subscribe to a belief that nature mirrors the currents of higher law emanating from God. This view of nature as transcendental force inspires the highly influential writings of John Muir, founder of the Sierra Club. In his writings on the western wilderness, composed in the last decades of the nineteenth century, Muir often restated the transcendentalists' case for wilderness, evoking the power of nature to lift humankind to a higher plane:

> The mountains are fountains not only of rivers and fertile soil, but of men. Therefore we are all, in some sense, mountaineers, and going to the mountains is going home. . . . Whatever the motive, all will be in some measure benefited. None may wholly escape the good of Nature, however imperfectly exposed to her blessings. . . . Fresh air at least will get into everybody, and the cares of mere business will be quenched like the fires of a sinking ship (1918/1994, 34).

River guides in Dinosaur National Monument echo Muir's views:

> The person coming away from the river [is] kind of feeling a little bit of transcending force or changing force through their river trip (River guide, WM in his 40s).

As shown in some additional interview texts, consistent with themes in Thoreau's work, the wilderness servicescape, the canyons, and the river are sometimes viewed as repositories of transcendent forces revealed only through prolonged exposure:

> Maybe on the first day they see the river as a thing to conquer, but eventually, they come to see it as a real spirit (Guide, SWM in his 30s).

> Usually, usually they've got to . . . get out there swimming and get caught in the current or something, and get a little scared before they'll really respect it. . . . I think a lot of people don't

really know the power of it until they really get in there and feel
the power of it (Guide, SWM in his 20s).

While customers may experience this transcendent spirit temporarily, this transcendent immanence informs the everyday reality of
many river guides, or "boatmen":

> People that work on the rivers have developed a respect for
> water because it's so powerful. 18,000 cfs [cubic feet per second]
> was the other day we put in? Can't fight that stuff; there's no
> way! It's so much bigger and stronger than you that it really
> does start to become this god, for people that are there all the
> time. It's probably as close to a religion for these people as anything (Guide, SWM in his 30s).

Wilderness as a Molder
of Human Character

Implicit in Muir's writings was a view elaborated in Frederick
Turner's writing on the frontier and adopted by President Theodore
Roosevelt and his advisers. Roosevelt, responsible for the creation
of Yosemite and Yellowstone National Parks, was an advocate of big
game hunting who viewed nature as a source of a distinctive American vital élan. In this view, nature is central to the American character and has a special role to play in molding it. Through
confrontation with the forces of nature in the unalloyed wilderness, Americans may resist the "vital exhaustion," "nervous irritation," and "constitutional depression," together identified as the
unavoidable curse of urban civilization by Frederick Law Olmsted
(Nash 1982, 155). In other terms, part of the value of the wilderness trip is its value as "a test, a measuring of strength" and "an
assurance of man's highest potency, the ability to endure and take
care of himself," as Stewart Edward White wrote in 1903 (quoted
in Nash 1982, 154).

This more agonistic view of the human wilderness interaction
manifests in the ongoing American love affair with hunting. Modern nature writers such as Wallace Stegner restate a view articulated
by the expansive Rough Rider, when he writes of wilderness as an

original, formative influence in North America: "An American, insofar as he is new and different at all, is a civilized man who has renewed himself in the wild" (Nash 1982, 261). The view also surfaces to some extent in the organizational visions of businesses like Outward Bound and the National Outdoor Leadership School (NOLS), which are active in Dinosaur National Monument (DNM).

The guides' belief in nature as an essential formative influence, not something to be conquered, but nevertheless something to be "withstood," is evident in many of their descriptions of the wild:

> Getting out in the wild has that kind of vitality that I think I missed in religion. Um, it has the kind of vitality where when you're out there and sometimes you realize to yourself, well, I'm fifteen miles from the nearest road and if I break my leg here, I'm in bad . . . I'm in big trouble. But it's a sense of kind of independence and self-sufficiency, and you get out there and you have to, uh, you know, control your environment from within. It's . . . it's . . . there isn't backup mechanisms that are easily used (Guide, SWM in his 20s).

Guides reiterate this Rooseveltian theme in their own ways, pointing out that the wilderness servicescape is a place where a person can be remade if he or she chooses:

> I think it opens people up. And also, I think, they're totally undefined out there; they don't know who they are or what they are in the wilderness (River guide, SWM in his 30s).

Guides talk explicitly about the positive impact on customers of "taking on nature" as illustrated in one story about an early-season trip through Warm Springs rapids:

> He could not believe it that we made it through this. He didn't want to go . . . and I said, "Come on, I need your help." And I had to talk him into it. He came on, and he's . . . when we got off the river, he thanked me for making him go. He said, "I'm glad you made me do that." And I didn't really make him. . . . It . . . it made him feel great 'cause he was out in nature, taking on nature (Guide, SWM in his 20s).

In addition, this theme of the wilderness as a molder of human character is important in how guides justify and interpret situational influences. For example, one guide notes:

> Stormy isn't necessarily bad because, I mean, you know, there's that challenge thing there (Guide, SWM in his 20s).

Other guides explain that they believe customers will go home and talk about how they withstood the elements, and because of this, even five days of rain, cold, wind, or even snow will be remembered in a positive way:

> And they were just like . . . and they went through the mud and moaned and complained about it. But I think that, too, will add to their experience. When they get home, and they can tell their friends at the office, oh, it was rainy and it was cold and we went on this hike and we slipped and slid . . . you know, in the mud. . . . I think it adds to their—it makes it seem like they were that much tougher to be out there (Guide, SWF in her 30s).

Customers also echo this construction of wilderness, often noting in posttrip responses that "taking on nature" strengthened their character, confidence, etc.

Wilderness as a Restorative, Healing Power

A third theme, intertwined with the two already mentioned, emphasizes nature's restorative powers. Describing visitors arriving on Mount Shasta aboard the new train in the 1870s, Muir wrote,

> Many are sick and have been dragged to the healing wilderness unwillingly for body-good alone. . . . Were the parts of the human machine detachable like Yankee inventions, how strange would be the gatherings on the mountains of pieces of people out of repair (1918/1994, 33).

Muir's theme resurfaces in the wilderness therapy literature. Wilderness therapy came to increasing prominence in the mental-health literature of the 1970s. A considerable scholarly literature has developed around wilderness therapy, with various cultural, evolutionary, and information-processing rationales enlisted to account for the restorative power of natural environments and analyze the restorative effects themselves (e.g., Hartig, Mann, and Evans 1991; Kaplan and Kaplan 1989; Ulrich et al. 1991; Hull and Michael 1995). For many psychologists, a wilderness challenge—even one as simple as carrying a pack and following a trail—can generate self-confidence, provide restoration, and reinstate alertness (Nash 1982). These beliefs are central to the work of Outward Bound, NOLS, and other wilderness training programs.

River guides often express their belief in the restorative power of the wilderness servicescape, sometimes articulated as a return to something basic:

> I think, river magic . . . I see it all the time . . . I saw it when I guided. Just the *spell* that the river environment can cast on people, and just bring them—pulling away from that urban nine-to-five lifestyle that most people live—and, you know, just bring them back to the *basics*. . . . The moonrise, listening to the water, sitting on a sandy beach and a warm breeze blowing through the cottonwoods, seeing wildlife. That, to me, is river magic. And I've seen it a lot (Guide, SWM in his 40s).

> When you're out in the canyons and you're kinda one with what's around you and, um, it feels like that's sorta where the human condition belongs. People really shine when they get out there, for the most part. It really seems to bring out the best in all kinds of different people. Putting them in a natural state. Like getting them "back to nature" (River guide).

In the environmental psychology literature, four interrelated factors are associated with the restorative effects of being in a natural environment: being away, extent, compatibility, and soft fascinations (Kaplan and Kaplan 1989). Informants' commentary suggests that each of these can be a part of their experiences of the wilderness servicescape examined here, and each may contribute to customer satisfaction.

Being Away

The first factor, that of "being away," implies involving oneself in cognitive content different than the quotidian. Being away affords distance from the world of pressures and obligations, and in this sense enables restorative stress relief (Hartig, Mang, and Evans 1991; Ulrich et al. 1991). In our river-rafting data, this aspect of the experience is often referred to as providing a "perspective on life":

> But there's something very simple about eliminating, um . . . you get away from the city stress and all the things that you thought were really important, like your Public Service bill is gonna be late or, you know, just little things. I don't know, it kinda helps you. It changes people's state of mind and helps them put themselves and their lives in *perspective* (River guide, SWF in her 30s).

> A lot of what I do is try to give people . . . through the river, I try to give people sort of a different *perspective on life* to some degree, a little bit, because I think that when you take people out of the setting that they're in—the city or whatever—and to an unknown, that they're sort of dependent on someone else, and it happens to be me at that point. I think that a lot of growth can occur; I think that they can really grow emotionally. I think they can really get a *different perspective* on their life and gain a little bit more from their life (River guide, SWM in his 20s).

Extent

A second factor that comes easily in the wilderness environment is "extent." Extent involves both a feeling of the interrelatedness of the immediate elements of the environment so that they constitute a portion of a larger whole, and the promise of a continuation of the world beyond what is immediately perceived. Extent heals by providing a perspective that matches some sort of intuition of the way things ought to be or really are below the surface of culture and civilization.

Variety and physical scale in the wilderness servicescape contribute to a feeling of extent. Extent is evident in many comments in our data:

And on a river trip, it's, you know, as soon as you shove off, you're five feet from the bank, and you're exactly where you're supposed to be. And it's that way for the whole trip. You're right where you're supposed to be. There's no way to go or to get there. Every . . . every step of the way, you're there. And I think that's what helps people relax so much because there's nowhere that they're trying to be (River guide, SWF in her 30s).

But more often than it seems that they [customers] really appreciate the times when they just float around a corner and see something really spectacular. I think they sort of feel a little bit of peace and harmony in the world that they don't often feel back in the city, and I think that's a real emotional point with them (River guide, SWM in his 20s).

Floating down the last mile and a half of Ladore, where you come down and all of a sudden you see a big fault line where the strata has been completely tilted vertical, and you come around the corner, and you float down into Echo Park where the Yampa comes in, and the geology changes really quick, and there's, you know, big towering cliffs coming out of the river, and it's open and parklike—that, and then floating the loop through and exiting Echo Park—there is, I love it (River guide, SWM in his 30s).

Compatibility

Another aspect of the restorative power of nature is compatibility—a feeling combining relatedness, awe and wonder, and the absence of environmental nuisances (Hartig, Mang, and Evans 1991). It may involve belief in what William James defined as an unseen order and harmony. Compatibility also refers to the congruence between opportunities for action provided by the environmental setting, the constraints on behavior it imposes, and individuals' purposes and intentions. This feeling is frequently in evidence in our field notes and survey data:

And he was just always, you know, going, "it's so amazing how . . . how nature can just be this beautiful." And he was . . . he was just like . . . "And how the rocks form in such an arch, how can it be so perfect?" And every day he was just in awe. Just going, "How . . . how can it be? How can it be this perfect? How can it be this beautiful?" (River guide, SWF in her 30s).

And I really think it all has to do with people being in a natural environment. Oh, we've gotten so far away from that, it's real easy, I think there's, like, this memory in your soul that kinda wakes up. I don't know. I don't want to sound too cosmic, but I think there's something in everybody's being that says, "Oh, yeah, this is how it's supposed to be. It's supposed to be simple like this" (River guide, SWF in her 30s).

[Magical moments in my experience included] entering Echo Canyon in complete silence early in the morning and seeing wildlife and the beauty of the rock formations for at least one hour (with no human or mechanical sounds) (Respondent to a posttrip survey).

I have many. . . . One [magical thing was] . . . when my friend and I were in the double ducky [inflatable kayak] for the second time, and something clicked. . . . We did every stroke together; we became one (Respondent to a posttrip survey).

Soft Fascinations

Finally, natural settings afford "soft fascinations" that hold the attention involuntarily but allow introspections and reflections. Fascination may be related to Bitner's (1991) concept of emotion-arousing complexity in the servicescape. The exploration of thoughts, including confusing or stressful feelings and memories, is made more tolerable by the presence of pleasurable stimuli. Fascination comes into play when, out of interest or curiosity, certain objects (e.g., a kayak, a canyon, wild animals) or processes (e.g., exploration, mastering new skills) capture and hold attention. According to environmental psychologists, as fascination is engaged, demands on depleted voluntary attentional capacity are diminished. Restoration then becomes possible (Hartig et al. 1991; Kaplan and Kaplan 1989).

The perception that fascination with the wilderness servicescape provides restorative benefits is evident in our data:

You're kinda one with what's around you, and, um, it feels like that's sorta where the human condition belongs. People really shine when they get out there, for the most part. It really seems to bring out the best in all kinds of different people. Putting them in a natural state. Like getting them "back to nature" (River guide, SWF in her 30s).

I remember thinking to myself, even as a child, "Look at how untouched that is," and [I would] look, and it was really calm, and the trees just seemed to almost blow, and it just all this magic air around them, they looked so calm and everything. It overwhelmed me from that day, and I still get that same feeling when I go and look at the canyon. I look back quite often, and I think, "Yeah, there's the trees." . . . There is something new every time (River guide, MWM in his 20s).

Because I'll go out there, and it's hard for me now, 'cause I just got married, so it's like it's really hard for me, because I love my wife to death, and I'll find it—hours and hours and hours will go by, and I don't think about her, and then I feel guilty. I really feel guilty about it, but it's because you're in that magical environment out there in the wilderness that just sucks you in, and it just absorbs you. And, you get absorbed in it, and you just don't think about anything else but what's around you and what's going on. And, sometimes, you're not even thinking about that; it's just that you're gone, you know? You're just out there (River guide, MWM in his 40s).

Wilderness as a Last Refuge Essential to Conserve and Preserve

Contemporary views of the wilderness bear the mark of the new ecology-oriented environmentalism. In this view, wilderness is a reminder of our biological origins and our continued membership in and dependence on the biotic community. For modern evolutionary biology and population ecology, it is axiomatic that wild environments are biologically diverse and that their diversity contributes to their stability. Wilderness, then, is the refuge of countless species among whom there is a kind of biological aesthetic order, and it is at the same time essential to human survival. In this vein, physicist A. J. Rush writes, "When man obliterates wilderness, he repudiates the evolutionary force that put him on this planet. In a deeply terrifying sense, man is on his own" (quoted in Nash 1982, 260).

Sometimes, however, the conservation and preservation ethic eschews Romanticism. For example, for the late godfather of "deep ecologists," Edward Abbey, wilderness is free of anthropogenic value; it stands as the antipode of civilization and all its myths, including those concerning wilderness. Yet its preservation is essential to the maintenance of modern civilization (Nash 1982, 270–271). This view inspires a range of organizational forms from Greenpeace to Earth First; deep ecology is its extreme expression (Turner 1995).

As with the other themes discussed above, ideals of conservation and preservation are found in our data:

> Um, I heard a couple talking about how when they used to camp, which was probably about twenty years ago, they could walk anywhere and not worry about it. And I've heard them talking about that, like around the campfire, like how nowadays you have to stay on a trail. And they know what, like [inaudible], and how not to walk on it. And, you know, even little flowers or whatever, they'll step over instead of just tramping through it. And it seemed like, you know, they have definitely a lot more respect for the environment than they did twenty years ago (River guide, SWM in his 20s).

> I think that's really the big impact that we have is, I haven't done a trip yet this year where people haven't said, "Well, what do you do with the ashes from the fire? And what do you with this and that?" And, it's just like we take everything out, you know; we leave nothing behind at all. Try to leave the smallest trace. And people will sit there and go, "How do people camp here?" They realize that these are designated campsites, and they're named, and they have campsites. And they look around, and they don't see one cigarette butt on the ground or any piece of trash. And I think that has more of an impact on them than anything else we can teach them. They're just really amazed that that many people can come through, and you really don't have the evidence (River guide, SWF in her 30s).

> They know this is a national monument; they've read the brochure, they go through it, and they know that it's protected. But when you start telling them about dams and geology and litter and all this stuff, that seems to me that it just goes, something clicks in their head, and they're going, "I understand now." This is a natural resource, the Park Service, a lot of people aren't fond of the Park Service for one reason or another. Any federal agency, it seems like the general public always has some kind of

problem with, and I think they understand a little more what
the Park Service is trying to accomplish by protecting the natural resource. . . . They don't realize how important the natural
resource is to them, and it plays a big role; I think it really affects
them (River guide, SWM in his 30s).

In the aftermath of the trip, responses to an open-ended projective question on the posttrip survey revealed that wilderness often
became associated with conservation values. Over half of the
responses to the prompt "An especially meaningful thing I learned
about the wilderness environment was . . ." included references to
preservation values, as shown in Table 12.1.

So far, we have shown how the wilderness servicescape is a site
for the elicitation of narrative themes drawn from several traditions
of thought about the wilderness in North America. Sometimes
guides and customers experience the transcendental qualities of
nature. Sometimes contact with the moral force experienced in the
wilderness servicescape—experienced as the highs, the flow, the
adrenaline rushes—are highlighted (Arnould and Price 1993; Privette 1983). Sometimes customers also find themselves transformed
by the experience of contact with the wilderness servicescape. And,
in many cases, people come away with a new or reinforced sense of
the desirability of preservation and conservation of the wilderness.

COMMUNICATIVE STAGING
OF THE WILDERNESS SERVICESCAPE

Building on common cultural constructions of the wilderness, commercial service providers present and interpret the servicescape for
the participants. Wilderness sites are selected for their potential to
deliver a sequence of experiences matched to narrative ideals, such
that, as one rafting customer put it in a posttrip survey, rapids are
"perfectly ordered from easier to more difficult."

Many service providers emphasize the role of wilderness in
delighting their customers, while deemphasizing their own communicative staging and emotion work (consistent with a theme of

TABLE 12.1   Posttrip Impressions of the Wilderness Environment

Case Number	Response
001	The effort required to maintain the "wild" river
004	It must be treated with great care
005	The cryobionic [sp?] soil sensitivity—avoid stepping on it
006	It must be protected
010	Its fragility
012	To be respectful of it so it can be enjoyed by future generations
016	Our national parks, monuments are well kept up and should be for future generations
019	About the delicate crust—the thin vegetation on the ground [cryptogamic soil]
021	How important our impact can be on it
023	It needs to be preserved
024	It needs to be protected and nurtured
027	How important it is to preserve and protect it
028	One small change can ruin the whole environment
029	The web of the numerous ecosystems Micro/Macro
031	Always appreciate it and NEVER take it for advantage
032	To keep it clean and treasure it forever
033	That everyone can share it with wildlife
034	It's beautiful, especially when you're surrounded by it
035	Our mere presence is destructive, so it's important to leave it as though we were never there. ADRIFT was very persistent in pointing this out to all of us—*Very good!*
037	The *respect* I gained for the river & its surroundings
039	How important water is in the West
040	Its fragility
042	This type of area needs to be protected for future generations
043	How odd the "state line" looks from the river—not a natural line!
046	How fragile it is
049	Protect it!

wilderness as a transcendental force). Other guides, however, have an intuitive sense that their communicative behavior channels the customers' experiences:

> The person coming away from the river kind of feeling a little bit of transcending force or changing force through their river trip. I think a lot of that comes from a kind of instructor's attitude toward it (River guide, WM in his 30s).

There is a strategic dimension to this; sometimes the guides use their customer knowledge to channel customers' experiences:

> You know, in the Grand Canyon, where I started working, you'd do like fourteen to twenty-day trips, and by the end of the trip, you knew those people inside and out, you know? You knew what made them tick, you knew what pleased them, you knew their buttons—their hot buttons, you know? (River guide, SWM in his 20s).

Further, some guides recognize there is sometimes a selective process in which clients desirous, however unconsciously or inchoately, of a particular kind of emotional experience partner with guides who are able to deliver this experience, and vice versa. This pairing between guide and customer facilitates the staging of particular experiences. Successful staging and pairing are linked to the guides' construction of the wilderness environment as an appropriate place for experiences that clients desire. The four wilderness narrative themes previously described, in turn, frame these experiences:

> And it's interesting, too, that people will . . . they sort of get the feel for the different guides, and if they want to really meet a party guide, they're going to find a party guide; and if they really want to learn and study, they're going to find a person that's most knowledgeable. And if they really want to work through some emotional stuff, they find a person's that's . . . they just wind up with them. And so I wind up having a lot of talks; people sort of find me. We get into these talks, and . . . back in California . . . this one guy came to me, and his life was getting a little tough, and his marriage was getting a little tough, and he was out there with the boys . . . and we sort of sat 'round one

night real late, . . . and he was telling me what was going on with himself and where his life was going. That's when some of the river analogies sort of flew. . . . And because they're out of their environment, it throws away all of the shields that they've had and all the sort of roles that they've played, and they can be someone different (River guide, SWM in his 30s).

Finally, some guides also recognize the contingent effectiveness of communicative staging. Most often it works:

But I think within the environment it's the perfect environment just to meet people, learn from them, and you can actually teach them. And it blows me away that—less and less it's blowing me away, 'cause I'm realizing it—but I'm twenty-two years old, and I can talk to a fifty-year-old man about his wife, you know, and they listen to me. Like I have something to say. And it blows me away, and then you start to realize that you do, maybe. And that's like the best part (River guide, SWF in her 20s).

We always make it a point, I make it a point, to speak really clear, really loud, really forceful talking, because that's a liability. I learned that from a liability insurance guide, and really it's helped me out a lot. It's pulled a lot of things off in terms of making a trip go smoother, too. So you do have their attention there, and you can calm their fears by talking about safety issues, in my opinion (River guide, MWM in his 20s).

Sometimes the communicative staging is less effective:

Gotta watch it. I've had some boatmen act real nervous when they give the leader speech, thus the people are gonna . . . they pick up on it. My very first commercial trip, I didn't give the leader speech, but my people knew it. I never told them it was my first commercial trip, but they knew it, and I was nervous, and they could see that. We get to Warm Springs Rapids; they really had a rough time (River guide, MWM in his 20s).

Three fundamental themes emerge as part of the communicative staging in which guides engage. These themes resonate with references to four cultural constructions of wilderness that are prominent in American culture.

Communicative Staging Themes

In this section of the manuscript, we develop three themes that characterize the guides' communicative staging of the wilderness servicescape (Cohen 1989). These themes are built on and around the prominent cultural constructions of the wilderness. Figure 12.1 illustrates the relationship between the communicative staging themes and the cultural constructions of wilderness.

Leisure and Work

Outfitters are differentiated by the degree to which they frame the servicescape as a leisure environment versus an environment of productive labor and personal growth For example, for some whitewater rafters, "The very meaning and experience of leisure [is] defined and circumscribed by the images and rhythms and oral valuations of work" (Cerullo and Ewen 1982, 30). Consistent with the theme of wilderness as source of American élan vital, personal skill building is a benefit commonly elicited from multiday white-water river rafters (Price and Arnould 1993). Customers appreciate this work for self-improvement.

Work in nature is also seen as better, more meaningful than activity in the city:

> When you're out in the backcountry, if you've forgotten something, then you have to use more of your mind to improvise, figuring out how to do things. If you break something, you've got to fix it instead of running out to a shop to have it repaired, or just going out and buying a new one. . . . Just a different way of dealing with things, and it's just out there. You know, it's just you're more involved in your own life, 'cause you're doing more stuff than you normally would do to take care of yourself (River guide, WM in his 40s).

This valuation is also reflected in consumer responses to a posttrip query about something meaningful they learned about themselves: "I can do anything I set my mind to"; "I can KAYAK!"; "I actually want to learn how to kayak now—it was a blast!"

FIGURE 12.1   Cultural Constructions of Wilderness and Communicative
Staging of a Natural Servicescape

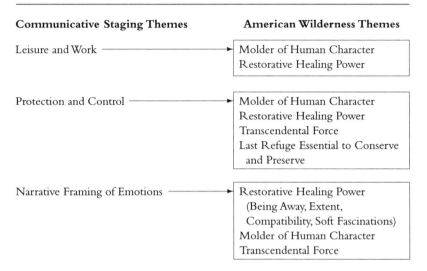

Communicative Staging Themes	American Wilderness Themes
Leisure and Work	Molder of Human Character Restorative Healing Power
Protection and Control	Molder of Human Character Restorative Healing Power Transcendental Force Last Refuge Essential to Conserve and Preserve
Narrative Framing of Emotions	Restorative Healing Power (Being Away, Extent, Compatibility, Soft Fascinations) Molder of Human Character Transcendental Force

Protection and Control

Essential to effective communicative staging in DNM, customers
come under considerable "surveillance" and control (Foucault 1977;
Turner 1995, 334). In river rafting this takes two forms; one form
is protection. Guides and clients alike (see Price and Arnould 1993)
see the guides as keeping them safe—protecting them, in other
words, watching over them:

> Especially when you're working, you feel a whole lot of respon-
> sibility because you're dealing with passengers and you're kind
> of responsible for them (River guide, SWF in her 30s).

> I know what to wear and how to dress, and I'm used to it. But
> I get real concerned about my passengers' comfort, and I worry
> about them if they're not properly dressed (River guide, SWF in
> her 30s).

In fact, some guides, operating with the cultural theme that contact
with the wilderness is restorative or character-building, think they
protect their customers too much:

Well, I don't know if [we're] held responsible for the weather, but held responsible for them getting wet, yeah. They think that you should be there baby-sitting them, you know. We baby-sit 'em enough (River guide, SWM in his 20s).

And sometimes, guides suffer fatigue or become frightened by the role that clients put them in (Hochschild 1983; Singh et al. 1994). Sometimes the customers transfer their sense of the wilderness as a transcendent force to the guides themselves:

I think it's scary. Really scary . . . I think that people end up with this, the river god being the guide, and somehow they think that you are this incredible otherworldly strong thing that somehow, that pilots you safely through these rapids and cooks your dinner in the rain over fire and, just, . . . you're so out of bounds of what they are accustomed to (River guide, SWF in her 30s).

In addition to protection, negative controls are also exerted to preserve the integrity of the trip by ensuring a safe run, and to reinforce the cultural theme that the wilderness is an untouched or untouchable preserve:

There is that side of river running you have, that you have to tell people, "Please don't put your leg out of the boat." And then they always turn around and, instead of just putting their leg in the boat and saying, "Oh! I'm sorry," . . . you don't expect an apology, but instead they'll turn around and say, "Why?" Well, because it's a danger, it's a hazard, and it's not a good idea to do that (River guide, MWM in his 20s).

GUIDE (SWM in his 20s): I don't know. I've seen people on my trip litter, you know?

INTERVIEWER: You have to get on their case?

GUIDE: Yep. I mean, especially, cigarette butts. They'll be smoking a cigarette and just flip it into the river. Nope, stop the boat, row over, make 'em pick it up. And that's something that we stress in the beginning. If you smoke, you know, you've got to strip it out and stick the butt in your pocket, or give it to me or one of the other guides, who will put it somewhere.

Narrative Framing of Emotions

Multiday river-rafting trips provide a linear, narrative framing that facilitates the creation of certain expectable emotional outcomes on each day of the trip. Following a Romantic subtext model of emotion, guides encourage customers to view their emotional response to the servicescape as natural—as energizing, true, unique, and shared. Movement through the servicescape, including both its substantive and communicative elements, provides a fundamental source of emotional moments (Arnould and Price 1995).

For many customers, day one is an anxious, confused, busy, and uncertain day. Customers from different groups feel like strangers, and their interactions are informed by norms governed by an urban social context. Suddenly they find themselves in uncomfortable proximity to the norms found in the rafting subculture. Much of their discomfort stems from aspects of the servicescape, which may appear very alien and remote. Communicative staging is critical at this point in order to get people over their stress and into a more relaxed mode that is safer and begins to reshape the experience as an enjoyable one. Much of the communicative staging at this point is directed at shaping how customers interact with the servicescape. Guides recognize that they engage in a certain channeling of emotions but frame this too simply as a matter of appropriate communications with customers:

> I think the most important thing you can do at a safety speech, aside from your basic safety issues that have to be covered, is to let people know this is . . . they're there to have fun, and to encourage people to have a really good time and explore and check it out. Sometimes people need a little shove in the right direction. . . . So, I think you can set a tone for a whole trip just by the way you greet people (River guide, SWF in her 30s).

Guides work hard to figure out how to get the group to relax and have fun by day two. A significant aspect of their emotion work at this stage is enabling customers to relax in and appreciate the servicescape.

By the third day of the trip, certain activities have become routine, and a certain camaraderie has been built: "And you notice," remarked one guide (a married white male in his 20s), "at least I notice, that somewhere around the third day, everyone has gotten into the flow of the river." Movement through the servicescape is designed to provide big excitement on the third day. Day three is about the tension and thrill of real rapids:

> Day three it's incredibly beautiful, but sort of the big excitement at the end is Warm Springs, at the end of the day. But I just notice that people are, everybody knows each other, the anxiety is gone for the most part, except that Warm Springs gives you that excitement. But there's still interaction. Yeah, something to really look forward to; people are dying, they've heard about Warm Springs (River guide, MWM in his 30s).

Of course, consciously or not, the guides contribute to the feelings that are experienced. For example, guides compliment customers on skills demonstrated, camaraderie promoted, wildlife spotted, plants identified, or stories told:

> Whenever you do something good or good for the group, the guides always congratulate you and say, "Good eye," or, "Thanks," something like that. It's just really second nature to them (p.o. notes).

Communicative staging by the guides reinforces how to see and interpret. This, in turn, validates and even accentuates customer excitement, as seen in this exchange that took place just before running the Warm Springs rapid:

> CUSTOMER: That's the [recirculating] hole [in the rapid] that makes me nervous; it probably doesn't bother you.
> GUIDE: It scares the shit out of me, John, is what it does, to be perfectly honest with you.

By the fourth day, the guides' efforts have often paid off, as seen in feelings of aesthetic pleasure, compatibility, control, camaraderie, and communitas that emerge. At this point there is much more convergence between guides and customers in their interpretation of the servicescape. Also notable is that by the fourth day, customers themselves have begun to enunciate the rules for interpreting and interacting with the servicescape; that is, they have become participants in communicative staging:

> At one point, . . . before we went through a bunch of waves . . . Teresa [a customer] said, "This is where we're supposed to whoop." And I said, "Well, go ahead. You start." And so she did. It was interesting, since Teresa comes from a very controlled, Catholic background. As she told me, she's trying to learn to give herself permission to do things, to like things (p o notes)

Teresa's case is not unusual in showing that even a relatively repressed sort of person may learn to mirror the "feeling rules" implicit in the guides' communications. Other examples of this shift in feeling rules are easy to find in our field notes.

While other emotional experiences also may be engaged in, on the last day of the trip, some guides suggest a silent float through a flat, sinuous stretch of water before a long, last series of waves and white water. People often acquiesce to this opportunity for aesthetic (even transcendent) wilderness experience. On one trip, a guide articulated feelings that dovetailed with those experienced by one of the researchers:

> And, uh, we had a half hour quiet rowing on our boat that stretched to an hour. During which time we just listened and, uh, [the guide] even wrote some in his journal. He announced afterward that it was perhaps the best hour he'd spent on a trip. I watched a heron fly against the hillside during much of this time. It was wonderful. I was just listening to the birds, and the air, and the water, the sounds of a natural symphony. Wonderful. Watching the water, glinting and running off the sandstone blocks way up above us as they emerge up out of Whirlpool Canyon (p.o. notes).

As shown in Table 12.2, this silent float often surfaces as one of customers' most compelling memories in posttrip survey responses to questions about the most magical moment of the trip:

TABLE 12.2   Magical Moments in the Servicescape

Case Number	Response
010	The magical float up to Steamboat Rock [Echo Park]
012	Entering Echo Canyon in complete silence early in the morning and seeing wildlife and the beauty of the rock formation for at least one hour (with no human or mechanical sounds)
025	A two-hour silent float through canyons one morning
035	The silent float—it was nice that everyone stopped talking and just listened to the sounds of the canyon for one-half hour
048	Early-morning silent float with light rainfall

The last day often elicits exhilaration associated with the theme of wilderness as a source of élan vital, as in the following example:

> Sinead and Dr. Evets went on and on, and on talking about their ride [in a two-person kayak]. They got really pumped, says Sinead, because they fell out of the boat. They went up a wave, and the wave picked 'em right up and stood 'em on end, knocked them out of the boat. . . . They're talking about the angle and what happened and why, and Mike was talking about how he saw them and how he thought he was in trouble, 'cause he saw them go in, and he was going right for it [in a single-person kayak]—there was no way out. . . . They were all very anxious to go over it several times—big excitement, big excitement (p.o. notes).

Consistent with belief in the restorative, transformative, and transcendent virtues of the wilderness, one guide's communicative staging on the last day of the trip imparts the idea that what is experienced is basic and authentic:

> One of the most telling moments on the float down from lunch to the takeout—I was sitting in the oar boat with D, looking downstream in A's oar boat—and I was watching Ely, the pediatric surgeon, bailing out A's boat. So, here's a middle-aged male

pediatric surgeon bailing out the boat of a female 22-year-old, kind of spacey river guide, and I remarked to D, "Look at that; isn't that something?" He says, "Yes, it's beautiful. Out here things like that [status differences] don't matter" (p.o. notes).

The last day is also tinged with nostalgic regret associated with the leaving the servicescape and reentering the ordinary world.

In the aftermath of the trip, other feelings emerge. Sometimes these are subtle feelings associated with the restorative theme of wilderness experience, as the following comments suggest:

I think . . . I remember somebody on my last trip saying, uh, you know, "I'm gonna go back to work, and all those things it seemed like they were, you know, things that were stressing me out aren't gonna be stressing me out anymore." You kinda . . . you keep that feeling with you. Keep that feeling of . . . it just kinda keeps things in perspective a little bit. Things that we let disturb us so much in our lives that really aren't . . . problems (River guide, swf in her 20s).

In other cases, the transformative theme of wilderness experience is evidenced, as in these comments on a posttrip survey:

I realized when I got back that I had taken few pictures, but it clearly demonstrated that I didn't have time to take many pictures—a good sign. I've decided to move to Salt Lake upon completion of my master's program [in New England] this coming June '96. The trip helped me to ultimately get my priorities in order and to stop putting things off "till the time is right." The time is now! (Pre-med student, swf in her 20s).

Some guides mythologize this transformative potential of the whitewater experience. Stories like the following are often elicited:

I have known people . . . I knew a woman who was a Ph.D.— I believe she was a tenured psychology professor or something—and took some river trips and loved it—quit her job and became incredibly active with river conservation. I've known a . . . I know a doctor who ran a commercial rafting company on the side (River guide, swm in his 20s).

In this section we have outlined the role of communicative staging in offering wilderness as a servicescape. Although companies are differentiated by their substantive staging, the most important source of differentiation is in the way the site is presented and interpreted by the service provider.

The strategic dimensions of communicative staging are complex. For example, the staging itself, which is rich with the metaphors of cultural constructions of the American wilderness, foregrounds the servicescape and deemphasizes the guide role (e.g., nature is powerful, transcendent, restorative, healing). Further, the effectiveness of communicative staging is contingent; sometimes it works and other times it doesn't. Certain themes characterize the communicative staging that the guides engage in. We have detailed themes of leisure and work, protection and control, and emotion management as customers move through the servicescape.

DISCUSSION AND CONCLUSION

Our paper is suffused with ironic tension. In postmodernity, the wilderness seems to provide a refuge from the artifice, pastiche, and hyperreality that afflict us to varying degrees. And yet we concur with serious students of landscape that wilderness is itself a cultural construction. That it is perceived as authentic is perhaps a confirmation of its subordination to the logic of postmodernity. It is quite clear that the surreal pastiche world influences the rafting experience. The canyons were "surreal, seemed fake, they were so huge," someone says in a posttrip survey. Children say they don't miss TV "too much"; customers compare the vistas to built Disney landscapes; some even ask if the river circles back around to the put-in! (Price, Arnould, and Tierney 1995b). River-rafting customers experience the river canyons of DNM as pristine, clean, liberating, and natural, yet their existence is linked to a regime of discipline and control policed by the National Park Service and the river outfitting companies.

There can be no doubt of the experiential reality of aesthetic and hedonic pleasures experienced, of the recentering and life transformations that customers sometimes recount. The researchers themselves are far from immune to these experiences. Yet we must disagree with Edward Abbey's view of wilderness as an empty, unresponsive, and inhumane immensity. *Tant bien que mal,* it is clear that even wilderness is now a part of marketing culture (Cohen 1988; MacCannell 1973).

Our focus on wilderness servicescape makes salient a number of aspects of servicescapes overlooked or taken for granted in other contexts. Our detailed multimethod, multiyear investigation of a complex, elaborate servicescape, to use Bitner's (1991) typology, provides a basis for proposing a number of additional areas for elaborating servicescape theory and research.

One crucial area for additional research is the experienced servicescape. In contrast to much previous work, in this paper we argue that both service providers' and customers' interactions with each other and experience of the servicescape are significantly affected by their *cultural constructions of the servicescape.* Even emotional scripts for the service encounter are guided by their construction of the servicescape. Future research could focus on understanding how cultural constructions of the servicescape influence customer–service provider behaviors and outcomes. For example, based on this research, we expect that when cultural constructions are complex and many interpretations of the servicescape are plausible, perceptions of the servicescape will be heavily dependent on communicative staging. How different communicative staging strategies affect servicescape perceptions could be systematically studied using field experiments and/or observation methods.

Another fruitful area for future research and theory building is the relationship between substantive and communicative staging in the experienced servicescape. *Communicative staging* is a vital aspect of the experienced servicescape in our research, yet it has received little or no attention in the servicescape literature. An important question is what kinds of services would benefit from communicative staging of the servicescape. Especially in services where the servicescape is foregrounded, communicative staging can add value.

A second and related question is, What are the conditions under which communicative staging will add value? Based on our research, we would expect that one of the most important factors influencing the *success of communicative staging* would be that providers and customers share cultural frameworks for action and interpretation. As hilariously demonstrated in a recent article (Gopnik 1995) about an American trying to get a workout in a Parisian health club, if provider and customer are operating from different cultural frameworks, communicative staging can frustrate the service experience for both customer and provider. In our data, guides sometimes question customers' tendency to view all Native American sites as "sacred." Some guides view this as a way of overexoticizing the ordinary, daily life of the now-vanished Fremont and Anasazi peoples. As a result, they are sometimes unwilling to visit certain sites. Similarly, critical studies of the Polynesian cultural center in Hawaii and Heritage Village in South Carolina have pointed out how raising impolite questions about colonialism on the one hand, and American history and biblical scripture on the other, can frustrate the experience that providers seek to create in these servicescapes (Gopnik 1995; O'Guinn and Belk 1989; Stanton 1989). Thus, anytime customers wish to impose a different cultural construction on the servicescape than management wishes to impose, communicative staging may be ineffective.

Phrased in another way, when the servicescape is foregrounded, communicative staging may be effective when there is a matchup between the persona of the service provider and the experienced servicescape. What we have in mind is an extension of McCracken's (1989) ideas about the transfer of cultural meanings from celebrity endorsers to customers via products to the service context. Thus, consistent with the meanings both of the locale and the boutiques, shoppers on Rodeo Drive may reasonably expect a certain cosmopolitanism, elegance, and fashion sophistication from service providers at the Gucci or Fred boutiques. In a similar fashion, the substantive staging of the Nike Town servicescape could be enhanced by the presence of specialized, "just do it" athletes in each department. In our research, highly effective guides convey meanings consistent with those associated with the cultural construction of the wilderness:

> Noticing the Hatch [River Outfitters] guides, who are . . . in their late 20s, maybe early 30s, some of them, healthy, rosy, tanned, muscular, and with flyaway hair—they do all seem to radiate something! Like a lot of endorphins and a lot of energy. They're very pretty people in general, too. Maybe it's air-like, maybe it's physical beauty, I'm not sure (p.o. notes).

In this quote from field notes, the notion that the wilderness is a restorative source of vital energy is conveyed through a match between provider and servicescape.

A third area in which useful research could be conducted concerns the experience of *natural versus built servicescapes.* By studying natural servicescapes, we can identify some elements of environments that provide important emotional benefits to people. For example, consistent with previous work in psychology, our research showed that qualities of being away, extent, compatibility, and soft fascination in the wilderness provide restorative, even transformative benefits. These qualities, already evident in numerous vacation and leisure servicescapes, might be designed into other built servicescapes to a lesser degree. Many personal service servicescapes could benefit from more strategic consideration of how these qualities could be built in. Psychologists, massage therapists, spas, and other similar services are especially appropriate examples, since the benefits they provide typically focus on restoration and transformation. A productive example of the use of nature for restorative benefits in a built environment is a courtroom in Chicago that has added a child-care center designed around the use of nature. According to the designer, the intent is to incorporate nature to help the children relax and feel whole.

One important feature of natural servicescapes is their inherent *dynamism.* Built servicescapes also can be dynamic. But so focused has been the service literature on ways of meeting customer expectations that this quality has not been discussed in strategic ways. Evident in our research are the benefits of spontaneity, surprise, authenticity, and behavioral freedom associated with the wilderness servicescape. Of course, static servicescapes also offer advantages, so service providers must be careful when deciding to create a dynamic servicescape. Some conventional retailers do use this quality to their advantage. For example, Sherry and McGrath (1989) describe two stores that constantly rearrange merchandise, claiming that this is "at once a display strategy, a provision of challenge and suggestion to the problem-solving gift shopper, and a kaleidoscopic sensory experience" (p. 159). Perhaps other retailers might benefit from injecting greater dynamism into their servicescapes.

Finally, our research makes it clear that natural servicescapes introduce many *uncontrollables* into the service encounter, and this creates certain challenges for the service provider. We would expect that delivering value in natural servicescapes requires flexible roles for both providers and customers. As we have elsewhere suggested, the presence of uncontrollable, and perhaps unfamiliar, situational factors in natural servicescapes places considerable responsibility on the service provider to provide satisfactory framing for customers by creatively building on shared cultural frameworks for action and interpretation (Arnould and Price 1993). Natural servicescapes may also require providers to engage in more customer socialization to counter perceptions of risk.

BIBLIOGRAPHY

ARNOULD, ERIC J., AND LINDA L. PRICE. 1993. "'River Magic': Hedonic Consumption and the Extended Service Encounter." *Journal of Consumer Research* 20 (June): 24–45.
———. 1996. "High Water, Low Water: The Emotional Moments of River Rafting." *Working Paper,* University of South Florida, Tampa, FL.
BITNER, MARY JO. 1991. "Servicescapes: The Impact of Physical Surroundings on Customers and Employees." *Journal of Marketing* 56 (April): 57–71.
CERULLO, MARGARET AND PHYLLIS EWEN. 1982. "'Having a Good Time': The American Family Goes Camping," *Radical America* 16:13–43.
COHEN, ERIC. 1988. "Authenticity and Commoditization in Tourism," *Annals of Tourism Research* 15:371–386.
———. 1989. "'Primitive and Remote' Hill Tribe Trekking Thailand." *Annals of Tourism Research* 16:30–61.
CRONON, WILLIAM. 1995. "The Trouble with Wilderness." *New York Times Magazine* (August 13): 42–43.
DEIGHTON, JOHN. 1992. "The Consumption of Performance." *Journal of Consumer Research* 19 (December): 362–372.

DUBIN, ROBERT. 1976. "Theory Building in Applied Areas." In *Handbook of Industrial and Organizational Psychology,* edited by Marvin D. Dunnette. Chicago: Rand McNally, 17–39.

FOUCAULT, MICHEL. 1977. *Discipline and Punish: The Birth of the Prison.* New York: Vintage Books.

GOPNIK, ADAM. 1995. "The Rules of the Sport." *New Yorker* (May 27): 36–39.

HARTIG, TERRY; MARLIS MANG; AND GARY W. EVANS. 1991. "Restorative Effects of Natural Environment Experiences." *Environment and Behavior* 23 (January): 3–26.

HOCHSCHILD, ARLIE R. 1983. *The Managed Heart.* Berkeley: University of California Press.

HULL, R. B., IV, AND SEAN E. MICHAEL. 1995. "Nature-Based Recreation, Mood Change, and Stress Restoration." *Leisure Sciences* 17:1–14.

KAPLAN, RACHEL, AND STEPHEN KAPLAN. 1989. *The Experience of Nature: A Psychological Perspective.* Cambridge: Cambridge University Press.

LUTZ, CATHERINE, AND GEOFFREY M. WHITE. 1986. "The Anthropology of Emotions." *Annual Review of Anthropology* 15:405–436.

MACCANNELL, DEAN. 1973. "Staged Authenticity." *American Journal of Sociology* 79 (November): 589–603.

MCCRACKEN, GRANT. 1989. "Who Is the Celebrity Endorser? Cultural Foundations of the Endorsement Process." *Journal of Consumer Research* 16 (December): 310–321.

MUIR, JOHN. 1918/1994. *Steep Trails.* Edited by William Frederic Bade. Reprint, San Francisco: Sierra Club Books.

NASH, RODERICK. 1982. *Wilderness and the American Mind,* 3d ed. New Haven: Yale University Press.

NEUMANN, MARK. 1993. "Living on Tortoise Time." *Symbolic Interaction* 16(3):201–235.

O'GUINN, THOMAS C., AND RUSSELL W. BELK. 1989. "Heaven on Earth: Consumption at Heritage Village, USA." *Journal of Consumer Research* 16 (September): 227–238.

PRICE, LINDA L.; ERIC J. ARNOULD; AND SHEILA L. DEIBLER. 1995. "Service Provider Influence on Consumers' Emotional Response to Service Encounters." *International Journal of Service Industry Management* 6(3):34–63.

PRICE, LINDA L.; ERIC J. ARNOULD; AND PATRICK TIERNEY. 1995a. "Going to Extremes: Managing Service Encounters and Assessing Provider Performance." *Journal of Marketing* 59 (April): 83–97.

———. 1995b. "'The River Wild': Nature and Media." Paper presented at the 1995 Annual Meeting of the National Parks and Recreation Association.

PRIVETTE, GAYLE. 1989. "Peak Experience, Peak Performance and Flow: A Comparative Analysis of Positive Human Experiences." *Journal of Personality and Social Psychology* 45(6):1,361–1,368.

ROSALDO, MICHELLE Z. 1984. "Toward an Anthropology of Self and Feeling." In *Culture Theory: Essays on Mind, Self, and Emotion,* edited by Richard A. Shweder and Robert A. LeVine. Cambridge: Cambridge University Press, 137–157.

ROSALDO, RENATO. 1984. "Grief and a Headhunter's Rage: On the Cultural Force of Emotions." In *Text, Play and Story,* edited by Edward M. Brunner. Washington, DC: Proceedings of the American Ethnological Society, 178–195.

SHERRY, JOHN F., JR., AND MARY ANN MCGRATH. 1989. "Unpacking the Holiday Presence: A Comparative Ethnography of Two Gift Stores." In *Interpretive Consumer Research,* edited by Elizabeth C. Hirschman. Provo, UT: Association for Consumer Research, 148–167.

SINGH, JAGDIP; JERRY R. GOOLSBY; AND GARY K. RHOADS. 1994. "Behavioral and Psychological Consequences on Boundary Spanning: Burnout for Customer Service Representatives." *Journal of Marketing Research* 31 (November): 558–569.

STANTON, MAX E. 1989. "The Polynesian Cultural Center: A Multi-Ethnic Model of Seven Pacific Cultures." In *Hosts and Guests: The Anthropology of Tourism,* edited by Valene L. Smith. Philadelphia: University of Pennsylvania Press, 247–264.

SUPRENANT, CAROL, AND MICHAEL SOLOMON. 1987. "Predictability and Personalization in the Service Encounter." *Journal of Marketing* 51 (April): 86–96.

TILLEY, CHRISTOPHER. 1994. *A Phenomenology of Landscape.* Oxford: Berg Publishers.

TUAN, YI-FU. 1974. *Topophilia: A Study of Environmental Perception, Attitudes, and Values.* Englewood Cliffs, NJ: Prentice Hall.

TURNER, JACK. 1995. "In Wilderness Is the Preservation of the World." In *Deep Ecology for the 21st Century: Readings on the Philosophy and Practice of the New Environmentalism,* edited by George Sessions. Boston: Shambhala Publications, 331–339.

ULRICH, R. S.; R. F. SIMONS; B. D. LOSITO; E. FIORITO; M. A. MILES; AND M. ZELSON. 1991. "Stress Recovery During Exposure to Natural and Urban Environments." *Journal of Experimental Psychology* 11:201–230.

VAN MAANEN, JOHN. 1995. *Representation in Ethnography.* Thousand Oaks, CA: Sage.

13

DREAM ON

Projections of an Ideal Servicescape

MARY ANN MCGRATH

The realms of the popular press and consumer myth have presented polarized and stereotyped images of male and female shoppers. Men and women are portrayed as living (and shopping) in separate worlds. Women are "born to shop" and "shop 'til they drop" in pursuit of fashion, color, and variety, while men are stereotypically thought to avoid malls like a plague and to inhabit a gray and navy world of sports, trucks, and athletic clothing. Several comic strips, such as *Cathy* and *For Better or For Worse,* play on the gender difference scenario, while a popular book comparing communication styles proclaims that *Men Are from Mars; Women Are from Venus* (Gray 1992). While researchers have generally found women to be a group yielding rich insights on shopping (Otnes, Lowrey, and Kim 1992; Sherry and McGrath 1989; Otnes, McGrath, and Lowrey 1995), there has been restrained research interest both in explicating the shopping behaviors of men and in exploring commonalities and differentiations in service expectations between the genders within the retail context.

Mary Ann McGrath is Associate Professor of Marketing at Loyola University, Chicago.

THEORETICAL PERSPECTIVES
OF GENDER AND SHOPPING

Academic researchers have advanced the explanation of gender and accompanying differences beyond that of a biological dichotomy. Specific perspectives include both the sociological and the psychological, with accompanying cognitive, affective, and behavioral implications.

The work of the marketplace has traditionally been affiliated with the role of women. Fischer and Gainer (1991) demonstrate that shopping has been a traditional role for women since the early part of this century in North America and a major part of most middle-class women's lives. Department stores served as the female equivalent to men's clubs and created a setting for otherwise scarce leisurely social interaction with other women (Benson 1986). Women have also dominated the shopping venue through their roles as gift givers (Barnett 1954; Caplow 1982; Cheal 1987) and creators of ritual occasions (Smith-Rosenberg 1975). Through shopping in these contexts, women define and maintain their self-identities; maintain linkages with families, traditions, and histories; and conform to and excel in socially prescribed roles (Fischer and Gainer 1991).

Meyers-Levy (1988) demonstrated that men and women tend to process information differently, implying significant psychological and subsequent behavioral differences between the sexes. Fischer and Arnold (1990) show that differences in gift-shopping behavior are better predicted by the constructs of gender-role attitudes and gender identity than by biological sex. Gender-role attitudes include an individual's level of agreement with traditional stereotypical roles allocated to each sex, while gender identity relates to the level of identification with communally feminine traits and agentically masculine traits. Wardlow (1993) suggests that a series of additional constructs might contribute to an enlightened perspective on gender and related differences that includes gay men and lesbians. These include physiological sex, gender affiliation, and self-definition and self-construction.

Most definitions in the field of consumer behavior report gender differences as outcomes, while using a myriad of construct conceptualizations given above (cf. Costa 1991, 1993, 1996). The following study attempts to fill an empirical gap in the literature related to understanding the role and preferences of shoppers by comparing data from male shoppers with those of the better-explored female shopper. The context of what each group perceives to be an ideal of service, environment, selection, and experience serves as the anchor for such comparisons. In addition, the study also provides insight into how male and female shopping behaviors and service expectations are similar and differentiated in the ideal.

BACKGROUND OF THE STUDY

This research was conducted at Consumer Corners, the pseudonym for a regional outlet mall of formidable proportions. Fieldwork was completed between October 1993 and January 1994. During this period of time, the author and a research assistant observed and interacted with a variety of shoppers, both male and female, as the informants prepared for and observed the Thanksgiving, Christmas, and Hanukkah holidays and indulged in preholiday tasks and postholiday returns and markdowns.

The mall that provides the focal context is located approximately thirty miles from each of two major Midwestern metropolitan areas. The mall is approximately one mile in length, and is designed in a Z-shaped configuration with food courts at each major turn and anchor stores at each vertex. Although the tenant structure reflects about a 15 percent annual turnover rate, there are on average eleven anchor stores and about two hundred specialty stores. The majority of Consumer Corners' stores are factory outlet stores or outlet stores associated with well-known retailers. Merchandise is typically sold at prices 20 to 60 percent below full retail. The immensity of the mall and the large number of outlet stores renders appropriate Consumer Corners' slogan: "You'll be overwhelmed and undercharged" (Consumer Corners Mall Directory 1993).

To study the shopping behavior of Consumer Corners' shoppers and to specifically target the understudied male shoppers as well as their better-documented female counterparts, we used a multimethod approach using five qualitative techniques. This approach is similar to methods used for other interpretive studies within our discipline. These methods are detailed as follows:

1. Interviews with shoppers were conducted using a survey format. To this end, two forms of projective methodologies were employed with a sample of male and female shoppers contacted in a mall-intercept situation. McGrath, Sherry, and Levy (1993) detail both the theory and analysis of such projective methods. Detailed dream scenarios were elicited from a sample of 15 male and 15 female informants. As an incentive to cooperate, each participant was given a $5 coupon for use at any of the mall's restaurants—in essence, a free lunch.

2. Within the confines of the mall, shoppers were observed and those observations documented, with special attention being paid to male shoppers and to interactions between consumers and retail personnel.

3. The research followed the Shopping With Consumers protocol (Otnes, McGrath, and Lowrey 1995). Two male and two female informants each allowed the author to accompany them on two shopping excursions and participated in three in-depth interviews related to their shopping behavior.

4. Interviews were conducted with 12 store managers to supplement survey, depth interview, and observational data and to serve as a form of member check.

Only part of the results of this in-depth study of shopping are reported here. Of current interest are the results of one projective instrument in which informants were asked to detail a dream that they had about their "ideal" store. To induce some detail into their stories, researchers gave informants the following probe:

What I would like you to do now is to use your imagination and describe a dream that you have had about shopping in an ideal store. Describe the beginning, the middle, and the end of this dream.

DETAILED FINDINGS

Both men and women responded without hesitancy to the query for a description of an ideal store. Related dreams included both activities and descriptions of the ideal context for performing such behaviors. Specifically, the descriptions of retail service venues provide insight into how consumers negotiate the space within their construction of an ideal context. These descriptions also uncover attributes and specifics that contribute to making these contexts ideal.

Male Dream Stores

Counter to the pervasive stereotype and results of projective techniques in general, most male informants expressed positive fantasies concerning the atmosphere and task of shopping in their ideally constructed service venue. In contrast, a single male informant reinforced the "men hate shopping" stereotype by expressing his reluctance to even enter the retail setting:

> My ideal shopping experience is to have a bar at the entrance [of the mall] or a movie theater at the entrance, so guys could sit there and drink (Married male, age 57).

All other male respondents, however, conjured up specific visions of an ideal store. Many envisioned a large department store or mall, while others imagined specialty stores or departments that carried items of interest to them and, in general, signified the hobbies and interests of many men. Popular fantasies revolved around automotive supplies, tools, computers and software, sports equipment, and novelty items.

In aggregate, the men envisioned their shopping as restricted to a single or limited category of products. The following excerpts illustrate this tendency:

> I love shopping in a tool store—looking for new tools, seeing what they have, and looking for tools that I don't have. I wish I could own all the tools in the store (Married male, age 67).

The store would have computers, automotive supplies, and software. There would be computer stations around, showing software. It would be very hands-on and well lit. There would be no sound, and the salespeople would be technicians (Married male, age 54).

The store would be big. There were computer shops, sports shops, and baseball card shops. It would not be really busy. Salespeople would be really nice (Single male, age 18).

A frequent scenario involving the ideal stores of males is the ability to perform one-stop shopping and to allow a man to "have in mind what [he] want[s] to buy, and the first store would have what [he] want[s]."

But in addition to the product line, retail ambience also is detailed with salience in the ideal store scenarios. In several male dream descriptions, lighting, background music, and salespeople were identified as important attributes. The "lighting has to be good; it has to be bright"; there has to be "plenty of light on things I'm buying—focused on merchandise"; and, "Halogen lamps give a nice pattern [of light]." The background music was described with specificity: "instrumental jazz"; "quiet"; "rap"; and "instrumental . . . a little more upbeat."

In the ideal stores of most male respondents, they would shop alone and would be unencumbered with social interaction with other customers or with sales personnel. The retail service would be better than the norm they experience in reality. Men suggest that in the ideal there "wouldn't be a lot of [salespeople]" and those present would be "very helpful . . . not pushy . . . acknowledge the customer . . . attentive" and "very courteous."

The dream scenarios also provide insight into male shopping activities, interests, and behaviors within ideal stores. One man, whose ideal store was an antique-automobile store, described his actions and demeanor inside this store:

[I would] take the lay of the land [and] have an idea of what [I] want to buy beforehand—will have research done. [I would] get under the car, look for technical difficulties, check the serial number, make sure the car is in good shape. [The car] is a major purchase. [You] want to know what you're buying is good (Married male, age 56).

A respondent whose ideal store carried a variety of tools had this fantasy:

> [I] can spend a lot of time looking around a tool store. My wife gets mad because [I] spend so much time. I look around, see if there's something I want or need. I pick up, look at [the tool]. I generally have a good idea of what the tool does before I pick it up (Married male, age 68).

Another man detailed an actual retail experience from recent history as his "dream":

> I spent four hours in Brookstone [in the Mall of America]. Different things are there like metal playing cards on a magnetic plate—just the types of things you could not find anywhere else. . . . It was very spacious, with categorized displays, open shelves, wide aisles. There was lots of room to try things out. It was very hands-on. You could feel it, test it—the quality. I was playing and buying. It was the neatest store I've ever been in (Married male, age 56).

Men's descriptions of how they would or do shop in their ideal stores mirror stereotypical and empirically documented female shopping behaviors (Sherry and McGrath 1989; McGrath 1989). These men take their time within the ideal store. They browse, touch, even "pick" at items, while attuned to auditory, visual, and tactile stimulations. They "play" with the merchandise. In short, males assume traditional female shopping behaviors when they are shopping in their "ideal" stores or in stores that are similar to their ideal stores. This finding was further tested and corroborated through observations in the mall of males shopping in stores similar to these "ideal" descriptions and through interviews with managers of the types of stores described by our informants.

Female Dream Stores

Female dream scenarios frequently dwarfed the traditional department or specialty stores described by males. Like the men surveyed, most women enumerated specific merchandise as well as physical characteristics of their ideal store, but the ideal descriptions of females did not converge as parsimoniously as did those of their male counterparts. The reason may be that most existing retail settings are in reality designed around the tastes, preferences, and shopping styles of women. Thus, ideal descriptions of women suggest only marginal tweaking of existing shopping settings. The traditional department store appears to serve as an anchor for such fantasizing by women.

For example, several women described their ideal stores as containing clothing, frequently in substantial quantity. The specific merchandise and characteristics, however, were very individualized. For one informant, an ideal clothing store also included other specific merchandise, all evocative of her child-sized stature:

> Petite Sophisticates and a toy store combined. It would have clothes that fit me, and I like to shop in toy stores. It would also have a candy store (Widowed female, age 64).

Other informants requested "all Guess? and Garbed clothes" or "lots of shoes in all colors from Europe and all over; lots of fur and leather clothes" or a store with "a lot of neat clothes for my age category . . . name-brand clothes." Erotic self-indulgence found in a study of self-gifting in women (Sherry, McGrath, and Levy 1995) was reflected in one woman's description of a store for women only:

> [I would like to] shop for clothes [where] only women can go in. They can run around in their underwear and try everything on. There would be every type of women's clothes—boots, shoes, accessories, everything. And plenty of them. . . . Limit the number of people who can enter to something like three people per square yard (Married female, age 33).

This closely parallels an actual scene from Filene's Basement in the 1960s, in which women shed their outer clothing without inhibitions to try on designer bargains in short supply while male managers were ignored as eunuchs in a harem.

Many women commented on an ideal store ambience. They demonstrated a sensitivity to light and sound, suggesting that lighting should be "bright," "moderate," "sunny," "natural," or with "sun roofs" and "skylights for lighting." A calming, quiet environ-

ment was generally suggested, again coupled with erotic intimacy—
"like a bedroom." Background music was detailed as an important
part of ambience, with choices ranging from "soft music . . . piano
playing" and "classical music" to "no noise." One woman included
an olfactory element in her fantasy, a "light perfume." Personal space
was emphasized; notably, "no crowds" could powerfully enhance
the ideal. For some women, this especially included "no kids."

At the other extreme and similar to the ideals of some male
informants, some women chose a more energized store atmosphere
with contemporary gospel and rap music. Active participation in
the retail setting was envisioned through access to "a karaoke
machine [where] you could choose oldies or music from today—no
classical or elevator music." For these people, crowds were not problematic—"just no mean people."

The female respondents were more verbal and specific than
males about the inclusion and role of the salesperson in their fantasized retail setting. In the ideal, salespeople would be "knowledgeable and friendly" with "good service—just like the old days."
Salespeople should "know things when you ask them questions and
would be there when you need them." They would be at once attentive and invisible. One woman gave the following specifications:

> There would be a way to know salespeople. You could pick
> them out; they would not have special clothing, but a band
> or something. Salespeople would not approach customers;
> customers would approach salespeople (Widowed female,
> age 42).

Unlike the male respondents, women did not provide specifics
as to how they would shop in their ideal stores. They were more
intent on what an ideal store should contain and what physical contextual attributes it should have. Overall, dream scenarios detailed
ideal female stores that contained merchandise and attributes that
could be individually configured to meet the specific or personalized
needs of female shoppers. Ironically, as retailers try to discern the
"science of shopping" (Gladwell 1996), these women were describing shopping as an art form, with both canvas and palette available
in the store to enable the women to create their own masterpiece.

Observations of women shopping in stores that approached their ideal corroborated a female shopping style that involves tactile, visual, nonlinear discovery. Women tend to maintain their general shopping demeanor and turn to an idealized store setting for ease in assembling outfits or personalizing their shopping as an individualized contextual experience.

INTERPRETIVE SUMMARY AND THEMES

Through the use of a projective storytelling technique, a number of male and female shoppers at a large regional mall detail their ideal retail service venue. These consumer fantasies demonstrate limited gender differences, provide insight into how people shop within the construction of their ideal context, and describe attributes and specifics that make these stores "ideal." Most intriguing is the finding that, although men and women fantasize significantly different types of settings as ideal, and there is evidence of gendered shopping behavior, when projected into their individual ideal formats, men and women tend to behave and explore the retail ambience in a similar manner.

A series of themes is repeated in the stories of both men and women. The themes shed light upon characteristics and consumer behaviors in an idealized retail setting. The following discussion summarizes these themes and, where appropriate, highlights gender-related differences.

Abundance

Shopper dreams are filled with a cornucopia of goods. Stores are envisioned as containing not only exactly what shoppers want, but the mother lode of whatever they might desire. The profusion of merchandise yields a plethora of choices, even a glut of materiality. Such plenty in the retail context alludes to personal opulence and prosperity, given the fantasized resources to acquire them. Although all shoppers eschew a dearth of goods, men and women envision them organized in different ways. Males appear to describe and gravitate toward simpler, less busy-looking settings, while women envision a myriad of merchandise available to them all at once which they can reconfigure into their personal mosaic.

Ambience

All shoppers appear to be sensitive to the nuances of the immediate retail environment, and several expressed preferences for specific surroundings. In general, men and many women expressed a preference for environs that exuded a feeling of comfort, solace, and peace. Perhaps this was a direct reaction to the marketplace stereotype of crowds and rushed acquisition, although other respondents characterize as their ideal such a frenetic, energized setting. The description of a servicescape in which the informant receives soothing succor and peaceful repose characterizes an idealized home environment. These modern shoppers, as involved and harried citizens of the nineties, appear to creatively fantasize a marketplace that sells a snippet of contentment and serenity that they may be unable to find in their private lives and domiciles. Rather than "coming home" to escape distress, they are willing to search the public sector for places less chaotic than their domestic alternatives. Fitting this image as well is the growing appeal of shopping from the home using catalogs and other self-paced interactive media.

At the other extreme, a notable group of women dreamers and one male idealized a frenetic and sensually stimulating retail environment. They enjoyed and were energized by a high level of activity and vitality in the marketplace. These shoppers drew both strength and amusement from an animated and vigorous setting. The current notion of mall as entertainment complex fits this idealized conceptualization.

Play

Descriptions of an idealized shopping experience contain elements of a frolic or romp through a setting respondents imagine has been designed to amuse shoppers. They toy and trifle. The task of acquisition is frequently secondary to amusement, enjoyment, and entertainment. In fact, informants do not relate any instances of purchasing; they are shopping. They play with merchandise, salespeople, and sometimes other shoppers. Any "work" of shopping, in the sense that there are tasks are to be accomplished, appears to be quickly set aside in their ideal shopping environment. Once in situ, they focus on adventurous exploration. In these ideal retail settings, both men and women shoppers are nostalgically transformed into the role of children in resolute pursuit of fun.

Although the process is similar for all respondents, a gender difference emerges with the choice of toys. Women play with clothes, echoing the childhood games of "dress up" and "Barbies"; men trifle with tools and similar devices related to *manual* pursuits.

Self-Indulgence

The ideal stores of both men and women are replete with creature comforts, evidence unconstrained behaviors, and generally condone the unconventional. As would be expected in such dream scenarios, the respondents' personal wants and whims are the focus of and central to the story. These ideal descriptions posit the construct of retail service to the extreme, in which the individual respondent represents an ultra-niche to be served in an unquestioning, unrelenting, and organizationally undisciplined manner. It is women, rather than men, who project an intimate eroticism in the retail setting. Their discovery and manipulation of "stuff" and their perceived dominance over the situation touches on orgasmic.

Service in a Servicescape

The overall conceptualization of service in the ideal retail venue of these respondents is at once attentive yet invisible. Consumers appear to abhor greeters and hovering sales personnel. Rather, they prefer to pursue their fantasies alone while retaining complete control of the retail setting. When a shopper decides that he or she requires some form of service, such assistance is expected to appear instantaneously. This idealized type of assistance, more realistically related to catalog browsing and ordering than to traditional in-store shopping, may explain the explosion in mail-order and interactive shopping services.

Price as a Nonissue

In the context of a price-sensitive, competitive retail scene, respondent narratives are notable for their lack of concern about or mention of price-related issues. Dreams that could have incorporated fantastic value, promotional deals, or even free merchandise were surprisingly silent on this issue. While the use of projective methods quickly elicits negative reactions and produces instant candor with informants (McGrath, Sherry, and Levy 1993), no such reactions were found in this study. It can be hypothesized that either value issues are so deep-seated and implicit to the discussion of shopping as not to require articulation, or they disappear when consumers are given every other dream option.

CONCLUSION

In summary, the findings of this preliminary exploratory study indicate that many commonalities and some notable differences exist between the way men and women react to and behave in a traditional retail setting, and how they characterize their projected ideal shopping and service settings. When either gender is in a store characterized as "ideal," shoppers linger, browse, enjoy touching and "playing" with merchandise, while at the same time savoring visual and aural atmospherics. All shoppers yearn for individualized attention and a level of service that may lie beyond the conventional, the possible, or the appropriate. Ideal stores for men and for women can differ significantly in atmosphere and product array. While many men choose to streamline the average shopping setting, women tend to want to fill stores to overflowing. At the same time, many women accept existing shopping settings as the mean, and they dream of only marginal changes to the real that would allow them to examine and incorporate greater numbers of items with greater facility into their personalized shopping agenda. In addition, most shoppers yearn for a level of emotional satisfaction, even pleasure, that traditional retail planners may find difficult to comprehend, much less appease.

Gender was not a discriminating variable in this study, but more a label for shopper types. Some women shopped "like a man" both in dreams and in reality, while several men displayed the attitudes, emotions, and behaviors of stereotypical women shoppers. Most interesting is that, given an ideal retail setting, happy shoppers found a universal form of enjoyment.

This study has offered a small glimpse at a major marketing exchange in the form of the interaction between consumers and the retail venue. What might be superficially assessed as gender differences in the retail setting may more likely be a dichotomy that characterizes two very different types of retail shoppers. These may loosely correlate with gender but may relate to other variables such as gender role attitude, gender identity, shopping expertise, task definition, time available, comfort level with visual stimulation, sociability, self-confidence, and a myriad of other variables. What is significant, however, is that both of these shopper types—better labeled masculine and feminine, or perhaps linear and diffuse— demand the same levels of service, stimulation, recreation, and aesthetic attractiveness that are frequently unavailable and possibly unattainable in the traditional retail venue.

BIBLIOGRAPHY

BARNETT, JAMES H. 1954. *The American Christmas: A Study in National Culture.* New York: Macmillan.

BENSON, SUSAN PORTER. 1986. *Counter Cultures: Saleswomen, Managers and Customers in American Department Stores 1890–1940.* Urbana: University of Illinois Press.

CAPLOW, THEODORE. 1982. "Christmas Gifts and Kinship Networks." *American Sociological Review* 47(3):383–392.

CHEAL, DAVID. 1987. "'Showing Them You Love Them': Gift-Giving and the Dialectic of Intimacy." *Sociological Review* 35(1):151–169.

COSTA, JANEEN ARNOLD, ED. 1991. *Gender and Consumer Behavior.* Proceedings of the First Conference. Salt Lake City: University of Utah Printing Service.

———. 1993. *Gender and Consumer Behavior.* Proceedings of the Second Conference. Salt Lake City: University of Utah Printing Service.

————. 1996. *Gender and Consumer Behavior.* Proceedings of the Third Conference. Salt Lake City: University of Utah Printing Service.

FISCHER, EILEEN, AND STEPHEN J. ARNOLD. 1990. "More than a Labor of Love: Gender Roles and Christmas Gift Shopping." *Journal of Consumer Research* 17(3):322–332.

FISCHER, EILEEN, AND BRENDA GAINER. 1991. "I Shopped Therefore I Am: The Role of Shopping in the Social Construction of Women's Identities." In *Gender and Consumer Behavior,* edited by Janeen Arnold Costa. Salt Lake City: University of Utah Printing Service, 350–357.

GLADWELL, MALCOLM. 1996. "The Science of Shopping," *New Yorker* 72(33):66–75.

GRAY, JOHN. 1992. *Men Are from Mars; Women Are from Venus.* New York: Harper Collins.

MCGRATH, MARY ANN. 1989. "An Ethnography of a Gift Store: Wrappings, Trappings and Rapture." *Journal of Retailing* 65(4):421–449.

MCGRATH, MARY ANN; JOHN F. SHERRY, JR.; AND SIDNEY J. LEVY. 1993. "Giving Voice to the Gift: The Use of Projective Methods to Recover Lost Meanings." *Journal of Consumer Psychology* 2(2):171–191.

MEYERS-LEVY, JOAN. 1988. "The Influence of Sex Roles on Judgment." *Journal of Consumer Research* 14(4):522–530.

OTNES, CELE; YOUNG KIM; AND TINA LOWREY. 1992. "Christmas Shopping for 'Easy' and 'Difficult' Recipients: A Social Roles Interpretation." *Journal of Consumer Research* 15(3):422–433.

OTNES, CELE; MARY ANN MCGRATH; AND TINA LOWREY. 1995. "Shopping with Consumers: Usage as Past, Present and Future Research Technique." *Journal of Retailing and Consumer Services* 2(2):97–110.

SHERRY, JOHN F., JR., AND MARY ANN MCGRATH. 1989. "Unpacking the Holiday Presence: A Comparative Ethnography of Two Gift Stores." *Interpretive Consumer Research,* edited by Elizabeth Hirschman. Provo, UT: Association for Consumer Research, 148–167.

SHERRY, JOHN F., JR.; MARY ANN MCGRATH; AND SYDNEY J. LEVY. 1995. "Monadic Giving: Anatomy of Gifts Given to the Self." *Contemporary Marketing and Consumer Behavior: An Anthropological Sourcebook,* edited by John F. Sherry, Jr. New York: Sage, 399–432.

SMITH-ROSENBERG, CARROLL. 1975. "The Female World of Love and Ritual: Relations Between Women in Nineteenth-Century America." *Signs* 1(1):1–29.

WARDLOW, DANIEL L. 1996. "Gender 2000: Panel Remarks." In *Gender, Marketing, and Consumer Behavior,* Proceedings of the Third Conference, edited by Janeen Arnold Costa. Salt Lake City: University of Utah Printing Service, 179–181.

14

COMMERCIAL ACTIVITY AT HOME

Managing the Private Servicescape

KENT GRAYSON

Sociologists have long recognized that consensus about social rules is necessary for successful social interaction (Goffman 1959, 1974; Schutz 1970; Thomas 1966). For example, it is generally accepted that, when having a conversation, participants will take turns speaking. If one of the participants breaks this rule and interrupts frequently, then the conversation is unlikely to run smoothly. In consumer behavior contexts, agreements about interactional rules result from a negotiation among three forces: (1) what the marketer wants, (2) what the consumer wants, and (3) what the broader social world will allow (Deighton and Grayson 1995). Often in our everyday consumption, this negotiation process is not salient because tensions among the three forces have already been resolved as part of our socialization as consumers. For instance, a young child at a restaurant may find it frustrating to wait for the waiter to bring over a piece of chocolate cake from the dessert tray. But over time

Kent Grayson is Assistant Professor of Marketing at London Business School, Regent's Park, London. The author thanks the London Business School's Centre for Marketing for its support of this project, and is grateful to Cathy Goodwin, Stewart Brodie, and Richard Berry for their helpful comments on earlier drafts.

we all learn that at a sit-down restaurant, the waiter (not the patrons) brings the food. That's just "the way we do things" and, as a result of socialization, it becomes part of our implicitly accepted social reality. Implicit agreements allow us to go to the movies, fill up at the gas station, and stay at a hotel without having to negotiate the rules every step of the way.

But there are so many rules for so many situations! For instance, at some hotels, it is appropriate to complain if your television has a bad picture, while at others you are lucky to have a television at all. How do we know when to complain, to whom, and in what manner? The answer comes in great part from servicescapes. As Goffman (1959) emphasized nearly forty years ago, we often look to the social environment's physical elements for clues about what to expect in a situation, and for instructions about how to behave (see also Rapoport 1990). A doorman stationed in front of a hotel tells us that the hotel is service-conscious and that we will probably get a quick response if we complain to the front desk about our television. A play area near the front of a furniture store suggests that young families may feel comfortable bringing children along. Classroom chairs arranged in a circle tell students that discussion during class will be encouraged.

The foregoing commentary captures the essence of a social truth but also exaggerates the simplicity of social life. In practice, social rules are flexible; they allow for multiple interpretations. Because of this, interactants may sometimes disagree about the social rules that apply to a situation. Even the most taken-for-granted social rules can be challenged by someone who does not know them or who wants to operate under a different social consensus. In situations like these, the social negotiation process moves from the background into the foreground (Garfinkel 1967). Consider the following examples:

> A European friend of mine recently visited the USA for the first time. While waiting at the airport for a connecting flight, he pulled out his pack of cigarettes. Perplexed by not seeing any ashtrays, he went from gate to gate and came eventually to a small airport bar, where he lit a cigarette. Still not seeing an ashtray, he asked the bartender for one. When the bartender

explained that smoking was not allowed anywhere in the building, my friend was astonished. Only after this incident did he notice all of the No Smoking signs around the airport.

One warm evening last spring, I had a dinner engagement with some colleagues and a job candidate at a fine restaurant across town. Because of the nice weather, I decided to walk from work to the restaurant. So I set off, removing my coat and rolling up my shirtsleeves as I went. When I arrived at the restaurant, I was greeted by a well-dressed maître d', who stood at a large and well-polished podium near the front door.

"Hello," I said to him, "has the Grayson party arrived?"

He checked his reservation book. "Not yet, sir." Then he inclined his head toward a plush waiting area. "Perhaps you would like to wait?"

I nodded, but as I started to turn, he gave me a tight-lipped smile. "And you may find that our air-conditioning is rather cool, sir, so you may want to put on your coat."

I recently chaperoned three children to a new "indoor playland" at a nearby shopping mall. Neither I nor the children knew what an indoor playland was, but it had been recommended by some neighbors, so we decided to give it a try. When we arrived, paid for entry, and walked inside, we were confronted by a colorful landscape of slides, ladders, bridges, a pool of soft balls, a child-sized castle, and a jungle of huge stuffed animals.

My three charges walked tentatively through the separate play areas, carefully watching other children play and occasionally touching some of the playland's soft surfaces. Finally, the oldest of the three jumped into a play area and began to climb a ladder to a treehouse. "C'mon!" he yelled to the other two as he climbed. "It's like a playground, only it's puffier!"

One day while working in Manhattan, I stopped at a busy restaurant to get some pizza to go. It was during the lunchtime rush, so there were a lot of people waiting to give their orders to the man at the counter. But because the line moved quickly, I still hadn't decided what kind of pizza to have when I reached the counter.

"Yeah?" the man asked, a white paper plate already in his left hand, a pizza spatula in his right.

"Ummmmm," I said, looking at the menu board.

"Listen," he said sharply as he pointed me to the end of the line, "if you don't know what you want, don't get in line. Now, who's next?"

These examples illustrate what can happen when the marketer, the consumer, and the broader social reality do not share a consensus about what rules do (or should) apply to a particular situation. The purpose of this chapter is to explore the strategies that marketers employ in such situations to influence the social consensus. To do so, I have chosen a consumption situation in which the rules for behavior are not well established. That situation is network marketing, a retail selling approach that is sometimes also known as multilevel marketing.[1]

One of the reasons that the social consensus about network marketing is not broadly shared is that its salespeople tend to use their homes (and the homes of others) as central retail selling venues. As this chapter will argue (and as many readers will already appreciate), today's broader social world does not generally consider the home to be an appropriate servicescape. Business is not usually welcome in the household. How, then, does a home-focused network marketer work within (or around) this social consensus? To answer this question, I first briefly outline the social history of the Western home and emphasize why, as a servicescape, it is not currently conducive to retail selling. Following this, I describe the results of exploratory research into the strategies used by network marketers who must negotiate within and around the home servicescape every day.

Implicit Social Agreements About the Home

Research on domestic life in the Western world has documented a number of significant transformations in the home's structure and

---

[1] Readers unfamiliar with network marketing may nonetheless be aware of prominent network marketing companies such as Amway, Mary Kay, Herbalife, and Cabouchon. Although network marketing companies take a similar approach to sales and distribution, they can differ greatly in terms of the type of product they market. Cosmetics, insurance, fragrances, health food, telephone services, vitamins, jewelry, water filters, and household cleaning products have all been offered by network marketing organizations. For a more detailed description of this industry, see Grayson (1996).

meaning since the Victorian era of the nineteenth century. One of these, which affected many socioeconomic groups throughout the West, was an increased clarification of the boundary between the public and private spheres of social life. Although, a division between public and private domains did exist before the 1800s, it was graduated; it blurred distinctions at the margin and therefore placed less emphasis on differences between the two domains. In contrast, social rules governing the twentieth-century home have been influenced by a much clearer line between public and private, a line that is drawn both physically and socially. This section describes the ways in which this transformation took place.

Preindustrial social life was characterized by a number of features that both reflected and contributed to what Daunton (1983) describes as "an ambiguous boundary" or "an uncertain threshold" between public and private domains. The home was a much more active location for commerce, so there was less reason for distinguishing between a person's profession and his or her home life. A cobbler worked in one part of the house, stored materials in another, sold finished products from a third, and ate and slept in yet another (Barley 1963, 13). Those who did not have freestanding houses were likely to live in apartment-type buildings that centered around enclosed courts or alleys. Here, courtyards, dead ends, and communal landings were used not simply for traveling from the street to the home, but also for socializing, exchanging goods, and doing household chores (Lawrence 1990). This physical melding of public and private was mirrored socially. As Shorter's (1976) research suggests, the preindustrial family was "pierced full of holes," which allowed

> people from outside to flow freely through the household, observing and monitoring. The traffic flowed the other way, too, as members of the family felt they had more in common emotionally with their various peer groups than with one another. In other words, the traditional family was much more a productive and reproductive unit than an emotional unit (Shorter 1976, 5).

The resulting relationship between public and private domains is illustrated in Figure 14.1. Although people did have areas that they

FIGURE 14.1   The Preindustrial Western Conception of Public and
Private Space

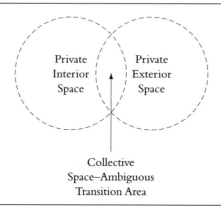

Collective
Space–Ambiguous
Transition Area

Source: Adapted from Lawrence (1990).

considered to be private as well as those they did not, a transitional
area existed that was both private and public (Lawrence 1990).

A change in the distinction between public and private was
catalyzed in large part by two related societal trends experienced
throughout the West during the nineteenth century: a rapid increase
in population and a wave of industrialization. Social scientists have
offered four general explanations for why these trends encouraged
greater separation between public and private spheres:

1. When humans (and some other animals) are placed in
   close proximity, they experience sensory overload, higher
   stress, and higher intraspecies aggression (Evans 1974;
   Hediger 1950). To avoid these tensions when placed in
   close urban proximity, city dwellers may have developed a
   more defined personal space (see Altman and Chemers
   1980; Taylor and Brooks 1980).

2. A society's built environment is assumed to reflect its
   social, political, and economic structure (Hillier and
   Hanson 1984). The increasing complexity of social life
   during industrialization may have been mirrored by a
   more segmented use of space (Kent 1990; Rapoport
   1990).

3. Growing public controls were imposed on individuals during the Victorian period, and a rising spirit of individualism was associated with the rise of capitalism. These almost paradoxical forces may have encouraged individuals to create an individualistic private sanctuary from the more controlling public sphere (Lawrence 1990; Shorter 1976).

4. On a practical level, home workshops were put out of business by larger factories, and the remaining cottage industries were quickly centralized. Barley (1963, 13) argues that this trend "revolutionized" homes in the Victorian era, transforming them into "merely machines for living in."

While no one factor or explanation can account for the dramatic change in perspective on public and private space during the course of the nineteenth century, there is little doubt that the boundary between public and private became "less ambiguous and more definite, less penetrable and more impermeable" (Daunton 1983, 12).

The result was a sense of public and private resembling that pictured in Figure 14.2. Here, private and nonprivate areas are separated by transitional space. In addition, divisions between areas are clearly defined at each point of contact. What is most relevant to this research is that business was socially banished from the home environment, and inhabitants became less and less comfortable when

FIGURE 14.2   The Industrial Western Conception of Public and Private Space

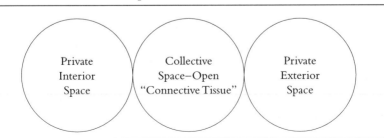

Source: Adapted from Lawrence (1990).

matters of commerce crossed the threshold from public to private. The home became a place where individuals had ultimate control, and where those seeking to persuade, influence, or otherwise diminish domestic autonomy were not welcome.

The social rules of the Victorian age maintain a strong influence on the Western conception of the home. The household still defines personal territory (Saile 1985; Taylor and Brower 1985), marks a clear distinction between public and private (Korosec-Serfaty 1985), and provides a basis for individual (as opposed to social) identity (Bachelard 1964; Lee 1976; Taylor and Brower 1985; Trilling 1971). For this reason, those who market to consumers in their homes are vulnerable to concerns about invasion of privacy (McLean 1994; Miller and Gordon 1994). In addition, people feel more relaxed in their own space (Edney 1975), emphasizing that one's home environment is more informal and fluid than the public arena. Perhaps because of this, people often face difficulties when trying to combine home duties and work responsibilities (Hochschild 1989). Telecommuting (or working from the home) has been criticized by some because the rules governing the home are too unstructured and undisciplined (Connelly 1995). Thus, network marketers, who make extensive use of the home as a selling and servicing environment, sometimes find that their business goals conflict with the prevailing social consensus.

An Exploratory Study of Network Marketing Sales Strategies

Almost without exception, network marketing companies market their products exclusively through independent household-based distributors. These distributors work from their own homes, distribute products to other people's homes, and often give sales and training presentations in the home environment. Furthermore, unlike other types of direct-selling agents, network marketing distributors are rewarded for encouraging others to become not just customers, but also successful distributors. Network marketers must therefore convince others that they, too, can operate a home-centered business. As a result, distributors face the challenge of operating in a social environment where the established rules of conduct do not support their endeavors, and where they must convince others to do the same.

Method

For this exploratory research, I conducted semistructured interviews with 17 network marketing distributors (7 women and 10 men). These data were collected as part of ongoing research on the network marketing industry, so my analysis was also informed by other interactions with network marketing practitioners and customers, attendance at sales presentations, and examination of previous research on the industry (e.g., Biggart 1989; Butterfield 1985; Peven 1968). Three different network marketing companies were represented in the sample of informants for this chapter, all three of which had an international presence that included both the United Kingdom and the United States.[2] Nearly half of these informants lived and worked in heavily populated urban areas, while slightly more than half lived and worked in smaller towns and suburban areas. Informants' level of experience with network marketing ranged from just under 1 year to over 11 years. The informants are identified by their gender and their years of experience as a network marketing distributor.[3]

During the interviews, I asked open-ended questions about informants' selling experiences, asking them to pay particular attention to the advantages and disadvantages of different selling environments. The following questions are typical examples:

- "What has your experience been with making presentations in other people's homes?"

---

[2] Although three companies were represented, a majority of the informants worked for only one of the three.

[3] Those with the same gender and years of experience are further distinguished by the letter *A, B,* or *C.* Thus, two men with seven years of experience would be identified as (Male A, 7 years) and (Male B, 7 years).

- "How does this compare with your experience presenting in other environments?"
- "What strategies do you recommend to your new recruits about presenting in a home environment?"

Informants reported that their decision to use the home environment as a place for selling is sometimes influenced by practical considerations. For example, if the prospect and the distributor live too far apart, then they will often agree to meet at a public location halfway between their homes. While recognizing these practical concerns, this chapter focuses on the more sociological issues raised during the interviews. As reflected in the remainder of this chapter, every informant focused considerable attention on how he or she uses and manipulates the social environment to guide the rules operating within the situation.

General Themes

Because many Westerners still distinguish between public and private—and between business life and personal life—network marketing does not fit neatly into a recognizable social category. Thus, new network marketing prospects face a situation similar to the one that the children and I faced at the indoor playland: We needed guidance about the consensus that was operating within that somewhat unfamiliar social setting. For this study, informants described two related approaches to guiding prospects in this way. These approaches are illustrated in the columns of the matrix in Figure 14.3. The first approach is to arrange the selling environment so that *physical cues* offer signals for the social rules that should be followed. Secondly, they orchestrate the selling process so that *procedural cues* offer similar types of signals. While procedural cues are themselves rules for behaving, they also indicate to interactants that other rules must be followed as well.

Within these strategic similarities, distributors differed in terms of the *type* of social consensus that they hoped to encourage with their cues. Three different types were described by informants and are illustrated in the rows of Figure 14.3. First, distributors can

FIGURE 14.3   Examples of Cues Used to Signal Different Types of
Social Consensus

		Type of Cues	
		Environmental	Procedural
	Business-Oriented Consensus	Chairs lined up in rows in front of stage area	Not serving beverages before the presentation
Type of Consensus Signaled	Home-Oriented Consensus	An informal living room setting with sofas	Serving beverages before the presentation
	New (Mixed) Consensus	Business materials laid out in the middle of the kitchen	Answering personal phone calls during the presentation

emphasize that the social rules for network marketing are the same as those that govern a professional business, and that network marketing should therefore be viewed as being distinct from other home activities. Second, they can foster a consensus that network marketing is similar to many other personal and home-based activities, and that it therefore fits easily into one's home life. Lastly, they can try to break through the social distinction between home and business, and instead foster a consensus that network marketing successfully integrates the public and private domains within a single activity. While most of the informants for this study fell clearly into one of these three categories, a few pointed out that they may try to foster a different consensus in different situations.

The next three sections examine these three approaches (i.e., the rows in Figure 14.3) individually, and each section focuses on the physical and procedural cues (i.e., the columns in Figure 14.3) offered by distributors. Before moving on, however, it is useful to note one theme that emerged in a number of interviews, regardless of approach. Overall, informants tended to show a sensitivity toward *territoriality* when describing their use of space for selling and servicing. In particular, informants generally recognized that people have more control over guiding the social consensus when they are in their own personal space. All things being equal, informants preferred *not* to present in prospects' homes, and instead preferred their own homes or more public spaces. "You're not in control, unfortunately," said one informant (Male C, 8 years) about presenting in other people's homes. "There could be pets, there could be children, . . . a television going on, and you can't ask people to turn their television off." Note that it is only social consensus that keeps a distributor from taking control of the situation—for example, asking a prospect to turn the television off. The social rules of the home dictate that the homeowner has every right to organize the environment as he or she wishes, and that the guest has little prerogative to suggest alterations.

FOSTERING A BUSINESS-ORIENTED CONSENSUS WITH PHYSICAL AND PROCEDURAL CUES

Although network marketing is generally home based, some distributors view a home orientation as a threat to their business. To them, the relatively casual environment of the home can encourage prospects to take a too-cavalier attitude toward the business. Thus, some distributors downplay the social implications of working in the home and instead make explicit attempts to foster a consensus in which the rules for network marketing are similar to those for operating any other small business. This consensus management often begins during a distributor's initial contact with a prospect. For example, although some distributors use the word *party* to refer to in-home presentations (see below), one informant (Female, 4 years) makes sure *not* to use this word and instead makes a point of calling it an "in-house presentation." This gives an initial indication to the prospect that formal rules will apply to the upcoming interaction.

Physical Cues That Emphasize a Business-Oriented Consensus

Given the casual and informal social environment of the home, one of the best ways to emphasize the business aspects of network marketing is to make presentations outside of the household. One informant (Male A, 4 years) described this as meeting on the "neutral ground" of a moderately nice restaurant, a hotel meeting room, or a formal pub. Neutral ground refers to the fact that individuals have more control over the social consensus when they are in their own homes, but in a public place, neither the prospect nor the distributor has more control.

However, an out-of-home environment is hardly neutral. It emphasizes to the prospect that network marketing should be regarded as part of the public domain, where commerce "appropriately" occurs. By making a sales presentation outside of the home, a distributor can diminish the effects of the more informal home environment, and can emphasize a more professional approach. One informant (who also uses the phrase *neutral ground*) explained his strategy for using public spaces as follows:

> [If] the person is really looking at the top sort of business angle, then I like to meet on neutral ground and make it a very professional—as professional as I can, being a relative newcomer at it. As professional as I can by meeting, you know, being the part and making it a, a proper business presentation. When I'm in the home, it tends to be a bit more chatty (Male B, 3 years).

There are other ways in which distributors can manage the physical cues of an out-of-home environment. Many informants mentioned that not just any out-of-home environment will do; many prefer a restaurant or pub that is quiet and tasteful to one that is noisy and casual. Alternatively, distributors working in the same geographic area will sometimes combine their resources and rent a hotel function room for weekly presentations. These rooms, with their plush carpeting, chandeliers, and presentation technologies, are beyond the financial reach of most individual distributors. By cooperating with one another, distributors can purchase an environment whose physical cues suggest a more formal professionalism than would be suggested by a home environment.

In these hotel function rooms, distributors augment the existing environmental cues. A welcome desk is often placed at the door, where prospects are asked to sign in. Chairs are arranged in rows in front of a speaker's stage or podium. Distributors presenting at these events tend to wear business suits, just as if they were holding a conventional corporate meeting. A small amplification system with a microphone can bring further attention to the presentational aspects of the gathering. All of these environmental cues signal to the prospect that, even though network marketing is home centered, "the way we do things" in network marketing is to treat it like a professional business.

However, business-oriented presentations do not always occur outside of the home. Although many distributors see the advantages of public presentations, some also prefer the more individualized one-on-one attention that they can give prospects in a home environment (Coughlan and Grayson 1994). Yet those wishing to foster a business-oriented consensus sometimes find it challenging to present in a home environment, which tends to signal more casual and informal behavior. To counteract these signals, distributors present other physical cues to signal a formal businesslike consensus. These cues help the distributor to carve out a social consensus within the home environment where, for the moment, the rules that generally apply to the home are no longer accepted.

Perhaps the most explicit strategy for doing this is to give the presentation in an area that is clearly defined as "a place for doing business." As one informant (Female, 6 years) advised, "Move them to an area where it's going to be more professional, like an office." When prospects arrive at this informant's house, she immediately ushers them upstairs to her office, where she has chairs waiting for them as if they were meeting her for a job interview. Another informant lamented that the environmental signals in his living room encouraged prospects to behave more informally than he would like:

> I have to use my front room because of a space problem I've got. But I'd like to have a specific area where I actually did it (Male B, 3 years).

Regardless of whether the presentation occurs in a separate office, distributors fostering a business-oriented consensus tend to arrange the furniture so that it sets the stage for a more professional consensus. If several prospects are coming to visit, distributors will arrange the furniture just as they would for a hotel conference room, with rows of chairs facing the presenter's area. The presenter's area will sometimes have a white marker board or a flip chart. If only one or two prospects are visiting, the distributor will still set up an area that requires the prospects to focus on the presentation:

> Get them sat 'round the table, and have your products on the table or whatever, so that you're away from them wanting to sort of lounge and take up your time. Because if they're sitting comfortably in their chair and you provide them with coffee, they may say, "oh, this is a nice evening out . . . ; I'll stay here for the rest of the evening" (Female, 6 years).

Just as an airport removes ashtrays from the environment to signal that smoking is not allowed, a network marketer removes comfortable seating from the environment to signal that casual interaction is not allowed.

Procedural Cues That Emphasize a Business-Oriented Consensus

While social gatherings tend to be fluid and improvised, business gatherings are focused and efficient. Thus, in contrast with distributors who foster a home-oriented consensus, business-oriented distributors ensure that their presentations have clear beginnings and endings. When a room is arranged as previously described—with a stage area placed in front of rows of chairs—this gives the presenter procedural control over the way in which the presentation will progress. When the presenter steps up to a podium or presentation table, this indicates the start of the presentation; when the presenter steps down, that is the end. However, this strategy is not always as effective as distributors would like:

> We would sometimes have a problem that people wouldn't quiet down when the presentation started. And sometimes worse, they might stay around too long after the presentation. You know what I mean, just chatting and enjoying themselves without any intention of signing up. And the hotel staff would be asking us when we were planning to leave (Male A, 4 years).

One group of distributors addressed this problem by playing loud music when prospects first arrived. The music was then shut off to indicate the beginning of the presentation, only to be started again to signal the presentation's end. Other distributors darken the room to use 35 mm slides or computer presentations. Darkening the room is of course a necessary step to ensure the visibility of such presentations, but it also helps to put procedural boundaries around the event. Note also that these technologies are used primarily by distributors fostering a business-oriented consensus and are rarely used in the home.

In the home, what a distributor does *not* do can give procedural cues that foster a business-oriented consensus. For example, one informant tells new distributors not to follow the conventional social rules for invited guests:

> I also tell them not to—although they never listen because people are nice and they want to entertain people—but I try and ask them not to serve any drinks or food or anything until I finish. Because, you know, nobody's going to concentrate. If they start having a glass of wine, then they're all going to be chatting amongst themselves, and it's going to be a big social event. And this is my work. This to me is work. You know, there's plenty of things I could be doing on a . . . Friday, Thursday night, eight o'clock, rather than go to talk to these people. So I don't want their attention taken away from me. . . . I think making them feel relaxed, you can make them too relaxed, and the whole thing is a waste of time. You know, it's got to be serious (Female, 9 years).

By not serving drinks before the presentation, a distributor can procedurally signal that the situation is not a social home environment, and that the rules to be followed are more akin to those of a formal business presentation.

The Challenges of Signaling a Business-Oriented Consensus

Perhaps the biggest challenge for a distributor who wishes to foster a business-oriented consensus is attempting to do so in a prospect's home. Because the homeowner has control over the consensus, and because the home is a more casual and informal environment, a distributor is likely to face a situation in which the prospect will be following rules that are not conducive to a business-oriented consensus. To address this, some distributors will initiate the social negotiation process as soon as they arrange to meet with the prospect. For example, one informant (Male A, 4 years) described how he uses questions to suggest that the presentation environment be more formal and businesslike: "You can say to them, 'Look, would it be quiet to come around and talk to you that night? I mean, would there be a bit of space for us?'" Another informant emphasizes procedural boundaries with prospects by making several telephone calls in advance and by laying out specific rules for behavior:

> On the phone I will say, "Allow an hour . . . ." I tell them that I can give them an hour of my time, is that all right? And I also confirm it, and I say, for example, if they're coming tomorrow or the next two days, if there's any reason they can't make it, to let me know because I'm extremely busy and I'd rather give that appointment away to someone else. And I treat them as though they're a very professional interview, but relaxed. I don't let them think they can waste my time or that, you know, it's OK to not turn up (Female, 5 years).

Here, the marketer makes the social negotiation process very explicit and is firmly guiding the rules for behavior in a direction that best serves her needs. If the prospect is not willing to follow these rules, then the distributor is not interested in doing business. In other words, if you don't know what kind of pizza you want, don't get in line.

FOSTERING A HOME-ORIENTED CONSENSUS WITH PHYSICAL AND PROCEDURAL CUES

While business-oriented distributors put social fences around network marketing to keep it from being defined by the home, others believe that these social fences raise more difficult hurdles in prospects' minds. "The minute I start to use offices and too much high technology," said one informant (Male C, 8 years), "the average person says, 'It's OK for him because he's got that. It's OK for him because he's got this.'" Another informant gave the following reasons for preferring home presentations to hotel presentations:

> It's fairly duplicatable. In other words, it's something that they can do later. In other words, it may not be suitable for them to go and set up a hotel meeting. You know, I mean anybody can either get someone to their home or go and visit them in someone else's home (Male, 11 years).

Still another informant described how difficult it was for her to recruit once she opened an office in the city:

> I think people got the impression that we were successful because we had an office in the West End. Therefore they got the message, "Well, I can't do this because it's beyond my reach" (Female, 7 years).

Thus, while business-oriented distributors foster a consensus that network marketing is a business and should therefore be viewed as being separate from the home, home-oriented distributors foster a consensus that network marketing is home-based and should therefore be viewed as being different from a business. "It's like inviting people to a dinner party," said one distributor about his in-home presentations (Male A, 3 years), "and that is quite successful." Another (Male A, 8 years) described the home selling situation as like "inviting friends 'round for a game of Monopoly." Still another (Female C, 1 year) said, "A new distributor, he's invited his friends, or her friends, to his home. So they are more relaxed in their friend's home." By fostering agreement that network marketing is like visiting a friend's home for a dinner party, network marketers can integrate their business into the home environment while deflecting the concerns that might otherwise arise from bringing a business into the home arena.

Physical Cues That Emphasize a Home-Oriented Consensus

One of the ways in which a distributor physically emphasizes the similarities between home life and network marketing is by giving sales presentations in a home environment—either his or her home or the home of a fellow distributor. (Later on, I will discuss the unique difficulties of presenting in the *prospect's* home.) This is successful because, when visiting someone else's home, a prospect already accepts the consensus that this environment is casual, informal, and not businesslike. To further foster this social consensus, network marketers strive to make their presentation environment as homelike as possible. Just as a polished podium and a well-dressed maître d' can set the stage for a formal dinner, a fireplace and casually dressed distributors can set the stage for casual interaction.

One might question whether such physical cues reflect a strategy at all. After all, the space is already in a home, so the distributor does not have to do much to make it homelike. While this is true, the informants who pursued this strategy recognized that they could alternatively take a more businesslike approach to their presentations, and emphasized their conscious decision to foster a different orientation. One informant described his approach as follows:

> You arrange the furniture [so] that it's not too formal, that it's, you know, they're in a relaxed frame of mind right from the word *go*. You don't have rigid chairs and tables, or whatever. Have it informal (Male, 9 years).

Another distributor (Female, 7 years) described her choice of selling location as follows: "I personally always like to do it in my living room, and my living room does *not* look like an office" (emphasis hers). While home-oriented distributors do not usually have to alter the physical cues of their environment as much as business-oriented distributors do, their decisions about physical cues are no less strategic.

473

Procedural Cues That Emphasize a Home-Oriented Consensus

Whatever the room arrangement, prospects generally know that they have been invited to the distributor's home for a business presentation. Therefore, to further emphasize that "this is just like home," network marketing distributors make it a point to begin the interaction as if it were a social visit. Both distributors and prospects know that the rules governing such situations require the host to offer food and/or drink to guests, and to talk with them informally and personally. As one informant (Male, 11 years) said, "I mean, invariably when you go to someone's house, you offer them a cup of tea. You know, or a cup of coffee or something." Another informant made a similar point:

> We create an atmosphere so we get to know each other. So I start off—I don't talk business. I just start off by telling them about myself, from a personal viewpoint, get to know me as a person, and then they usually open up and talk about themselves. So that's the first thing; we create a rapport before we start talking about the company and the business (Male B, 8 years).

Still another informant (Male, 9 years) asserted, "Generally, social chat for five or ten minutes is well worth doing." To be sure, most experienced salespeople recognize the value of informal interaction before the sales presentation begins. However, in this study, informants who take a business orientation to network marketing did not mention the importance of social interaction, either before or after the presentation. While it may occur, they did not view it as an important element of their sales strategy.

While business-oriented distributors will give formal procedural signals about the presentation's beginning and end, home-oriented distributors sometimes seek the opposite extreme. They instead emphasize the relaxed and friendly nature of the business by not making a formal business presentation at all. Instead of arresting the informal interaction in order to make a presentation, they instead integrate the product into the social situation. For consumable products, this is relatively easy: Distributors will serve protein shakes, filtered water, or weight-loss drinks when guests arrive. This often prompts prospects to ask about the products, just as they might ask about a host's recipe for an interesting meal. Those selling non-consumable products will place their wares around the room like books on a coffee table, knowing that this will capture the interest of prospects. One distributor described a similar approach as follows:

> I just simply welcome the people in. Tell them, "There's a full catalog." Tell them, "There's the product; if you've got any questions, ask me." To keep the whole thing relaxed. Um, rather than this, you get everybody 'round, then you say, "We're going to start the presentation now" (Male B, 4 years).

The Challenges of Fostering a Home-Oriented Consensus

As with fostering a business-oriented consensus, those fostering a home-oriented consensus face the biggest difficulties when presenting in a prospect's home, rather than in their own. At first, it seems counterintuitive that presenting in someone else's home would present difficulties for the home-oriented distributor. Prospects should feel perfectly at home in their *own* household, and should therefore welcome a more informal and casual approach to network marketing. However, a distributor visiting a prospect's home is not generally seen as a friendly neighbor visiting for dinner, but as an economic interloper entering the prospect's personal territory. Thus, as many distributors discover when they arrive at a prospect's home, the hosts have already defined the encounter as a business visit, regardless of the fact that it is occurring in their own home. One informant explained that this is one of the reasons she moved from a home orientation to a business orientation for her presentations:

> Everything you said, you'd get a negative result from people like, "Yes, but you're here to sell us." And I'd say, "Well, but you did invite me." . . . They have a preformed idea that you are there to sell, or there to get them involved into something

which they don't really think they want to become involved in (Female, 6 years).

Rather than allow prospects to fully define the social consensus, some distributors take an active role themselves. They feel that they must do this so that they can renegotiate the social consensus more in the direction of a casual visit than that of a business meeting. One distributor had the following advice:

> You must take control of the situation in the nicest possible way. You know, don't let them ask too many questions [about the business]. What you have to do is, you know, make yourself at home in that sense. You know: "Hi. How are you? Thanks for inviting me to your house" (Male A, 3 years).

Just as a restaurant maître d' must sometimes—in the nicest possible way—actively indicate to male patrons that a suit coat is required, a network marketing distributor must sometimes indicate to prospects that a casual and informal social consensus is preferred.

FOSTERING A COMBINED CONSENSUS WITH PHYSICAL AND PROCEDURAL CUES

While most of the strategies described by informants fit neatly into the business-oriented category or the home-oriented category, a few comments were not easily categorized. While these data are not as rich as for the preceding categories, as a group they hint at a third option for distributors. Rather than emphasize either the home orientation or the business orientation, some distributors challenge the Victorian distinction altogether. These distributors foster a consensus that network marketing is neither fish nor fowl, that the rules for running a business and the rules for running a household can work in concert. Just as the child at the indoor playland helped his friends by saying that it was "like a playground, only puffier," these distributors help prospects by saying that network marketing is like a business, only homier.

To accomplish this, distributors invite prospects to their home, where they can see firsthand how a business can integrate into the home environment. One informant (Male C, 8 years) invites prospects to his home by saying, "Look, you can see how I run my business from my back bedroom. And I'm running a multi-million-pound business from home with no overhead." Another informant (Female, 5 years) makes her presentations in the middle of her kitchen, telling prospects that this is where she started her successful business. By locating the presentation in the middle of the home's most active room, she indicates that her business is part of her home life. By making her presentation at a table, she avoids the casual atmosphere that is fostered by those presenting in a living room.

Procedurally, distributors balance a business consensus and a home consensus by simultaneously engaging in activities from both realms. Business-oriented distributors will avoid the casual cues of a home environment, and home-oriented distributors will avoid the formal cues of a business environment, but these distributors will welcome both:

> They see everything going on—the phone ringing, my daughter needs dinner (Female, 5 years).

> We try and have some activity going on. Maybe the wife comes on, gets involved (Male B, 8 years).

> If people see that . . . we can work from home, quite relaxed—you know, I've got the dishwasher on and the phones ring and there's stuff happening all the time—people actually get the idea that it is something that they can do from their home (Female, 7 years).

CONCLUSIONS

This chapter highlights a number of issues regarding the role of servicescapes in guiding the behavior of consumers and marketers. First, it has isolated the importance of not only physical cues such as the arrangement of chairs in a room, but also procedural cues such as beginning a sales situation with social conversation. In this chapter, the two types of cues have been discussed separately because procedural cues are often more explicit than physical cues in establishing rules for behavior. However, in terms of fostering a more general social consensus, they both often serve the same function. Putting a desk at the door of a hotel meeting room (a physical cue) serves much the same function as having prospects sign in at that desk (a procedural cue); they both suggest that the rules to be followed in this situation will be businesslike. Marketers should therefore note that the required procedures for interacting in a servicescape can have an impact above and beyond the procedures in question. Having to ring a bell before entering a jewelry store, put on a name tag before getting on a cruise ship, or be chosen by a doorman to enter a nightclub are all procedures that help to foster a social consensus for the entire service experience.

In terms of the specific cues mentioned by informants in this study, it was certainly not surprising to learn that presenting in a living room encourages a more casual approach than presenting in a hotel function room, or that business suits foster a more businesslike environment than casual clothing. The appropriateness of these sales strategies is obvious, but the fact that they are self-evident underscores one of the key lessons about servicescapes: When customers enter a store, a restaurant, or a hotel, they bring with them a well-developed ability to "read" the environment and therefore to understand the implied instructions for behavior in the social situation. Because we all have this servicescape literacy, many servicescape strategies seem obvious, and this is perhaps why informants for this study found it so easy to discuss their servicescape strategies. Yet, if they were *not* obvious, this would undermine the main purpose of environmental cues: to present interactants with signals that they can rely upon for guidance regarding the expected consensus.

A corollary is that inappropriate cues will offer the wrong guidance to consumers and may negatively affect their evaluation of the marketing experience. This is important to recognize because, like network marketers, many other marketers embark upon new businesses with certain situational factors already in place. For example, a hotel investment company may take over an older hotel property, a doctor may set up practice in a skyscraper, or a fast-food restaurant may set up a joint venture with a gas station. In cases like these, management will always wonder what level of investment should be made in servicescape alterations or refurbishment. This research suggests that managers must not underestimate the impact that existing servicescape cues will have on the social consensus. Recall the frustrations of the business-oriented distributors who found that selling in a living room with beverages resulted in a social situation where the consensus was too informal. The impact of the casual living room environment was too difficult for these distributors to completely overcome. The hotel company, the doctor, and the fast-food restaurant mentioned likewise must pay careful attention to the impact of their existing servicescapes, and must make careful investments to counteract—or capitalize on—the consensus that they foster.

What is additionally notable about network marketing is the way in which marketers can use the *established* cues to clarify what is otherwise an *ambiguous* exchange proposition for the consumer— ambiguous because it breaks with the generalized consensus that business and personal spheres are distinct. As I indicated at the outset, agreements about rules of conduct for marketing result from a negotiation among three forces: (1) what the marketer wants, (2) what the consumer wants, and (3) what the broader social world will allow. Undoubtedly, the network marketer would prefer that consumers and the broader social world simply accept network marketing at face value. However, because the broader social world has drawn clear distinctions between public and private spheres and because the consumer generally subscribes to this consensus, some explicit negotiation must occur. When negotiating, the network marketer has two general options: to work within the existing consensus or to try to foster a new one. The data collected for this chapter indicate that network marketers find it easier to adapt their approach to network marketing to the existing consensus than to attempt to get the existing consensus to adapt to them. What is particularly illustrative about the network marketing example is that distributors go to such different extremes to define exactly the same business. This emphasizes the ambiguity of the exchange proposition and highlights the ability of servicescape cues to help resolve this ambiguity.

Lastly, given the apparent influence of servicescapes and the existing social consensus about the home, one wonders how any distributor can find success by taking the middle ground, where home and business are shown to be intermingled. For marketers, the cost of violating an established social consensus—e.g., allowing a patron to smoke in a no-smoking area—can be significant, so why do some network marketers risk this?

There are two potential answers to this question. The first is that a broad social consensus is flexible enough to allow divergent private agreements within it, especially if those agreements are insulated from the broader social world (Deighton and Grayson 1995; Schouten and McAlexander 1995). Despite the international success of several network marketing companies, the industry itself is still thought to be on the fringe of conventional business activity, and some marketers may therefore be able to develop their own subcultures of consumption.

The second possible explanation is that, even though it is difficult for individuals to influence a broad social consensus (Berger and Luckmann 1966), such a consensus is not immutable. Just ten years ago, the idea of a completely smoke-free airport would have seemed as ludicrous to Americans as it did to my European friend. In terms of the social consensus about the home, the past two or three decades have witnessed a technological transformation that may rival the Industrial Revolution in its influence. Greater penetration of computers and modems in the household has made shopping from the home much easier for customers (Baig 1995, Strnad 1994). These same technologies have encouraged more and more workers to telecommute—to work at home instead of traveling to the office (Ford and McLaughlin 1995; McQuarrie 1994). A similar trend is the growing prevalence of SOHOs (small office/home offices), indicating that many people feel comfortable managing and patronizing businesses based in the home (Donath 1995). This trend may be pushing the generalized consensus about personal and commercial domains back toward a relationship like that pictured in

Figure 14.1, and thus facilitating some new opportunities for home selling in general and network marketing in particular.

BIBLIOGRAPHY

ALTMAN, IRWIN, AND M. CHEMERS. 1980. *Culture and Environment.* Monterey, CA: Brooks/Cole.

BACHELARD, GASTON. 1964. *The Poetics of Space.* Translated by Maria Jolas. New York: Orion Press.

BAIG, EDWARD. 1995. "Taking Care of Business—Without Leaving the House." *Business Week* (April 17): 106–107.

BARLEY, MAURICE W. 1963. *The House and Home.* London: Vista Books.

BERGER, PETER L., AND THOMAS LUCKMANN. 1966. *The Social Construction of Reality.* New York: Anchor.

BIGGART, NICOLE WOOLSEY. 1989. *Charismatic Capitalism: Direct Selling Organizations in America.* Chicago: University of Chicago Press.

BUTTERFIELD, STEPHEN. 1985. *Amway: The Cult of Free Enterprise.* Boston: South End Press.

CONNELLY, JULIE. 1995. "Let's Hear It for the Office." *Fortune* 131 (March 6): 221–222.

COUGHLAN, ANNE, AND KENT GRAYSON. 1994. "1993 Multi-Level Marketing Executives Survey." *Downline News* (April): 1–5.

DAUNTON, MAURICE J. 1983. *House and Home in the Victorian City: Working-Class Housing 1850–1914.* London: Edward Arnold.

DEIGHTON, JOHN, AND KENT GRAYSON. 1995. "Marketing and Seduction: Building Exchange Relationships by Managing Social Consensus." *Journal of Consumer Research* 21 (March): 93–108.

DONATH, BOB. 1995. "SOHO? Oh, No!" *Marketing News* 29 (February 27): 32–35.

EDNEY, J. J. 1975. "Territoriality and Control: A Field Experiment." *Journal of Personality and Social Psychology* 31:1,108–1,115.

EVANS, G. W. 1974. "An Examination of the Information Overload Mechanism of Personal Space." *Man-Environment Systems* 4:61.

FORD, ROBERT C., AND FRANK MCLAUGHLIN. 1995. "Questions and Answers About Telecommuting Programs." *Business Horizons* 38 (May/June): 66–72.

GARFINKEL, H. 1967. *Studies in Ethnomethodology.* Englewood Cliffs, NJ: Prentice Hall.

GOFFMAN, ERVING. 1959/1973. *The Presentation of Self in Everyday Life.* (Woodstock, NY: Overlook Press).

———. 1974/1986. *Frame Analysis.* Boston: Northeastern University Press.

GRAYSON, KENT. 1996. "Network Marketing." In *Networks in Marketing,* edited by Dawn Iacobucci. Thousand Oaks, CA: Sage, 325–341.

HEDIGER, H. 1950. *Wild Animals in Captivity.* London: Butterworth.

HILLIER, BILL, AND JULIENNE HANSON. 1984. *The Social Logic of Space.* Cambridge: Cambridge University Press.

HOCHSCHILD, ARLIE. 1989. *The Second Shift: Working Parents and the Revolution at Home.* London: Judy Piatkus.

KENT, SUSAN. 1990. "A Cross-Cultural Study of Segmentation, Architecture, and the Use of Space." In *Domestic Architecture and the Use of Space,* edited by Susan Kent. New York: Cambridge University Press, 127–152.

KOROSEC-SERFATY, P. 1985. "Experience and Use of Dwelling." In *Home Environments,* edited by I. Altman and C. M. Werner. New York: Plenum, 65–86.

LAWRENCE, RODERICK J. 1990. "Public Collective and Private Space: A Study of Urban Housing in Switzerland." In *Domestic Architecture and the Use of Space,* edited by Susan Kent. New York: Cambridge University Press, 73–91.

LEE, T. 1974. *Psychology and the Built Environment.* New York: Methuen.

McLEAN, E. 1994. "Privacy Big Issue for Marketers." *Advertising Age* (July 4): 14.

McQUARRIE, FIONA A. E. 1994. "Telecommuting: Who Really Benefits?" *Business Horizons* 37 (November/December): 79–83.

MILNE, G. R., AND M. E. GORDON. 1994. "A Segmentation of Consumer Attitudes Toward Direct Mail." *Journal of Direct Marketing* (Spring): 45–52.

OLSON, MARIANNE E., AND MARJORIE J. SMITH. 1992. "An Evaluation of Single-Room Maternity Care." *Health Care Supervisor* 11 (September): 43–49.

PEVEN, DOROTHY E. 1968. "The Use of Religious Revival Techniques to Indoctrinate Personnel: The Home Party Sales Organizations." *Sociological Quarterly* (Winter): 97–106.

RAPOPORT, AMOS. 1990. "Systems of Activities and Systems of Settings." In *Domestic Architecture and the Use of Space,* edited by Susan Kent. New York: Cambridge University Press, 9–20.

SAILE, D. G. 1985. "The Ritual Establishment of Home." In *Home Environments,* edited by I. Altman and C. M. Werner. New York: Plenum, 87–107.

SCHOUTEN, JOHN W., AND JAMES H. McALEXANDER. 1995. "Subcultures of Consumption: An Ethnography of the New Bikers." *Journal of Consumer Research* 22 (June): 43–61.

SCHUTZ, ALFRED. 1970. *On Phenomenology and Social Relations.* Edited by Helmut R. Wagner. Chicago: University of Chicago Press.

SHORTER, EDWARD. 1976. *The Making of the Modern Family.* London: Collins.

STRNAD, PATRICIA. 1994. "Work at Home, Shop at Home." *Advertising Age* 65 (January 10): S-7.

TAYLOR, RALPH B., AND D. K. BROOKS. 1980. "Temporary Territories: Responses to Intrusions in a Public Setting." *Population and the Environment* 3:135–145.

TAYLOR, RALPH B., AND S. BROWER. 1985. "Home and Near-Home Territories." In *Home Environments,* edited by I. Altman and C. M. Werner. New York: Plenum, 183–210.

THOMAS, WILLIAM I. 1966. *On Social Organization and Social Personality.* Edited by Morris Janowitz. Chicago: University of Chicago Press.

TRILLING, L. 1971. *Sincerity and Authenticity.* Cambridge, MA: Harvard University Press.

PART IV

THE SERVICESCAPE CONTEXT: CONCEPTS AND ISSUES

In this section, we explore the interpretation of individual-level folk phenomenologies of place and broader thematic issues in the cultural transformation of space. The reader may regard this section as the capstone of the book insofar as its chapters synthesize and integrate concerns raised throughout our treatment of servicescapes. Here we explore the successes and failures of design in the realms of person, segment, and society. In particular, at the personal level, we attend to issues of variety seeking, satisfaction, and sense of self. At the social level, we address specific normative and ethical dimensions of design. Servicescapes may reinforce dysfunctional stereotypes, perpetuate inequality among consumers, compromise the privacy of individuals, and inappropriately commoditize relations between people.

If Morris Holbrook's chapter has a counterpart or analogue in the marketing literature, beyond his own voluminous work, it is likely to be Rose's (1995) autoethnography of product use or Sherry's (1996) introspective *silva rerum* treatment of gift-giving phenomena. Holbrook provides us with an essay—a hybrid of creative nonfiction and experimental ethnography—that immerses the reader directly in the heart of product involvement. The author, a self-confessed jazz "fanatic," employs an existential-phenomenological vehicle to convey to us his own experience of servicescapes as they impinge upon his search, acquisition, consumption, and animation of products. His native evocation of sense of place answers a cross-disciplinary call for such emic accounts, and his choice of introspection to explore deeply this sense is an appropriate one. Marketers striving to understand product involvement and place attachment could wish for no more comprehensive and eloquent a starting point.

Dawn Iacobucci describes a servicescape condition that the reader will readily, if unfortunately, recognize: the service encounter as a verbal duel. Many, if not most, of our Western market transactions are devoid of a condition recognized in a host of African languages, perhaps best captured by the Nguni term *ubuntu:* the quality of being human. Iacobucci recognizes industry- and organization-level shortfalls in servicescape design, even as she concentrates on the interpersonal dimension of failed service delivery. Hochschild (1983) has documented some of the stressors of "emotion-work" in service encounters that Iacobucci usefully examines in light of antecedents, consequences, and corrective interventions. Her analysis, and its accompanying recommendation to infuse the servicescape with motivating gamelike characteristics, invites elaboration in light of the chapters that have preceded hers. Culture shapes the degree to which marketplace relations will be humane, and marketing is embedded in human relations to a degree most westerners would find surprising. It is telling that the Japanese require loanwords (*marketingu, sabis*) to express servicescape dimensions arising effortlessly from their web of interpersonal relationships. Further, Iacobucci's game metaphor should cause us to consider how we might infuse the servicescape with ludic qualities that would delight, rather than merely satisfy, consumers.

Cathy Goodwin examines the influence of the servicescape on consumers' access to physical and informational privacy; she also explores a variety of ways in which privacy influences consumers' experience of service. She classifies our experience of servicescapes into four categories, whose essence she succinctly captures with root metaphors—retreat, dressing room, depot, prison—and examines place variations within each category. The possibilities consumers are able to enact in managing the boundary between public and private domains are provocatively considered. Goodwin concludes her meditation on privacy by inviting marketers to seek an appropriate metaphor for organizing their conception and delivery of servicescape elements.

Gender is the focus of the chapter written by Eileen Fischer, Brenda Gainer, and Julia Bristor. Like the earlier effort by McGrath (Chapter 13), their investigation employs projective tasks, but it takes a tack revealing significant socially constructed differences across servicescapes. Such differentiation is increasingly apparent as consumer research moves into the cultural sphere (DeGrazia 1996; McCracken 1995) to explore the interiority of objects and the production of consumption. The authors ground their study in the evocative power of ambient environments, focusing in particular on the role that people— patrons and clients—fulfill as servicescape elements. That consumers are complicit, if unwitting, cocreators of retail theater is revealed in their responses to the authors' projective tasks as handily as in the Nike Town and wilderness ethnographies presented in Chapters 4 and 12. This account makes it evident that consumer fantasy is as potent as either direct perception or physical existence. What emerges between the lines of their investigation is the notion that places are imbued with a sense of abiding rightness that is culturally conditioned, and that servicescape design cues frequently fail to moderate this sense or to extend it effectively to an optimal spectrum of consumers. The tacit knowledge harbored by consumers is, if properly elicited, of inestimable value to marketers.

Part IV concludes with Elizabeth Chin's comparative ethnography of inner-city children's experiences of servicescapes. Her account is embedded in the larger commercial ecology of urban economic zones and explores the consequences of the collision of aspiration with differential access to resources. She explores the impact of the social situatedness of the entrepreneur upon the servicescape and examines characteristics of the servicescape that contribute to its becoming either a kind of "third place" (Oldenburg 1989) within cultural constraints on the one hand, or a species of gated community on the other. She demonstrates how target hardening can be accomplished with and without recourse to ethnic marking. She also shows how consumer socialization unfolds apace with childrens' exposure to racism, and how fascination with acquisition and inequality intensify each other. That servicescapes are sites of consumer disempowerment is all too frequently ignored in the marketing literature but insightfully addressed in this final chapter.

BIBLIOGRAPHY

DEGRAZIA, VICTORIA. 1996. *The Sex of Things: Gender and Consumption in Historical Perspective.* Berkeley: University of California Press.

HOCHSCHILD, ARLIE. 1983. *The Managed Heart: Commercialization of Human Feeling.* Berkeley: University of California Press.

MCCRACKEN, GRANT. 1995. *Big Hair: A Journey into the Transformation of Self.* Toronto: Viking.

OLDENBURG, RAY. 1989. *The Great Good Place.* New York: Paragon House.

ROSE, DAN. 1995. "Active Ingredients." In *Contemporary Marketing and Consumer Behavior: An Anthropological Sourcebook,* edited by John F. Sherry, Jr. Thousand Oaks, CA: Sage, 51–85.

SHERRY, JOHN F., JR. 1996. "Reflections on Giftware and Giftcare: Whither Consumer Research?" In *Gift Giving: A Research Anthology,* edited by Cele Otnes and Richard Beltramini. Bowling Green, OH: Bowling Green State University Popular Press, 217–227.

15

THE RETAILING
OF PERFORMANCE AND THE
PERFORMANCE OF SERVICE

The Gift of Generosity with a Grin and the Magic of Munificence with Mirth

MORRIS B. HOLBROOK

Disciples of semiotics like to point out that the precondition of meaning is difference. From this, it follows that one might best understand one's own most cherished moments—in service encounters, retail environments, other consumption experiences, or elsewhere—by considering how they contrast with one's own personal nemeses. To begin in this vein with some occasions that stand for me as the apotheosis of fear and loathing, I do not believe that I have ever hated anything so much as I hated playing football.

Morris B. Holbrook is the W. T. Dillard Professor of Marketing in the Graduate School of Business at Columbia University, New York City. The author thanks John Sherry, Kent Grayson, and an anonymous reviewer for their helpful comments on an earlier draft of this chapter and gratefully acknowledges the support of the Columbia Business School's Faculty Research Fund.

At age fifteen, roughly five feet ten inches tall, weighing a flabby 185 pounds, I should have spent my time reading diet books, studying aerobics, practicing weight reduction calisthenics, or jogging around the track at the Milwaukee Country Day School. But, with only twenty-five boys in our sophomore class and with the more talented of those pressed into service on the real varsity team, the M.C.D.S. Junior Varsity needed my corporeal bulk to occupy the center position, where galloping offensive backfielders would routinely crash into me on what would otherwise have been their unobstructed path through the line of scrimmage. I felt obliged to play this ignominious role of human tackling dummy partly out of some sort of misplaced school spirit, but mostly to stop my classmates from thinking me a hopeless sissy and ridiculing me accordingly.

But, in my efforts to adopt an attitude of bravery, I failed completely. Frankly, I found it terrifying to stand there waiting to be bowled over by some firmly muscled fullback, who would viciously sink his sharp knees into my soft stomach. I did not possess the dexterity to get out of the way, nor the brains to hit the opponent with my shoulder instead of my abdomen, formidable as the latter weapon of defense might otherwise have seemed. So, as my JV year dragged on and on, as the Wisconsin autumn grew colder and colder, as first the sleet and then the snow began to fall, and as the turf on the football field at Country Day gradually froze solid as a rock, adding greatly to the pain of belly flopping onto it when trounced by the opposing lineman, I increasingly mourned the day that I had agreed to make my overweight and undercoordinated self a human sacrifice to the gods of the gridiron.

I still have dreams in which I sit in my afternoon mathematics class, bored out of my mind, miserably gazing through the glass windowpanes at the blizzard outside and dreading the rapidly approaching hour when I must suit up for the afternoon's scrimmage. I would call them nightmares except that they are all too realistic. Almost forty years after the fact, they simply perpetuate the agony of my football phobia. At the time, these events seemed all the more painful because I had begun to fancy myself something of a jazz pianist and therefore felt intensified fear at the prospect of subjecting my unprotected hands, already throbbing with the cold, to the pounding footsteps of the thundering fullback.

SERVICE AS BALM: A MAGICAL GIFT

After football practice on Tuesdays, with surpassing irony worthy of what you might expect at a small midwestern prep school for boys, I would take my numb and often sprained fingers a few blocks to the nearby Bay Shore Shopping Center, where I would enjoy the restorative ministrations of my weekly piano lesson. Those with a penchant for oversimplification might view piano instruction as an ordinary service encounter. But, to me, my wondrously sensitive piano teacher, Tommy Sheridan, was more like a doctor to the soul. During football season, Tommy would go easy on me because, having instructed other victims of Country Day football, he knew that the pigskin consumed hours of practice that I should be devoting to the ivories and that hurt muscles or broken bones could not play sweet music.

Tommy—father figure to many an M.C.D.S. athlete manqué before me—cheered me up and encouraged me not to worry excessively about my painful symptoms of digital damage. Indeed—in the spirit of such fun-inspired jazz heroes as Louis Armstrong, Fats Waller, or Dizzy Gillespie and by the demonstrative force of his own extraordinary example—Tommy proved to me again and again that the joy of music is the best possible boon to nimble fingers. He also showed me that, as elsewhere, true friendship in the performing arts can—indeed, usually does—emanate not from one's equals (who are potential competitors) but from one's vast superiors (who are secure in their status and therefore unthreatened). One finds the same principle at work in a profession such as teaching where a contemporary might strive to think up a put-down while a senior colleague might dream up some words of kindness. In my own experience as a fledgling jazz player, fellow students would often make derogatory comments behind each other's backs, whereas someone with the eminence of, say, Dizzy, would further enhance his already lofty stature by finding ways to say something nice. Similarly, what probably sounded like crap would evoke nothing but words of encouragement from Tommy Sheridan: "Yeah, play it, Morris. . . . Blow!"

The alliteratively inclined might call this Service with a Smile. To anticipate my comments on the connection between (retailing) service and (artistic) performance, I would call it the Gift of Generosity with a Grin or the Magic of Munificence with Mirth.

RETAILING AS A SERVICE SUBLIME

After my piano lesson, I would leave Tommy's studio and go downstairs to wait at the Bay Shore Drugstore for my mom to pick me up. On cold days it made sense, of course, to stand inside the drugstore and, while there, to browse through the little bin of record albums that the owner had thoughtfully provided for neighborhood kids who, like me, had nothing better to do while they waited for their mothers to come and fetch them. This pathetically tiny record rack held about as many albums as a cardboard box of a size that, years later, we would come to associate with Xerox paper. But, again by today's standards, what it lacked in quantity it more than made up for in quality. It contained nothing but discontinued, out-of-print, or poor-selling stuff that the druggist could purchase cheap and offer for resale at cut-rate prices like $1.99 or $2.49, precisely because no one wanted them in the first place—in other words, the best music that money could buy—that is, recordings whose lack of popular appeal reflected their artistic excellence and which consisted of some samples from the classical repertoire, a little high-brow singing, and mostly a cornucopia of first-rate jazz.

Though mass popularity may not necessarily constitute a proof of poor quality, the converse strikes me as almost always true—that is, artistic excellence virtually guarantees a tiny audience appeal. Thus, spectacularly unpopular in the United States (though, paradoxically, not in the rest of the world), jazz has commanded roughly 2 percent of the musical market in America during the latter half of the twentieth century. Traditionally, even first-rate jazz recordings find only a small number of customers, fail commercially, and immediately go out of print. Generalized across other media of the arts and entertainment, this principle constitutes a virtually ironclad marketing law. At any rate, in the case of jazz recordings, the more estimable the music, the more dismal the failure and the sooner the extinction.

To my profound delight, the proprietor of the Bay Shore Drugstore had somehow managed to corner the local market on such rarities and to put them on display for my delectation. Sometimes I knew not what treasures lay before me and would sneak over to a pay phone on the wall in the back of the store to call my friend Peter, who would obligingly read to me from old record reviews printed in the dog-eared copies of *down beat* that he stashed under his bed. Blessed with a nearly photographic recall of details from *db*'s enlightened jazz criticism, Peter unerringly steered me toward many purchases that have proven to be true collector's items.

Via this retailing route (as well as one or two other stores of a similar type that I also frequented at about the same time but which, in my mind's eye, merge and blur with the aforementioned friendly pharmacy), I acquired such masterpieces as the Teo Macero/Art Farmer version of *Guys and Dolls;* a reworking of *Porgy and Bess* by the Mundell Lowe All-Stars; the Jackie & Roy vocalizations on *Free and Easy;* the first Diz and Bird recording I ever owned, containing their version of "Slim's Jam"; and Manny Albam's tribute to *West Side Story,* featuring the likes of Al Cohn, Gene Quill, Jimmy Cleveland, and Bob Brookmeyer. As just illustrated and as further indicated in the works of such novelists or playwrights as Nick Hornby (1995) and Terrence McNally (1986/1990), the record collector falls naturally into the habit of making lists—lists of personal favorites, lists of recordings by a particular artist, lists of albums purchased long ago at the Bay Shore Drugstore. Doubtless, all the items on the latter list are now impossible to find and, I would venture to guess, worth their weight in gold—but none more than my personal favorite among the set of recordings that I discovered in this manner—namely, *Cross Section: Saxes* on Decca by Hal McKusick.

Hal McKusick was a favorite saxophonist of mine during the late 1950s, when he shined brightly on a series of fine albums in the company of such worthy sidemen as Al Cohn, Art Farmer, Kenny Burrell, and Bill Evans. Two of these recordings have recently reappeared on compact disc. Others have long been out of print and—like prisoners of war in Korea, passengers on a plane lost at sea, or mountaineers who never returned home—might be feared lost forever. Happily, both still grace my shelf of ancient LPs. And my favorite—*Cross Section,* which contains a fabulous reworking for saxophones of Charlie Parker's famous solo on "Now's the Time"—came to me in exchange for some paltry fraction of my lunch money at age fifteen (enough to buy, say, a couple of Twinkies that I should not have been eating anyway) by the good graces of the beneficent proprietor at the drugstore in the Bay Shore Shopping Center.

Surely, from the customer's point of view, this was Real Soul Food—that is, goods and services capable of fueling one's musical imagination and feeding one's aesthetic experiences for years or even decades—in my case, so far, almost forty years. This was Durables with a capital *D.* This was Spiritual Sustenance by the grace of Righteous Retailing. Indeed, this was Merchandising via the Magic of Munificence with Mirth.

Nostalgic Update

During the summer of 1995, while writing the present essay, I returned to Milwaukee to see my mother and had the occasion to visit the Bay Shore Shopping Center. Tommy's piano studio and the pharmacy in the space below it have disappeared. Apparently, both were torn down to make room for a gigantic Sears, Roebuck, which now occupies the former domain of artistic civility and thereby profanes what was once sacred ground. But, in 1958, I had no reason to foresee that the march of progress would wreak such destruction upon the center of my personal civilization.

Even more recently—during the summer of 1996, while waiting to rewrite the present essay—I found that Decca had reissued Hal McKusick's *Cross Section* on compact disc. That's the trouble with using concrete examples. The real world keeps changing. But, relentless in its quest, nostalgia always finds new targets.

Doctors Indeed

A couple of years after my formative days at Bay Shore—after I had turned sixteen, had learned to operate a car, and had finally managed to get my long-awaited driver's license—my mother would sometimes let me take the family Oldsmobile to downtown Milwaukee, where I would cruise a seamy section of Wells Street to visit a remarkable record store called Radio Doctors. If Bay Shore had the smallest selection of nonetheless high-quality jazz recordings in the Midwest, Radio Doctors had perhaps the largest. The rule of thumb at Radio Doctors was that if it was jazz and if it was obtainable, the store would stock it, very often with the option to purchase it in either monophonic or stereophonic sound (at $3.98 or $4.98, depending on whether you wanted to pursue what was then a new and still slightly suspect technology). Sometimes my friend Peter would accompany me, and we would spend hours pawing through the thousands of jazz recordings filling every nook and cranny of this musical pharmacopoeia, stopping frequently to audition the many that looked interesting.

Today, we would call a place like Radio Doctors—essentially a family business presided over by the energetic and endlessly patient "Dr. Stu" Glassman—a mom-and-pop specialty store. Considering the inveterate lack of hipness displayed by the typical resident of Milwaukee, Wisconsin, one finds it astounding that this store managed to stay in business. But it succeeded by appealing powerfully to a small but loyal clientele. Indeed, I am not the only academic writer who has publicly paid tribute to this amazing emporium. Recently, Jerome Klinkowitz (1991) from the University of Northern Iowa began his scholarly work on the music of Gerry Mulligan with the following encomium:

> My most personal affectionate gratitude is shared by everyone who buys jazz records—gratitude for the clerks and owners who keep shops stocked, who are often archivists themselves, who think of digging out an odd album that includes one's favorite, and—in the case of selling records to a kid just barely into his teens with collecting ambitions far deeper than his

pockets—who give a break on the price. To . . . Ron and Gordy at the old Radio Doctors Shop downstairs on Wells Street in the lost Milwaukee of my childhood, I'm thankful for making such listening possible (p. xii).

Imagine how I felt when I stumbled onto this paean for my all-time favorite record retailer from a kindred spirit who, nearly half a century later, nostalgically recalls its vanished charms. In reading such a panegyric, an old introspectionist like me feels about as happy as an ethnographer who has just completed a satisfactory member check. To celebrate, I promptly wrote a sappy, syrupy, sentimental letter to Professor Klinkowitz to tell him that he was not alone in his reverence for the old store and that I, too, was there.

COMING OF AGE IN SLOW MOTION

Perhaps one reason I recall Radio Doctors so fondly is that it served as the locale for one of my most memorable coming-of-age experiences as a consumer. Specifically, it was there that I had to make one of the most difficult buying decisions of my life. Milt Jackson's long-awaited new album with Benny Golson and Art Farmer (*Bags' Opus* on United Artists) had just come into the store. Despite the fact that I knew I would purchase this potential gem on that day no matter what, I foolishly risked playing some of the LP on the clunky old machine used by customers in those days of 33 rpm to audition new recordings. During this maiden voyage of the virgin vinyl, I accidentally bumped the turntable's tone arm to send it flying into the air. I saw the scene unfold as if in slow motion—the arm rising like a well-balanced seesaw and then plunging mercilessly downward toward the delicate record grooves. I grabbed, but to no avail. The brutally sharp diamond needle (comparable in force to having one's toe stepped on by a woman's high heel) gouged the fragile disk in the most disastrous possible place—namely, at the peak of the climax in Jackson's solo on "I Remember Clifford." After that, the recording would skip a few bars of Bags's pure improvisatory genius whenever it came to that triumphant passage in the music—the passage where the harmony seems to have strayed perilously far from the home key but suddenly modulates back to safety through an abrupt series of rapid chord changes that Jackson executes effortlessly with a wrist-flicking turn of phrase.

Realizing the enormity of my destructive clumsiness, I had to debate with myself whether to do the honorable thing by buying the damaged album (to live henceforth with a defaced masterwork) or to sneak the record back into the jazz bin whence some unsuspecting customer would purchase it (leaving me to abide forever with my resulting guilt). With dismay, I opted for the former and, as a result, did not hear the true majesty of Jackson's work on "Clifford" until thirty years later, when I finally bought a reissue of the album on CD. Some might feel that—granting the miraculous nature of Bags's magnificent performance—I might have been better off to live with the guilt. Or, perhaps, my little self-sacrificial concession to altruism might eventually shorten my stay in an otherwise endless purgatory. In the latter connection, when a retailer has served its clients as faithfully as Radio Doctors had served me, they would have to be pretty callous to betray this trust.

NOSTALGIC UPDATE TWO

Inevitably, in the face of the dominant crass commercialism that has increasingly characterized the record industry, Radio Doctors changed over the years. The last time I visited the store—during the early 1970s, if I recall correctly—Dr. Stu was still in charge. But he had moved into larger quarters in a new location on Wells, had brightened up the place, had introduced innumerable newfangled displays featuring performers like the then-popular Beatles and the Beach Boys, and had cut back the jazz selection to a bare-bones minimum that scarcely left room for the opportunistic reissues-of-reissues packages that were then flooding the market.

Twenty years later—on my most recent trip to Milwaukee in August 1995—I tried to find Radio Doctors. But, by then, Wells had become a one-way street in a distressingly congested part of the downtown area, and I could not begin to figure out how to get onto this thoroughfare going in the right direction. After driving in circles for a while and growing increasingly frustrated, I finally gave up.

While rewriting this essay in September 1996, I succumbed to another fit of nostalgic curiosity. I picked up the phone, dialed 414-555-1212, and asked the operator if she had a listing for Radio Doctors on Wells Street. "No, I have nothing under that title at this time," she replied in a familiar Milwaukee twang. For her, a polite midwestern apology. For me, instant heartache.

IN SEARCH OF LOST INNOCENCE

In the days since Radio Doctors, I have searched in vain for perfection in record retailing among various East Coast music stores that have served a larger clientele of hip customers and that have therefore tended to offer a larger selection of merchandise than you could hope to find at even the most enlightened outlet in the Midwest. At college, I frequented a place in Cambridge, Massachusetts, called Minute Man. Indeed, I considered it my haunt and would audition every new jazz album that came into the store in its entirety before I replaced it in the racks (a rare event) or bought it (the usual outcome). On the day that John Kennedy died in Dallas, looking for comfort or meaning, I went straight to Minute Man, buried my head in earphones, and did not emerge until the owners closed their shop several hours later.

Apparently, I regarded Minute Man—or wanted to regard it— as a sort of port in a storm or a home away from home. A real home is supposed to provide a safe harbor where you can retreat from the world's hurricane-like tribulations and trials (a place, somebody said, where when you go there, they have to take you in). But, at times like this, the attitude of the Minute Man proprietors did not strike me as either generous or munificent. I would say that—in the Bostonian tradition of extreme politeness—they tolerated me. In other words, though they scowled at me while I made use of their auditioning services, they did not actually say anything rude, probably for fear of losing the generous pile of cash that I would inevitably spend. I did not mourn Minute Man when, a few years after I left Cambridge, it starved from lack of business and was replaced by one of those ugly top-40 chain stores.

MECCA ANALYSIS

Then I moved to New York. Musical Mecca. Where else? The place that was and is the undisputed record-retailing capital of the world (unless you count Los Angeles, where good music flourished in the 1950s but has since fallen into general disuse). In the Big Apple during the late 1960s, I found the twin towers of record retailing— King Karol's and Sam Goody's.

Ben Karol had the well-deserved reputation for never discontinuing any recording, out of print or not. And there I ferreted out many jewels not available elsewhere (such as Alicia De Larrocha's first renditions of *Goyescas* by Enrique Granados on Epic, not exactly jazz, though certainly jazzy enough in its own way). But, despite Karol's refreshing eclecticism, Goody's was the place for me.

Every week, Sam Goody ran special sales on two or three record labels, whose entire catalogs of albums with list prices of $5.98 he would make available (in stock) for $3.49 (a substantial saving to a young and struggling Ph.D. candidate in marketing). Besides, throughout, the Goody's store on 49th Street near Eighth Avenue conveyed a carefully cultivated atmosphere of offering the broadest and hippest selection at bargain prices. Guys with authentic-sounding British accents would more or less *tell* you which albums to buy. Thus, after the reign of stereo had emerged and Verve decided to ditch its supply of monophonic pressings, I was politely but firmly steered toward an assortment of now-priceless collectibles at 99 cents apiece—including *The Tal Farlow Album,* still one of my most prized musical relics.

Sometimes Goody's salespeople would give me a price reduction even if the recording was not officially on sale. For example, during a brief infatuation with rock, I once carried a new Rolling Stones album to the cash register in the mistaken belief that I could buy it for $3.49. When the cashier tried to charge me the going rate of $5.98, I smiled beatifically and gave him the finger. To my delight, he responded by granting me the sale price that I had hoped for. Such acts of service inspire one with visions of Greatness in Retailing. One prepares to worship at the Shrine of Merchandising Genius. And, for a time during the 1960s and 1970s, Goody's did win a famously loyal clientele.

TOOTH AND CLAW IN RECORD RETAILING

Unfortunately, such acts of service also cost money and tend to drive record retailers out of business when they must compete with giant cost-efficient operations on the order of J&R (warehouse-like and located in a slightly sleazy but well-populated low-rent district much farther downtown) or when they must contend—more recently— with powerful record-retailing chains like Tower Records, HMV, and Virgin (which has opened the world's largest record store in Times Square). Thus, the estimable King Karol's has bit the dust, while Sam Goody's has devolved into a low-inventory, high-turnover, reduced-access, déclassé purveyor of CDs that—with astonishingly inept disregard for its former customers' browsing habits—the store once tried to display, like books on a shelf, with only the ends showing so that anyone interested in searching the stacks had to cock his or her head and try to read the tiny little CD-sized labels sideways. This disastrous change in Sam Goody's retailing formula introduced a flaw in service design comparable to the misbegotten decision to save a few bucks by altering the recipe for Schlitz beer. And, like Schlitz, Goody's has paid a heavy price via the loss of its formerly devoted customers.

PARADISE LOST

Meanwhile, CDs have generally spelled the death of store-haunting, record-browsing music-shopping experiences as we knew them in the days of twelve-inch 33 rpm LP albums. In those happy days of yore, the record jacket artist had a 144-square-inch canvas on which to practice the fine art of album cover design. Nowadays, CDs afford only 25 square inches—one-sixth the surface area—in which to work. With such a paltry window of opportunity, nobody bothers trying to create anything memorable. Further, compact discs are so sensitive to the slightest smudge or scratch that customers insist on having their music sealed in shrink-wrapped or cellophane-covered jewel boxes, often with those incredibly annoying little silver patches across the seams to prevent *anyone* (including the owner) from getting the damned things open without the help of a penknife, razor blade, or some other potentially blood-letting implement of destruction. As a result, stores seldom offer the customer a chance to listen before buying. At about fifteen dollars a pop for a list-priced CD, record retailing has become a (gambling) game that jazz lovers play at their own (high) risk.

We old fans of browsing through the illustrious cover art found in the photographs by William Claxton for the Pacific Jazz label on the West Coast, in the designs by Reid Miles for Blue Note Records on the East Coast, or in the ink drawings by David Stone Martin for the various Norman Granz labels featuring music from both coasts must turn for solace to the emerging plethora of coffee-table-worthy books intended to celebrate the virtues of jazz album cover art from the glory days of the LP era. My current collection contains six such oversized compendiums—with titles like *Jazz West Coast* (Claxton and Namekata 1992), *California Cool* (Marsh and Callingham 1992), *New York Hot* (Marsh and Callingham 1993), *The Album Cover Art* (Marsh, Cromey, and Callingham 1991), or *Jazzical Moods* (Mukoda 1993)—representing Claxton, Blue Note, West, East, and other types of jazz covers. (Though I have seen similar volumes devoted to CD artwork, I would not seriously consider buying them. Supporting such publications would be tantamount to extolling the virtues of the photography found on Topps baseball cards.)

Besides poring over these published evocations of nostalgia, I have surrounded myself with genuine mementos of my past as a collector of 33 rpm twelve-inch jazz recordings. The walls of my small study display over thirty such designs, ranging from the humorous (*The Clown* by Charles Mingus on Atlantic) to the scenic (*The Mod-*

ern Jazz Quartet at Music Inn, Volumes 1 and 2, on Atlantic) to the historic (*The Genius of Art Tatum* and *The Oscar Peterson Quartet* on Verve) to the classic (the aforementioned *Bags' Opus* by Milt Jackson and *Modern Art* by Art Farmer on United Artists) to the erotic (*Playboys* by Chet Baker and Art Pepper on Pacific).

Leaning in the last direction, three of my prizes—now regarded as legendary by savvy collectors but sure to appall devotees of political correctness—feature the same beautiful female model in dazzling color photographs by Hal Adams or Peter James Samerjan shown on covers designed by the inimitable Robert Guidi for the illustrious Contemporary label. On *Coop!* (presenting the music of saxophonist Bob Cooper), her brightly painted lips form the third red letter of the album's title. On *Double Play!* (with tune titles related to baseball performed on dueling pianos by André Previn and Russ Freeman), she wears only a blue baseball cap and crosses her arms over both breasts in a thumbs-up gesture that resembles the umpire's "you're out" signal. And, speaking of double entendres, on *You Get More Bounce With Curtis Counce* (featuring Jack Sheldon, Harold Land, and Carl Perkins), she has unbuttoned her white blouse to the waist and rapturously tilts back her head as she listens to her own well-endowed chest through a stethoscope.

Every time I contemplate these ancient trophies—if still alive, that beautiful woman who has given me so much pleasure is at least seventy years old by now—I marvel at the loss that the switch to CDs has incurred. To you, Dear Reader, my enumeration of cover art masterpieces might sound like a laundry list. But to me, they represent irreplaceable evocations of the dear departed past. In retrospect, I am surprised that I did not devote even more time to my adolescent wanderings through the record bins at the old Radio Doctors on Wells Street in Milwaukee.

THREE BLIND MICE

But the art or science of record retailing—which shapes the whole shopping experience surrounding the acquisition of musical recordings in general and jazz albums in particular—has undergone a sea change that places it aeons away from the Radio Doctors of my misspent youth. In February 1995, when I wrote the first draft of this essay, I habitually traded most of my spare cash (in much larger quantities than when I was a boy) for compact discs purchased on the Upper West Side of Manhattan in the stupendously uncomfortable atmosphere of the Tower Records store on the west side of Broadway at 67th Street. Located just north of Lincoln Center, across the street from the Juilliard School of Music, this store catered to perhaps the hippest community of record shoppers anywhere on the face of the earth—Juilliard students with their long hair flying, patrons of the New York Philharmonic still clutching their concert programs, opera lovers killing time during an intermission by looking for James Levine's new recording of *Aida,* and global travelers who had come all the way from Amsterdam with a list of target purchases a foot long. The Tower chain in New York may be the only large-scale record retailer in the world today in which the jazz and classical sections dwarf the rock inventory in size, departing from the standard tradition—found at every shopping mall in America—where massive pop arrays vastly overshadow minuscule representations of music at the high-culture end of the spectrum.

To cater to its fanatic clientele (read "fans"), Tower at 67th crammed its store full of a terrific assortment of what record retailers nowadays call "product." CD bins were filled so tightly that one could scarcely flip through the jewel boxes to see the pictures on their tiny covers. Below the bins, disorganized shelves contained massive volumes of replacement inventory. Computer readouts from the cash register told the busy clerks (much too busy, say, to answer questions about the location of albums for which you had searched in vain) when to scamper out and replace discs in the display racks (all the while ignoring customers who might have questions about where to find things). These clerks—indifferent itinerants who could not care less whether you-the-customer did or did not exist—clogged the narrow aisles and choked the surging traffic of global shoppers to a standstill. Those trying to examine the selections for sale by particular artists found themselves elbowed, jostled, pushed aside, and otherwise inconvenienced in the merchandising gridlock that resulted. Generous? Munificent? Hardly. The atmosphere was claustrophobic, frenzied, and indeed almost manic in its intensity.

Six blocks uptown, also on the west side of Broadway, the HMV chain had recently opened an equally large store that—according to earnest if dubious reports in the *New York Times*—offered an equally impressive selection of "product." But shopping at HMV presented a stark contrast to the Tower experience just described. Rather than the jumbled clutter found at Tower, HMV conveyed the impression of being almost empty—bare walls, a bare floor, a barren and cavernous sense of spaciousness, relatively little merchandise on display, and hardly anybody in the store. Especially if you had just visited its competitor, HMV seemed a rather desolate place—something like a warehouse for a failing toy manufacturer or a showroom for a bankrupt car dealer. Certainly the sales staff appeared lonely. You no sooner entered their terrain than they would rush up to you—obliging, obedient, pitiably anxious to please—importunately wanting to know if they could help. Invariably, the answer—no matter how simple your request—was that they could not. All they could really accomplish was to finger the keys on their computers and to report disconsolately that, whatever it was you wanted, they didn't have it. On repeated occasions, I failed to find an album of interest at Tower, walked up to HMV, and was equally unsuccessful there.

The same problem did *not* generally occur in reverse. That is, if HMV did not have something on hand, Tower often did. Hence, though HMV was six blocks closer to where we live and therefore easier to reach on a lunch hour stroll, I increasingly seldom entered its forlorn doors. Viewing HMV as far from generous or munificent, I tended to regard it as a modern merchandising marvel—a stupendously spacious store on prime New York real estate with astronomical costs of rent and other overhead that has somehow managed to stay in business despite its conspicuous lack of any visible customers.

This observation leaves even more inexplicable the sudden appearance in late 1994 of a new branch of Coconuts located directly across from Tower Records on the other side of Broadway.

As a student of marketing with some interest in retailing, I could not fathom how any sane person(s) could have conceived this misbegotten entry in the Upper West Side record store sweepstakes. First, Coconuts chose to situate itself on what every self-respecting New Yorker knows is the deprived side of Broadway—the east side; the side across from Zabar's and Citarella and Fairway and Lincoln Center and Barnes & Noble; the side where hardly anyone ever went except to see a movie at one of the several multiplex theaters over there on the wrong side of the IRT subway tracks.

Even worse—far worse—Coconuts entered the competition with a selection that was conspicuously dominated by both Tower and HMV. To reach this paltry inventory, you descended two floors on an Escalator to Nowhere that deposited you underground in a Temple of Vacuity—a bargain basement bereft of bargains. Thus, if Tower was small and crowded while HMV was big but empty, Coconuts managed to combine the worst of both possible worlds: Coconuts was small but empty. Alas, it almost defied belief that anyone would try to compete in the marketplace with this merchandising mistake as the third music retailer to be found within a radius of less than three blocks.

BIGGER BUT NOT BETTER

Shortly after I had composed the comments just presented, I heard that a big real estate developer had bought the three-story office building at 67th Street that housed Tower Records, planning to gut it, build above it, and thereby replace it with a high-rise apartment house (perhaps with some retail outlets, including a restored Tower, on the ground floor). At first, to my joy, Tower intended to move into new quarters located at 83rd and Broadway—across from Zabar's and Barnes & Noble—just a few short blocks from our apartment at 87th and Riverside Drive. But unfortunately, for reasons that (again) mystify me, Tower chose instead to move (at least temporarily) to a vacant space in a building called The Ansonia at 73rd and Broadway—a mere one block north of HMV—thereby keeping the average distance between the three major competitors roughly constant (namely, three blocks), but placing Tower at the periphery of the trading area encircling Lincoln Center. With panache, even while promising to reopen in two years at its old location, Tower issued a flyer boasting that its new store is "full of improvements that create an enhanced shopping experience for our customers." These "benefits" include "an even bigger selection of the music you want"; "50 listening stations with over 600 of the latest CD's in all styles of music for you to sample before you buy"; "wider shopping aisles . . . to accommodate all of our customers more comfortably"; "more accessible computer terminals . . . to find what you're looking for"; and "more . . . customer service."

These claims—with the exception of the first and last—appear to be generally true. Specifically, the new Tower does feature listening stations where one can audition new CDs preselected for special presentation by the store (rarely the ones of interest to the likes of me). The new Tower does contain marginally wider shopping aisles (though they are often blocked by people who have donned the headphones required for the auditioning just described and who therefore cannot hear one's requests to please move out of the way). And the new Tower does maintain two or three computer terminals that list available recordings of an artist or piece of interest (though waiting in line behind some stubborn completist intent upon compiling every available version of the *Jupiter* Symphony can sometimes seem rather tedious).

But I do question whether the new Tower provides a bigger selection of music than formerly. For example, with supreme irony, I recently found a rack of old-fashioned 33 rpm LPs in the Tower of Today. It contained some of the same artists and albums that I might have seen in that tiny bin from the old pharmacy at Bay Shore (*Art Pepper Meets the Rhythm Section; Chet Baker in New York*). But, if anything, it was somewhat smaller than the record rack that yielded *Cross Section: Saxes* so long ago.

And I emphatically deny that the new Tower offers more customer service than the old Tower, than its two major competitors on the Upper West Side, or than any other store on the planet Earth. Instead, its employees—when not rooted behind the happily singing cash registers—continue to remain largely invisible, inaccessible, and inviolable. If you somehow manage to corner one of them, their prevailing attitude seems to be one of supreme indifference.

Perhaps for this reason, combined with its injudicious geographical repositioning farther from Coconuts but closer to HMV (in the wrong direction from Lincoln Center), the fortunes of the Upper West Side Tower appear to have declined somewhat in the wake of its relocation. On May 20, 1995, the *New York Times* reported that, after the change, HMV's UWS sales had grown by 15 to 18 percent, while Tower's had shrunk by 20 percent (p. 29).

RETAILING SERVICE AS PERFORMANCE; PERFORMANCE AS SERVICE

Clearly, whether on Broadway or in some other more conventional shopping center, the provision of retail services often involves events that bear a strong resemblance to aspects of artistic performance. This common observation concerning the hedonic or even aesthetic nature of the shopping experience strikes one with particular force during an epoch wherein shopping centers such as the famous Mall of America near Minneapolis or its slightly larger cousin in Edmonton rival amusement parks like Walt Disney World or Six Flags in their capacity to provide thrills and adventures, ranging from swimming in artificial surf to skating on regulation-sized hockey rinks to bungee jumping, and wherein every self-respecting New Yorker knows that Bloomingdale's is really a form of off-Broadway theater. Indeed, according to unverified rumors, when someone asked William Dillard if he intended to purchase the flashy but financially troubled Bloomie's, the owner of the commercially successful but more low-key Dillard's chain replied, "No way! I am in the retailing business. Bloomingdale's is in the entertainment business." What Mr. Dillard forgot to add is that everybody knows (though many do not like to admit) that much retailing is a form of entertainment. Meanwhile, some have begun to argue that, conversely, artistic performance is a form of retailing. Fundamentally, this experiential conflation of retail services with the performing arts provides one conceptual basis for the present paper (cf. Williamson 1992).

This viewpoint also pervades a recent anthology entitled *The Authority of the Consumer* (Keat, Whiteley, and Abercrombie 1994). The contributors to this volume focus on a phenomenon that appears widely in our contemporary culture of consumption—namely, the empowerment of the consumer and the conceptualization of participants formerly regarded as clients, patients, students, viewers, patrons, audiences, parishioners, or even criminals as customers for the offerings produced by such professional services as social work, health care, education, the arts, museums, theaters, religion, and even law enforcement. Unfortunately, the authors of *AOC* adopt what strikes me as a rather narrow-minded and even wrongheaded view of consumption as nothing but a sort of passive ingestion of products valued primarily for their hedonic, materialistic, or utilitarian benefits. This unnecessarily pejorative conception of consuming leaves little room for the finer aesthetic, ludic, moral, or sacred aspects of consumption that many consumer researchers have recognized as fundamental to the human condition.

Yet—nestled among the chapters tending to demean the nature of consumption—we find an essay by Baz Kershaw (1994) entitled "Framing the Audience for the Theatre." Kershaw acknowledges the transparently obvious ways in which theater performances resemble retail services:

> British theatre [is] a paradigm for other productive realms, especially in the service industries. In this respect theatre and performance today offer rich pickings, as they are areas of cultural production in which commodification is chronically pervasive (p. 168).

As examples, Kershaw evokes familiar images of theater lobbies filled with merchandise for sale—T-shirts, cassette tapes, hats or caps, pennants or posters—in short, those "countless objects, the consumption of which might magically recapture the moment of gazing at the stars onstage" (p. 173). Here, "the possession and use of spin-off artifacts may become a potent substitute for the experience itself" (p. 174).

From this perspective (with relevance also to museum gift shops, Grateful Dead tours, virtual reality machines, and other forums for vicarious experience), the theater becomes a giant merchandising scheme that invites Kershaw to exfoliate a hegemonic interpretation based on the dominance of a capitalist ideology whereby "in consuming theatre as a service we are more or less implicitly consuming the ideologies of the society which built it" (p. 177):

> That is to say, the contract constructed by the modified conventions of the theatre experience implicitly underwrites commodification. In a sense, the audience's bodies embody the ideology of the theatre as a commodity form because by their compliance they consume its meanings (p. 179).

But, as Kershaw also points out, Walter Benjamin anticipated an important distinction between (live) theater and other kinds of (canned) artistic performance in his celebrated essay on "Art in the Age of Mechanical Reproduction." In this essay, Benjamin (1936) explained how the "aura" or "authenticity" of a performance disappears when it is captured by a mechanical device and trapped on tape or frozen on film. Exactly the same point divorced from its political trappings reappeared recently in a panel discussion at New York's 92nd Street YMCA, in which the playwright Terrence McNally described the difference between watching one of his scripts performed live and seeing it presented in a movie. For McNally, as for Benjamin, the live performance contains endless possibilities waiting to be developed, whereas the version reduced to celluloid or Mylar is entombed and therefore dead. From this, it also follows that—in live performance by contrast with the case of mechanical reproduction—the audience plays an active participatory role in the unfolding of the theatrical event or the progress of some other artistic happening.

Similarly, Kershaw argues that live theatrical performance can *resist* commodification by virtue of the process whereby the audience senses itself to participate actively in the production of the theatrical experience. In this, members of the audience escape their role as merely passive consumers: "The audience . . . become producers rather than consumers. . . . Audiences of performance gain power . . . through *not* being consumers" (p. 184). Analogously, Kershaw takes this active role of theatrical audiences as a metaphor for the empowerment of consumers in other service industries (such as retailing):

> If we view theatre/performance as a paradigm for the more widespread service industries, it may enable us to locate the sources for a radically democratized empowerment of 'consumers'. . . . If we are searching for the potential of radical resistance to the commodifications of post-industrial, service-based economies, then we may find it in the billions of human interactions which are encouraged, especially, and ironically, at the point of sale of the commodity or service in the performative society (pp. 184-185).

In other words, we may find a resistance to commodification—comparable to the generosity or munificence once enjoyed at the Bay Shore Drugstore or at Radio Doctors—in the occasionally pleasant sales encounter or in the often vividly meaningful shopping experience in which (to borrow a distinction suggested by Stephen Brown) one's sense of a merchandising "space" gives way to the feeling of a service-oriented retail "place." Or, as suggested by my earlier account of the phenomenological contrast between football practice at Country Day and piano lessons with Tommy Sheridan, we may find it in the singular interaction that characterizes certain remarkable communions that occasionally occur between the performing artist and the engaged consumer. In this light, service and performance—for example, retailing and musicality—interpenetrate. What enlivens one ennobles the other. And the best advice we could offer a retailer wishing to commune with a consumer would be to emulate an artist like Hal McKusick or a performer like George Carlin.

THE GIFT OF GENEROSITY WITH A GRIN

During cold, gray weekends in the late fall at Montauk Point, the eastern tip of Long Island, where we spend long Saturdays at a recuperative distance of about 120 miles from the Upper West Side of Manhattan, we like to put on old comfortable clothes and head for places like Amagansett or East Hampton, where the browsing in bookstores and antique shops (but not much in the way of record bins) helps take the chill off the premonitions of winter in the air. On one such recent outing in December, we visited the Old Whaler's Church in Sag Harbor to attend an evening concert by the Hal McKusick Jazz Quartet, featuring the legendary Clark Terry on trumpet and flügelhorn.

As noted at the outset, Hal McKusick was a favorite saxophonist of mine during the late 1950s, when he glistened on some of my beloved jazz albums, at least one of which came from a happily recollected better world of record retailing once found in days of yore but now lost to us forever. Recalled from a perspective deepened by the intervening forty years, McKusick's style might be described as showing touches of cool (West Coast) restraint à la Lester Young fused with the basically hot (East Coast) sensibilities of a Charlie Parker disciple. I had never seen McKusick in person— indeed, after the 1950s, he more or less disappeared into the New York radio, television, and recording studios—but I have always admired his classic LPs and certainly looked forward to finding out how the last few decades had treated his music.

After a long day of wandering through the shops in Amagansett and East Hampton en route to Sag Harbor, my first priority upon arriving at the Old Whaler's Church dictated a rather urgent trip to the rest room. There I encountered a long line of gentlemen who struck me as unusually well dressed for people about to attend a jazz concert. Here I stood in my most casual blue jeans, running shoes, and a ragged sweater behind two or three dapper fellows wearing dark business suits, dress shirts, and elegant neckties. Indeed, I was preoccupied with feeling somewhat self-conscious about my relatively shabby appearance and perhaps squirming a bit due to my physical exigencies, when it came time for the white-haired, fashionably attired, soft-spoken man in front of me to use the bathroom. To my surprise and delight, he graciously stepped aside, flashed me a winning smile, and said that I could go first because he was in no particular hurry and did not mind waiting.

Thus relieved, I found myself all the more ready to enjoy the excellent concert that followed. The years have not dimmed Hal

McKusick's energy or dulled his command of the saxophone. Indeed, he scorched his way through Thelonious Monk's "Straight No Chaser" and, later, Dizzy Gillespie's "Night in Tunisia." On the more tender side, he played a lovely version of Monk's "'Round Midnight" on alto and a gentle rendition on tenor of Mal Waldron's "Soul Eyes," after which someone in the audience called out, "Bird would have loved that." "I hope so," Hal McKusick replied modestly.

After this, Clark Terry lit up the stage with a blistering rendition of "Secret Love," a constantly shifting "Mood Indigo," and a couple of his trademark tunes—"On the Trail" and "Squeeze Me"—before calling McKusick back for some jams on "Perdido" and "Caravan" plus a very soulful blues in B-flat. When he returned to the stage, Hal McKusick the host gave his guest Clark Terry a big kiss on the cheek. And, after the former's gutsy tenor solo on the blues, the latter commented cheerfully, "I think Hal's been eatin' some chitlins."

Throughout the evening, a large audience of local residents appeared happy to have these fine musicians come to play on their end of Long Island. At one point, while announcing a tune, Hal McKusick strained his voice to be heard and commented that the packed church—overflowing with people who had paid premium ticket prices to benefit the Bridgehampton Child Care Center—soaked up so much sound that he could not hear himself bouncing off the back wall. "Thank God," he added appreciatively.

Meanwhile, the concert left at least one visiting jazz fan feeling glad to learn that this seventy-year-old proto-bopper still swings so hard and continues to sound so fine. With special relevance to my key theme concerning the retailing of performance and the performance of service, I have further concluded that, beyond his remarkable talents as a jazz musician, the master saxophonist is also a very nice guy. As he walked out onto the stage, I realized at once that Hal McKusick had been that dapper, amiable, white-haired gentleman who graciously stepped aside to let a younger and rather shabbily dressed stranger use the bathroom ahead of him. Indeed, after his first solo, Hal McKusick looked right at me, pointed his finger as if to acknowledge my moment of epiphany, and smiled.

A customer-oriented breakthrough in the retailing of artistic performance? Far more than that, I believe. More even than service with a smile. Indeed, the Gift of Generosity with a Grin.

THE MAGIC OF MUNIFICENCE
WITH MIRTH

Over the years, in the face of a diminished stream of recorded output from the jazz community, my tastes in albums have necessarily broadened. As one manifestation of these wider interests, I have occasionally pursued my favorite humorists into the record bins. In this connection, an especially happy discovery was an album by George Carlin entitled *An Evening with Wally Londo,* which includes part of his classic piece on what I regard as the "beauty" and the "beast" of the sports world—namely, baseball and football (Little David LD 1008).

George Carlin's work draws heavily on aspects of how we use language and shows us lessons that we can learn through the bemused inspection of our own verbal habits. Thus, in "Baseball-Football," he plays implicitly and with great subtlety on the theme with which this essay began. Specifically, like war, football is a "technological struggle" characterized by helmets, penalties, kicks, fouls, unnecessary roughness, the blitz, the shotgun, bullet passes, long bombs, and (if needed) sudden death. By contrast, like music and other performing arts, baseball is pastoral, nostalgic, or lyrical in nature and is characterized by parks, caps, making errors, sacrifices, play, stretching, and the desire to be "safe at home."

I find George Carlin's masterful unpacking of the homologies in the symbolic meanings of these two sports as profound as any set of binary oppositions constructed by, say, Claude Lévi-Strauss or his many structuralist followers. But the real point of my story concerns what happened when I asked to quote the material from Carlin's recording in one of my own essays (Holbrook 1995, 176-177). In writing that essay, I had been required to request numerous permissions from several authors and publishers. To my consternation, I had ascertained that the going rate for such permissions ranged from a relatively modest $5.00 per citation for short quotes from the *New York Times* to a rather intimidating $4.17 per *word* for a short snatch of poetry from T. S. Eliot. Suffice it to say that such fees imposed by several publishers promised to more than swallow any pitiable royalties that I might otherwise have earned.

In the midst of coping with this state of affairs—on *Christmas Eve*—I received a jolly message on my answering machine from none other than my hero George Carlin. After politely apologizing for calling me at a late hour (as if I might have cared), he mentioned that the recording of "Baseball-Football" I had quoted was an old version and said that he would like to send me a more up-to-date, amended, revised, and improved rendition. Toward that end, he left his home phone number, invited me to let him know where he could fax me the new material, and closed with beneficent wishes for a happy holiday. In due course, he sent me his own typed copy of this magnificent piece and free permission to quote it in my own work.

This spectacularly kind gesture by a genuine comedic genius strikes me as the apotheosis of a "service" encounter between a consummate performing artist and his ardent admirer. Service with a smile from George Carlin? A friendly demonstration of the Christmas spirit? Light-years beyond that, I would say. Beyond even the Gift of Generosity with a Grin—reminding me of those cold afternoons long ago when I would flee the agonies of the gridiron for the warmth of the piano studio and the record bin in the drugstore downstairs—George Carlin has shown me the true Magic of Munificence with Mirth.

BIBLIOGRAPHY

BENJAMIN, WALTER. 1936/1969. "The Work of Art in the Age of Mechanical Reproduction." In *Illuminations,* edited by Hannah Arendt. Translated by Harry Zohn. Reprint, New York: Schocken Books, 217–251.

CLAXTON, WILLIAM, AND HITOSHI NAMEKATA. 1992. *Jazz West Coast: Artwork of Pacific Jazz Records.* Tokyo: Bijutsu Shuppan-Sha.

HOLBROOK, MORRIS B. 1995. *Consumer Research: Introspective Essays on the Study of Consumption.* Thousand Oaks, CA: Sage.

HORNBY, NICK. 1995. *High Fidelity*. New York: Riverhead Books.

KEAT, RUSSELL; NIGEL WHITELEY; AND NICHOLAS ABERCROMBIE, EDS. 1994. *The Authority of the Consumer*. London: Routledge.

KERSHAW, BAZ. 1994. "Framing the Audience for the Theatre." In *The Authority of the Consumer,* edited by Russell Keat, Nigel Whiteley, and Nicholas Abercrombie. London: Routledge, 166–186.

KLINKOWITZ, JEROME. 1991. *Listen: Gerry Mulligan*. New York: Schirmer.

MARSH, GRAHAM, AND GLYN CALLINGHAM, EDS. 1992. *California Cool—West Coast Jazz of the 50s & 60s: The Album Cover Art*. San Francisco: Chronicle Books.

———. 1993. *New York Hot—East Coast Jazz of the 50s & 60s: The Album Cover Art*. San Francisco: Chronicle Books.

MARSH, GRAHAM; FELIX CROMEY; AND GLYN CALLINGHAM, EDS. 1991. *Blue Note: The Album Cover Art*. San Francisco: Chronicle Books.

McNALLY, TERRENCE. 1986/1990. "The Lisbon Traviata." In *Three Plays by Terrence McNally*. Reprint, New York: Plume, 3–88.

MUKODA, NAOKI. 1993. *Artwork of Excellent Jazz Labels: Jazzical Moods*. Tokyo: Bijutsu Shuppan-Sha.

WILLIAMSON, JANICE. 1992. "Notes from Storyville North: Circling the Mall." In *Lifestyle Shopping: The Subject of Consumption,* edited by Rob Shields. London: Routledge, 216–232.

16

CUSTOMER SERVICE INTERACTION

Poor Customer Service and Prescriptions for Improvement

DAWN IACOBUCCI

Every single person every single day has an experience with a vendor that treats them with contempt.
— CBS *Evening News,* June 29, 1995

The expert commentator describing the status quo of customer service in the opening quotation was reacting to a case involving a customer who had purchased a defective coffee machine from a popular coffee retail outlet. Upon attempting to return the machine, the customer received a dissatisfactory response to his complaint. The expert commented that the customer no longer wants simply a replacement machine, but now also wants an apology. The vendor's televised response was, "Customer service is not about servitude." The expert then stated that in such cases customers want an

Dawn Iacobucci is Professor of Marketing at the Kellogg Graduate School of Management, Northwestern University, Evanston, Illinois. She wishes to thank the National Science Foundation for research support (NSF grant #SES-9023445) and Dave Messick and John Sherry for comments on an earlier draft.

indication of respect and further suggested that it is a customer fantasy to "embarrass the heck out of the company that embarrassed and humiliated me." The newscaster concluded with the quip, "Never before has an espresso machine produced so much steam."

Most of us would probably agree that poor customer service is pervasive. As consumers, we are occasionally positively surprised by the service provider who goes above and beyond the call of duty, but more typically we are bitterly disappointed or angered by inane, unempowered, unmotivated, unintelligent, unyielding bureaucratic frontline workers. Knowing that repeat business is profitable, it would serve a firm well to minimize such service failures.

Observations regarding poor customer service might be made informally as consumers (see Albrecht and Zemke 1985), but certainly this phenomenon could be studied scientifically as well. The purpose of theory is to explain and predict phenomena (Popper 1959; Sternthal, Tybout, and Calder 1987). If it can be agreed upon that the observation of poor customer service is at least an occasional phenomenon, then a useful pursuit would be the inquiry into how well certain theories might explain and predict it. It seems prudent and parsimonious to verify the fit of extant theories before attempting to create a new one, so the next step is the determination of which theories might be applicable.

There may be several different classes of explanation, depending on how the phenomenon is defined precisely. If generalizations were made about industries that tend to provide especially bad customer service, *industry systemic* explanations would be sought. For example, if the airline industry were considered one that typically provided dissatisfactory service, an industry-level explanation would be created that considered features of the service not completely under the control of the provider (weather delays, rising fuel costs) that nevertheless influence customer satisfaction (time schedules, price).

To any generalization, there are exceptions. Even in industries fraught with complaints, such as the airlines, there are exceptional carriers noted for their superior customer service—e.g., British Air, SAS, Southwest Airlines (Albrecht and Zemke 1985; Zemke and Schaaf 1989). Sometimes the exceptions may have common properties, which assists theoretical development regarding the common factors. For example, the retail industry is large and heterogeneous, but several direct-order participants (e.g., Lands' End, L. L. Bean, Eddie Bauer) are known for excellent customer service (Zemke and Schaaf 1989). Given this observation, the focus would be on whatever factors seem likely distinguishing features of direct-order retail, e.g., minimal contact with service personnel, convenience of home shopping.[1]

A second class of explanation for poor customer service by some providers and excellent service by others may involve factors inherent to the focal *organization*. For example, a currently popular model called the cycle of success emphasizes the interdependent nature of a firm's employees and its customers (Schlesinger and Heskett 1991; Heskett et al. 1994; Hart, Heskett, and Sasser 1990). Schlesinger and Heskett (1991) illustrate the importance of a firm keeping its employees happy and competent (i.e., well paid and well trained) so that they may in turn keep the customers happy. For example, Marriott is known for comparatively satisfied employees (high retention rates) and customers (high room occupancies), and the "cycle of success" argument is that each drives the other; there is a relationship between a customer and a service provider. Organizational cultures with no employee appreciation or empowerment provide little extrinsic incentive for creatively solving customer problems or responding to customer requests (see Bowen and Lawler 1992).

A more micro class of explanation regarding customer-employee interactions would focus on examining the *individuals* involved as the cause of poor service. A good portion of customer service moments of truth are attributable to the service provider, including his or her competence, empathy, and ability to anticipate customer needs or recover from service failure (Bitner, Booms, and Tetreault 1990; Brown and Swartz 1989; Solomon et al. 1989; Surprenant and Solomon 1987). Recall the introductory coffee example: the customer was disappointed with the coffee machine, but

---

[1] The prediction then would be that if the same conditions could be created in a non-direct-order retail outlet, similarly good customer service behavior could be expected.

he did not get angry until the service provider reacted in an uninterested manner. While good or poor interpersonal interactions between the customer and employee might not compensate for poor or good core service delivery, interpersonal interactions certainly contribute to customer satisfaction and attitudes regarding the quality of the service-providing firm (Crosby and Stephens 1987; Lovelock 1996; Oliver 1980; Parasuraman, Berry, and Zeithaml 1985; Price, Arnould, and Tierney 1995). Thus, if one defines "servicescapes" more broadly than a service's literal physical setting (Bitner 1992), then the customer-employee relationship is one aspect within which service encounters occur and against which service encounters are evaluated.

Given this importance of customer-employee interactions as a determinant of customer perceptions of quality and satisfaction, which in turn are linked to repurchase behavior and a company's financial indicators, this chapter focuses on the interpersonal aspect of customer service. Thus, while industry-level and organization-level explanations are likely to be fruitful, this chapter seeks to evaluate the explanatory power of theories intended to explain interpersonal behavior. Industry and organizational factors will still prove useful to the extent that they describe the environment within which the service provider and customer interact.

Even with a narrow focus on interpersonal explanations, many theories potentially apply. Most social and behavioral research disciplines have offered multiple perspectives on interpersonal behaviors and norms prescribing desirable forms of social interactions. This richness suggests there are many opportunities for examining possible explanations for the phenomenon at hand—indeed, too many to consider exhaustively in this single chapter. Thus, I will focus primarily on one perspective.

In particular, a theoretical metaphor useful to behavioral researchers in a number of disciplines is the idea that parties interact in ways that may be described as gamelike, combining rules and strategies of playing with consequences of selected behaviors (Brandenburger and Nalebuff 1995). Game theory has been used to examine phenomena involving "power, bargaining, cooperation, and trust" (Mandel 1994, 44), in social psychology, sociology, political science, interorganizational behavior, military strategy and international relations, and history. Game theory figured prominently in work capturing the 1994 Nobel Prize for economics. Given the evident widespread utility of game theory, this chapter uses it as a conceptual framework.

GAME THEORY BASICS

Zagare (1984) and Van Lange et al. (1992) provide lucid introductions to game theory that are particularly well suited to behavioral and managerial readers, considering that this area of research quickly becomes complex mathematically and difficult for the novice to follow. Zagare (1984) points to von Neumann and Morgenstern (1944) as the fundamental work establishing the field of game theory, and Van Lange et al. (1992) credit Luce and Raiffa (1957) for introducing the concepts on a large scale to the social sciences.

The canonical assumptions of game theory are these. First, the simplest interesting games require only two players. Even with only two players, Rapoport and Guyer (1966) presented seventy-eight classes of games, undoubtedly the most familiar of which is the prisoners' dilemma game, described shortly. Certainly researchers have extended games to more than two players, as in studies of social dilemmas (e.g., Messick and Brewer 1983; Wiener 1993) and coalition formation (e.g., Komorita and Tumonis 1980), possibilities considered later in the paper, but the focus is primarily on the two-party game, given that it is most characteristic of the customer-employee dyad.

Second, the two players' actions are interdependent; the choices made by each party affect the outcomes of both players. If one actor's behaviors neither affected nor were affected by the other's, then the two players would not so much be playing a game with each other as contesting against an embedding environment.

Third, each player is expected to be motivated to maximize his or her outcomes. This so-called assumption of rationality requires players to be "utility maximizers," at least contingent on their available information. Particularly because of this assumption, game theory has been used both in normative and descriptive capacities. While the initial attraction to game theory may be for its potential in explaining and predicting phenomena, in subsequent applications to customer service, managerial attempts to improve service would be of a normative nature (e.g., how should a service provider act?). Prescriptives are discussed later in this chapter. For the moment, the rationality assumption is useful for its prediction of how an actor would behave in any given circumstance.

Fourth, each player selects a choice of how to behave. For simplicity, games are typically restricted to decisions between two choices. (Multiple choices are usually a function of iterated dyadic interactions.) Depending on the research questions at hand, the choices take on different guises, but one choice can generally be referred to as cooperative (commonly labeled *C*) and the other as competitive (labeled *D* for "defect from cooperation").

Fifth, as a result of both parties choosing to behave in one manner or the other, both parties obtain their outcomes. The outcomes are a function of the joint dyadic choices (given the previously described interdependence). The taxonomy of games mentioned previously depends on the structure of these outcomes. The zero-sum (or constant-sum) games are those for which one party must win at the expense of the other party losing completely (e.g., two advertising firms vying for the same account from a manufacturer). While these games are relatively simple in structure and yield nice mathematical properties, most behavioral researchers are more interested in the class of games referred to as non-zero-sum or mixed-motive games. For example, in the prisoners' dilemma game, the conflict of interest is that between maximizing one's own outcomes and maximizing the joint dyadic outcome—i.e., individualistic versus collectivistic rationality.

Before describing more precisely the prisoners' dilemma game, it may be useful to review the intuitive motivations of the players in the game. Dawes (1980, 182) describes the background as follows:

> [The name *prisoners' dilemma*] derives from an anecdote concerning two prisoners who have jointly committed a felony and

who have been apprehended by a District Attorney who cannot prove their guilt. The D.A. holds them incommunicado and offers each the chance to confess. If one confesses and the other doesn't, the one who confesses will go free while the other will receive a maximum sentence. If both confess they will both receive a moderate sentence, while if neither confesses both will receive a minimum sentence.

These outcomes are diagrammed in Figure 16.1. One suspect's choices (confess or not) define the rows of a 2 × 2 matrix; the other's define the columns. The elements in the body of the matrix describe the valuation of the possible outcomes for each party. The first number in each pair corresponds to the outcome for suspect A; the second number corresponds to the outcome for suspect B. Higher numbers represent better outcomes. For example, if A confesses and B does not, A receives the best outcome (4) and B the worst (1), and vice versa if B confesses and A does not. If both confess, the outcomes for both are worse than if both resist confessing.

These observations capture the essence of the individual versus collective optimization. For both A and B, confessing yields better outcomes for themselves than not confessing, regardless of what the other chooses to do. That is, from A's perspective, if B does not confess, A's higher value corresponds to A confessing (4 versus 3). If B does confess, A's higher value still corresponds to A

FIGURE 16.1   Outcomes for the Prisoners' Dilemma Game

		Suspect B	
		Do Not Confess (C)	Confess (D)
	Do Not Confess (C)	3,3	1,4
Suspect A	Confess (D)	4,1	2,2

Note: The first number in each pair corresponds to the outcome for suspect A; the second number corresponds to the outcome for suspect B. The higher the number, the better the outcome.

confessing (2 versus 1). (The same holds true for B.) Thus, confession is said to be a "dominant" strategy for the individuals involved.[2]

Unfortunately, if both players select their dominant strategy (i.e., both confess), a nonoptimal collective outcome results, because each player could have done better as an individual under a different choice (i.e., not confessing). Note, too, the reverse situation. If both players choose not to confess, neither achieves his or her absolute best outcome, but the joint solution (3,3) is superior to their both confessing (2,2). Van Lange et al. (1992) describe this dilemma as a conflict arising due to two definitions of rationality: individual rationality prescribes noncooperation, whereas collective rationality prescribes cooperation.

Given the superiority of the collective outcomes for mutual cooperation, and the implications for social interactions and welfare more generally, much research has been devoted to determining how cooperative behavior might be enhanced (Pruitt and Kimmel 1977). Three strategies seem especially effective. First, the payoff structure might be modified; i.e., the incentive to cooperate can be increased and/or the incentive to not cooperate can be decreased. Second, if the parties are allowed to communicate, they can promise to cooperate with each other and therefore be less tempted to defect from cooperation (Misumi 1989). Third, for games with multiple trials, each player can adopt the so-called tit-for-tat strategy whereby a player chooses C or D at time t to mimic the other's choice at time $t - 1$ (Axelrod 1980). Thus, a cooperative choice is answered by subsequent cooperation, and a competitive choice is reciprocated with competition (Komorita, Parks, and Hulbert 1992). This responsive strategy is thought to encourage cooperation because neither party is taken advantage of and neither party makes a first strike; accordingly, each player shapes the other's behavior.[3]

---

[2] The dominant strategies for A and B appear as analysis of variance-like main effects in the matrix.

[3] Interestingly, that these results suggest that the most effective means of encouraging both players to "turn the other cheek" (Matthew 5:39) is to institute a policy of "an eye for an eye" (Exodus 21:24).

These are the basic assumptions and findings of the prisoners' dilemma game. *N*-person games are those with more than two persons, and Van Lange et al. (1992, 13) describe several means by which they differ. First, in two-person games, an actor's competitive action is directed against only one other player, whereas in an *N*-person game, the outcome of a competitive action is spread over *N* − 1 others. Second, reciprocated choices (i.e., the tit-for-tat strategy) are less effective in attempting to shape or control the behavior of multiple others. Lastly, in a two-person game, one's choice is never anonymous, but in an *N*-person game, the anonymity allows a player to behave destructively (continually competitively), to the detriment of the collective group outcome, without sanction or retribution. Each of these distinctions might be classified essentially as effects of diffusion of responsibility (Latane and Darley 1968), which in this context means that simply adding players allows each individual player to be less directly accountable for the group's collective actions.

Finally, research on games for which the players are groups rather than individuals indicates that groups tend to cooperate less than individuals playing the same game structure. The explanations seems to be that groups tend to be more afraid of being exploited by others, and more likely to choose self-protecting options (Insko et al. 1990; McCallum et al. 1985).

IMPLICATIONS FOR CUSTOMER SERVICE

Let us now evaluate the appropriateness of each of the aforementioned assumptions to the arena of customer-employee interactions. Identifying the conceptual places of lack of fit can be informative; game theory has prescriptions for encouraging good interpersonal behavior (i.e., cooperation), so if customer service interactions can be made more gamelike, then there would be clear directions to pursue to improve customer service relations. This approach is in the classic tradition of mathematical logic, which attempts to solve a problem by framing it to resemble another problem that has already been solved. Whatever properties of game theory that are diagnosed as *not* seeming to fit well have direct implications for actions that managers might take to increase the likelihood of good customer service relations on the part of their frontline personnel. If some assumption does not hold, the service encounter might be reshaped so the assumption appears to hold better (if it makes sense to do so without destroying other positive aspects about the service), or the lack of correspondence about the properties of the service encounter may be the driving source of the poor service. Such diagnostic information would be valuable in considering how one might possibly redesign the service operation so as to enhance better interaction.

Application of Game Theory Assumptions

Recall that the basic assumptions of game theory were five: (1) two parties interact; (2) they are interdependent; (3) each actor is expected to maximize his or her outcomes; (4) each actor may choose to behave cooperatively or competitively; and (5) as a result of their joint choice, each actor receives an outcome. The outcomes were characterized as being maximized for the individual or for the collective good. Let us examine each of these assumptions.

Two Parties Interact

At first glance, it appears that the property of two parties would hold true for the focal phenomenon; there is a customer and a service provider, seemingly composing a dyadic interaction. To the extent that a two-person interaction characterizes many service encounters, this assumption appears generally valid. There may be other circumstances, however, for which the customer service situation is somewhat more complex. Let us consider both sides of the dyad.

The evaluation of services is thought to be influenced, at least in part, by the other customers involved (Lovelock 1996). For example, a play is often thought to be more enjoyable with more people in the theater, while an airline trip is usually thought to be more enjoyable with fewer people in the plane. Thus, for some services, the customer may in fact be a body of customers. Sometimes the interactions between a single service provider and multiple customers may be characterized as a series of dyadic interactions; if only one customer is served at a time, then the service encounter essentially remains dyadic, even in the presence of multiple customers. For other services, multiple customers may be treated as a single unit. For example, a waiter might deal with two or more friends dining together, or a realtor might interact with two or more members of a family seeking a home, interactions more complex than dyads.

Conversely, for the purchase of many services, a customer encounters multiple service providers. For example, during the extended service experience of an airline flight, a customer interacts with an airline ticket agent, a baggage handler, a flight attendant, and others. That is, from the customer's perspective, the service provider may be a collection of service providers. If the employees are well trained, the customer is handed from one provider to another in a seamless manner, presumably emulating more closely a one-to-one interaction, a customer with a unified and organized firm.

Thus, a customer–service provider interaction may be one-on-one, or individual-to-group, or group-to-group. It is intriguing to consider the asymmetries between these bodies of persons. Even with the simple dyad (i.e., a single customer and a single service provider), there may be some power imbalance between the parties because the service provider carries the credibility and authority of being a firm's representative. This asymmetry may be compounded if the customers and providers are groups. The service providers represent a firm, or a collective institution, and accordingly may demonstrate greater cohesion than the group of customers (Iacobucci and Ostrom 1996). As a result of either the cohesion or the authority, the providers are likely to carry more implicit power to the interaction.

These possibilities amount to two interesting deviations from the simple prisoners' dilemma game: asymmetry and groups. Some researchers have examined games in which there are role variations among the players, such as when the power of different actors is manipulated. Komorita and Tumonis (1980) found that in iterated game playing, more powerful actors exercise their muscle early but with time treat others more equitably, as all actors learn that the strong players need the weak players as much as the weak need the strong.

Considering the property regarding groups, recall the diffusion of responsibility described previously. If a customer interacts with multiple service providers, it should never be surprising—in fact, the prediction would be—for service providers to regularly say, "It's not my job." This literal indication of lack of felt responsibility may be due, at least in part, to the existence of multiple alternative providers.

Recall also the finding that groups tend to cooperate less than individuals. Suppose an airline flight is delayed, and the customers start to grumble together, beginning to function more as a unified group, and the frontline employees start to similarly band together in defense. A negatively reciprocal cycle of interaction between these two ad hoc groups is more likely to begin than a series of cooperative and understanding behavioral iterations.

To prevent such downward spiraling, customers and employees alike must break out of a group mentality. However, the service-providing firm has direct control only over its employees; intervention in customer behavior is more difficult. Employees can be trained to identify such situations and begin to act less mindlessly and more decisively, counter to the group movement. Nonconforming behavior should help break the cycle of mutual group competitive iterations.

Note also that, presumably on each side, the multiple parties would share roughly common utilities (e.g., customers want to get the best service possible). However, to the extent that the goals of the members within the groups demonstrate heterogeneity (e.g., customer segments), the functional group cohesiveness may dissolve, making a group appear to be more like disassociated players.

A means of purposefully breaking the group mentality on the part of the customers might be literally taking a customer aside, apart from the group, and treating his or her concern individually. Doing so, of course, could create a dilemma of its own, because greater time spent with one particular customer would mean less time for others.

More generally, if the service delivery system is designed so as to enhance the customer's perception that the service is one-on-one, the firm may enjoy many benefits. First, this individual-versus-group issue is addressed. In addition, the customer may experience greater satisfaction simply because the service encounter appears more personalized (Surprenant and Solomon 1987). Unfortunately, tailored service might be prohibitively expensive in certain mass-service industries.

In sum, to enhance the emulation of service provision to a familiar two-party game, here are five derived managerial prescriptions:

1. Depending upon the service provided, recognize that the customer–service provider interface may be one-to-one (e.g., doctor-patient), one-to-many (e.g., traveler–airline front line), many-to-one (e.g., household–realtor), or many-to-many (e.g., consultant team–manufacturer).

2. If customers see multiple providers, train the front line to be consistent, providing a coherent front, in order to emulate a single entity.

3. Recognize that employees will carry greater power due to their representation of a firm, so customers may initially feel disadvantaged and frustrated. But before management gets cocky, recall that over time, the "stronger" players (the firm) come to learn that they need the weaker players (the customers) as much as the weak need the strong.

4. Understand the reasons underlying the "it's not my job" attitude on the part of some workers (i.e., it might not be just laziness), and do not allow frontline employees to diffuse their responsibilities—each worker must be held accountable.

5. Because groups are less likely to cooperate (i.e., behave well) than individuals, service provision must proceed by breaking extant group mentality. Service providers must not band together in mindless solidarity but rather

occasionally break out of trained, scripted interactions with their customers. The empathy of a service provider is merely his or her ability to act like a caring individual. In addition, responding to customers as individuals will carry the added benefit of a personalized feeling for the customer, and therefore greater customer satisfaction.

The Two Parties Are Interdependent

The interdependence assumption of game theory would seem to describe quite well the nature of the service encounter exchange. The interdependence between the customer and employee is the heart of the "cycle of success" model described previously (Schlesinger and Heskett 1991). For most services, a customer certainly needs a service provider to help execute the desired purchase (e.g., a checkout person in a store, an attorney to write a contract).[4] Conversely, a company certainly needs customers to continue in business, and so—at least indirectly—employees need customers. If their firm went out of business, they would lose their jobs. Again, the assumption appears to fit generally. In truth, the situation may be more complex.

Most customers know they are dependent on service personnel. When they experience poor service, many customers threaten to "take their business elsewhere." However, this threat is rarely satisfactory comfort to the customer making it. Sometimes the customer cannot take his or her business elsewhere (e.g., no competition, high switching costs, no time). In such situations, the customer is literally entirely dependent on the service provider. In addition, the customer knows that he or she is only one of many customers, and the withdrawal of a single customer rarely has substantial impact on a firm.[5] Finally, many industry studies indicate that customers

---

[4] Exceptions would be the so-called self-service purchases, but these by definition do not involve a provider and so are not really in the realm of the phenomenon considered in this paper, given the focus on interpersonal interactions.

[5] There are exceptions, such as the tale of the bank customer with a large account who was treated badly. He asked for, but did not receive, an apology and subsequently took his business elsewhere (Hart, Heskett, and Sasser 1990).

usually do not report their dissatisfaction to the offending firm, in part because they feel that there is no point in doing so (Wilson 1991). Thus, with no apparent, meaningful recourse, customers are frequently left feeling frustrated in a state of learned helplessness.

Service providers are also well aware that losing one customer rarely has substantial impact on their volume of business or profitability; a service provider demonstrates that knowledge when he or she treats a customer inconsiderately. In addition, the currently popular movement of "relationship marketing" suggests that while some customers are extremely valuable, and nearly everything should be done to please them, other customers are extremely costly, and they should be let go (Reichheld 1993). However, this philosophical stance is fairly strategic and is likely to be implemented only at high management levels, not by the frontline service provider (the person conducting the interpersonal interactions with the customer).

Moreover, while it has been acknowledged previously that employees are dependent upon customers, the connection is often only indirect. That is, while the employee needs his or her job and so needs the employer firm, and therefore indirectly the customers, this link may be so long and indirect that the employee does not bother to appreciate the customer. Rarely does an employee lose his or her job just because a single customer was dissatisfied.

Certainly there are services for which the association between customers' satisfaction and employees' job security is more direct. For example, waiters are tipped in a fairly timely manner as an evaluation of their services. Small-business owners would also likely feel more proximal feedback, given that the loss of one account would represent a greater percentage of their business. Professional service providers obtain feedback with more immediacy, given their greater inherent involvement with their customers. Thus, interdependency or its greater recognition might be increased by enhancing the immediacy of the reciprocity, as in these examples of timeliness, impact on accounts, and intensity of interactions.

The servicescape contains interdependencies; customer service may benefit from highlighting the connections to both parties. It would behoove firms to make their employees more aware of this linkage (e.g., the importance of happy customers), such as in the form of employee incentives, or even education about such concepts as the value of a "lifetime" customer. On the other side of the dyad, customers ought to speak up more (giving feedback to the firm and generating negative word of mouth), and they should follow through on their threats to take their business elsewhere, because if a firm's employees are consistently incompetent and rude, then sooner or later the numbers of defecting customers will be substantial and impactful.

Managerial prescriptions therefore include the following:

6. While it is true that customers feel dependence upon the service-providing firm, they are free to take their business elsewhere. The offending firm might not feel the pinch with a single dissatisfied customer, but the firm will feel it when the droves leave en masse. Customers should be encouraged to be vocal in their displeasures, whether contacting Better Business Bureaus or generating negative word of mouth.

7. The interdependence should be made clearer to the front line—that frontline employees' jobs are dependent upon the firm, which is quite directly dependent upon customers' purchase behavior. Interdependence is enhanced by proximal cues—either more immediate rewarding of desired actions or more spatial closeness such as in high provider involvement.

Each Party Acts to Maximize Own Outcomes

It can probably be safely assumed that customers are typically looking to obtain a good outcome from their service encounters (e.g., good price, value, quality). However, for purchases in which customer involvement is low, motivation for obtaining "the best outcome" would also be low, so customers might not be true utility maximizers. In addition, it is known that individuals do not always behave in a manner that appears rational; i.e., in ways that optimize their outcomes. Thus, for example, even in the face of an incompetent and rude employee, some customers can coolly and kindly hold their ground and continue to "cooperate" (e.g., "be nice"), even when it means that the service provider is thereby taking advantage of their good nature.

The picture is even less clear for the employee. An employee may indeed wish to maximize his or her utility, but the question is, What objective is sought? The employee seeking career advancement will behave differently from the employee who seeks to minimize effort.[6] As with the property of interdependence, the small-business owner or other service providers who are integrally involved in the firm may be more inclined to align their objectives with satisfaction of the customer. The objectives sought by minimum-wage-earning frontline representatives of a large firm serving many customers may or may not be aligned with the customer because these employees may not feel the same level of ownership of the firm and its policies. Even if the frontline provider wishes to be a good employee, his or her desires may not translate into customer-satisfying behavior, as in the case of the frequently inflexible reactions by nonempowered employees of many large, bureaucratic firms.

Add one more managerial prescription:

8. Recognize that utilities are complicated, multidimensional, and subjective, so that simple economic predictions based on price (for customers) or wages (for employees) will rarely capture the essence of interactions.

Each Party Chooses to Act Cooperatively or Competitively

This aspect of game theory might best be thought of as a property rather than an assumption. One modification that may be desirable is to characterize the available options of behavioral choice on a continuum, or at least with more than two choices. However, two

---

[6] An economist would presumably attach a monetary-like utility value to such "subjective" benefits, and the arguments still hold.

choices, especially those as extreme as competition and cooperation, are sufficient for making interesting theoretical comparisons.
One issue for the applicability to customer service might simply be
the naming of these categories, e.g., nice versus mean, or interper-
sonally supportive versus opportunistic, rather than cooperative versus competitive per se (cf. Dant and Schul 1992; Heide and John
1992). Another issue might be the education of both parties—the
customers and employees—about the benefits of collectively good
outcomes (i.e., win–win solutions).

Joint Outcomes Are Obtained

As just previewed, it may be helpful to inform the parties involved
as to distinctions between individual and collective optimization.
Collective good might be particularly salient for customers or
employees who wish long-term relationships with each other, compared with the short-term, transactional orientation that characterizes some marketing exchanges (see Dwyer, Schurr, and Oh 1987).
Further, only for such long-term relationships are reciprocating
cooperation effects possible.

The finding described earlier, that actors play games differently in the beginning of a long-term relationship compared with
later (Komorita and Tumonis 1980), was that earlier in sequences
of games, players are more likely to act powerfully and competitively, but with experience they learn about the mutual dependence and so behave more cooperatively. (The same effect from
trial t to trial $t + n$ is also seen for novice bargainers versus experts,
a nice conceptual parallel.) Thus, a desire to have a long-term relationship may provide sufficient motivation to begin a cooperative
reciprocation, which may then be sustained by the very long-term
nature itself.

A managerial derivation follows from this:

9. A desire for a relational (i.e., long-term) orientation
   toward customers may be self-fulfilling; a firm will act
   more cooperatively (e.g., more generously) toward the
   customers, which in turn clearly will bring them back.

Means of Encouraging Good Behavior

In general, game theory holds that the collective good is enhanced by mutual cooperation. This cooperation is induced via three primary means: (1) changing the payoff structures; (2) allowing communication between the parties; and (3) encouraging each party to adopt reciprocating strategies.

The first option, to change the payoff structure, seems promising in its likelihood to enhance better customer-employee interactions. Increasing the employee's incentive to cooperate (e.g., be nice to customers) is easy to do, and it is consistent with other suggestions to make rewards contingent upon good customer relations (including the previously discussed issue of making the interdependency more immediate). The flip side, decreasing payoffs to the front line for competitive behavior, is presumably simply punishment. It is less clear how a manager might affect the customer's behavior (i.e., increasing payoffs for behaving cooperatively or decreasing payoffs for competitive behavior).

The second suggestion, to allow for communication between the customer and employee, would seem to be useful managerially because it is easy to implement and seemingly free. However, the ability to communicate is typically already in place in service encounters. Certainly it can often be improved. For example, if service providers are busy and harried and/or customers are similarly troubled, the communication may be nonexistent, cryptic, or impatient. Further, sometimes customers might wish direct communication with someone "more important" at the firm, and such personnel are often less accessible. Thus, firms could train their frontline employees in communication and empathetic skills, and make management more visible to customers. Nevertheless, given that communication abilities usually exist in some form, it is not likely that this direction holds much potential for improved customer relations.

The third option, adopting a reciprocal strategy over multiple trials, may be executed as long as a sequence of interactions occur. That condition may characterize many services, but certainly it is an irrelevant option to one-stop service encounters, unless both customers and employees can be educated about fairly abstract notions such as generalized reciprocity.

It is also possible that reciprocal strategies (for longer-term service relationships) might be less successful at inducing cooperation in commercial settings. The assumption is that if both parties start out nice and cooperative, and the other's previous behavior is imitated, the series of dyadic interactions will continue to be pleasant. If either party breaks the "nice" momentum, however, and the other party then mimics the more negative behavior, game theory predicts the dyad will spiral downward, seemingly never to return. Both of these predictions seem apparently reasonable at first glance. Particularly to the extent that much of classic marketing may be moving toward relationship marketing, the potential for longer-term encounters may be increasing, seemingly implying great fit for the findings of such reciprocal gaming behavior.

However, as for many of the game theory assumptions and findings, when they have been applied to customer service, the situation appears more complex. It is possible, for example, that there is less of an opportunity to see complete continued reciprocation in service encounters. Service providers are employed by a firm, so they must answer to someone at the firm for their behavior; thus, they may have less freedom to act competitively (e.g., meanly). While it does not seem fair or humane for service providers to have to occasionally tolerate abuse from customers, that appears to be more acceptable than expecting a customer to ever tolerate a ranting service provider. Perhaps this norm exists because of the pervasive attitude that "the customer is always right," but it could be due to the simpler fact that the customer is paying for the service, and no customer in his or her right mind would pay for abuse.

Those thoughts lead to some final managerial prescriptions:

10. It is not news to suggest rewarding one's best employees, but, as in the prescriptions regarding interdependencies, the rewards should be more proximal to the exemplar behavior.

11. Establishing communication is critical. Firms should prefer that the complaining customer not do so via word

of mouth, but more constructively directly to the company. Unfortunately, few firms have any such feedback systems in place. Recent 800 numbers are a beginning, but customers would be most satisfied if they thought their feedback would be heard by top management, rather than the frontline or intermediary bureaucratic layers.

12. Both the customer and the service provider should be encouraged to adopt reciprocating strategies for positive behaviors. Negative reciprocation is a derivation from the game theory metaphor that might best be avoided.

CONCLUSION

This chapter has examined only the tip of an iceberg in trying to develop an understanding of sources of poor customer service. The focus was on interpersonal aspects of the service encounter, because of the importance of this component of the service experience. However, clearly it would be beneficial to integrate the industry- and organization-level factors and whatever other systems may be relevant, such as business environments or national cultures. Within the examination of interpersonal aspects of the customer-service provider interaction, the choice of game theory was defended by its seeming centrality, but it is important in these concluding statements to mention again the existence of many other possibilities.

Even so, this chapter has pointed to antecedents of poor customer service. If a service delivery system environment can be created in which the encounter simulates individual-to-individual relations that appear directly interconnected, with cooperative choices mutually well rewarded, etc., the service encounter will be more gamelike. If, in turn, the encounter is more gamelike, then the interactions can be made more pleasant by modifying payoff structures, enhancing communication, and inducing reciprocal behavior.

One might argue that if game theory was of such enormous applied value, there would be no more warring nations. However, the theory is clear in its normative directives, and it cannot be blamed for the lack of, or improper, institution. The struggle for improved customer service is a battle, too, and the service manager would do well to take heed of these interpersonal interactive prescriptives. Poor customer service is so pervasive and so enormously frustrating that managers must pursue meaningful strategies for improvement. The ideas generated in this chapter could be operationalized and implemented toward this goal.

BIBLIOGRAPHY

ALBRECHT, KARL, AND RONALD ZEMKE. 1985. *Service America!* New York: Warner Books.

AXELROD, ROBERT M. 1980. "Effective Choice in the Prisoner's Dilemma." *Journal of Conflict Resolution* 24:3–25.

BITNER, MARY JO. 1992. "Servicescapes: The Impact of Physical Surroundings on Customers and Employees." *Journal of Marketing* 56:57–71.

BITNER, MARY JO; BERNARD H. BOOMS; AND MARY STANFIELD TETREAULT. 1990. "The Service Encounter: Diagnosing Favorable and Unfavorable Incidents." *Journal of Marketing* 54:71–84.

BOWEN, DAVID E., AND EDWARD E. LAWLER III. 1992. "The Empowerment of Service Workers: What, Why, How, and When." *Sloan Management Review* (Spring): 31–39.

BRANDENBURGER, ADAM M., AND BARRY J. NALEBUFF. 1995. "The Right Game: Use Game Theory to Shape Strategy." *Harvard Business Review* (July–August): 57–71.

BROWN, STEPHEN W., AND TERESA A. SWARTZ. 1989. "A Gap Analysis of Professional Service Quality." *Journal of Marketing* 53:92–98.

CROSBY, LAWRENCE A., AND NANCY STEPHENS. 1987. "Effects of Relationship Marketing on Satisfaction, Retention, and Prices in the Life Insurance Industry." *Journal of Marketing Research* 24:404–411.

DANT, RAJIV P., AND PATRICK L. SCHUL. 1992. "Conflict Resolution Processes in Contractual Channels of Distribution." *Journal of Marketing* 56:38–54.

DAWES, ROBYN M. 1980. "Social Dilemmas." *Annual Review of Psychology* 31:169–193.

DWYER, F. R.; P. H. SCHURR; AND S. OH. 1987. "Developing Buyer-Seller Relationships." *Journal of Marketing* 51:11–27.

HART, CHRISTOPHER W. L.; JAMES L. HESKETT; AND W. EARL SASSER, JR. 1990. "The Profitable Art of Service Recovery." *Harvard Business Review* (July–August): 148–156.

HEIDE, JAN B., AND GEORGE JOHN. 1992. "Do Norms Matter in Marketing Relationships?" *Journal of Marketing* 56:32–44.

HESKETT, JAMES L.; THOMAS O. JONES; GARY W. LOVEMAN; W. EARL SASSER, JR.; AND LEONARD A. SCHLESINGER. 1994. "Putting the Service-Profit Chain to Work." *Harvard Business Review* (March–April): 164–174.

IACOBUCCI, DAWN, AND AMY OSTROM. 1996. "Commercial and Interpersonal Relationships: Using the Structure of Interpersonal Relationships to Understand Individual-to-Individual, Individual-to-Firm, and Firm-to-Firm Relationships in Commerce." *International Journal of Research in Marketing* 13:53–72.

INSKO, CHESTER A.; JOHN SCHOPLER; RICK H. HOYLE; GREGORY J. DARDIS; AND KENNETH A. GRAETZ. 1990. "Individual-Group Discontinuity as a Function of Fear and Greed." *Journal of Personality and Social Psychology* 58:68–79.

KOMORITA, SAMUEL S.; CRAIG D. PARKS; AND LORNE G. HULBERT. 1992. "Reciprocity and the Induction of Cooperation in Social Dilemmas." *Journal of Personality and Social Psychology* 62:607–617.

KOMORITA, SAMUEL S., AND TONI TUMONIS. 1980. "Extensions and Tests of Some Descriptive Theories of Coalition Formation." *Journal of Personality and Social Psychology* 39:256–268.

LATANE, BIBB, AND JOHN M. DARLEY. 1968. "Group Inhibition of Bystander Intervention in Emergencies." *Journal of Personality and Social Psychology* 10:215–221.

LOVELOCK, CHRISTOPHER H. 1996. *Services Marketing,* 3d ed. Englewood Cliffs, NJ: Prentice Hall.

LUCE, ROBERT D., AND HOWARD RAIFFA. 1957. *Games and Decisions: Introduction and Critical Survey.* London: Wiley.

MANDEL, MICHAEL J. 1994. "Commentary: How Game Theory Rewrote All the Rules." *Business Week* (October 24): 44.

McCALLUM, DEBRA M.; KATHLEEN HARRING; ROBERT GILMORE; SARAH DRENAN; AND J. P. CHASE. 1985. "Competition and Cooperation Between Groups and Individuals." *Journal of Experimental Social Psychology* 21:301–320.

MESSICK, DAVID M., AND MARILYNN B. BREWER. 1983. "Solving Social Dilemmas: A Review." In *Review of Personality and Social Psychology* vol. 4. Beverly Hills, CA: Sage, 11–44.

MISUMI, KAZUTO. 1989. "Communication Structure, Trust, and the Free Rider Problem." *Journal of Mathematical Sociology* 14:273–282.

OLIVER, RICHARD L. 1980. "A Cognitive Model of the Antecedents and Consequences of Satisfaction Decisions." *Journal of Marketing Research* 17:460–469.

PARASURAMAN, A.; LEONARD BERRY; AND VALARIE ZEITHAML. 1985. "A Conceptual Model of Service Quality and Its Implications for Future Research." *Journal of Marketing* 49:41–50.

POPPER, KARL. 1959. *The Logic of Scientific Discovery.* New York: Basic Books.

PRICE, LINDA L.; ERIC J. ARNOULD; AND PATRICK TIERNEY. 1995. "Going to Extremes: Managing Service Encounters and Assessing Provider Performance." *Journal of Marketing* 59:83–97.

PRUITT, DEAN G., AND MELVIN J. KIMMEL. 1977. "Twenty Years of Experimental Gaming: Critique, Synthesis, and Suggestions for the Future." *Annual Review of Psychology* 28:363–392.

RAPOPORT, ANATOL, AND M. GUYER. 1966. "A Taxonomy of 2 × 2 Games." In *General Systems: Yearbook of the Society for General Systems Research.* 11:203–214. Cited in Zagare (1984).

REICHHELD, FREDERICK F. 1993. "Loyalty-Based Management." *Harvard Business Review* (March-April): 64–73.

SCHLESINGER, LEONARD A., AND JAMES L. HESKETT. 1991. "Breaking the Cycle of Failure in Services." *Sloan Management Review* (Spring): 17–28.

SOLOMON, MICHAEL R.; CAROL SURPRENANT; JOHN A. CZEPIEL; AND EVELYN G. GUTMAN. 1989. "A Role Theory Perspective on Dyadic Interactions: The Service Encounter." *Journal of Marketing* 49:94–111.

STERNTHAL, BRIAN; ALICE M. TYBOUT; AND BOBBY J. CALDER. 1987. "Confirmatory versus Comparative Approaches to Judging Theory Tests." *Journal of Consumer Research* 14:114–125.

SURPRENANT, CAROL F., AND MICHAEL R. SOLOMON. 1987. "Predictability and Personalization in the Service Encounter." *Journal of Marketing* 51:86–96.

VAN LANGE, PAUL A. M.; WIM B. G. LIEBRAND; DAVID M. MESSICK; AND HENK A. M. WILKE. 1992. "Social Dilemmas: The State of the Art." In *Social Dilemmas: Theoretical Issues and Research Findings,* edited by Wim B. G. Liebrand, David M. Messick, and Henk Wilke. Oxford: Pergamon Press, 3–28.

VON NEUMANN, JOHN, AND OSKAR MORGENSTERN. 1944. *Theory of Games and Economic Behavior.* Princeton, NJ: Princeton University Press.

WIENER, JOSHUA L. 1993. "What Makes People Sacrifice Their Freedom for the Good of Their Community?" *Journal of Public Policy and Marketing* 12:244–251.

WILSON, JERRY R. 1991. *Word of Mouth Marketing.* New York: Wiley.

ZAGARE, FRANK C. 1984. *Game Theory: Concepts and Applications.* Newbury Park, CA: Sage.

ZEMKE, RONALD, AND D. SCHAAF. 1989. *The Service Edge: 101 Companies That Profit from Customer Care.* New York: NAL Books.

17

PRIVACY AS A DIMENSION
OF SERVICE EXPERIENCE

CATHY GOODWIN

A regular at a neighborhood bar says, "This is home! I can break furniture here!" (Katovich and Reese 1987).

A hospital CEO suggests that hospital and prison experiences have much in common (Heskett, Sasser, and Hart 1990).

Retail outlets for pornographic films and videos are designed to offer anonymity in a public setting (Donnelly 1981; Sundholm 1973).

"Only her hairdresser knows for sure," promises an advertisement for Clairol products.

These examples demonstrate a critical aspect of services: the degree to which an encounter allows consumers to balance public and private domains in their lives. In contemporary culture, the public domain has been associated with technology and objectivity, the private domain with "romanticism . . . intentions, feelings and sentiments, the sphere of the irrational and subjective" (Brown 1987, 132). Private domains traditionally are associated with family, close friends, intimacy, and noneconomic exchange, while public

---

Cathy Goodwin completed this chapter while visiting at the Great Valley campus of Pennsylvania State University, Malvern, Pennsylvania. She acknowledges support of the Social Sciences and Humanities Research Council of Canada.

domains require interaction with strangers, often accompanied by monetary transactions.

Historically, private homes served as venues for business meetings and entertainment. Today, these activities take place in the arena of commercial services, such as restaurants, bars, and hotels (Rybczynski 1986, 27–28), while home-centered grooming rituals are performed at salons and spas. Other services bring public domains into the home; examples are computerized banking services and mobile veterinary clinics. This transformation of domains may enhance a consumer's experience: the consumer who views a Borders bookstore as an extension of her living room (Reilly 1996) enjoys being able to experience a formerly private activity—reading, talking—in a public setting. On the other hand, a service may lower the quality of a consumer's experience by denying opportunities to balance these domains.

The topic has been addressed indirectly, primarily in the context of environmental psychology. Shopping behaviors are influenced by the presence or absence of others (Bell 1967; Granbois 1968; Wells and LoSciuto 1966). The servicescape encourages approach or avoidance behaviors (Bitner 1990, 1992), sometimes simply by arranging the furniture (Mehrabian 1976). This chapter extends this research to suggest that consumers' ability to achieve desired privacy levels figures importantly in commercial service encounters, which by definition incorporate at least minimal elements of the public domain; any commercial transaction invites scrutiny beyond levels appropriate to interactions with family and friends.

Altman (1976) noted that too much privacy results in loneliness, while too little privacy creates vulnerability. I define two dimensions of privacy, drawing on earlier work (Goodwin 1991), which in turn derives from Altman (1976). The first dimension, physical privacy, describes the consumer's control over the degree to which he or she is physically observed by others as well as control over intrusive stimuli, such as sounds or smells. The second dimension, informational privacy, represents the customer's control over information disseminated about him- or herself. After defining these dimensions, I discuss the way privacy influences the consumer's service experience and the way services allow the consumer to balance public and private domains.

DIMENSION OF PRIVACY

Following Goodwin (1991), this article shares Altman's (1976) view that privacy involves regulation of boundaries, but redefines the dimensions as physical or informational privacy. The two dimensions identify four categories of privacy (see Figure 17.1), each of which was illustrated by one of the examples opening this chapter. The neighborhood bar exemplifies a service that offers a *retreat,* high in both dimensions, where customers enjoy freedom for self-expression. When a service is low in both physical and informational privacy, the experience resembles a *prison,* where inmates have little control over access to their bodies or their dossiers. High information control but low physical control enables anonymity in public places—the *depot,* such as a bus or airline terminal—where neither provider nor fellow customers know one's name. Finally, hair salons and spas offer discreet backstage environments (Goffman 1961), *dressing rooms* where customers can prepare their masks in private. The next section considers each dimension separately.

Physical Privacy

Physical privacy offers control over seeing and being seen, hearing and being heard, smelling and being smelled. Physical privacy particularly offers freedom from "noxious stimuli," such as noise,

FIGURE 17.1   Categories of Privacy

		Physical Privacy	
		No	Yes
Informational Privacy	Yes	The Depot	The Retreat
	No	The Prison	The Dressing Room

541

which is difficult for the brain to ignore (Toch 1992, 36). Unremitting exposure to high levels of multiple stimuli creates "load," which has been associated with exhaustion in retail settings (Donovan and Rossiter 1982). Christmas shopping at the Mall of America (near Minneapolis) or King of Prussia Mall (in a Philadelphia suburb) will exhaust the senses as shoppers rub against strangers, hear music chosen by retailers, and smell a mixture of gasoline and fast-food grease.

Physical privacy has been associated with more general forms of control in service encounters. Hui and Bateson (1991) identified crowding as a loss of control that leads to dysfunctional information-processing and consumption behaviors. Sensations of crowding may be derived not from numbers of people present in the environment, but from their ability to frustrate the consumer's achievement of purpose (Proshansky, Ittelson, and Rivlin 1972) or demand responses that "are alien to us" (Toch 1992, p. 36). In a library, the presence of only one other person at a large table can seem intrusive. A French sociologist described the annoyance created by a single consumer drumming his fingers at a restaurant counter, "without any thought for the effects of his gestures on the physical environment." (Guillaumin 1993, 51). The opportunities for mutual annoyance multiply when people of different socioeconomic statuses, ethnic backgrounds, and values are pushed together to create a reluctant melting pot. Motor vehicle bureaus and coach class on major airlines offer examples of short-lived but stressful experiences.

These annoyances occur because cultures differ both in defining the type of stimuli that are considered as disturbing and in the norms providing protection from disturbance. For example, Arabs tolerate high density of contact in public spaces—but in private spaces, "friends may sit in quite large rooms often at opposite ends of it to talk" (Rodaway 1994, 59). Because trust is based on sense of smell, distance is tolerable once trust has been established. In contrast, Americans prefer distance in public places but closeness at home. They seek physical distance on park benches and buses but are comfortable with tighter quarters at home; the lounge where visitors are entertained is usually the largest room in the house (Rodaway 1994, 60). The Dutch live behind large, clean picture windows, allowing a degree of visual intrusion that would be uncomfortable in other cultures (Schama 1993). At the same time, cultures offer different variations of "circuit breakers" (Moore 1984) to obtain physical privacy. For a tribesman of West Africa, taking cattle to the salt licks represents a request for privacy (Kottler 1990), while the wearing of a veil can serve as a symbol of withdrawal (Murphy 1964).

These cultural norms will be reflected in the way services are delivered. In some locations, hotels are expected to be noisy, and complaints from guests receive little attention. In others, an individual guest or couple may be joined by a stranger in a restaurant. Sleeping cars are shared by strangers in many countries. American consumers may find these experiences strange or even stressful. At the same time, foreigners can contribute to intrusiveness by not understanding cultural behaviors or symbols that allow members of the culture legitimate ways to obtain privacy. Examples include speaking to strangers or directing one's gaze. Such topics offer rich areas for future cross-cultural research.

Informational Privacy

Like physical privacy, informational privacy can be placed in historical and cultural context. Preliterate societies offered few opportunities to dispense information about others, while in small societies, people already have access to full information about one another. Thus, the "attitude that there is some part of life that does not belong to public society" belongs to our cultural era (Baumeister 1987, 63). Services offer informational privacy in two ways: anonymity permits disclosure among strangers in the public domain, while confidentiality protects disclosures when one's identity is known by those in the public domain.

Anonymity
The ability of services to offer anonymity is due to two cultural forces: role separation and mobility. Historically, business and family roles overlapped; today, self-concept may be situational (Belk 1984), so that people interact with each other based on social role

categories (Lofland 1989). To the clerk whose attitude communicates, "I just work here" (Brown 1987, 133), the consumer may be happy to respond, "I just shop here." While the resulting depersonalization can be viewed negatively (Surprenant and Solomon 1987), the resulting anonymity will be welcomed by some customers, who may not want friends or family members to know they're buying cigarettes, candy, a McDonald's Happy Meal, or even certain kinds of underwear (Goodwin 1992). Role separation has been institutionalized among providers of deviant services; for instance, staff of pornographic bookstores are trained not to look at customers (Donnelly 1981).

Mobility, historically associated with wealth and freedom, allows consumers to create situational roles that are separate from such historical identities as family and status (Belk 1984). Hotels and motels offer faceless lodging experiences, although few go as far as the No-Tell Motel in facilitating illicit trysts; guests are allowed to bypass the lobby and remain unseen by staff and other guests (Lilly and Bell 1981). A hero in one of the Dick Francis murder mysteries demonstrates the use of mobility to play different roles to different audiences. Harry lives in the family mansion, which is so large that he can easily conceal the equipment needed for his aviation hobby. Harry's family knows nothing of his flying activities, while those at the airfield have no idea that Harry comes from a wealthy family. Indeed, the aviation hobby symbolizes access to freedom and anonymity: pilots can move about easily, identified only by aircraft number.

In this novel, the airfield offers Harry a location where people come together based on mutual personal interests, without revealing their identities. A number of services recognize the desirability of these features. Club Med incorporates both role separation (casually dressed people interact on a first-name basis) and mobility (customers often fly off to exotic islands). Willow Creek Church allows new members to remain anonymous until they feel comfortable with a deeper commitment. Urban coffee shops, such as Starbucks and Borders, allow people to carry on intensely personal conversations without whispering; patrons enjoy open space, sunlight, and good coffee, secure that their words will be meaningless to strangers.

Confidentiality

Confidentiality codes among professionals can bring informal secrecy norms of family and friends into the public domain of commercial services (Oyen 1982, 2). Formal codes of professional services cover emotionally loaded situations, such as illness, bereavement, and divorce. Yet less emotionally loaded situations tend to be protected by design, location, and informal norms. The old Clairol advertising slogan "Only her hairdresser knows for sure" expresses cultural norms of secrecy associated with preserving appearance: the best hair looks natural. Some readers will remember the controversy created when news media asked President and Mrs. Reagan's hairdressers to disclose their hair color formulas.

In recent years, attention has been drawn to dissemination of computer-generated information collected during the course of doing business (Goodwin 1991). While disclosure of a single telephone number or travel report may seem innocuous, this information can be aggregated to yield knowledge of an individual's calls and travels over a period of time (Ware 1985). In this environment, seemingly innocent data can do harm. Farrell's ice cream store held birthday parties for young children. Data from the store's record of birthdays was used to enforce Selective Service enrollment (Baker et al. 1986). An individual can be profiled from a record of videotape or library book rentals (Wolter 1989). The Internal Revenue Service has used data from list compilers, including demographic and lifestyle data, to enforce compliance (Baker, Dickinson, and Hollander 1986; Betts 1984; Werner 1983). In this environment, assurances of confidentiality can facilitate consumer balance between public and private domains.

FORMS OF SERVICE EXPERIENCE

Service encounters can be classified based on the consumer's ability to obtain these two forms of privacy, physical and informational. A retreat offers both physical and informational privacy. A dressing room creates physical but not informational privacy; those using the service are free from observation and/or unwanted intrusion, but they cannot prevent others from learning that they used the service and, sometimes, other personal details disclosed to the provider. A depot provides informational but not physical privacy; people can be seen, but nobody knows who they are. Finally, the fourth category resembles a prison, where neither form of privacy is possible. I will describe each of these in turn, along with the managerial and research implications summarized in Table 17.1.

It is important to understand that what is being classified is the consumer experience, not the service category. The same service may be a retreat to one customer (the coffee shop regular) and a depot to another (the coffee shop visitor from another city). People also respond to services in terms of their own traits and experiences; for some, a plane ride will be a retreat, an opportunity to get away from family and job, while others will be far more sensitive to restriction on movement and inability to escape close physical presence of strangers. It is also important to understand that privacy has been defined as control, which is not always equivalent to solitude. For example, commune members may experience little solitude, yet are protected from scrutiny of nonmembers. Joining a commune

TABLE 17.1   Implications of Privacy Levels in Service Encounters

Consumer Experience of Service Encounter	Customer Benefit	Provider Benefit	Downside
Retreat	Self-expression; freedom from possible sensory intrusion	Intense loyalty	Customer too familiar; entitlement
Dressing room	Transformation behind closed doors	Appreciation from customer	High unmet demands; low tolerance for error
Depot	Efficient service; novel stimuli	Customers spend more	Irritable customers
Prison	Efficiency or safety	Control	Abusive customers

enables them to have some control over sensory inputs and informational outputs.

Service as Retreat

Metaphors of home, sanctuary, and retreat recur frequently in discussions of privacy, as in the following examples (emphasis added):

> "We need a sanctuary or *retreat*, in which we can drop the mask" (Benn 1971, 24–25).

> "[We need] a *zone of immunity* to which we may fall back or *retreat*, a place where we may set aside arms and armor needed in the public" (Duby 1987, viii).

Denzin (1970) suggests identity has *"lodged"* when individuals no longer need to actively negotiate their identity with others. Lyman and Scott (1967, 238) define *home territories* as "areas where the regular participants have a relative freedom of behavior and a sense of intimacy and control over the area." Cohen and Taylor (1976, 94–95) suggest there are times when life scripts seem dysfunctional, when we realize a lack of "a sector of life" in which we are *"really at home, ourself, free"* (p. 95).

Services may be experienced as retreats when they offer an escape, a separation from everyday, "mundane" role requirements (Cohen and Taylor 1976). Among Israeli military parachutists, a long period of training featured intense group participation, while each jump was preceded by a brief confinement within the airplane. The jump phase symbolized escape, as each parachutist experienced intense personal freedom. Many reported shouting or singing loudly during the jump (Aran 1976).

Several services serve as escape valves, releasing people from previous roles and interactions. Examples include Club Med and river-rafting excursions (Arnould and Price 1993), where participants are screened and nonparticipants barred from the setting. In Heritage Village, limited access created a "sacred refuge or retreat" (O'Guinn and Belk 1989, 230) that allowed participants to enact religious behaviors that would be ridiculed in the outside world. Rituals sometimes remove former identities and/or add new identities, as in the case of reenactments of the Civil War or medieval jousting tournaments.

Boundaries are less clearly established among the "third places" of Oldenburg (1989), such as neighborhood bars and coffee shops. These commercial settings offer "areas where the regular partici- pants have a relative freedom of behavior and a sense of intimacy and control over the area" (Lyman and Scott, 1967, 238). Privacy derives from control enacted not by providers, but by the regulars. Within the third place, regulars can disappear into close fraternal relationships; in one bar, the regulars even brought ethnic food for "Christmas dinner with the family" (Katovich and Reese 1987). Like family members, regulars are free to break rules, yet also per- form chores to symbolize intimacy and belonging. As regulars dive into the third place, they escape from their everyday family and job environments by assuming place-specific roles and statuses.

Implications

Customers benefit from retreats as opportunities to express them- selves freely, feeling secure and peaceful away from their usual home or work environments. Customers who view services as second homes tend to be ferociously loyal (Goodwin and Gremler 1995), while escape experiences tend to be addictive (Celsi et al. 1993), encouraging customers to return to the same provider or industry. Fraternal experiences create strong emotional ties through shared secrecy. For providers, the downside would appear to come from the regular customers' sense of entitlement, i.e., a feeling that they own the place (Katovich and Reese 1987). Providers who create a retreat can anticipate and even encourage this sense of appropriation. While the service customer has been viewed as a partial employee (Mills and Morris 1986), consumers of retreat settings may want to become partial managers of outcomes. To achieve success and avoid conflict, providers need to understand and manage this dynamic.

Service as Dressing Room

Other services offer a place for people to put on masks and cos- tumes before going onstage. These services screen customers from visual observation yet do not offer enough role separation to allow informational privacy. Almost any service that can be obtained by telephone would fit this category, as would hotels and rental cars that require a credit card or other identification. Retail services include services designed to enhance the physical image (such as beauty salons) or mental well-being. To receive medical services, consumers often must grant permission to release information to insurance companies and medical colleagues.

Individuals may achieve physical privacy by being alone, but they may also share a dressing room as a group, the way team members share a locker room. Services designed as dressing rooms often bring together consumers who share common problems, creating commercial versions of what Turner (1968) calls "cults of affliction." Burdick (1990) found that Brazilian women felt comfortable discussing marital conflicts in Pentecostal or *umbandu* (mediumship) religious settings because everyone there was "full of troubles" (p. 162). The women were more reticent in neighborhood Bible study groups, where membership was based on geographic proximity.

The experience of groups isolated for a specific shared purpose may require or encourage self-disclosure on topics related to the core service. For example, Wiseman (1979) describes friendly interactions of women in a used-clothing store. Health club members often converse freely in the locker room. In contrast, consumers of services categorized as retreats are free to withhold information or even create a service-specific identity.

Implications

Consumers benefit from the opportunity to manage their audiences. The backstage created by the service allows them to put on masks or costumes, surrounded only by supportive helpers. From a provider's perspective, customers will pay a premium to the backstage crew; thousands of people find a way to pay for plastic surgery that is not covered by insurance. Repeat customers develop special bonds with providers such as hairdressers, ranging from comfortable friendship to admiration (McCracken 1995). Sharing of a common purpose and restricted access may facilitate self-disclosure.

On the other hand, customers can bring high expectations to this experience. They may see the provider as a maid or valet rather than a skilled professional. After all, a dressing room is usually occupied by a star. While customers often appreciate the outcome and enjoy the experience of being taken care of, anticipating an uncertain outcome can be stressful; such stress may be expressed in negative behaviors toward providers or other customers.

To deal with these customers, providers often realize that customers may come to view them as psychologists (Barbieri 1983; Cowen et al. 1979). Lawyers, bankers, and financial advisers often interact with people during some of their most difficult life crises, such as divorce or bankruptcy (Gold 1983). Divorce lawyers have indicated that up to 50 percent of conversation with clients involves discussion of personal psychological problems, not legal issues, yet often felt inadequate to their task; some offered to participate in a ten-session program to enhance their skills (Doane and Cowen 1981). Other providers of dressing room services will need to be aware of the potential to be viewed as a counselor and to address the consequences, both positive and negative.

Service as Depot

Some services offer customers the opportunity to be an anonymous face in the crowd, allowing them to try new roles, free from the gaze of friends, employers, or family members. A dressing room allows access only to those whose identities have been verified; a depot permits access and exposure among strangers. In airport retail outlets or shopping malls, the lack of disclosure may derive from the presence of large numbers of strangers who simply don't care about each other, and whose interactions with providers are limited to brief, one-time encounters.

Implications
Both providers and customers benefit from efficient people-processing options and may experience anonymity as a source of freedom from critical reference groups. On the other hand, depot

experiences usually include heavy load, due to the complex, differentiated, changing, and often unfamiliar stimuli generated by shopping malls or transit stations. The combination of load and anonymity can generate customer affect ranging from crankiness to aggression; deindividuation encourages venting of anger and disregard of customary norms of courtesy. In pornographic retail sites, anonymity is constructed deliberately while clients remain under the provider's surveillance (Sundholm 1973).

Services fostering anonymity can encourage robotic behavior rather than creativity or freedom. Relph (1982) describes "parcel people" who are processed through railway stations and airports. While the system functions, parcels ignore their surroundings. Passengers tune out ugly or bland surroundings, selectively paying attention to signs and flight announcements. Anonymity creates deindividuation (Zimbardo 1969), which in turn encourages aggressive, even self-destructive behavior. The anonymous consumer can choose to express frustration in deviant ways, such as yelling at rude clerks or service providers. Service providers often need special training to cope with people in these situations (Hochschild 1983; Lovelock 1994).

More generally, service businesses may alleviate these conditions by reducing load or offering escape settings. Providing an escape may represent a public service (the airport chapel) or marketing opportunity (Admirals Club). Recently, airport vendors have offered tiny cubicles for rent by the hour, where travelers can rest or read or get work done in a quiet place. The proliferation of these offerings suggests opportunities may exist in other services typically experienced as depots, such as shopping malls.

Service as Prison

Some services resemble total institutions, demanding that the customer give up both physical and informational privacy. McEwen (1980) identifies three charactcristics of total institutions:

1. *Organizational scope, or degree of contact with the outside world*—Intensity is associated with isolation.

2. *Involuntariness of membership*—Some unions and government organizations have involuntary membership, and some total institutions, such as drug rehabilitation programs, seem voluntary.

3. *Bureaucratic elements*—Inflexibility, regimentation, depersonalization, and social distance are measures of bureaucratic management of inmates.

Medical services represent a strong example: large systems attempt to maintain detailed computerized records that (like prison records) will be readily shared with official personnel from any jurisdiction. Just as prisoners are known as inmates, not guests (except in jest), the involuntary nature of medical consumers is suggested by the term *patients*. Erie Chapman, CEO of the U.S. Health Corporation, has identified similarities between patients and prisoners: interminable sessions of questioning, removal of familiar clothing and possessions, forced dependency on others for simple needs, and limited access to visitors (Heskett, Sasser, and Hart 1990, 7).

Airplane rides also have been compared to short-term incarceration in total institutions (Zurcher 1979). Just as prison inmates may have limited information about each other but are registered with authorities, passenger identities are verified by airline officials but disclosed selectively to fellow travelers. Those who create problems in flight can be held in custody or tracked down subsequently more easily than, say, a shopper at a mall. Holbrook (1992) used vivid imagery to make this point, comparing the passenger to a numerical digit (p. 97) and a captive (p. 98), with the ride itself resembling both a roller coaster ride and a term in a concentration camp (p. 100). Although a roller coaster ride tends to be experienced as pleasurable, participants are strapped into small, enclosed spaces, with complete loss of control over exit opportunities.

Economy-class seating arrangements and the crowded conditions that fit descriptions of prison experiences are reported in the literature. Seating arrangements resemble "strict spatial partitioning" that Foucault (1979, 195) associates with plague cities; the "syndic" locks each house from the outside, controlling access. If people have to leave, they'll take turns and avoid meeting each other or communicating with each other.

Toch (1992) quotes a prison inmate who complains that he hasn't been able to put his elbows on the table and waits up to twenty minutes after eating before he can leave the table (p. 39). Anyone who has experienced a meal served in economy class of a commercial airline, particularly from the vantage point of a middle seat, can draw a comparison. Toch also notes that regulations allow public activity to interfere with desires of prisoners who have particularly high privacy needs (p. 43). Similarly, those who attempt to sleep or read on long flights will be disturbed by card playing, loud conversations, and intrusions by crew members attempting to sell duty-free items or highlight scenic attractions visible only to the few nearest the window.

Implications

Customers accept entry into prisonlike systems in order to achieve a larger goal, such as a discounted vacation or improved health. As discussed earlier, those who feel imprisoned can behave like prisoners, perhaps basing their behavior on images derived from literature, media, or word of mouth. Service providers sometimes justify creating a prison experience in order to gain control of diverse populations who are brought together, particularly in stressful circumstances. Yet stressful prison experiences can unleash antisocial behaviors. Customers often feel not merely deindividuated, as in the depot, but depersonalized. Flight attendants, nurses, and other "wardens" have reported abusive behaviors, and reports of irrational behavior on airplanes appear frequently in the media. Responses to confinement tend to be negative and antisocial (Toch 1992), creating difficulties when service delivery depends on cooperation among consumers. Inmates lack a sense of responsibility to their guards, often refusing to offer even minimum courtesies.

Unlike prisons, services often encourage consumers to reframe their negative experiences. Medical personnel frequently deny that clients are experiencing pain or discomfort, as in the famous "This won't hurt a bit." Flight attendants advise passengers to "sit back, relax, and enjoy the flight," when none of these options is remotely possible.

Rather than simply encouraging consumers to reframe an obvious reality, a few firms have transformed the nature of the service. Southwest Airlines creates a culture of informality and fun on its point-to-point routes; Shouldice Hospital encourages extensive customer participation among hernia patients. These services mitigate the prison experience by reducing load. Shouldice assigns compatible roommates and encourages people to be ambulatory, while Southwest gets people to laugh, and the employee attitude is contagious.

When load cannot be reduced, consumers will seek ways to escape. Ironically, many of the recent safety restrictions on the use of electronic devices further reduce passenger escape options. Firm-created recreation often fails to create the desired escape experience, as the film or music selection may bore or even offend large segments. Northwest Airlines has announced an intention to build electronic games into seat backs; while some passengers may be able to escape into those games, others will experience increased sensory load from the noise and movement. A similar complaint has been made about in-flight phones: those who reach across for a phone and those who hold long conversations will interfere with the physical privacy of several other passengers.

In some service experiences, there may be little the provider can do to increase privacy levels. Still, an understanding of the prison environment should help providers avoid innovations that further reduce passengers' privacy.

Providers also need to be aware that their own behavior will influence consumers: if they act like guards, they may find themselves dealing with prisoners. I can recall two flights when passengers seated near me had to make a second request for items they requested, such as cream for their coffee. On one major carrier, the flight attendant responded to a reminder by handing the passenger the item without a word. On another, the flight attendant said, "Oops, I'm sorry," and made a little joke. In the first case, the passenger responded with a sarcastic remark, compounding the tension; in the second, the passenger smiled back. The difference between the two flight attendants may be transitory (a rough day). Yet in the long run, employee attitudes require more than a quick fix. There is considerable evidence of congruity between employee and consumer climate perceptions (Schneider 1980). The Stanford prison experiment suggests that depersonalization will contribute to a degradation of behavior among both prisoners and guards. The effects of bureaucracy are not straightforward: when outcomes are measurable, some bureaucracies can enhance outcomes and enhance satisfaction.

DIRECTIONS FOR FUTURE RESEARCH
Demographics

The ability to obtain privacy through services can be influenced by gender and economics, which are not unrelated; Zelizer (1989) has documented that nineteenth-century husbands rigidly controlled their wives' spending money. Social norms also influence access. Jacobs (1981) noted that, for Jewish women, the *mikvah,* or ritual bath, foreshadowed contemporary health clubs, offering a setting where physical openness encouraged psychological self-disclosure. Going to a bar alone still remains a male prerogative in many locations, while females have significant relationships with hairdressers (McCracken 1995).

Disposable income allows consumers access to a greater variety of services and, hence, privacy management opportunities. Privacy can be bought in the form of first-class tickets, single rooms, or airline VIP room membership. Upscale beauty salons may offer booths to special customers. The sanctuaries available in tense urban settings—museums, quiet restaurants—tend to target consumers of higher socioeconomic status. As privacy management options (such as resorts) or the means of obtaining these options (such as airfares) are discounted, more citizens gain access, but the nature of the experience changes for everyone.

It is likely that the association of services with privacy will be related to public and private meanings. Consider the following examples:

- A neighborhood bar will be viewed differently by women, regulars, and casual drop-ins. A variety of demographic variables are potentially relevant.
- The community created by health clubs and coffee shops would appear to have special meaning to the unmarried and the childless, particularly those living in urban areas.
- Those in transition appear to utilize services to fill gaps in their lives (Goodwin and Gentry 1996).

Therefore, researchers can draw on previous studies of symbolic and experiential consumption. Traditional laddering techniques can be supplemented by metaphor elicitation approaches (Coulter and Zaltman 1994) to understand how meanings might be gendered or otherwise influenced.

The Provider's Privacy

The consumer's experience will be altered by the way the provider him- or herself experiences privacy during service delivery. Many service employees, such as bus drivers, have no physical privacy throughout the duration of the service encounter. Some, such as flight attendants, receive attention as if they are athletes or film stars. Service providers retain a certain degree of informational privacy; customers rarely even know the home address of their doctors or dentists, unless they seek and find a listing in a telephone directory.

Providers working out of their homes remain particularly vulnerable to privacy loss, and many need to separate work from family domains (Christensen 1994). Those whose offices are on display also reveal a great deal about themselves by choice of decor, photos, and items inadvertently left on a desk or table. Buttenwieser's (1981) novel *Free Association* describes a psychoanalyst whose office is in his thin-walled apartment in Manhattan. Patients pick up tantalizing hints of their analyst's private life as they wait. They also run into him in Laundromats, art museums, and restaurants.

Psychotherapists deal openly with issues of self-disclosure, but the topic remains problematic among other occupations, where role occupants remain on display and sometimes fend off personal questions. For instance, I have heard passengers ask flight attendants where they live and what they do on layovers. On some airlines, flight attendants can request assignment to galleys belowdecks to escape the incessant pattern of interactions. Such control mechanisms would appear to be reinforced by interpersonal styles, such as programmed responses to questions and nonverbal behaviors that discourage inquiry.

Service Quality

Quality frequently has been defined in terms of SERVQUAL dimensions, including empathy, responsiveness, and reliability (Parasuraman, Zeithaml, and Berry 1985). Recent research suggests that perceptions of quality will be influenced by the consumer's response to the larger environment. For instance, a messy office influences attributions for service failures (Bitner 1990), while an intense outdoor experience influences satisfaction (Arnould and Price 1993). An understanding of the privacy dimension of experience will contribute to an understanding of the way consumers respond to services, which in turn contributes to an understanding of evaluation processes and satisfaction outcomes. Qualitative methods, such as depth interviews and participant observation, seem essential to identifying dimensions salient and important to customers. Because experiences are often reported metaphorically ("It was like a dream" or "It was like being robbed"), methods designed to evoke metaphors and images seem particularly appropriate in this context (Coulter and Zaltman 1994).

Loneliness

Altman (1976) identified two negative consequences from a lack of boundary regulation: intrusion and loneliness. Like a great deal of privacy research, this chapter has focused on the ability of services to protect the consumer from intrusion, ranging from noise to crowds to critical comments that demand a response. Yet services also influence feelings of loneliness. Hospitality services, such as restaurants and hotels, tend to be designed for couples. A widow taking her first solo trip described a series of insults at the hands of restaurant staff, motel clerks, and gas station attendants (Ginsburg 1990). Other services attempt to reduce loneliness, with tactics ranging from outright matchmaking to creating nonthreatening social environments. Attempts of well-meaning providers may backfire: customers resisted joining twelve-person group tables set up by a New York bar owner (Schoolsky 1990).

Urbanization and family life cycle trends suggest that increasing numbers of people will be living alone. During times of life crisis, there is evidence that consumers will turn to service providers for support, due to unavailability of family and friends (Gentry and Goodwin 1995). Consumers are particularly vulnerable during those times, and those with limited personal support networks will be particularly susceptible to service provider influence. The loneliness construct has been studied extensively, and issues of measurement have been addressed by social psychologists (Maragoni and Ickes 1989). Among consumer researchers, the topic remains taboo and even trivial: an unwanted phone call represents an intrusion; an insulting remark from a restaurant host or motel clerk is considered, at most, a breach of etiquette. Therefore, a first step in research would involve identifying the extent and seriousness of the problem. Loneliness may indeed constitute a significant source of vulnerability.

CONCLUSION

A great deal of research on services has focused on what services are *not*. Introductory lectures often describe services as intangible. This chapter emphasizes that services play a unique role in the consumer's life experience by allowing him or her to create and manage the boundary between public and private domains. The separation of domains has been addressed in a variety of disciplines. Korosec-

Serfaty (1984) sees the home as metaphor for public and private aspects of self. Attics and cellars offer space for secrecy but are also connected to the public living area. Douglas and Isherwood (1979) suggest that local culture is expressed by "[w]hom she [the house-wife] invites into her house, what part of the house she makes available to outsiders" (p. 56). Thus, if the home is a metaphor for the private domain, a service may be viewed as a door or a porch.

The door has been viewed as mediator between public and private, sacred and profane (Cooper 1971). In seventeenth-century Dutch art, doorways separate the very clean "inside" from the outside, which is less clean both morally and literally (Schama 1993). Some firms offer services that allow people to remain behind their doors. Mobile veterinary clinics and delivery services from high-quality restaurants allow clients to get their cats vaccinated or to eat chef-prepared food while remaining at home. Other services thrust the consumer into the public arena, with little protection from exposure.

In contrast to the door, the porch creates a middle ground between an intimate home setting and an impersonal public realm. The porch "lets casual encounters remain casual and the private stay private" (Mugerauer 1993, 111). The porch can be a metaphor for any service that allows people to interact closely and self-disclose freely while retaining the option of leaving the scene to go to one's real home, i.e., to balance public and private domains. The consumer who chooses to meet a new acquaintance in a wine bar or a Borders cafe will be managing her privacy: she will be able to converse intimately but avoid creating unwanted intimacy by inviting the friend to her living room.

By viewing the door or the porch as a metaphor for service encounters, we can explore the servicescape from the perspective of function. Does the consumer have a place to retreat if the public becomes intrusive? Can he or she control who is invited into the more intimate sections of the home? By addressing these questions, we recognize that privacy has a larger role than as a component of the service encounter and a contributor to quality. Rather, a key element of the core service involves allowing the consumer to balance domains, an opportunity that today's society offers predominantly within the context of service offerings.

BIBLIOGRAPHY

ALTMAN, IRWIN. 1976. "Privacy: A Conceptual Analysis." *Environment and Behavior* 18 (March): 7–29.

ARAN, GIDEON. 1976. "Parachuting." *American Journal of Sociology* 80(1):124–152.

ARNOULD, ERIC J., AND LINDA L. PRICE. 1993. "River Magic: Extraordinary Experience and the Extended Service Encounter." *Journal of Consumer Research* 20 (June): 24–45.

BAKER, R. C.; ROGER DICKINSON; AND STANLEY HOLLANDER. 1986. "Big Brother 1994: Marketing Data and the IRS." *Journal of Public Policy and Marketing* 5:227–242.

BARBIERI, SUSAN M. 1981. "Shrinks Who Work for Tips." *Chicago Tribune* (December 8): sec. 5, p. 12.

BATESON, JOHN E. G. 1985. "Perceived Control and the Service Encounter." In *The Service Encounter,* edited by John A. Czepiel, Michael R. Solomon, and Carol F. Surprenant. Lexington, MA: Lexington Books.

BAUMEISTER, ROY F. 1987. "How the Self Became a Problem: A Psychological Review of Historical Research." *Journal of Personality and Social Psychology* 52 (January): 163–176.

BEARDSLEY, ELIZABETH. 1971. "Privacy: Autonomy and Selective Disclosure." In *Nomos XIII: Privacy,* edited by J. R. Pennock and J. W. Chapman. New York: Atherton Press, 56–70.

BELK, RUSSELL W. 1984. "Cultural and Historical Differences in Concepts of Self and Their Effects on Attitudes Toward Having and Giving." In *Advances in Consumer Research,* vol. 11, edited by Thomas Kinnear. Provo, UT: Association for Consumer Research, 754–760.

BELL, G. D. 1967. "Self-Confidence and Persuasion in Car Buying." *Journal of Marketing Research* 4:46–52.

BENN, STANLEY I. 1971. "Privacy, Freedom and Respect for Persons." In *Privacy,* edited by J. Roland Pennock and John W. Chapman. New York: Atherton Press, 1–26.

BETTS, MITCH. 1984. "IRS Chief Defends Use of Mailing Lists in Matching." *ComputerWorld* 18(25) (June 18): 24.

BITNER, MARY JO. 1990. "Evaluating Service Encounters: The Effects of Physical Surroundings and Employee Responses." *Journal of Marketing* 54 (April): 69–82.

———. 1992. "Servicescapes: The Impact of Physical Surroundings on Customers and Employees." *Journal of Marketing* 56(April): 57–71.

BRISTOR, JULIA M., AND EILEEN FISCHER. 1993. "Feminist Thought: Implications for Consumer Research." *Journal of Consumer Research* 19 (March): 518–536.

BROWN, RICHARD HARVEY. 1987. "Personal Identity and Political Economy: Western Grammars of the Self in Historical Perspective." In *Current Perspectives in Social Theory,* vol. 8. Greenwich, CT: JAI Press, 123–159.

BURDICK, JOHN. 1990. "Gossip and Secrecy: Women's Articulation of Domestic Conflict in Three Religions of Urban Brazil." *Sociological Analysis* 51(2) (Summer): 153–170.

CELSI, RICHARD L.; RANDALL L. ROSE; AND THOMAS W. LEIGH. 1993. "An Exploration of High-Risk Leisure Consumption Through Skydiving." *Journal of Consumer Research* 20 (June): 1–23.

CHEAL, DAVID. 1987. "'Showing Them You Love Them': Gift Giving and the Dialectic of Intimacy." *Sociological Review* 35(1):150–169.

CHRISTENSEN, KATHLEEN. 1994. "Working at Home: Frameworks of Meaning." In *Women and the Environment,* edited by Irwin Altman and Arza Churchman. New York: Plenum, 133–165.

COHEN, ABNER. 1971. "The Politics of Ritual Secrecy." *Man* 6(3):427–429. Reprinted in John Friedl and Noel J. Chrisman, eds. *City Ways: A Selective Reader in Urban Anthropology.* New York: Thomas Y. Crowell, 298–324.

COHEN, STANLEY, AND LAURIE TAYLOR. 1976. *Escape Attempts: The Theory and Practice of Resistance to Everyday Life.* Middlesex: Penguin.

COOPER, CLARE. 1971. *The House as Symbol of Self.* Institute of Urban and Regional Development, Working Paper #120 (May).

COULTER, ROBIN, AND GERALD ZALTMAN. 1994. "Using the Zaltman Metaphor Elicitation Technique." In *Advances in Consumer Research,* vol. 21, edited by Chris T. Allen and Deborah Roedder John. Provo, UT: Association for Consumer Research, 501–507.

COWEN, E. L.; E. L. GESTEN; M. BOIKE; P. NORTON; A. B. WILSON; AND M. A. DeSTEFANO. 1979. "Hairdressers as Caregivers: A Descriptive Profile of Interpersonal Help-Giving Involvements." *American Journal of Community Psychology* 7(6):633–648.

DAVIES, EIRLYS E. 1988. "Public Intimacy: The Language of Valentines in the National Press." *Language and Communication* 8(2):95–107.

DENZIN, NORMAN K. 1970. "Symbolic Interactionism and Ethnomethodology." In *Understanding Everyday Life,* edited by J. Douglas. Chicago: Aldine.

DOANE, JERI, AND EMORY L. COWEN. 1981. "Interpersonal Help-Giving of Family Practice Lawyers." *American Journal of Community Psychology* 9(5):547–558.

DONNELLY, PAUL. 1981. "Running the Gauntlet: The Moral Order of Pornographic Movie Theatres." *Urban Life* 10(2):239–264.

DONOVAN, ROBERT, AND JOHN ROSSITER. 1982. "Store Atmosphere: An Environmental Psychology Approach." *Journal of Retailing* 58 (Spring): 34–57.

DOUGLAS, MARY, AND BARON ISHERWOOD. 1979. *The World of Goods.* New York: Basic Books.

DUBY, GEORGES; DOMINIQUE BARTHELEMY; AND CHARLES DE LA RONCIERE. 1987. "Portraits." In *A History of Private Life,* vol. 2, edited by Philippe Aries and Georges Duby. Cambridge, MA: Belknap Press of Harvard University, 33–310.

FENNELL, GERALDINE. 1986. "Extending the Thinkable: Consumer Research for Marketing Practice." In *Advances in Consumer Research,* vol. 13, edited by Richard J. Lutz. Provo, UT: Association for Consumer Research, 427–432.

FOUCAULT, MICHEL. 1979. *Discipline and Punish.* Translated by Alan Sheridan. New York: Vintage Books.

FRANCIS, DICK. 1966. *Flying Finish.* New York: Harper and Row.

FRIED, MATTHEW L., AND VICTOR J. DiFAZIO. 1974. "Territoriality and Boundary Conflicts in the Subway." *Psychiatry* 37 (February): 47–59.

FRY, VIRGINIA H.; A. ALEXANDER; AND DANIEL L. FRY. 1989. "The Stigmatized Self as Media Consumer." In *Studies in Symbolic Interaction*, vol. 10B, edited by Norman K. Denzin. Greenwich, CT: JAI Press, 339–350.

GINSBURG, GENEVIEVE DAVIS. 1990. "Hers: Life After Death." *New York Times Magazine* (December 2): 34ff.

GOFFMAN, ERVING. 1961. *Asylums.* Garden City, NY: Doubleday Anchor Press.

GOLD, GEORGE M. 1983. "True Counselors: Helping Clients Deal with Loss." *ABA [American Bar Association] Journal* 69 (February): 141.

GOODWIN, CATHY. 1991. "Privacy: Recognition of a Consumer Right." *Journal of Public Policy and Marketing* 10(1):149–166.

———. 1992. "A Conceptualization of Motives to Seek Privacy for Nondeviant Consumption." *Journal of Consumer Psychology* 1(3):261–284.

GOODWIN, CATHY, AND DWAYNE GREMLER. 1996. "Friendship Over the Counter." In *Advances in Services Marketing and Management*, vol. 5, edited by Stephen Brown, Teresa Swartz, and David Bowen. Greenwich, CT: JAI Press, 247–282.

GRANBOIS, D. H. 1968. "Improving the Study of Customer In-Store Behavior." *Journal of Marketing* 32:28–33.

GUILLAUMIN, COLETTE. 1993. "The Constructed Body." Translated by Diane Griffin Crowder. In *Reading the Social Body*, edited by Catherine B. Burroughs and Jeffrey David Ehrenreich. Iowa City: University of Iowa Press, 40–60.

HESKETT, JAMES L.; W. EARL SASSER, JR.; AND CHRISTOPHER W. L. HART. 1990. *Service Breakthroughs: Changing the Rules of the Game.* New York: Free Press.

HIRSCHMAN, ELIZABETH C. 1993. "Ideology in Consumer Research, 1980 and 1990: A Marxist and Feminist Critique." *Journal of Consumer Research* 19 (March): 537–555.

HOLBROOK, MORRIS. 1992. "Morris Fears Flying." In *Postmodern Consumer Research: The Study of Consumption as Text*, edited by Elizabeth C. Hirschman and Morris B. Holbrook. Newbury Park, CA: Sage.

HOLBROOK, MORRIS B., AND ELIZABETH C. HIRSCHMAN. 1982. "The Experiential Aspects of Consumption: Consumer Fantasies, Feelings and Fun." *Journal of Consumer Research* 9 (September): 132–140.

HUI, MICHAEL K., AND JOHN E. G. BATESON. 1991. "Perceived Control and the Effects of Crowding and Consumer Choice on the Service Experience." *Journal of Consumer Research* 18 (March): 174–184.

JACOBS, RUTH H. 1981. "Out of the Mikvah, into the Sauna: The Role of Women's Health Clubs." Working Paper #78, Wellesley College Center for Research on Women, Wellesley, MA.

JOURARD, SIDNEY M. 1966. "Some Psychological Aspects of Privacy." *Law and Contemporary Problems* 31:707–718.

KATOVICH, MICHAEL A., AND WILLIAM A. REESE II. 1987. "The Regular: Full-Time Identities and Memberships in an Urban Bar." *Journal of Contemporary Ethnography* 16 (October): 308–343.

KEYES, RALPH. 1973. *We the Lonely People: Searching for Community.* New York: Harper and Row.

KOROSEC-SERFATY, PERLA. 1984. "The Home from Attic to Cellar." *Journal of Environmental Psychology* 4:303–321.

KOTTLER, JEFFREY A. 1990. *Private Moments, Secret Selves.* Los Angeles: Jeremy P. Tarcher.

LILLY, J. R., AND BELL, R. A. 1981. "No-Tell Motel: The Management of Social Invisibility." *Urban Life* 10:179–198.

LOFLAND, LYN H. 1973. *A World of Strangers: Order and Action in Urban Public Space.* New York: Basic Books.

———. 1989. "Social Life in the Public Realm: A Review." *Journal of Contemporary Ethnography* 17(4) (January): 453–482.

LYMAN, STANFORD M., AND MARVIN B. SCOTT. 1967. "Territoriality: A Neglected Social Dimension." *Social Problems* 15:236–249.

MARANGONI, CAROL, AND WILLIAM ICKES. 1989. "Loneliness: A Theoretical Review with Implications for Measurement." *Journal of Social and Personal Relationships* 6(1):93–128.

MARKS, STEPHEN R. 1994. "Studying Workplace Intimacy: Havens at Work." In *Gender, Families and Close Relationships,* edited by Donna L. Sollie and Leigh A. Leslie. Thousand Oaks, CA: Sage, 145–168.

McCRACKEN, GRANT. 1995. *Big Hair.* New York: Viking.

McEWEN, C. A. 1980. "Continuities in the Study of Total and Nontotal Institutions." In *Annual Review of Sociology,* vol. 6, Greenwich, CT: JAI Press, 143–185.

MEHRABIAN, ALBERT. 1976. *Public Places and Private Spaces.* New York: Basic Books.

MILLS, PETER K., AND J. J. MORRIS. 1986. "Clients as 'Partial Employees' of Service Organizations: Role Development in Client Participation." *Academy of Management Review* 11(4):726–735.

MOORE, BARRINGTON, JR. 1984. *Privacy: Studies in Social and Cultural History.* Armonk, NY: M. E. Sharpe.

MUGERAUER, ROBERT. 1993. "Toward an Architectural Vocabulary: The Porch as a Between." In *Dwelling, Seeing and Designing: Toward a Phenomenological Ecology,* edited by David Seamon. Albany, NY: SUNY Press, 103–128.

MURPHY, R. F. 1964. Social Distance and the Veil. *American Anthropologist* 66:1,257–1,274.

NATHE, PATRICIA A. 1976. "Prickly Pear Coffee House: The Hangout." *Urban Life* 5(1) (April): 75–104.

OLDENBURG, RAY. 1989. *The Great Good Place.* New York: Paragon House.

OYEN, ELSE. 1982. The Social Function of Confidentiality. *Current Sociology* 2 (Summer): 1–41.

PARASURAMAN, A.; VALARIE A. ZEITHAML; AND LEONARD L. BERRY. 1985. "A Conceptual Model of Service Quality and Its Implications for Future Research." *Journal of Marketing* 49 (Fall): 41–50.

PROSHANSKY, H. M.; W. H. ITTELSON; AND L. G. RIVLIN. 1972. "Freedom of Choice in and Behavior in a Physical Setting." In *Environment and the Social Sciences: Perspectives and Applications,* edited by J. F. Wholwill and D. H. Larson. Washington, DC: American Psychological Association, 29–43.

REILLY, PATRICK M. 1996. "Street Fighters: Where Borders Group and Barnes & Noble Compete, It's a War." *The Wall Street Journal* (September 3): A1, A8.

RELPH, EDWARD. 1982. "The Landscape of the Conserver Society." In *Environmental Aesthetics: Essays in Interpretation,* edited by Barry Sadler and Allen

Carlson. Western Geographical Series, vol. 20. Victoria, BC: University of Victoria, 47–65.

RICHARDSON, LAUREL. 1988. "Secrecy and Status: The Social Construction of Forbidden Relationships." *American Sociological Review* 53(2):209–219.

RODAWAY, PAUL. 1994. *Sensuous Geographies: Body, Sense and Place.* London: Routledge.

ROOK, DENNIS W. 1984. "Targeting the 'Solo' Consumer." Paper presented at the 11th International Research Seminar in Marketing, June 13–15, Aix-en-Provence, France.

RYBCZYNSKI, WITOLD. 1986. *Home: A Short History of an Idea.* New York: Viking Penguin.

SAMDAHL, DIANE M. 1992. "Leisure in Our Lives: Exploring the Common Leisure Occasion." *Journal of Leisure Research* 24(1):19–32.

SCHNEIDER, BENJAMIN. 1980. "The Service Organization: Climate Is Crucial." *Organizational Dynamics* (Autumn): 52–65.

SCHOOLSKY, ROBERT. 1990. "Bar Associations." *Restaurant Hospitality* 74 (April): 174–176.

SUNDHOLM, C. A. 1973. "The Pornographic Arcade: Ethnographic Notes on Moral Men in Immoral Places." *Urban Life and Culture* 2:85–104.

SURPRENANT, CAROL F., AND MICHAEL R. SOLOMON. 1987. "Predictability and Personalization in the Service Encounter." *Journal of Marketing* 51 (April): 86–96.

TOCH, HANS. 1992. *Living in Prison: The Ecology of Survival.* Washington, DC: American Psychological Association.

TOLICH, MARTIN B. 1993. "Alienating and Liberating Emotions at Work: Supermarket Clerks' Performance of Customer Service." *Journal of Contemporary Ethnography* 22(3) (October): 361–381.

TOURNIER, PAUL. 1963. *Secrets.* Translated by Joe Embry. Richmond, VA: John Knox Press.

WARE, WILLIS H. 1985. *Emerging Privacy Issues.* Rand Paper Series P-7145. Santa Monica: Rand Corp.

WELLS, WILLIAM D., AND LOSCIUTO, A. 1966. "A Direct Observation of Purchasing Behavior." *Journal of Marketing Research* 6:227–233.

WERNER, TOM. 1983. "Despite Industry Outcry IRS Still Wants Lists." *ZIP/Target Marketing* 6 (November): 10, 12.

WISEMAN, JACQUELINE P. 1979. "Close Encounters of the Quasi-Primary Kind: Sociability in Urban Second-Hand Clothing Stores." *Urban Life* 8 (April): 23–51.

WOLTER, RICHARD C. 1989. "Task Force Examines Self-Regulation." *Direct Marketing* 51 (March): 104.

ZELIZER, VIVIANA. 1989. "The Social Meaning of Money: 'Special Monies.'" *American Journal of Sociology* 95:342–377.

ZIMBARDO, PHILIP G. 1969. "The Human Choice: Individuation, Reason, and Order Versus Deindividuation, Impulse and Chaos." *Nebraska Symposium on Motivation* 17:237–307.

ZURCHER, LOUIS A. 1979. "The Airline Passenger: Protection of Self in an Encapsulated Group." *Qualitative Sociology* 1 (January): 77–99.

18

BEAUTY SALON AND BARBERSHOP

Gendered Servicescapes

EILEEN FISCHER, BRENDA GAINER, AND JULIA BRISTOR

Imagine yourself moving to a new city, badly in need of a haircut upon the day of your arrival. You have no time to ask anyone where you ought to go. You wander by a few places and choose the first one that seems appropriate for you. You are greeted by the proprietor, seated in a chair, asked what kind of cut you want, and seated facing a mirror. You glance around, and although you can't be sure of the kind of cut you'll get, you already have some assurance that this is an acceptable place for you to get your hair cut.

Now ask yourself, What is it about the shop front and/or the environment inside the store that makes you feel it is appropriate for you? Or what can make you walk on by—or get up and leave after being seated—thinking that this place isn't suitable? Chances are good that at least one factor in your "try/no-try" decision is the

Eileen Fischer is Associate Professor of Marketing at York University, North York, Ontario. Brenda Gainer is Associate Professor of Marketing and Director of the Non Profit Management Program at York University. Julia Bristor is Manager of Market Research at Aire Liquide America.

assumptions you make about whether this is predominantly a men's or a women's space (or neither). What cues lead to these assumptions? Why might you not risk going to a place that primarily caters to people of the opposite sex? And what, if anything, can service providers do to make you more likely to feel at ease, regardless of your sex?

This paper explores what it is that makes servicescapes feel more (or less) gendered.[1] It also considers the implications of the gendering of servicescapes for both consumers and service providers.

We begin by tracing the roots of our research questions and then highlight the literature in which the study is grounded and the a priori assumptions that derive from this literature. We next describe the research undertaken and provide an analysis and interpretation of our findings. We conclude by drawing out the implications of our findings for both research and practice.

WHY CONSIDER GENDERED SERVICESCAPES?

Recent years have seen a steady stream of interest in the roles that sex and gender play in consumer behavior (e.g., Bartos 1989; Buss and Schaninger 1987; Costa 1994; Fischer and Arnold 1990; Gentry and Doering 1977; Kahle and Homer 1985; Schmitt, LeClerc, and Dube-Rioux 1988) and a small amount of interest in marketing issues related to the sex or gender of service customers and service providers (e.g., Burnett, Amason, and Hunt 1981). One topic that is consistent with these streams but has as yet received no direct attention concerns the ways that servicescapes may be gendered, and the impact this may have on female and male consumers.

Both reason and personal experience lead us to expect servicescapes might be gendered, by which we mean both that there

---

[1] Throughout this paper, the word *gender* will be used when referring to socialized or socially constructed phenomena, (e.g., gender roles); the word *sex* will be used when referring to biological phenomena (e.g., a person's sex).

are cues in the environment that resonate differentially with females or males and that different expectations might hold for males versus females in a given service setting. Logical reasons for expecting such gendering are numerous. First, in practice, a number of service settings are explicitly labeled as being "for men," "for women," or for both (e.g., barber shops versus beauty parlors versus unisex salons). Second, many retail service providers sell products primarily for one sex or the other (e.g., women's versus men's clothing stores). Third, at least until recently, much of the work of shopping has been regarded as "women's work" (see Bristor and Fischer 1993; Firat 1994) and many retail settings as the domain of women (Sparke 1995). Fourth, literature outside consumer research argues that many spaces—both private and public—have been and/or are gendered (e.g., Moore 1996; Rose 1989, 1993; Spain 1992). While this literature largely talks about how shared spaces are organized in a way that reflects and reinforces patriarchy, it raises our sensitivity to the possibility that the ways spaces are organized, decorated, and used may reflect both male-female distinctions and the values socially assigned to these distinctions.

Personal experience adds to our curiosity. In our lives as consumers, we have each experienced some environments in which we feel at ease and others in which we feel uncomfortable. Often, our experiences of discomfort have occurred because we perceived ourselves to be unwelcome or not respected women in "men's environments." Our male partners and colleagues have reported similar feelings of discomfort at being men in "women's environments." While some obvious factors have undoubtedly contributed to our experiences and those of our partners and colleagues, others have been less obvious and have eluded systematic identification. We believed, therefore, that investigation of this topic might lead to insights that would contribute to our theories and models concerning servicescapes. Moreover, such research might eventually benefit consumers who occasionally feel unwelcome in servicescapes they cannot avoid, as well as marketers who wish either to target women *and* men effectively or to design service settings that appeal to one versus the other.

WHAT MAKES A SERVICESCAPE?

Researchers have long argued that physical environments in which services are performed both contribute to the image of the service and influence behaviors in the service setting (e.g., Kotler 1973; Shostack 1977). Recent evidence suggests that cues in the environment influence customers' satisfaction with services (e.g., Bitner 1990). The disparate research on elements of servicescapes has given rise to at least two notable attempts to provide a conceptualization of the elements and impact of servicescapes, one from Baker (1987) and one from Bitner (1992).

Bitner's contribution, grounded in environmental psychology, focuses on the built environment, excluding the social environment. As such, her framework points to what she terms "objective physical elements," including ambient conditions (e.g., temperature, air quality, noise, music, odor); spatial layout and functionality (e.g., layout, equipment, furnishings), and signs, symbols, or artifacts (e.g., signage, personal artifacts, style of decor). The outcomes she identifies are positive and negative emotions, cognitions, and physiological responses.

Baker's typology, though earlier, is more inclusive of factors relevant for our purposes. She identifies two similar categories of elements (ambient conditions and design), as well as a third category that she labels "social." Under this heading she discusses the "human component" of the environment, which arises from both customers and service providers. She notes in particular the importance of the number of people in the setting, their appearance, and their behavior. The outcomes she notes include approach and avoidance behavior.

While Baker's work does not pay specific attention to the observed or expected sex of service providers and other customers, her focus on the human component is useful. It points out how people in the service setting may be experienced as aspects of the space that contribute to consumers' interpretations and understandings.

The research questions for our study thus derived in part from the services literature and in part from our belief that servicescapes may be gendered. We decided to look at whether the following variables contribute to differentially gendered servicescapes:

- Ambient conditions
- Spatial layout and functionality
- Signs, symbols, and artifacts
- The number, appearance, and behavior of people in the service setting

We also considered *how* each might contribute.

THE RESEARCH PROCESS

Prelude

This project began with what might be regarded as a "false start" but was in fact an instructive undertaking. Given the first reason outlined for expecting servicescapes to be gendered (i.e., that some service providers cater primarily to men or to women), we decided to focus our observations on two hair salons catering primarily to women (one for younger women and one for older women) and one barbershop catering primarily to men (of all ages). After each coauthor had made multiple visits to research sites and recorded her observations, we met to compare notes.

To our initial surprise (and puzzlement), we found very few tangible elements of the environments that were strikingly different. Despite our expectations that we would find clear, if not overwhelming, gendered contrasts, the ambient conditions, spatial layout, and functionality were far more similar than different when we compared each hair salon with the barbershop. Moreover, the differences between the two salons in terms of these elements was at least as great, if not greater, than the differences between the salons and the barbershop. We did observe more differences with respect to signs, symbols, and artifacts, but these were so superficial as to be obvious: in their waiting areas, the hair salons had magazines targeted primarily to women (e.g., women's fashion magazines), whereas the barbershop had general-interest publications (e.g., a daily newspaper); on their walls, the hair salons had far more pictures of women than of men, whereas the barbershop had only pictures of men. Areas of difference that we expected—for instance, in color schemes, simplicity, warmth, or homeyness of decor; personal nature of artifacts displayed; or degree of clutter versus tidiness— were not apparent.

In fact, one coauthor noted that in walking past an empty hair-cutting place at night, it was impossible to determine whether it was primarily for men, for women, or for both. The name of the salon was not instructive. There were no pictures on the walls to indicate the expected sex of the clientele, and the magazines discernible from outside were of general interest. This chance experience underlined for us the ambiguity with respect to gender of the objective physical elements of the space alone.

Only under the category of human elements were the observable differences readily interpretable. These differences seemed very simple and basic. As expected, the customers in the hair salons were primarily women, though cutters and colorists of both sexes were employed. The customers in the barbershop were virtually all men (with the exception of one young girl who received a trim while her father had his hair cut); the cutters in the barbershop we observed were all men. Beyond this, the similarities by far outweighed the differences. Behavioral differences that we expected— specifically in the amount and intimacy of discussions between customers and service providers, or among customers—simply were not apparent.

At this juncture, we questioned in what sense gendered spaces could be said to exist. In light of our own experiences and those of people close to us, the phenomenon seemed both real and powerful, yet we were finding little in the actual built environment that could account for our beliefs. If we were guided by Bitner's model alone, we might have been forced to conclude that gendered spaces did not exist, i.e., that there was nothing in the built space that made it gendered. One possibility is that the barbershop/beauty salon venue was an inappropriate place to look; perhaps other service settings might yield more clues as to how artifacts and other aspects of the built space "create" a gender.

Rather than pursue this possibility using the same means we had already employed (i.e., observation), we chose to adopt a strategy that would allow us to examine the following questions:

- To what extent is the perception that some servicescapes are gendered shared by consumers who frequent similar sets of service environments?

- What cues (including ambient conditions; spatial layout and functionality; signs, symbols, and artifacts; and the number, appearance, and behavior of people) in the service environment are regarded as contributing to it being gendered?

This focus necessitated an alternate method.

Method

The means we chose to explore whether and how some servicescapes are gendered was to gather and interpret open-ended responses using a projective technique. Projective techniques have been used previously in consumer research by, for instance, Rook (1985). They have also been much used in marketing research (Malhotra 1993). A projective technique was chosen because we believed people might be unable or unwilling to respond to more direct approaches such as depth interviewing or oral history taking.

We believed respondents might be unable to shed light on the subject if interviewed because, as Lorber (1994) has noted, people are largely unaware of the ways in which gender is socially constructed. Gendered signs and signals are so ubiquitous that people may fail to note them unless, by accident or design, they challenge assumptions that are taken for granted (see Lorber 1994). We thought people might be unwilling to respond to more direct approaches because they preferred not to reveal what might be regarded as personal insecurities. The artifice of the projective technique allowed us to create a verbal scenario where gender cues could be manipulated so as to challenge taken-for-granted assumptions, and where students could assign perceptions and feelings to someone other than themselves.

Accordingly, we asked masters-level students to respond to a short verbal scenario. Three sets of scenarios were created (see Table 18.1). The first set of four scenarios was designed to elicit from consumers their sense of whether particular servicescapes were gendered. To examine this, we asked for reactions to service settings that were not explicitly labeled male or female, but that seemed likely to be perceived as gendered. The second set of four scenarios was designed to probe more explicitly the elements of the servicescapes that people interpreted as contributing to any sense of being gendered. The third set explored further what elements within the environment contributed to gendering, and attempted to unearth how open to reshaping these interpretations might be.

The actual wordings of the scenarios, and the number and age ranges of respondents of both sexes, are listed in Table 18.1. Respondents were recruited from M.B.A. classes at a large northeastern university during May 1995. They were given class time to write their reactions to the scenarios and were told that their participation was completely voluntary. Each person received and responded to a single scenario. Note that there are roughly equal numbers of people responding to each scenario within and across sets, but there is not an equal number of men and women responding to most scenarios. Our goal, as previously stated, was not to compare men and women; thus, we tried only to ensure that each scenario was responded to by nearly equal numbers of people.

All responses were read and interpreted by each author. The responses to individual scenarios were first examined separately to identify key words and themes; later, responses within and across sets of scenarios were compared to help form an overall interpretation of the texts. Responses from men and women were not analyzed separately, again because the study was focused not on sex or gender differences between customers but on perceived gender differences in service settings.

TABLE 18.1

Scenario Wording	Number (Age Range) of Female Respondents	Number (Age Range) of Male Respondents
Set 1		
a. Jennifer is about to enter a garage to have her car repaired. Please write a short story about what you expect will be her experiences in this service setting. What will the place look like? Who will be there? What will they be like? What will happen? How will she feel about her experience?	3 (23–32)	3 (25–33)
b. Jennifer is about to enter a hardware store to make a purchase. Please write a short story about what you expect will be her experiences in this service setting. What will the place look like? Who will be there? What will they be like? What will happen? How will she feel about her experience?	1 (26)	3 (24–39)
c. Scott is about to enter a fabric store to make a purchase. Please write a short story about what you expect will be his experiences in this service setting. What will the place look like? Who will be there? What will they be like? What will happen? How will he feel about his experience?	2 (25–31)	3 (23–35)
d. Scott is about to attend an aerobics class. Please write a short story about what you expect will be his experiences in this service setting. What will the place look like? Who will be there? What will they be like? What will happen? How will he feel about his experience?	1 (25)	4 (24–39)

continued

TABLE 18.1 continued

Scenario Wording	Number (Age Range) of Female Respondents	Number (Age Range) of Male Respondents
Set 2		
a. Jennifer is about to enter a garage to have her car repaired. Many people consider this to be a traditionally masculine service setting. What is it that makes garages masculine? Consider decor, layout, other patrons, the service providers, and any other factors that contribute to the ambience. Be as specific as possible.	1 (26)	5 (22–32)
b. Jennifer is about to enter a hardware store to make a purchase. Many people consider this to be a traditionally masculine service setting. What is it that makes hardware stores masculine? Consider decor, layout, other patrons, the service providers, and any other factors that contribute to the ambience. Be as specific as possible.	2 (23–25)	4 (34–36)
c. Scott is about to enter a fabric store to make a purchase. Many people consider this to be a traditionally feminine service setting. What is it that makes a fabric store feminine? Consider decor, layout, other patrons, the service providers, and any other factors that contribute to the ambience. Be as specific as possible.	3 (23–31)	4 (23–37)
d. Scott is about to attend an aerobics class. Many people consider this to be a traditionally feminine service setting. What is it that makes an aerobics class feminine? Consider decor, layout, other patrons, the service providers, and any other factors that contribute to the ambience. Be as specific as possible.	0	7 (23–37)

Scenario Wording	Number (Age Range) of Female Respondents	Number (Age Range) of Male Respondents
Set 3		
a. We are designing a new hair studio. Many people consider this to be a traditionally feminine setting. However, we want to target this service to men too. How would you design this hair studio to make men feel welcome and comfortable? Consider decor, layout, other patrons, the service providers, and any other factors that contribute to the ambience. Please be as detailed and specific as possible.	10 (21–37)	13 (22–35)
b. We are designing a new auto repair facility. Many people consider this to be a traditionally masculine setting. However, we want to target this service to women too. How would you design this repair facility to make women feel welcome and comfortable? Consider decor, layout, other patrons, the service providers, and any other factors that contribute to the ambience. Please be as detailed and specific as possible.	5 (23–30)	12 (23–39)

ANALYSES AND INTERPRETATIONS

We first address the two questions presented earlier: the extent to which some servicescapes are perceived as gendered and the cues perceived as contributing to servicescapes being gendered.

To What Extent Are Servicescapes Perceived as Gendered?

Analyses of the texts that were created from all sets of scenarios suggested that many respondents did perceive the service settings about which they wrote to be gendered. Consider the following excerpt from a response to scenario 1(a), which concerns a woman entering an auto repair shop:

> I imagine Jennifer to walk into a garage where the workers are mainly male (90%+), and for the most part are all wearing overalls that are full of grease. [She may be] overwhelmed by all the male employees who seem to be leering and looking at her. She'll tell them what's basically wrong with her car and agree with everything the employee tells her, so that she can get out of there as soon as possible (Female, age 23).

In this case, it is clear not only that men are expected to be numerically dominant in the setting, but that it is anticipated the service setting will be one where a female will feel "overwhelmed."

Similar, although less intense, are the feelings one respondent expected men to have in a female-gendered service setting. For instance, in response to scenario 1(c), concerning a man entering a fabric store, a respondent wrote:

> Scott may have some trouble because it may be likely that the fabric store doesn't have many male customers. The place will be sort of disorganized with colorful bolts of cloth everywhere, some rolled up and some not. . . . He will leave feeling dissatisfied with his purchase and more confused than when he started (Female, age 25).

The respondent indicates that the setting is expected to be gendered so strongly that a man will feel out of place.

Even in cases where the imagined customer was made welcome, there is an anticipated feeling of "otherness," as is expressed in the following response to scenario 1(d), which describes a man entering an aerobics class:

> Scott will not be treated negatively, but he will be aware that he is not the "norm." [An aerobics studio] is often a fashion conscious setting and Scott will probably feel as though he is dressed "sloppily" (Female, age 25).

To put these assertions in context, we note that in response to the first set of scenarios, where the gender we thought might be associated with the environment was not explicitly mentioned, a number of respondents gave no indication that they thought the environment was associated more with one sex than the other. At the same time, however, in responses to the later two sets of scenarios, where we did indicate what gender we associated with the environment, no respondents stated that they thought the servicescape was a neutral one. On balance, the notion that a servicescape may be gendered seems to resonate with the perceptions of the informants we queried.

What Cues Contribute to the Gendering of Servicescapes?

Consistent with our own observations in the barbershops and hair salons, the responses to all sets of scenarios indicated that the most salient cue to the gender of a service environment is the observed—or anticipated—sex of customers and service providers.

In response to scenario 2(a), which asks, "What is it that makes garages masculine?" responses included having "men all around" (Male, age 29) and the fact that "garage workers/mechanics tend to be male" (Male, age 30). Likewise, we were told that what makes a hardware store masculine is that "you see mainly males going into hardware stores" (Male, age 34) in response to scenario 2(b). Similarly, in response to scenario 2(d), which asks, "What makes an aerobics class feminine?" one informant stated, "Instructors [are] predominantly female—mostly female participants" (Male, age 37), while another said, "An aerobics class is feminine primarily because most of the other patrons are female" (Male, age 23). And a respondent to scenario 2(c) stated simply, "I have never seen a man in a fabric store" (Female, age 31).

The next most prominent reason for perceiving a service setting as masculine or feminine arises from notions about who should buy/use the product (goods or services) or who is best suited to buying or using it. One respondent to scenario 2(a) suggested, that "Cars and auto repairs have traditionally been areas of interest dominated by males; high school shop classes were usually all male students" (Male, age 32). A respondent to scenario 2(b) made the similar claim that hardware stores are masculine because they "sell products specific to activities traditionally carried out by men" (Male, age 34). A respondent to scenario 2(c) asserted that what makes fabric stores feminine "is the nature of the product and not the setting/ decor/layout" (Female, age 23). Similarly, we were told, in response to scenario 2(c), that "what makes an aerobics class feminine is [that] . . . only females are concerned about their bodily fitness in terms of measurement and . . . the type of exercise is not vigorous enough for aerobics to classify as masculine" (Male, age 36).

These observations from respondents are worthy of comment for two reasons. First, they indicate that the people we studied carry well-formed expectations and/or understandings of who will be in the service settings we described and who should use the products retailed there. Given the large role played by expectations regarding services generally (see Berry, Zeithaml, and Parasuraman 1990), it is reasonable to posit that gender-specific expectations exist. This is important, since it speaks to the possibility that particular servicescapes may be perceived as gendered by consumers *prior to their having had exposure to a particular space.* While we cannot know for certain whether or not each of our respondents had been in the service setting about which they wrote, chances seem good that a portion of them had not. Yet, perhaps based on personal prior experiences in *other* settings, or perhaps based on cultural beliefs and norms about who buys or uses what products, it appears that people "construct" servicescapes in their own mind without necessarily having experienced them.

Second, as we suggest below, these expectations lead to other inferences that reinforce notions that servicescapes are gendered. For example, several respondents indicated they expected auto repair garages to be dirty and that this is part of what makes them masculine. A typical response stated, "The first thing that makes [a garage] masculine is the general decor of the place—it is usually dirty and greasy" (Male, age 22). Both garages and hardware stores were characterized by many as masculine because they were expected to look utilitarian. One informant explained what makes a hardware store masculine this way:

> There is little creativity associated with hardware aisles. Everything is placed in a logical order (nails with hammers, automotive goods near tires, etc.). Aisles are not decorated. There are few creative displays. Salespersons are uniformed in boring and old-fashioned outfits (Female, age 23).

In describing servicescapes they assumed to be frequented by women, informants made parallel inferences. For instance, a respondent to scenario 2(c) stated fabric stores are feminine because they "are usually decorated in the traditionally feminine pink, yellow, and light greens. Also use of lace is typically seen in decor" (Female, age 24). Many told us that the music playing in aerobics studios made them feminine. In response to scenario 2(d), one stated, "Music is a major factor. Dance music is usually enjoyed more by females" (Male, age 35).

Our analyses of these responses leads us to two observations. First, some of the "gendered" elements of servicescapes anticipated are unlikely to exist in fact. For instance, our own observation of fabric stores suggests they are plainly decorated and rarely feature the anticipated pastels and lace, while our observations of garages suggest that they are often both clean and tidy. We posit that informants' expectations that these environments are gendered may be prompting them to imagine they would find—or have observed—elements of the servicescape that fit with cultural gender stereotypes. It is interesting that the plainness/functionality associated with, for instance, hardware stores and the frilliness/frivolity linked to, for instance, fabric stores are resonant with the polarity between the culturally more valued "design" versus the culturally less valued "decoration" associated with masculinity versus femininity in modernity (Sparke 1995).

Second, it seems that informants may have a tendency to ascribe gendered connotations to aspects of the environment they have interpreted quite selectively. For instance, consider the level of decoration of a servicescape. In our observation, plain decor is as apt to characterize fabric stores as it is hardware stores. However, while some respondents noted that fabric stores may be plainly decorated, in no case did anyone suggest that this made them masculine (or even less feminine). Yet in a number of cases people stated the plain decor of both hardware stores and garages made them masculine. It appears that gender associations are so strong that they may lead people to interpret selectively those aspects of the servicescape that reinforce their preexisting perceptions. We posit that either informants attend differentially to aspects of the servicescape that "fit" with the gender they expect it to manifest, or they selectively interpret those aspects of the objective physical environment that they observe so as to make the experienced environment fit with preexisting notions.

To extend this discussion of what cues contribute to the gendering of a servicescape, it is useful to consider postmodern analyses of signifiers (which would include both goods and those elements of servicescapes identified by Bitner and Baker). At least some such analyses stress that signifiers have no fixed meaning and may at any given time be ascribed multiple conflicting meanings (see, for example, Featherstone 1990). Consider that the categories "male" and "female" are, in the culture being studied, as in every other, one of the primary organizing principles for domains of social life (see Ortner and Whitehead 1981). What we observe in the case of servicescapes as they are being studied here is probably that the decor signifiers take on meanings associated with gender when this primary cultural organizing principle is salient or is cued. Thus, it should not be surprising that whatever decor is anticipated or observed in a service setting is susceptible to being interpreted consistent with whatever gender is associated with that setting.

Emergent Themes: Reactions to Gendered Space

Although we did not articulate any prior expectations regarding possible reactions to gendered servicescapes, our interpretations of the responses to the scenarios yielded a number of themes that seem to offer useful insights. In fact, statements regarding reactions dominated the responses in terms of both volume and vehemence.

The conceptual literature might have led us to anticipate that reactions would be either positive/approach or negative/avoidance. Perhaps because most of our scenarios asked people to consider the case of a person entering an environment frequented by people of the other sex, most types of reactions we inferred were of a negative nature.

One theme related to negative reactions concerned feeling *alien and unwelcome*. For instance, one respondent to scenario 2(b) said this about hardware stores:

> Patrons, on average, are mostly male and often are rude to female patrons. That is, they often stare as a female walks in, as if to say "what is she doing invading this male sanctuary!" (Female, age 25).

Another, responding to scenario 2(d), described what he had actually felt in an aerobics class:

> Peer pressure often excludes men. In my experience, the other attendees of the class have not made me feel welcome. They are letting their hair down and don't want me to be there (Male, age 30).

Often such feelings of being alien and unwelcome were attributed to the anticipated behavior of other customers, as above. In other cases, the feelings were linked to anticipated behaviors of service personnel. For instance, in fabric stores, it was suggested, "The staff is geared to serve females. Often men entering on their own are given an initial funny look" (Male, age 30, scenario 2(c)). Reactions to scenario 2(a), the garage scenario, were particularly strong in this regard, as in the following example:

> Men working in garages [can be] sexist towards women—thinking they don't know anything and therefore shouldn't be in this field. [Women] may be talked down to (Female, age 26).

A number of remarks similar to the following also were made:

> Service people talk down to women, assuming they won't understand auto repair. Service people talk to men as if they understand (even though we don't) (Male, age 30).

Feelings of being alien and unwelcome also were attributed to anticipated elements of the decor in some servicescapes. A number of respondents made comments such as the following in response to scenario 2(a):

> There may well be posters of scantily clad females hung in the [auto repair] area, which is offensive to many women but not men. Men therefore "belong" there more than women. [It's] not designed to make women comfortable (Female, age 26).

A second, related, theme pointing to negative reactions concerned feelings of *confusion and mystery*. Our informants anticipated that people of both sexes would find the servicescape dominated by people of the other sex to seem disorganized and impenetrable.

Remarks that made this evident concerned apparent lack of order, or undecipherable organization, in layout. For instance, one informant responding to scenario 2(b) speculated that hardware stores are masculine because "layout is not always apparently obvious—do logical associations of men differ from women?" (Male, age 34), and another responding to the same scenario noted they had "somewhat jumbled stock, sale items known by arcane names," adding "A certain mythology is involved here, too, by the way" (Male, age 36). Similarly, regarding fabric stores, a respondent to scenario 2(c) stated:

> Men tend to be less detail oriented and therefore will not spend time searching aisles for perfect patterns/fabrics. They need the [hardware store] approach where everything is titled, explained and ticketed (Male, age 23).

Regardless of whether the respondents were given a scenario of a man in a female-gendered servicescape or of a woman in a male-gendered setting, they seemed to believe that the customer would feel him- or herself to be facing undecipherable merchandise, layout, and behavioral norms. In essence, respondents imagined that consumers entering servicescapes not usually frequented by people of their sex might find themselves confronted with an impenetrable web of socially constructed practices and meanings in which, as an interloper, they could only become entangled. The complexity of the codes and practices to which the outsider is not privy may exceed that which we, as marketers or as consumer researchers, normally assume to be operative in a service environment. And, as the next theme indicates, significant risk may be associated with blundering into this set of unknowns.

The final theme related to negative reactions concerns *fear*. Under this heading, we need to separate the fears anticipated for men in women's space from those anticipated for women in men's spaces. The fears anticipated for women are largely those of lack of information and lack of control, and are related to the confusion and mystery just noted. So, for instance, a respondent to scenario 3(b) describing how to target an auto repair facility to women made these comments:

> I know that many women are uncomfortable visiting these facilities because [they] do not have expertise in auto repair. They feel that the mechanics/service people will take advantage of this lack of knowledge, perhaps repairing things that don't need repairing or even charging them too much (Female, age 25).

To a lesser extent, there seemed to be physical fear associated with women in male-gendered servicescapes. This became apparent in that several respondents suggesting how to target women noted that repair shops would be more welcoming if they were better lit and had more windows.

The fears anticipated for men in female-gendered environments focused more on "contamination." That is, several respondents suggested directly or indirectly that men's masculinity might be threatened or contaminated if they were overexposed to feminine service settings. In response to the suggestion of a man entering an aerobics studio in scenario 1(d), one stated, "He's a little uncomfortable because some of his peers still see this as a female activity" (Male, age 29); another asserted that only homosexual men would attend.

Responses to scenario 3(a), which asked how to target a hair studio to men as well as women, signaled similar concerns. Many suggested that having female service providers would be a plus, since "many men seem to be uncomfortable with other men washing their hair" (Female, age 24), but a number insisted that men would want to be private from the female customers. A few suggested that a hair salon simply could not appeal to both men and women, as in the following comment:

> I'm afraid you couldn't [target a studio to men and women]. Any studio is associated with women (in my mind at least). I am only comfortable in barbershops. . . . Maybe if you put sports jerseys in the windows and the televisions were always tuned to a sports channel, then you might be able to attract men. But I think you would have zero client"elle" [sic] (Male, 22).

Several respondents, like the one just quoted, hint that any ambiguity about the gender of a space renders it uncomfortable for men who are concerned about signals concerning their sexuality. Not only spaces that are frequented by females, but those that are suspected of being frequented by homosexual men, are "dangerous" and appear to inspire fears in some respondents.

In response to this variety of negative reactions, informants suggested a customer would either avoid the service setting altogether or leave it as quickly as possible. Many also indicated that the overall assessment of the service was destined to be unsatisfactory.

In summary, gendered servicescapes seem to be socially constructed rather than physically constructed, but are nevertheless very real to consumers. Our study suggests that gendered servicescapes arise from customers' expectations of the environment, and these expectations are shaped by broader cultural norms and stereotypes. Cues—expected *or* observed—in the environment are interpreted in light of the gender of the consumer (and, in some cases, the service provider) associated with the goods or services being offered.

LIMITATIONS AND DIRECTIONS FOR FUTURE RESEARCH

Our study, inevitably, has many limitations and points toward some potential avenues for future research. With respect to limitations, we must note that some of our observations and inferences may hold only for imagined or anticipated encounters with service settings and may be less relevant in actual encounters with servicescapes, where a host of other cues can come into play to reinforce or undermine associations with gender. A further limitation is that the scenarios we developed were restricted to servicescapes we had reason to suspect might be gendered. We cannot know whether they apply to other servicescapes we did not study. Our study used only one method of data collection and did not allow for detailed probing of some of the more interesting findings.

Obviously, a fuller and more systematic investigation of the nature and implications of expectations regarding gender in particular service settings would be useful. On-site interviews, and possibly a participant observation study informed by some of the insights we have formed here, would provide greater depth than the current study has afforded.

Some of our findings point to specific issues that deserve to be explored in future research. For instance, the finding that some respondents expected certain service environments to be distinctly uncomfortable places for some customers suggests that more work could be done on understanding factors (including, but not limited to, gendered expectations) that contribute to such anticipated discomfort. Further, although our focus here was not male/female differences per se, but rather the gendering of built space, our study does indicate that future research might fruitfully explore socialized male/female differences in, for instance, service-setting ideals.

Another question of interest is whether certain servicescapes are uniformly perceived as gendered while others are sometimes, often, or usually devoid of gender-related expectations. It seems likely that the servicescapes most susceptible to gendering are those that feature merchandise or artifacts that are used exclusively or primarily by persons of one sex. But it is possible that servicescapes that are more consciously "decorated" versus those that are less so are also more susceptible to gendering—probably feminine gendering—because of the association between femininity and decorating (see Sparks 1995). Other dimensions might also be identifiable and subject to inquiry. Future research could also address the circumstances under which the sex of other consumers is the most salient cue versus those under which the sex of service providers is most critical. Another question is whether there may be segments among men and among women who are more sensitive than others to the gendering of servicescapes. One such segmentation basis may be the generation of the consumer. If socially constructed gender divisions are blurring, as some believe (cf. Lorber 1994), consumers born more recently may differ from those born longer ago in what they expect and how they perceive what they encounter in service settings.

MANAGERIAL IMPLICATIONS

Our study, limitations notwithstanding, does raise some implications for managers. The following discussion addresses three major groups of these implications.

Do Managers Know
What Customers "Know"?

It is doubtful that many contemporary retailers have purposely designed spaces that are meant to alienate or even intimidate people of one sex, even if their primary target market is people of the other sex. Yet our study suggests customers may "know" some service environments are not "women-friendly" and others are not "men-friendly." Gendered associations linked to the servicescape appear likely to affect how consumers feel before, during, and after their service encounters. Customers may anticipate with dread entering an environment they feel is inappropriate for someone of their sex; once in the environment, they may very well interpret elements of the servicescape as reinforcing their prior beliefs.

These expectations, however formed, might come as a surprise to some managers, and as a frustration to those who believe they are serving customers of both sexes equally effectively. One simple implication of this study, then, is that service-setting owners and operators may want to learn two things: (1) whether their current customers of one sex or the other are in any way intimidated by the service environment; and (2) whether customers of one sex are routinely patronizing *other* service providers in part because of ungrounded expectations that they will be less than welcome in a particular setting.

How Can Consumer (Mis)Apprehensions Be Addressed?

Managers seeking to signal to customers of either sex—or of both sexes—that they are welcome and will be comfortable in a given service setting must recognize that they may face a significant challenge. Customers' socially acquired expectations may operate in a given service setting regardless of how that particular servicescape is designed and peopled.

If any one feature of the servicescape is going to challenge customers' prior expectations and put them at ease, it seems likely to be disconfirmation of expectations that they are the only one of their sex in the environment (e.g., men are more likely to feel at ease in an aerobics class if there are other men present). However, even this may not allay feelings of alienation, confusion, and fear if gendered associations with the product being sold or serviced are overwhelming (e.g., cars are so male-gendered that it may be extremely difficult to put women at ease in auto repair shops or car salesrooms, regardless of the number of other women there).

Developing communications that directly confront gendered stereotypes may be one option for managers. For example, recent ad campaigns for Saturn automobiles have sketched the story of a woman who was condescended to by men selling other cars but treated with respect by those selling Saturns; in the end, she herself becomes a salesperson for this type of car. This ad series explicitly acknowledges the expectations many women have in the auto industry, and tries to undermine them at least insofar as Saturn dealerships are concerned.

Opportunities for Targeting and Positioning

Some service providers might wish to work with the status quo of people's expectations regarding which sex "should" shop or be served in which settings. Managers in service industries where some customers have a discernible preference for segregation by sex could design service settings targeted only to one sex or the other (assuming sufficiently large groups would welcome such an approach). For instance, high-quality haircutting services targeted at men could be attractive to a significant number of males, though McCracken's (1995) observation that men are reluctant to admit their involvement in the hair care category may prove an obstacle. The positioning for such settings would stress not that one sex or the other is unwelcome, but rather that, in the service environment designed for them, the targeted sex will be made to feel comfortable, their distinct preferences will be understood, their distinct tastes reflected.

Alternatively, as with the Saturn example, some service providers may stand to benefit by positioning themselves as the provider that will make people of both sexes feel comfortable despite stereotypes to the contrary. It must be said, however, that the deep-rooted and pervasive effect of prior expectations derived from social stereotypes is not likely to be undone quickly or permanently by the actions of a single marketer. Customers "know what they know," and encouraging them to believe that certain servicescapes are equally friendly for people of both sexes will take time and effort. Customers may be quite dubious about the truthfulness of claims such as those suggested in the Saturn campaign. Achieving a "gender-neutral" servicescape in which all feel welcome may require undermining a host of entrenched cultural notions.

BIBLIOGRAPHY

BAKER, JULIE. 1987. "The Role of the Environment in Marketing Services: The Consumer Perspective." In *The Service Challenge: Integrating for Competitive Advantage,* edited by John Czepiel, Carole Congram, and James Shanahan. Chicago: American Marketing Association.

BARTOS, RENA. 1989. *Marketing to Women Around the World.* Boston: Harvard Business School Press.

BERRY, LEONARD; VALARIE ZEITHAML; AND A. PARASURAMAN. 1990. "Five Imperatives for Improving Service Quality." *Sloan Management Review* 29 (Summer): 29–38.

BITNER, MARY JO. 1990. "Evaluating Service Encounters: The Effects of Physical Surrounding and Employee Responses." *Journal of Marketing* 54 (April): 69–82.

———. 1992. "Servicescapes: The Impact of Physical Surroundings on Customers and Employees." *Journal of Marketing* 56 (April): 57–71.

BURNETT, JOHN; ROBERT AMASON; AND SHELBY HUNT. 1981. "Feminism: Implications for Department Store Strategy and Sales Clerk Behavior." *Journal of Retailing* 57(4):71–85.

BUSS, W. CHRISTIAN, AND CHARLES M. SCHANINGER. 1987. "An Overview of Dyadic Family Behavior and Sex Roles Research: A Summary of Findings and an Agenda for Future Research." In *Review of Marketing,* edited by Michael Houston. Chicago: American Marketing Association, 293–324.

COSTA, JANEEN ARNOLD. 1994. *Gender Issues and Consumer Behavior.* Thousand Oaks, CA: Sage.

FEATHERSTONE, MIKE. 1990. *Consumer Culture and Postmodernism.* London: Sage.

FIRAT, A. FUAT. 1994. "Gender and Consumption: Transcending the Feminine." In *Gender Issues and Consumer Behavior,* edited by Janeen Arnold Costa. Thousand Oaks, CA: Sage, 205–228.

FISCHER, EILEEN, AND STEPHEN ARNOLD. 1990. "More than a Labor of Love: Gender Roles and Christmas Gift Shopping." *Journal of Consumer Research* 17 (December): 333–345.

GENTRY, JAMES, AND MILDRED DOERING. 1977. "Masculinity-Femininity Related to Consumer Choice." In *Advances in Consumer Research,* vol. 5, edited by Keith Hunt. Ann Arbor, MI: Association for Consumer Research, 423–437.

KAHLE, LYNN, AND PAMELA HOMER. 1985. "Androgyny and Midday Mastication: Do Real Men Eat Quiche?" In *Advances in Consumer Research,* vol. 12, edited by Elizabeth Hirschman and Morris Holbrook. Ann Arbor, MI: Association for Consumer Research, 242–246.

KOTLER, PHILIP. 1973. "Atmospherics as a Marketing Tool." *Journal of Retailing* 49(4):48–64.

LORBER, JUDITH. 1994. *Paradoxes of Gender.* New Haven: Yale University Press.

MALHOTRA, NARESH. 1993. *Marketing Research: An Applied Orientation.* Englewood Cliffs, NJ: Prentice Hall.

McCRACKEN, GRANT. 1995. *Big Hair: A Journey into the Transformation of Self.* Toronto: Penguin.

MOORE, HENRIETTA. 1996. *Space, Text and Gender: An Anthropological Study of the Marakwet in Kenya.* New York: Guilford Press.

ORTNER, S., AND H. WHITEHEAD. 1981. *Sexual Meanings: The Cultural Construction of Gender and Sexuality.* Cambridge: Cambridge University Press.

ROOK, DENNIS. 1985. "The Ritual Dimension of Consumer Behavior." *Journal of Consumer Research* 12 (December): 251–264.

ROSE, G. 1993. *Feminism and Geography: The Limits of Geographic Knowledge.* Cambridge: Polity Press.

SCHMITT, BERND; FRANCE LeCLERC; AND LAURETTE DUBE-RIOUX. 1988. "Sex Typing and Gender Schema Theory." *Journal of Consumer Research* 15 (June): 122–128.

SHOSTACK, G. LYNN. 1977. "Breaking Free from Product Marketing." *Journal of Marketing* 41 (April): 73–80.

SPAIN, DAPHNE. 1992. *Gendered Spaces.* Chapel Hill, NC: University of North Carolina Press.

SPARKE, PENNY. 1995. *As Long as It's Pink: The Sexual Politics of Taste.* San Francisco, CA: Pandora.

19

SOCIAL INEQUALITY AND THE CONTEXT OF CONSUMPTION
Local Groceries and Downtown Stores

ELIZABETH CHIN

Natalia and Tionna, a pair of ten-year-old African-American girls, have entered Claire's, an inexpensive accessory and jewelry store on the second floor of the downtown mall in New Haven, Connecticut. It is early December, and the girls are wearing their winter coats unzipped and sagging backward halfway down their arms, the better to ventilate their overheating bodies. They wander throughout the store for more than twenty minutes, touching everything, it seems. They pull earrings off display racks to look at them; they paw through bins of sale items—flattened hair bows, bent hoop earrings,

Elizabeth Chin is Assistant Professor of Anthropology at Occidental College, Los Angeles, California.

This research was supported by fellowships from the Wenner-Gren Foundation for Anthropological Research; the National Science Foundation, grant number DBS-9209313; and the Kenneth B. and Mamie Phipps Clark Fellowship from the City University of New York Graduate Center. Insightful comments and suggestions for improvement have come from Eric Arnould, Robert Gardener, John Sherry, Monique Taylor, Mary Weismantel, and an anonymous reviewer. I have remained, in some cases, obstinate or obtuse in response to those comments, but where I have not, this work has improved immeasurably. As ever, my greatest acknowledgment is to the children and families of Newhallville.

scratched bracelets—holding them up for inspection and at times trying them on. They come upon a section of earrings, necklaces, and rings that are adorned with the distinctive squat bodies, squashy faces, and fluffy hair of Troll Dolls. "They are going too far with that mess now," Natalia remarks, moving on to a display of key chains. Pulling one off the rack, she reads the message printed on the decorative tag in a ringing voice: "If it weren't for boys, I'd quit school." A moment later she remarks, at an equal volume, "That white lady's following us around." She is referring to one of the store's salesclerks, who is indeed keeping a close eye on the girls. Though the clerk has undoubtably heard this last remark, she registers no response.

Natalia and Tionna live in a predominantly black neighborhood in New Haven known as Newhallville. While they visit downtown shops like Claire's only infrequently, neighborhood groceries are an almost daily pit stop. In contrast to the long visits, loud discussion, and sometimes frenetic behavior typical of these girls' visits to Claire's downtown, their visits to these small groceries are remarkably quiet and directed. When Natalia and Tionna bustle into Bob's Market one summer afternoon, accompanied by Natalia's cousin Asia, they settle down after a step or two inside the store, speaking to each other quietly. They do not handle the merchandise, most of which is not interesting to them in any case. After scanning the cooler for drinks and considering the large packages of cookies at the back of the store, they decide to buy candy and gum, which Bob keeps in a glass case behind which he is stationed. The girls come up to the counter in a bunch. "Can I have a Twix bar?" Tionna asks. "I want Juicy Fruit," says Natalia. "A glazed doughnut," Asia adds. The girls dig into the deep pockets of their oversized jeans and pull out bills and warm coins. Bob dispenses candy, picks up the money, and counts out change, all the while holding a conversation with another customer. Throughout, Bob has kept as much of an eagle eye on the girls as did the "white lady" at Claire's, but this attention does not elicit comments—or discomfort—from them, either inside the store or later.

This chapter ethnographically examines the differences between Bob's and Claire's in order to analyze the consumer experience of a group of African-American ten-year-olds in the neighborhood and downtown. Children's experiences in and understanding of these two consumer sites are entwined in multiple ways, not only with children's consumer activities, but also with their identity and experience as social beings. Race, gender, class, and age are forms of social inequality that represent significant dimensions of consumer experience and opportunity. The forms of social inequality that come to bear upon children in different consumption sites are a primary factor in shaping their experience of and understanding those places; in that process, children also build apprehensions of themselves and the society in which they live. For the Newhallville girls who are the main subjects of this paper, being black, young, female, and poor is an experience that is at once widely various and fundamentally similar in Claire's and Bob's. This variety of experience not only is the result of the obvious differences in the stores' merchandise and geographic locations, but also arises from the ways in which these stores, their merchandise, and personnel are enmeshed in the understanding, maintenance, and resistance of social inequality.

The effects and impact of social inequality are central to the ways in which Claire's and Bob's exist as servicescapes for Newhallville children and other children like them. The stores themselves do not create these inequalities, or experiences thereof, in a vacuum; Bob's and Claire's are not worlds unto themselves, whose borders end with the square footage identified in the lease or deed. In New Haven, state and local policies are profoundly implicated in the formation and maintenance of an urban landscape characterized by various forms of social inequality, especially along lines of race, labor, and economy. Thus, the city and state are also servicescapes themselves; housing and residential policies, taxation, employment, and education opportunity shape urban geography and social experience, including those taking place in and with relation to Bob's and Claire's.

CONSUMPTION AND SOCIAL INEQUALITY

Inequality as a part of consumption has been addressed primarily in terms of "disadvantaged consumers" and "ghetto consumers" (Andreasen 1970, 1975, 1976, 1986, Cady 1976). These studies have admirably documented the economic conditions and commercial limitations often found in urban areas with populations that are typically minority and poor. These areas are characterized by high prices, low quality of merchandise, and small amount of variety or choice in products or brands. Faced with these conditions, consumers living near or below the poverty line often find themselves having to choose whether to pay utilities or rent, for example, stealing from Peter to pay Paul to meet even their basic needs (Jeffers 1967).

The role of social inequality in shaping consumer opportunity is a fundamental underlying concept in the work on disadvantaged and ghetto consumers. However, consumption has not often been examined as being itself a medium through which social inequality is engendered; ethnographic studies directly addressing these issues have been few (Hill 1990; Honeycutt 1975; Nightingale 1993). This paper aims to build on previous work by considering not only the internal workings of the neighborhood, but also what happens as neighborhood residents venture beyond local boundaries to shop, in this case going to the local downtown mall. This focus on consumers as they move between servicescapes—within the larger servicescape of the city itself—can illuminate the larger complexities of consumption faced by those who are constrained not only in the neighborhoods where they live, but in the stores and spaces that are most often interpreted as providing consumers with new freedoms. In joining recent and ongoing theoretical and methodological perspectives in anthropology with social geography, this study formulates an ethnographic understanding of the political economy of consumption, social inequality, and their impact on individual lives.

New work in social geography has examined the social, political, and economic processes involved in the production and maintenance of spaces such as malls, housing developments, and parks (Jackson and Thrift 1995; Miller 1995; Sherry 1995). From this perspective, places like Bob's and Claire's are not "just there," but instead represent the coming together of social, economic, and political processes. It is these same processes that have in recent history given rise to the notion that urban neighborhoods with minority populations constitute the "inner city," a new sort of urban space characterized by a range of social and economic woes. Similarly, and concurrently, malls have become the emerging and dominant form of civic space, replacing the public and accessible (if mythological) "main street" or public square with spaces that are privately owned, developed, and monitored (see essays in Sorkin 1992). Malls and urban minority neighborhoods are joined at the hip, so to speak. Urban planning and redevelopment, federal funding, residential segregation, and changing employment and production vistas are among the factors that have led to Newhallville's ghettoization as well as to the rehabilitation of New Haven's downtown. By the same token, these larger processes are at work in Bob's enduring presence on the corner of Highland and Winchester and Claire's opening up next to Lane Bryant in the Chapel Square Mall.

THE RESEARCH

Part of a larger study on the role of consumption in the lives of poor and working-class minority children (Chin 1996), the data for this chapter were gathered during a two-year period from September 1991 to August 1993. My discussion centers around a core group of 25 children from 22 households. One child in each of 20 families was a member of a fifth-grade class, which I observed and with which I participated intensively for an academic year. (The children in the 2 additional families were good friends of children from the main study group.) My research was concerned primarily with the 20 fifth-grade children (a number of whom I met when they were in fourth grade), but as I came to know families more intimately, I got to know these children's siblings as well, and over 50 children were included in these households altogether.

Eleven of the 22 households, or half the study group, depend on public assistance as their primary source of income; the remainder of heads of household are pink- and blue-collar workers, typically holding union jobs or, if retired, receiving union pensions. One family is quite well off, with a combined income of $90,000. This is the only family where both parents have college degrees. Eleven families own one car, and 2 families own two cars (I do not have this information for 3 households). Even when taking individual complexities into account, the majority of families discussed here are poor or working class. Most live from paycheck to paycheck, and homeowners seem to be hardly better off than families who rent. These families are typical of Newhallville in general. Like most families, their households are intergenerational, heads of household must make do with too many expenses and tight funds, and caretakers worry about the children's well-being in school and in the neighborhood.

The primary methodology was participant observation, undertaken in a variety of settings and placing me in several roles in the Newhallville community. These included teaching in an after-school program (conducting a project in which kids learned to do anthropology and completed an ethnographic project); volunteering in these children's fifth-grade classroom; and tagging along behind children as they shopped independently downtown, sat on stoops, or wandered through the neighborhood. I engaged with their families as well, accompanying them on shopping trips for groceries and clothes, watching television, eating meals, and going to church. Other methods included conducting inventories of children's possessions; taking children on shopping trips; and conducting formal and informal interviews with children, parents, teachers, police, community activists, and city officials.

The breadth of my focus, combined with a long period of field research, allows a perspective impossible to attain in research projects with more narrow goals. The reverse is also true; this study can make few claims in the area of statistical reliability. The material discussed here, though dealing directly with mall stores and local groceries and children's experiences in and in relation to these places, is interpreted in the context of what Malinowski (1922) has called "the imponderabilia of daily life." It is through this engagement with daily life that ethnographers learn the small, and at times apparently insignificant, snippets of information that later prove to be central in allowing them to interpret, understand, and examine a given culture.

THE FIELD SITE: CITY AS SERVICESCAPE

Located eighty miles northeast of New York City on the shore of Long Island Sound, New Haven is a medium-sized city of about

130,000. It is the seventh poorest city of its size in the United States (U.S. Bureau of the Census 1980); for cities over 100,000, New Haven ranks first in the nation in infant mortality (Reguero and Crane 1994).[1] The city also possesses a hefty illegal drug trade, a bankrupt shopping mall, a struggling downtown area, and deeply troubled public schools. Once a bustling manufacturing-based town producing guns and other munitions, tires, beer, paper, caskets, apparel, and bagels, New Haven has seen its population shrink by over 20,000 since its peak economic activity in the 1950s. Today the primary employment sector is dominated by local hospitals, educational institutions such as Yale University, and retail stores, utilities, and restaurants (New Haven Downtown Council 1992). New Haven, then, can be considered a sort of regional servicescape, providing medical, educational, and commercial services not only for city residents, but for much of the state and the nation as well.

With a reputation as one of the poorest and most problem-ridden areas of the city, Newhallville and its residents are isolated from the rest of New Haven geographically, socially, economically, and commercially. Newhallville has a minority population of 91.7 percent; 26.6 percent of Newhallville residents live in poverty, as do half of all children aged 5 years and under (U.S. Department of Commerce 1993). This residential and socioeconomic segregation is hardly the result of such processes as individual preference; rather, it can be seen as the not wholly surprising outcome of programmatic urban restructuring undertaken by successive New Haven political administrations and city agencies.

The history of urban redevelopment in New Haven provides one example of how, as a servicescape, the city appears to be less and less amenable to its minority population. Residential segregation, already well under way in the first half of this century, was given

---

[1] In New Haven there are 18.5 infant deaths per 1,000 live births. Some argue the infant mortality rate in the city is inflated because Yale–New Haven Hospital has one of the nation's premier neonatal units, and thus a higher concentration than normal of women with high-risk pregnancies and seriously ill infants. However, one New Haven neighborhood had an infant mortality rate almost three times higher than that of the city as a whole, with 66.7 deaths per 1,000 live births (Reguero 1994), among the highest rates in the world.

a big boost in the years during which New Haven emerged as the nation's "model city" in the Great Society years and during the War on Poverty. From the late 1950s to the early 1970s, over half a billion federal dollars funded urban redevelopment projects to improve economic and living conditions in New Haven. These projects had a debilitating impact on the black community, eventually displacing almost 40 percent the city's African-Americans from frame homes into housing projects, from ethnically diverse neighborhoods into racially homogeneous areas (Minerbrook 1992). Thus, the social isolation of neighborhoods such as Newhallville may be seen as being primarily a product of urban redevelopment, not of social factors internal to the Newhallville community.[2]

The fortunes of Newhallville and its residents have depended largely on those of the Winchester Repeating Arms plant. It employed 12,000 during the war years, by the late 1970s that number was only about 1,400 (City of New Haven 1982). Only 475 people worked at Winchester in 1992. During the past several years, the city has been engaged in transforming the former site of the Winchester plant into an industrial park, called Science Park. This success has been tentative at best (City of New Haven Blue Ribbon Commission 1990); currently the facility is unfinished and only partly occupied. In an ironic twist, one of the most visible occupants of Science Park is the New Haven Family Alliance, a nonprofit organization devoted to helping dysfunctional families and troubled youth. Neighborhood residents must ask security guards for permission to enter the former site of their (or their parents') employment in order to visit an organization whose purpose is to help families deal with stress and behaviors related to their poverty and underemployment.

The site of the Winchester plant powerfully embodies the changing nature of New Haven as servicescape in the experience of Newhallville residents. Redevelopment has not only shut them out,

---

[2] Recent city attempts to rectify this situation have met with sometimes violent response from other city residents. When the city notified one neighborhood that it intended to use some properties to house Section 8 families, the houses were burned to the ground.

except as the recipients of social services related to dysfunction, but the gated and guarded borders are also a reminder that they are to some extent shut in as well. One Newhallville resident, a youth of about 18 years, had a deeply apocalyptic view of the New Haven servicescape, and described in great detail a plan—supposedly a secret pact between Yale University and the city administration— to cut off electricity, water, and food delivery to black neighborhoods should race riots ever occur. As he said, "They'll starve us out." Whether or not such a plan exists is to some degree irrelevant in the face of the widely held belief that such a plan has, indeed, been laid. It is these deep-seated tensions that provide the backdrop for Newhallville children's consumer experiences both within the neighborhood and in the downtown shopping mall.

LOCAL GROCERIES

When I asked kids where they spent their money in the neighborhood, they'd answer, "B and K," or "Bob's," or "Moody's," the main small groceries in the area. But when I asked them what they did there, much in the same way that they often refused to talk about school because it was a "boring" topic of conversation or because "we didn't do anything," Newhallville kids rarely waxed poetic on the subject of Bob's. Their silence was, in fact, significant and shows to what degree Bob's is part of their daily and hence unremarkable landscape. In contrast, kids could at almost any moment, it seemed, launch into vivid descriptions—real or imaginary—of downtown shops and shopping.

Bob's store has two aisles and a refrigerator case, and Bob also sells cold cuts and subs, which he makes fresh and to order; there is a grill for making hot items like steak-and-cheese sandwiches and Jamaican beef patties. There is only one brand of nearly every item: Heinz mustard, Morton salt, Domino sugar, Ragú spaghetti sauce. Much of the shelf space is half filled or simply empty. Bob rules over his small store with a stern, paternalistic benevolence, and while dispensing advice about purchases, life, education, and love, makes his strict standards for hard work and upright living no secret. While some shopkeepers may occasionally extend credit to customers, letting children who are known to them repay small sums (fifty cents or a dollar) if they are short one day, Bob does not. He does not disdain the food stamps that many of his customers pay him with, but neither does he bend any of the rules—allowing them to make small purchases with stamps worth ten or twenty dollars in order to get cash change in return, for instance.

Bob is often caught between his roles as social network member and entrepreneur. There are two video game machines at the front of the store. The machines bring in about $300 a week; he gets half. Bob told me that he feels he is doing something to keep kids busy and off the street by having the games there. In the next breath he compared playing these games to having a dope habit. He is not so dedicated to the profit he receives, however, that he is willing to jeopardize his standing in the community. When one boy was stealing money from his mother's purse to come down to Bob's store to play the games, she called Bob and told him to refuse to let her son near the machines.

Storekeepers like Bob have a great deal at stake in maintaining the goodwill of residents, and up to a point, commercial imperatives can often take second place to community imperatives. As a result, children can expect Bob's to be if not quite a home away from home, a place that is in many respects homelike. Children can use the phone to call home, and caretakers call the store to see if their children are there. Bob is often asked to keep an eye out for certain kids and to tell them to go home when he spots them. Continuing a tradition that many say was once the norm in Newhallville and the southern communities from which many of its older residents come, Bob, like many storekeepers, takes a personal interest in neighborhood children. Often, this interest takes the shape of his giving kids assistance on purchases, particularly if they have been sent there on an errand and cannot quite remember what they were supposed to buy. The following story is from my field notes:

> A girl came into the store, having been sent to buy batteries. Bob asked her, "What size?" She didn't know, and so Bob let her

come behind the counter to use the phone to call home. On the phone for a minute or two, uttering half-finished sentences that were being both misunderstood and interrupted at the other end, the girl used her most reasonable voice, saying, "Mom, will you *please* let me speak to Duane?" She repeated this entreaty several times. Meanwhile, Bob was both tending to other customers and directing a steady stream of advice and interrogation to the girl behind him. "What size do you need? Double A? Let me talk to your mother!" "Mom, put Duane on the phone, *please!*" "What size do you need?" "Mom!" Finally, Duane got onto the other end of the line, and told the girl to get double-A batteries.

At $2.95 for a package of two, they were very expensive; Toys "Я" Us sells a pack of four for $3.99. Toys "Я" Us, however, can only be reached from the highway and is in the next town.

Kids can expect Bob to treat them not with the stylized deference that is characteristic of customer service interactions downtown, but with a no-nonsense familiarity they see plenty of at home. This allows certain prickly aspects of Bob's enterprise to be submerged in everyone's experience; for instance, the fact he lives in a significantly more upscale neighborhood about half a mile away is rarely discussed. Because children's relationships to Bob are shaped most overtly along lines of generation and race, he often appears like an irascible grandparent. Children are not necessarily fans of such treatment, but they surely are used to it and find it unremarkable. It is a relationship that in the context of the general social scene in New Haven, where racial lines are often starkly drawn and maintained, makes Bob an "us," rather than a "them."

The store's doorjamb and a post stationed at the middle of one of the aisles serve as community bulletin boards. A notice taped to the post at eye level reads, "Three bedroom apartment for rent, section eight accepted." Other announcements include a flyer for a talent show and a photocopy of a photocopy of a letter warning about new types of racism. Children are well aware of Bob's views on everything from a good tomato to gospel singing, and are well aware also that they may become the objects of his opinionated banter. It is a stream of opinion with which children are intimately familiar, if, like Bob, their grandparents came up from the southern states in the 1940s and 1950s. I recorded the following conversation between Bob and an elderly woman resident in my field notes:

> They get on the subject of kids, and how they don't have any manners today. The woman says, "Today when I ask a little boy, 'Do you want to go to the store for me?' well, it used to be, 'Do you have a quarter?' Now it's a dollar!" "Inflation?!" I say. "Kids today just don't have any manners," they reply.
>
> "You got to talk to that baby, even when it's in your stomach," says the woman. "Then they know that voice. And then when the baby's born, you got to hold it and kiss it and let them know: 'Mommy loves you.' Then that baby could be, like in the back of the store here, and nobody can get it to quiet down, but the mommy says, 'What's that?' and the baby is quiet because it knows that voice. I used to spank that baby even in my stomach," and she demonstrates by patting her middle vigorously. It doesn't look like a spank to me at all.
>
> "I was born depressed," Bob says, "Because I was born in a depressing time, 1936. We weren't getting nothing to eat!"
>
> "But the babies, they still eat the same," the woman interjects.
>
> "Not me; my mother couldn't nurse me," Bob answers. "She was nursing the baby of the people who owned the plantation, and she didn't have enough for both of us, so I got left out!"
>
> "That's right, and up in that house, your mother probably got so angry, she spit in their food, too," the woman says.
>
> "She made all their food," Bob goes on. "That's what she did."

Stores like Bob's remain on the whole free from the class and race tensions that characterize Newhallville children's relationships with stores outside the neighborhood. Rather, they are places to discuss and air these tensions, to recount stories that illustrate the ways in which the boundaries of race and class, in particular, are erected and maintained in shops outside the neighborhood. Kids do not enter Bob's on the defensive, expecting him to single them out because they are black or because they do not have money. Rather, they can expect to enter into an atmosphere that speaks of and to the experience of being black in America, whether to see a notice about racism taped to a post or to hear a story about conflict between plantation owners and black household servants. Though Newhallville children are reminded of "their place" by Bob as he asserts his right to monitor and control their behavior, he exercises that right from a position understood by both children and their parents to be located within the community.

Places like Bob's, all of which are black owned and operated, are not generally regarded by older residents as contributing to the area's downslide, though limited stock and high prices for food staples, household supplies, and tobacco constitute serious shortcomings from the adult consumers' point of view. These issues are much less problematic for children who, when making purchases for themselves, primarily buy snacks and drinks. Not only are these items inexpensive, each costing less than a dollar, but their prices throughout the city are fairly consistent. In contrast, at the time of my research, cigarettes cost $1.20 downtown and $1.60 in Newhallville.

Bob's, like other local markets, is strategically located within a couple of blocks of the neighborhood elementary and junior high schools, and nearly all neighborhood children walk to school. Kids stop in to buy candy, chips, and drinks both on their way to school in the morning and when returning home in the afternoon. Accessibility to kids is a centrally important aspect of these stores as servicescapes for urban minority children. My research has shown that children are not often included in the shopping excursions of their caretakers, whether to the supermarket or further afield; even back-to-school clothes-shopping trips rarely include the children (often teenagers) for whom the clothes are being bought. Bob's is the store that children visit most often and with which they have the most familiarity. Children as young as five or six, if they live within a couple of blocks, may go there alone during the day on errands or to buy something for themselves. Certainly, by the time children are ten years old, they go to local stores at least once or twice a week, if not every day.

It might appear at first that Bob's is a magnet for children because he stocks the candy, chips, and drinks they buy so often.

However, many local businesses, such as barbershops, also sell candy and drinks. In addition, at other locations throughout the neighborhood, people sell commercially produced or homemade treats from their homes, dispensing ice cream and candy from their back doors or out their kitchen windows. What makes Bob's different from local barbers or kitchen-window ice-cream shops is that Bob's is a public meeting place for children or can be a group destination for kids. And yet, one of the striking things about children's visits to Bob's is their brevity; Bob does not allow kids to linger either inside the store or on the sidewalk outside. It might seem that Bob's tactics would discourage youthful patrons, rather than encouraging them to make their purchases in his store. Yet it is Bob's vigilance in preventing people from hanging out around his store that is an important factor in attracting younger children.

In comparison to other local markets, which are similarly stocked and laid out, Bob's differs most dramatically in the atmosphere right outside the door. The sidewalks in front of two other local groceries in Newhallville are thronged daily by kids of junior high and high school age, whether school is in session or not. Younger children know that when they go to Bob's they will not have to navigate through a clump of "big kids" who might tease or intimidate them. These corners have a reputation for being filled with kids who are involved in the illegal drug trade at one level or another; one of these spots is a fairly well known drug pickup spot for those driving in from the suburbs to make purchases. The presence of older kids and teenagers, especially when there is actual or potential drug trade in evidence, is threatening for younger children on a number of fronts. The threat for younger children is real. Tarelle, who lives across the street from one such corner, told me of being offered money by older teenagers who were trying to enlist her in street business, where children as young as eight can work as runners or lookouts. Moreover, younger children seek to avoid these spots because they have erupted periodically in violence. In the summer of 1992, a small riot broke out in front of the store across from Tarelle's home, a confrontation between teenagers and the police.

Local groceries like Bob's and B and K have a lively, intimate, and almost homey atmosphere. Kids are well known to store proprietors, who not only sell them goods but keep them in line, give them advice, do them favors, and even communicate with their parents about their behavior. The central communal role played by such stores is made vividly clear by the discussion between Bob and one of his older customers—aimed in large part at the children who were in the store at the time—which was an oral continuation of narratives of slavery and life in the South which have been passed down for generations in this African-American community. A similar encounter in a store like Claire's is hard to imagine.

CLAIRE'S AND THE
CHAPEL SQUARE MALL

A small store selling inexpensive jewelry and accessories, Claire's is very popular among Newhallville girls. Racks of earrings are particularly enticing for these girls, who are just on the edge of being allowed to wear larger hoop earrings, rather than the small studs and drop earrings caretakers prefer for little girls. They play with the idea of purchasing jewelry they know their caretakers will disapprove, holding up a pair of huge, bamboo-patterned "door knocker" earrings while proclaiming, "My grandmother would never let me wear these!" This playful dynamic is a striking contrast to children's subdued demeanor at Bob's.

These girls' behavior is not just playful, however. Kids are often also markedly loud, provoking or anticipating direct and indirect confrontation of store employees, in some instances pointedly ignoring salespeople's concerns or talking about them as if they weren't able to hear. Children seem to view these visits not just as an opportunity for enjoyment and excitement, but as a challenge of sorts as well. One afternoon as we neared Claire's, Asia recounted her most recent experience there:

> "Last time I was in there, the lady was laughing because I didn't have enough money. The other day I went in, and I bought all this stuff, and the lady said, 'That will be forty dollars.' I pulled out a fifty-dollar bill and said, 'Here.'" Asia demonstrated, and

the look on her face was both self-satisfied and challenging. "I swear I was about to say, 'Keep the change,' until my grandmother came up," she said.

Asia's story captures the pressures many Newhallville kids face in having to assert their right to be in the mall by demonstrating their ability to buy. In Asia's story, when she is at first unable to pay for what she wants, she is sure that the saleslady is laughing at her. As she recounted the incident, the pleasure she took in later being able to present this woman with a fifty-dollar bill was palpable, as was her frustration in not being able to add insult to injury by imperiously directing the woman to keep the change. Despite this experience, however, Asia apparently did not consider the possibility of avoiding Claire's or of refusing to go in again. Rather, she returned there, armored with defiance of a fifty-dollar bill and toting a hefty measure of distrust.

Unlike in Bob's, children's experiences in the mall and in stores like Claire's are shaped by tensions around issues of race. These tensions, in turn, are conflated with problems related to class. Situations and interactions in which kids like Asia are made to feel inadequate or even nonexistent often make shopping an undertaking fraught with difficulty, and their response is often to don their street-tough personas. Such problematic interactions—where black shoppers are assumed to be unable to make purchases, where they are steered toward inferior merchandise, or where they are treated as if giving them attention is a waste of time—are a kind of received knowledge in Newhallville. Residents dress up when they go downtown to shop; they want to appear respectable to store personnel, to appear to have money in their pockets or purses, and thus to be treated with attention and respect. In New Haven's social and political culture, black has come to be equated with poor, and this development has had far-reaching repercussions for Newhallville children's experiences in the servicescapes of downtown.

On April 1, 1992, newspaper buyers were startled by a *New Haven Register* headline that read, "White Person Slips, Falls! Shoppers Shudder; Is Downtown Safe?" A closer look revealed that the headline was an April Fool's Day joke published not in the *Register,* but in a parody by the *New Haven Advocate,* a local weekly tabloid that emulates the *Village Voice.* The headline and spoof article that followed baldly stated what was more often merely hinted at in the *Register:* that the mall is an unsafe place for white shoppers, and African-American kids are the reason why whites feel uncomfortable there. The *Advocate's* sharp parody of the *New Haven Register* front page encouraged readers to call in and answer the daily "soundoff" question, a regular *Register* feature: "Would anyone except a suicidal moron on drugs shop in downtown New Haven?" The text of the article added further ironic flames to the fire:

> The shopper . . . said he will stick to patronizing suburban malls from now on, "like everybody else around here who's scared to death of the city." . . . Sources say police may call a key suspect in the incident, identified as Javan Reed, a/k/a Dwayne Black Person, who lives in a black neighborhood where everybody deals drugs, in for questioning. Sources wouldn't say on the record whether Reed a/k/a Person is guilty as hell.

To retain white, middle-class, suburban-dwelling shoppers, malls in Connecticut, including those in New Haven, have been aggressive in attempting to reduce the presence of minority youth. Trumbull Shopping Park, another Connecticut mall, fought a legal battle in order to gain the right to ban public transit from making stops on its property on Friday and Saturday nights. Their express reason for making this decision was security problems arising from teenagers—most of whom were minority youth from nearby Bridgeport ("Mall Wins Ruling" 1995). In the early 1980s New Haven had employed a similar strategy, moving bus stops from directly in front of the mall to relocate them across the street on the town green. This move was not as obstructive as that employed by Trumbull Shopping Park, but involved a considerable increase in discomfort for bus riders and was widely thought to be racially motivated. The original bus stops, located in front of the mall, were placed on a covered walkway open to the street that provided at least some protection from rain and snow. Across the way on the green, two rather small bus shelters hardly provide the same amount of protection from harsh weather conditions.

Regardless of the reasons for which consumers who are older, more affluent, or lighter-skinned have abandoned Chapel Square, it is primarily minority youth and teens who now constitute the mall's most important market ("A Teen-Age Pall at the Mall" 1993). Shop owners have had to develop subtle means of discouraging young people from spending too much time in the mall's public spaces, while attempting to continue to entice them to spend their money in its commercial venues. These strategies include an increasingly visible uniformed security force and the use of piped music featuring genres thought to be unappealing to undesirable youth. In a variation of what Russell Baker (1992) jokingly called "the Beethoven defense," the New Haven mall often features songs by the likes of Frank Sinatra.

The Chapel Square Mall is not unusual in its attempts to maintain a profile as a safe, communal servicescape that exists in distinct opposition to the chaotic, violent city beyond. The maintenance of this image spurs, in part, the attempts to limit or prevent young people's presence there, since they are perceived by some to threaten the pacific atmosphere. Such consumer community building, the proffering of togetherness through shopping, is most evident in the yearly Christmas spree of conviviality and community events from the perennially popular picture on Santa's knee to caroling and dance performances. Halloween, in particular, has emerged as a time when the mall is supported as a healthy alternative to the New Haven streets and all their dangers. This perception of the mall as an alternative to the city itself as a site of communal activity is supported not only by its own publicity efforts but also by institutions such as the public schools. For several years running, mall shopkeepers have distributed candy and Halloween balloons to hordes of costumed kids who trick-or-treat their way around the two-story concourse on a weekend near the thirty-first of October. Significantly, this event is designed to appeal to young children and their families (segments of the population that mall management finds amenable), not problematic older children and teens. During my fieldwork, the principal of the school where I conducted research sent a note to each child's family, encouraging caretakers not to allow their children to trick-or-treat door-to-door. Instead, the memo advised, caretakers should either take children only to family members' homes or go trick-or-treating at the mall.

From the time they are very small, Newhallville children accompany their families—parents, older siblings, cousins, aunts and uncles, grandparents—on downtown shopping excursions. As mentioned earlier, these visits may not be all that frequent, but they are important and memorable. When Newhallville children are about ten years old, many are allowed to go downtown unaccompanied by older relatives or friends. They are by this point familiar enough with downtown from earlier experience that they can find their way around the mall with ease, heading directly for their favorite stores. Among the children from the main study group, girls go downtown alone more often than do boys, who prefer to spend much of their unsupervised time riding bikes in and around the neighborhood.

Being able to explore the city and the mall on their own is not just an expansion of children's horizons as shoppers or individuals, but a mark of maturity—one intrinsically opposed, for girls at least, to the vulnerability of childhood and playing with dolls at home. Tionna explained that at the mall, "We try not to act like kids. When we're here, at home, then we act like kids, we play, we play with our dolls." While Newhallville girls who were visiting the mall independently did not ignore the toy store by any means, it was Claire's that was an inevitable pit stop. Going to this store, where more "grown-up" merchandise such as large hoop earrings and sunglasses could be purchased, was part of not acting like a kid in the mall.

Despite widespread feelings in New Haven that the mall is not a particularly safe or comfortable space to be, the statements and behavior of Newhallville children indicate that for them, the mall offers freedoms unavailable elsewhere, while also imposing particular forms of restraint. "Kids come here to stay out of trouble and to shop," said sixteen-year-old Cherie Lee in an interview with the *New York Times* ("A Teen-Age Pall at the Mall" 1993). Yet even as a store like Claire's offers an opportunity for independent, grown-up shopping, it also exposes children to another grown-up experience: being directly confronted with racism.

At the New Haven mall, pointed efforts at constraining the activities and limiting the presence of minority youth permeate the atmosphere. Security guards, which at once help provide the safety kids seek, ensure that safety in part through an intense monitoring of minority kids. Children are hardly unaware that they are at best only temporarily welcome in most mall spaces—and then only under certain circumstances—and that they are almost if not wholly unwelcome in others. Natalia's sudden and loud announcement in Claire's that "That white lady is following us around," is an acknowledgment of this state of affairs as well as an overt challenge to them. Natalia may have had the gumption to make this challenge because she did, in fact, have a twenty-dollar bill in her pocket. Similarly, Asia's insistent conviction that a salesclerk in Claire's was laughing at her because she had no money could only be defused by returning to the store to brandish money and retrieve her self-confidence.

Kids generally do not, however, have large sums to spend downtown, and store clerks know or suspect this. When kids plan a downtown trip, which they often do several days in advance, it is not unusual for caretakers to save up to give them some spending money, perhaps ten dollars or so. On other occasions, children may save up some money from baby-sitting or allowance to take on a trip downtown.[3] What kids like Natalia and Tionna want at the mall is not to go shopping, in the sense that they intend to go and spend their money. In fact, children never talked about "going shopping" but rather, "going downtown." This distinction implies that for these kids, the importance of going downtown lies in its social nature, rather than in the prospect of buying things or spending money.

In Natalia's trip, described at the outset of this chapter, even though she did have twenty dollars to spend, she only spent three dollars in Claire's. Ultimately, the point of the time spent in Claire's

[3] My research among Newhallville families showed that even families on federal assistance provide their children with a regular monthly allowance, sometimes as much as twenty dollars. One mother, however, sometimes required her children to assist in paying for groceries with part of this allowance.

was not choosing the appropriate item to buy—in this case, a small child-sized ring with a pink rhinestone. The point was being in the store, touching the merchandise, picking up giant door knocker earrings and imagining her grandmother's response, consulting with Tionna about the relative merits of a key chain that said "If it weren't for boys, I'd quit school," and announcing that the Troll Doll fad had gotten out of control. In the moments where the roving eye of the store owner or clerk was either forgotten or ignored, these girls' time in Claire's appeared to consist of "playing grown-up," rather than "going shopping."

It is undeniable that kids can be loud, rambunctious, clumsy, and annoying to other people in the store, especially when they are not accompanied by their elders. The most commonly observed response on the part of store employees, as noted loudly and pointedly by Natalia, is to observe such children carefully. Newhallville kids immediately suspect that such monitoring is aimed at preventing them from stealing, an assumption that they resent highly. Successive experiences of this type prime children for confrontation. I once observed a mall store's proprietor place herself in the midst of a group of African-American kids who were examining a display, arms folded and demanding loudly, "Can I help you?" The effect of this intervention was to silence almost immediately the buzz of commentary the children had been directing at the items. The kids retreated from the woman, without ever directly acknowledging her presence. The woman remained there, arms crossed, until they turned their backs on her and walked away. Though I never observed anything so overt in Claire's, kids are always ready for such an encounter, even as they invite such intervention with their behavior.

Claire's is a servicescape for Newhallville girls that is chock-full of complexity and conflict, where their race marks them—at least in their own minds—for monitoring and judgment. The loud and often disruptive behavior of Newhallville kids in the mall can be seen, in part, as an assertion of their right not only to be where they are, but to have a presence in the world that exists outside the borders of their neighborhood. Their shouts and suspicions point to their growing awareness that to be black in this world, unlike in

Newhallville, is to be other and to be suspect; to be black in Newhallville, however, is to be shut out from places like downtown and hemmed into a neighborhood with pleasures and dangers of its own.

CONCLUSION

[R]acial, economic, legal and social disempowerment can be condensed into a glance or a tone of voice. . . . The store is a key site where this multiaxial disempowerment is put into practice. It is where racial power can be redirected along economic and legal axes. . . . Store counters are the furniture of capitalism, the equivalent in the sphere of consumption of the workbench in that of production.

—Fiske (1994, 481)

This chapter has analyzed some of the contextual factors shaping the ways in which a store is thought about, used, and understood by children like those from Newhallville. Shoppers are not anonymous, historyless individuals when they walk in the door, and stores are not monolithic spaces that affect all who enter in uniform and predictable ways, as has often been assumed in the literature (see, for example, Halton 1992; Reece 1986; Williams 1982; Willis 1991). In the confrontation between historically situated people and socially constructed spaces, people are repeatedly reconstructed as particular people *in that space.*

Newhallville children are different kinds of people when they are in Claire's than when they are at Bob's, and the difference lies in part in the ways in which they engage with the social spaces they occupy. It does not matter much when kids are at Bob's that they might be poor. There is not much to buy, the merchandise changes very little from week to week, and everybody in the neighborhood knows a lot about everybody else in any case. Neither is their blackness a problem issue at Bob's; it is instead a point of common ground. At Claire's and in the mall, the confluence of poor, working-poor, working-class, and middle-class blacks and whites can at times serve to fuel their fantasies about each other more than anything else, as the *Advocate*'s April Fool's Day front page illustrates.

Being black at Claire's is problematic, but the excitement of the atmosphere is worth the price.

The disparaging glance or tone of voice directed at Newhall-ville children in Claire's and in the mall is part and parcel with the social inequality they experience in other aspects of their lives, as black children attending a racially segregated school, living in a pre-dominantly black neighborhood, in an area that is beset by poverty and struggling with the drug trade and related violence. The tension that these children feel, tension over being observed and judged when off their home turf, is particularly pronounced in downtown stores, but surfaces even on the street the minute they are over the neighborhood's informally maintained but universally recognized border line. One afternoon, as I stood with two girls on a corner at the neighborhood's edge, Tionna yelled at a passing car, "What are you looking at, you white people?" One wonders what they might have answered.

Tionna's question, shouted out at the retreating image of a passing car, is very much like Natalia's loud pronouncement that "that white lady is following us around." Both suggest that in New Haven, whites and blacks view each other through a distorting lens. The larger structural issues at work in creating neighborhood and downtown spaces are themselves implicated in the creation and per-petuation of social inequality; any significant transformation of these children's experience must also involve fundamental changes in New Haven's geographic, as well as social, scene. Nevertheless, small changes in the consumer experiences of children, particularly downtown, can work to transform what Fiske (1994) refers to as the "multiaxial disempowerment" that can be the result of the transactions taking place across the store counter, between clerk and customer. It is not the aim of this chapter to suggest what those changes might be, but rather to illustrate the far-reaching implica-tions of children's consumer experiences in important servicescapes. The focus has been primarily upon places like Bob's and Claire's, but the primary issues to be addressed concern society at large. If these servicescapes are to be transformed so as to challenge, rather than perpetuate social inequality, critical engagement with and under-standing of these larger social processes is required.

Both the 1992 uprising in Los Angeles and the growing power and popularity of figures like Louis Farrakhan attest to the centrality of consumption as a political arena, and of the store as the battlefield where the struggle is bound to be waged. This is what Fiske is getting at when he describes store counters as "the furniture of capitalism." In Los Angeles, it was to some extent a festering resentment between local blacks and Korean store owners—one that mingled understandings of race and class—that fanned the flames of community outrage over the police beating of Rodney King. Against the backdrop of a changing economy that had left the working class increasingly without work and local businesses floundering, the riots were what Fiske calls "loud public speech by those whose voices are normally silenced or confined to their own media" (p. 484).

In contrast, Farrakhan speaks publicly, loudly, and often. The organization that he heads, the Nation of Islam, explicitly points to the economic realm as an arena of oppression of blacks and urges its followers to start their own businesses and to patronize stores that are black owned and operated. In the words of one minister I recorded during a service at a Nation of Islam temple in Connecticut in August 1992:

> We all got to be teachers of the poor and underprivileged out there. What you going to do, sit here and run around with a puff head and keep it all to yourself? That's what the white man does. The white man just keeps it all to himself. If you sit there and let that happen, you're acting like a slave. You are afraid to go out and take what belongs to us. The honorable Elijah Muhammad said that nothing's going to happen to you. You can go to work and not worry, let God protect you. But he's not going to come out of the sky with a machine gun every time somebody calls you nigger. He's going to come out of you!

This field note excerpt from this minister's much longer social and spiritual analysis of American society elides the social and cultural with the material and economic. What the "white man just keeps all to himself" is a little unclear—is it knowledge, resources, jobs, money? The vagueness may be intentional and meant to indicate all of the above. Moreover, as is often the case, class and race seem to be given some equivalency in this speech, with blacks being "poor and underprivileged" and the white man having everything.

Tionna asked what was perhaps the defining question for my work: "What are you looking at, you white people?" Her question shows that at ten years old she already is well versed in negotiating the divisions of race and class that shape New Haven's social, geographic, and consumer spheres. As participant observers, ethnographers look long and hard at those they study. In the case of consumption among racial minorities, among children, and among the poor and working class, a lot more looking needs to be done before Tionna's question can be answered in a way that might satisfy both her yearning and her defiance.

BIBLIOGRAPHY

ANDREASEN, ALAN R. 1975. *The Disadvantaged Consumer.* New York: Free Press.
———. 1976. "The Differing Nature of Consumerism in the Ghetto." *Journal of Consumer Affairs* (Winter): 179–189.
———. 1986. "Disadvantaged Consumers in the 1980s." In *The Future of Consumerism,* edited by Paul N. Bloom and Ruth Belk Smith. Lexington, MA: Lexington Books, 113–128.
———, ED. 1970. *Improving Inner-City Marketing.* Chicago: American Marketing Association.
BAKER, RUSSELL. 1992. "The Beethoven Defense." *New York Times* (July 23): L19.
CADY, JOHN F. 1976. "Competition and Economic Dualism in the Ghetto Marketplace." In *Minorities and Marketing: Research Strategies,* edited by Alan R. Andreasen and Frederick D. Sturdivant. Chicago: American Marketing Association, 56–71.
CHIN, ELIZABETH. 1996. "Fettered Desire: Consumption and Social Experience Among Minority Children in New Haven, Connecticut." Unpublished dissertation, Anthropology Department, Graduate School of the City University of New York.
CITY OF NEW HAVEN. 1982. *Inside New Haven's Neighborhoods: A Guide to the City of New Haven.* New Haven, CT: New Haven Colony Historical Society.
CITY OF NEW HAVEN BLUE RIBBON COMMISSION. 1990. "Final Report of the Blue Ribbon Commission Appointed by Mayor John C. Daniels." New Haven, CT: City of New Haven.
FISKE, JOHN. 1994. "Radical Shopping in Los Angeles: Race, Media and the Sphere of Consumption." *Media, Culture, and Society* 16:469–486.

HALTON, EUGENE. 1992. "A Long Way from Home: Automatic Culture in Domestic and Civic Life." In *Meaning, Measure and Morality of Materialism,* edited by Floyd Rudmin and Marsha Richins. Provo, UT: Association for Consumer Research, 1–9.

HILL, RONALD PAUL. 1991. "Homeless Women, Special Possessions, and the Meaning of 'Home': An Ethnographic Case Study." *Journal of Consumer Research* 18:298–310.

———. 1992. "Homeless Children: Coping with Material Losses." *Journal of Consumer Affairs* 26:274–287.

HILL, RONALD PAUL, AND MARK STAMEY. 1990. "The Homeless in America: An Examination of Possessions and Consumption Behaviors," *Journal of Consumer Research* 17:303–321.

HONEYCUTT, ANDREW. 1975. "An Ethnographic Study of Low Income Consumer Behavior." Unpublished dissertation, School of Business, Harvard University.

JACKSON, PETER, AND NIGEL THRIFT. 1995. "Geographies of Consumption." In *Acknowledging Consumption,* edited by Daniel Miller. New York: Routledge, 204–237.

JEFFERS, CAMILLE. 1967. *Living Poor: A Participant Observer Study of Choices and Priorities.* Ann Arbor, MI: Ann Arbor Publishers.

MALINOWSKI, BRONISLAW. 1922. *Argonauts of the Western Pacific.* London: Routledge and Keagan Paul.

"Mall Wins Ruling on Limiting Bus Service." 1995. *New York Times* (August 27): sec. 1, 36.

MILLER, DANIEL. 1995. "Consumption as the Vanguard of History: A Polemic by Way of an Introduction." In *Acknowledging Consumption: A Review of New Studies,* edited by Daniel Miller. New York: Routledge, 1–57.

MINERBROOK, SCOTT. 1992. "Why a City Alone Cannot Save Itself: The Story of New Haven Shows How Big Social and Economic Forces Overwhelm Local Leaders." *U.S. News and World Report* (November 9): 36–40.

NEW HAVEN DOWNTOWN COUNCIL. 1992. "Major Employers in New Haven County." New Haven, CT: New Haven Downtown Council.

NIGHTINGALE, CARL. 1993. *On the Edge: A History of Poor Black Children and Their American Dreams.* New York: Basic Books.

REECE, BONNIE B. 1986. "Children and Shopping: Some Public Policy Questions." *Journal of Public Policy and Management* 5:185–194.

REGUERO, WILFRED, AND MARILYN CRANE. 1994. "Project MotherCare: One Hospital's Response to the High Perinatal Death Rate in New Haven, CT." *Public Health Reports* 109:647–652.

SHERRY, JOHN F., JR., ED. 1995. *Contemporary Marketing and Consumer Behavior: An Anthropological Sourcebook.* Thousand Oaks, CA: Sage.

SORKIN, MICHAEL. 1992. *Variations on a Theme Park: The New American City and the End of Public Space.* New York: Farrar, Straus and Giroux.

"A Teen-Age Pall at the Mall: After-School Gatherings Please Youths but Are Worrying Many Others." 1993. *New York Times* (November 13): B1, B5.

U.S. BUREAU OF THE CENSUS. 1980. "1980 Census of Population and Housing." Washington, DC: U.S. Government Printing Office.

U.S. DEPARTMENT OF COMMERCE. 1993. "Detailed Housing Characteristics: Connecticut." Washington, DC: U.S. Government Printing Office.

"White Person Slips, Falls! Shoppers Shudder; Is Downtown Safe?" 1992. *New Haven Advocate* (April 1): 1.

WILLIAMS, ROSALIND H. 1982. *Dream Worlds: Mass Consumption in Late Nineteenth-Century France.* Los Angeles: University of California Press.

WILLIS, SUSAN. 1991. *A Primer for Daily Life.* New York: Routledge.

INDEX

About the Authors

Eric J. Arnould is an anthropologist and Associate Professor of Marketing at the University of South Florida, Tampa. His research interests include channels structure and market organization in West Africa, household consumption rituals, services marketing, and scientific representation in postmodernity.

Julie Baker is an Assistant Professor of Marketing at the University of Texas at Arlington. Her areas of research interest include the store/service environment, internal marketing, and product (goods/services) quality.

Julia Bristor is Manager of Market Research at Air Liquide America. Her interests are in organizational buying behavior and feminist issues in consumer behavior.

Elizabeth Chin is Assistant Professor of Anthropology at Occidental College in Los Angeles. Her research in the United States is focused on the ethnography of children's consumption. She also conducts research on Haitian popular and folkloric dance, performing professionally in the United States and in Haiti.

Millie Creighton is Assistant Professor of Anthropology at the University of British Columbia, Vancouver. Her research interests include Japanese culture and society, aesthetics and popular culture, and concepts of gender, identity, and self.

Eileen Fischer is Associate Professor of Marketing in the Schulich School of Business, York University, North York, Ontario. She is interested in the influence of gender roles on consumers' behaviors, and more broadly in the effects of experiential learning on consumers' and entrepreneurs' behaviors.

Brenda Gainer is Associate Professor of Marketing and Director of the Non Profit Management Program in the Schulich School of Business at York University. Her interests are in sociocultural influences, particularly those related to gender, on consumer behavior.

Cathy Goodwin completed Chapter 17 while visiting at the Great Valley Campus of Pennsylvania State University, Malvern, Pennsylvania. Her research interests include services marketing, privacy, stress and social support, and consumption symbolism. She acknowledges support of the Social Sciences and Humanities Research Council of Canada.

M. Gottdiener is Professor of Sociology and Chair of the Department of the State University of New York at Buffalo. Among his many research interests are urban affairs and cultural studies.

Kent Grayson is Assistant Professor of Marketing at the London Business School. He researches deception and trust in marketing, and the status of marketing as a performance. He has also implemented a number of studies on the network marketing industry.

Morris B. Holbrook is W. T. Dillard Professor of Marketing in the Graduate School of Business at Columbia University, New York City, where he teaches marketing strategy, sales management, research methods, consumer behavior, and commercial communication in the culture of consumption. His research focuses on issues related to communication in general and to aesthetics, semiotics, hermeneutics, advertising, the media, arts, and entertainment in particular.

Douglas B. Holt is Assistant Professor of Marketing at Pennsylvania State University, in State College, where he teaches courses in consumer behavior and international marketing. He is interested in the sociology of culture. Among his research interests are consumption practices and lifestyle dynamics.

Dawn Iacobucci is Professor of Marketing at the J. L. Kellogg Graduate School of Management, Northwestern University, Evanston, Illinois. Her research interests include modeling dyadic and network relations, services marketing, and multivariate statistics. She teaches marketing research and services marketing courses to M.B.A. students and statistics to Ph.D. students.

Annamma Joy is Associate Professor in the Marketing Department of Concordia University, Montreal, and a visiting scholar at the Hong Kong University of Science and Technology. She is an anthropologist whose research interests include art and marketing in Canada and China.

Joan Lindsey-Mullikin is a Ph.D. student in the Department of Marketing at the University of Arizona, Tucson. She was previously employed by McDonnell Douglas Corporation.

James H. McAlexander is Associate Professor of Marketing at Oregon State University, Corvallis. His research focuses on consumer ethnography.

Mary Ann McGrath is Associate Professor of Marketing at Loyola University of Chicago and Director of the Loyola Center for Values in Business. Her teaching and research interests include consumer behavior and marketing communications.

Cele Otnes is Associate Professor and Fellow of the Cummings Center for Advertising Studies at the University of Illinois at Urbana-Champaign. Her research interests are primarily focused on the ways advertising and marketing shape consumer rituals in American culture.

Ron Pimentel is Assistant Professor of Marketing at the University of Central Florida, Orlando. His research focuses on visual aspects of marketing: preference for visual images and meanings associated with visual images.

Linda L. Price is Associate Professor of Marketing at the University of South Florida, Tampa. Her research interests include experiential consumption, decision making, information processing, innovativeness, and interpersonal dynamics.

Ozlem Sandikci is a doctoral candidate in the Department of Marketing at Pennsylvania State University. Her research interests include gender and advertising and cultural aspects of consumption.

John W. Schouten is Associate Professor of Marketing at the University of Portland in Portland, Oregon. His research focuses on consumer ethnography.

John F. Sherry, Jr., Professor of Marketing, is an anthropologist who teaches graduate courses in marketing behavior, international marketing, and consumer research at Northwestern University's J. L. Kellogg Graduate School of Management. His research interests include symbolic communication, cultural analysis, and consumer experience. He is currently President-Elect of the Association for Consumer Research and was formerly Associate Editor of the *Journal of Consumer Research*.

Michael R. Solomon is Human Sciences Professor of Consumer Behavior in the School of Human Sciences, Auburn University, Auburn, Alabama. His research interests include consumer behavior and lifestyle issues, the symbolic aspects of products, fashion and image processes, and services marketing.

Patrick Tierney has a joint appointment in the Departments of Recreation and Leisure Studies and Hospitality Management at San Francisco State University, where he is Professor and Coordinator of the Commercial Recreation and Resort Management Program. Pat has been co-owner for seventeen years of Adrift Adventures, an ecotourism adventure recreation business.

Alladi Venkatesh is Professor of Management at the University of California–Irvine, and Research Associate at the university's Center for Research on Information Technology in Organizations (CRITO). His broad research area is technology and social change. He specializes in the impact of information technologies on families/households. He is also interested in postmodernism and its relevance to marketing theory and practice.

Melanie Wallendorf is Professor of Marketing and of Comparative Cultural and Literary Studies at the University of Arizona. Her research focuses on the sociological aspects of consumer behavior. She is currently Associate Editor of the *Journal of Consumer Research*.